Handbook of Procurement

How can organizations ensure that they can get best value for money in their procurement decisions? How can they stimulate innovations from their dedicated suppliers? With contributions from a number of leading academics and professionals, this handbook offers expert guidance on the fundamental aspects of successful procurement design and management in firms, public administrations, and international institutions. The issues addressed include the management of dynamic procurement; the handling of procurement risk; the architecture of purchasing systems; the structure of incentives in procurement contracts; methods to increase suppliers' participation in procurement contests and e-procurement platforms; how to minimize the risk of collusion among sellers and of corruption of procurers' agents; pricing and reputation mechanisms in e-procurement platforms; and how procurement can enhance innovation. Inspired by frontier research, it provides practical recommendations to managers, engineers and lawyers engaged in private and public procurement design. It will also be a key reference text for MBA courses related to procurement design and supply chain management.

Nicola Dimitri is Professor of Economics at the University of Siena and Senior Consultant at Consip SpA.

Gustavo Piga is Professor of Economics, University of Rome Tor Vergata, and OECD-Sigma Procurement Expert.

Giancarlo Spagnolo is Head of Research at Consip SpA and Associate Professor of Economics at the Stockholm School of Economics.

Handbook of Procurement

EDITED BY

NICOLA DIMITRI,

GUSTAVO PIGA

AND

GIANCARLO SPAGNOLO

CAMBRIDGE
UNIVERSITY PRESS

CAMBRIDGE UNIVERSITY PRESS
Cambridge, New York, Melbourne, Madrid, Cape Town, Singapore, São Paulo

Cambridge University Press
The Edinburgh Building, Cambridge CB2 2RU, UK
Published in the United States of America by Cambridge University Press, New York

www.cambridge.org
Information on this title: www.cambridge.org/9780521870733

First published 2006

Printed in the United Kingdom at the University Press, Cambridge

A catalogue record for this publication is available from the British Library

ISBN-13 978-0-521-87073-3 hardback
ISBN-10 0-521-87073-9 hardback

Contents

Part VI Dynamic Forces and Innovation

Figures

Tables

List of Contributors

Gian Luigi Albano is Senior Economist at the Consip Research Unit, Italy.

Lawrence Ausubel is Professor of Economics at the University of Maryland, USA.

Patrick Bajari is Professor of Economics at the University of Minnesota, USA.

Paolo Buccirossi is Director of LEAR (Laboratory of Economics, Antitrust, Regulation), Italy.

Luis Cabral is Professor of Economics and Management at New York University, USA.

Giacomo Calzolari is Associate Professor of Economics at the University of Bologna, Italy.

Laura Carpineti is Junior Economist at the Consip Research Unit, Italy.

Guido Cozzi is Professor of Economics at the University of Macerata, Italy.

Peter Cramton is Professor of Economics at the University of Maryland, USA.

Chrysanthos Dellarocas is Professor of Information Systems at the University of Maryland, USA.

Vincenzo Denicolò is Professor of Economics at the University of Bologna, Italy.

Nicola Dimitri is Professor of Economics at the University of Siena, Italy.

Federico Dini is Junior Economist at the Consip Research Unit, Italy.

Andreas Engel is Consultant at TWS Partners, Germany.

Josè Ganuza is Associate Professor of Economics at Pompeu Fabra University Spain.

Veronika Grimm is Assistant Professor at the University of Cologne, Germany.

Esther Hauk is Associate Professor of Economics at Pompeu Fabra University, Spain.

Elisabetta Iossa is Professor of Economics at the Brunel University, UK.

Bruno Jullien is Research Director at the CNRS (DR1), GREMAQ, University of Toulouse, and Research Director at the IDEI of Toulouse, France.

William Kovacic is a Commissioner of the Federal Trade Commission.

Yvan Lengwiler is Professor of Economics at the University of Basel, Switzerland.

Tracy Lewis is Professor of Economics at the Fuqua School of Business, Duke University, USA.

Robert Marshall is Professor of Economics at Penn State University, USA.

Leslie Marx is Associate Professor of Economics at Duke University, USA.

Riccardo Pacini is PhD student in Economics at the University of Rome Tor Vergata, Italy.

Marco Pagnozzi is Assistant Professor of Economics at the University of Naples, Italy.

Isabelle Perrigne is Associate Professor of Economics at Penn State University, USA.

Gustavo Piga is Professor of Economics at the University of Rome Tor Vergata, Italy.

Matthew Raiff is Managing Partner at Bates White LLC, USA.

Giancarlo Spagnolo is Head of the Research Unit at Consip, Italy, and Visiting Associate Professor of Economics at the Stockholm School of Economics, Sweden.

Steve Tadelis is Associate Professor of Business School at the University of California at Berkeley, USA.

Tommaso Valletti is Reader at Tanaka Business School, Imperial College London, UK, and Associate Professor of Economics at the University of Rome Tor Vergata, Italy.

Achim Wambach is Professor of Economics at the University of Cologne, Germany.

Elmar Wolfstetter is Professor of Economics at Humboldt University, Berlin, Germany.

Huseyin Yildirim is Assistant Professor of Economics at Duke University, USA.

Matteo Zanza is Consultant at Arthur D. Little Global Management, Italy.

Preface

The present volume originates from the interaction between top public procurement practitioners and economists working at, and with, the Research Unit of the Italian Public Procurement Agency, Consip.

It is based on the belief that procurement, while representing a large share of the GDP of developed and less developed economies and occupying a substantial share of employment in the private and public sectors, suffers still from a limited variety of discussions, outside of the academic arena, on strategic economic choices regarding the optimal set-up of a tender for purchasing.

Economic research on optimal procurement design has made gigantic steps in recent decades. Still, public and private procurement centres around the world, that are often involved in a large number and variety of acquisitions, can seldom afford to hire expert consultants to allow for an optimal case-by-case procurement design (informed by frontier research). In the many relatively small acquisitions where time and financial constraints make expert economic advice and ad hoc design impossible, practitioners take crucial decisions on procurement design without guidance from recent research in the field, most of which is phrased in too technical terms to be accessed by non-researchers.

This is why in 2002 Consip, the centralized Italian Agency for Procurement of Goods and Services, created an internal Research Unit dedicated to both research and internal consulting on procurement design. To perform and facilitate both these tasks, the unit started 'translating' into accessible 'best practices' the most robust findings of recent theoretical, empirical, and experimental economic research on procurement design. This handbook grew somewhat unespectably out of this much less ambitious project, mostly thanks to the enthusiastic encouragement and hard work of the group of top-notch external experts that ended up co-authoring it.

The activity of Consip's Research Unit comprises scientific support and internal consulting focused on the practical problems of everyday procurement design, including the choice of scoring rules in different forms of competitive tendering, the determination of number and size of lots into which to divide each supply, optimal incentive contracting to ensure quality and cost-effectiveness, methods favouring participation and preventing collusion, the management of risky bids, and issues related to market structure evolution. This focus on practical procurement issues is directly reflected in the structure of the volume, as all chapters are motivated by major problems in practical procurement design and management. Consip's Research Unit coordinates the activities of the European Union Learning Lab on Public Procurement, whose members, Europe-wide procurement organizations, regularly meet to discuss strategic choices to foster competition and carry out benchmarking exercises.

Consip and a number of top-level external world experts strongly supported the idea of a volume that could help bridging the gap between advanced research and the practice of procurement, and support practitioners when expert advice, the best choice whenever possible, is not feasible. They all readily saw how valuable could be such a reference for Consip's professionals, for all other procurement managers employed in the public and private sector, and for undergraduate and MBA students and teachers engaged in strategic procurement/sourcing courses. For these reasons the editors are extremely grateful to Consip, and even more to the authoritative external experts who kindly agreed to contribute to what later turned out to be a quite ambitious project.

All chapters are original, unpublished work containing non-technical analysis of procurement design problems and practical recommendations – summarized in 'practical conclusions' – that procurers may want to consider to support decision making in their professional activity when they believe the relevant circumstances apply. Given the complexity of procurement decisions, our practical conclusions should not be used as mechanical rules, as this might lead to serious mistakes. Rather, they should be intended as an inspiration and help for intelligent and responsible procurement design, where optimal choice cannot be based on a passive implementation of recipes, but must be the outcome of a smart and creative act.

The book is intended mainly for professionals, economists, and lawyers. The volume can also be used as reference for MBA courses in procurement or, in general, courses related to supply chain management. Advanced undergraduates and first-year graduate students in economics and in law can also find in the book an interesting and useful reference for courses related to procurement design.

Procurers and other readers are likely to find in the chapters of this handbook many instances and examples of which they have had some significant experience they can share with or question the authors about. We welcome and encourage interaction with procurers, who can write to us at ufficiostudi.consip@tesoro.it.

Enjoy the reading!

PART I

Preliminary issues

1 Introduction

Nicola Dimitri, Gustavo Piga and Giancarlo Spagnolo

1.1. Why a handbook on procurement?

Procurement represents a very large fraction of total economic activity. The value of public procurement transactions in EU countries is about 16 percent of their GDP, while in the United States it is around 20 percent.[1] In the private sector, the value of transactions is even larger and is steadily increasing, due to the current trend towards outsourcing all non-core business activities.

Efficient procurement is therefore a core necessity for firms' profitability and survival, and for the public sector's effectiveness in obtaining resources for social spending and/or lower taxes. Procurement design directly and substantially affects firms' and countries' performance in the short and in the long run: in the short run, most obviously by immediately determining the costs and quality of inputs in the private or public supply chains; in the long run, most importantly by determining suppliers' and more generally firms' incentives to invest in R&D and to innovate in general.

Procurement design and management is a complex issue though, as contractual problems directly interact with competitive screening and risk management problems. Moreover, procurement is most often a dynamic, repeated activity, with short-term objectives often conflicting with long-term ones. Strategic procurement decisions must be taken with a focus on the future dynamics of the demand–supply relationship. Neglecting the importance of repeated relationships with potential suppliers and the effects of procurement choices on an industry or a district dynamic could have very undesirable consequences for a large buyer, in terms of both price and quality. This dynamic distinguishing feature of procurement also greatly enlarges the role for reputational forces.

---

[1] See http://europa.eu.int/comm/internal_market/publicprocurement/index_en.htm.

Unfortunately, there is not a one-size-fits-all measure for effective procurement design: the variety and complexity of situations in which procurement decisions are made means that appropriate purchasing procedures must take into account many aspects, and be tailored to each single situation. Nevertheless, some key forces driving effective procurement design are common to most procurement decisions, and it is on these kinds of driving forces that this handbook is focusing, providing a toolkit for how to take them into account in different situations.

Strategic procurement decisions require rational and competent decision makers, especially when procuring innovative goods or services. The need for competence obviously relates to the specific ability to gauge market developments, but cannot leave aside more general skills that have to do with legal and, particularly, strategic issues.

It is with regard to this latter strategic need that this handbook hopes to bridge a gap between economists and procurers. Indeed we believe that, also thanks to many excellent existing books, legal professionalism in procurement has progressed faster than knowledge on the topics this handbook is concerned with. Strategic and efficiency issues, however, are no less urgent or important than legal consistency ones. If anything, they need to be studied also by legal experts of procurement to enable them to structure contracts appropriately and suggest modifications to laws that sometimes prevent full implementation of sensible procurement strategies.

Therefore, the main goal of the volume is twofold. It wishes to inform professionals involved in practical activity of the more robust indications coming from advanced economic research in the field, to help them solve the main problems arising in practical procurement design. At the same time, the book will also inform researchers of the most important problems that arise in procurement practice, in so doing providing important inspiration for new fertile research efforts in the field. This is why particular emphasis has been given to examples and case studies, through which the specifics of different procurement situations will be illustrated and discussed.

1.2. Terminology and definitions

Procurement is characterized by lack of uniform terminology; different terms, in different countries or contexts, are used to describe identical or very similar situations, and these differences can sometimes generate confusion and misunderstandings.

Differences are particularly noticeable in the terminology of competitive bidding procedures. A main source of difference is given by the community of reference. For example, while economists normally refer to both sealed-bid and dynamic competitive bidding procedures as auctions, procurers by auctions typically intend dynamic, descending-in-price competitions, while sealed bidding is often referred to as sealed-bid tendering. The language used in legislation can also be different: for instance, the 2004 EU Directive on public procurement refers only to 'electronic auctions' and never mentions sealed bids or sealed bidding, which is instead used by the US Federal Acquisition Regulations.

Given such diversity of terminology, we found it compelling to attempt to harmonize language through chapters. The choice we made turned out to be a compromise among the terminologies used by most of the potential readers of the volume, so that all of them could feel sufficiently familiar with the language adopted. With very minor exceptions, throughout the book the terms *procurer* and *buyer* will be used interchangeably, as will the terms *bidders* and *suppliers* (sometimes *sellers*). By *contractor* we shall mean a supplier who has been awarded a supply contract. Moreover, we shall often use the term *competitive tendering* as a general expression for competitive bidding procedures, to mean what economists refer to as *auctions*. More specifically, we shall adopt the term *sealed bid tendering* (procedure) or simply sealed bidding for what economists refer to as *sealed bid auctions*, and use the term *dynamic (descending-reverse) auctions* or simply *auctions* for what economists name *open-dynamic auctions*. Finally, the term *tender* will be used to mean a *price/technical offer*. The glossary provides more detailed support and we encourage the reader to spend some time to glance through it.

1.3. Book structure and content

This book is organized in six parts, each of them covering a major theme of interest for effective procurement practice. After the preliminary section setting the stage, the following ones will discuss some general strategic principles in procurement, the design of competitive tendering procedures, criteria to attract and select participants, methods to prevent collusion and corruption, and procurement and innovation in a dynamic perspective.

1.3.1. Part I Preliminary issues

This part introduces the reader to the main themes concerning procurement, motivating the volume and its structure.

Chapter 2 contains a discussion on the *variety of practices in public procurement*. It concentrates on evidence gathered from a survey conducted by Consip, mostly from European but also from some non-European countries. The authors point out that a large degree of heterogeneity emerges across countries in the procedures that are followed by public purchasers. This finding is crucial in that it gives the reader possible methods to approach the chapters of the book. The reader will find it interesting to compare the indications emerging from the survey with the practical conclusions proposed in this volume, on themes such as the choice of competitive tendering formats, scoring rules, etc.

1.3.2. Part II General strategic principles

This part contains three chapters, each of them dealing with a general aspect of procurement design.

The first important decision to make in designing the procurement system of a complex organization concerns its *degree of centralization*. The point falls within the general theme of delegation, a topic widely investigated, though not very extensively in procurement. In Chapter 3 the authors argue that evidence from practice is very heterogeneous showing a wide array of patterns of procurement design. While, in recent years, the public sector has exhibited a tendency towards more centralized systems, the private sector has showed much more variety, with a considerable presence of mixed models where elements of decentralization and centralization co-exist. The main effort of the chapter is devoted to identifying the most important reasons supporting centralized and delegated procurement.

After the overall design and the extent of delegation in a purchasing system are defined, the buyer has to tackle another crucial aspect, that is, the *structure of supply contracts.* These must be tailored to achieve the desired quality at the lowest possible price compatible with suppliers' cost. Chapter 4 discusses the main categories of contracts that could be adopted in procurement. The authors observe that a major element of distinction among them is whether standards of quality are contractible, namely well specifiable in the formal agreement. The point is very important because when the procurer cannot introduce clauses in the contract that unambiguously describe the desired quality standards, then the procurer is bound to rely on non-contractible incentives.

Another fundamental dimension of procurement that buyers should carefully choose in order to deliver value for money is the *awarding procedure.* Chapter 5 deals with the issue by comparing advantages and disadvantages of competitive tendering procure with respect to negotiations. In a competitive tendering procurement compete for a contract by submitting offers to the procurer, who chooses the most economically advantageous tender. In a negotiation procedure the buyer interacts individually with one, or more, selected suppliers to obtain the best contract conditions. Competitive tendering procedures are typically more impersonal, accountable, and transparent than negotiations, though they normally prevent communication between buyers and sellers which could improve price and quality. Negotiations can instead allow the procurer to exchange information with potential suppliers and utilize their expertise when designing the project. The authors discuss the implications of these features for procurement design.

1.3.3. Part III Competitive tendering strategies

Having opted for a competitive tendering awarding procedure, the buyer faces two major decisions: she first has to select which competitive bidding format to adopt and then the number of contracts lots. This section is dedicated to these two very important aspects of procurement design.

Competitive tendering procedures fall within two main categories: sealed-bid tendering and dynamic reverse auctions.[2] In a sealed bid tendering

---

[2] For more on the main types of sealed-bid competitive tendering procedures see the glossary.

suppliers submit offers without observing the tenders made by the opponents, while in dynamic auctions prices are disclosed in the course of the competition so that suppliers have the opportunity to outbid their rivals before the auction ends. In procurement activity both formats are used, but on what elements can a buyer decide which one to opt for? Chapter 6 deals with this point, arguing that the choice should mostly depend on the nature of uncertainty for serving the contract. The authors notice that a possible problem with dynamic auctions is that they might last for too long and discuss how the auction length could be kept under control without the procedure losing effectiveness for the buyer.

Choosing how to split the supply is another major decision that buyers have to face. This determines the *number of supply contracts*, or lots, which bidders will compete for. Chapter 7 examines how the number and size of contracts to procure could emerge from the resolution of a trade-off. On the one hand, with few, large lots the buyer could better exploit the advantages of bidders' economies of scale and scope and would be likely to pay low prices for the awarded contracts. However, large lots could also preclude small business enterprises from submitting tenders, and have undesirable consequences for the buyer. A possible negative implication of this concerns the level of competition taking place in the competitive tendering as well as in the market where suppliers operate. The authors contend that if only few, large suppliers can participate in the tender, then it could be easier for them to collude. Moreover, reducing the number of competitors in a bidding competition could also have a negative impact on the outcome of future competitive tendering procedures and on the long-run sustainability of the level of competition in the suppliers' market.

When the buyer splits the supply into more than one lot, she has to determine which *multi-contract competitive tendering* format to opt for. The general choice between a multi-contract sealed bid format and a dynamic reversed auction is still based upon the general principles discussed in Chapter 6 for the single contract case. However, the presence of multiple lots introduces some new elements in procurement design; in particular, the format can vary depending upon whether lots exhibit so-called positive or negative complementarities. For a supplier, a set of contracts exhibit positive (negative) complementarities when the cost of serving all the contracts in the set is lower (higher) than the sum of the costs of each single contract. With either kind of complementarities allowing for package bidding would enchance competition. Chapter 8 focuses only on sealed bid formats, leaving the treatment of multi-contract dynamic auctions to Chapter 9, and discusses competitive tendering designs to take into account both positive and negative complementarities.

Multi-contract dynamic auctions are studied in Chapter 9, where, in particular, the authors concentrate on the following three main formats: simultaneous descending auctions, simultaneous clock auctions, and the clock proxy auction. These innovative auction formats have been proposed in recent years to deal with auctions with many related items, where the most desirable allocation of items requires price discovery. The authors argue that selection among these three models should depend upon the nature of complementarities among contracts and the extent to which the supply can be split into multiple contracts. As the three models proposed are dynamic auctions, they are well suited to mitigate the problems of the so-called winner's curse, and could also help simplify the bidders' decision problem when the number of contracts is high.

1.3.4. Part IV Attracting and screening participants

A widely accepted view in procurement is that a key element of a successful competitive tendering for buyers is large and qualified suppliers' participation, a point which this section elaborates upon. This can be true in a variety of situations, some of the most important of which are discussed in the ensuing four chapters.

The advent of Information and Communication Technology (ICT) stimulated the development of so-called *e-procurement platforms* as electronic mediators enhancing transactions in two-sided markets. For instance, e-marketplaces in the public sector are e-platforms; they function as intermediaries between suppliers, exhibiting their catalogues, and public administrations, which can access the catalogues and order the products they need. In Chapter 10 the author argues that e-platforms are successful if they can find proper incentives to attract the two sides of the relevant market to enter as many transactions as possible. In particular the price charged by the platform to customers, at participation or usage level, is a major policy instrument to favour participation. In this context, prices should depart from costs to allow for cross-subsidies between the two sides of the market. The chapter deals also with non-price policy instruments.

Looking more closely now at the competitive tendering design, how could a buyer *foster the desired participation* by suppliers? Chapter 11 discusses some of the main elements inducing a desirable pool of participants to submit offers. The authors first consider which competitive tendering formats could be more favourable for the buyer, in particular to attract both large and small firms to participate. They argue this would occur when small firms believe they are not systematically outbid by stronger rivals. Besides the competitive tendering format, the authors discuss other important aspects of procurement design that can affect participation, such as the choice of the reserve price.

When bidders are asked to submit both an economic and a technical offer, buyers can take account of their own preferences by introducing a *scoring rule* assigning a score to the two components of the proposal, and awarding the contract to the supplier who obtains the highest overall score. This is calculated by giving weights to the technical as well as to the economic score. By varying the weights a procurer can fine-tune the right incentives for suppliers to satisfy his preferences. For example, if a procurer cares more about quality than price, then he could assign a higher weight to the technical part of the formula; by so doing he may attract suppliers providing higher quality standards. Based on the notion of 'economic value of a point', as the fundamental element for bidders to choose the composition of their offers, Chapter 12 suggests how a buyer could proceed to select the most appropriate scoring rule to meet her desiderata.

A main concern related to qualified participation is bidders' effective ability to deliver the desired performance. Indeed, it is not infrequent for suppliers facing financial difficulties to participate in a competitive tendering, with the precise goal of winning the contract to try to survive in the market. Hence, a contract awarded at an *abnormally low price* is not necessarily good news for a buyer; indeed, the price may have been submitted by a risky bidder who will be unable to serve the contract appropriately, or to serve it at all. But how can buyers prevent this kind of risk? In Chapter 13 the authors discuss how limited liability can change suppliers' attitude towards risk and influence the possibility of risky bids. They also suggest how procurement design could take into account the possibility of abnormally low tenders, and compare these measures with the relative advantages of third-party guaranteed financial instruments, such as letters of credit and surety bonds.

1.3.5. Part V Preventing collusion and corruption

For a buyer a successful competitive tendering, in terms of low price and high quality standards, is fundamentally related to the degree of competition that develops among participants. If bidders soften price quality competition then the final outcome of a competitive tendering would hurt the procurer's objectives.

Chapter 14 presents a general discussion on how to *prevent collusive agreements*. The authors observe that many elements can influence cartel formation, some of the most important of which are the number of participants, barriers to entry for suppliers, the timing of information disclosure concerning the outcome of a competitive tendering, firms' asymmetries in capacities and costs, and market shares when the supply is split into homogeneous lots. The authors also observe that, with sealed bidding, first- and second-lowest-price tendering procedures operate differently in preventing the risk of collusion. With reference to an important case study, the authors finally discuss how a procurer should behave when she suspects the existence of a cartel.

The formation of *anti-competitive bidding rings* could be fought by either reinforcing measures to prevent cartels or by increasing punishment once a cartel is detected. These two strategies have relative merits, which Chapter 15 examines by presenting some important case studies taken from cartel prosecution. The authors discuss when prevention policies could be more effective with respect to the more commonly adopted punishment measures. They also notice that cartel formation can take specific forms, which might depend upon the type of competitive tendering format adopted. Due to the availability of a large and interesting body of evidence for sales auctions, and given that the logic of cartel formation is similar in sales and procurement, the authors consider both scenarios. Based on evidence, they also discuss the relation between collusion and subcontracting.

Corruption can also be a major element generating distorted and undesirable competitive tendering outcomes for the procurer. Since corruption can occur when the buyer is purchasing on behalf of a third party, it can takeplace both in the public and in the private sector. The fundamental problem induced by a corrupt buyer is that she could award a contract to an inefficient firm, possibly at a high price, in exchange for a bribe. In Chapter 16 the authors observe that bid rigging, bid orchestration and distortion of quality ranking are the three main instruments of corruption in competitive tendering procedures. Among other things, they note that the scope for corruption may also depend on the complexity of the tenders, and on the possibility that bids are forwarded to the procurer by use of an electronic format. They discuss a number of devices that can minimize the risk of corruption in procurement.

1.3.6. Part VI Dynamic forces and innovation

This section focuses on some aspects related to procurement dynamics, a main distinguishing feature of purchasing procedures.

An important characteristic of dynamic procurements is given by the buyer's potential *cost of switching* from one contractor to another. As soon as the current contract expires, in deciding the awarding procedure for the new contract the procurer might wonder whether it would be preferable for her to keep the same contractor rather than selecting a different one. If the incumbent contractor has been fully satisfactory in serving the contract, then the procurer might prefer to award the new contract to him again, although the fact that the incumbent was a good one does not necessarily mean that a new contractor could not provide an even better product. But there could be costs for the buyer to change suppliers that should be properly taken into account. Chapter 17 examines the optimal strategies in dynamic procurements settings when there are switching costs. The authors also explore policy implications for adoption of technology and firm organization.

The parties involved in repeated interactions may build up a *reputation* for a certain quality of service, since their behaviour can be observed. If the buyer knows how well potential bidders served analogous contracts in the past, then she can gauge the expected level of efficiency of the contractor. By reducing the risk of opportunistic behaviour, good reputation enhances trust and favours the development of transactions. In electronic markets with many and often anonymous participants, the possibility of con-structing a good reputation is particularly important. In Chapter 18 the authors identify the main properties of simple and effective reputation mechanisms in e-procurement platforms and e-markets in general, including their role in attracting entry of new participants. Given the importance of reputation, they also examine how to prevent the possibility of untruthful feedback that could destroy the value of reputational mechanisms. Finally, they suggest how to implement reputation mechanisms in public procurement.

Innovation has become a crucial competitive determinant for firms and countries as a whole. Chapter 19 discusses optimal procurement design for direct acquisitions of innovative knowledge and goods, and indirect procurement methods that stimulate innovation among a firm's network of suppliers, or in a region, industry or country. As for direct methods, it discusses and provides guidance on whether a procurer should use *ex ante* or *ex post* prizes rather than a contest or the award of intellectual property rights to obtain a certain innovation or a highly innovative good. Regarding indirect methods, the authors discuss how the choice of a new technological standard from a large buyer can and should be made; how procurement risk management techniques should be modified when innovation is a crucial concern; and a number of other practical procurement design methodologies that can foster innovation among suppliers, at both the macro and micro levels.

2 The variety of procurement practice: evidence from public procurement

Laura Carpineti, Gustavo Piga and Matteo Zanza

2.1. Introduction

Efficient procurement practices, both private and public, play a key role in modern economies as they ensure reduction of wasteful activities. Achieving such efficiency is an ambitious task, as procurement faces numerous challenges, especially due to the market structure, the legal framework, and the political environment that procurers face.[1]

Although reaching efficiency always implies experimenting with new methods and techniques of tendering, and although at a single point in time these might also vary depending on the level of development of institutions, market and the economic well-being of the given country, one should expect that procurement practices would tend to converge after controlling for all these factors.

Indeed, in recent years public and private procurement players have set up several initiatives and networks aimed at sharing best procurement practices. Some examples are the International Federation of Purchasing and Materials Management (IFPMM),[2] the International Purchasing and Supply Education and Research Association (IPSERA),[3] the Public

---

[1] K. V. Thai (2004).

[2] The IFPMM is the union of forty-two national and regional purchasing associations worldwide, private and public. Its objective is to facilitate the development and distribution of knowledge to elevate and advance the procurement profession, thus favourably impacting the standard of living of citizens worldwide through improved business practices.

[3] IPSERA is a multi-disciplinary network of academics and practitioners dedicated to the development of knowledge concerning purchasing and supply management.

Procurement Network (PPN)[4] and the EU Public Procurement Learning Lab (EU Lab).[5]

Box 2.1. The EU Public Procurement Learning Lab (2003–2005)

The EU Public Procurement Learning Lab is an informal network among public procurement entities across Europe. The objective of the initiative is to exchange best practices and experiences in the field of public purchases and strengthen networking activities. The kick-off meeting took place in Rome in November 2003 and three working groups were created to develop the following topics: 'Procurement and Small and Medium Enterprise', 'Technical Issues of Procurement', 'Competitive Tendering Design and Competitive Issues'.[6] A description of the working groups' activity is given in Appendix 2.1. Each working group was expected to provide an overview of the EU practices on the topic developed, supported by data, cases, examples, etc. Information collected in this chapter results from the activity of the third working group. Detailed questionnaires were distributed to collect data on key aspects of procurement design (see Appendix 2.3). The success achieved in 2004 induced participants to carry on the EU Lab Initiative also in 2005, by advancing the studies on competitive tendering design and on SMEs and developing a new benchmark on procurement strategies for specific product categories. The study on 'Competitive Tendering Design', relevant for the case studies of this chapter, was more focused on the topic of purchasing of specific product categories, namely paper for printers.[7]

Overall, thirty-five institutions representative of twenty-seven countries participated in the seven meetings organized between 2003 and 2005 (taking place in Italy [2], the United Kingdom, Sweden, France, Cyprus, and Belgium [1]).

This chapter aims at pointing out similarities and differences in public procurement practices. We leave the issue of evaluating these practices to the other chapters of this book; nevertheless the reader will find some links to

---

[4] The PPN is an international cooperation network of public procurement expert officials involving European states. The PPN's aim is to strengthen the application of the EU procurement rules through a mutual exchange of experience and benchmarking and to promote problem solving in cross-border cases relating to public procurement. Noteworthy is the PPN's report on 'Public Procurement in Europe'.

[5] See Box 2.1.

[6] See G. Piga and M. Zanza (2004).

[7] EU Lab Report on 'Purchasing of Fix-line telephone services and Paper for Printers'.

these chapters in order to understand the issue of what is best practice according to accepted economic principles. The chapter does not describe private practices, which are generally less regulated and might vary even more.

We focus on the main aspects of procurement design, stressing the differences in procedures across countries and pointing out, where possible, the rationale behind each choice. We base our analysis on the results of a benchmark analysis conducted in 2004 among a group of European and American public procurement institutions, also taking advantage of the wave of centralization in public procurement that occurred in the late 1990s (see Chapter 3 for more on this). In some cases, a comparison between European and US legislation is provided. Appendices 2.1 and 2.2 at the end of the chapter describe the European and American procurement institutions involved in the survey, while Appendix 2.3 describes the questionnaires distributed in 2004 and 2005.

Practices adopted in public procurement point to substantial differences that might not be justified by the different economic conditions of each country, particularly in the light of the international legislative actions (eg., the 2004 EU Directive or the 2005 US Federal Acquisition Regulation) aimed at streamlining and harmonizing the procurement processes.

The chapter is organized as follows. In section 2.2. we describe the general principles of procurement: the tendency to centralize and the mechanisms to achieve quality in procurement relationships. Section 2.3. provides data about the procurement design chosen by the surveyed institutions, with emphasis on tendering processes, electronic tendering, lots, reserve price, and disclosure policy. Section 2.4. deals with mechanisms adopted to attract and screen participants such as joint bidding, subcontracting, abnormally low tenders and awarding constraints. Section 2.5. finally illustrates the practices to increase competition and to avoid collusion in competitive tendering. Concluding remarks are in section 2.6. Paragraphs are grouped together to best fit the Handbook organization.[8]

2.2. General principles

2.2.1. Centralization

The choice between centralizing or decentralizing purchases is a new strategic topic that raises several questions and challenges for both the public and

---

[8] Issues studied in Part V of this Handbook are not covered here as they were not considered in the relevant questionnaires.

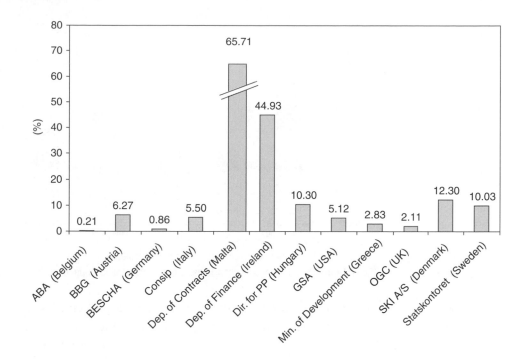

Figure 2.1. Purchased value as a percentage of total public procurement, 2003
Sources: Purchased values relative to 2003: Questionnaires; data for GSA refer to 2004 and have been provided directly by the institution.
We adopted the total public procurement which is openly advertised as a percentage of GDP relative to year 2003: EUROSTAT. Data are based on information contained in the calls for competition and contract award notices submitted for publication in the Official Journal of the European Communities. Data on total public procurement for Department of contracts (Malta) and for Directorate for public Procurement (Hungary) have been provided directly by the institutions. GDP 2003: EUROSTAT.

private practices of procurement. Chapter 3 of this volume shows that partial centralization is becoming the prevailing strategy.

Figure 2.1 shows the ratio between the surveyed central procurement bodies' purchased value and the total public procurement in different European Countries and in the United States – that is, purchases of goods, services, and public works by governments and public utilities. It makes clear that surveyed institutions award different shares of national public procurement.

2.2.2. Contract execution through qualified suppliers

Competitive procurements are usually open only to qualified suppliers, to guarantee good contract execution. To screen participants, the procurer can

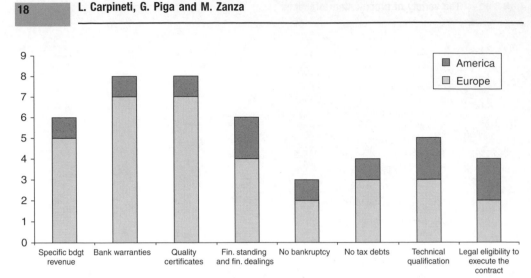

Figure 2.2.   Number of surveyed countries that adpted a given participation requirement
Notes: America: GSA from the USA and the Brazilian Federal Government (see Appendix 2.2).

use participation requirements that aim at guaranteeing participants with sufficient legal and technical qualifications, excluding at the same time the inadequate ones. For information about quality in the procurement contract see Chapter 4. Almost all organizations surveyed restrict participation to the bidding phase by requiring technical, economical and legal qualifications. However, the type and the number of qualifications requested of suppliers varies across procuring institutions and countries. This may be explained on the ground of different procurement legislation but also, and most important, on the ground of different strategies in terms of type (figure 2.2) and/or number (figure 2.3) of required qualifications.

More than half of the institutions surveyed require suppliers to satisfy three to five parameters in order to enter the competitive tendering. Moreover, requirements vary according to (i) the nature of the good/service being procured and (ii) the degree of desired participation in the competitive tendering (e.g., weaker participation requirements may facilitate participation of SMEs).

But what can a procurer do in the case of a poor performance during the execution of the contract? Several institutions declare that in case of contractors' poor performance the contracting authority can cancel the contract. However, often the contracting authorities do not apply this clause because re-tendering the object of the contract is too expensive.

In this context, a bidder's reputation and past performances may represent an important element for the selection of suppliers. This aspect is treated in Chapter 4. A specific participation requirement may be the use of a bidder's reputation in the awarding phase. The French institution disqualifies

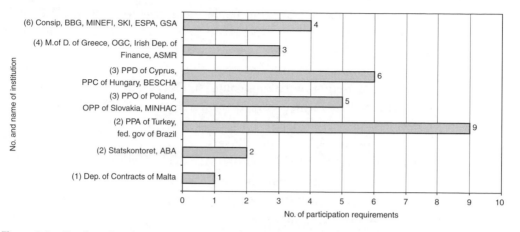

Figure 2.3. Number of participation requirements requested (Europe and America)
Notes: America: GSA from the USA and the Brazilian federal government (see Appendix 2.2).

candidates on the basis of poor performance in previous contracts. This practice is also adopted by the American Federal Acquisition Regulation, which requires the government to do business only with 'responsible contractors', defined to mean those who have, among other requirements, a satisfactory record of past performance.[9] For a more detailed analysis of bidders' reputation as a tool to stimulate better performance see Chapters 13 and 18.

2.3. Procurement design

2.3.1. Tendering processes

2.3.1.1. Sealed bid tendering

There are many kind of competitive tendering formats available to procurers, as explained in Chapters 4, 5, and 6.

All organizations involved in the survey, both European and American, usually award contracts using paper-based sealed bid tendering.[10] They do so for two main reasons:

---

[9] FAR 9.104–1 (d).

[10] Suppliers submit bids in sealed envelopes; the bidder submitting the best bid, i.e., the highest discount or the best offer, wins the contract and pays what it bids; as explained in section 2.3.1.4, sealed bid single round tendering can be performed also on-line (bids are submitted in secured files). The electronically based sealed-bid tendering presents the same advantages of paper- based sealed-bid one.

- *Process simplification*: sealed bid tendering is easy to implement; the less complicated the tendering process, the lower will be the probability that losing participants appealing in court will win.
- *Competition*: some institutions explicitly recognize the advantage of sealed bid tendering in making collusion less sustainable with respect to other competitive formats (e.g., descending auctions). See Chapter 14 for a detailed analysis on this.

It is important to underline that buyers may use other types of tendering processes, such as second-price tendering.[11] Some institutions consider this format potentially useful, but they never adopt it because of legal constraints; in Italy, for instance, second-price tendering cannot be adopted since the law prescribes that the winner must pay the price it bid. Apart from legal restrictions, there are also economic reasons for not using second-price tendering. In fact, under some circumstances, it may favour corruption, as explained in Chapter 16.

2.3.1.2. Combinatorial tendering process

Only few institutions surveyed apply this process, and for different product categories. For instance, the Procurement Directorate of Cyprus performs combinatorial tendering with package bidding mainly for commodities (e.g., laboratory consumables), while the Brazilian federal government adopts this format especially for works and services. Consip, the Italian-procurement agency, decided to perform combinatorial tendering for telecommunication services, furniture and fresh fruits and vegetables. From collected data we are not able to define the reason these institutions apply this particular tendering format. However, combinatorial tendering formats may present advantages and disadvantages with respect to traditional sealed bidding procedures. For a detailed analysis of this see Chapter 8.

2.3.1.3. Two-stage sealed bid tendering Process

Some administrations allow the procurement of goods using a two-stage tendering process whereby in the first stage all n suppliers are evaluated on the basis of some criterion and in the second stage $(n-i)$ $(0 \leq i \leq n-2)$ suppliers compete again for the contract award.

The US Federal Acquistion Regulation (FAR) allows two-step sealed bidding (Article 14.5). It is 'a combination of competitive procedures designed to obtain the benefits of sealed bidding when adequate specifications are not

---

[11] See the Glossary.

available. "Step one consists of the request for, submission, evaluation, and (if necessary) discussion of a technical proposal, without involving pricing. The objective is to determine the acceptability of the supplies or services offered." Step two involves the submission of sealed price bids by those who submitted acceptable technical proposals in step one.'

The French organization, MINEFI, recently implemented a two-stage multi-awarding system for PCs and paper for printers (two-stage tendering process). In the first stage (open competition) several suppliers are selected on the basis of quality only. Admitted suppliers regularly compete over price in the second stage (restricted competition).

Recently, the new EU Directive allowed the use of a new two-stage tendering format, the framework agreement, where in the first stage several suppliers are selected on the basis of price and possibly quality (open competition) and in the second stage only admitted ones (or a subset of these) regularly compete over price and/or quality (restricted competition).[12]

2.3.1.4. Online (descending) auctions

Besides sealed bid single-round and two-stage tendering formats, procurement institutions may also opt for a multi-round tendering format, the so-called descending auction, which can also be performed online. Different from standard paper-based tendering, it is a common feeling among the surveyed institutions that an online auction is very useful because it allows the use of different kinds of auction formats (see Chapter 6). A noteworthy case of US procurement agency adopting online auctions is the federal General Service Administration (GSA).[13] This procurer set up a website[14] offering to registered suppliers the opportunity of bidding electronically on a wide array of products. Auctions are completely web-enabled, allowing participants to bid on a single item or multiple items (lots) within specified timeframes.

Besides electronic sealed bid competitive tendering, the institutions surveyed adopt two different formats: dynamic auctions and multi-round

---

[12] We abstract from the cases allowed by the Directive (i) that the first stage selects only one supplier, in which case there is no second-stage competition; (ii) that at the first stage the procurer fixes the price and quality parameters for all suppliers without allowing a second stage.

[13] A description of GSA is given in Appendix 2.2.

[14] www.gsaauctions.gov.

descending auctions.[15] These solutions provide the procurer different functionalities, such as:

- Bid decrements: the minimum level by which a supplier can reduce the bid compared with the previous lowest one. From the survey it emerges that an institution establishes the maximum amount of discount that the bidder may submit at each stage.
- Extensions: this aspect is related only to the descending auction format. This auction can have a fixed time period (e.g., two hours), or it can operate with extensions. Two institutions run online auctions of a certain planned duration (e.g., thirty minutes), but if any bids are received within the last five minutes then the online auction is given a five-minute extension. This continues until there is a five-minute period of inactivity.
- Weightings: more complex online auctions will allow suppliers to update their bids with respect to any component, that is, both price and quality, when the latter is objectively measurable.

2.3.2. Electronic tendering procedure

ICT development has increased the scope for electronically based procurement. The new EU Directive on the coordination of procedures for the award of public works contracts, public supply contracts and public service contracts, adopted in March 2004, acknowledges the application of online auctions and affirms that 'Since use of the technique of electronic auctions is likely to increase, such auctions should be given a Community definition and governed by specific rules' (Whereas n. 14 of the EC Directive). In the United States, e-procurement tools started to be adopted in the mid-1990s. A recent study[16] points out that e-procurement tools are rapidly spreading over US states, but reverse auctions in 2001 were utilized by only one state out of ten.

Our survey indicates that electronically based procedures are becoming important; in fact ten institutions have taken advantage of at least one

---

[15] See the Glossary. In particular, one institution designed online auctions with a limited or unlimited number of rounds: in the multiple-round format the number of rounds can be decided before the beginning of the procedure or can depend on the bidding activity of participants. In this case it will be very important to fix a bid decrement in order to reduce the possible number of rounds. See Chapter 6 for a more detailed analysis.

[16] M. J. Moon (2005).

electronic competitive tendering (both one-shot and/or reverse).[17] The institutions surveyed explain their choices differently. First, they are claimed to be useful to improve procurement performance – process simplification and innovation, quickening of the tendering process, costs savings – particularly for the awarding of standardized products (goods that can be specified very clearly and that are often evaluated only in terms of price). Indeed, this mechanism guarantees an automatic scoring of the received tenders where there is no need of a discretional evaluation by a commission of experts.[18]

Second, one institution considers the adoption of online tendering procedures useful because it reduces entry barriers, since participants may submit an offer without being physically present. This statement is only partially true because technological tools can also be an entry barrier, when bidders are not confident about ICT solutions.

2.3.3. Lots

It is common practice among institutions surveyed to divide the contract into lots.[19] Only two institutions do not usually split procurement contracts into lots.

This choice is crucial because it may have very important consequences in terms of competition in the short and long run (for a more detailed analysis of the relationship between the number of lots and competition see Chapter 7). However, even though the majority of institutions split contracts into lots, the main reasons behind this choice vary among them (see figure 2.4).

Institutions split contracts into lots to (i) promote participation in a competitive tendering[20] and in future procurements (having more lots means increasing the probability of awarding lots to more than one supplier, and thus the potential to optimally manage competition on procurements over

---

[17] Three institutions performed electronic tenders below and above the threshold defined in the Official Journal of the EC; instead the German institution ran online auctions only below the EU threshold.

[18] Some examples of products and services that usually need to be evaluated by a commission are consultancy services and global services. Nevertheless, the World Bank Group implemented an e-procurement solution for the selection of consultants (K. Leipold, J. Klemow, F. Holloway, et al. 2004).

[19] Two institutions award 50% of their frame contracts through multiple-lots competitive tendering; Consip splits 40% of its frame contracts into lots; one institution states that usually large supply contracts are divided into lots.

[20] Smaller lots give suppliers the opportunity to bid on just a part of the contract.

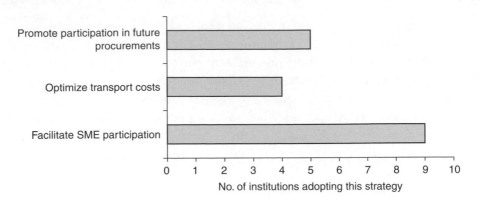

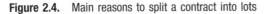

Figure 2.4.   Main reasons to split a contract into lots

time);[21] (ii) to optimize transport costs in the presence of relevant geographical dispersion of suppliers; (iii) to facilitate SME participation.

To favour the participation of SMEs, the US legislation allows for set-asides. The FAR (19.5) states that 'the purpose of small business set-asides is to award certain acquisitions exclusively to small business concerns. A "set-aside for small business" is the reserving of an acquisition exclusively for participation by small business concerns.' Moreover, in the United States there is specific legislation supporting SMEs through the Small Business Administration (SBA) founded in 1953.

Contrary to the United States case, the EU Directive does not allow for set-asides. Therefore, in the light of the increasing centralization of procurement activity pervading the European Union, SMEs have to face even more difficulties to be awarded a public procurement contract.[22]

Finally, even if almost all institutions divide the frame contracts into lots, they do not follow a common strategy when deciding the number and the type of lots. Five institutions surveyed state that the decision is influenced by market structure. One institution declares that the number of lots should be lower than the number of suppliers expected to bid, as suggested by the national Antitrust Authority. This should prevent bidders from 'splitting the cake' through collusion. However, as explained in Chapter 7, this may not be always true.

Case study 2.1 describes how European institutions chose different strategies in terms of number and kind of lots for the same product category. Norms also matter in understanding national choices. For example,

---

[21] See Chapters 7 and 11.

[22] Further information on 'the Access of SMEs to Public Procurement Contracts' in Europe is provided by a report edited by EIM Business and Policy Research and commissioned by the EU Commission.

Consip and the Austrian organization, BBG varying operate under a normative framework that, although varies over time, has required Italian and Austrian purchasing units to either buy from the institutions or take their prices as reference. In this case, political and competitive considerations might have prompted the institutions' officials to enlarge the number of lots, not to restrict further the number of suppliers for the public sector.

Case study 2.1. Division into lots for the paper for printers procurement

During 2005, a benchmark procurement design applied to a specific product category was implemented within the EU Lab (see Box 2.1).

Table 2.1 reports the number and type of lots designed by the procurement agencies when procuring paper for printers: lots can be quantitative (lots containing the same product and referring to the same geographical area), geographical (lots that refer to different geographical areas), and qualitative (lots containing different types of product).

Table 2.1. Strategies adopted by the institutions in choosing number and type of lots

Institution	No. of lots	Geographical lots	Qualitative lots	Quantitative lots
ABA	1	—	—	—
BBG	3	x	—	—
Consip	12	x	—	—
Irish GSA	2	—	—	x
Hanse	12	—	x	—
MINEFI	1	—	—	—
OGC	3	—	x	—
PPD	2	—	x	—
SKI	1	—	—	—
Statskontoret	1	—	—	—
UMIC	4	x	x	—

The table shows the variety of strategies adopted. In fact, four institutions opted for a sole source, while Consip split the contract into twelve lots. According to the type of lots, three institutions divided them by adopting a geographical rationale, four institutions opted for a qualitative one, and only the Irish GSA divided the frame contract in two quantitative lots. UMIC from Portugal is the only institution that awarded both geographical and qualitative lots.[23]

---

[23] The first two lots were for virgin A4 paper, while lots number 3 and 4 contained standard A3 paper. Geographical lots considered the 'Lisbon Area' and 'rest of the country'.

For a more detailed analysis of the effects of lot division and lot awarding see Chapters 7, 11 and 14.

2.3.4. Reserve price

The reserve price is the maximum amount the procurement entity is willing to pay for a certain good or service. Setting the reserve price at a high or low level can have different consequences in terms of participation and awarding price (for more details see also Chapters 11, 14 and 15).

Many organizations surveyed do not publish the reserve price (thus they do not use it) since they consider it an estimate that does not necessarily have to be disclosed to bidders, and as an internal expectation of the price that the result of a competitive mechanism should not exceed. For instance, some institutions claim that the publication of the reserve price could facilitate collusive behaviour. In contrast, seven institutions publish the reserve price before the competitive tendering, and some of them do so in order to avoid cartels. The publication of the reserve price can also have consequences for the procurer in terms of participation and awarding price. For instance, five institutions fix the reserve price at a sufficiently high level, with the objective of attracting more bidders to the competitive process and, consequently, of fostering competition among them. A more detailed analysis of the consequences of reserve price setting is presented in Chapter 11.

Concerning the procedure adopted to calculate the reserve price (or the expected price), the institutions exploit

- Information from the suppliers' side and from previous contracts awarded. Usually, the value of the reserve price is calculated on the basis of the average price that prevails in the market at the awarding date (resulting from internal market analysis), economic indicators, and, when available, the previous awarding price. In other cases, it can result after a discussion with the suppliers invited to the competitive bidding (as established for instance by the EU Directive within the competitive dialogue).
- Information from the demand side. Two institutions cooperate with public administrations in order to ascertain their purchasing costs. In Italy, these data are provided by the National Institute of Statistics (ISTAT).

2.3.5. Disclosure policy

The amount and the kind of information disclosed on the competitive tendering may have positive or negative effects in terms of risk of collusion among bidders (see Chapters 6, 14, and 15 for a more detailed evaluation). The US FAR states that 'Contracting officers must publicize contract actions in order to (a) Increase competition; (b) Broaden industry participation in meeting Government requirements; and (c) Assist small business concerns, etc.'[24]

The survey shows that each country has specific rules about information disclosure polices. As a general result, the information about tender features disclosed before the awarding of the contract is similar among the institutions surveyed. For instance, the number of expected bidders is rarely published before the competitive bidding. Only one institution does it to stimulate competitive offers since, with a high number of expected bidders, giving out this information encourages bidders to be more aggressive.[25]

In contrast, institutions behave differently in terms of information disclosed after the bidding phase takes place. In 2005, a new survey about disclosure policy was conducted. The institutions were sent a questionnaire asking what information is disclosed before and after the awarding of the contract. Figure 2.5 indicates that there is no common strategy in dispatching information after the bidding phase.[26] In fact, some institutions dispatch only information about the winner, while others disclose data about losing participants too. This is the case for the American institution, which, by law, discloses the number of offers solicited, the number of offers received, the quantities and unit price (in general terms) of each award, and, in general terms, the reasons for a bidder's proposal not being selected (FAR 15.503(b)).

---

[24] FAR 5.002.

[25] The institution recognizes that, in the case of a low number of expected bidders, publishing the number of expected participants could keep their offered prices higher. This is why it does not commit to publishing the number of expected participants.

[26] Thirteen institutions answered the new questionnaire, namely, ABA (Belgium), BBG (Austria), BESCHA (Germany), Consip (Italy), Department of Contracts (Malta), MINEFI (France), Ministry of Development (Greece), Department of Finance (Ireland), PMB (Latvia), PPD (Cyprus), PPO (Serbia), SKI (Denmark), UMIC (Portugal).

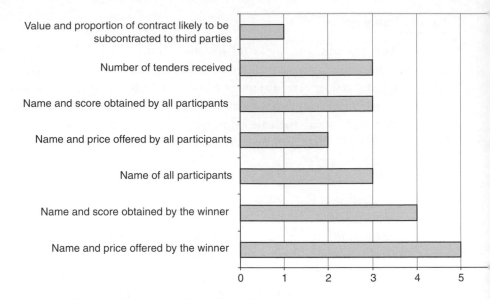

Figure 2.5.   Information disclosed after the awarding of the contract

2.3.6. Awarding criteria

Procurement contracts can be awarded on the basis of two broad criteria: the lowest price and the most economically advantageous tendering (MEAT). In the latter, non-price aspects are also taken into account (for more on this see Chapter 12). Responses pointed out that for the majority of institutions price is not sufficient to identify the best offer; in fact, there are other relevant aspects to be considered, usually characteristics of the item or additional related services that improve the overall quality of the supply. In other words, the higher the complexity of the supply, the more non-price attributes become important in the offer evaluation process.

In contrast, the lowest-price procedure is very suitable for procurement of products where price is the only relevant factor (e.g., in some cases energy procurement, food and office equipment).

Case study 2.2. Awarding criteria for the paper for printers procurement

The survey conducted on paper for printers shows that, for the same product categories, three institutions out of eleven chose the lowest price, and the rest adopted the MEAT. Among these, the weights assigned to the price and technical aspects differ substantially.

Table 2.2. Awarding criteria adopted by the institutions

Institution	Awarding date	Price	Quality	Others
ABA	May 2005	50%	30%	Ecological aspects: 20%
Consip	June 2005	96%	4%	
Irish GSA	June 2003	32%	68%	
Hansel	November 2004	75%	10%	Services: 15%
MINEFI	October 2003	First stage: 0	First stage: 100%	
		Second stage: 100%	Second stage: 0	
OGC	February 2005	40%	60%	
SKI	September 2003	70%	30%	
Statskontoret	January 2003	50%	50%	

Scoring rules are necessary when non-price attributes are relevant elements of the supply. The responses to the questionnaires point out that in many circumstances, institutions adopt a specific scoring rule for different procurements. However, scoring rules adopted vary across countries.

Example 2.1. Formula usually adopted by Consip (Italy)

$$\mathrm{TP} = \mathrm{PE} + \mathrm{PT}, \quad \text{and}$$

$$\mathrm{PE} = n * \frac{P_B - P_o}{P_B - P_S},$$

where PE = economic points (obtained as a function of offered price), PT = technical points; n = maximum economic points available, P_S = threshold price (price that assigns the maximum number of points), P_O = price offered, P_B = reserve price.

Example 2.2. Formula usually adopted by PPD (Cyprus)

$$\text{Total score} = \frac{\mathrm{TP}_x}{\mathrm{TP}_{\max}} + \frac{\text{Minimum price}}{P_x},$$

where TP_x = technical points of bidder x, $\mathrm{TP}_{\max}$ = technical points of the best technical offer, Minimum price = lowest price offered, P_x = price offered by bidder x.

The choice of the scoring rule is crucial in designing competitive tendering procurement, as different scoring rules have different features that may affect the competitors' behaviour. For a more detailed analysis of scoring rules see Chapter 12.

2.3.7. Single awarding or multiple awarding

An important strategy that a procurer should take into account when designing a competitive procurement mechanism is the choice of the number of winning bidders. Both the FAR and the new EU Directive seem to formalize the concept of multiple awarding. In some cases the FAR gives to public entities the possibility of setting up 'Multiple Award Scheduling'.[27] European procurement agencies may award a 'framework agreement'[28] to more than one supplier (at least three). The Danish, the French, the

---

[27] FAR 8.401: 'Multiple Award Schedule (MAS)' means contracts awarded by GSA or the Department of Veterans' Affairs (VA) for similar or comparable supplies, or services, established with more than one supplier, at varying prices.

[28] A framework agreement is an agreement between one or more contracting authorities and one or more economic operators, the purpose of which is to establish the terms governing contracts to be awarded during a given period, in particular with regard to price and, where appropriate, the quantity envisaged. The awarding of contracts based on framework agreements is in general more flexible than that of frame contracts; in fact in framework agreements there can be a choice between multiple operators and/or a 'second-stage competition' on one or more economic variables that in frame contracts tend to be fully pre-determined. According to EU Directive 18/2004 the second-stage competition for framework agreements must comply with the following procedures: 'Where a framework agreement is concluded with a single economic operator, contracts based on that agreement shall be awarded within the limits of the terms laid down in the framework agreement. For the award of those contracts, contracting authorities may consult the operator party to the framework agreement in writing, requesting it to supplement its tender as necessary.' 'Contracts based on framework agreements concluded with several economic operators may be awarded either – by application of the terms laid down in the framework agreement without reopening competition, or – where not all the terms are laid down in the framework agreement, when the parties are again in competition on the basis of the same and, if necessary, more precisely formulated terms, and, where appropriate, other terms referred to in the specifications of the framework agreement, in accordance with the following procedure: (a) for every contract to be awarded, contracting authorities shall consult in writing the economic operators capable of performing the contract; (b) contracting authorities shall fix a time limit which is sufficiently long to allow tenders for each specific contract to be submitted, taking into account factors such as the complexity of the subject-matter of the contract and the time needed to send in tenders; (c) tenders shall be submitted in writing, and their content shall remain confidential until the stipulated time limit for reply has expired; (d) contracting authorities shall award each contract to the tenderer who has submitted the best tender on the basis of the award criteria set out in the specifications of the framework agreement.'

Swedish, and the UK institutions have already adopted parallel framework agreements signed with a number of competitively selected suppliers.[29] The public administrations may then (i) directly purchase from one of the suppliers, after previously justifying the necessity of excluding the others or (ii) reopen the tendering process among suppliers in order to obtain a better result. See Chapter 4 for a more careful evaluation of these aspects. Results make it clear that institutions do not follow the same strategy.

For a more detailed analysis of single and multiple awarding see Chapters 7 and 11.

2.3.8. Contract duration

The choice of supply contract duration may reflect particular features of the good being procured (see Chapters 4 and 14), taking into account national legislation (for instance the EU Directive states that 'The term of a framework agreement may not exceed four years').[30] However, responses to the questionnaire show that institutions are free to optimally fine-tune the duration according to the characteristics of the good/service being procured. In fact, the practice shows that framework duration may vary from a minimum of one year to a maximum of five.[31]

> **Case study 2.3.** Contract duration for the paper for printers procurement
>
> In the specific case of paper for printers, the benchmark analysis shows that the institutions decided to fix a different duration for the contract, even though the product category procured is the same. In fact, the duration varies from three months to thirty-six.

---

[29] The Danish institution usually selects between three and ten suppliers, while in Sweden this number strictly depends on the goods purchased. For instance, for PCs there are about six or seven suppliers, while they may reach fifty in the case of IT consultancy. In the French case of PC purchasing three suppliers were selected for each lot. Every three months the competition is reopened among them. The French institution does not procure for other public administrations. Framework agreements set up by this institution are described in section 2.3.1.3.

[30] Article 53.

[31] The institutions involved in the survey award mainly goods and services. For public works the duration may turn out to be longer than five years.

Table 2.3. Contract duration

Institution	Duration of the contract (months)
ABA	36
BBG	3
Consip	18
Hansel	36
MINEFI	24
Irish GSA	36
OGC	36
PPD	4
SKI	30
Statskontoret	36
UMIC	12

2.4. Attracting and screening participants

2.4.1. Joint bidding

Joint bidding allows two or more suppliers to group together and bid as a single larger entity. This is particularly useful for small and medium-sized enterprises wishing to compete for large procurement contracts. Moreover, joint bidding enables small (very often financially weak) specialized suppliers to pool resources and skills to service more complex procurement (such as facility management, IT projects, etc.).

The survey shows that the majority of procurement agencies allow joint bidding. Differences, however, emerge in relation to the restrictions applied to suppliers that group together, which are usually meant to increase competitiveness during the tendering process. This is confirmed by the fact that two institutions follow the indications provided by national antitrust authorities, prescribing that the level of competition in the competitive tendering is enhanced if grouping is prevented between two or more suppliers capable of submitting individual bids, while allowing it between suppliers that cannot on their own fulfil the requested services. For other institutions, grouping of suppliers is not regulated and suppliers may group even if they are able to bid by themselves as long as the aim or the effect of grouping is not a restriction of competition; genuine bidding consortia are allowed, whereas collusive bidding is subject to challenge and legal proceedings.

The regulation of grouping is clearly important in order to optimize the procurement strategy. A bad regulation of joint bidding can have significant negative consequences in terms of bidders' collusive behaviour and competition (for a more detailed analysis see Chapter 14).

2.4.2. Subcontracting

Subcontracting is an important factor of procurement design. In principle, it may facilitate the participation of minor suppliers. For example, the recent European Directive states that 'in order to encourage the involvement of small and medium-sized undertakings in the public contracts procurement market, it is advisable to include provisions on subcontracting' (Whereas n. 32).

In the United States, FAR regulates subcontracting and specifically included clauses aimed at involving the Small Business Administration in the programme (FAR 19.7).

Procurement agencies rely on subcontracting practice. Nineteen out of twenty-one institutions grant the possibility of subcontracting to winning suppliers.

2.4.2.1. Ceiling to subcontracting

The institutions surveyed regulate and design subcontracting in different ways. Some require suppliers to specify the fraction they will subcontract before bidding, while others allow it after bidding. Further, the fraction suppliers can subcontract varies across countries, as does the way monitoring of subcontracted activities takes place.

The survey shows that institutions approach subcontracting in different ways. For instance, in terms of the fraction of the contract that can be subcontracted,

- Among those institutions that allow for subcontracting, sixteen do not impose any ceiling;
- Only three institutions impose ceilings on subcontracting; two of them allow contractors to subcontract no more than 50 percent of the value of the contract. In the Italian case, the ceiling is 30 percent of the value of the supply contract, and in public works the winner can subcontract only complementary services and/or goods;

- As recommended by the Italian Antitrust Authority, subcontracting to large suppliers that are eligible to enter the competitive tendering (but that do not) as well as to those that have competed in the competitive mechanisms is forbidden. Similarly, in Sweden it is required that suppliers that bid for a framework contract in the first stage but that failed to receive it are not allowed to become subcontractors.
- One institution stated that the quota depends on the type of contract to be awarded.

2.4.2.2. Subcontracting before or after the competitive tendering

In the context of subcontracting it is important to consider when the decision is made. In fact, when subcontracting is decided after the framework contract, in the absence of specific regulation collusion can occur among participants (e.g., the winner subcontracts to losers). Among the institutions surveyed the possibility of subcontracting only before the competitive tendering is present in eleven cases, while six institutions grant the possibility of subcontracting before and after the competitive mechanism.

2.4.2.3. Monitoring of subcontracting

It is important to understand how monitoring of the subcontract is managed in a centralized context where frame contacts or framework agreements have been signed. Two possible solutions are available: central institutions that sign the frame contract can directly monitor how the subcontract is executed or leave this responsibility to the purchasing entity. Answers to the questionnaire show that the latter is more common among institutions. In fact, nine institutions leave it to the purchasing units to monitor subcontracting. Only five do it directly, especially for IT products. Finally, one institution grants the whole responsibility to execute the contract and to manage the subcontractors to the prime contractor.

2.4.3. Abnormally low tenders

Article 51 of the 2004 EU Directive states that 'If, for a given contract, tenders appear to be abnormally low in relation to the goods, works or services, the contracting authority shall, before it may reject those tenders, request in writing details of the constituent elements of the tender which it considers relevant'. According to the US FAR, offers are abnormally low if they do not seem 'fair and reasonable' compared with the expected price.[32]

Abnormally low tenders are a concern for procurers since the contractor may under-perform or even go bankrupt.

Example 2.1. Identification of abnormally low tendering in Brazil

Step 1: Suppose that the estimated price of the procurer is $120 US. First, the procurer calculates 50 percent of this value ($120 × 50% = $60).

Step 2: It then identifies the offers that are higher than $60 and calculates the average ($65 + $80 + $110)/3 = $85.

Step 3: It selects the lowest between the average price, resulting from step 2 ($85), and the estimated price ($120). Then it calculates the value that is 70% below this amount ($25.5).

Step 4: Offers that are lower than $25.5 are considered abnormally low. In our example, bid 1 is abnormally low; bid 2 is not.

Bids received	$
Bid 1	22
Bid 2	40
Bid 3	**65**
Bid 4	**80**
Bid 5	**110**

From the questionnaires what emerges is that when a competitive tendering results in an abnormally low price compared with other offers, market prices, or the institution's own costs estimation, the contracting authority (or the evaluation commission) is obliged to invite the bidder to justify its price quotation; if the supplier is not able to justify its offer, the offer is considered abnormally low and rejected. In fact there is great variety across countries as to how abnormal offers should be evaluated. For instance, the Brazilian institution defines a complex mechanism[33] (other

---

[32] The FAR does not define the term 'fair and reasonable' but the US Office of the Under Secretary of Defense for Acquisition, Technology, and Logistics considers 'fair' those offers in line with (or below) either (i) the fair market value of the contract deliverable or (ii) the total allowable cost of providing the contract deliverable that would have been incurred by a well-managed, responsible procurer using reasonably efficient and economical methods of performance plus a reasonable profit. Those offers that a buyer would be willing to pay, given available data on economic forces such as supply, demand, general economic conditions and competition, are called 'resonable'.

[33] Other methods adopted to prove that bids are unrealistic are provided by A. R. Engel and A. Wambach (2005). For example, in Peru the procurement agency calculates the average and then

examples are given in Chapters 13 and 19): the procurer should request justification when a supplier presents a price that is 70 percent lower than the lowest of the following values: (i) the arithmetic average between tendering prices that are higher than 50 percent of the estimated price set by the administration; (ii) the estimated price set by the administration.

Evaluation and exclusion of abnormally low offers may be conducted in such a way as to turn down a truly innovative and convenient offer or distort offers by procurers. There are also other useful instruments to prevent risk, such as surety bonds. An analysis of the risk associated with abnormally low tenders and the best methods to deal with them is presented in Chapter 13.

2.4.4. Awarding constraints

An awarding constraint limits the fraction of supply (or the lots) that each participant can be awarded. The potential effects of using awarding constraints in terms of participation, competition, and collusion are discussed in Chapter 7. The survey revealed that many agencies do not use awarding constraints, while those deciding to use this clause (six institutions), provide different reasons leading to this choice:

- Avoiding lock-in. Awarding constraints are used with the positive intent of preventing monopoly in the market or to promote the creation of new markets, because they guarantee the procurement fom more than one supplier. In the United States the procurer may impose awarding constraints in order to avoid lock-in (FAR 6.202).[34] In contrast, the EU Directive does not regulate this specific aspect (see also Chapters 7 and 17).
- Increasing participation, in particular for SMEs which can afford to participate only in small lots.[35]

---

eliminates those bids that lie 10% above and below this average. The average of the remaining bids will be calculated again and the contract will be awarded to the bidder whose bid is immediately below the second average.

[34] The article states that 'Agencies may exclude a particular source from a contract action in order to establish or maintain an alternative source or sources for the supplies or services being acquired if the agency head determines that to do so would'.

[35] According to the theory, limiting the number of lots one can win prevents big suppliers from being awarded the whole supply. Consequently, SMEs have more possibilities of being awarded a lot and thus may be attracted to enter the competitive bidding. As a result, participation of SMEs increases expected competition by attracting more participants. However, by lowering the chances to win, all participants may be induced to submit more aggressive bids. Hence, the buyer can realize more savings.

2.5. Mechanisms to prevent collusion

In order to achieve a successful tendering process the procurer has to promote competition and deter collusive behaviour among participants in competitive tendering. Therefore, the procurement design should optimally account for such elements in order to obtain efficient outcomes (see Chapters 14 and 15).

The survey shows that procurement institutions approach the problem of deterring collusion mainly through the adoption of the sealed bid tendering format. In fact, this format reduces the possibility that each participant may have information about the offers of other participants. The surveyed institutions appear to be aware that sealed bidding can – other things being equal – reduce collusion.

In general, the fact that descending auctions make it possible to observe (even anonymous) deviations from pre-arranged collusive agreements among bidders and therefore make a cartel even more stable is not always understood. For instance, one agency considers online auctions a useful tool to prevent collusion because they have the effect of increasing the visibility of collusive behaviour, on the grounds that each participant has online information only about his bid.

Institutions adopt different strategies to minimize the risk of collusion in the competitive tendering:

- Forbidding controlled or affiliated suppliers from taking part in the offer;
- Establishing a number of lots not greater than the number of expected participants;
- Increasing the duration of contracts to avoid rotation among suppliers;
- Limiting/regulating the grouping of enterprises;
- Trying to facilitate the entry of SMEs, for example, by splitting the contract into lots;
- Examining bids with respect to expectations based on prior knowledge of the marketplace;
- Using available media to communicate tender notices so as to stimulate participation;
- One institution considers the reputation that the contracting authority has in professional circles (no hesitation to lodge a complaint with the antitrust authority in case of suspicions) to be the most effective strategy to avoid collusion among participants;

- Finally, one institution does not have a specific strategy to avoid collusion, since the detection process is based on denunciations (social control).

2.5.1. Interaction with the national antitrust authority

Interestingly, some institutions rely on interaction with the national anti-trust authorities to better deal with cartels. Cooperation between antitrust authorities and procurement agencies may be of great importance in order to prevent collusive behaviour, as explained in Chapter 15. Our survey shows that eleven institutions interact with the national antitrust authority.

Different approaches to interaction emerge:

- Advising: before performing a competitive tendering, some institutions ask the antitrust authority to give an opinion about the proposed tendering or about similar past ones. Even if the antitrust opinions are not binding, institutions take them into account while designing competitive mechanisms;
- A steering group shared between the two institutions looking at procurement strategy design;
- Sharing of information related to national or supranational guidelines;
- Cooperation aimed at identifying whether collusive behaviour took place in a competitive tendering.

2.6. Concluding remarks

This chapter pointed out similarities and differences in the public procurement sector by focusing on the main aspects that a responsible procurer should take into account in the design of procurement mechanisms.

Our survey showed the great variety of approaches to procurement design. Similarities also emerge, but very often the reasons provided to support one tool or strategy instead of another seem to be different and not fully consistent with optimal choices.

Certainly, it is important to underline that the survey did not control for the peculiarities of each country/contest, such as level of competition, legal and political frameworks, level of innovation in and centralization of public procurement, and geographical structure of the country. However, differences emerge even among some important procurement agencies operating in similar overall economic contexts (European Union) and under the same supranational regulation (European Directive).

Appendix 2.1. The 'EU Lab' initiative and participants

Description of the initiative

During the Greek Presidency of the European Union the 10th meeting of Ministers and the 40th meeting of Directors General of the Public Administration took place. Participant ministers considered it of vital importance to meet on a regular basis, in order to exchange practices and ideas in the areas of cooperation and give overall direction to activities within the network. In this context the 'EU Lab' instrument was considered the ideal tool to promote informal exchange of information and to establish a network among participants. During the Italian Presidency, the Italian Department of Public Administration, jointly with the Ministry of Economy and Finance, launched an EU Lab on public procurement, named the EU Public Procurement Learning Lab.

The objective of this initiative is to compare activities and to share useful knowledge among European procurement entities, in accordance with the resolution of the 11th meeting of European Ministers responsible for Public Administration. The kick-off meeting took place on 28 November 2003 in Rome and nineteen institutions, representative of sixteen countries, participated in the meeting. In 2004 participants focused their activities on three specific topics: 'Small and Medium-sized Firms,' 'Technical Issues', 'Competitive Tendering Design and Competitive Issues'. Every topic was developed by a working group in which institutions decided to participate according to their interest, and each group was coordinated by a 'Leading Country.' Consip took the role of 'General Coordinator' of the whole initiative.

The EU Lab in 2004

The EU Lab's activity is defined by the work of three working groups that focus on the main strategic aspects and issues related to public procurement.

The working group on 'Technical Issues' aims at sharing information among EU Lab members about technical, mainly ICT-related, aspects of public procurement. The main objective of the working group is to collect information about requirements that are necessary in each country for the suppliers willing to participate in electronic tendering. Examples of technicalities analysed are the introduction of digital signatures in e-tendering and the coordination of platform mechanisms to achieve cross-country compatibility.

The working group on 'SMEs' aims at identifying problems that different EU Lab members have experienced in terms of participation of small and medium-sized enterprises in public procurement tendering. In fact, the coordination of government procurement and purchasing activities may create entry barriers for SMEs, which is problematic since one of the most important aspects of procurement design is to promote entry. Are frame contract systems, framework agreements and other forms of tendering poor in this respect? What are the experiences of the different EU countries with regard to this issue? How can the design of public procurement using frame contracts, framework agreements and other mechanisms be improved to promote entry of small and medium-sized enterprises? These are some of the questions that the working group on public procurement and SMEs focuses on.

The working group on 'competitive tendering design and competitive issues' aims at studying how different member institutions apply procurement tenders, with the objective of sharing best practices. In order to achieve this result, this working group analyses every aspect that a procurement entity should consider in designing competitive tendering. Moreover, this group considers the consequences of competitive mechanisms for public procurement in terms of competition among bidders.

Participants in the working group on competitive tendering design and competitive issues

The questionnaire on competitive tendering design and competitive issues (see Appendix 2.3) was sent to thirty-one members of the EU Lab, representing twenty-five countries, and nineteen European institutions responded: ABA (Belgium), ASMR (Czech Republic), BESCHA (Germany), BBG (Austria), Consip (Italy), Department of Contracts (Malta), ESPA (Romania), MINEFI (France), MINHAC (Spain), Department of Finance (Ireland), Ministry of Development (Greece), Office for Public Procurement (Slovakia), OGC (UK), Public Procurement Authority (Turkey), PPD (Cyprus), Public Procurement Council (Hungary), Public Procurement Office (Poland), SKI (Denmark), Statskontoret (Sweden).

The EU Lab in 2005

The activities carried out in 2005 by the EU Lab focused on the topics 'Involving SMEs in Public Procurement' and 'Purchasing of PC Desktop,' 'Purchasing of Fixed Line Telephone Service' and 'Purchasing of Paper for Printers'.

To the survey on paper for printers, eleven European institutions responded: ABA (Belgium), BBG (Austria), Consip (Italy), Hansel (Finland), MINEFI (France), GSA (Ireland), OGC (UK), PPD (Cyprus),

SKI (Denmark), Statskontoret (Sweden), UMIC (Portugal). The most relevant results achieved are reported in the case studies in this chapter.

Appendix 2.2. Participants from the United States and Brazil

Two American institutions contributed to the 2004 survey:

- *US General Service Administration (GSA).* The institution provides products and services to support federal government agencies and employees, buying for the central Administration. All purchases (products and services) are governed by the Federal Acquisition Regulation (FAR), and its implementing regulation, the General Services Administration Manual (GSAM). Approximately 13,000 employees work at the GSA, and the institution performs on average 696,385 actions per year. The list of product categories covered by the institution covers telecommunication, energy, IT, goods and services (office furniture, stationery, paper, credit cards, cars, buses, ambulances), real estate (cleaning services, asset management, financial services).

- *Brazilian Department of Logistic and General Services* (DLGS) of the Brazilian federal government. In the Brazilian federal government, the DLGS belongs to the Ministry of Planning, Budget and Administration, and is the central agency responsible for formulating and promoting public policies and directives related to the activities of the administration of goods, works and services, transportation, internal and external communications, and procurement tendering and contracts, for the entire federal administration; promoting the system of rules and norms in the federal government for procurement tendering and contracts, and orienting the federal administration with respect to legal practices in procurement tendering and public contracts; and providing and managing the procurement tendering electronic systems within the federal government. Since the DLGS does not handle procurement contracts, the information provided in this chapter refers to the practices of the Brazilian federal government.

Appendix 2.3. Structure of the questionnaires distributed

Questionnaire on competitive tendering design and competitive issues (2004)

The Questionnaire focused on two main issues:

- Competitive tendering design, containing questions about the main aspects that a procurement entity has to consider when designing competitive tendering. We submitted questions focused on eight aspects: (i) Tendering processes; (ii) Number of lots; (iii) Duration of the contract; (iv) Reserve price; (v) Participation requirements; (vi) Awarding criteria; (vii) Policies; (viii) Subcontracting.

■ Competition, containing questions related to the level of competition registered by the institutions, methods to avoid collusion, and own experiences about participants' collusive behaviour.

Questionnaire on paper for printers (2005)

The questionnaire contains six main parts:

■ Contract features. We were interested in knowing the awarding date, the monetary value and the duration of the last and the previous frame contract/framework agreement awarded.

■ Competitive tendering format. In this section we aimed at collecting information about the tendering process used, open or restricted, and on the format applied: sealed bid single-round, multi-round, or combinatorial tendering process. The same questions were posed when an online auction was performed.

■ Number of lots and participants per lot. First of all we investigated whether the supply contract was divided into lots. Then, we collected information about the feature of the lots auctioned off. Lots can be quantitative (two lots that differ in value), geographical (lots that refer to different geographical areas), or qualitative (lots containing different types of product). Finally, for each lot, we requested the number of participants, the prices offered, and information about the bidding firm.

■ Quality. We selected seven specific features of quality: paper basis weight, thickness, ISO white, opacity, coarseness, moisture, permeability. These features constitute the EU standard requirements.

■ Prices. In this section we focused on awarding prices as well as market prices.

■ Awarding criteria. We collected data about the awarding criteria used – the lowest bid or the most economically advantageous offer – and the relative formula applied.

Bibliographical notes

Since this chapter is devoted to analysing procurement practices, the main formal contributions or empirical studies on each topic can be found in the specific chapters of this handbook. In exploring differences and similarities across institutions, we referred to the procurement legislative frameworks for Europe and the United States, namely, the recent EU Directive 2004/18 and the FAR (2005).

Interesting insights into public procurement practices in the United States are provided by Thai (2004) and Moon (2005). An initial benchmarking, mainly focused on legislative aspects of European public procurement, is the PPN Report (2005), while a preliminary explorative analysis on the economic aspects in Europe is given in the EU Lab Report (2004). Other documents on European countries' procurement profiles are available at the web page dedicated to the EU Lab initiative.

References

EC (2004). On the coordination of procedures for the award of public works contracts, public supply contracts and public service contracts, Directive 2004/18/EC of the European Parliament and of the Council, 31 March, 2004.

EIM Business and Policy Research (2004). The Access of SMEs to Public Procurement Contracts.

Engel, A. R. and A. Wambach (2005). Risk Management in Procurement Auctions, *Quaderni Consip*, 10, Rome, Italy.

EU Public Procurement Learning Lab (2005). Report on Purchasing of Fix-Line Telephone Services and Paper for Printers.

General Services Administration, Department of Defense, National Aeronautics and Space Administration (2005). Federal Acquisition Regulation.

Leipold, K., J. Klemow, F. Holloway and K. Vaydia (2004). The World Bank e-Procurement for the Selection of Consultants, Challenges and Lesson Learned, *Journal of Public Procurement*, 4.

Moon, M. J. (2005). E-procurement Management in State Government: Diffusion of e-Procurement Practices and its Determinants, *Journal of Public Procurement*, 1, pp. 54–72.

Piga, G. and M. Zanza (2004). An Exploratory Analysis of Public Procurement Practices in Europe, ch. 10 pp. 179–206 in Khi Thai et al. Eds., *Challenges in Public Procurement: An International Perspective*, PrAcademics Press.

Public Procurement Network (2005). *Public Procurement in Europe*, Final Report.

Thai, K. V. (2004). Challenges in Public Procurement, in Khi Thai et al. Eds., *Challenges in Public Procurement: An International Perspective*, PrAcademics Press.

Websites

Defense Procurement and Acquisition Policy:
http://www.acq.osd.mil/dpap/contractpricing/vol1intro.htm#I.2.1

Small Business Administration (SBA): *http://www.sba.gov/*

General Services Administration (GSA): *www.gsaauctions.gov*

Eurostat: *europa.eu.int/comm/eurostat*

International Federation of Purchasing and Materials Management (IFPMM): *http://www.ifpmm.org*

International Purchasing and Supply Education and Research Association (ISPERA): *www.ispera.com*

Public Procurement Network (PPN): *http://www.minefi.gouv.fr/daj/marches_publics/ppn/ppn-anglais/ppn-anglais-summary.htm*

EU Public Procurement Learning Lab:

http://www.consip.it/sc/uff_studi_ini_eu_ing.htm

PART II

General strategic principles

3 When should procurement be centralized?

Nicola Dimitri, Federico Dini and Gustavo Piga

3.1. Introduction

Technological and organizational innovations can make it possible to have more cooperation and more initiative simultaneously. Information technology is an obvious source of such movements. By allowing finer performance measurement and better communications, it facilitates getting more initiative (through lowering the cost of providing incentives) and more cooperation (by making coordination easier and increasing contacts among units). (Roberts 2004, p. 112)

Motivated by the need to control costs and streamline processes, the issue of centralization versus decentralization has captured the interest of researchers, practitioners and public administrators from a variety of perspectives and is becoming increasingly important for many organizations. An efficient procurement policy is arguably one of the key activities in private companies, international institutions and governments. In this chapter we discuss purchasing systems from the specific point of view of their degree of centralization.

Given the considerable volume of resources involved, firms and governments always seek to optimize procurement so as to deliver value for money to business units and taxpayers.[1] In pursuing such a goal often the first important choice is to choose between centralized and decentralized purchasing; profitability, performance and budget control within a private company or a public institution can vary considerably according to how purchases are organized and managed.[2]

---

[1] Some estimates suggest that private procurement is about 50% of revenues. See http://www.purchasing.com/article/CA605712.html. In Europe and in the United States public procurement is about 16% and 20% of GDP, respectively (see also Chapter 2). More data can be found in Moon (2005), Thai and Grimm (2000), Jones (2002) and Andersen et al. (2003).

[2] Centralized procurement is estimated to save 15–20% on purchases of materials and services. See http://www.purchasing.com/article/CA273586.html.

Prior to discussing the main aspects of the issue, it is convenient to define what we mean by centralized versus decentralized procurement; we do so by distinguishing three broad types of procurement set-ups:[3]

Full centralization: Procurement is fully centralized when all the relevant decisions (what, how and when) to purchase products, whether by competitive tendering procedures or by negotiations, are in the hands of a company headquarters or a central public unit dedicated to buying products to satisfy the needs of the company or public offices. Furthermore, the contract conditions for the products acquired are the same throughout a firm's local branches or local public administrations.

Full decentralization: Procurement is decentralized when divisions or local administrations are delegated the power to decide how, what and when to procure.

Hybrid models: In between full centralization and full delegation there is a wide range of intermediate procurement models where central and local purchasing units share the power on purchasing decisions.

Hybrid models appear to be prevailing in both private and public procurement with central units playing the key role of defining some common strategies and polices. For instance, the 2004 Assessment of Excellence in Procurement by A. T. Kearney, made on 275 international companies, shows that *centre-led procurement* models, by which strategic decisions are taken centrally but transactional activities are executed locally are becoming increasingly popular.[4]

Though hybrid models are being increasingly adopted, at present there is no clear evidence of a prevailing structure and contractual arrangement in the private sector. In public procurement frame contracts/agreements (see Chapter 2), stipulated by central procurement agencies on behalf of public administrations, appear instead to be quite common. In such a mildly centralized arrangement, contracts make available to all public administrations several items for a given period of time at a certain (often renegotiable) price. Public administrations are recommended to use such contracts, unless

---

[3] McCue and Pitzer (2000) provide a definition of centralized and decentralized procurement. An extreme one is represented by a central purchasing station to which end users send their requests/needs. The station approves the requests, selects the contractors, negotiates prices and makes the purchasing decision. In the opposite, decentralized, extreme, the local end user retains decisions over all these elements.

[4] See Chapter 3 of the study, available at http://www.atkearney.com/main.taf?p=5,3,1,115,1.

what they need is not available or local suppliers are able to provide the relevant items under better price-quality conditions.

There is no doubt that in recent years many countries have increased their degree of centralization. For example, after an initial period of skepticism, where centralized procurement was seen as a factor of monopsonization and decreased competition, the new EU Directive 2004/18 explicitly recognizes the possibility of central procurement bodies.

And indeed, centralization of public procurement appears as a clear trend in Europe, as well as in the United States, Southern America and Asia. Examples of central procurement agencies established in Europe over the past decade are OGC Buying Solutions (UK, see Box 3.1), UGAP and the new project Opache (France), Consip (Italy), Hansel (Finland), SKI (Denmark), Satskontoret (Sweden) and BBG (Austria).[5] The American GSA (General Service Administration, see Box 3.2), created in 1949 to provide several services to the federal government, is arguably one of the most advanced centralized public marketplaces in the world.[6] It provides a

---

Box 3.1. The case of UK Office of Government Commerce

The Office of Government Commerce (OGC) was founded on 1 April 2000. The aim of the project was to achieve substantial value-for-money improvements in the government's procurement budget, amounting to over £13 billion. The merger of procurement services, previously provided by The Buying Agency (TBA), the Central Computer and Telecommunications Agency (CCTA), the Property Advisers to the Civil Estate (PACE) and procurement units from the Treasury, created OGC Buying Solutions on 1 April 2001. This larger organization today provides public administrations with access to more than 500,000 goods and services through framework agreements, as well as professional assistance in purchasing fully managed telecoms services, energy and secure e-mail, intranet, data transfer and publishing services.

---

[5] These agencies centralize purchases for amounts ranging from 0.04 to 1.84% of the total public procurement. Malta and Hungary have quite centralized structures with more than 10% and 67%, respectively. Such heterogeneity in the degree of centralization can, of course, be explained by differences in national procurement legislation. See Chapter 2 Piga and Zanza (2004).

[6] See Chapter 2 for more on GSA.

Box 3.2. The case of US Federal Procurement (GSA)

The GSA was established on 1 July 1949 to provide a wide variety of management and related services to the federal government. The Federal Property and Administrative Services Act of 1949 (63 Stat. 379), which created the GSA, stemmed from recommendations contained in the first Hoover Commission report and other studies aimed at improving management practice. The Act grouped functions formerly assigned to various agencies, including real estate management, records management, transportation and public utilities management, procurement and management of the stockpile of strategic and critical materials. Later, additional and related programmes were assigned to the GSA, such as management of federal information technology (to include automated data processing and telecommunications), expansion of productive capacity, production and supply of materials and facilities necessary for national defence, motor vehicle management, representation of government agencies in proceedings before federal and state regulatory bodies, and the operation of Presidential libraries.

---

huge variety of goods and services for the US federal government. In addition, between 2002 and 2004 several states (such as Florida with My Florida Marketplace, North Carolina with NC E-Procurement@Your Service and more recently California with the California Performance Review programme) implemented e-procurement platforms providing centralized state term contracts to all public administrations within the state.

Evidence of centralization can also be found in Asia and South America. Since 1949 Korea has had a centralized procurement agency (PPS) which today accounts for 30 percent of Korean public procurement.[7] In 2003 the government of China enacted the first national regulation on government procurement, called Government Procurement Law (GPL), which applies to the purchase of goods, services and construction projects by state bodies, public institutions and social organizations at all government levels. Mexico (with Compranet, 1996), Brazil (with Comprasnet, 1997), Chile (with

---

[7] The Public Procurement Service (PPS) is Korea's procuring agency. It is a central administration purchasing and providing goods and services needed for the operation of the various government agencies and public organizations.

ChileCompra, 2003), and other governments in Latin America have recently developed centralized (e-)procurement systems.[8]

In the 1990s many private companies also experienced significant changes in their organizational structure; some of them successfully decentralized decisions, including procurement. Among others, this was the case with Motorola, General Electric, United Technologies and Fiat.[9] However, a big company such as Honda (and more recently General Motors) followed the opposite direction. In 1973 Honda adopted a decentralized decision system, whereby authority over major decisions was spread among thirty senior executives. The company profitably expanded until the late 1980s. Since then when there was a crisis; cars were no longer meeting Japanese expectations, with the company experiencing a consistent reduction in profits and market share, falling behind Mitsubishi, Nissan and Toyota, its major national competitors. Centralization of decisions allowed Honda to streamline processes and revert the negative trend.

The wave of changes in organizational arrangements that occurred in the 1990s testifies that firms are always seeking the optimal organizational structure, and that in pursuing such a goal they continuously adapt over time to economic and technological evolution.

The sector of IT infrastructures followed a trend similar to that in the car industry.[10] During the 1970s and early 1980s IT systems were highly centralized; it was thought that the entire company had to be supported by mainframes. In the mid-1980s distributed computing environments became dominant and IT departments much more diffused. As a consequence IT staff was much more decentralized to support geographically spread business units. Today centralization is again becoming more attractive, since a single IT organization is more cost-effective, can better assure consistent technology standards throughout the company and avoids duplicating the same solutions, systems or applications in response to similar problems occurring in separate business units. Moreover, compared with decentralized systems, a centralized IT function can better support business processes or functions (e.g., the whole supply chain).

---

[8] For more information on emerging central public procurement stations in Latin America see http://www.undp.org/surf-panama/egov/docs/programme_activities/bpractices/profiles_e-govenrment_purchase.pdf.

[9] Brickley et al.(2004) present in great detail the case study of Honda and discuss in depth several issues concerning the optimal design of organizations.

[10] See the following contributions published in *CIO Magazine*: http://www.cio.com/archive/091501/centralization.html and http://www2.cio.com/analyst/report860.html.

Centralization appears attractive for international organizations with a key role in certain fields. For example, recently it has been argued that in food security more centralized European food safety policies, as opposed to the actual multilevel governance, would be more effective to enhance consumer trust in EU food supply, making the system less sensitive to crises.[11] According to this view, centralization would help create a much more stable regulatory and market environment, increasing transparency and accountability. In the health care sector, a recent volume from the Board on Global Health (BGH) illustrates the benefits of a centralized international system for the procurement of antimalaria drugs – though, in this area, centralization is not a new idea. Indeed, UNICEF centralized procurement for childhood vaccines, and the WHO (World Health Organization) did so for tuberculosis and proposed to do the same for malaria and HIV/AIDS.[12] Other institutions, such as the UN, still retain a largely decentralized procurement system.

It is no surprise that increased centralization came with the rise of the ICT revolution. In the public sector, procuring a certain item for all public administrations (local and central) in a given country could have an extremely high coordination cost until as recently as twenty years ago. E-mail and web portals, where tenders are posted and orders can be made in real time, lower communication costs dramatically between the centre and the periphery before and after submitting a tender. Centralization, in turn, reduces unitary fixed costs of expensive IT infrastructures.

The debate on procurement centralization, however, started before the ICT revolution, and is likely to continue in the future. Indeed, some benefits associated with centralization are independent of the communication infrastructure; for example, economies of scale lower unit costs of qualified personnel (IT, legal, strategic and sourcing) working for a procuring unit; the buyer's bargaining power increases, and his transaction costs (e.g., competitive tendering committees, official journal publications) tend to decrease. Notwithstanding the availability of ICT, other disadvantages of centralization remain, in particular those related to the physical distance between the local procurer and the central unit.

The rest of this chapter is organized as follows. In section 3.2 we identify some main themes involved in choosing between more centralized and

---

[11] See Bernauer and Caduff (2004).

[12] The social impact of effective procurement of antimalaria drugs and the variety of reasons suggesting that a centralized structure would be highly desirable were the main motivations for our case study, which is presented at the end of this chapter.

decentralized procurement systems; section 3.3 contains some concluding remarks. Finally, we present a case study.

3.2. Centralized versus decentralized procurement systems: some major themes

Centralization is becoming more and more attractive for institutions operating in different sectors and pursuing different goals. The trade-off between centralizing and delegating happens at various levels, and final decisions emerge after careful examination of several elements that we discuss in the next sections. As we shall see, sometimes neither complete centralization nor complete decentralization appears as an optimal arrangement, and hybrid/flexible models seem to be more appropriate.[13]

Regardless of their public/private nature, when organizations have to decide whether to centralize procurement in the hands of a single body (top management, central government) or delegate it to substructures (divisions/branches and local public administrations) they need to consider many aspects. In what follows we identify and discuss some of the main themes that may guide the choice between the two possibilities:

- Efficiency: savings and cost control;
- Product standardization;
- Favouritism;
- Strategic procurement;
- Network effect and standards;
- Market dynamics;
- Emergencies;
- Decision information costs;
- Bargaining power;
- Monitoring contractors' performance;
- E-procurement.

---

[13] A form of hybrid system that can occur is when different items are centralized in different locations, originating a mixed kind of procurement framework where central and local procurement units share the power over procurement decisions; the case of General Motors (see Section 3.2.4.1) is illuminating in this sense. Another example is the 'flexible purchasing' of the TBS (Turner Broadcasting System Inc.), so called by Sheila Johnson, TBS's manager of strategic sourcing. This model is said to combine the advantages of two approaches, since neither full centralization nor full decentralization suit well the procurement needs of the company. See the discussion by William Atkinson at http://www.purchasing.com/article/CA451871.html.

Though listed separately, the following paragraphs will show that many of the above issues are highly related. For example, savings and cost control induced by economies of scale can be achieved more easily when centralization involves the procurement of more standardized items. At the same time, large-scale acquisition of standardized items may also increase the buyer's bargaining power.

3.2.1. Efficiency: savings and cost control

Savings and cost control are key issues in public and private procurement.

Everywhere, governments need to control public spending. Fairly often this is done by rationalizing public spending for goods and services, which accounts for a considerable amount of monetary resources and appears an easier target for budget cuts than pension or health expenditure.

Controlling for purchasing costs is also fundamental for private companies to compete in the global economy. Cost control is crucial for firms to remain in business when economies do not grow, or grow very little, since demand is likely to be weak and firms' revenues low. But also with more sustained growth, cost control could be very important as a competitive factor.

In the automobile industry, it is argued that in order to succeed in today's economic environment, companies need to focus more on developing and/or preserving several critical abilities to reduce costs today and in the future. Areas in which the ability to reduce costs should be employed are sourcing and procurement, but also administration and, more generally, supply chain management.[14] The recent study by A. T. Kearney on the procurement practices of major international companies mentioned earlier shows that cost reduction and management are essential and strategic for companies. The study also illustrates some advanced cost-management techniques.[15]

Centralization is obviously an issue for organizations of a certain size and geographical presence. When organizations become large, controlling the costs of decentralized branches may become more difficult. This can be tackled by assigning budgets to decentralized units, which, however, does not necessarily imply efficient spending.

---

[14] See http://www.oracle.com/industries/automotive/AutomotiveSupplierExcellence(c14223–01).pdf

[15] The '2004 Assessment of Excellence in Procurement' is the fifth research study in a series that began in 1992. It puts emphasis on the importance of cost and sourcing management as a way to cut costs but also to create value from supply markets. The study elicited responses from procurement and supply chain executives of leading companies around the world. The study group was composed of 275 companies, with average revenues of nearly US$10 billion in 2003. For more on the study see http://www.atkearney.com/main.taf?p=1,5,1,154.

Could centralization help to control costs and deliver the desired quality? Gene Richter, former Chief Procurement Officer at IBM, commenting on the book *Who Says Elephants Can't Dance* by Lou Gerstner, former CEO of IBM, argues in favour of centralized procurement for large corporations: 'most companies with centralized procurement are able to significantly reduce a division's purchase costs and still be responsive to a division's need to have world-class sources'.

Hence centralization can help reduce costs, even considerably, with its benefits essentially being due to (i) synergies (economies of scale, no effort duplication), (ii) specialization, and, (iii) knowledge and resource sharing.

Synergies As we will see in the next section, product standardization is one of the key elements favouring more centralized procurement. Since decentralization activates multiple purchasing procedures, it is in standardized items that duplication costs can be most reduced and economies of scale open up opportunities for considerable savings. If the product is provided by a natural monopolist (e.g., phone services, electricity, gas) then centralization brings greater bargaining power on the demand side that can reduce the contractor's rent.

In public procurement centralization can save other kinds of duplication costs also, such as costs for advertisements in official journals and litigation.

The likelihood and costs of controversies over documents related to procurement transactions may decrease with centralization: first, because qualified human resources involved in centralized procurement should improve the clearness, transparency and measurability of the procurement procedures and, more generally, the overall 'quality' of documents; second, because centralization reduces the number of procurement contracts for any purchased item; finally, because it is more likely for litigations to be concentrated in the hands of one court whereas decentralization, in case of controversies, would involve the courts associated with each local administration.

Specialization Centralized procurement helps to concentrate skilled human capital and expertise. As well as legal experts producing high-quality documents, category managers, market analysts/specialists and other procurement professionals are recruited and trained to develop highly specialized competence, optimizing procurement design. This way specialized teams can be formed to better design procurement strategies and improve them over time through continuous learning and experience.

Hiring experts can be expensive, and so in general more difficult, for small decentralized units; this is why privileged financial status puts large agencies in a better position to recruit professionals, create very competent teams and more efficiently pursue cost-effective procurement.

Knowledge and information sharing   Knowledge and information sharing is a key externality in an organization, as it can enhance efficiency via the use of more up-to-date information, problem-sharing and common solutions. Often markets are connected (e.g., printers with PCs, insurance with banking); because of product line diversification, some firms can meet repeatedly in different procurement competitions.[16] For instance PC producers (but also retailers) such as Siemens, HP and IBM can participate in a competitive procurement tendering for PC desktops as well as for laptops. IBM can also bid for mainframes, data warehousing, and other IT service contracts. This makes information and knowledge sharing among groups of purchasing specialists very important to design effective procurements. Teams specialized in different supply categories can work together to solve common problems such as the choice of the appropriate scoring rule or the best contractual arrangement, and to share information about markets, potential bidders and other important elements.

This is why knowledge and information sharing, among highly competent teams, is more likely to arise and to be effective within central, rather than local, procurement units.

A final point is in order. As described in more detail in other chapters of this book (see section 11.3), 'risk-averse' firms might be induced to bid more aggressively if the negative consequences associated with losing the competitive tendering turn out to be too high. Centralization obviously increases the risk of negative consequences, everything else being equal, as the market share that can be lost in a single competitive tendering is higher. It is possible that buyers, who must decide whether or not to centralize, consider this effect. Although this would favour centralization for the higher savings, one should keep in mind that more aggressive bidding might also

---

[16] This phenomenon is also known as 'multimarket contact'. One standard problem connected to such a phenomenon, first noted by Bernheim and Whinston (1990), is that in general it facilitates collusion among firms. Firms 'meeting' in different markets face more chances to 'talk' and may collude more effectively to share their control over different markets. Preventing collusion, and thus minimizing the risks of bad performance of auctions, is one key element of the design of any procurement strategy. Therefore information sharing among teams on this point can be quite important.

induce firms to implement dumping strategies and price goods under costs (or reduce non-contractible quality) if they believe that monitoring will be minimal during the life time of a contract. As quality control might be an issue with centralization (see section 3.2.10), buyers should be careful to credibly communicate their ability to monitor quality effectively and to sanction irregular misbehaviour on the part of the supplier.

3.2.2. Product standardization

A natural case for increasing the degree of centralization is when the characteristics of the product being procured are standardized. Typical examples are ICT equipment, IT servers, stationery and paper, meal coupons, fuel, credit cards and car engine components. Such products can have some degree of differentiation but, on the whole, they may satisfy common needs/preferences of a large number of purchasing units/end users with very little necessity for variety.

And, indeed, standardized items are procured by central public agencies in several countries. For instance, many public procurement agencies that were mentioned in the introduction (GSA, OGC, Consip, Statskontoret, My Florida Marketplace, North Carolina E-Procurement@Your Service, Comprasnet) procure on behalf of public administrations products such as fax machines, laptops, desktops, document management software, printers, projectors, web servers, natural gas, electric power, fuel oil, fuels, fuel cards, office furniture, stationery, paper, credit cards, cars, buses and ambulances.[17]

Observing central agencies favouring competitive procurements, rather than negotiations, supports the conclusions of Chapters 4 and 5, where it is argued that competition is preferable when products are less complex/standardized.

Standardization favours centralization for two main reasons. First, standardization facilitates information gathering and processing. Products can be described quite precisely and unambiguously since the variety of models is limited (low heterogeneity of product), local requirements are similar (low heterogeneity of needs) and the risk of incorrect, incomplete,

---

[17] Some procurement agencies (e.g., Compranset, GSA, Consip) also purchase less standardized products such as real estate and health services. Yet, their centralized procurement can be successful in exploiting significant economies of scale that can emerge when one contractor provides a whole package of services, as opposed to when the buyer resorts to many specialized single interventions from different suppliers.

information processing on the part of the central purchasing unit is low. For example, paper sheets are a fairly standardized product and related requests coming from different areas are very similar. Analogously, IT servers, though they can come with different characteristics and power (e.g., scalability, availability and number of concurrent users), are essentially standardized machines.

Second, standardization allows suppliers to exploit significant economies of scale in producing high volumes of the same product. This, in general, lowers unit costs and opens up the opportunity for the buyer to pay lower prices for the supply contracts awarded. Savings in production costs should exceed the higher effort the contractor incurs in serving a supply contract across many dispersed local units.[18]

At the regional, national and sometimes continental levels, standardization seems to favour procurement centralization; yet some organizations may experience difficulties in centralizing procurement procedures. For example, supply contracts for electricity provision are typically made with country-specific suppliers and multinational companies may find centralization problematic. Despite electricity being a standardized commodity, the geographical distance among the various procurement units, together with possible legal barriers to suppliers operating in different countries, may discourage or even prevent full centralization. Therefore, even if a multinational firm could fully centralize all electricity procurement contracts, the difficulty, or even impossibility, of suppliers to compete on multiple lots would seriously reduce the advantages of centralized procurement. Since energy cost control is strategic at the corporate level, even if energy was purchased locally, the central unit could retain control over certain main procurement strategies. We discuss later why and how goods and services with strategic importance for the organization call for increasing centralization in procurement.

3.2.3. Favouritism

Local purchasing units are typically better informed than the centre on the product characteristics that they need but sometimes may find it costly, or inconvenient, to transfer this information to the centre. Take for example

---

[18] It is interesting to note that public procurement frame contracts/agreements often require public administrations to order a minimum number of items. This is typically done to avoid orders of just one or a few units of the item limiting suppliers' ability to cover fixed costs (and to exploit economies of scales), by shipping the item to many dispersed local purchasers.

cleaning services, asset management or road cadastre. Since these services often incorporate local specificities, it could be very difficult or expensive for a central purchasing unit to collect more accurate information than the local unit. Local privileged information can also concern the characteristics of local suppliers such as their quality standards, reliability in delivery performance and financial status. More precise information can therefore be an element favouring decentralized procurement.

Local choices, however, might not always follow the 'best value for money' principle. Sometimes decentralized selection of contractors can be less efficient than centralized selection since a local unit may be more inclined, than the centre, to favour *local* suppliers. Decentralized decisions may bring local suppliers closer to the buyer, and the potential for local lobbying activity to influence purchasing decisions can have a serious negative impact on procurement efficiency.

This, however, does not exclude favouritism also occurring at the central level, though the higher visibility of central units would make corruption more difficult to entertain (for more on corruption see Chapter 16).[19] This last argument appears consistent with evidence and indications from public and private procurement practice. For example, the International Consortium on Government Financial Management (ICGFM) recently issued the results of its 2005 *Worldwide Survey* on corruption entitled *Resisting Corruption in the Public Sector*. To reduce corruption the ICGFM survey recommends several actions for governments to take. Among them are to 'cure corruption-prone procurement by centralizing purchases'. In public procurement, a larger competitive tendering requires by law a higher degree of public visibility and more open procedures, which reduces the scope for discretion by purchasers. Insofar as centralization facilitates e-procurement (see section 3.2.11), and the latter is a safer method to assure no-tampering with received offers (see Chapter 16), corruption may be further curbed by aggregation of demand.

Centralization can also provide incentives to improve communication. Especially at the start of a centralization process, communication between periphery and the centre could be problematic. This is either because local units may experience genuine difficulties in providing appropriate descriptions of their requests or because they want to keep control over local decisions and so they are reluctant to release information to the centre.

---

[19] See Celentani and Ganuza (2002).

Of course, since centralization often requires some degree of product standardization, items procured centrally may not match exactly the needs of a local unit, which could create additional problems within organizations. However, when quality is very important, the local incentive to conceal procurement requirements from the centre can decrease, or even disappear. In this situation decentralized local units would no longer have the power to favour local firms, so they should be more interested in revealing as much information as possible to the central unit, as it would suit them better that the centre selects a high-quality rather than a low-quality contractor. Box 3.3 below illustrates how favouritism can have an impact on price and quality.[20]

Box 3.3. The effects of favouritism in procurement: an example

Favouritism may be costly when quality is important. In a competitive tendering with scoring rule (see Chapter 12) this could also have a negative impact on the economic part of a tender, since it can lead to over-valuation of some suppliers' quality, allowing them to submit less competitive economic offers. For example, if a scoring rule assigns 0.6 weight to the quality score S_Q and 0.4 to the economic score S_E, then $S = (0.6) S_Q + (0.4)S_E$, with the supplier obtaining the highest score being awarded the contract. If both S_Q and S_E can at most be 100 then S too can at most be 100. An overall score of, say, 50 points can be achieved with an infinite number of pairs (S_Q, S_E), determined by the following expression $S_E = 50/(0.4) - (3/2) S_Q$, where to each level of S_Q there is a corresponding value of S_E. Suppose the true S_Q is low, say 40, but in a competitive tendering a firm is discretionally favoured and its quality overestimated, at say 60; then S_E can be 35 rather than 65. This would imply a less attractive economic offer on the part of the contract winner. In return for this saving the firm could, for example, pay a bribe to the procurer. Therefore, overall such procurement competitive tendering would result in both low quality and low savings too.

Centralized procurement, however, can bring about dissatisfaction and unrest among some potential suppliers, which might generate political costs, especially in the public sector. For example, with few, large lots small businesses can face difficulties in accessing centralized procurement competitions; this could induce discontent, and related political pressure for

---

[20] See Vagstad (2000).

alternative procedures. A form of centralized procurement, with many lots and package bidding, can mitigate this effect (for more on this see Chapters 7 and 8).

To conclude, in choosing whether to delegate procurement decisions to local units the buyer should also compare possible decentralization costs, associated with local favouritism that might select lower-quality firms, with the possible political costs of centralized procedures.

3.2.4. Strategic procurement

One important dimension for deciding which procurements should be centralized is the strategic importance of the goods, or services, for the company or the public institution. Procurement is strategic when it involves items/activities with a considerable impact on business or policy. The greater the importance of these activities, the more centralized decisions tend to be.[21] Indications from private procurement practice emphasize that major suppliers of core goods or services need a consistent and highly competent counterpart; the strategic importance of such items suggests that, everything else being equal, they should be more centralized since decisions which involve them can have important consequences on the whole organization. A recent survey conducted by the Boston Logistic Group on international companies from many sectors confirms this view: 'Companies will use scale to drive more production and distribution economies by centralizing strategic procurement, forming purchasing councils, and rationalizing the supplier base'.

3.2.4.1. Centralization of strategic products and activities in the private sector

The view that centralization is likely to involve items/activities that are strategic for business is supported by procurement practice. Here we discuss two cases. The first refers to General Motors, one of the world's largest car manufacturing companies, and the second relates to the business model of franchising.

General Motors (GM) As already mentioned in the introduction, GM started centralizing the procurement of car components, which are clearly part of the core business of the company. In 'Ward's Auto World' (July, 2005), Brian Corbett writes, 'After decades of numerous GM purchasing

---

[21] For instance, see Aghion and Tirole (1997) and Dessein (2002).

agents buying different versions of the same component from multiple suppliers, there now is one manager for each Global Creativity Team exclusively responsible for sourcing one type of part for every GM vehicle worldwide.' Bo Andersson, GM vice president-global purchasing and supply chain, states, 'Every purchasing decision for clutches, seat components and glass now is made by team leaders in Germany, forgings by a leader in India, regulators in Sweden, fasteners and rubber sealing in Spain, compressors in Brazil, radios in China and seatbelts and heating-ventilation-air conditioning systems in Mexico.' In so doing, GM centralized the procurement of car components by function; though this is not a fully centralized model, centralization is complete component wise.

Franchising One interesting example of core activities centralization is franchising.[22] Franchising is a contractual arrangement between two parties whereby the franchisee pays the franchisor for the right to open a shop, sell the franchisor's good and use his trademark. The shop and the business will be his own, but subject to some rules dictated by the franchisor. The franchisor imposes on the franchisee certain qualitative standards; for instance, building design, menus and overalls are decided centrally by the franchisor. On the other hand, the franchisee is delegated the right to hire people and to decide some local advertisement policies. Quality, building design, menu, overalls etc. are crucial for business success, and consistent policy standards on these elements are believed to be necessary for good performance. Indeed, by allowing all franchisees to use his trademark the franchisor uses his *reputation* everywhere franchisees operate and merchandise his products. Moreover, since the franchisor can exert close control over these key elements it is natural and effective for the centre to take charge of them. All other, possibly less important, decisions are more costly to monitor centrally by the franchisor. For instance, it is certainly more efficient for a multinational franchise company to delegate recruitment policy to a local franchisee (since culture, labour-market-specific conditions, skills etc. vary considerably across areas).

---

[22] Many large companies operating in different sectors around the world work with the franchising model, among them, Accor, McDonald's, Midas, Merle Norman Cosmetics, Allegra Print & Imaging, Frannet. Visit the World Franchising website for more resources and listings of the most important worldwide franchisors. For a discussion on franchising and centralization see Macho-Stadler and Perez-Castrillo (1998).

3.2.4.2. What is core in the public sector?

Governments and public institutions may consider some activities/products to be strategic to pursuing certain social or national goals. Defence procurement typically falls within this category; indeed, due to secrecy reasons, purchasing in this area is normally centralized as less information is likely to be divulged. In the United States defence procurement is mostly centralized in the hands of the Department of Defence, though it allows for some degree of decentralization. And in fact, the *Defense Acquisition Guidebook* establishes that the Defense Acquisition System is the

management process by which the Department acquires weapon and automated information systems. Although the system is based on centralized policies and principles, it allows for decentralized and streamlined execution of acquisition activities. This approach provides flexibility and encourages innovation, while maintaining strict emphasis on discipline and accountability.

Military procurement in China was recently centralized. The State Council Information Office published in December 2004 a white paper entitled 'China's National Defence in 2004'. The document describes China's national defence policies and the army's modernization process, including procurement approaches. Military procurement, which includes 'computers and network devices, vehicle chassis, generating sets, shelters and other types of general-purpose equipment, has changed from separate to centralized procurement. . . . Now procured in a centralized way are more than 1,000 kinds of materials in twenty-four categories needed in the development, training, scientific research and daily life of the armed forces.'

Procurement in the health care sector can be another important social-strategic goal. The case study on antimalaria medicines discussed at the end of this chapter represents an interesting example, especially when certain types of vaccines need to be purchased rapidly.

Green procurement is another aspect of increasing importance. Green procurement policies aim at purchasing products with mild, or no, impact on the environment. Since public procurement represents a considerable share of government expenditure, in both developed and developing countries, this has considerable implications and state/international organizations are now facing increasing responsibility to take the environmental impacts of their activities into account. A move towards favouring products whose manufacture, use and disposal limit the negative environmental impacts not only has direct environmental benefits, but also sends a strong message to producers and suppliers that the issue is now important for procurers.

In part, this centralization occurs at a higher level, through laws passed by parliaments setting minimum environmental standards for production to be included within all public and private tendering competitions.

Other environmentally sensitive choices are made by procurement laws. This is also demonstrated by the recent European Directive 2004/18 allowing purchasing bodies to include environmental sustainability criteria in the award of public contracts, whereby some important 'green goals' can be introduced into the definition of strategies for the procurement of several items such as gasoline, paper, printers and photocopiers.[23]

Since environmental management and protection is a major challenge for societies, and can now be considered core for many governments, centralization can play a key role in promoting green procurement policies and establishing appropriate common standards. The positive effects (externalities) produced by purchasing environmentally sustainable items through local units can be magnified by large-scale centralized procurement. Since a small local procurement unit may not give sufficient importance to the environmental impact of its tendering competitions, the more procurements are centralized, the more this negative externality is reduced.

3.2.5. Networks and standards

Network industries are an important part of the economy. Some notable examples of networks are telecommunications, Internet providers and computer software and hardware. Other important networks are present in the transport industry (e.g., airlines), banking and finance (markets for bonds, equities and derivatives, ATM networks) and e-markets (e.g., B2B, B2C and B2G platforms). The main characteristic of a network is that, for a member, the value of being part of it increases with the total number of members; the larger the network the more valuable it is to join it. Take for instance the case of computer operating systems or software: using the same system, people can exchange many different types of files and easily process

---

[23] For example, the Government of Denmark, like many others in European countries, is particularly sensitive to environmental issues and its effort in green public procurement started in 1994. The Danish central procurement station (SKI) has also created *Greennet*, a website dedicated to green procurement issues and related policies.

other users' documents. In other words, members of a network 'speak the same language'.

Therefore, centralized procurement can have a fundamental role in fostering coordination and expanding networks.

The following example, is a case in point. Consip recently ran a procurement competition for the acquisition of 12,000 licences for the third release of the operating system Sun Star Office for Italian public administrations. This competitive tendering will contribute significantly to expanding the Star Office network of users in Italian public administrations, thus increasing the value of the operating system for single members.

Centralized procurement can also be used to introduce and promote innovative common standards in the public sector. For example, in September 2004 the Brazilian government and IBM agreed to expand the LINUX computer operating system as an alternative to Microsoft Windows. This strategy allows the development of common standards but should also stimulate Microsoft to be more competitive to avoid falls in market share. Chapter 19 discusses this case in particular and the relation between procurement and innovation in general.

3.2.6. Market dynamics

In procurements where markets change rapidly and across geographically dispersed local units, information held by top managers/officers may become incomplete or obsolete rather quickly.[24] Decentralized decisions then appear to favour timely adoption of new opportunities coming from local markets. For instance, local procurement units close to innovative industrial districts or, more generally, to dynamic productive areas may see the release of new, cheaper, higher-quality items which can be purchased immediately if the unit is allowed to do so. Also, the presence of local units distributed in segmented markets calls for more decentralization to exploit fully and in a timely manner local innovations/dynamics on which information is usually unavailable (or available at very high costs) from the centre.[25]

---

[24] See Aghion and Tirole (1997), Dessein (2002) and Brickley et al. (2004).

[25] Local information can be rather important when markets are segmented. For instance, cleaning services and food markets are typically segmented and populated by many small enterprises. In such contexts, market dynamics can differ according to the geographical area.

While centralized procurement may lack specific local market information, it is likely to have a superior overall systemic market vision owing to highly skilled and experienced human resources and international networks. Central procurement agencies may more easily account for national and international market dynamics (changes in the trend of prices, market structures, business models etc.) in the definition of procurement strategies, which could be exceedingly costly at the local level.

Here again, hybrid, flexible procurement systems appear quite attractive. While centralization can capture key national and international market dynamics and trends, decentralization could take advantage of possible favourable conditions of the local market.

A widespread example of a hybrid procurement model in the public sector is given by so-called framework agreements and frame contracts (see chapter 2 for more details). These contracts reflect a common approach to procurement governance; they are often stipulated by a central agency on behalf of public administrations, but public administrations are allowed to procure on their own in case local suppliers offer better economic or quality conditions.

3.2.7. Emergencies

By emergency we mean an urgent need for an item or service that does not allow time to solicit and organize a competitive tendering. Urgency can, for example, concern purchases required to deal with damage caused by natural disasters, as well as acquisitions necessary to address immediate safety and security issues.

In these circumstances it is not always clear whether centralized or decentralized procurement would perform better. Many factors can influence performance in both cases, such as whether the emergency occurs at the local or central level, and the kind of items involved.[26] A key point is, of course, the type of emergency. Decentralization may perform better in day-to-day purchasing, since local units can deal quickly with local suppliers, reducing the risk of delay or default or else unexpected events such as over-consumption and inadequate quality. With day-to-day purchasing, emergencies may also be dealt with through centralized frame contracts/agreements. This is when local units might find, within the conditions

---

[26] Corruption and/or malpractice, a typical risk of emergency procurement, is unlikely to be more probable in either of the two set-ups.

specified by the contract, goods and services with the characteristics that they are searching for.[27]

When instead emergencies are disasters, things are rather different. In this case some degree of centralization may be highly desirable, since planning activities are essential to define the scope and require at least some coordinated central intervention. In a dramatic emergency, the government may need to buy goods and services for workers, equipment to save lives, mitigating the risk of delays that could compromise the public interest. Furthermore, given a certain territory and a time unit (say one year), the probability of a negative event at a particular location of the territory is clearly smaller than the probability of the same event within the whole territory. This makes the setting up of competence at each local unit extremely costly and wasteful and centralization much more desirable, compensating the greater costs that a centralized unit is likely to face to deliver equipment to the site of the emergency.

For instance, the government of Canada established contractual policies to ensure that procurement meets this need.[28] Another interesting example is the Afghanistan Reconstruction and Development Services (ARDS) created in May 2002 by the Transitional Islamic State of Afghanistan (TISA) in order to cope with the urgent task of reconstruction. The ARDS appointed a country's central procurement consultant (PC) to put in place emergency procurement capacity. Among his main goals, the PC should (i) facilitate rapid and transparent utilization of donor resources for reconstruction and development; (ii) improve procurement efficiency, (iii) disseminate to all eligible suppliers from developed and developing countries the same information and equal opportunities to compete; and (iv) encourage development of domestic contracting and manufacturing industries in the borrowing country.

A further important case of a centralized approach to emergencies is given by the role played by the GSA in the United States. The agency is empowered to support government efforts by (i) providing guidance on appropriate asset (e.g., aircraft, motor vehicles and personal property) management in response to hurricane support efforts; (ii) selecting vendors, from a special list, as sources for emergency procurements (selection can be done on-line using the GSA's e-tools); and (iii) assisting emergency

---

[27] See Bolton and Farrell (1990) for a discussion of urgencies and examples of military procurement.

[28] See the following article for more information about emergencies procurement in Canada (http://www.findarticles.com/p/articles/mi_qa3993/is_200509/ai_n15639963).

acquisitions of goods and services with GSA Smart Pay, a special card allowing purchasers to procure at lower costs.[29]

3.2.8. Decision information costs

Centralized and decentralized procurement arrangements have advantages and disadvantages. Centralization, whether full or mild, allows the centre to retain authority and control over procurement decisions. However, in order for procurement to be successful, the centre should be aware of the end user's needs and require local units to provide information about them that the centre typically lacks. This implies that the centre incurs decision information costs[30] or information-gathering costs. Such costs tend to increase when procurement is more centralized.

In the past decentralization was a necessity since existing communication lines prevented efficient (fast and precise) and reliable information flows.[31] Therefore, companies working at the global level favoured decentralized functions. Today, ICT innovations allow cheaper and faster worldwide mail/ web communication. These changes have introduced some new perspectives on centralization and decentralization.[32] New arguments for centralization are the role of IT in speeding up decision information processes, reducing their costs via automated workflows and e-tools for learning about local needs. More generally, e-procurement systems appear to support centralization. At the same time, however, IT can also be favourable to decentralization as monitoring and agency costs are reduced. The final decision emerges as a resolution to this trade-off.

The informational gap between central and local procurement units is what generates the cost of collecting and processing local information efficiently, especially for large private companies with many branches located around the world.[33] Therefore it is clear that in order to centralize

---

[29] Visit the GSA Disaster Recovery and Relief Support website. Several US public agencies were involved in responding to the Katrina devastation in 2005. Among them were the GSA, the DoD, the Department of Homeland Security and the Department of Transportation. See Pool and Welch (2005) for further insights into procurement contracting during Katrina.

[30] This definition is given by Gurbaxani and Whang (1991).

[31] See Meyer (1998).

[32] See Somasundaram (2003) for an interesting discussion of information costs for centralized and decentralized (web based) procurement systems.

[33] See Brikely et al. (2004) for more on centralization and decentralization in organizations.

procurement any organization must set up a reliable communication process.[34] This process must be as efficient as possible to allow central purchasing units to undertake timely and appropriate procurement decisions.[35] Decision information costs depend on two main factors:

- The organizational features, such as department fragmentation;
- The nature of the good/service to be procured as well as the characteristics of the market.

The Organizational features can affect decision information costs in two ways. First, for given technology standards, costly communication may arise in deeply hierarchical and fragmented organizations since information has to come from the bottom of the hierarchy, through many steps, up to the top management. The higher the number of steps the more expensive it is to transfer information across organizational layers. Second, the same problem occurs when local purchasing units are geographically dispersed and far from the procurement headquarter; in this case, correct information and communication of data about needs, market conditions and possible future scenarios may become complicated. Therefore, the larger the horizontal/vertical expansion of the organization, the more likely it is for information flows to be less accurate with respect to the needs of the local units; this, of course, can undermine the effectiveness of centralized procurement systems.

With respect to the second point, it is quite evident that transferring and processing information is much easier, faster and cheaper on simple standardized goods than on more complex goods. Take for instance the two polar cases of sheets of paper and facility management. Since there are only a few types of paper sheets (e.g., A3, A4, recycled A3 and A4), and needs are extremely homogeneous across end users, transferring information concerning the paper required is not a concern. The case of facility management instead includes building management services (among others, maintenance of electric systems, management of heating, cleaning and gardening), accounting services and financial consultancy. These services are performed to suit the characteristics/needs *specific* to the local unit. For instance, wiring

---

[34] For a contribution on communication and centralization see Melumad and Reichelstein (1987), Aghion and Tirole (1997) and Dessein (2002).

[35] Communication can also be an important factor for the central procurement unit to control and provide the needed incentives to local procurement units. Some research shows that communication should not be seen only as a cost for organizations, but also as a tool to guide local purchasing units' activities and to transfer values and goals. On this point see, for instance, Melumad and Reichelstein (1987).

and water management depends on size, structure and many other technical and building-specific aspects. Moreover, some services may be useful only to some administrations; for example, elevator maintenance (or asset management) is probably required by (or more valuable to) large municipalities/ministries (in general, big offices), but not necessarily by schools or small offices. In other words, technical aspects and heterogeneity of demand can make information gathering and processing costly at the central level. As a result, procurement may turn out to be largely ineffective.[36]

Box 3.4. Public procurement: OGC buying solutions

The OGC decision on whether and how to set up a frame contract relies heavily upon dialogues with local entities. OGC works jointly with the Customer Programme Board (CPB) to define, frame contracts/agreements. The members of the CPB represent all public administrations, including central civil government, local authorities, defence, etc. Public administrations are presented several scenarios about the actual situation and potential evolution (in terms of new products, solutions and contractual conditions) of the marketplace and about the needs of the local administrations. OGC identifies 'gap' areas; it asks public administrations whether the findings are correct and whether OGC should set up a framework for the areas in the gaps. OGC also asks whether local administrations would buy from that framework.

3.2.9. Bargaining power

Large, decentralized companies, as well as public administrations, often buy the same products from multiple suppliers (e.g., stationery, electricity, PCs), and in so doing fail to take advantage of economies of scale and volume price discounts. Demand aggregation can pool this volume, increase bargaining power and generate lower unit costs.

With a highly pooled demand the buyer's power can be strong; however, this is less the case the fewer the firms that could potentially supply the product. Bargaining power can also be based on a reputation, for instance,

---

[36] Notice that this problem is potentially common to all procurements which heavily bundle contracts.

for being a prompt/reliable payer or for establishing comfortable relationships with suppliers during the execution of the contract.

The first point, however, is more important, which relates the issue of bargaining power to savings induced by economies of scale. When local units are delegated to purchase products they can organize several, and usually independent, procurement competitions or negotiations. But the ability of companies/institutions to obtain a 'good' contract typically increases with the quantity of products being procured, which then entails greater bargaining power. As a consequence, economies of scale may allow the buyer to pay a lower price and/or, at any given price, achieve higher quality or better contract conditions.

Since with centralization the volume of purchased products typically becomes larger, bargaining power tends to increase. And, indeed, centralized purchasing can be particularly advantageous when the buyer is the major customer for a certain product. For example, in many countries, public procurement dominates in the health care and defence sectors.

Within the health care sector public procurement may be almost monopsonist, in some specific markets for sophisticated medical equipment such as MR, ecotomography; this induces considerable contracting power. Decentralizing procurement at the level of single (or groups of) hospitals may not fully exploit this potential bargaining power.

Buyers, however, should pay attention to their dominant purchasing positions. In particular, if not appropriately designed, large procurements can favour big suppliers and discriminate against smaller firms; this can have adverse effects on the short-term, as well as on the long-term, degree of competition in the relevant market (for more on participation, lot division and dynamic competition see Chapters 11 and 17).

Furthermore, large suppliers (as is the case in many sectors of the oligopolistic market for health) may coordinate and 'sink' centralized, non-mandatory, arrangements such as a frame contract, by not participating in the relevant competitive tendering, trusting that this will keep their stronghold on smaller local procurement units that are easier to 'capture'. Mandatory purchasing of health-related products through a centralized agency, however, is often not politically feasible. A gradual approach, where the volume of centralized purchasing is below its potential, might then create a system that slowly evolves towards more competitive conditions.

In the defence sector governments are clearly dominant, and the buyer's power increases with centralization. As illustrated in section 3.2.4.2, the procurement function in China has been moving rapidly towards more centralized arrangements. The National Defence Policy (2004) report indicates that the switch from negotiations to multiple ways of procurement, such as open bidding procedures, invited bidding and competitive bargaining, and the substantial move to centralized procurement 'has raised the overall cost-effectiveness of armaments procurement and ensured the procurement at reasonable prices of weapons and equipment advanced in performance, superior in quality and complete as a set.'

Buyers' concentration and demand coordination can sometimes be important to attract new large suppliers and increase competition. For instance, the move from a situation in which buyers are fragmented and can place only low-value orders to a situation in which all these buyers are coordinated to aggregate purchases may stimulate the entry of new suppliers that would have faced high costs in serving fragmented markets. It is on the basis of this argument, that is, more buyers' power, that the European Commission approved the joint venture ABB/Daimler-Benz (M. 580, 1996) in the sector of transportation.[37] In the sector of paper and board manufacture, the Commission also approved the merger between Enso and Stora (M. 1225, 1999). The main reason here was the existence of a countervailing buying power and increased competition. The European Commission clarified that

The European Commission has decided to authorise the merger between the Finnish paper and board company Enso OYJ (Enso) and the Swedish paper and board manufacturer, Stora Kopparbergs Bergslags AB (Stora). The merger will create the number one paper and board manufacturing company in the world. However, the Commission's investigation showed that the merger will not create or strengthen a dominant position on the newsprint and magazine paper markets. As to paper board for the production of materials to package liquids ('liquid packaging board'), the merged entity will face countervailing buying power from packaging materials producers. This power will be increased by Enso's divestiture of links with one producer, Elopak, and by the parties' agreement not to treat any one producer more favourably than others unless warranted by objective cost justifications. Moreover, third-country imports will further increase competition on the market. The merger will not therefore create or strengthen a dominant position on the liquid packaging market either.

---

[37] This case and related topics are widely discussed in Fumagalli and Motta (2001).

There are other recent cases in which the European Commission approved mergers with motivations based on the benefits from increased buyers' power.[38] Important examples are the mergers of Carrefour and Promodes (M. 1684, 2001), Alcatel and Telettra (M. 42, 1991) and Valeo and ITTI (M. 1245, 1998).

3.2.10. Monitoring contractors' performance

Quality and performance are considered crucial for procurement, and unsatisfactory results are usually punished by excluding suppliers from current and future business (see also Chapter 4 on this point).

Centralization may increase the ability of the buyer to deter post-contractual opportunism.[39] As we saw in section 3.2.9, strong (large) buyers can have considerable bargaining power. Larger procurements may enhance the effectiveness of suppliers' actions, raising non-contractible quality (for more on this see chapter 4) and customer satisfaction compared with small procurements run by local units. This reasoning seems to apply without particular caveats to large buyers purchasing for themselves (and probably for not-too-large private central units purchasing in the interest of local branches) since monitoring may be effectively done centrally.

But it is not clear whether buyers' power driven by centralization, would indeed allow the achievement of higher quality via the threat of contractors losing large volumes of business. Given the level of non-contractible quality of the procurement, monitoring costs appear to increase with centralization if monitoring is also centralized. This is because a contractor's performance information needs to be collected and processed from many dispersed public administrations/end users. When costs increase, incentives for (and effectiveness of) central monitoring may decrease. This may be the reason monitoring is often decentralized. This is so, for example, with the FAR (Federal Acquisition Regulation, 2005), regulating the US federal public acquisition procedures, which specifically requires all agencies to evaluate

---

[38] See http://europa.eu.int/comm/dgs/competition/buyer_power.pdf.

[39] However, as pointed out in Chapter 4, large and long-lasting procurement contracts may provide suppliers with weak incentives to perform well over unverifiable aspects of quality in the absence of appropriate contractual arrangements (bonuses, renewals, etc.) or procurement strategies (dual sourcing). The buyer may end up locked in. See Chapters 7 and 17 for more details about the problem of lock-in.

contractors' past performance (for contracts above $100,000) and use such information for selection purposes.[40] The FAR also provides guidelines on (i) how and what type of information agencies should collect to evaluate contractors and (ii) how agencies should use such information for selection purposes. The US experience suggests that even when procurement can be successfully centralized, monitoring might not be centralized.

Centralization implies shifting decision-making power from the periphery to the centre of the organization. It is therefore possible that those local units which are not in favour of centralization may have the incentive not to monitor appropriately the quality of products which they have not procured, to claim that centralization is ineffective and possibly regain power. If centralization is still deemed optimal, this calls either for centralized monitoring or strong support to local units from the centre in terms of technical and professional assistance.

3.2.11. Centralization and e-procurement

In Section 3.2.8 we noted the importance of ICT infrastructures in enhancing efficient communication among parties involved in a procurement process. We also argued that they help in standardizing purchasing procedures agreed upon by making them more impersonal, less subject to discretionary individual decisions and fully accountable (due to the electronic protocols followed). The importance of e-procurement is shown by the rapid increase in on-line transactions in recent years. The European Commission states that

Modernising and opening up procurement markets across borders – including through the expansion of electronic procurement – is crucial to Europe's competitiveness and for creating new opportunities for EU businesses. Using information technology appropriately can contribute to reducing costs, improving efficiency and removing barriers to trade, which will ultimately result in savings for taxpayers. The Directives adopted in March 2004 as part of the public procurement legislative package provide a legal framework aimed at boosting the development and use of electronic procurement. The Commission has issued an Action Plan in order to help Member States implement the Directives correctly, so as to release the full potential of electronic public procurement.

---

[40] FAR requires past performance to be used only if considered important in awarding the relevant good/service. If this is the case, it must carry a fair weight (no less than 5–10%). If past performance is crucial it must be given a weight no lower than 25%, or at least equal to the weight attached to other non-monetary attributes.

E-procurement increases efficiency by reducing the cost of human resources in purchasing offices and administrative (time-consuming) paper-based procedures. It also allows the buyer to employ a large variety of procurement tools such as requests for quotation, on-line auctions and many other e-sourcing solutions.

Therefore, e-procurement and centralization are closely linked. On the one hand e-procurement favours centralization, since it helps central purchasing bodies successfully manage acquisition processes along the supply chain, while providing sufficient flexibility to local units to satisfy some specific needs.[41]

On the other hand, centralization magnifies the benefits of e-procurement. Web-based sourcing increases efficiency when procurement is more centralized since it affects larger volumes of transactions. However, purchasing systems which were already largely centralized before implementing web-based procedures will obtain fewer benefits than those systems which had most of their procurement decentralized, since they had already exploited many of the gains from centralization. Therefore, one important conclusion is that the value of web-based procurement systems is higher for business units which, by introducing e-procurement systems, can now undertake centralized procurement activities that they did not have before.[42] This view that e-procurement has a considerable impact on centralization is consistent with purchasing practice and recent studies. As discussed in the introduction, several governments and private firms have successfully implemented (or are willing to implement) centralized e-procurement systems.

These movements clearly tend to further centralize procurement and to maximize all the benefits offered by the Internet and, more generally, ICT technologies. A high level of control over procurement policies is positively correlated with the use of e-procurement.[43] In the United States e-tools are used more intensively by large, innovative and highly centralized

---

[41] Somasundaram (2004).

[42] This important conclusion is provided by Subramaniam and Shaw (2003).

[43] See Moon (2005) and Neef (2001) for a discussion on the benefit of e-procurement. Moon (2005) argues that data and analysis are also consistent with the general view that innovations are more likely to be undertaken by large administrations with sufficient financial resources and strong political pressure to find alternative ways to provide public services. Chang and Shaw (2005) describe a roadmap to adopt emerging technology in e-business. In their view, at the initial stages, when the use of e-business technology is limited, production planning, logistics planning and procurement are decentralized and disconnected, so the efforts may be duplicated or inefficient across the network. These considerations suggest that a move to more centralized systems not only is allowed by technology but it appears as necessary to ensure effective communication and processes within

administrations. A survey of forty-seven states showed that in 2001 91.5 percent of the states were allowing electronic competitive bidding, 89.4 percent were using automated procurement systems, 85.1 percent were using purchasing cards and 68.1 percent were running electronic ordering.[44]

We conclude by observing that e-procurement is highly related to the development of e-platforms; for more on this see Chapter 10.

3.3. Concluding remarks

The choice between centralized and decentralized procurement systems has gained importance in recent years for private companies, governments and international institutions. Traditional arguments supporting centralization have been based on product standardization, economies of scale, buyers' power and process streamlining. The ICT revolution and developments in e-sourcing technologies, together with the need to control costs, introduced further elements into the debate on the degree of centralization of a procurement system, and evidence appears to be in favour of more centralized purchasing.

In this chapter we discussed the main factors to be considered while choosing the degree of centralization of a purchasing system. We have seen that emergencies, favouritism, bargaining power and other factors are important determinants in the optimal design of a procurement system, but that product standardization and product strategic role are the crucial elements supporting more centralized procurement systems. However, extreme centralization (or decentralization) is not always an ideal procurement arrangement. The size and characteristics of firm/government activities, market conditions and dynamics suggest that hybrid procurement systems may often be preferable since they allow exploitation of both the efficiency of centralization and the flexibility of decentralization. Recent trends appear to indicate that hybrid models are indeed becoming quite attractive and pervasive for private companies and public procurement agencies.

independent business units and to suppliers (e.g. through centralized design data source and electronic data interchange [EDI]).

[44] See Moon (2005).

We conclude these remarks with the following practical conclusion.

Practical conclusion 1

Benefits from centralization are likely to offset costs when procurement involves standardized, strategic, urgent or very essential products.

Net benefits from centralization increase when procurement is web-based.

Case Study 3.1. Centralized procurement of antimalaria drugs

In what follows we discuss procurement of antimalaria drug. As we shall see, centralization in this field is motivated by many of the elements discussed in the previous sections. Standardization, coordination, bargaining power, quality assurance and concentration of skilled human resources are all aspects suggesting the high desirability of a supranational centralized vaccines procurement body.

In September 2003 the Committee on the Economics of Antimalaria Drugs, jointly with the World Bank and the Roll Back Malaria Partnership, sponsored a meeting aimed at discussing how to procure and finance ACTs (artemisinin-combination therapies). Discussions held at that meeting, and related reports, are the basis of a chapter in the book *Saving Lives, Buying Time – Economics of Malaria Drugs in an Age of Resistance* published by the World Bank/Institute of Medicine in 2004.

That chapter debates the advantages and disadvantages of different levels of international procurement of ACTs, as well as some possible institutional arrangements, among which a more centralized system is proposed. The book argues that some form of centralized, coordinated procurement is widely acknowledged and relatively uncontroversial; this could make effective antimalaria drugs largely accessible and arrest the current trend of increasing deaths from drug-resistant malaria. Since the newer drugs are more expensive than those they are replacing the affected populations, among the world's poorest, cannot afford them. There was a proposal to create an international system for procuring antimalaria drugs, arguing that centralization is not new in this field. The following quotation from the book identifies some of the reasons centralized purchasing is advantageous for this particular problem:

Supranational centralized procurement is attractive because it allows countries to participate in and benefit from a more focused and efficient effort than any single country could individually mount. Even if their drug policies differ, all malarious countries face common challenges. Every country with endemic falciparum malaria will need at least one ACT as first-line treatment for uncomplicated cases. The number of available ACTs in the short-to-medium term will probably number half a dozen, produced by 10–20 manufacturers capable of delivering ACTs of acceptable quality.

Coordination, product standardization, economies of scale, bargaining power and quality assurance of drugs are key elements inducing procurement centralization in this very important sector. In this particular case, centralization is supported by other important factors such as (i) the greater ability of an international procurement institution to get subsidies from other international organizations and to use them promptly to buy the drugs (timing, in this area, is crucial to save lives; accordingly, the proposed procurement system should organize only procurement, not shipping);[45] (ii) the greater ability of supranational organizations to forecast demand. The demand for ACTs is hard to estimate, but estimation is essential to run appropriate procurements. It could be easier for an international central procurement institution to have the right human and financial resources to conduct reliable forecast activity.

Bibliographical notes

The economic literature on centralization and optimal organization design is quite extensive. For a broad discussion on the theme, as applied to organizations, see the book by Brickley, Smith and Zimmerman (2004). The volume also considers several interesting case studies and patterns in the private sector. A more detailed analysis on communication and decision information costs can be found in Bolton and Dewatripont (1994), Gurbaxani and Whang (1991) and Melumad and Reichelstein (1987). Dessein (2002) and Aghion and Tirole (1997) examine decision information costs with an emphasis on strategic decisions and market dynamics.

Research on centralization, as applied to procurement, is quite recent. McCue and Pitzer (2000), which provides a definition of centralized procurement, contains an interesting overview of recent trends concerning centralized/decentralized purchasing systems. More on public procurement trends can also be found in Thai and Grimm (2000), Neef (2001) and Piga and Zanza (2004).

---

[45] The book reports that 'ACTs currently have a short shelf-life roughly estimated at 2 years. Therefore, one practical consideration for a procurement agency will be organizing the direct delivery of ACTs from producer to customer with as little delay as possible. This precludes the procurement agency from physically warehousing ACTs and shipping them.'

For insights into emergencies, duplications and delay issues see Bolton and Farrell (1990). Favouritism and corruption are examined in Celentani and Ganuza (2002) and Vagstad (2000). The relation between e-procurement, IT architecture and centralization is discussed in Chang and Shaw (2005), Somasundaram (2004), Subramaniam and Shaw (2003), Subramaniam, Qualls and Shaw (2002) and Moon (2005).

References

Aghion, P. and J. Tirole (1997). Formal and Real Authority in Organizations, *Journal of Political Economy*, 105, 1–29.

Andersen, K. V., N. C. Juul, S. Korzen-Bohr and J. K. Pedersen (2003). Fractional Institutional Endeavors and e-procurement in Local Government. Proceedings of the 16th Bled Electronic Commerce Conference, Bled, Slovenia 961–973.

Bernauer T. and L. Caduff (2004). European Food Safety: Multilevel Governance, Re-Nationalization, or Centralization? Working Paper No 3 CIS ETH Zurich.

Bernheim, D. B. and M. D. Whinston (1990). Multimarket Contact and Collusive Behavior, *RAND Journal of Economics*, 21 (1), 1–26.

Besley, T. and L. Jewitt (1991). Decentralizing Public Goods. *Econometrica*, 56 (6), 1769–1778.

Bolton, P. and M. Dewatripont (1994). The Firm as a Communication Network, *Quarterly Journal of Economics*, 4, 809–839.

Bolton, P. and J. Farrell. (1990). Decentralization, Duplication and Delay. *Journal of Political Economy*, 98, 803–826.

Brickley J., C. Smith and J. Zimmerman (2004). *Managerial Economics and Organizational Architecture*, McGraw Hill-Irwin.

Cabral, L. and S. Greenstein (1990). Switching Costs and Bidding Parity in Government Procurement of Computer Systems. *Journal of Law, Economics and Organization*, 6, 453–469.

Celentani M. and J. Ganuza (2002). Organized vs. Competitive Corruption, *Annals of Operations Research*, 109, 293–315.

Chang, H. L. and M. J. Shaw (2005). A Roadmap to Adopting Emerging Technology in E–Business An Empirical Study. College Business Working paper, University of Illinois.

Committee on the Economics of Antimalarial Drugs, Board on Global Health (2004). *Saving Lives, Buying Time (Economics of Malaria Drugs in an Age of Resistance)*. K. J. Arrow, C. B. Panosian and H. Gelband, Eds., The National Academic Press.

Dessein, W. (2002). Authority and Communication in Organizations, *Review of Economic Studies*, 69, 811–838.

Directive 2004/18/EC of the European Parliament and of the Council of 31 March 2004 on the coordination of procedures for the award of public works contracts, public supply contracts and public service contracts. Official Journal L. 134, 30/04/2004 p. 0114 − 0240.

Fumagalli C. and M. Motta (2001). Buyers Coordination and Entry, CEPR Discussion Paper No. 2908, Mimeo.

Gurbaxani, V. and S. Whang (1991). The Impact of Information Systems on Organizations and Markets. *Communications of the ACM*, 34 (10), 23.

Government Accountability Office, *United Nations Preliminary Observations on Internal Oversight and Procurement Practices*, Statement of Thomas Melito, Director International Affairs and Trade, Testimony Before the Permanent Subcommittee on Investigations, Committee on Homeland Security and Governmental Affairs, U. S. Senate, United States, GAO-06–226T, 10/31/2005.

Hart O. and J. Moore (2005). On the Design of Hierarchies: Coordination versus Specialization, *Journal of Political Economy*, 113, 675–702.

Jones, D. S. (2002). Procurement Practices in the Singapore Civil Service: Balancing Control and Delegation. *Journal of Public Procurement*, 2 (1): 29–53.

McCue, C. P. and J. T. Pitzer (2000). Centralized vs. Decentralized Purchasing: Current Trends in Governmental Procurement Practices. *Journal of Public Budgeting, Accounting & Financial Management*, 12 (2), 400–420.

Macho-Stadler I. and J. D. Pérez-Castrillo, (1998). Centralized and Decentralized Contracts in a Moral Hazard Environment, *Journal of Industrial Economics*, 46 (4), 489–510.

Melumad, N. D. and S. Reichelstein (1987). Centralization versus delegation and the value of communication. *Journal of Accounting Research* 25, supplement, 1–18.

Melumad, N. and T. Shibano (1991). Communication in Settings with No Transfers, *Rand Journal of Economics*, 22, 173–198.

Melumad, N., D.Mookherjee and S. Reichelstein (1995). Hierarchical Decentralization of Incentive Contracts, *The Rand Journal of Economics*, 26, (4), 654–672.

Meyer, N. D. (1998). *Decentralization: Fantasies, Failings and Fundamentals*, NMDA Publishing.

Moon, M. J. (2005). E-procurement Management in State Governments: Diffusion of E-procurement Practices and its Determinants, *Journal of Public Procurement*, 5, (1), 54–72.

Neef, D. (2001). *E-procurement: From Strategy to Implementation*, Prentice Hall.

Piga, G. and M. Zanza (2004). An Exploratory Analysis of Public Procurement Practices in Europe, ch. 10 in K. V. Thai, A. Aranjo, R. Y. Carter, G. Cullender, D. Prabkin, R. Grimm, K. R. E. Jense, R. E. Lloyd, C. P. Mecue and J. Telgen (Eds.), *Challenges in Public Procurement: an International Perspective*, PrAcademic Press, 227–247.

Pool, C. and B. Welch (2005). Responding to Katrina: Contracting in an Emergency Situation – Version 2.0. Acquisition Direction Advisory http://summitinsight.com/femakatrina.pdf.

Roberts, J. (2004). *The Modern Firm*, Oxford University Press.

Somasundaram, R. (2004). *Diffusion of e-Procurement in the Public Sector: Revisiting Centralized vs. Decentralized Debates As a Twist in the Tale*, Proceedings of the 13th European Conference on Information Systems.

Subramaniam, C. and M. J. Shaw (2003). A Study on the Value and Impact of B2B E-commerce: The Case of Web-Based Procurement, *International Journal of Commerce*, 6 (4), 19.

Subramaniam, C., Qualls W. and M. J. Shaw (2002). Impact of B2B E-Procurement Systems; A Summary Report-College of Business.

Thai, K. V. and R. Grimm (2000). Government Procurement: Past and Current Developments. *Journal of Public Budgeting, Accounting & Financial Management*, 12 (2): 231–247.

Vagstad, S. (2000). Centralized vs. Decentralized Procurement: Does Dispersed Information Call for Decentralized Decision-Making? *International Journal of Industrial Organization*, 18, 949–963.

4 Procurement contracting strategies

Gian Luigi Albano, Giacomo Calzolari, Federico Dini,
Elisabetta Iossa and Giancarlo Spagnolo

4.1. Introduction

Well-designed supply contracts are essential to effective procurement.[1] By
fixing obligations and promises, contracts protect each party in a procurement transaction against the risk of unexpected changes in the future
behaviour of business partners, thereby allowing safe and efficient planning,
investing, and production in decentralized supply chains. Contract obligations ensure, for example, that a buyer will receive the right service or good
when and as needed, as promised by her supplier, and that the supplier's
investment specific to a particular procurement will not be 'wasted,' in the
sense that the buyer will indeed buy what she ordered at the agreed terms.

There are several types of contracts and very many dimensions along
which apparently similar contracts differ, so that choosing the right contracting strategy is not always easy for a buyer. And a bad choice of contract
can have very negative consequences for a buyer in terms of cost and quality
of supply. However, economists and practitioners would agree on considering *contract flexibility*, the *incentives for quality and cost reduction*, and
the allocation of procurement risk as the most important dimensions influencing the buyer's choice of the procurement contract.

In this chapter we offer simple and practical indications on how to
choose among different types of procurement contracts. We focus on
situations where the needs of the buyers are unlikely to change during
the execution of the contract, so that renegotiation of the initial
contract specifications, which is generally costly for the buyer, is unlikely to

---

[1] The origin of the word contract is the Latin *contractus*, from *contrahere*, to draw together, while
dictionary definitions of the term include 'an agreement between two or more parties, especially one
that is written and enforceable by law', or more specifically 'an agreement between two or more parties
that creates in each party a duty to do or not do something and a right to performance of the other's
duty or a remedy for the breach of the other's duty' (Dictionary.com).

occur.[2] In these situations, contract flexibility plays a limited role in the choice of the procurement contract whilst incentives for quality and cost reduction as well as procurement risk allocation remain central. The issue of contract flexibility will be analysed in depth in Chapter 5. Also, we will discuss only briefly how the choice of the procurement contract can affect the characteristics of the suppliers that decide to participate in the procurement process. For an in-depth discussion of issues related to how to select the most efficient supplier, see Parts II and III of this handbook.

The present chapter is organized as follows. In the first part we focus on *explicit contracts*, that is, on written and legally binding contracts that can be enforced by courts of law and therefore can govern dimensions of the procurement that can be monitored and verified by a court at a reasonable cost. Within this framework, in section 4.2 we explain the importance of choosing the allocation of procurement risk and the relevance of creating incentives for quality provision and for cost reduction. In section 4.3 we describe the features of the most frequently used contract types. We discuss how these contracts differ in the allocation of procurement risk and in the provision of incentives on cost and quality dimensions that are hard to contract upon explicitly. We also discuss the procurement context in which a contract type may work best. In the second part of the chapter we turn to *implicit contracts*. When important aspects of a procurement transaction are not verifiable by third parties, implicit/relational agreements sustained by the threat of losing reputation and/or future business in case of non-compliance can be very effective in inducing the contractor to maintain promises and in general to respect the terms of the (implicit) agreement made with the buyer. In section 4.4 we then discuss different types of implicit contracts and the procurement context in which they can be effective.

4.2. The choice of the procurement contract

4.2.1. The role of procurement risk

Procurement risk refers to those events that may affect the realization of the contractual performance, and whose occurrence cannot be accurately

---

[2] A brilliant, in-depth treatment of the economic effects of explicit procurement contracting is in Laffont and Tirole (1993). An equally brilliant and in-depth discussion of the achievements of contract theory is Bolton and Dewatripont (2003). Both these contributions are rather technical. Some non-technical synthetic discussions of contracting issues are offered by an interesting book by McMillan (1992). As for the practice of procurement contracting, see FAR (2005, part 16) and Office of Government Commerce guidelines, both of which we mention in the next section.

predicted and *influenced* by contracting parties. In large and complex acquisitions, such as the construction of a new tunnel, risk may refer, among other things, to the discovery of a particularly resistant rock that needs a specifically designed drilling machine. In less complex procurements, such as the supply of milk to schools, risk may refer to late deliveries caused by bad weather conditions, or to the sudden increase in fuel price (which raises the actual delivery cost with respect to the level estimated by the contractor before the tendering process). Procurement risk affects actual production costs and it can affect the quality of the performance, be it on-time delivery of ink cartridges for laser printers or the brightness of paper for photocopiers. Most important, the buyer and the contractors care about 'extreme' events such as the risk of contractor default that may disrupt the service altogether. The degree of fear of (procurement) risk is also called *risk aversion*.[3]

In procurement contracts, it is unlikely that a contractor will be able to immunize himself (say, through an insurance contract) against all unpredictable events. However, the breadth and the nature of a contractor's activities may provide useful *proxies* for his ability to 'insure' himself against the vagaries of a specific procurement contract. Possible internal 'insurance policies' are thus provided by the value of the contract being only a tiny fraction of the contractor's turnover, a high degree of diversification of the contractor's activities, and, more generally, by the contractor's ease of access to the credit market.

The absolute capacity of each contracting party to bear the procurement risk is not, however, the most relevant factor for selecting the contractual form. What really matters is the contracting parties' *relative* attitude toward risk: other things being equal, efficient risk sharing calls for risk to lie with the party that is able to manage it best. The first relevant case then arises when the buyer is more concerned about risk than the supplier. This is exactly the environment studied in Chapter 13. The second relevant case arises when the buyer and the supplier are both indifferent to risk. In this

---

[3] We clarify the concept of risk aversion with the following example. Suppose that a firm has to choose between two possible investment decisions, A and B. Option A yields €100 for sure, option B yields zero with probability 1/2 and €200 also with probability 1/2. A firm is said to fear risk (or be risk averse) if it prefers option A to B, that is, if it prefers a riskless investment whose (certain) monetary value is exactly equal to the expected monetary value of the risky investment, where the latter is a weighted average of the risky outcomes whose weights are given by the probabilities that each outcome occurs (1/2 * €0 + 1/2 * €200 = €100). Indifference to risk (or risk neutrality), instead, arises when the firm is indifferent between A and B. In other words the firm is indifferent between a sure bet and a risky bet whose expected monetary value is equal to the one of the sure bet.

case, it is, in principle, efficient for the buyer to shift all the risk to the contractor to maximize the performance incentives. This objective can be pursued by selecting a contract in which the contractor takes on the cost reducing activities, and thus bears most of the risk.

This chapter analyses the case in which the supplier is at least as concerned about risk as the buyer, as is frequently the case in procurement.[4] In this case, efficient risk sharing would call for the buyer to bear all the risk. As we shall see, though, this might have a negative impact on incentives.

4.2.2. The role of incentives for cost reducing activities and quality provision

In a procurement market for standardized goods/services, quality parameters can be measured at some cost. For instance, the relevant quality parameters of a laptop are the nature and type of the screen, processor, memory and external connection devices. Moreover, on-time delivery can be easily checked. Cleaning services for hospital rooms also have many verifiable quality dimensions. It is indeed easy to measure the bacterial concentration in the air and on the floor.

When quality is verifiable, it is always advisable to specify a quality standard in the contract, and then to impose penalties when quality falls below that standard and possibly bonuses when quality is above the standard. The penalty imposed must be such that it is convenient for the contractor to supply the quality promised at the selection stage rather than violate the contract and save money. Since suppliers may have different costs of reducing the quality agreed upon and since these costs are likely to be unknown to the buyer, establishing the level of penalty that induces the contractor to provide quality is not often an easy task. Also, in case of a dispute, penalties that are too high may not be enforced by the court, because it may consider enforceable only reasonable damage actually

---

[4] Competition for procurement contracts very often involves small and medium enterprises, which by features and size may fear risk more than large firms. An additional potential source of risk arising in public procurement is the (typical) delayed payment of public administrations. In contrast to large firms, who benefit from diversification of activities and/or more general financial solidity, small firms incur very high costs when buyers do not pay on time, since their current production/activities/ investments can rely heavily on those cash flows. This is a clear source of risk, but also a potential entry barrier to the market for procurement contracts. Another potential source of uncertainty is that very often small suppliers group together to bid for a public contract (or are subcontracted part of the supply), but grouping/subcontracting makes the performance of each single supplier depend on the performance of all others. Default/poor performance of a single supplier can compromise the others' performance and overall results.

suffered by the party (see Chapter 12 for further discussions on penalty levels).[5,6]

In procurement markets for non-standardized goods or services, such as clinical and educational services or complex infrastructures such as high-tech IT projects, there are dimensions of the exchange that cannot be explicitly considered in the contract even if they are observable by the contracting parties.[7] This occurs because these dimensions cannot be verified by third parties such as courts of law. The quality of the goods or services procured often comprises some unverifiable dimensions.

In this chapter we shall consider both verifiable and thus contractible and non-verifiable and thus non-contractible quality and we shall discuss the incentive problem that arises because the contractor might wish to choose to deliver low quality in order to reduce its production costs or its effort.

As to production costs, the aggregate costs of producing a certain good or service are in most procurement situations verifiable from accounting data. In most of this chapter we will then restrict our attention to situations where accounting data are reliable and aggregate costs are verifiable. This allows the buyer to link the payment mechanism to the realization of aggregate costs – a possibility whose pros and cons we shall discuss in depth. However, whilst aggregate costs are generally verifiable, specific actions, including the contractor's effort, undertaken by the contractor may not be. How to induce the contractor to undertake valuable cost-reducing activities that lower the possibility of cost escalating will be a central issue in what follows.

Before concluding this section, we wish to point out that different contracts are associated with different contract management costs, such as verifying the reliability of the contractor's accounting costs, measuring different levels of quality standards, computing and enforcing penalties, and in general monitoring compliance with the terms specified in the original contract. Whilst for brevity we will not discuss these costs explicitly, we wish

---

[5] This is the principle of 'liquidated damage' actually informing the contracting laws in the United Kingdom. An interesting discussion on the topic is provided by Anderlini and Felli (2005).

[6] Suppose the penalty for not providing what was promised on a certain quality dimension is €100, and that there are three competing suppliers, A, B and C, who can save €20, €90, €150, respectively by providing less than the promised quality. While A and B always prefer delivering what was promised, C does not since it could earn €50 if it violates the contract. However, if the buyer could in some ways learn such costs, she could fix the penalty at €160 and induce all suppliers to keep promises.

[7] For instance, in the case of consultancy services, even though the contractor promises to employ highly qualified and referenced professionals, their ability to perform required tasks may be lower than expected. This dimension is hard or even impossible to specify in the contract.

to emphasize that as a general principle more complex contracts tend to be associated with higher management costs, and that there cannot be efficient procurement without efficient contract management.[8]

4.3. The most commonly used categories of procurement contracts: explicit contracting

The US Federal Acquisition Regulation (FAR, part 16) pays considerable attention to contracting issues. The FAR describes a large variety of contract types that may be used in acquisitions, prescribes policies and procedures and provides guidance for selecting the appropriate contract depending on the circumstances of the procurement. The Department of Trade and Industry (DTI) and the Office of Government Commerce (OGC) in the United Kingdom provide indications on contracting choices for all procurements over £10,000 in value. Similar to FAR, the DTI describes many types of contracts and provides indications useful to teams, consultants, professional advisers, senior management (who need quick overviews of key principles), but also to suppliers (who can learn what the departments will expect of them).

The practice of procurement contracts distinguishes three broad categories of contracts: fixed-price, cost reimbursement or cost-plus, and incentive contracts (the most commonly used forms are fixed prices and incentive contracts). Many procurement contracts are in fact a combination of the three broad categories, specifying incentives on some aspects and fixed-prices on other aspects, and combining contract types in order to adapt the contract to the specific circumstance faced by the buyer.

4.3.1. Cost-reimbursement contracts

The distinguishing feature of cost-reimbursement contracts (CRCs) is that the buyer agrees to reimburse all (documented) production costs related to the project and to pay a fee for supervision (also defined as cost-plus-fixed-fee contracts according to the FAR). Thus the contractor does not have to worry about the possible discrepancies between estimated and actual

---

[8] Iossa and Legros (2004) show for example how it might be desirable to choose the procurement contract in such a way as to induce information acquisition and revelation on the contractor's performance from future potential contractors.

production costs; hence he is fully insured against any cost overrun. However, for the same reason, CRCs have the disadvantage of not providing the contractor with incentives to undertake cost-reducing activities or effort in order to limit costs. However, if the contractor's actions in cost-reducing activities have no bite because, say, unpredictable events adversely affect the completion of the project, he cannot be held responsible for discrepancies between estimated and actual production costs.[9]

A special form of CRC is the capped price contract (CPC), which is frequently used by the UK Department of Trade and Industry, particularly for professional and consultancy services. These contracts are similar to cost-reimbursement contracts in that a daily fee, which includes also a profit component, is agreed for a certain number of capped days. For instance, the contract would specify a fee of £500 per day at a maximum of thirty days, so the cap is fixed at £15,000. The cap is clearly indicated in the contract/purchase order. If the contractor is able to complete the task within the stipulated number of days then his bill will be less than the capped amount. If, however, the contractor needs additional days to complete the task, he has to make the case for the cap to be increased. The rationale behind such a contract is that the buyer is sometimes unable to estimate how much work is needed to produce, say, a financial report. However, it is necessary to explicitly include a cap otherwise the contractor would always have an incentive to put in little effort, thus stretching the duration of the project and raising the bill.[10]

Unit price contracts (UPCs) are similar to CPCs in that the buyer asks suppliers to submit offers specifying a separate unit price for each input factor, but does not include any cap. Moreover, the buyer announces an estimate of the quantity of the input factors needed to complete the project. For each incoming offer, the buyer evaluates the overall expected cost, or the 'score' of this offer. The buyer awards the contract to the firm with the lowest score (cost), but is obliged to pay for the input factor needed to complete the project.[11]

---

[9] Practical guidelines are explicit in restricting the use of cost-reimbursement contracts to special circumstances, that is, 'when uncertainties involved in contract performance do not permit costs to be estimated with sufficient accuracy to use any type of fixed-price contract'. See FAR (2005, 16.301–3).

[10] This simple observation is consistent with the OGC's guidelines stating that the capped price contract should never be drawn up solely on the basis of an agreed daily (or other period) fee, without including a cap on time or cost.

[11] Ewerhart and Fieseler (2003) analyse the consequences of suppliers' strategic bidding in a UPC competitive tendering.

The above variants to CRCs attenuate the incentive problem typical of CRC contracts, but do not fully solve it. Thus, CRC contracts are not suitable in situations where the total costs of a procured project greatly depend on the incentives of the contractor to contain project costs, and lack of adequate incentives for the contractor to contain cost could easily result in cost escalating during the project realization.

Another drawback of CRCs is that they affect the screening process at the tendering stage. More precisely, when the buyer faces a reasonably large pool of potential contractors and is truly uncertain about their intrinsic efficiency levels, the use of cost-reimbursement contracts may not select the most efficient supplier. Since all costs are reimbursed, efficient and non-efficient suppliers will have an incentive to submit the same offer at the selection stage, thus preventing the buyer from selecting the most efficient supplier. The prospect of being fully reimbursed once the project is undertaken provides the least efficient supplier an extra incentive to bid aggressively for the contract.[12] This observation implies that CRCs should never be awarded through a competitive tendering process since they may jeopardize the buyer's goal of selecting the most efficient supplier.[13]

There are, however, cases where CRCs can perform well. In particular this is the case when contract flexibility is important. As pointed out in Chapter 5, when important design changes are likely to occur *after* the contract is signed and production begins – because of design failures, unanticipated site and environmental conditions, changes in regulatory requirements – then CRCs can be a suitable contractual form because they reduce (or even eliminate) the costs of renegotiating the contract.

CRCs can also be suitable in situations where quality is non-verifiable and it plays an important role in the procurement market. This is because CRCs have the advantage of not giving the contractor incentives to cut quality in order to save on the monetary cost of quality provision. As we have seen, with a CRC cost savings do not accrue to the contractor. Thus, the lack of incentives for cost reduction that characterizes CRCs may actually work well in terms of provision of non-verifiable quality. However, under a CRC, the contractor will generally still have incentives to cut quality in order to save on the non-monetary dimensions (e.g., time and effort) of the cost of quality provision. See Chapter 5 for more on this point.

---

[12] McAfee and McMillan (1986) on this point.

[13] We refer the reader to Chapter 5 for an in-depth analysis of the circumstances under which the buyer may prefer negotiation to a competitive tendering process for selecting the contractor(s).

4.3.2. Fixed-price contracts

A fixed-price contract (FPC) is a contractual agreement whereby the contractor is paid a fixed price for realizing a project that satisfies a predetermined quality standard. The fixed price usually comes out of a competitive tendering process. While the contractors receive no additional payment for achieving higher quality standards, penalties are typically included in the contract to be levied if the delivered quality is below the agreed standard. Clearly, in order to deter the contractor from opportunism, penalties have to be high enough relative to the value of the contract; otherwise they have no bite in preventing quality reduction on the part of contractors.[14]

Under an FPC, the contractor bears all the costs incurred in providing the good or service specified in contract. The contractor then fully enjoys the benefits of possible cost savings realized in implementing a project with the agreed quality standard. It follows that FPCs spur the contractor's investment in cost-reducing activities. However, under an FPC the contractor fully bears the risk of sustaining higher production costs than those estimated before submitting his bid, and it is then crucial that the contractor is able to control production costs, that is, that unexpected events do not play a crucial role in determining actual production costs. Such a situation typically arises when the project is not very complex and markets for the relevant production input do not suffer much from unexpected potentially adverse shocks.

The class of fixed-price contracts comprises also some variants. One example is provided by fixed-price contracts with economic price adjustment (FPCPAs) that take into account fluctuations of inputs prices (labour and material) used by the contractor. Adjustments typically take place according to indexed prices that are explicitly indicated in the contract.[15] The logic behind such a contract is to reduce the risk faced by the contractor.

FPCs are then appropriate for projects involving little complexity and uncertainty, that is, for standardized products/services. If the actual production costs of the projects depend heavily upon the contractor's actions/investments to reduce costs (or to increase quality) and very little on events

---

[14] In Italy, for instance, the value of penalties cannot exceed 10% of the overall contract value.

[15] FPCPAs may become an appropriate solution when there is uncertainty about the stability of market or labour conditions during the period of contract performance and when 'contingencies that would otherwise be included in the contract price can be identified and covered separately in the contract'. See FAR (2005, 16.203–2).

out of his control, the buyer may find it profitable to make the contractor bear all the burden for cost savings, thus providing an incentive scheme that reconciles both the buyer's and the contractor's interests.[16] The following example, borrowed from a procurement competition organized by the Italian Procurement Agency (Consip), illustrates some of the circumstances under which a fixed-price contract may become the appropriate contractual form.

Example 4.1. Standardized software package and helpdesk service

A group of local public authorities wished to procure a software package for treating financial data (e.g., cash flows), together with a centralized helpdesk service. The features of the software package as well as the related costs (e.g., licences) were considered sufficiently predictable. It was not a contract for the development of a new software, rather for the provision of an existing, standard application software for end users.

Potential suppliers were believed to be heterogeneous with respect to their ability to provide a certain quality level of the *bundle* of software and helpdesk. The sources of potential opportunism were mainly concentrated in setting up and running the helpdesk service. Suppose indeed that a user suddenly found it difficult to activate one particular command of the software. She then decides to ring up the helpdesk. How long is she going to wait to talk to the operator?

Upon designing the contract, the procurement agency was in a position to take these contingencies into account by establishing *ex ante* a minimal quality standard for the helpdesk service. For instance, queries had to be answered within x minutes. Not only could such contingencies be observed by both parties (contractor and user), they could also be verified; that is, it was feasible to conceive, at a reasonable cost, a monitoring mechanism producing pieces of evidence (e.g., phone call records) that could be brought to a court of justice had a formal complaint arisen from either party.

---

[16] The contractual practice in the United States is consistent with our main conclusion. The Federal Acquisitions Regulation (FAR) advises the contracting officer to adopt a (firm-)fixed-price contract for 'acquiring commercial items or for acquiring other supplies or services on the basis of reasonably functional or detailed specifications when the contracting officer can establish fair and reasonable prices at the outset, such as when – [...] available cost or pricing information permits realistic estimates of the probable cost of performance; or performance uncertainties can be identified and reasonably estimates of their cost impact can be made [...]' (16.202–2).

The nature of such a contract has now become clear enough to draw some practical conclusions. The intrinsic features of the software package being standard, production costs were predictable and reasonably unaffected by unexpected events. The minimal quality standards of the helpdesk service being observable and verifiable, each potential supplier could reasonably estimate the cost of running such a service. Thus the overall cost of supplying both the software and the helpdesk service could be estimated *ex ante* quite accurately by competing suppliers. It was then decided to adopt a fixed-price contract to be awarded through competitive tendering. The contract consisted of a fixed price for the bundle of services (software and helpdesk line), plus a series of penalties to be levied if the *ex post* quality of the service had fallen below the contractual minimal standards.

Example 4.2. Public-private partnerships in the construction industry

A common form of public–private partnership (PPP) for the provision of public services in the United Kingdom involves the purchase of services associated with a facility (e.g., a school, a hospital or a road) for a fixed number of years. The contractor, commonly a consortium of firms, takes responsibility for all stages of the project – typically, the design, building and operation of the facility and the finance of the project against a fixed fee for a certain number of years. The contractor therefore fully bears the risk of cost overruns, but also enjoys the benefit of any cost reduction that a better facility or project design generates. As reported by the National Audit Office (2005), PPP construction projects are about two-thirds better (in percentage of projects) in terms of delivering on time and within budget than conventionally procured projects.

The above examples emphasize the advantages of FPCs in terms of incentives for cost reduction. However, precisely because of these incentives, FPCs may be unsuitable in situations where quality is unverifiable. Strong cost-reduction incentives can induce the contractor to save on non-verifiable activities, at the (buyer's) cost of quality degradation. If the contractor has something to gain from providing unverifiable quality (e.g., reputation), and would indeed provide it if he were not under pressure to reduce cost, then FPCs may not be the most suitable procurement contract, unless, as we shall see in section 4.4, there are other ways (namely, implicit contracting) for the buyer to induce the contractor to supply non-verifiable quality.

4.3.3. Incentive contracts

In between the two extremes of CRCs and FPCs lie incentive contracts (ICs). Incentive contracts typically include a target cost, a target profit and a profit adjustment formula which ensures that (i) actual cost or quality that meets the target will result in the target profit or fee; (ii) actual cost (quality) that exceeds (is below) the target will result in downward adjustment of target profit or fee; and (iii) actual cost (quality) that is below (exceeds) the target will result in upward adjustment of target profit or fee. While the amount of profit or fee payable under the contract is related to the contractor's performance, the contractor is never left entirely responsible for fluctuations in production costs.[17]

4.3.3.1. Linear incentive contracts

ICs have been extensively used in complex procurements in the construction industry and in the US defence industry as an alternative to CRCs. ICs often take the form of *cost* incentive contracts. The most common form of cost incentive contracts is linear and can be described by the following compensation scheme for the contractor:

$$T = P + bC,$$

where T is the total transfer to the contractor, P is a (fixed) base payment, C is the realized (verifiable) cost and b is a positive constant between zero and one representing the share of cost borne by the buyer. In the extreme cases of b=0 and b=1 IC becomes a fixed price and a cost-reimbursement contract, respectively.

Analogous incentive contracts can also be used to stimulate quality provision of the good/service rather than cost reduction. In this case, an IC normally specifies a base payment P for minimum performance q_{min} (e.g., shipping the good within a certain date), typically a quality measure, and additional higher target levels $q_1, \ldots, q_n$ with corresponding bonuses $B_1, \ldots, B_n$ so that if target q_i is reached (delivery takes place x_i days before the deadline), the buyer pays an additional bonus B_i.

---

[17] 'Most incentive contracts include only cost incentives, which take the form of a profit or fee adjustment formula, and are intended to motivate the contractor to effectively manage costs. No incentive contract may provide for other incentives without also providing a cost incentive.' See FAR (2005, 16.402–1).

4.3.3.2. Balancing risk sharing and incentives

An incentive contract stimulates the contractor to limit costs by leaving him a fraction of cost savings, but at the same time it reimburses him some money in case of cost overrun. Similarly, a quality incentive contract stimulates the contractor to provide better quality by including (possibly increasing) bonuses if the achieved quality levels are higher than the minimal performance. In both cases, the incentive scheme designed in the contract balances risk sharing and incentives.

As explained above, the cost-sharing parameter b plays a crucial role in the contractor's incentives to reduce cost. The higher b, the less the contractor is responsible for cost overruns and the less the contractor benefits from cost reduction; thus the higher the cost-sharing parameter b, the lower the incentives of the contractor to reduce cost (that is, using economics terms, the lower the 'power of the incentive scheme').[18]

What criteria should the buyer adopt to set the cost-sharing parameter b? Atleast, three factors affect the choice of b:[19] the ability of the contractor to bear the procurement risk, the predictability (i.e., the variability) of the shock affecting production costs and the responsiveness of the actual production cost to cost-reducing activities (investment, effort, care).

The first factor, as we explained earlier in this section, becomes relevant if the contractor is unable to insure himself against unexpectedly high production costs; thus it measures the contractor's aversion to receiving variable payments. The higher the contractor's risk aversion, the less willing he is to agree on a contract that is sensitive to the difference between the estimated and the realized production costs. The second factor captures the extent to which the contracting parties are able to predict shocks that might affect productions costs. When such shocks are highly unpredictable, then the contractor is less willing to accept a high-powered incentive contract, that is, a low cost-sharing parameter b.[20] The third factor provides a measure of the contractor's return from investing in (costly) activities to keep production costs low. More concretely, when uncertainty about shocks is low, when the contractor is moderately concerned about risk (his business activities are sufficiently diversified, the value of the procurement contract is small with respect to the contractor's turnover), and when the expected impact on project costs of cost-reducing activities or effort by the contract is

---

[18] McMillan (1992) provides an interesting non-technical discussion on performance incentives.

[19] See Weitzman (1980).

[20] In US defence procurement contracts, b typically varies between 0.1 and 0.3 (see Laffont and Tirole 1993, ch. 1).

large, then b can be optimally set closer to 0. Instead, when the expected impact on project costs of cost-reducing activities or effort by the contractor is low, when shocks are highly unpredictable and when the contractor's risk aversion is high, then the cost-sharing parameter b should be set closer to 1.

In a procurement environment where both unpredictable events and the contractor's actions/investments affect the level of actual production costs, but neither of them is the crucial dimension, ICs can be a good choice for the buyer for they (i) motivate the contractor to undertake cost-reducing actions, and (ii) offer the contractor a form of insurance against adverse exogenous events.

The following example describes an incentive contract in which the quality of the performance can be easily measured in monetary units.

Example 4.3. Real estate management

The contractor undertakes the conversion of a series of buildings into commercial outlets and rents them on behalf of a local buyer. The contractor binds himself to guarantee a minimum level of rent per year (minimum performance). The incentive scheme takes the form of a percentage on the difference between the actual rental price the contractor agrees with tenants and the minimum rental price the contractor has to guarantee to the owner. The higher the actual rental price, above the guaranteed minimum level, the higher the payment to the contractor. Obviously, the higher effort (intensity of search) the contractor expends in looking for (possibly wealthy) tenants, the higher the probability that the actual rent will be above the guaranteed minimum level, which, in turn, generates a high profit share to the contractor. However, the actual outcome is also affected by events that escape the contractor's control: sudden slowdown of demand in the real estate rental market, lower transaction costs that favor the selling market etc. Given that the contractor is less able than the buyer to bear the risk linked to those events, it is optimal that the buyer share with the contractor their effects through an IC.

4.3.3.3. Incentive contracts and transaction costs

How costly is it to manage an incentive contract? The incentive contract just described looks quite easy to handle. Both the procurer and the contractor need one piece of information: the actual rental price. However, in many contractual environments, especially those where the incentive schemes rely on the difference between actual and estimated production costs, the contractor bears the brunt of providing precise accounting measures of realized production costs while the procurer has to measure quality levels. These pieces of information are necessary for the computation of the incentive component or fee specified by the contract.

All costly activities related to the management of an incentive contract constitute in fact transaction costs. Sizeable transaction costs may undermine the feasibility of incentive contracts. If the expected benefits of adopting an incentive contract, namely an efficient risk-sharing between the contracting parties, are outweighed by the value of transaction costs, the procurer may find it in her interest to adopt a different class of incentive schemes that is easier and thus less costly to manage: a fixed-price contract. While a fixed-price contract shifts completely the procurement risk to the contractor's side, it allows the procurer to ignore possible discrepancies between estimated and realized productions costs and requires a minimal amount of information collection on her side.

Moreover, lack of reliable accounting measures may further undermine the effectiveness of incentive contracts, particularly in industries or countries where accounting and auditing standards are low. Auditors have traditionally emerged as market institutions certifying the reliability of audited firms' accounting data. However, it has recently become clear that, even in more developed economies, the reliability of auditors' certificates becomes questionable when the auditors themselves are stakeholders in an audited firm's business. Unreliable accounting data may then induce the procurer to opt for a fixed-price contract that does not rely on information produced by the contractor.

4.3.3.4. Multiple performance dimensions and task heterogeneity

Another important issue with ICs is to identify the key aspects/variables on which to design performance incentives. As a general rule, the buyer should base incentives on all measurable aspects that provide information about the effort the contractor exerts in the various tasks implied by the contract.[21]

---

[21] This idea relates to the *informativeness principle*, which states that any measure of performance that provides information about the effort level should be included in the compensation contract (Holmstrom, 1979). For instance, in a contract for IT help desk services, the performance of interventions on workstations might be measured in terms of the restoring speed, which is usually traceable and thus verifiable.

Procurement contracts usually include many heterogeneous tasks, and the effort put by the contractor into some activities may be more reliably measured (subject to lower exogenous uncertainty) than that put into others, so that an analogous IC has a stronger impact on the former than on the latter.[22] An efficient incentive contract makes the power of incentives over highly measurable dimensions necessarily stronger than that designed for less measurable ones. An immediate consequence of this is that a contractor facing high-power incentives on better measurable tasks will tend to allocate most of his efforts and abilities to these, thus depriving the remaining tasks of quality even though these may be very important for the buyer.

For example, consider a contract for the procurement of PCs plus assistance and maintenance services. The effort put into delivery of the machines is more likely to influence the actual performance on that task than the effort put into services does. Great effort put into the supply services may not ensure that results are as good as in the case of the supply of machines, since in the former case the contractor may take much time to solve (or to learn how to solve) particular technical problems and/or the machines may respond badly to initial, possibly imperfect, corrections.

One possible solution to this problem, when technologically feasible, is *unbundling with split award*, which consists in grouping tasks into contracts/lots as homogeneous as possible in terms of measurability and awarding them to different suppliers.[23] In other words, more measurable tasks should all be included in one contract/lot and awarded to one supplier, while less measurable tasks should all be included in a separate contract/lot and awarded to another supplier. This would enable the buyer to elicit the 'right' effort on each task, by designing incentives in an efficient manner, namely by placing high-powered incentives on the former contract/lot and low-powered incentives on latter contract/lot.

In some cases, splitting tasks can be rather easy. Apart from duplication contract management costs and possible economies of scale, the supply of PCs can in principle be kept separate from the provision of the services so that the buyer can design appropriate incentive schemes. Even when

---

[22] The importance of ensuring effort on all incentive aspects is underlined by the US federal procurement regulation (FAR, 16.402-4), which establishes that 'a properly structured multiple-incentive arrangement should motivate the contractor to strive for outstanding results in all incentive areas'.

[23] Note that lot division should also account for other important factors such as competition and market structure. See Chapter 6.

unbundling differently measurable tasks and re-grouping them in internally homogeneous bundles/contracts is technologically feasible at low cost, the fact that the newly created bundles differ significantly may hamper the buyer's ability to compare them and give suppliers' incentives based on their *relative* performance.

In other circumstances the nature of the procurement makes unbundling extremely costly or even impossible. In this case provision of efforts on all incentive areas may be achieved by lowering the intensity of incentives (increasing b) over the more measurable tasks relative to what would be optimal if tasks were not bundled, although this solution comes at the cost of reducing the incentive for effort in general.

Similar problems of task design also arise when cost, instead of effort, can be the object of 'arbitrage' by the contractor, that is, when the contractor is allowed to allocate the *common production costs* among several differently powered contracts/lots. The problem is as follows. When the production/ supply of goods/services involves some common (indirect) costs, since by standard accounting practices these costs are split among the goods produced (usually on basis of labour intensity), the contractor may switch the burden of these costs from most powered to least powered contracts to increase reimbursements. This phenomenon has been emphasized in defence procurement,[24] where often suppliers are asked to produce several related weapons. For instance, we expect a government procuring a new missile and a traditional type of tank to treat the former as a CRC (due to R&D investment and production schedule uncertainty) and the latter as an FPC. To avoid the cost substitution effect, the government may simply allocate the lots/contracts to different contractors, just as in the case of effort substitution described above.

4.3.3.5. Incentive contracts and tendering procedures

Incentive contracts trade off the buyer's need to provide appropriate incentives to the contractor to handle high-quality (or low-cost) projects and the latter's demand for insurance against unpredictable events affecting the realization of the project. Such a feature of incentive contracts is relevant *after* a contractor has been selected. A crucial question for any buyer is also how the provision of incentive schemes, be it in the form of a linear incentive contract or in the more extreme form of a fixed-price contract, is likely to affect the competitive bidding for such a contract. In other words,

---

[24] See Rogerson (1992).

what is the impact of the choice of different incentive schemes on the buyer's screening process for the intrinsically most efficient (best price/quality combination) contractor?

In order to answer this crucial question let us abstract from the potentially higher transaction costs of ICs. Consider first a scenario where the buyer wishes to select the most efficient supplier from a pool of quite heterogeneous firms whose efficiency levels are known only to themselves. Efficiency here is to be interpreted as the supplier's ability to perform the contract at a low cost, although exogenous events may affect the actual level of production costs. The buyer manages a large variety of procurement contracts so that she is less concerned about the procurement risk of the single specific supply, whereas suppliers are small and conduct rather undiversified activities, and hence dislike risk. Then a *linear*[25] *incentive contract* with an appropriately chosen cost-sharing parameter *b* ensures that (i) the most efficient supplier is selected and (ii) the right trade-off is achieved between giving the contractor an incentive to limit cost and sharing risks. In other words, a linear incentive contract in which the power of the incentive scheme is set by the buyer at the outset while suppliers submit tenders for the fixed part, *P*, yields the appropriate balancing between selecting the lowest-cost (or best price/quality) supplier, providing him the right incentives to control *ex post* supply costs and quality performance while leaving the buyer to bear part of the risk.

Even when suppliers are indifferent to risk, so that risk sharing is not an issue, the buyer may still find it in her interest to stick to a linear incentive contract since the latter remains instrumental in selecting the most efficient supplier. Hence suppliers' indifference to risk does not completely justify the adoption of the most extreme form of incentive contract, that is, a fixed-price contract, unless screening at the tendering stage is not a relevant issue for the buyer. If the buyer is reasonably confident that suppliers are not too heterogeneous in terms of intrinsic efficiency, the adoption of a fixed-price contract efficiently allocates the procurement risk to a risk-insensitive contractor.

Suppose now that suppliers' efficiency refers not only to their ability to perform at a low cost, but also to the effectiveness of their cost-reducing investments/actions. If suppliers are indifferent to risk, thus risk-sharing is not a problem, the buyer may find it in her interest to let suppliers choose their most preferred cost-sharing fraction *b* at the tendering stage. Why?

---

[25] This result is obtained by McAfee and McMillan (1986).

Intuitively, more efficient suppliers are more confident of the effectiveness of their cost-reducing efforts, so they prefer to cash in on a higher fraction of cost savings (low b). If they are allowed to do so at the tendering stage, they can be more aggressive on the fixed part of the contract, thus benefiting the buyer through a lower awarding price.

Let us wrap all this up. A buyer wishing to minimize the awarding price of a contract while (i) selecting the most efficient contractor from a pool of potential suppliers indifferent to procurement risk and (ii) inducing the highest possible level of cost-reducing (or quality-enhancing) effort from the selected contractor can indeed reach this goal. All the buyer has to do is to let bidders compete for an incentive contract in which both the fixed part (P) and the cost-sharing fraction (b) are chosen by suppliers at the tendering stage.[26]

We are now in a position to summarize the discussion of the first part of the chapter in the form of a practical conclusion.

Practical conclusion 1

Favour fixed-price contracts when suppliers are relatively insensitive to procurement risk and when they appear rather homogeneous in their ability to control production cost. Fixed-price rules are also appropriate when contract management costs are expected to offset the benefits of risk sharing in incentive contracts.

Use incentive contracts when (i) procurement risk is important (ii) suppliers are more sensitive to it than the buyer and (iii) accounting costs are fully reliable. If a linear IC is adopted, the cost-sharing parameter(s) should be larger:
- the higher is the contractor's fear of risk;
- the less predictable are the shocks affecting production costs;
- the lower is the contractor's ability to control cost;
- the more cost-reducing activities can be detrimental to aspects of quality that are not perfectly measurable.

When suppliers are insensitive to procurement risk and appear quite heterogeneous in terms of their ability to control production costs, they should be allowed to choose the cost-sharing parameter(s) at the tendering stage.

Reduce the power of incentives if there are important tasks that are hard to monitor.

---

[26] This result is analytically derivered by McAfee and McMillan (1987), and, slightly differently, by Laffont and Tirole (1987). Riordan and Sappington (1987) independently derived similar results.

4.4. Non-contractible quality and implicit contracting

Until now we have focused our attention on *explicit contracts*. However, when quality is observable but unverifiable and therefore non-contractible (for brevity, in the following we will generically indicate non-contractible dimensions with the single term 'non-contractible quality' [NCQ]), implicit contracts can be powerful tools to ensure that the contractor delivers the good or service at desirable quality standards. The main underlying idea for implementing NCQ is to build *implicit contractibility* based on self-enforcing promises by the two parties, the buyer and the seller(s). The term 'implicit' here refers to the fact that if incentives for NCQ are put in action, they automatically or implicitly emerge as optimal actions on the part of contractors and not as formal obligations enforced by a contract. This broad idea will be widely analysed in this part of the chapter.

Implicit contractibility may come in by linking observable but NCQ to credible promises on the buyer's behaviour with the supplier. The buyer can credibly announce to the supplier(s) she will make use of her discretion outside contractual terms so as to penalize observable opportunism and/or reward observable NCQ.

4.4.1. Implicit contracting methods for NCQ

There is certainly no unique way of grouping and organizing the (luckily) numerous methods of implicit contractibility. Here we propose a classification which groups them on the basis of the different moments in which the buyer's behaviour induces firms' incentives to procure NCQ. We can then identify:

1. **Selection or pre-contractual methods**, which are activated when designing the environment for contract assignment, for example, by limiting competition for the contract and in general by discriminating between competitive tendering and bilateral negotiation.
2. **Within-contract methods**, which operate during the contract execution and refer to the buyer's exercise of discretionary power to induce within-contract competition, for example, selecting more than one supplier (which is called dual sourcing).

3. **Post-contract methods**, which affect the profits the suppliers can expect from future contracting with the buyer (such as exclusion from future procurements).

All these methods can be combined in different ways. We will list them according to the previous classification, illustrating their costs and benefits for the buyer, and suggesting when and how they should be used independently or together.

4.4.2. NCQ and procurement discretion

Before proceeding to a detailed analysis of the methods, it is worth investigating the need for discretion to implement them. The power to penalize or punish observable opportunism or reward observable but NCQ requires ability to act/react to changes in observable but non-contractible variables with some *degree of discretion* by the party that observes non-contractible dimensions. In the absence of some discretionary power, no implicit contracting method can be effectively put in action.

Notice that, if discretion is necessary for implicit contracting, it also opens the door to opportunistic behaviour by whoever is in charge of observing non-verifiable variables, the buyer herself or some party to whom the buyer delegates observation. Since third parties such as courts cannot observe quality, a buyer may not give the promised bonus or may inflict penalties although quality was at the desired level. However, it is clear that if a buyer abuses her discretion in administering bonuses and penalties, she will lose any credibility with the consequence of avoidance by serious contractors and of making implicit contracting methods ineffective, at best. These methods will then be effective only if the buyer is able to build her own reputation for fair behaviour; reputational forces are generated both for the buyer and for suppliers by frequent and repeated interactions.

Limiting the cost of discretion. It is also important to notice that, when the buyer is an agent of a final user or consumer of the procured service or good, as frequently happens in public procurement and within large firms, the buyer can use her discretion in a self-interested way, that is, exchanging a discretionary bonus against a 'bribe' from the contractors. In this respect, the buyer's discretion can be reduced by publicly conditioning bonuses/penalties on measures of 'customer satisfaction' that should be correlated with the level of NCQ provided. Still, two important problems emerge, both linked to 'customer satisfaction' surveys, which are collectively subjective,

and therefore not auditable evaluations.[27] If an end user of a supplied good/
service declares that he is satisfied not because the good/service is actually of
good quality but because the supplier 'bribed him' with a favor or money,
there is no way to demonstrate that the end user was lying (unless hard
evidence of the bribery is produced). Thus, in general, we can identify two
types of issues related to the correct use of discretionary bonuses and
penalties on the basis of 'soft' information.

Conflicts of interest. The first problem is linked to the need to limit the
buyer's discretion by conditioning bonuses/penalties on the (soft) information of 'customer satisfaction' surveys. This issue is one of *conflict of
interests* and credibility, and is typical of situations where the end users of
the procured good/service are also those who pay for the good/service.
Conflict of interest arises if the person who assesses the contractor's performance is the same person who pays the bonus because then the evaluator
has incentives never to assess a good performance, thereby avoiding paying
the costly bonus. Customer satisfaction collects soft information about the
perceived quality of the good/service from end users. If these users are also
paying for the good/service, they will have incentives to always untruthfully
report unsatisfactory performance in order to avoid having to pay the
bonus, as there is no risk that their report can ever be proved to be
untruthful. Anticipating this, rational suppliers will provide minimal levels
of NCQ. However, this problem can be partly overcome by linking customer satisfaction to *in-kind* bonuses (e.g., as we shall see, contract renewal is
a form of in-kind bonus) instead of monetary bonuses, since it will always
be in the interest of the buyer to renew the contract of a good and efficient
supplier.

Corruption. The second problem linked to limiting the buyer's discretion
by conditioning bonuses/penalties on 'customer satisfaction' surveys is one
of *corruption* and is relevant in situations in which the one who pays for the
procured good or service is not its end user. When the users of the good/
service are not those who pay for it, as is often the case in public procurement and frequently also in large firms where the sourcing function is
'far' in organizational terms from headquarters, the risk of corruption – i.e.,
of the contractor trying to 'bribe' end users to report high satisfaction that
triggers the bonus – is serious. In private procurement, instead, the buyer is
generally also the final user of procured goods and services so that discretion

---

[27] This kind of information is often called 'soft' by economists. The benefits and cost of more flexibility
in public procurement are the focus of Banfield (1975) and Kelman (1990).

can be eased. In this respect, implicit contracting may prove more effective in private than in public procurement.

In the next pages we will discuss implicit contracting methods with the understanding that they are certainly applicable to private procurement, while for public procurement their applicability depends on national legislations and the associated discretion which is in the end left in the hands of the public buyer. It should be clear that the various methods we will discuss are generally not mutually exclusive and some of them may be pooled to form a corpus of instruments aimed at stimulating provision of NCQ.

4.4.3. Selection or pre-contractual methods

When all dimensions relevant to the procurement relationship are contractible (in the sense discussed in the previous section), strong price competition in the awarding process of the procurement contract is always desirable. Indeed, with full contractibility the formal agreement controls all the relevant ingredients in the relationship and strong price competition is always desirable because it helps the buyer obtain any given quality aspect at lower prices, or a better balance between price and properties of the supply (in case a scoring rule is used).[28]

The desirability of price competition at the contract-awarding phase becomes much less clear when some variables of the procurement relationship fall into the category of non-contractibles. In some cases the object of procurement is a complex project, for example, when it consists of supplying a large IT infrastructure or when it involves several complex and interacting tasks and requires highly customizable goods/services (typical in the defence sector), or when it consists of a complex real estate to be built. In all such cases strong price competition may not be the best solution, since price is not necessarily the most important factor and quality can be highly non-contractible (for an in-depth discussion of this point see Chapter 5). In this case, the price-squeezing effect of competition generally increases the likelihood of selecting low-quality suppliers (which face lower costs and can therefore offer lower prices) and may induce contractors to further reduce non-contractible and costly quality at the execution stage. This may become particularly relevant when some R&D activity is necessary to finalize procurement (e.g., in defence or hospital contracting). Indeed, R&D for

---

[28] See Chapter 12 on scoring rules for more on the optimal balancing between price and non-price attributes.

innovative projects is often non-contractible because it refers to activities that are at the frontier of technological knowledge and effort towards improvement is difficult to measure. This interpretation of R&D in terms of what we here identify as NCQ brings us to the analysis of procurement of innovation and R&D, which is extensively discussed in Chapter 19. Here, we simply note that high-tech procurement that involves R&D may well require a reduction of competition at the final tendering phase. The problem is that competition that is too strong at the production stage tends to undermine incentives for investment at the preceding R&D stage.[29] Indeed, we observe that in some innovative procurement projects for the defence sector, a maximum of two firms are often admitted at the competitive phase that awards the contract. The idea is that a pre-selection phase limiting the number of firms in the pool of potential providers reduces price competition and increases the chances of winning the contract, inducing participants to invest more before the competition stage and leaving the selected contractor with higher (expected) margins to employ/invest in NCQ provision or R&D.[30] Nevertheless, it is obvious that restricting competition does not mean no costs for the buyer. First, larger market power in the hands of a few competing firms tends *per se* to induce price increases. Second, larger prices are also a consequence of less effective selection of the most efficiently producing firm from a restricted pool of competitors.

Our brief discussion and the deeper investigations in Chapters 5 and 19 illustrate that softening price competition and creating larger margins on contractors' profits is very often a necessary precondition for NCQ provision. However, nothing, at the moment, assures that contractors will indeed find the right incentives to use those margins (or part of them) to provide quality. After all, those margins could be kept by contractors as extra profits induced by softened competition, unless this opportunistic behaviour induces some negative consequences that the contractor may want to avoid. Here is exactly where all the other methods for implementing NCQ based

---

[29] See Rob (1986) for a discussion on similar arguments for defence procurement.

[30] Sometimes lessening competition can take the form of a two-stage selection procedure. The first stage is open to all suppliers; the buyer then negotiates with the most preferred (reputable) in the second stage. In public procurement two-stage procedures seem to be increasingly attractive. For instance, FAR (14-502) establishes that the two-step procedure 'may be used in preference to negotiation' when the acquisition requires technical proposals and/or it is referred to complex items. In the FAR view, the first step selects the best-quality proposal, while the second step is for price bidding. Further, the recent European Directive explicitly introduces 'online auctions', which may follow the pre-qualification stage for suppliers' price and/or quality offer.

on within-contract or post-contract incentives come in to help the buyer, as we show below.

Practical conclusion 2

When the procurement involves very important non-contractible dimensions such as R&D it may be useful to soften price competition at the selecting stage, for example limiting the number of competing suppliers.

4.4.4. Within-contract methods

4.4.4.1. Dispensing 'sticks and carrots' within contract execution

Rewards or penalties to be delivered within the contract (and/or after its completion) could be introduced on the basis of observed quality, where bonuses and penalties may be monetary or in-kind, as we illustrate next. The threat of losing bonuses or having penalties inflicted should discipline the contractor to provide NCQ. As we have pointed out in section 4.4.2, buyer's discretion can be reduced by publicly conditioning rewards/penalties on measures of 'customer satisfaction' that should be correlated with the level of NCQ provided.

A tactic sometimes employed to motivate the supplier on NCQ is the threat of early unilateral contract termination. It should now be clear that contract termination is not based in this case on explicit contractual infringements. Rather, when the procurement selection process is being designed, it can be established contractually that if during contract execution non-contractible quality performance – as measured by some customer satisfaction indicators – falls below a predefined threshold, the buyer is free to renege on the contract and find alternative procurement channels. Finding an alternative supplier may be costly, however, and the higher this cost, the less likely it will be that the buyer will renege when facing low performance, and the less effective will be the threat of reneging in terms of eliciting a satisfactory performance from the contractor initially selected. The role of the methods we are now going to discuss will be mainly one of reducing the cost of finding an alternative supply channel, so as to increase the credibility of the threat of reneging and switching to an alternative supplier, and hence its effectiveness in stimulating high NCQ provision.[31] Note, though, that all these methods will naturally tend to increase the price

---

[31] Managing dynamic competition is also extensively treated in Chapter 17, though the focus there is on the costs of switching to a different supplier after the 'natural' expiration of a contract.

at which suppliers will be willing to execute a contract, because they anticipate that they will need to provide better NCQ, and because there is some uncertainty about the actual duration of the contract.

4.4.4.2. Within-contract competition

One main way to put pressure on the contractor to induce desirable levels of NCQ consists of keeping open the possibility of shifting to different suppliers within contract execution in case NCQ is too low. Again, this form of competition during the execution of a procurement contract requires a considerable amount of discretion on the part of the buyer, but may be effective for NCQ because the entire procurement contract or subparts of it remain subject to the threat of switching to an alternative supplier. Within-contract competition in procurement with its several forms that we will illustrate next has been and is currently employed, for example, in the automotive industry by important carmakers in the United States, Europe and Asia.[32]

Switching to lower-ranked offers. One simple way for the buyer to replace a contractor is switching directly to the second-best supplier selected in the initial competition. This allows the buyer to save time and to avoid the costs of a new competition in case of switching to an alternative supplier. Once the first procurement selection process is performed,[33] the buyer ends up with a ranking of potential suppliers and chooses the top-ranked one as contractor (or more of them in case of multisourcing), also establishing that if during contract execution NCQ does not satisfy some predefined requirements, the buyer is free to fire the first contractor and ask the second ranked supplier if he wants to step in on the conditions of his initial offer during the selection process. If the second ranked supplier does not want to step in, the buyer may ask the third ranked one, then the fourth, and so on; if offers are not good enough, it may always choose to incur the cost of arranging a new procurement competition.[34]

---

[32] To quote a famous example, Toyota uses dual-sourcing awards to different firms for the same parts (e.g., wheels) on different models (e.g., Toyota Corolla, Toyota Carina).

[33] It can be either an open competitice tendering or a restricted procedure or any other negotiation with more suppliers.

[34] Of course a new competition may be also desirable when the item being procured is subject to high obsolescence, as with IT products, and the contract is almost expired. In this case, a new competitive tendering allows the buyer to procure possibly more advanced and cheaper items with respect to those offered at 'obsolete' conditions by the second best supplier.

The contractual option to switch to the second or third-best supplier in case customer satisfaction falls below a minimal threshold level can be seen as a special case of what is called *second sourcing*.[35] The low cost of switching to other suppliers without running a new selection process implied by this contractual option makes the threat credible, and should in turn discipline the top-ranked supplier to offer a good service, so that a switch never actually occurs. In addition, rational suppliers then have no incentive to underbid at the selection process with a view – in case of victory – to cut back on NCQ, because they know they would lose the contract at a later stage by doing this.[36]

Some drawbacks and applicability limits of this procedure are worth emphasizing. Reneging may involve discontinuing procurement that in certain cases may be impossible. In fact, unforeseen interruption of the contract can be very costly for the buyer so that unilateral reneging is not credible, not least because finding and establishing a supply relation with a substitute provider requires always a minimum lag and some adjustments. In some cases interrupting provision of the good or service even for a very short period may be very costly, if not totally unfeasible, for the buyer (e.g., in case of procurement for hospitals, production chains etc.). Further, it should be clear that if a switch occurs during provision, the contract will be carried out at worse economic/technical conditions because typically a supplier ranked second in the contract-awarding process is asked to supply at the condition he offered at the selection stage.[37] Hence, if the conditions proposed by non-first-ranked suppliers are particularly onerous for the buyer, she may rather prefer to run a new selection process. These difficulties and costs reduce the effectiveness of the threat to renege early and replace the contractor.

---

[35] This is the definition of second sourcing provided by Lyon (2006). It fits the idea of switching to the second-best supplier. However, second sourcing can take several different forms. In the seminal work of Anton and Yao (1987), second sourcing takes place when the buyer announces that she will re-open the competition between the incumbent contractor and a rival supplier at some point of the supplying phase.

[36] This method of within-contract reneging and switching to second-ranked firms is already established by the Italian law for public works when the procurement does not involve discretionary bid evaluation and it has also been recently proposed for acquisitions of goods/services managed by Consip, the Italian Public Procurement Agency. See Guriev and Kvasov (2005) for a theoretical argument. See also Ellman (2005).

[37] Alternatively, at the beginning of the procurement process the buyer could ask this second-ranked supplier if he is ready to commit the conditions offered by the first supplier in case he is named for procurement. However, suppliers may well refuse this proposal when first-ranked conditions are too demanding.

In addition, if reneging takes place after some completion of the procurement process, the buyer and the stepping-in supplier have to find an agreement on how much the incoming supplier should serve, either the remaining part for completing procurement or the whole. In the presence of economies of scale the second solution is of course optimal in terms of making the acceptance by the second-ranked supplier more likely and the threat to renege more effective, and should therefore be pre-announced and established contractually in order to induce the supplier to take full account of it at the initial tendering stage. Note that if non-first-ranked suppliers systematically deny the buyer's offer to step in, the threat of contract termination loses its power and the first-ranked firm regains room for opportunistically reducing NCQ.

Full-fledged dual or multisourcing. If the option to renege and switch to non-first-ranked suppliers still hinges on a single supplier at any point in time (whose identity can nevertheless change over time, as we have seen), an alternative method to encourage suppliers to provide NCQ is to have two or more suppliers active at the same time. This within-contract method is known as *dual or multisourcing* (depending on how many suppliers are involved at the same time, this is also known as 'split-award procurement'). This method has been used for example in defence procurement by the US Department of Defence (DoD), such as for air force engine contracts and in missile systems procurement.[38,39] Dual sourcing means having the supply contract split between two contractors, who then supply simultaneously (substitute) products. Even if it is not exactly seen as second sourcing, the presence of alternative suppliers reduces the potential for contractors opportunism because the buyer is free to choose whether she can have both of them active or which part of procurement should be allocated to whom, depending on the NCQ level each of them provides. Dual sourcing may then serve to discipline suppliers when doing so contractually is simply not feasible.[40]

---

[38] See Lyon (2006) for more details.

[39] See Chapters 6 and 17 for more details about dual sourcing.

[40] Nevertheless, dual sourcing is applied with success by public and private procurement agencies. Consip, the Italian central procurement agency, adopted dual sourcing in a contract for the procurement of complex IT infrastructures (mainframes) run on behalf of the Italian Ministry of Economy and Finance. Other examples of agencies using dual sourcing are the DoD, US Department of Defense, for the procurement of missiles, Solectron, a leading provider of electronics manufacturing and integrated supply chain services and Toyota. It should be noted, however, that

However, dual sourcing does not come without costs. In particular, splitting procurement (i) reduces the economies of scale of each supplier, implying a duplication of the fixed costs, including those linked to setting up and managing two contractual relationships instead of one, and (ii) by increasing uncertainty in procurement almost certainly includes one supplier that is not at least cost.

Continuous 'contestability'. Another close alternative to reneging and switching to other providers has been proposed recently.[41] The idea in this case is to award a long-term procurement contract that is continuously, under threat of competition from new potential suppliers even if these were not present at the time of the initial tendering (this is also known as *contestability*).[42] The buyer awards a contract that specifically contemplates the possibility that a competitor of the current contractor may make a better offer to the buyer than the ruling contract. If this happens, the current contractor has the option to match the competitive offer or withdraw, letting the competitor to step into his place.

For contestability to work as a disciplining device it is necessary that the buyer accords her preference to the current contractor instead of an *equally good* competitive offer if the current contractor has always offered acceptable NCQ. This simple and reasonable preference accorded to the ruling firm is capable of making the contractor provide high quality and aim to be unmatched by rival suppliers (irrespective of whether they plan to offer high quality or to cheat on quality) so that substitution of supplier does not occur in practice. One positive side of this method is that whenever incentives to provide NCQ are assured by competition, the buyer may also increase the power of incentives on contractible dimensions without the risk of the buyer trying to save on costs by cheating on quality. A possible drawback of the same procedure we can argue is that continuous competition produces a more uncertain environment for the contractor and this may backfire on the

---

while dual or multisourcing can be freely adopted by private companies, procurement laws may restrict the use of it on the part of public agencies.

[41] See Neeman and Orosel (2004).

[42] Despite both terms identifying a competitive environment, 'contestability' and 'competition' are different concepts. A market is said to be contestable (i.e., competitive) even though there is just one (or few) incumbent firm(s) in the market, which is (are), however, constantly put under the pressure of a potential new entry of a rival firm. The simple credible threat of a new entry, coupled with the absence of entry barriers, makes the market as competitive as one composed of many incumbent firms. For further details on contestability see the seminal contribution of Baumol et al. (1986).

buyer in terms of higher prices and reduced incentives to invest. However, the buyer clearly expects to pay more to obtain higher levels of NCQ.

Practical conclusion 3

When using within-contract methods, balance the goal of higher NCQ with

- increased uncertainty in contract duration/quantity supplied,
- the cost of interrupting the contract and switching to worse price/quality conditions in case of second sourcing and
- economy of scales and contract management costs in case of dual sourcing.

4.4.5. Post-contractual methods

The last set of tools that we investigate refers to the buyer's possibility of reacting *after* the execution of the contract in case low quality has been provided, or in general to take decisions concerning future contractual relationships on the basis of the past performance of suppliers.[43] These methods are close in spirit to the idea of reneging on the contract and switching to alternative suppliers in case of low-quality procurement. However, it should be noted that relying on post-contractual discretionary decisions might produce fewer litigations with respect to within-contract actions on the basis of non-contractible dimensions.[44]

---

[43] Past performance is widely used in private procurement. Although policies are different across countries for legislative reasons, past performance is receiving increasing attention also by public buyers. For instance, Article 48 of the 2004 European Directive establishes that the supplier can prove his ability to perform by a list of references regarding the most important works carried out in the past five years. The International Bank for Research and Development considers experience and past performance on similar contracts one of the key element of suppliers' evaluation, especially for large, complex projects (guidelines provided to institutions using the funds of the Bank, 2004). In Australia, the Department of Finance and Administration also provides guidelines for Australian public agencies. In the section 'Principle of Value for Money', the Commonwealth Procurement Guidelines (2005) state that among costs other factors must be considered when assessing suppliers. One of these is 'the performance history of each prospective supplier.' In the United States the FAR specifically regulates the issue of past performance for all US federal agencies. In particular the FAR suggests to agencies how and what type of information should be collected to evaluate contractors' past performance.

[44] For an analysis of evaluation of past performance in US public procurement see Guerrero and Kirkpatrick (2001). For a discussion on past performance and an overview of recent evolutions of public procurement in the United States see Kelman (2002).

Considering these methods based on past performance will also allow us to discuss an ingredient that has been partially neglected in our previous analysis, namely, the effect that the 'shadow' of future interactions has on today's decisions by contractors. When procurement is inherently a dynamic process, because the buyer needs to be served repeatedly overtime, specific dynamic methods can be employed to cope with NCQ. In this dynamic context suppliers' profits are not limited to the ones coming from the current contract, but also include profits potentially accruing to suppliers from future contracts (i.e., the flow of expected future discounted profits). It is material to realize that if the perception of these future profits for suppliers' present decisions is sufficiently important, then future profits may well play a crucial role in the provision of NCQ.

The novelty we are introducing in this part of the analysis with respect to the previous discussion relies on the possibility that repeated interactions between the buyer and suppliers open the door to reciprocal reputations for 'correct' behaviour. On their side, suppliers have the possibility of building a good reputation that is of value for the buyer's decisions in future interactions. On the part of the buyer, repeated interaction may make credible her discretionary decisions regarding outperforming or poorly performing firms. As an example of this mechanism, in the United States a part of the past performance information refers to customer satisfaction and it is used to select suppliers in public contracts. Interestingly, in the United Kingdom, within the context of the newly developed PPPs for the provision of public services, the National Audit Office has recommended that customer satisfaction surveys become part of the evaluation process aimed at testing the contractor's performance following the commencement of the service.

We now discuss some simple instruments that the buyer can use to penalize badly performing suppliers or favor well-performing ones on the basis of future repetition of procurement. Similar to the within-contract methods discussed earlier, these instruments will induce suppliers to require higher compensation to cover the costs of providing higher NCQ and, being based on non-verifiable performance measures or non-auditable customer satisfaction reports, may increase the potential for conflicts of interests and collusion.

4.4.5.1. Contract renewals and contract length

An important way to reward a performing contractor or to punish a cheating one hinges on contract renewals. For example, IBM stimulates chip manufacturers to maintain high quality with the 'carrot' of contract renewal (or the threat of non-renewal).[45] This method also has the mentioned advantage of moderating the problems generated by monetary incentives linked to observable but non-verifiable performance measures as it uses *in-kind* rewards for good performance (in terms of an extension of the supply contract or an automatic renewal of it).

The effectiveness of renewals as performance incentives can be reinforced by substantially shortening the basic duration/size of the supply contract, which can be seen as a tryout period, and then by allowing the buyer to renew the supply contract several times if the supplier's performance is satisfactory. The fact that the buyer within the contract duration can only procure from the selected contractor even if the contractor decides to degrade NCQ is generally refereed as within-contract or static lock-in (see Chapters 6 and 17 for more on this point). Shortening contract duration then reduces lock-in by increasing the ability of the buyer to react to a contractor's low performance.

However, shortening the contract duration is not without cost. Large/long-lasting contracts can be good since the contractor can exploit economies of scale and recoup investment costs, which then translate into higher efficiency for the contractor and larger savings for the buyer. Cost savings from large production are clearly relevant also in a dynamic context, where, in addition, there are elements of future uncertainty playing an important role. Indeed, a small supplier winning a ten-year procurement contract will face much less uncertainty over his future profitability than if he were awarded a one-year contract. Depending on the ability of managers and owners to bear the procurement risks, this smaller uncertainty may well translate into a lower price for each single unit of procured good or service. At the same time one should also remember that searching for (the most preferable) procuring partners is always a costly process (e.g., the sheer costs of organizing and advertising the competitive tendering). It may then be difficult to credibly commit to replacing the actual contractor for poor performance. Switching costs must therefore be kept sufficiently low (see Chapter 17 for more on this). In this respect note also that reputation on past performance may become a barrier to entry because newcomers arrive with no reputation and are thus ill favored. This can be avoided with neutral valuation for newcomers.

---

[45] See McMillan (1992) for more examples. The book also offers an interesting discussion on the instruments to stimulate contractor's performance and how to design incentive schemes.

Second, the try-out period should be chosen carefully. In fact, especially for complex products/services, the contractor needs time to learn how to work and how to deal with the difficulties that may arise in the execution of the contract and in the relationship with the buyer. If the try-out period is not sufficiently long, temporary lower-than-expected performance is 'unfairly' punished and this will be reflected in higher price and possibly also lower quality offered by contractors.

Renewals conditioned on customer satisfaction indicators have been recently used in public procurement, for example, for the procurement of IT services in the Italian Procurement Agency (Consip S.p.A.). One of the reasons for their adoption was that as a form of implicit contract, contract renewals conditioned to customer satisfaction are less subject to the problems of conflict of interest and corruption discussed in section 4.4.2. If bonuses are in the form of contract renewals and the end users of the good/service untruthfully report good performance in exchange for a 'bribe' from the supplier, this will result in another period of bad supply, and the endusers will therefore require a much higher bribe or – more likely – report truthfully that the supplier performed badly and must be replaced. This ensures that the cost of misreporting performance is borne exactly by the one who reports the performance. Similarly, by untruthfully reporting bad performance when performance was good, the buyer cannot gain anything, and incurs the cost of losing a well-performing supplier.

Practical conclusion 4

Choose the contract duration so as to optimally balance the goal of NCQ with economies of scale and incentives to invest.

4.4.5.2. Past performance scores, exclusion, consortia and negotiation

Past performance scores, exclusion. Very close in spirit to contract renewal is the possibility of the buyer penalizing suppliers that performed poorly in the past in terms of a lower score, or even complete exclusion from future contract-awarding contests. Clearly, the supplier rationally anticipates that the cost savings which materialize by compromising on quality (and the associated increase of profits) have to be traded off against future profits that are lost because of exclusion from future contracting.[46] A sufficiently

---

[46] See Kim (1998), Doni (2005) and Calzolari and Spagnolo (2005).

long exclusion period paired with not excessively high/costly required quality is then clearly capable of breaking the tie of this trade-off in favor of quality provision. It is self-evident that all this is effective in inducing quality provision only if future exclusion of the erring supplier is feasible for the buyer, if it can be anticipated by suppliers and, ultimately, if it is credible. Shortening contract duration will have positive effects on the effectiveness of this mechanism, much as for renewals, though in stable, repeated contexts it may facilitate suppliers' collusion, besides generating the costs discussed in the previous section 4.4.5.1.[47] Of course, if the buyer uses exclusion of badly performing suppliers she should avoid being left with very few suppliers who can be admitted at the selecting phase in consequence of several exclusions. If this happens, additional exclusions may become very·costly for the buyer (in terms of reduced competition) and then not credible, thus undermining all the reputational incentives for quality provision.

Consortia. We have argued that when reputational forces are at play in NCQ provision, then competitive procuring mechanisms may not be desirable for a buyer who cares a lot for the quality of the goods or services, for example, in health procurement. Further exploring this point, there are other methods which can be even more effective by mediating the need for larger profits through more efficient production. It may be desirable from the buyer's standpoint to stimulate the formation of consortia among suppliers that may otherwise compete with each other. Even if the formation of consortia tends to increase the prices for procurement, this very same fact would also make the consortia's profit high, so that the incentives to cheat on quality would be reduced by appropriate threats of termination following bad performance. It is interesting to notice that consortia are often blocked in standard procurement on the basis that they behave very similarly to illegal cartels. When NCQ is a crucial success factor for the procurement the buyer should be ready to pay higher prices even if they result from agreements between suppliers because high prices also imply lower incentives to cheat on quality and then larger implementable quality.[48] Consortia may be even better for NCQ and reputation than limiting the number of competitors *tout court*. In fact, frequently interacting

---

[47] See again Calzolari and Spagnolo (2005). The buyer might even ask the contractor to put in its hand some 'hostage bonds' (or guarantees) that will not be given back in case of poor performance. Such a method may be a disciplining one only if the buyer is able to build a reputation for fairness, which is difficult to obtain if the provided quality is not observable outside the contractual relationship.

[48] Calzolari and Spagnolo (2005) illustrate this point with a formal model.

suppliers (e.g., in the 'big market' for office equipment, such as PCs, laptops, printers) very often know each other, their technologies, their costs and production advantages much better than a buyer, so that a pre-selection phase performed by a less informed buyer (with the aim of reducing competition for quality concerns) may well be dominated by informed decisions of suppliers. Consortia have the information and all the incentives to maximize their overall profits also by ensuring the most efficient allocation of production among their members. This means that consortia have the potential to pair larger reputational concerns necessary for high NCQ provision with more efficient procurement.

Negotiation. Our previous analysis on reputational incentives for procurement has clearly highlighted a positive relationship between the future rents a supplier may expect and the NCQ it is ready to provide. This idea can be further exploited to yield some extreme implications. In fact, it is clear that with dynamic procurement the largest future profits for a firm materialize when the buyer is ready to renew the contract with a contractor that has supplied the desired amount of NCQ without going to the market at all. It is evident that this type of bilateral contracting can be very costly in terms of (lost) efficiency (and then of high prices paid for procurement) if the buyer is stuck with an inefficient supplier. On the other hand, when quality is very important, the buyer may prefer to build a long-lasting relationship assuring future rents and incentives for quality provision, even though the supplier is not the most efficient one.[49] This desirability of bilateral *negotiations* over competing mechanisms creates a link to the discussion on competing mechanisms versus negotiations in procurement in Chapter 5.

Finally, we conclude this analysis of *reputational mechanisms* for NCQ emphasizing again that the key factor for these mechanisms is suppliers' expectation of future profits.[50] This helps identify an instance where reputational incentives may fail, namely, when a supplier has a very short horizon for his activities, as may happen in case of financial distress possibly

---

[49] Fehr et al. (2004) show experimentally how in a dynamic exchange environment, when non-contractible aspects become important, agents do not search for the best offer each period but rather stick to the same partner and cooperate with him as long as possible.

[50] Very often feedback (or reputation) mechanisms are used in marketplaces and e-procurement platforms to improve trade efficiency. eBay, Amazon, Yahoo and many other well-known e-markets use feedback systems to cope with a high level of non-contractibility (or even with the absence of any formal contract) and opportunism in transactions. See Chapter 18 for an in-depth analysis of feedback mechanisms.

leading to bankruptcy. In this situation the supplier has nothing to lose from disappointing the buyer and saving on costs for quality provision. It follows that when the buyer intends to implement reputational incentives for quality, she may want to envisage a pre-selection phase not only limiting participation to increase suppliers' future profits but also excluding from the pool of participants all suppliers in financial distress, who may be insensitive to reputational forces.[51]

4.5. Conclusions

In this chapter we reviewed the theory and practice of procurement contracting with the aim of offering simple practical indications on how to arrange procurement contracts in different situations. In the first part we have seen how the variety of contracts available makes the choice of the appropriate contractual setting not easy to make for any buyer. We illustrated the conditions in which some types of contracts are likely to work better than others, and where general linear incentive contracts are an effective compromise between providing the contractor with the incentives to be efficient and risk sharing for *ex post* unforeseen events.

We then proceeded by illustrating the tools the buyer can use to obtain adequate control over the non-contractible dimensions at the different stages of the procurement process, namely, in the selection phase (e.g., by limiting price competition) and during the execution of the supply (e.g., with bonuses, renewals, reputation, dual sourcing and other competitive devices). These methods come with their costs though, and must be used with care, when non-contractible dimensions of the procurement are really important.

Bibliographical notes

A general, although technical, analysis of optimal explicit procurement contracting is Laffont and Tirole (1993). A more recent study encompassing

---

[51] It is worth noting that reputational incentives may also work when suppliers are uncertain about their future interaction(s) with the buyer. The simple possibility of future profits issued from this relationship may be sufficient to discipline suppliers' behaviour, such as for NCQ provision. Also note that a supplier which plans to shut down his activities may prefer to sell its good reputation, namely, its goodwill, instead of destroying it to save on costs for quality provision.

technical treatment of advances in the theory of optimal contracting, including incomplete and implicit contracts, is by Bolton and Dewatripoint (2004). Implicit contracting and optimal contract duration is the focus of recent contributions by Guriev and Kvasov (2005) and Calzolari and Spagnolo (2005), among others. Dual sourcing as an instrument to improve performance is discussed in Richardson (1993), while Dalen et al. (2004) investigate the role of renewals. Kelman (2002) offers an informal but thorough discussion of the role of past performance and reputation in US public procurement. For practical guidelines on contracting policy in US public procurement see the FAR (2005).

References

Anderlini, L. and L. Felli (2005). Should Courts Always Enforce What Contracting Parties Write? *mimeo*.

Anton, J. J. and D. A. Yao (1987). Second Sourcing and the Experience Curve: Price Competition in Defense Procurement, *RAND Journal of Economics*, 57–76.

Banfield, E. C. (1975). Corruption as a Feature of Governmental Organization. *Journal of Law and Economics*, 58, 587–605.

Baumol W. J., J. Panzer and R. D. Willig (1986). *Contestable Markets and the Theory of Industrial Structure*, Harcourt Brace and Jovanovitch.

Bolton, P. and M. Dewatripoint (2004). *Contract Theory*, The MIT Press, Cambridge, MA.

Calzolari, G. and G. Spagnolo (2005). Reputational Commitments and Collusion in Procurement, mimeo, University of Bologna and Consip.

Dalen, D. M. Moen, E. R. and Riis, C. (2004). Contract Renewal and Incentive in Public Procurement, CEPR Discussion Paper No. 4540.

Doni N. (2005). L'affidamento mediante gara di contratti pubblici: l'importanza della reputazione (with English summary), *Politica Economica*, 21 (2), 307–335.

EC (2004). On the coordination of procedures for the award of public works contracts, public supply contracts and public service contracts, Directive 2004/18/EC of the European Parliament and of the Council, 31 March 2004.

Ellman, M. (2005). The Optimal Length of Contracts with Application to Outsourcing, manuscript, Universdad Pompeu Fabra.

Ewerhart C. and K. Fieseler (2003). Procurement Auctions and Unit-price Contracts, *RAND Journal of Economics*, 34 (3), 568–580.

General Service Administration, Department of Defense and National Aeronautics and Space Administration (2005). Federal Acquisition Regulation, vol. I.

Fehr, E. M. Brown and A. Falk (2004). Relational Contracts and the Nature of Market Interactions, *Econometrica* 72 (3), 747–780.

Guerrero, J. C., C. J. Kirkpatrick (2001). Evaluating Contractor Past Performance in the United States, *Public Procurement Law Review*, 10, 243–259.

Guriev, S. M. and D. Kvasov, (2005). Contracting on time, *American Economic Review*, 95, (5), 1369–1385.

Holmostrom, B. (1979). Managerial Incentive Problems: A Dynamic Perspective, Review of Economic Studies, 66 (1), 169–182.

Iossa, E. and P. Legros (2004). Auditing and Property Rights, *The Rand Journal of Economics*, 35, 356–372.

Kim, I. G. (1998). A Model of Selective Tendering: Does Bidding Competition Deter Opportunism by Contractor?, *The Quarterly Review of Economics and Finance*, 38, 907–925.

Kelman, S. (1990). *Procurement and Public Management: The Fear of Discretion and the Quality of Government Performance*, Washington, DC: American Enterprise Institute Press.

Kelman, S. (2002). Remaking Federal Procurement, Working Paper No. 3, Visions of Governance in the 21st Century Program, Kennedy School of Goverment. Published as Remaking Federal Procurement, *Public Contracts Law Journal* (Summer 2002).

Laffont, J. and J. Tirole (1987). Auctioning Incentives Contracts, *Journal of Political Economy*, 95 (5), 921–937.

Laffont, J. and J. Tirole (1993). *A Theory of Incentives in Regulation and Procurement*, Cambridge, MA: MIT Press.

Lyon T. (2006). Does Dual Sourcing Lower Procurement Costs?, *The Journal of Industrial Economics*, Vol. 54 (2), 223–252.

Lyon T. P. (2000). Does Dual Sourcing Lower Procurement Costs?, mimeo Kelley School of Business, Indiana University.

Manelli A. and D. R. Vincent (1995). Optimal Procurement Mechanisms. *Econometrica*, 63, (3), 591–620.

McAfee, R. P. and J. McMillan (1986). Bidding for Contracts: A Principal–Agent Analysis, *The Rand Journal of Economics*, 17 (3), 326–388.

McAfee, R. P. and J. McMillan (1987). Competition for Agency Contracts, *The RAND Journal of Economics*, 18 (2), 296–307.

McMillan, J. (1992). *Games, Strategies and Managers*, New York, NJ: Oxford University Press.

National Audit Office. (2005). Improving Public Services through Better Construction. National Audit Office, HC 209.

Neeman A. and G. Orosel (2004). Contestable Licensing, *Contributions to Economic Analysis & Policy*, 3 (2004), 3, (1), Article1, http://www.bepress.com/bejeap/contributions/vol3/iss1/art1.

Office of Federal Procurement Policy (Office of Management and Budget Executive Office of the President) (2000). Best Practices for Collecting and Using Past Performance Information. www.acqnet.gov/Library/OFPP/BestPractices/ pbsc/library/OFPPbp-collecting.pdf.

Richardson, J. (1993). Parallel Sourcing and Supplier Performance in the Japaneese Automotive Industry, *Strategic Management Journal*, 14 (5), 339–350.

Riordan, M. H. and D. E. M. Sappington (1987). Awarding Monopoly Franchises, *American Economic Review*, 77 (3) 375–387.

Rob, R. (1986). The Design of Procurement Contracts, *American Economic Review*, 76 (3), 378–389.

Rogerson, W. P. (1992). Overhead Allocation and Incentives for Cost Minimization in Defence Procurement, *The Accounting Review*, 67 (4), 671–690.

Weitzman, M. L. (1980). Efficient Incentive Contracts, *The Quarterly Journal of Economics*, 94 (4), 719–730.

5 Incentives and award procedures: competitive tendering versus negotiations in procurement

Patrick Bajari and Steven Tadelis

5.1. Introduction

Manufactured goods, such as computers, TVs and automobiles are mass produced, have standardized characteristics and are typically purchased at list price. Other goods, such as new buildings, fighter jets, custom software or consulting services are tailored to fit a procurer's specific and often unique needs. To procure these customized goods, the procurer hires a contractor who supplies the goods according to a set of desired specifications. We call this the *procurement problem*.

The procurement problem has attracted much attention both in policy and in academic circles. The main focus of academic economists has been on procurement by the public sector, in part because of its sheer importance to the economy.[1] For example, procurement by federal, state and local government accounts for more than 10 percent of Gross Domestic Product in the United States. Many private sector transactions are also governed by procurement contracts. Prominent examples include electronics components, custom software, automobile production and building construction.

When considering the procurement of goods and services, the procurer is faced with many challenges. First, she has to choose what exactly should be procured, and how to transmit her needs to the potential suppliers. Second, a contract must be laid out that includes contractual obligations and methods of compensation. Third, the procurer needs to decide how to award the procurement contract between the potential suppliers. Finally,

We thank the National Science Foundation for financial support.
[1] See also Chapters 1 and 3 for more facts on procurement in practice.

the award mechanism should result in the selection of a qualified and desirable supplier and in the implementation of a cost-effective final product.

Following up on these last two points, competitive tendering is widely recognized as an attractive procurement mechanism and is commonly advocated for several reasons.[2] Most notably it is viewed as a procedure that stimulates and promotes competition. By its nature, open competitive tendering invites potential suppliers from many venues. Furthermore, in the face of competition from many potential suppliers each one has strong incentives not to inflate his price. Indeed, fair market price discovery is often touted as a beneficial result of such tendering. Open competitive mechanisms are also known for their transparency, making it easier to prevent corruption both in the public and private sectors where procurement managers may have incentives to rig the system in return for bribes and other benefits. These characteristics, as well as arguments for equal opportunity, provide a justification for statutes such as the Federal Acquisition Regulations (FAR) that strongly favour the use of competitive tendering in the US public sector.

Interestingly, there is widespread use of *both* competitive tendering and negotiations in the private sector. For example, from 1995 to 2000, 44 percent of private sector non-residential building construction projects in Northern California were procured using negotiations, while *only 18 percent* were procured using open competitive tendering. The use of negotiations with single source suppliers is also common in high tech and software, and used for defence procurement as well. This chapter offers a framework to compare competitive tendering with negotiations and relate these award mechanisms to the payment procedures chosen in the contract. In particular, it tries to shed light on when competitive tendering with fixed price contracts will be preferred to negotiating cost plus contracts, and when not.

To put this chapter in perspective it is worth observing that most of the economic analysis describes the procurement problem as follows. The supplier has information about production costs that the procurer does not have. The procurer then has to consider clever ways to infer the suppliers costs, such as offering the supplier many potential projects to choose from, and having the supplier select the one that will be produced.[3]

---

[2] There has been a flurry of managerial and policy advice on using "reverse auctions" or "online reverse auctions" as these are referred to when online platforms are used. A search on the web for "reverse auction" will offer too many sites to mention.

[3] For an excellent summary of this literature see Laffont and Tirole (1993). Analysis along these lines is the focus of Chapter 19 in this handbook.

In contrast, scholars and practitioners of engineering and construction management argue that the central problem in procurement is not that suppliers know so much more than procurers at the onset of the project, but that instead both procurers and suppliers share uncertainty about many important design changes that occur after the contract is signed and production begins. These changes are usually a consequence of design failures, unanticipated conditions and changes in regulatory requirements.[4]

An illustrative example of the significance of *ex post* adaptation is the building of the Getty Center Art Museum in Los Angeles, which is a 24 acre, one billion dollar facility that took over eight years to construct (see Engineering New-Record 1994, 1997). The project design had to be changed due to site conditions that were hard to anticipate. The geology of the project included canyons, slide planes and earthquake fault lines, which posed numerous challenges for the team of architects and contractors. For instance, contractors "hit a slide" and unexpectedly moved 75,000 cubic yards of earth. More severely, in 1994 an earthquake struck. Cracks in the steel welds of the building's frame caused the contractors to reassess the adequacy of the seismic design standards that were used. The project design had to be altered also due to the regulatory environment – 107 items had to be added to the building's conditional use permit. These problems were very hard to predict, both for the procurer and the contractor. However, it seems reasonable that once problems arose, the contractor had superior information regarding the costs and methods to implement changes. A more recent and much more contentious example is the "big dig" in Boston, where 12,000 changes to more than 150 design and construction contracts have led to $1.6 billion in cost overruns, much of which can be traced back to unsatisfactory design and site conditions that differed from expectations.[5]

These observations suggest that the procurement problem may indeed be primarily one of smoothing out or circumventing adaptations after the project begins rather than information revelation by the supplier before the project is selected. In this chapter we argue that the form of contracts and award mechanisms can be tailored in a way to help mitigate this procurement problem. In particular, a trade-off between incentives to reduce cost

---

[4] See Bartholomew (1998), Clough and Sears (1994), Hinze (1993) and Sweet (1994).

[5] According to the *Boston Globe*, "About $1.1 billion of that can be traced back to deficiencies in the designs, records show: $357 million because contractors found different conditions than appeared on the designs, and $737 million for labour and materials costs associated with incomplete designs." Responsibility for these cost overruns is a subject of heated debate. See http://www.boston.com/news/specials/bechtel/part_1/

and incentives to facilitate changes and share information will be the key force in our arguments of contractual choice.

We argue that simple projects, which we define as easy to design with little uncertainty about what needs to be produced, ought to be procured using fixed-price contracts, should be accompanied by high levels of design completeness (to prevent the need for adaptations), and are best awarded through competitive tendering. In contrast, complex projects, which we define as hard to design with large scope for surprises in the final configuration, ought to be procured using cost-plus contracts, should be accompanied by low levels of design completeness (implying a high chance that adaptations to the contract will be needed), and should be awarded through a negotiation with a reputable and qualified supplier.[6]

The intuition for our prescriptions stems from a tension between providing incentives to lower costs and avoiding costly and wasteful renegotiation that follows requests for changes. The strong incentives to reduce costs that are offered by fixed-price tendered contracts will lead the parties to the transaction to dissipate valuable surplus when changes need to be renegotiated. This efficiency loss will often be due to haggling over prices when there is true lock-in of the current supplier who wishes to use the need for changes to his advantage. Cost-plus contracts, in contrast, discourage cost-saving efforts but ease the process of renegotiating changes and adaptation to the contract's original requirements.[7]

We continue to argue that the choice of payment procedures, such as fixed price and cost-plus contracts, is tied in with the follow-up decision that a procurer faces: whether to award a procurement contract by competitive tendering or by negotiating with a potential supplier.

While our research has been motivated by practices in the private sector, it offers implications for the public sector as well. In the United States the public sector statutes that govern procurement, typically based on FAR, strongly favour the use of competitive bidding. For example, from 1995 to 2000, 97 percent of public sector building construction projects in Northern

---

[6] See the first part of Chapter 19 for further discussions on contracting choices and contract types. The focus there is more adequate for simple procurement settings (standardized goods and services) where contingencies can be foreseen and controlled within the contract.

[7] In fact, Williamson expresses the idea that "low powered" incentives are good to accommodate adaptations and writes that "low powered incentives have well-known adaptability advantages. That, after all, is what commends cost plus contracting. But, such advantages are not had without cost — which explains why cost plus contracting is embraced reluctantly." (1985 p. 140). It turns out that in many cases cost-plus contracting is indeed embraced.

California were procured using competitive bidding. While competitive bidding does have the advantage of unbiased awarding of projects, it fails to respond optimally to *ex post* adaptation. This suggests that public procurement of complex projects are suffering from efficiency losses.

We begin our analysis in the next section with a simple framework to describe the procurer's choice of devising a contract that will govern the procurement relationship with a selected supplier. We then continue to describe how the contracts chosen will dictate the use of award mechanisms. We conclude with a discussion of implications for business strategy and public procurement.

5.2. The contracting framework

5.2.1. Contractual components: design and incentives

In this section we discuss and analyse the precursor to awarding a contract: devising one. Consider a procurer who wishes to procure a project (good or service) from a supplier. To facilitate the procurement and get what he desires, the procurer must provide the supplier with plans and specifications that describe the project. This is the procurer's first dimension of contractual choice: how much *design costs* to invest at the onset, where more investment (and hence costs) in design creates a more detailed set of plans and specifications. Clearly, a more detailed and accurate design of a project reduces the need to renegotiate changes after the project starts taking shape.

It is often prohibitively expensive to draft a complete design that includes all the relevant blueprints and instructions that fully describe the project exactly as the procurer's needs dictate. That is, there is always a chance that a contingency will arise for which there are no instructions, or for which the blueprints are insufficient. This in turn implies that the plan as specified may not result in the successful completion of the project, and the procurer may not obtain the value he initially expected. We refer to this problem as *contractual incompleteness* because it is generally associated with the design and specifications not being a complete description of what ought to be done, and how the supplier should proceed in all future contingencies.[8]

The contractual incompleteness of the project will depend not only on how much investment in design was initially performed, but will also depend on

---

[8] The second part of Chapter 19 discusses the impact of of non-contractible quality on the procurement problem.

how prone the type of project is to unforeseen changes. Such unforeseen changes can arise from technological or regulatory contingencies that are just too hard to predict or plan for, or alternatively too expensive to try and draft into the design. To capture this idea we define the *complexity* of the project as how expensive it is to provide a rather complete set of plans and contingencies. The more complex a project is, the more expensive it will be to try and prevent contractual incompleteness. Thus, the procurer's first choice is how complete a design to invest in while being aware of the costs of design and the amount of uncontrollable events that can affect the project's progression.

The procurer's second dimension of contractual choice is the payment structure of the contract. Most procurement contracts are variants of simple fixed-price or cost-plus contracts. In fixed price contracts, the procurer offers the supplier a pre-specified price for completing the project as specified, and any changes are negotiated separately at the stage in which they arise. A cost-plus contract does not specify a price, but rather reimburses the contractor for costs (time and material) with an additional stipulated fee (the "plus"). In cost-plus contracts the costs of changes are automatically built into the original contract.[9]

5.2.2. The costs and benefits of incentives

We are now in a position to highlight some trade-offs of using either payment structure. Let us start by ignoring first any changes to the original design, and assume that the project will be executed exactly as the design specifies. If a fixed-price contract is in place then the supplier bears all of the costs of providing the project. This, of course, implies that the supplier has strong incentives to lower the cost of production, and some of these would pass on to the procurer through competitive pressures (that we discuss more in section 5.3).

In contrast, if a cost-plus contract is in place then the supplier knows that any extra costs he incurs will be fully compensated for, and may even generate a small profit if the fee is based on a percentage of the costs. Thus, the supplier will have no incentives to reduce the costs of production, and no such costs savings can therefore be transferred to the procurer.

---

[9] An intermediate type of contract is an incentive contracts (see, e.g., the discussion in section 2 of Bajari and Tadelis, 2001). These reimburse only a fraction of the total cost to the supplier and can sometimes include quality performance incentives. See Chapter 19 for a detailed description of the features and the advantages of such a contract.

To set a benchmark imagine an idealized situation where the design and specification of the project leave no room for contractual incompleteness. For example, imagine that all the contingencies and specifications of the project are completely clear and well documented, and performance per specifications is easy to verify upon delivery. For this idealized case the observations discussed earlier lead to an obvious conclusion:

Practical conclusion 1

If contractual incompleteness is negligible and if performance is easy to verify then favour fixed-price contracts.

This simple observation is a direct consequence of the incentives provided by each of the two payment structures.[10] When the only dimension of interest to the procurer is the cost, then clearly one wants to achieve the lowest possible cost, and this is achieved by providing the supplier with the strongest possible incentives to lower costs.

Notice, however, that two qualifications were stated in practical conclusion 1. The first qualification is that contractual incompleteness is negligible. This means that the procurer can avoid the need to ask for any changes or modifications after the project commences, and no redrafting or renegotiating will be needed to complete the project according to the procurer's needs. The second qualification is that performance is easy to verify. This means that the procurer can easily detect any departures from the design and specification as well as any shortfalls that deviate from the specified requirements. Furthermore, the fact that performance can be verified means that any such deviations from the design and specifications can be used as a hold on payments to the supplier. This guarantees that if the supplier wishes to receive payment, he must satisfy all the requirements that meet the procurer's needs.

Now imagine that the second qualification is violated. For example, there may be performance dimensions that can either not be detected by the procurer or even if detected, can not be used as a reason to hold back payments because third parties such as courts or arbitrators cannot verify them. If, furthermore, the supplier can save costs by cutting back on these performance dimensions, then it is quite obvious that providing the supplier with

---

[10] This result, in fact, resurfaces in Chapter 19. Indeed, it is a rather obvious and intuitive conclusion that one would expect from a variety of approaches to this problem.

cost-cutting incentives will create a tension. Namely, by shaving back on certain areas of performance for which contractual ramifications cannot be enforced, the supplier can save on costs and increase his profits. This suggests the following:

Practical conclusion 2

If it is impossible or extremely costly to contractually verify important performance measures, and if the contractor can save on costs by cutting back on these performance dimensions, then favour cost-plus contracts.

Practical conclusion 2 resonates with the old saying of "you get what you pay for".[11] If the supplier is bound to a fixed-price contract he will, as mentioned earlier, have strong incentives to cut on costs. When cutting corners is one way to achieve costs savings, then it better be easy to deter such behaviour if the procurer is harmed by it. This simple observation is often recognized by practitioners, but when ignored, can lead to extremely undesirable outcomes. Thus, cost-plus contracts have merits by inhibiting a supplier's incentives to cut costs by cutting back on important, yet hard to monitor performance dimensions.

It turns out that cost-plus contracts have another appealing feature, which has been recognized at least by some scholars and practitioners in the area of construction management: facilitating changes and modifications to the original designs and specifications.[12] For example, the most common sources of changes in building construction are defective plans and specifications, changes in project scope and differing conditions than expected at the site of construction. In other words, *contractual incompleteness* will often lead to the need for renegotiating the original specifications of the project.

Conventional wisdom in the industry is that cost-plus contracts are better suited to facilitate such change and to reduce the amount of adversarial relations and frictions between the procurer and the supplier when such changes are required. To see why, imagine a situation where at some advanced stage of the project's development it turned out that the plans and

---

[11] This issue was broadly discussed in Kerr (1975) and analysed more completely and carefully by Holmstrom and Milgrom (1991) and Baker (1992). Again, it resurfaces in the first part of Chapter 19, that allows for a more flexible range of cost incentives.

[12] See Ibbs et al. (1986) who quantify the impact of 96 different contract clauses on project performance in building construction by surveying buyers and contractors for 36 building construction projects. They claim to verify aspects of cost-plus and fixed-price contracting that are discussed below.

specifications are defective, or lacking some directive for an unforeseen issue that arises.

Consider the effects of having a fixed price contract in place when the procurer asks the supplier to adopt some changes to the original plan. The original plans and fixed price compensation take the form of a specific-performance contract that binds the supplier to the original plans and does not oblige him to agree to the changes proposed by the procurer. Thus, the procurer will have to negotiate any changes with the supplier. The pro-curer's objective is to get the changes done in the most cost-effective way according to his needs while the supplier wishes to make as high a profit as he can from the potential windfall. The supplier would like to take advantage of this situation since he is in a unique position of being able to hold up the procurer as a consequence of being in the midst of the project, and has no competitive pressure to discipline his behaviour. Knowing this, the procurer may expect to be overcharged and the two parties are likely to engage in contentious adversarial negotiations.

Alternatively, consider the effects of having a cost-plus contract in place when the procurer asks the supplier to adopt some changes to the original plan. Unlike the specific-performance nature of a fixed price contract, a cost-plus contract effectively has a built-in mechanism to compensate the supplier for any changes that are required. Namely, any additional costs that the supplier incurs are automatically compensated for through the cost-plus structure.[13] In other words, the lack of cost-reducing incentives serves as a lubricant for smooth and cooperative implementation of changes when contractual incompleteness gives rise to the need for changes. Thus, we can conclude:

Practical conclusion 3
If contractual incompleteness is anticipated and the need for flexibility to implement changes is foreseen then favour cost-plus contracts.

We can now conclude this section with a recommendation that follows from the trade-offs identified above such that a procurer can follow before making the two contractual choices of investing in design and choosing a

---

[13] Furthermore, if the fee is a percentage fee then implementing costly changes includes a small increase to compensate the contractor for any opportunity costs of extra time and potential overhead. This, of course, adds the risk that the contractor has incentives to increase costs and get a higher fee, which favours fixed-fees. With fixed fees the procurer and contractor may need to bargain over a fair fee for the opportunity costs of time, but this is typically a fraction of the labour and material costs of change over which no bargaining is needed with a cost-plus contract.

compensation structure. Recall that a project is said to be *complex* if the procurer anticipates it to be difficult to describe, specify and monitor, so that a rather complete design will be exceptionally costly to provide (or maybe even impossible). In contrast, a project is *simple* if it is easy and rather inexpensive to design and it is straightforward to predict and monitor performance. Since the costs of design and engineering efforts are an integral part of the total project costs we can conclude our recommendations as follows:

Practical conclusion 4

For simple projects favour a complete investment in design and specification followed by a fixed-price contract, while for complex projects favour a low investment in design followed by a cost-plus contract.

It is worth explaining the reason for favouring savings on design for complex projects. At first it may seem that complex projects would require an extra effort in trying to provide more details into the design. However, the complexity of such projects implies that many changes are expected even if design efforts are high. Thus, if a cost-plus contract is in place to deal with such changes, the added benefits of extra design efforts are small. This follows because it will not be too costly to implement changes in the aftermath of unforeseen issues, which makes the benefits of a more complete design less pronounced. A caveat is that one would wish to avoid changes that will completely disrupt the projects production plan and cause expensive changes to the infrastructure as it develops. Thus, some initial investment in planning will be necessary to predict how complete the design ought to be to at least set the stage for proceeding with the project.

Now that we have set up the contractual framework and offered some insights about the trade-offs facing our procurer in designing the contract's structure, we turn to explore the connection between the contract's structure and the award mechanisms that the procurer can choose.

5.3. Competitive tendering versus negotiations

We proceed to argue that the choice of a contract's payment structure should be tied to the choice of award mechanism, namely, the choice between a process of competitive tendering and a negotiation with a selected supplier. To set the stage, recall the many known benefits of competitive tendering. First, it promotes competition among potential suppliers. Second, it offers a kind of transparency that helps mitigate favouritism and corruption. The question is then, what is the object over which bids are solicited and what form should these bids take?

Consider our contractual framework and imagine that a simple project is at stake where our procurer follows practical conclusion 4 and chooses to invest in a rather complete design that is accompanied by a fixed-price contract. This implies that our procurer is in a position to give a very detailed description of the project to potential suppliers, and all the procurer wishes to receive in return is a single price that will be paid once the project is completed according to the plans and specifications. In this situation a competitive tendering mechanism will offer the procurer all its benefits. Suppliers will have to compete their surplus away, and the procurer is getting exactly what he wants: a well-defined project at the lowest possible price. If the procurer instead chooses to negotiate a price with a single supplier, the competitive pressure is weak and the procurer will not achieve all the possible cost-savings that he can. Therefore we conclude:

Practical conclusion 5
For simple well-specified projects favour a fixed-price contract to be awarded by a competitive tender.

Now turn to the other case of a complex project with an incomplete design and which the procurer plans to award using a cost-plus contract. As most practitioners would readily agree, '[a] cost-plus contract does not lend itself well to competitive bidding,' and in the area of construction management, '[m]ost negotiated contracts are of the cost-plus-fee type.'[14]

To try and implement a competitive tender for a cost-plus contract one might suggest that bidders can bid over the 'plus' portion of the compensation. In this way the procurer can choose the supplier who requests the lowest compensation for his management, and the production costs of labour and material will be automatically paid for through the cost-plus structure. However, as the "plus" is often only a small fraction of the costs, this can be quite a disastrous way to select a contractor for what is in essence a challenging and complex project.

To see this we begin by considering what will determine a supplier's desired compensation when bidding for a contract. Clearly, a supplier will

---

[14] These quotes are from Hinze (1993, p. 144) and Clough and Sears (1994, p. 10) respectively.

not wish to settle for less than he could obtain in some alternative job. If, as one would imagine, more cost efficient and able suppliers have better alternative opportunities, then their bid for a fee in a cost-plus contract will be higher than less able and cost efficient suppliers. This argument implies that it is the *highest cost and least able* supplier who will win such a competitive tender for a cost-plus fee. Furthermore, if complex projects that are tied to cost-plus contracts require suppliers with more expertise, then hiring the least able supplier can be devastating.

Instead of using a competitive tender the procurer can search the market for those able and reputable suppliers and choose one to negotiate with in order to set the fee for the cost-plus contract. In this way the procurer guarantees himself a qualified and able supplier. Furthermore, since the fee is expected to be a small fraction of the costs, the lack of competitive pressure on the supplier will not have a large effect on final costs. Therefore we conclude:

Practical conclusion 6

For complex and incompletely specified projects favour a cost-plus contract to be awarded using a negotiation with a reputable supplier.

We have described a link between the choice of contractual payment structure and the way in which such contracts ought to be awarded. As it turns out, there is a complementary reason to favour negotiations with a reputable supplier over tendering when complex projects are to be awarded. Practitioners have recognized that competitive tendering stifles valuable coordination between the procurer and the potential supplier before the plans and specifications are finalized. To see this, note that the primary information that the procurer receives from suppliers in a competitive tender is their bid. A supplier has no incentive to offer the procurer advice on how to improve the plans or avoid certain pitfalls. In fact, a supplier would have the incentive to keep any findings of this kind to himself as they offer him a competitive advantage over his rivals in a competitive tendering process.

For example, it is widely believed in the construction industry that when competitive tendering is used to award a fixed-price contract, the contractors strategically read the plans and specifications to determine where they will fail. Suppose that some contractor sees a flaw in the plans that will cause a change leading to one million dollars of profits, and that the other contractors do not. Our savvy contractor will likely win the job since he would be willing to bid less than contractors who do not see the flaws in the plans. Competitive tendering may therefore lead to a problem of *ex-ante* opportunism that is more problematic when projects are complex. After he is awarded the project, the pitfalls he anticipated will materialize and he will be in a position to reap excessive profits from the required changes.

In negotiations, however, the procurer and supplier typically spend a good deal of time discussing the project before work begins. During such negotiations the procurer can elicit the supplier's views about where the designs and specifications can be improved, so that negotiations might be preferable to competitive tendering. The construction industry literature suggests that one merit of cost-plus contracting and negotiation is that procurers and contractors spend more time discussing the project and ironing out possible pitfalls before work begins.[15] Thus, we conclude:

> **Practical conclusion 7**
> For complex projects for which the expertise and input of an experienced supplier is essential at the design stage, favour a cost-plus contract to be awarded using a negotiation with a reputable supplier.

We conclude this section with some insights and recommendations for projects that are not clearly categorized as very simple or complex, and for which the choice of contract structure and award procedure is not obvious. First, consider the effects of market conditions on the choice of contracts and award procedures. It is well known that the benefits from a competitive tender will generally depend on the number of qualified bidders who will participate. In particular, the more potential suppliers are available for bidding, the higher the benefits from promoting competition. We have:

---

[15] As Sweet (1994) puts it, "[s]eparation of design and construction deprives the owner of contractor skill during the design process, such as sensitivity to the labour and materials markets, knowledge of construction techniques, and their advantages, disadvantages and costs. A contractor would also have the ability to evaluate the coherence and completeness of the design and, most important, the costs of any design proposed."

> ### Practical conclusion 8
> For moderately complex projects that can be specified at moderate costs, if there is more potential competition then favour a more complete design and a fixed-price contract to be awarded using a competitive tender. If potential suppliers are scarce then save on design costs and favour a cost-plus contract negotiated with a qualified supplier.

Finally, we consider the difference between an open competitive tender in which any supplier can submit a bid and the procedure of "invited bidders" in which only a handful of suppliers are invited to participate in the competitive tender. To analyse potential differences between these procedures consider the response of suppliers to a request for bids for a rather complex, but somewhat well-specified project. Preparing the bid will be more challenging and costly the more complex and large the project is. If qualified suppliers expect that less qualified suppliers may try to compete and offer low bids, then this may deter the qualified suppliers from exerting the time and costs of preparing the bids.

Hence, a procurer may not be able to attract qualified suppliers if price competition is expected to be fierce. If the procurer can prevent less qualified suppliers from bidding and in this way restrict competition to guarantee a reasonable rate of return then the qualified suppliers will have incentives to invest in preparing these bids and compete.[16] Thus,

> ### Practical conclusion 9
> For moderately complex projects for which several qualified bidders exist, and for which preparing bids includes significant costs on the suppliers, favour a fixed-price contract to be awarded by inviting a small number of qualified suppliers to a competitive tender.

5.4. Discussion

5.4.1. Lessons for business strategy

The widespread benefits offered by competitive tendering to set a project's price are well known: promoting competition and hampering corruption. We have shed some light, however, on some of the costs of using this

---

[16] Ye (2006) investigates the problem of costly bidding, and how restricting the number of bidders may help the procurer.

popular mechanism. In fact, in a recent study of contracts awarded in the construction industry in Northern California[17] we have shown that in the private sector there is widespread use of negotiations. Specifically, more than 43 percent of over 4,000 private sector contracts between 1995 and 2000 were awarded using negotiations with a sole supplier, while only 18 percent were awarded using open competitive tendering (most of the rest were awarded using a select group of invited bidders). An analysis of the data suggests that the choices made are consistent with the trade-offs we have laid out in our analysis above.

As we have argued, there are two channels through which cost-plus contracts awarded through negotiations can be more attractive than fixed-price contracts awarded through competitive tendering. The first is the need for flexibility and changes to incompletely specified designs of complex projects. A response to this problem is choosing a cost-plus contract that cannot be competitively tendered in a sensible way. The second channel, which has been emphasized by some industry participants, is using the knowledge and experience of a contractor before the designs are complete and construction begins. As we have argued, if a project will be awarded using competitive bidding then a contractor has an incentive to hide information about possible design flaws, submit a low bid, and recoup profits when changes will be required.

The procurement problem we investigate is generally applicable, be it that of an automobile manufacturer who needs to procure a braking system, an accounting firm that needs to procure information technology services, or a city government that needs to provide garbage collection and disposal services for its residents. This problem is also related to the 'make-or-buy' problem of the organization of production, which is the choice of which activities to produce oneself, and which to outsource to an external supplier. If we consider the procurement of goods and services that are repeated over time, then we can view internal organization and self-production as buying the time of employees and paying directly for the input materials, much like a sequence of cost-plus contracts (where the fee is not spent but absorbed as part of the organization's profits). Alternatively, outsourcing transactions for a predetermined price depend on output performance.[18]

Our analysis suggests that for long-term and steady provision, goods and services that are simple in our contractual framework should be outsourced

---

[17] See Bajari, McMillan and Tadelis (2006).

[18] See Chapter 16 on the design of repeat-purchase contracts.

with fixed-price contracts, while goods and services that are complex should be internally produced as if they are procured with a cost-plus contract. The benefits of internal production are also that the procurer retains control over the process, which may indeed be a valuable option when complex issues are at hand and direction and flexibility are needed throughout the process of production. Casual observation suggests that in many cases employees have directives that specify their work, but these are often verbal and not specified in a detailed contract. Outside contractors are subject to very detailed contracts and contractual compliance is measured vis-a-vis these formal specifications.

5.4.2. Lessons for public sector policy

In the public sector, statutes such as the US FAR (and the many statutes that are modelled after the FAR) strongly favour the use of competitive bidding, and particularly open competitive bidding when feasible. For instance, in our study of the building construction industry in Northern California mentioned above, 97 percent of the projects awarded in the public sector were awarded using open competitive bidding as compared to only 18 percent in the private sector. As private sector firms are more sensitive to cost minimization, it is reasonable to conclude that their behaviour is more responsive to optimal choices.

As mentioned above, competitive bidding is perceived to select the lowest cost bidder, prevent corruption and favouritism that are opposed to efficiency, and it offers a clear yardstick with which to compare offers. According to an Ohio Court, competitive bidding '... gives everyone an equal chance to bid, eliminates collusion, and saves taxpayers' money.... It fosters honest competition in order to obtain the best work and supplies at the lowest possible price because taxpayers' money is being used. It is also necessary to guard against favouritism, impudence, extravagance, fraud and corruption.'[19] This is the main rational for requiring competitive tendering in the public sector.

Our results suggest that for complex projects, there is a downside to the use of fixed-price contracts awarded through competitive tendering and that selecting a contractor and negotiating with him may be the favourable course of action. This downside of open competitive bidding can arise from a lack of input by contractors at the design stage, from the need to proceed

---

[19] See Sweet (1994, p. 379).

quickly without the ability to complete detailed plans and specifications, and from the expectations that ex post haggling and frictions might occur when changes are needed. An important practical question for public procurement is whether one can design a set of objective rules for awarding negotiated contracts that minimize transaction costs, but that are not easily subject to manipulation, corruption, or blatant favouritism.[20]

Indeed, there has been mounting criticism of the LOGCAP contracts awarded to Haliburton by the US Army that were no-bid cost-plus contracts. Whistle-blowers who worked at Haliburton claimed that there was no incentive or process to reduce costs when possible, and that the motto at the time in the company was 'Don't worry about price, it's cost-plus'.[21] The design of novel rules that on one hand allow the use of flexible cost-plus contracts while on the other hand offer some controls that reduce the possible scope of opportunistic behaviour is beyond the scope of this article. That said, our analysis suggests that there may be large gains and savings of tax-payers' money from designing and successfully implementing cost-plus negotiations in the public sector with better controls.

Bibliographical notes

The analysis provided above is based primarily on Bajari and Tadelis (2001) and Bajari, McMillan and Tadelis (2006). The implications of how complexity of a process may affect the choice to outsource or self-produce is analysed in Levin and Tadelis (2006) who apply their framework to procurement by local governments. An attempt to measure the transactions cost impact of changes to contracts in highway procurement was done by Bajari, Houghton and Tadelis (2006). Related to this agenda is a paper by Chakravarty and McLeod (2004) who show that current contracts used by the American Institute of Architects are helpful for the problem of procuring large, complex projects when unforeseen contingencies are inevitable. Corts and Singh (2004) show the relationship between contractual choice and project complexity in the face of repeat business. Banerjee and Duflo

---

[20] See Chapter 16 for more on corruption.

[21] This is documented in a letter from two members of congress, Henry A. Waxman and John D. Dingell to William H. Reed, Director of the Defense Contract Audit Agency. A copy currently exists at: http://www.house.gov/reform/min/pdfs_108_2/pdfs_inves/pdf_admin_halliburton_contract_inves_feb_12_-let.pdf

(2000) offer some evidence that correlates the choice of cost-plus contracting with reputable suppliers in the Indian software industry.

A classical analysis of competitive tendering versus negotiations was offered by Bulow and Klemperer (1996). They emphasize the competitive advantages of these procedures, and hence ignore the issues of adaptation due to changes. Manelli and Vincent (1995) introduce quality concerns, and show that sometimes competitive tendering will be dominated by sequential negotiations with suppliers. For a treatment of tendering contracts that are not fixed price contracts, see McAfee and McMillan (1986).

References

Bajari, Patrick and Steven Tadelis (2001). Incentives Versus Transaction Costs: A Theory of Procurement Contracts. *RAND Journal of Economics*, Autumn 32 (3), pp. 387–407.

Bajari, Patrick, Robert McMillan and Steven Tadelis (2006). Auctions vs. Negotiation in Procurement: An Emprical Analysis, working paper, UC Berkeley.

Bajari, Patrick, Stephanie Houghton, and Steven Tadelis (2006). Bidding for Incomplete Contracts, working paper, University of Michigan and UC Berkeley.

Baker, George (1992). Incentive Contracts and Performance Measurement, *Journal of Political Economy*, 100: 598–614.

Banerjee, Abhijit V., Duflo, Esther (2000). Reputation Effects and the Limits of Contracting: A Study of the Indian Software Industry, *Quarterly Journal of Economics*, 115 (3), August, 989–1017.

Bartholomew, Stuart H. (1998). *Construction Contracting: Business and Legal Principles*, Prentice-Hall, Inc.

Bulow, Jeremy and Paul Klemperer (1996). Auctions vs. Negotiations, *American Economic Review* 86, pp. 180–194.

Chakravarty, Surajeet and W. Bentley MacLeod (2004). On the Efficiency of Standard Form Contracts: The Case of Construction, USC CLEO Research Paper No. C04–17.

Clough, R. and G. Sears (1994). *Construction Contracting*, New York: Wiley.

Corts, Kenneth and Jasjit Singh (2004). The Effect of Relationships on Contract Choice: Evidence from Offshore Drilling, *Journal of Law, Economics, and Organization*, 20 (1): 230–260.

Engineering News-Record. "Getting to the Top: Getty Center Builders Say Elevating Art in L. A. Is No Small Task." December 12, 1994.

Engineering News-Record. "Getty Center Wraps Up Eight Years and $1 Billion Later." October 15, 1997.

Hester, Weston T., John A. Kuprenas, and T.C. Chang (1991). Construction Changes and change orders: their magnitude and impact, a report to the Construction Industry Institute, the University of Texas at Austin, under the guidance of the Cost/Schedule Task Force from University of California.

Hinze, Jim (1993). *Construction Contracts*, McGraw-Hill Series in Construction Engineering and Project Management. Irwin/McGraw-Hill.

Holmstrom, Bengt and Paul Milgrom (1991). Multitask Principal–Agent Analyses: Incentive Contracts, Asset Ownership and Job Design, *Journal of Law, Economics and Organization*, 7 (0) (Special Issue), 24–52.

Ibbs, C. William et al. (1986). *Determining The Impact of Various Construction Contract Types And Clauses On Project Performance*. Volumes I and II, The Construction Industry Institute, Austin, Texas.

Kerr, Stephen (1975). On the Folly of Rewarding A, While Hoping for B, *The Academy of Management Journal*, 18 (4), 769–783.

Laffont, Jean-Jacques and Jean Tirole (1993). *A Theory of Incentives in Procurement and Regulation*. MIT Press.

Levin, Jonathan and Steven Tadelis (2006). Contracting for Government Services: Theory and Evidence from the U.S. Cities, working paper, Stanford University and UC Berkeley.

Manelli, Alejandro and Daniel Vincent, Daniel (1995). Optimal Procurement Mechanisms, *Econometrica*, 63, 591–620.

McAfee, R. Preston and John McMillan (1986). Bidding for Contracts: A Principal Agent Analysis, *Rand Journal of Economics*, 17, 326–38.

Sweet, J. (1994). *Legal Aspects of Architecture, Engineering and the Construction Process*, Minnesota: West Publishing Company.

Williamson, Oliver E. (1985). *The Economic Institutions of Capitalism*, New York: Free Press.

Ye, Lixin. Indicative Bidding and A Theory of Two-stage Auctions, forthcoming in *Games and Economic Behavior*.

PART III

Competitive tendering strategies

6 Information and competitive tendering

Gian Luigi Albano, Nicola Dimitri, Riccardo Pacini and
Giancarlo Spagnolo

6.1. Introduction

As stressed in the previous chapter by Bajari and Tadelis, it would be
optimal for a procurer wishing to buy a sufficiently standardized, and
contractually well-specifiable, good or service to elicit competition among
potential suppliers. There are, however, many mechanisms she could use to
elicit such competition. This chapter discusses and provides practical
indications on how to choose between a sealed bid tendering and a dynamic
auction to allocate procurement contracts between competing suppliers. It
then suggests simple strategies to keep under control the duration of
dynamic procurement auctions when this is a concern for the procurer.

A crucial factor to consider in the optimal choice of a tendering format is
the nature of uncertainty and the size of different types of costs the selected
supplier will face when serving the contract. Therefore we begin with an
example of such uncertain costs.

Consider a procurement for cleaning services of a large company's or
public administration's buildings. The contract may specify a variety of
services including the cleaning of offices, corridors, halls and more
demanding tasks such as the sanitation of laboratories. The contract also
establishes that the contractor(s) will be paid a fixed amount of money per
unit of surface $(€/m^2)$[1] regardless of the nature of the building. Therefore
the unit price coincides across categories of surface, whereas the cost of

The authors would like to thank Eric Van Damme for discussions and constructive comments on earlier
versions of this chapter.

[1] This is an example of fixed-price contract. The conditions under which such a contractual form may
constitute the procurer's optimal choice are investigated in Chapter 4. To simplify the exposition,
throughout the chapter we shall also assume demand for service to be independent of the price at
which the contract is awarded.

performing the same task in different environments may vary substantially. The sanitation of a laboratory, for example, is presumably more time consuming and requires more expertise than cleaning an office furnished only with a desk and few bookshelves.

When estimating the cost of performing the contract in order to place a bid for it, each supplier has to consider at least two different dimensions. The first dimension concerns the supplier's efficiency in performing each single task specified in the contract. Efficiency results from the interaction of the personnel's experience in similar tasks, managerial skills and the quality of the cleaning equipment. Thus the supplier's efficiency captures a *private* component in his production cost. It is private in that it is entirely firm specific. The second dimension concerns the supplier's ability to correctly estimate the mix of different tasks in the contract: cleaning few, large buildings with administrative offices requires a different combination of material and human resources than sanitizing a large number of small laboratories. If suppliers are not completely informed about the composition of the demand for cleaning services at the time of bidding for the contract, they face a *common* uncertainty.

Uncertainty about the common component of the cost of serving a contract matters since the contractor may find out that the 'true' cost of performing the contract differs from his initial estimate. This may happen if the contractor submitted a bid on the basis of too optimistic a forecast of the common component. More generally, if a supplier does not take this possibility into account at the time of bidding for the contract, he may suffer from the 'winner's curse'; that is, he may realize that actual production costs are higher than estimated ones. On the one hand, the danger of running losses *ex post* may induce suppliers to bid too cautiously for the contract, which implies potentially high awarding prices for the buyer. On the other hand, the suppliers' inability to recognize the winner's curse may generate a too aggressive bidding that results in low awarding prices for the buyer, but may induce the contractor to cut production costs by lowering the quality of the performance.

In this chapter, we explain how the buyer can profit by inducing some 'information production' when uncertainty about the common component of the cost of serving a contract is relevant and when suppliers' pieces of private information about the common component are (statistically) linked or correlated. The simple information-producing device is a dynamic auction format (section 6.3). A dynamic auction format, be it increasing in discounts/scores or decreasing in prices, allows each bidder to observe the identities of active competitors at different prices[2] and, more important, the prices at which competitors quit the competition. Exiting times provide information about cost estimates of those bidders quitting the auction, thus helping remaining bidders revise their own estimates.

When the nature of uncertainty concerns almost exclusively the private component of production costs, suppliers elaborate their bidding strategies on the basis of their private information only. Since learning is not an issue, the buyer can then adopt a sealed bid format that requires lower human and financial resources, is less exposed to the risk that suppliers collude, and has a duration that is perfectly determined (section 6.2). Auction length may become indeed a crucial issue in a dynamic format when bidders increase discounts (or lower prices) very slowly. In section 6.4, we will investigate how the buyer can streamline a dynamic auction without losing the benefits of information production.

6.2. Private and common dimensions in the cost function

Several factors affect the cost of performing a procurement contract. Some of them are entirely firm specific while some others are common to all participating suppliers. A contract for supplying schools with heating oil involves different distribution costs depending on the distance between any single school and the location where a contractor stocks his oil reserves. Consequently, distribution costs are entirely firm specific. At the same time, when suppliers bid for the contract they are unable to predict the evolution of wholesale price for heating oil throughout the duration of the contract. Such an uncertainty is common in that it affects all suppliers.

One simple way of capturing the private and common dimensions in the suppliers' costs is by using the following general relation

Cost = C(Private, Common)

The relationship makes it clear that, in general, both components affect production costs, although the design of a procurement competitive tendering sometimes requires the buyer to establish which dimension is the more relevant, as we will see in the next two sections.

---

[2] We are implicitly assuming that the open format takes the form of a Japanese auction rather than an English auction. See section 6.5 for the main features of these mechanisms.

Table 6.1. PROPER's costs with known common component

	A	B
Reserve price	70	
Private value component		
Estimated cleaning costs: (€/metre^2)	40	80
Common value component with no uncertainty		
Surface to be cleaned: (metre^2)	30,000	10,000

6.2.1. The private component

We consider again the contract for cleaning services, briefly discussed in the Introduction, and further develop it in order to illustrate how the private component in the suppliers' production costs may affect their bidding for the contract. The contract for cleaning services comprises two main space categories; (A) offices and corridors and (B) laboratories. Table 6.1 summarizes the estimated costs per squared metre for PROPER Ltd (PROPER henceforth), one of the competing suppliers. The table also indicates the exact size of surfaces to be cleaned for both category A and B.1

Thus we consider the simplest bidding environment where each supplier perfectly knows the composition of the final demand for cleaning services. Hence PROPER's bid for the contract will depend only upon his (private) efficiency component and, arguably, upon his conjectures on other competitors' efficiency levels. The cleaning contract for the two types of surface is awarded through a single-lot sealed-bid tendering process, with a reserve price of €70/m^2, so that any bid above this level is rejected.

PROPER's cost for performing the contract is simply a weighted average of the two unit costs, where the weights reflect the fraction of each type of space in the contract,

$$\text{Unit Cost} = (€40 \times 30000 + €80 \times 10000)/40000 = €50/\text{m}^2$$

PROPER can safely submit prices between €50 and €70, without losing money. The exact bid will depend on his conjectures about other competitors' bids. For instance, if PROPER faces a group of rivals with large market shares and with an established reputation of high expertise in the business then he may anticipate intense competition for the contract. This would probably induce PROPER to bid closer to €50 than to €70.

Table 6.2. PROPER'S costs with unknown common component

	A	B
Reserve price		70	
Private value component		
Estimated cleaning costs: ($€/m^2$)	40	80
True demand for cleaning services		
Surface to be cleaned: (m^2)	30,000	10,000
Estimated common value component		
Surface to be cleaned: (m^2)	32,000	2,000

Table 6.3. Sample of buildings inspected by PROPER

Type	First building	Second building	Third building	Fourth building	Fifth building	Sample average SA	Estimated number of buildings to clean NB	Estimated surface SA*NB
A	1,000	2,200	1,600	500	2,700	1,600	20	32,000
B	80	120	100	140	60	100	20	2,000

6.2.2. The common component and the winner's curse

PROPER's bidding strategy becomes more complex when uncertainty affects the common component of production costs. The simplest way of illustrating this point in our example is to introduce some uncertainty about the composition of the final demand. Table 6.2 illustrates the situation in which both demand for type-A and type-B surfaces are unknown to PROPER and to all other suppliers. Imprecise information about the composition of final demand generally arises when the procurer awards 'frame contracts'. In this case, a contract may specify minimal and maximal quantities that public administrations can purchase. However, it is not known at the time of the competitive tendering whether and which particular administrations will make use of the frame contract. Hence, the composition of demand, that is, the mix of different surfaces is not known to suppliers at the bidding stage.

Suppliers may gather information about both types of surfaces by inspecting a sample of buildings. In fact, PROPER has inspected a sample of five buildings and recorded the surface occupied by offices, corridors and laboratories in each site. Table 6.3 reports the results of the inspection.

Table 6.3 says that PROPER observed 1,000, 2,200, 1,600, 500, 2,700 m^2 of type A of surface, so the resulting sample average is 1,600 m^2; he also observed 80, 120, 100, 140, 60 m^2 of type B of surface with a resulting sample average of 100 m^2. Moreover, data concerning a previously awarded contract and other similar contracts induce PROPER to believe that the contract will cover twenty buildings. Multiplying the sample average by the estimated number of buildings to be cleaned, PROPER estimates a surface of 32,000 m^2 for type A and 2,000 m^2 for type B. If PROPER were to predict the unit cost by using *only* the sample observations he would derive a unit cost equal to

$$(40 \times 32000 + 80 \times 2000)/34000 = 43.52 €/(m^2)$$

Sample observations induce PROPER to overestimate the task requiring the lower unit cost, but to underestimate the task with the higher unit cost. As a result, submitting unit prices between 43.52 and 50 will make PROPER lose money. The sample observation is to be interpreted as favourable information on the contract which can induce aggressive bidding, namely submitting offers below the price level at which PROPER's *actual* costs are equal to revenues.

In general, different suppliers may have different pieces of information concerning the composition of the demand which is easily explained by different samples of inspected buildings, but also by past experience concerning similar contracts. PROPER, for instance, belongs to the set of suppliers with almost no experience in similar contracts, while, say, CLEANFAST Ltd (CLEANFAST henceforth) has a long history of participation in procurement contracts for cleaning services and is able to reasonably predict the range of type-A and type-B surfaces to be cleaned.

If suppliers are similar in terms of intrinsic efficiency,[3] the winner is likely to be the one with the most favourable information on the contract, that is, the firm that most likely underestimates the impact of the high-cost task and overestimates the impact of the low-cost one. Why? Let us reconstruct the possible thought process adopted by PROPER. Suppose the latter were firmly convinced that all competitors, including himself, follow a very

---

[3] This means that the pool of competing firms have unit costs for the two types of surfaces lying in small interval around 40€/m^2 and 80€/m^2. Hence, uncertainty concerning the common component is more relevant to suppliers than the private component in determining their bids for the contract.

simple bidding strategy: the submitted bid is equal to the estimated cost, based on all available information, plus a constant mark-up, identical across all suppliers. This is only a heuristic bidding strategy, plausible in some respect, but without any ambition to illustrate an 'optimal' criterion. In general, some estimates of the 'true' cost for cleaning the different types of surfaces will be higher while some others will be lower than the 'true' cost. Given the heuristic bidding strategy just described, the contractor will be precisely the supplier who held the most optimistic estimate of the 'true' cost. Hence, it is possible that the contractor's winning bid (that is, his initial cost estimate plus a fixed mark-up) does not cover the 'true' cost of performing the contract.

To sum up, if a supplier ignores the possibility of holding too an optimistic piece of information about the composition of demand, he may end up suffering from the winner's curse as being awarded the contract eventually generates losses. This phenomenon was originally noticed in auctions for the sales of oil drilling rights[4] where winners paid sums that turned out to be higher than their revenues from oil sales.

How could a supplier avoid falling victim to the winner's curse? The intuitive answer is to bid cautiously! More precisely, he should modify the size of the mark-up to cover the additional cost that arises when he learns that he has been awarded the contract and, thus, that the 'true' cost is somewhat higher than his initial estimate. More succinctly, an accurate bidding strategy requires each supplier to anticipate the news of 'winning' and to adjust his bid upwardly.

From the buyer's point of view the winner's curse may then generate two kinds of problems.

1. *Underbidding:* If participants are aware of the winner's curse and are afraid of ending up suffering losses, they may adopt too a cautious bidding strategy which, in turn, generates high awarding prices.
2. *Overbidding:* If participants are unaware of the winner's curse, they elaborate their bidding strategy on the basis of their cost estimates only. Hence they may end up bidding too aggressively, thus submitting too low prices. Although this may benefit the buyer in terms of low awarding prices, it may also deteriorate the contractor's financial stability and induce the latter to adopt opportunistic cost-reducing actions that would

---

[4] Capen, Clapp and Campbell (1971) first noticed this problem. For a more sophisticated analysis of the winner's curse in a general model of competitive bidding see Milgrom and Weber (1982).

Table 6.4. Sample of buildings inspected by CHIEF

First building	Second building	Third building	Fourth building	Fifth building	Sample average SA	Estimated number of buildings to clean NB	Estimated surface SA*NB
160	240	200	280	120	200	20	4,000

result in a bad quality service. Even worse, the contractor may go bankrupt and disrupt the service altogether.[5]

Both underbidding and overbidding are explored in more depth in the next section.

6.2.3. Underbidding and overbidding

Underbidding. Suppliers may have access to an imprecise source of information about the common component of the cost function. If they anticipate the possibility of experiencing losses *ex post*, suppliers may adopt an extremely cautious approach to bidding for the contract. Caution protects firms from losses, but implies potentially high awarding prices.

Underbidding can be illustrated with the aid of table 6.4.

Data in the table represent the observations from five sampled buildings, concerning type-B surface, collected by CHIEF, a third company providing cleaning services. The available sample, however, which would lead to an estimate of 4,000 m^2 of type-B surface, is not the only available information to CHIEF on the composition of demand. Indeed CHIEF built up some experience, though less than CLEANFAST, in the sector which turned out to be useful for two major reasons. Thanks to his past experience CHIEF has become aware of the possibility of overbidding, and so of incurring the winner's curse. Then experience is also used to construct an interval estimate for the actual demand for type-B surface. CHIEF is reasonably convinced that the actual demand will lie somewhere between 8,000 and 38,000 m^2 (the true demand being 10,000). Therefore, the sample observations and the information coming from past experience are inconsistent. What could CHIEF do in this case? Both the observations from buildings inspection and the limited past experience do not entail CHIEF's full confidence in the available information. However, since CHIEF is aware of

---

[5] The problems arising from financially distressed contractors are dealt with in Chapter 13.

the winner's curse, he may prefer to be cautious and privilege information coming from previous experience, which provides a higher estimate of the more expensive surface B. In so doing he would disregard sample observations. Hence CHIEF would feel better insured against the risk that actual demand of type-B surface, the more expensive one, could be quite high. It is then reasonable that CHIEF would be inclined to choose the mid-point, 23,000 m^2, as an estimate for type-B surface. Assuming CHIEF estimates type-A surface to be 32,000 m^2, he would not be willing to submit an offer below

$$(40 \times 32000 + 80 \times 23000)/55000 = 56.7 \, €/m^2$$

This value might represent a safe harbour, but since the 'optimal' bid normally includes a mark-up component,[6] the minimum price CHIEF might be induced to offer is €60/m^2. Caution may then be caused by moderately reliable information, both private and public, about the common component of production costs. Indeed, once aware of the winner's curse thanks to experience, the less reliable the information, the more cautious the bidding (i.e., underbidding).

As we said CLEANFAST is also experienced, in fact more than CHIEF, and then fully aware of the winner's curse. Would the behaviour of the two suppliers be any different? Would CLEANFAST be also very cautious and significantly underbid? Because of his large experience and recent sample observations CLEANFAST feels confident about his demand prediction, which is also more accurate than the one by CHIEF. As a result, the minimum price CLEANFAST would be likely to bid is just above €50/m^2 (i. e., slightly underbid), the lowest price that could offer if he knew the true demand for the service. Therefore CLEANFAST's bidding behaviour would be much less conservative than CHIEF. The buyer is then likely to benefit from CLEANFAST's more confident bidding and thus less likely to suffer from underbidding.

Overbidding. This behaviour is caused by suppliers' inability to take into proper account the information of 'winning the contract' while they formulate their bids. The cleaning contract will provide again a useful framework to illustrate this point. Consider four competing suppliers whose

---

[6] The computation of the 'optimal' mark-up is far from being a straightforward task. Intuitively, PROPER has to weigh a higher mark-up that would generate higher profit, conditional on winning, and a lower probability of winning since the higher the mark-up the higher the chances that another competitor submits a lower bid.

Table 6.5. Bidders' estimates for lot B

Buildings→ Suppliers↓	First	Second	Third	Fourth	Fifth	Sample average SA	Estimated number of buildings to clean NB	Estimated surface SA*NB
1	500	1,000	800	500	600	680	20	13,600
2	450	900	850	450	650	660	10	6,600
3	400	950	750	550	750	680	10	6,800
4	550	1,100	700	500	650	700	20	14,000
Average estimate								11,075

demand estimates for lot B are illustrated in table 6.5. Each bidder has inspected a different sample of five buildings, and predicts a different number of buildings to be cleaned.

The row corresponding to each bidder contains five observations, their sample average, the same bidder's estimated number of buildings to clean, and the overall estimated surface. The average of the individual estimates is $11075 \, m^2$. So, if the four estimates were available to each bidder, they could all take the average to forecast the demand. The resulting estimation error, $11075 - 10000 = 1.075 \, m^2$, would be lower than the one they would derive by relying only on their individual estimate. However, if bidders compete independently from each other they have access only to their *own* sample observations. Hence, by relying only on the information available ex ante, each bidder would make a bigger estimation error (between $-3,400$ and $+4,000 \, m^2$).

If a bidder relies upon his piece of information only, and fails to take into account that the winner is the one who is most likely to have under-estimated the surface of lot B (higher unit cost) then he may submit too low a bid. Hence the bidder with the most optimistic information *ex ante* may experience losses *ex post*.[7]

Lack of experience[8] is sometimes considered a plausible explanation for bidders' inability to anticipate the information coming from 'winning the

[7] Kagel and Levin (2002) discuss experimental evidence showing that the magnitude of the winner's curse typically increases with the number of participants in sealed bid, common value sale auctions. The explanation rests in the increased level of competition and the higher likelihood that some bidders rely on private information (i.e., signals about the value of the object) which is far away from the 'true' common value.

[8] See again Kagel and Levin (2002). In particular, throughout the chapter we assume that 'experienced' means being both aware of the winner's curse and better informed, 'less experienced' being not so well

auction'. Consider, for instance, how PROPER's bidding strategy may differ from the one adopted by CLEANFAST. The latter has a long experience in similar contracts, whereas PROPER is little less than a novice in the procurement market. Even if the two firms had access to very similar information about the current contract and were not to differ much in terms of intrinsic efficiency, CLEANFAST would be able to integrate its current information with past evidence. More precisely, CLEANFAST, having been in the same market for, say, ten consecutive years, is able to construct an informative time series that contains the realized demands for type-A and type-B surfaces.[9] Hence, any piece of *current* information can be evaluated by integrating it with past observations. PROPER, instead, has to rely on its current information only. In order to reduce or avoid overbidding altogether, thus fine-tuning its bidding strategy, PROPER should know something about CLEANFAST's time series. In the next section, we will investigate more in detail what auction format may facilitate PROPER's learning process.

The inability to anticipate the effects of the winner's curse due to lack of experience may produce an even more dangerous outcome for the buyer. Suppose that more efficient suppliers are more likely to be experienced bidders because, say, they have participated and have been selected as contractors in previous procurement contracts. Hence, they are more likely to anticipate the effects of the winner's curse and bid more cautiously. If, for symmetric reasons, less efficient suppliers are more likely to be inexperienced and, thus, more prone to suffer from the winner's curse, they may end up bidding more aggressively than experienced suppliers. As a result, the competitive process may not allow the buyer to select the most efficient

informed but aware of the winner's curse, and 'inexperienced' being both unaware of the winner's curse and poorly informed. Accordingly, we argue that an experienced bidder (i.e., CLEANFAST) is expected to slightly underbid, a less experienced bidder (i.e., CHIEF) to underbid, and an inexperienced bidder (i.e., PROPER) to overbid. Then, our explanation of underbidding-overbidding depends on our definition of experience. For example, despite the availability of a long time series concerning previous awarded contracts, a very well informed bidder may wrongly use the data by not adjusting his bid upwardly for the winner's curse, thus overbidding. We could refer to such a bidder as being naïve. Alternatively a supplier, with very little information and no experience in performing a procurement contract, may underbid since he might have come to know about the possibility of the winner's curse from other sources, rather than personal experience, and adjust his bid accordingly. We could refer to such a bidder as being rational. However, we are fairly confident that our definition of experience is plausible and useful to explain underbidding-overbidding in procurement practice.

[9] In our illustrative example, an unpredictable, period-specific shock affects the demand for cleaning services. Thus observing the realized demand over 10 years certainly helps CLEANFAST form a better idea about, say, the variance of the shock.

contractor. As we will see in the next section, the buyer can minimize the occurrence of a 'bad selection' by designing a competitive process that allows less experienced suppliers to learn from more experienced suppliers' bidding behaviour, that is, to enrich their poor initial information about the common component with more experienced competitors' information revealed through the bidding process.

We conclude this section by observing that overbidding, that is, submitting too low a bid, can also be due to a strategic choice. Suppliers in financial distress, while struggling to remain in the market, may be tempted to offer particularly low prices to win the contract. They may aim at renegotiating better conditions once they have started performing the contract. This phenomenon, extensively studied in Chapter 13, has obviously nothing to do with aggressive bidding originated by lack of awareness of the winner's curse.

6.3. Costs and benefits of information circulation: choosing the competitive tendering format

The previous section has drawn a competitive environment in which two competitors, PROPER and CLEANFAST, rely on considerably different experiences. Moreover, the simple fact that PROPER considers CLEANFAST an 'expert' in the market may induce the former to believe that any positive information about the current contract (low estimated unit cost) makes it more likely that CLEANFAST has received positive information as well.[10] This situation captures a broad set of circumstances in which the buyer would benefit from adopting a dynamic, rather than a sealed bid tendering format. The latter would certainly leave inexperienced and poorly informed bidders such as PROPER fully exposed to the risk of overbidding. Why? The simple, almost obvious, reason is that such a bidder would have to rely on his very limited information and experience to make a fairly complicated inference on the 'true' demand for the cleaning service.

How would PROPER's bidding behaviour be affected by a dynamic format?[11] From the discussion in section 6.2.2 we observe that the

---

[10] This is a rather simple way of introducing 'affiliated' information among bidders. Affiliation is a particular form of statistical correlation. In their seminal paper on auctions with affiliated information, Milgrom and Weber (1982) show that the seller (the buyer in procurement) benefits more from an English than from a sealed bid, second-price auction.

[11] The dynamic format we consider here is not an English (reverse) auction, rather a descending clock auction in which the price is exogenously lowered by using a clock at a speed, say, of 0.5€/sec. Bidders

minimum price PROPER would be willing to bid, including a mark-up, is €45; above that price the bidder would expect non-negative profits, if it were to win the contract. Let us imagine the following scenario. Prices start at €70 (reserve price) and are gradually lowered. Suddenly, and unexpectedly, NODIRT Ltd, another expert in the market, quits the auction. This event becomes a very useful source of information to PROPER that *has* to revise upwards the expected cost for undertaking the contract. It is now likely that PROPER will not be willing to remain active if the price goes below, say, €55.

Information production during the auction helps bidders revise their estimates of the common component. In doing so, they may avoid becoming victims of underbidding when adjusting for the winner's curse (this is the case with CHIEF) or overbidding when relying only on their estimates of the common component (this is the case with PROPER). More confident bidders bid more aggressively than in sealed-bid formats, thus benefiting the buyer through a lower awarding price. Moreover, the winner discovers more frequently *ex post* that the cost of serving the contract is no higher than his *ex ante* estimate. Hence, it is less likely that the contractor will look for opportunistic cost-reducing actions that would undermine the quality of the service.

But what about the possible drawbacks of a dynamic format? There exist indeed two sources of concern for a buyer when opting for a dynamic auction.

1. Information circulation may increase the risk of collusion, especially in auction for multiple contracts (objects). Indeed, bidders can exploit the openness of the auction format to send signals (through prices) to each other in order to coordinate. Moreover, dynamic auctions allow members of a bidding ring to detect deviation from a collusive scheme and punish deviating bidders.[12]

2. The transparency and the openness of a dynamic format may induce some bidders to adopt bidding strategies (i) to conceal their information to rivals or, to the other extreme, (ii) to bluff, that is, to deceive rivals. The kind of strategies in (i), sometimes described as a 'snake in the grass', are more likely to take place in those dynamic formats in which the pace

---

are considered active as long as they keep a light switched on. Switching off the same light implies that the corresponding bidder has irrevocably quit the auction. The contract is awarded to the last active bidder at the price the last bidder quits the auction. See section 6.5 for more on the properties of both the English (reverse) and the Japanese formats.

[12] These issues are dealt with in depth in Chapters 14 and 15.

at which prices evolve over time depends entirely upon bidders' activity. A slow-moving bidding process may produce little valuable information and may result in an excessively long auction. Strategies in (ii) may take the form of 'jump bidding.'[13] This is the situation whereby a bidder submits a very low price early in the contest which is meant to 'persuade' competitors that he is in a position to get the contract at a very low price, thus deterring further competition.

The discussion developed so far leads us to the following

Practical conclusion 1

The buyer should prefer a sealed bid tendering procedure over a dynamic auction when
- the common component in the production costs is believed to be small or not very uncertain;
- bidders are likely to have relatively similar information about the common cost component.

The buyer should prefer a dynamic auction when the common component in the production costs is believed to be substantial and uncertain *and* it is reasonable to expect that bidders possess different, though linked, pieces of information and/or experience on the common component.

Adopting a dynamic format does not automatically solve the problems of underbidding and overbidding. The openness of the auction format is a necessary condition for some learning to take place. However, other aspects of information circulation during the auction are likely to affect bidders' learning process and, consequently, the extent to which underbidding or overbidding arises. In order to illustrate this last point suppose that a dynamic auction is used with a fixed-end rule. That is, the bidding process cannot last more than, say, two hours. In this environment, if bidders are allowed to raise discounts (or lower prices) by small amounts (ticks), they may opt for a snake-in-the-grass strategy. Experienced bidders may have a special interest in doing so in order not to disclose their information to less experienced or poorly informed bidders. Hence, bidding activity may become more 'lively' only in the last handful of minutes, thus leaving little time to inexperienced bidders for learning about the common component. However, if the auction end were extensible, the outcome might change substantially. Suppose that the auction has an initial duration of 2 hours,

[13] See, for instance, Fishman (1988) and Avery (1998).

but ends only if during the last ten minutes no price offer is received. Otherwise, it is extended by another ten minutes and so on until no bid is eventually submitted. Such a simple modification of the design might considerably affect the evolution of the bidding process and, consequently, the amount of information circulation during the auction.

Whenever the buyer is concerned with information production, she can take other actions that may be at least as effective as the appropriate choice of rules for a dynamic format. The buyer could actively gather and publicly release as much information as possible on the common component before the auction starts. The reserve price, for instance, may provide a useful benchmark cost to the bidders. If the procurement contract is split in several lots, uncertainty could be reduced by setting a separate reserve price for each individual lot.[14] More generally, in the effort of mitigating uncertainty, the procurer should include in the contract, and in the auction design, as many important aspects related to the market as possible. Together with the duration of the contract, the buyer can specify the geographical areas where the contract applies, maximum and/or minimum quantities to be supplied and any other aspect helping bidders properly evaluate the cost of the contract. This discussion leads us to

Practical conclusion 2

When uncertainty about the common component is believed to have a great impact in the bidders' production costs, the buyer should provide bidders with as much relevant information on the contract as possible.

6.4. Streamlining dynamic auctions

If allowing suppliers to observe and learn from each other's bidding behaviour is considered important, a dynamic auction should be preferred to sealed bid tendering. Learning takes time, however, and so do dynamic auctions. The higher the number of rounds in a multi-round auction, the more time to think is left to bidders between the rounds, the more bidders

---

[14] In our example of contract for cleaning services, there would be a reserve price for type-A surfaces and a different one for type-B surfaces.

can learn from each other's bids and the more likely it is for participants to avoid underbidding or overbidding, but the longer is the auction.

Long-lasting auctions, however, may substantially increase organizational costs for running the bidding process and wages/fees of the specialized personnel working on behalf of suppliers. If the buyer organizes a high number of auctions per year, it may be unfeasible to have many auctions running for a very long time at the same time. These considerations apply to standard dynamic formats as well as to online dynamic auctions. The latter have become increasingly more widespread, since in many instances they have proved to be a flexible and powerful way to conduct procurement activity. They allow auctions to take place while bidders are located in different places, thus inducing higher participation. However, the extensive use of new information and communication technologies to auctions may have played a crucial role in *stretching* auctions length.

We can summarize three main drawbacks associated with '*long*' dynamic auctions. We will then discuss how the buyer can overcome such problems by keeping the auction length under control.

Information circulation and collusion

Collusion can be sustained more easily in a dynamic auction for a single contract rather than in a sealed bid tendering since members of a bidding ring may punish immediately a defecting bidder. In the case of multiple contracts, bidders may also use bids as communication devices. In general, the longer a dynamic auction the easier coordination among bidders since they have a higher number of opportunities (e.g. in the various rounds) of agreeing on the allocation of contracts.

Bidders' psychological costs during the auction

Long-lasting auctions may be psychologically exhausting for participants, even when they are experienced and skilful.

Costs of specialized personnel

Public procurement activity typically contemplates the presence of an awarding committee[15] that is in charge of the regularity of the auction

---

[15] This is, for instance, the case in Italy.

procedure. Should a dynamic auction be too long such costs would increase as well as the costs of personnel specifically dedicated by the participants to the auction. This last point could make the auction too costly for some bidders, who may choose not to participate.

6.5. Shortening multi-round descending auctions

In this section we present and discuss a few dynamic formats among those most commonly observed in practice, and we suggest how their length could be kept under control. To concentrate on the main ideas we focus on the design of auctions with a single supply contract.

6.5.1. Multi-round descending auctions

Multi-round auctions are a combination of dynamic and sealed bid formats. They are normally run online by using an e-platform. At each round, and within a specified time interval, participants submit their offers to the system secretly, without knowing whether or not other bidders have made an offer. In order to be considered valid, bids have to be below a pre-determined price level. In the first round, the threshold is the buyer's reserve price. In subsequent rounds, the threshold may be each participant's bid submitted in the previous round minus a fixed amount, or tick. Alternatively, the threshold may be the same to all bidders and equal the lowest price submitted in the previous round minus the tick. In order to be considered active participants, bidders have to submit a valid bid at each round. If, at some round, they fail to submit a valid bid they can no longer bid.

At the end of each round, the buyer publicly reveals all valid offers keeping bidders' identities anonymous. Hence, each participant knows the whole set of valid offers but does not know who offered what. The auction ends when only one valid bid is received. This is the awarding price and the winning bidder is the participant who submitted the last valid bid. It is easy to see that this set of rules also comprises, as a special case, the English (reverse) auction in which the validity rule requires any bidder to outbid the standing lowest bid.

Since the number of rounds is undetermined the auction can be lengthy enough to let information circulate, thus favouring the learning process which helps mitigate problems related to the winner's curse. If delegates are under pressure, pauses between rounds can lower the risk of bidding mistakes. However, the auction can turn out to be too long, simply because the last two active bidders may decide to slow down the pace at which the auction evolves by submitting at each round bids just below the validity threshold. Moreover, if participation is costly, inexperienced and poorly informed bidders may be deterred from entering if they believe that more experienced and better informed ones will sooner or later outbid them. Tacit collusion may also arise since bidders can use prices to send signals to each other, although collusion-via-prices becomes more feasible to bidders in multi-lot (or multi-contract) dynamic auctions than in the single-lot (or single-contract) version.

6.5.2. How to shorten multi-round descending auctions

When length is a relevant concern, there are three possible ways to shorten the auction; they are not necessarily incompatible with each other.

6.5.2.1. Maximum number of rounds or fixed-end rule

One way to keep the auction length under control might be to introduce a maximum number of rounds, or to announce a fixed-end rule in an English (reverse) auction. Suppose the number of rounds is fixed *ex ante*. This choice is mainly driven by considerations concerning organizational costs, the nature of the contract being procured, the nature of the information possessed by participants and the risk of collusion among them.

The winner is the bidder submitting the lowest bid at the final round or at any previous round if there is no further lower bid. Due to the fixed number of rounds, auction length is now under full control. Moreover, the presence of a last round may increase the amount of uncertainty that favours participation by small suppliers, since they may think that if they can make it to the final sealed bid round they might have a chance to win the contract. However, information circulation is likely to be seriously undermined by the fixed-end or the last round effects. When bidding behaviour reveals part of the bidders' information about the uncertain common component, bidders may be tempted to behave like 'snakes in the grass' until the very last round of the auction in order to limit competitors' learning. In doing so, they transform *de facto* a multi-round dynamic auction into a (one round) sealed bid format. If uncertainty about the common component, and thus the risk related to the winner's curse, led the buyer to choose a dynamic auction, the adoption of a fixed number of rounds or a fixed-end rule may jeopardize the buyer's goal and worsen the winner's curse itself.

6.5.2.2. Increasing the tick size in the validity rule

Since a fixed number of rounds is most likely to be a counter-productive solution when the winner's curse is a serious concern, the buyer may opt for increasing the tick size in the validity rule in order to speed up the bidding process, thus shortening the auction. Although the auction length is not under full control bidding can be rather fast: the greater the tick size the faster the auction. Participation by small suppliers may become more difficult since they are likely to be systematically outbid by bigger ones.

Observing bidders' quitting times provides other participants with useful information. The accuracy of the learning process, however, decreases with the tick size. Suppose that the tick size is equal to Δ. Then a bidder, who has submitted a valid bid $b(t)$ at round t, and who does not submit at round $t+1$, reveals a less precise information about his experience and/or private signal on the common component than when the tick size is smaller, say, $\Delta/2$.

6.5.2.3. Anglo-Dutch

A third way to shorten a multiple round auction is its Anglo-Dutch modification. The Anglo-Dutch auction was first proposed by Paul Klemperer[16] to favour participation and deter collusion in the UK spectrum auction. Though keeping the auction length under control was not the major concern of the original proposal, the format has a natural connotation in this sense. The main innovation consists in interrupting the auction when only two bidders remain and calling a final sealed bid round between them. Thus if at some round only two valid bids are received, then the next round becomes the last one. The bidder submitting the lowest price at the last round is awarded the contract and receives a payment equal to his own bid.

The number of rounds is undetermined until only two bidders remain in the contest. The final round prevents lengthy auctions caused, possibly, by the two 'strongest' (that is, better informed and/or more experienced) bidders. The possibility of making it to the last stage may induce the participation of 'weak' bidders (i.e., poorly informed and/or more inexperienced), which may enhance competition and lower the risk of collusion.

---

[16] See Klemperer (1998, 2004).

Moreover, if the tick size is relatively small, the learning process throughout the auction may be rather accurate. The auction may nonetheless remain lengthy.

Based on the above considerations, we are able to formulate.

> **Practical conclusion 3**
>
> To shorten the time length of a multi-round descending auction the buyer may adopt the Anglo-Dutch modification with a moderate tick size. If auction length is the biggest concern, the buyer may further increase the tick size.
>
> Do not specify a fixed number of rounds.

We conclude this discussion with a warning. Although shortening a dynamic auction may be a desirable outcome for the buyer, observing a short auction is not necessarily 'good news' for the buyer. Short auctions may result from some bidders being very aggressive early in the auction in order to intimidate their rivals and force them to quit. This is the so-called 'jump, or pre-emptive bidding' phenomenon that some bidders may adopt to discourage rivals. A successful 'jump bidding' reduces the auction length, but limits the extent to which learning takes place since most participants quit just for fear of being unable to compete against jump bidders. To limit the occurrence of such a phenomenon, the validity rule can be changed to include both an upper and a lower threshold for a bid to be considered valid. If the interval is not too narrow the auction could still be quite fast, while the speed would remain under control to promote learning and competition.

6.6. Faster dynamic auctions

We now consider three additional auction formats that have recently caught the attention of researchers and practitioners alike.

6.6.1. Descending clock auction

The online version becomes a *button auction*. The buyer starts from a high price which is decreased continuously. In order to remain active participants have to bid continuously. Depending upon the rules, this may happen either by keeping the assigned button pushed until a bidder decides to drop out, or by pushing it at the start of the auction and a second time to signal the exit.

Each bidder knows at any time how many rivals are still in the auction, although participants' identities are normally kept anonymous. The auction ends when only one bidder remains; he is awarded the contract at a price equal to the one at which the last bidder has quit (see also Chapter 9).

The buyer has full control on the speed at which the price decreases; hence the bidding process may end very quickly. Since bidders can observe the exact prices at which rivals quit the learning process is, in principle, very accurate. However, if the speed is high, and the auction short, the specialized personnel bidding on behalf of interested companies may find themselves under strong time pressure and the probability of mistakes may increase considerably.

As in the case of multiple round and English (reverse) auctions with no predefined length, weaker bidders may be discouraged to participate and competition may be softened. It is also difficult to implement a descending clock format electronically by using Internet. Slow connections, analogous to the ones emerging in the e-Bay last minute bidding, may create legal problems. These are partially solvable by making time discrete, that is, every t minutes the price goes down by a tick diminishing in size; and by offering bidders a limited number of waivers they can use to interrupt the clock for some minutes (like 'Time-outs' in basketball) to think or communicate with headquarters about the developments in the auction.

The descending clock format may appear difficult to implement for scoring auctions of complex goods/services contracts where a thermometer, measuring the quality dimension, has to be lowered together with the price of the contract. However, the thermometer can represent directly the score, without the exact specification of how the score (price/quality ratio) is achieved.

Practical conclusion 4

In order to reduce the risk of bidding mistakes in a descending clock auction the buyer may modify the format in a series of dimensions, not necessarily incompatible with each other:

1. introducing a pause after each exit;
2. making exit revocable for a limited number of times;
3. introducing a number of waivers, that is, allowing bidders to be inactive for a limited period and to come back at a lower price;
4. decreasing price by using discrete ticks.

Practical conclusion 4 (163) provides some guidelines to correct the main drawbacks of the descending clock format.

6.6.2. Survival auctions

The survival auction is also organized in multiple rounds.[17] The number of bidders remaining active from one round to the next one is determined according to the so-called 'survival rule'. This keeps under full control its time duration. More precisely, at each round participants submit sealed bid tenders. A bid is considered valid if it is lower than a certain threshold: at the first round, this threshold is the buyer's reserve price; from the second round onwards the threshold is the highest bid submitted in the previous round. At each round, the buyer only announces the highest submitted bid and the bidder having submitted that bid is excluded irrevocably from the auction, while all other 'surviving' bidders proceed to the next round. Thus if N is the number of participants, the auction lasts $N-1$ rounds at most. The winner is the last surviving bidder who is awarded the contract at a price equal to the bid of the last excluded participant.

Since the number of rounds has an upper bound[18] of $N-1$, the auction length is under full control. Moreover, adopting a 'wait and see' strategy by submitting a bid marginally lower than the highest admissible one may be too risky. Indeed the most 'cautious' bidder would be irrevocably excluded from the contest.

Surprisingly enough, the strategic properties of the survival and the descending clock auctions are exactly the same.[19] Hence if the online version of the descending clock auction cannot be implemented because of, say, poor Internet connection among the participants, the buyer can safely adopt the survival design. In some countries, however, the survival auction may raise legal problems.

6.6.3. Two stage sealed bid tendering

This is an extreme case of survival auction in which all bidders, except those who submitted the two lowest prices, are excluded after the first round. The

---

[17] See, for instance, Fujishima, McAdams and Shoham (1999) and Kagel, Pevnitskaya and Ye (2004).

[18] The actual number of rounds could, in principle, be lower than $N-1$ if at some round two bidders submit the two highest offers, in which case both of them are excluded.

[19] The reader interested in the analytical details is referred to Fujishima et al. (1999).

Table 6.6. Submitted discounts in a two-stage sealed bid tendering

Rounds	Bidder 1	Bidder 2	Bidder 3	Bidder 4	Bidder 5
1	10%	8%	13%	15%	18%
2				20%	22%

two surviving bidders challenge each other in the second and final round. Such a design reduces the time length to a minimal number of sessions, a lower number of rounds being feasible only if the auction format is lowest-price sealed bid. Although the two-stage sealed bid tendering has been used in a variety of situations,[20] it is only recently that some of its properties have been understood. In particular, the two-stage tendering generates the same expected revenue of an English (reverse)[21] auction when bidders' private pieces of information about the cost of the contract are (statistically) correlated. The two-stage tendering may also be coupled with 'Indicative Bidding'.[22] This variant is frequently used for the sales of assets: participants are first asked to provide non-binding indications on their willingness to pay and then, on the basis of such information, the auctioneer selects a subset of bidders for the second and final sealed bid stage in which bidders' offers are binding.

Due to its potentials for practical applications, we conclude this chapter by illustrating in table 6.6 a one-object, two-stage sealed bid tendering with five participants. Bidders submit discount percentages with respect to a reserve price. Figures in the upper row are bidders' discounts at the first stage. The discounts of bidders 4 and 5 are the highest, so they proceed to the second round. As explained above, the two highest discounts are not disclosed at the end of the first round, whereas rejected bids are publicly announced. This information could be useful to bidders 4 and 5 in the next round. At the second stage, they cannot lower their first-round discounts. In our example, offers from bidders 4 and 5 at the second stage are valid only if higher than, respectively, 15 per cent and 18 per cent. Bidder 5 is awarded the contract at a 20 per cent discount of the reserve price (table 6.6).

The above discussion leads to our final.

---

[20] One noticeable example is the privatization in Italy of the formerly state-owned industrial conglomerate ENI.

[21] The technical details are in Perry, Wolfstetter and Zamir (2000).

[22] See Ye (2006).

Practical conclusion 5

When both winner's curse and time length are strong concerns, the buyer may favour the two-stage sealed bid tendering format. When length is a milder concern, the buyer may use the survival auction.

Bibliographical notes

The first (field) evidence of the winner's curse traces back to Capen, Clapp and Campbell (1971). The theory of optimal bidding behaviour in pure common value auctions was pioneered by Wilson (1977). Milgrom and Weber (1982) provide the most general framework to analyse standard auction formats. Their model introduces the concept of 'affiliated' information and admits, as special case, both the private value and the pure common value models. Krishna (2002) is an excellent textbook with an up-to-date analytical treatment of auction theory.

The bridge between auction theory and market design is explored by both Milgrom (2004) and Klemperer (2004). Auctions are also increasingly studied in laboratories. A thorough introduction to the experimental literature on common value auctions and the winner's curse is provided by Kagel and Levin (2002).

Many of our ideas on how to shorten auction length are inspired by Milgrom (2004) and by other reports written by the same author about the design of the Federal Communication Commission (FCC) spectrum auctions in the United States.

References

Avery, C. (1998). Strategic Jump Bidding in English Auctions, *Review of Economic Studies*, 65, 185–210.

Capen, E., R. Clapp and W. Campbell, (1971). Competitive Bidding in High Risk Situations, *Journal of Petroleum Technology*, 23, 641–653.

Fishman, M. J. (1988). A Theory of Preemptive Takeover Bidding, *Rand Journal of Economics*, 19, 88–101.

Fujishima, Y., D. McAdams and Y. Shoham (1999). Speeding up Ascending-Bid Auctions, *Proceedings of the 16th International Joint Conference on Artificial Intelligence*, 554–563.

Kagel, J. and D. Levin (2002). *Common Value Auctions and the winner's curse*, Princeton University Press.

Kagel. J., S. Pevnitskaya and L. Ye (2004). Survival Auctions, Ohio State University, *Working Paper.*

Klemperer P. (1998). Auctions with Almost Common Values, *European Economic Review*, 42, 757–769.

Klemperer P. (2004). *Auctions: Theory and Practice*, Princeton University Press.

Krishna V. (2002). *Auction Theory*, Academic Press.

Milgrom P. (2004). *Putting Auction Theory to Work*, Cambridge University Press.

Milgrom P. and R. Weber (1982). A Theory of Auctions and Competitive Bidding, *Econometrica*, 50, 1089–1122.

Perry M., E. Wolsfstetter and S. Zamir (2000). A Sealed Bid Auction that Matches the English Auction, *Games and Economic Behaviour*, 33, 265–273.

Wilson, R. (1977). A Bidding Model of Perfect Competition, *Review of Economic Studies*, 44 (3), 511–518.

Ye, L. (2006). Indicative Bidding and A Theory of Two-Stage Auctions, *Games and Economic Behavior*, forthcoming.

7 Division into lots and competition in procurement

Veronika Grimm, Riccardo Pacini,
Giancarlo Spagnolo and Matteo Zanza

7.1. Introduction

A buyer always has the choice to procure a good or service with a single contract or divide it into several contracts. On the one hand, large firms and centralized public procurement agencies often find it optimal to divide supply into smaller, local lots because of the transportation costs linked to geographical dispersion. On the other hand, complementarities between different parts of the contract would suggest advantages from bundling them. But the division into lots has other important effects. By specifying the size of each lot, the division of a supply contract determines which potential suppliers have sufficient capacity to participate in each separate competitive tendering (for at least one lot), and which do not. By influencing participation, the division into lots has an important impact on the participants' behaviour and on the final outcome. The division into lots also determines how a procurement contract can be 'split' among potential competitors, hence how easy it is for bidders to achieve and sustain implicit or explicit collusive agreements to share the supply at inflated prices.

Existing economic analysis provides only limited guidance when it comes to deciding the number of lots into which a supply contract should be divided, and deciding about their sizes. The reason is that standard textbooks usually consider cases with a fixed number of objects.[1] Still, two main prescriptions emerged from the literature:

1. *The number of lots should be smaller than the expected number of participants*

We would like to thank Gian Luigi Albano, Francesco Busato, Nicola Dimitri, Federico Dini, Gustavo Piga, Tommaso Valletti, Marina Venzo and all the Consip staff for valuable suggestions and help.
[1] See, e.g., section II in *Auction Theory*, Krishna (2002), or part II in Milgrom (2004).

Some competition authorities and procurement agencies use this as a simple rule to prevent bidders from colluding by sharing the lots.[2] This rule is indeed useful, but one should not forget its limits. The suppliers' ability to sustain collusion is not always positively affected by a higher number of lots. And even if the number of lots falls short of the number of bidders, collusive agreements may be implemented through rotation schemes, especially in procurement, where tendering processes are typically organized often and regularly. Moreover, since many firms operate in more than one market, collusion can be sustained by multi-market sharing agreements. Collusive gains can also be shared by taking turn to win procurements, or through side transfers, such as subcontracting: firms could agree on the winning firm in advance and on the condition of subsequent subcontracts to the others. There are definitely tendering processes in which the technical aspects of supply require a very large number of lots, which makes it impossible to follow the rule described above; as we will see, in those cases a large number of lots may even hinder collusive behaviour (see section 7.5).

2. *Define at least one lot more than the number of incumbents and reserve it to new entrants*

This precaution may promote participation of new bidders, and thus foster competition. It was a crucial feature of the British UMTS auction held in 2000.[3] At the beginning only four licences were envisaged. However, the market was shared by exactly four incumbents, such that a one-lot-each outcome was plausible. 'Weaker' rivals would have been discouraged from entering the tendering process, and a share-the-market non-competitive outcome was likely. Therefore, a design with five licences instead of four was chosen, where each bidder was allowed to win only one licence. Moreover, the most valuable licence was reserved to new participants to encourage the entry of weaker bidders. As a consequence, many more than five bidders participated, and even though the new bidders had practically no chance to win any other than the most valuable licence, their bids increased competition (as thus, prices) on other licences, too. The tendering process was a success and let the UK government raise around £23 billion.

Beyond those two basic rules, the discussion so far has not clarified how to choose the right number and size of lots. Even when both rules are

---

[2] These follow a general suggestion offered by Klemperer (2004).
[3] See Binmore and Klemperer (2002).

simultaneously satisfied and all technical and geographical constraints are taken into account, the procurer usually retains substantial freedom in choosing the number and size of lots. Depending on whether the buyer is a private firm or a public authority, the focus of the procurer may be on low prices and/or an efficient allocation, the latter meaning that those firms that have the lowest cost to supply a good or service should do so. The division into lots should serve those goals. The task is complicated because changing the division into lots not only changes the strategic behaviour of the participants in each single tendering process; it also affects the incentives of firms to participate in the competitive tendering and determines the scope for collusive agreements.

Another important issue is the level of market competition in the long run, which is not so obviously related to the one reached in a single tendering process. In certain sectors, particularly when the procurer represents a large fraction of total demand, maximizing competition in the short run might have negative effects on the level of competition in the long run. Current tendering design may affect the entry or exit of firms from the procurement market and, consequently, it may affect the number of participants in future tendering processes: strong competition today may, sometimes, imply weak competition tomorrow. The extreme – and worst – case of such a future reduction occurs when the procurer ends up locked in with one dominant supplier.

In what follows, we first discuss the optimal division into lots, taking participation as given and assuming that bidders do not collude (section 7.2). We go on describing two indices that help to capture the expected degree of competition in the competitive procurement for different divisions into lots (section 7.3). Then we focus on how the division into lots may affect the trade-off between participation and risk of collusion (sections 7.4 and 7.5). In the last parts of our article we analyse dynamic aspects of competition. We demonstrate how repeated market contact among firms influences participation and collusion (section 7.6) and finally we point out economic conditions that could lead to a situation where the procurer remains locked in with a sole supplier, the potential consequences and possible solutions (section 7.7).

7.2. Division into lots and revenue/efficiency considerations

In this section we take the number of bidders as fixed and assume that they do not collude. Under those assumptions we review what economic theory suggests concerning the division into lots. In our discussion we focus on the case that all individual lots are being procured by a procedure where the lowest bidder is awarded the contract and pays what he bid. This is the standard procedure in public procurement. Of course, the procurer could make use of more sophisticated rules that – for example – involve package bidding. For those issues we refer the interested reader to Chapters 8 and 9.

In order to analyse the question of optimal division into lots it is important to specify the goal of the procurer: this could be either the minimization of procurement cost, or achieving an efficient allocation (i.e., awarding the lots to the lowest cost firms), or some combination of both. Sometimes those two objectives coincide, sometimes there is a conflict between them. We will explicitly mention whenever the latter is the case.

In the economic literature the division into lots is being analysed from two different perspectives: some authors focus on the question whether to bundle contracts or to sell them separately, others characterize the *optimal* division into lots. Tendering rules resulting from the latter approach are much less standard than the implications from the first question.[4] In the following we first focus on the decision whether to bundle several lots (and if so which ones) or to procure them in separate tendering processes. When deciding the number and configuration of items the buyer should consider the following issues:

1. The cost structure of firms

   The most important reason to bundle several lots is to exploit synergies in production. Consider, for example, the procurement of (manufacturing and installation of) furniture for two nearby office buildings. A firm that furnishes both buildings certainly has a lower cost of doing so than two separate firms that furnish one building each. The reason is that many tasks have to be accomplished only once, independently of the order's size. However, if both contracts were being procured simultaneously but in separate tendering processes a firm's cost of providing one contract would depend on whether it is also awarded the other one. This exposes a firm to a high risk in the bidding process: if it bids lower than its cost for the single contract in one competitive tendering (speculating that it will be successful also in the other one), it may nevertheless end up being awarded only one contract – at a bid that is lower than its actual production cost (for more detailed clarifications on the 'exposure

---

[4] Optimal multi-object tendering processes are analysed by Armstrong (2000), Avery and Hendershott (2000), and Jehiel et al. (2003).

problem', see Chapter 8). A conservative bid (i.e., higher than the production cost for the single contract) guarantees a positive profit also if the firm wins only one tendering process. However, the chances to win are rather low if other firms bid aggressively in order to exploit synergies.[5]

Example 7.1

Consider two parallel competitive procurements for two lots, 1 and 2. Bidder A has production cost of €10 for each lot, 1 or 2, whenever he is awarded only one of them. If he is awarded both, he can exploit synergies in production which lowers his production cost to €15 for both lots together. Now suppose that firm A faces the competition from firm B, which is known to place a bid of €8 on lot 1 but will not bid for lot 2, and firm C that, with a probability of 50 per cent places a bid of €10 on lot 2, and with a probability of 50 per cent it places a lower bid, say €5 on lot 2. In this situation firm A can only make a profit from those tendering processes if it is awarded both lots since the price for each one will be lower or equal to €10. Thus, firm A is 'forced' to run the risk of bidding below its cost for lot 1 (i.e., place a bid slightly below €8 to win against firm B). In these kind of situations, bidders may be induced to bid too cautiously or not to participate.

The basic problem here is that if complementary lots are being procured in simultaneous tendering processes, a bidder cannot assure that he will be awarded those lots that guarantee a lower joint production cost than the sum of the single lots. Thus, if the number of bidders is not affected by the bundling decision, those lots should be procured in a bundle.

---

2. The number of bidders

Even without synergies in production, if there are only few bidders competing for several lots, competition among them can be increased by bundling the lots.[6] Let us illustrate this point by the following example: There are two lots, lot 1 and lot 2 and two bidders, firm A and firm B.[7] As pointed out at the beginning of the paragraph firms do not collude. Firm A's production costs are €1 for lot 1 and €10 for lot 2. Firm B's production costs are €9 for lot 1 and €1 for lot 2. To make the exposition

---

[5] This problem is discussed in much detail by Milgrom (2004).

[6] See Palfrey (1983) and Chakraborty (1999).

[7] This may represent a market with two stronger firms and other inefficient firms, whose presence does not affect the degree of competition in a substantial way.

simple we assume that both firms know the other's cost structure. It is easy to see that procuring the contracts as a bundle lowers the buyer's procurement cost: in separate tendering processes the price to be paid for lot 1 is €9, and the price of lot 2 is €10. Thus, the total procurement cost is €19 if the contracts are procured in separate tendering processes. In this case firm A would produce lot 1 and firm B would produce lot 2. If the bundle is being procured, the buyer would pay €11 for both, and firm B (the firm with the lower total cost) would supply both lots.

This example illustrates an important trade-off: bundling the two contracts in one competitive tendering increases the competition among the bidders and therefore lowers the price to be paid by the procurer. However, the allocation that is reached in the bundle tendering process is not efficient: the firms' total production cost would be minimized by awarding the first lot to firm A and the second one to firm B, as it happens in the two separate tendering processes. This example illustrates a general principle: in the absence of synergies, separate competitive procurements allocate efficiently, whereas bundling may allocate inefficiently, but decreases the price to be paid by the buyer if there are only few bidders. If there are many firms competing for both lots, separate sales are more profitable.[8]

3. The degree of heterogeneity of participants and aftermarket trade
Often potential providers of goods and services include large firms that are able to provide multiple products and small firms that can only provide a part of the goods and services to be procured (due to capacity constraints or because they are specialized). If this is the case, bundling may exclude certain firms from the competitive procurement. The issue of lot division and participation is discussed in detail in section 7.4. Here we discuss only the case where after the tendering process subcontracting takes place regularly at negligible costs among the firms, so that bundling does not exclude small firms from production, although it excludes them from the actual tendering process.

Again we observe a trade-off between revenue and efficiency: bundling the lots generally does not hurt from the revenue perspective in the presence of efficient aftermarket trade.[9] The reason is that large firms anticipate the additional expected cost savings from subcontracting parts of the project to small firms in their bids. Thus, the existence of small

---

[8] This follows results by Palfrey (1983) and Chakraborty (1999).
[9] In the sense that many smaller firms are in the market.

low-cost firms lowers the price although they are not able to bid in the competitive tendering. The price paid for the desired goods and services by the procurer may actually be lower than the total price paid in separate competitive procurements, depending on the resale procedure used in the aftermarket. However, since subcontracts usually do not reallocate the items in an efficient manner, the items should be sold separately in case efficiency is the main goal.[10]

However, when considering this point one has to analyse carefully the incentives of large firms to delegate parts of the project to small firms: they might well have an incentive to drive small firms out of the market in order to face less competition in future tendering processes. In which kind of market environment this is likely to happen is discussed in more detail in section 7.7.

4. Buy all distinct components as late as possible

Often an order comprises of many parts that may have quite different time limits for delivery. Firms usually face higher uncertainty with respect to their cost for projects that lie further ahead in time. For example the cost of an office building is much better known to a firm if construction should take place soon than in case construction is scheduled for some time in the future. The reason is that prices for a variety of input factors may vary considerably. Thus, when unbundling the lot, one should care to sell those lots separately that have very distinct scheduled delivery dates. An exception from this rule should probably be made if there are strong complementarities between two projects with different delivery dates.

Practical conclusion 1 (Lot division)
- Bundle those lots where strong synergies in production/provision are expected (due to production procedures, transportation cost, etc.).
- If you focus on revenue
  - Bundle lots if the number of bidders is small, and sell separately if the number of bidders is large.
  - Bundling is more attractive (i.e., less risky in terms of lost participation) if you expect aftermarket trade among firms than if firms do not subcontract.
- If you focus on efficiency
  - Divide the item into small lots if synergies play no role.

---

[10] See Grimm (2006).

The results suggest that dividing the procurement into many lots is more attractive if the number of bidders is high. Roughly speaking, the reason is that in order to achieve a low procurement cost, there needs to be sufficient competition on each lot. Bundling is only desirable if this is not the case, that is, if the number of bidders competing for each lot is too low, or if there are strong synergies between contracts. In the following section we introduce two ratios that may serve as indicators of expected competition in the tendering process(s) and explain how they should be used to evaluate the design.

7.3. The competition ratios

We propose two simple ratios as partial indices of expected competition in a competitive procurement under different scenarios regarding the number and size of lots in which the procurement is divided. The first we call *Optimistic Ratio*, since it builds on the hypothesis that firms do not collude; the second one, called *Pessimistic Ratio*, is especially meaningful if firms are prone to implementing 'share-the-lots' collusive agreements as soon as favourable circumstances arise.[11] The ratios are of course to be computed before the tendering process takes place, when the expected number of participants is still an estimate and the tendering design incomplete. They must be evaluated together to provide guidance regarding the decision how to divide supply into lots. The competition ratios are based on the following variables:

adjusted number of individual participants (n): this is the expected number of individual firms in the tendering process, where each firm is counted as many times as the number of lots for which it can bid given its capacity;

number of distinct participants (N): this is the absolute expected number of individual firms in the tendering process. Each individual firm is counted only once, independently from the number of lots it can bid for.[12]

number of lots (L): this variable counts the number of lots the supply contract is divided in.

---

[11] Whether the market is highly competitive or prone to collusion should be judged according to standard market analysis, including consideration of market history, concentration, and further characteristics described in Chapters 14 and 15.

[12] Note that the number of lots on which a firm can bid is different from the number of lots that a firm can win.

The **Optimistic ratio**, OR, is defined as the ratio between the *adjusted number of participants* (n) and the *number of lots* (L):

$$\text{OR} = \frac{n}{L}.$$

OR implicitly assumes that tendering process participants behave competitively for each lot, without colluding or making agreements with others to share the lots at high prices. If OR increases, the level of expected competition is higher and vice versa. In OR, if a firm is large enough to bid for two lots, it is counted twice in the numerator. This means that OR gives prominence to the effect of an increase in the number of lots on the participation decision of firms, whereas it does not take into account the potential negative effect on the strategic behaviour of those firms active on more lots. If the number of lots increases and there are no new entrants, OR does not change, even though the possibilities of sharing the market increase. On the contrary, if there are new entrants OR increases.

The **Pessimistic ratio**, PR, is defined as the ratio between the *number of distinct participants* (N), and the *number of lots* (L):

$$\text{PR} = \frac{N}{L}.$$

PR assumes that bidders have high propensity to collude; that is, that they try to share the lots without competing for them whenever possible. As for OR, if PR increases the expected level of competition is higher and vice versa. Contrary to OR, PR underlies the hypothesis that larger firms behave strategically in the sense that their behaviour is coordinated with the aims of sharing lots with the other large competitors. In PR, a firm that is large enough to bid for two lots is nevertheless counted only once at the numerator. Thus, the index rather reflects a scenario where each firm is willing to avoid aggressive bidding on a lot in exchange for the same behaviour from its competitors on other lots. If an increase in the number of lots does not trigger sufficient entry of new participants, then PR decreases.

Example 7.2

This example demonstrates the differences between the two ratios and the nature of information they provide in terms of competition and/or collusion. Consider two scenarios with the same number of lots but a different market structure.

Scenario 1 (High risk of collusion): Six lots and six large potential participants, each of them able to bid on all lots. At the numerator, OR counts each firm six times, whereas PR only once: $OR_1 = (6 \times 6)/6 = 6$, $PR_1 = 6/6 = 1$. **Scenario 2 (Low risk of collusion):** Six lots and thirty-six small firms, each one able to bid for only one lot. In this case both, OR and PR, coincide: $OR_2 = 36/6 = 6$, $PR_2 = 36/6 = 6$.[13]

The optimistic ratio OR gives the same value in both scenarios since it is not able to distinguish between the two cases ($OR_1 = OR_2$). Thus, OR is more informative when it is likely that bidders will behave competitively. If bidders are prone to collusive behaviour, however, it is likely that the six large firms in scenario 1 try to share the lots (focusing on one lot each), whereas the thirty-six small firms in scenario 2 would still compete heavily. The pessimistic ratio PR recognizes that the market structure of scenario 1 is characterized by a number of firms equal to the number of lots, assigning the value '1' to it ($PR_1 < PR_2$).

Practical conclusion 2 (Competition ratios)

When bidders are expected to behave highly competitively, focus more on OR. When you suspect that bidders might try to cooperate or even collude, focus more on PR.

7.3.1. How to Read the Ratios

Complementarity The ratios measure the minimum (PR) and maximum level (OR) of expected competition related to a given number of lots and participants. The actual level of competition may vary between what PR and OR suggest. So the two ratios can be considered complementary and they should be used jointly in order to have a clear picture of the level of expected competition depending on the tendering design.

Relativity The values of OR and PR under any given division into lots should be compared with the values they indicate with different numbers of lots. Given a proposed distribution of lots and related expected number of participants, OR and PR indicate the expected competitiveness of the tendering process. If it is not considered appropriate/sufficient, the number of lots should be increased and reduced and OR and PR should be calculated and confronted for all scenarios.

---

[13] Factors that should be taken into account in the evaluation of collusion are discussed in Chapters 14 and 15.

7.3.2. Limits of OR and PR

In competitive procurements where – due to technological or geographical constraints – the expected number of bidders has to be less than the number of lots, PR is not very informative. Thus, one should focus on OR when analysing the competitiveness of the situation. In order to prevent collusive behaviour, the tendering design should put small firms in a position to trouble the larger ones. The following example illustrates that especially if PR cannot be meaningfully used, it is also important to look at the effects of a bundling decision in very much detail. In the situation we outline, bundling reduces procurement cost if firms behave competitively but is a fatal error if firms tend to behave cooperatively.

Example 7.3

Suppose there are three firms that could bid for four lots, two big firms (A and B) that could bid for all lots, and one small firm (C), that can only bid for one lot (but is indifferent which one it gets). The agency announces in advance that it will not accept any price higher than €25 per lot (or, alternatively, €50 for two lots). Firm A is quite efficient for lots 1 and 2, while firm B is efficient for lots 3 and 4. Firms have no synergies in production. The following table summarizes the production costs of the three firms for each single lot and for two bundles of two lots each:

	A	B	C
1	1	6	5
2	1	5	5
3	5	1	5
4	6	1	5
1&3	6	7	insufficient capacity
2&4	7	6	insufficient capacity

Suppose that, in order to reduce procurement cost, the agency thinks about bundling lots 1 and 3 and lots 2 and 4, respectively. This decreases only marginally OR from 9/4 to 8/4.[14] The success of bundling, however, depends crucially on whether the two large firms behave competitively or are likely to behave cooperatively in the bundle tendering processes

---

[14] PR increases from 3/4 to 1 but we already explained that when there are more lots than bidders PR should never be taken into account.

where bidder C cannot participate. If they behave competitively in both situations, bundling indeed would lower the price from €20 (€5 per lot) in case of four lots to €14 (€7 per lot) in case of two lots. If, however, the two large firms behave cooperatively, the price would increase by bundling from €20 (€5 per lot, because firm C would claim one of the lots at any higher price) to €100 (the highest possible price accepted by the agency on each lot).[15]

The example illustrates that the ratios have to be handled extremely carefully, always having in mind the effects of bundling on participation and the scope for collusive behaviour. Especially in situations where bidders are rather asymmetric they might not give the right intuition, while they provide rather useful insights if bidders are alike. We will focus on these issues in more detail in sections 7.4 and 7.5.

7.4. Division into lots and participation

In what follows we discuss how the lot division may promote or hinder participation. Participation is desirable since usually more intense competition leads to lower prices for the procurer (see also Chapter 6 for an exhaustive treatment of this issue). In general we should expect a firm to participate in the competitive procurement if its expected profit from the tendering process is high enough compared to its bidding cost and its outside options. Thus, the question we try to answer is: how should the lots be divided in order to increase the expected profit of potential new bidders – without, however, decreasing expected profits of established bidders too much?

Most problems arise because firms are heterogeneous, and therefore have quite different incentives to participate. Firms can be distinguished by their size (large/small) and by whether they already have an established position in the market or not (incumbent/entrant). In the following we discuss several entry-promoting features of the tendering design that are important to foster the participation of (i) small firms (that may be well established or new to the market) and (ii) potential new entrants (that may be large or small).

1. Small (low capacity) firms

Small firms usually do not have sufficient capacity to accomplish the

---

[15] See section 7.5, for a more detailed analysis on coordination and collusion.

entire contract on their own. Thus, by designing rather big lots, the buyer excludes small firms from the competitive procurement. However, in many cases the participation of small firms is desirable. Often specialized small firms are more efficient than large firms in providing certain parts of the project. Moreover, they increase competition on the lots they bid on, which lowers the expected price to be paid by the procurer. Finally, the existence of small bidders may complicate attempts by large bidders to 'share the pie'. Those arguments favour the division of the procurement into many small lots.

However, keep in mind that there are several reasons not to divide the procurement in too many lots. In the presence of complementarities between lots, bidders would face the exposure problem (i.e., they have to bid on one lot not knowing whether they would receive its complement). Moreover, a design with multiple lots may facilitate cooperative behaviour, and thus, may increase the price to be paid. Thus, when dividing the procurement into many lots, this has to be done in a smart way, accounting for complementarities and choosing configurations that offer no obvious way to 'share the pie' (more on this issue in section 5.3).

When considering the effect of the number and size of lots on competition, one should account also for hidden participation, that is, whether there are active resale markets or not. It is less severe to exclude small bidders from the actual tendering process, if they later on have the possibility to participate in the production process due to an active resale market. Usually, in this case, lower cost of small bidders will be reflected in the price, since large bidders account for the potentially lower cost of production in their bids. Whether large firms have an incentive to subcontract parts of the project to small firms depends on dynamic aspects, such as the possibilities to drive small competitors out of the market in the future by excluding them from production today. Those aspects are discussed in more detail in section 7.7.

2. New entrants and disadvantaged bidders

If among the potential competitors there are both well-established firms and new entrants, the tendering process should be designed such that new entrants or disadvantaged firms face a reasonable probability of success. Even if it is expected that in the short run new entrants are less efficient than established firms, the former should enter to improve the procurement outcome. On the one hand this drives down the price, even if entrants are not successful in the end. On the other hand, in the long run some of the entrants become experienced and thus, their participation today guarantees fiercer competition in the future (this relates to dynamic competition as discussed in section 7.7).

Firms that have no realistic chance to be successful, however, have no incentive to enter the competitive tendering. Entry is costly for each firm and will only happen if a firm faces a high enough expected benefit. As we have mentioned in the introduction, a main prescription that emerged from the literature is to *'define at least one lot more than the number of incumbents and reserve it to new entrants'*.

7.5. Coordination and collusion

Collusion in procurement consists in an implicit or explicit agreement among potential competitors to share the supply contracts cooperatively and at prices higher than competitive ones, rather than compete for them. Collusion therefore requires coordination among all potential competitors on one, common sharing rule. In order to have an incentive to participate, each member of the cartel has to receive a 'slice of the cake' that is being divided; coordination is needed to decide how to divide and allocate the shares of the contract.

Firms entering a competitive tendering may agree on the way of sharing the procurement contract either explicitly or implicitly. Explicit collusion means that firms communicate and agree on the way of bidding and sharing the lots before the tendering process takes place. Implicit collusion prevails if firms coordinate their behaviour without explicitly communicating. They individually consider their features and those of the procurement contract, and still reach a non-competitive outcome.

7.5.1. Number of participants and coordination

The presence of many competitors generally makes it more difficult for firms to coordinate their actions in order to share the contract. Thus, given the number of lots, the larger the number of participants the lower the risk of explicit or implicit collusion.

Example 7.4

The procurer splits the procurement contract in ten smaller lots and only two eligible firms are in the market: the two firms may easily coordinate to split the 'cake' (i.e., five lots per firm). Now suppose participation requirements become less restrictive, so that eight more firms can participate in the tendering process: it is still feasible to split the market (one lot per firm), but it may be more complicated for ten firms to coordinate on who should get which lot.

7.5.2. Number of lots and coordination

Independently of the number of bidders, 'sharing the pie' only works if each bidder receives a 'slice.' Thus the first rule in order to prevent coordination (which we already mentioned in the introduction) is that *the number of lots should be smaller than the expected number of participants.* As we already mentioned at the beginning, this intuitive rule is useful, but has also limits. Colluding firms may operate in many markets, and split directly the markets where to participate or win, they can take turns in winning, or use side transfers to divide the collusive pie (in particular subcontracting). Moreover, there are procurements in which the technical aspects of supply require a very large number of lots (e.g., medicines), which makes it impossible to follow the rule described above; and then a larger number of lots may even hinder collusive behaviour. Given the number of participants, the higher the number of lots, the easier it is for firms to split the supply cooperatively. However, when the number of lots is already higher than the number of participants, a further increase in the number of lots increases the number of possible collusive allocations. In this case, firms may find it more difficult to coordinate their bids for sharing the procurement contract.

Example 7.5

Consider a market with two similar firms, A and B, and a competitive tendering with two identical lots, lot 1 and lot 2. In this case, the firms' coordination is relatively simple since there are only two possible collusive outcomes: either firm A bids only on lot 1 and firm B only on lot 2 or vice versa, both firms offering a very high price. Now consider the same context but with 44 identical lots. In this case the number of possible collusive divisions of supply is very high, and firms may find it much more difficult to coordinate without directly communicating (and so risking antitrust prosecution).

The example illustrates that, given the number of firms in the market, a higher number of lots may well complicate firms' coordination and hence, be pro-competitive. Of course, the increase of the number of lots and the resulting reduction of their size could also enable smaller firms to participate in the tendering process, which further increases competition.

7.5.3. Symmetry and coordination

The ratios PR and OR measure expected competition by relating the number of participants and the number of lots. However, they do not take into account two other important factors: suppliers' distribution in the market (in terms of turnover, geographical location, etc.) and the numerical and dimensional distribution of lots. Economic analysis[16] shows how firms' asymmetry in costs and in capacity may influence the sustainability of collusive agreements, but it does not analyse how such an agreement may be affected by the number and the sizes of lots. In this section we demonstrate how the number and the sizes of lots may affect coordination and collusion among firms, given the firms' characteristics and geographical distribution.

Example 7.6

- Consider three identical firms on the market and two different lot distributions: (i) three identical lots, (ii) four identical lots.

  Moving from three to four lots here may hinder collusion because each firm is then likely to bid or bargain for more than one lot.
- Consider three different firms, a large firm and two small ones, and again two possible lot distributions: (i) three identical lots, (ii) four identical lots.

  Moving from three to four lots may facilitate collusion because coordination among firms becomes easier: smaller firms will be awarded one lot each, while the large one will get the other two.

  The example points out how the possibility of (implicit) collusion may depend on the composition of firms in the market and the exact configuration of lots.

---

[16] See, e.g., Ivaldi et al. (2003).

Practical conclusion 3 (Collusion)

- Given the number of lots, maximize participation to make the bidders' coordination harder (this is a general practical conclusion that is also addressed in the chapter on participation).
- Given the number and identities of the participants
  - The number of lots should be lower than the number of participants.
  - If this is not feasible, further increasing the number of lots makes coordination more difficult.
- Taking into account the firms' distribution (in terms of turnover, geographical location, etc.) and all other characteristics useful to predict the likely behaviour of others in an auction, avoid division into lots that give prominence to a specific sharing criterion.

7.6. Multi-product firms and multi-market contact

If there are multi-product firms participating in several competitive procurements, a procurer should not restrict the focus to a specific tendering process, but rather be aware of possible collusive agreements that could take place across markets/tendering processes. Economic literature and several procurement agencies suggest to reduce the number of lots in a tendering process in order to hinder participants from cooperatively sharing the 'cake'.[17] However, in the presence of several firms acting in more than one market, reducing the number of lots may not be enough to avoid collusion, because:

1. Large firms participate in different markets and, therefore, can still share a (bigger) 'cake';
2. Small firms may not be able or eligible to participate anymore (for the larger lot), which further facilitates it for large firms to win the tendering process with non-competitive bids.

In such a context having more lots of smaller size may enable participation by small firms and increase the overall level of competition.

---

[17] Klemperer (2004); OECD (1999).

Example 7.7

Consider three different markets (e.g., PC desktops, PC laptops and prin-ters), three large firms, and two small ones, all of them producing the three product categories.

- **Case 1**: For each product category the supply contract is divided into three smaller lots. This may allow the two small firms to participate and bid, which may prevent large ones from sharing supply at collusive prices.
- **Case 2**: A single lot is procured for each product category. The two small firms cannot enter the tendering process because of insufficient capacity. Without the small firms, the three large firms might find it easy to collude and split the three markets one each, at non-competitive prices.

Restricting focus on the single procurement auction would be terribly misleading in this example: PR, which assumes a collusive behaviour of par-ticipants, improves in Case 2 relative to Case 1 (e.g., from 5/3 to 3). The example points out that the reduction in the number of lots, highly recom-mended by PR, may not prevent large firms that are active on many markets from making collusive agreements across different markets, while it may have the negative effect of excluding smaller bidders. With less competitors in each market, collusion becomes easier to sustain for the large firms.

Practical conclusion 4 (Multi-market contact)

In presence of large multi-product firms active in several procurements, do not restrict the focus on single auctions when deciding the number of lots: take into account all auctions where these firms meet.

7.7. Lock-in

Lock-in captures a situation in which the buyer (in this case the procurer) ends up being 'caught' by only one supplier, because of the absence of alternative suppliers, the existence of high switching costs,[18] or the incompleteness of

---

[18] Switching costs arise when a buyer has to pay a specific cost passing from one supplier to another.

contracts. Lock-in can be categorized into two main types: (i) over recurring procurements: when the supply contract is awarded to a sole supplier, other firms may exit from the market, which reduces the level of competition in subsequent competitive procurements; (ii) within the contract: when the buyer is exposed to the opportunistic behaviour of the current supplier. The second case is discussed extensively in Chapter 4. Thus, here we focus on the first type of lock-in.

7.7.1. The lock-in over recurring procurements

The lock-in over recurring procurements is a dynamic problem that may occur over several repeated competitive procurements. Not all markets are subject to this kind of lock-in, but only those characterized by specific technical-economic conditions. These are:

1. **Presence of learning by doing**, that is, firms learn how to reduce production cost while fulfilling the supply contract. In future competitive procurement they then have a comparative advantage with respect to the firms that did not produce.
2. **Dominance of the buyer on the market**. When the procurement absorbs a relevant market share, the winning firm becomes the only one able to improve the production process.
3. **Presence of idiosyncratic investments**. Participation in these markets requires specific investment which is sunk at the time the competitive procurement takes place. Thus, if one dominant supplier is already present in the market, incentives to enter may be low.

In all the above cases, an one lot-tendering process could

- trigger the **exit** of all suppliers but one from the market in the medium-long term. The number of potential suppliers may reduce the tendering process by lowering the level of competition. Being confronted with one monopolistic supplier is not a desirable situation for a procurer.
- cause high **switching costs** for the buyer, should he decide to change the initial supplier. This usually happens when, after having bought a certain technology, the buyer makes durable investments in complementary goods.[19]

Therefore, the procurer should identify those markets with a high risk of lock-in and choose an appropriate tendering design.

---

[19] For example, when purchasing the computer 'X', the buyer will also purchase a printer, some specific software and other complementary peripherals which are not often compatible to computer 'Y'.

7.7.2. How to avoid lock-in

To avoid the situation that a supplier becomes dominant and to reduce the risk of lock-in, the procurer has to maintain competition high in future competitive procurements. For this purpose economic theory suggests to split the supply contract in two or more lots and to fix a limit (as a fraction of supply) that each firm can be awarded. Technically, this is called co-sourcing (or dual sourcing) if there are two suppliers that should each get a fraction of the contract, and multi-sourcing if more than two firms should supply a fraction each.[20] This procedure ensures that more than one firm has the chance to improve its technical skills while carrying out the contract. Thus, competition in future tendering processes remains relatively high.[21]

An alternative strategy to avoid lock-in is to rotate suppliers. As a consequence several firms have the chance to improve their technical skills while carrying out supply contracts, which also maintains competition high in the long run.

7.7.2.1. Splitting the supply contract

If the procurer fears to be locked in with a dominant supplier it can use several procedures to mitigate this firm's market power. The most obvious solution is to implement the so-called awarding constraint.[22] An awarding constraint consists of a clause which rules out any allocation where one single firm is awarded with more than a certain (fixed) part of the supply contract. The supply contract is then usually split among those firms that presented the best offers. This ensures a minimum number of suppliers (that depends on the constraint as well as the firms' bids). If the procurer only wants to split the supply contract when the second best firm is not too

---

[20] Differently, the term second-sourcing is used when the supply is transferred from a first supplier to a second more efficient one. This is usually obtained with a re-procurement process: first there is a competitive bidding for the development contract. A system is thought to be ready for re-procurement when a technology has achieved a stability of design such that further development work is minimal. Then technology is transferred to a second source and another competitive stage is introduced through a re-procurement stage (Anton and Yao, 1987). Another kind of competitive sourcing is used by Japanese automobile producers: Toyota, for example, does not have only one supplier but several ones (Richardson, 1993).

[21] Shepard (1987) and Farrel and Gallini (1988) were amongst the first economists who studied how to limit the supplier opportunistic behaviour after the tendering process, using dual sourcing.

[22] American Defence policy encourages the use of dual sourcing to reduce procurement costs. Defence programme managers are 'required by law and regulation to incorporate effective competition in the acquisition of weapon systems, whenever practicable.'

inefficient, it may use a 'split-award tendering process'.[23] In this competitive procurement, each supplier submits bids for a share of the contract as well as for a sole source award. The contract is awarded to the best offer on the whole supply (sole source) or to the combination of the two 'partial' offers (dual sourcing). The buyer may choose the solution that minimizes the procurement price or favour either bundling or separate sales.

The minimum number of firms that should be awarded a share of the contract should be carefully chosen in the light of the specific market structure. Choosing more than two firms is recommendable for new markets that are at the initial stage. A tendering design that leads to more than two suppliers can strengthen the supply structure and support market development still in its infancy. Winning firms then have an incentive to invest in specific know-how they need in order to remain in the competition in the future.[24]

It has been showed[25] that dual sourcing:

- simultaneously allows both winning firms to learn and to gain experience, resulting in a steeper overall product-specific learning curve.
- only produces procurement cost savings to the government when it is followed by a winner-take-all tendering process[26] (however, again the danger of lock-in, which implies higher cost in the future, would have to be weighed against potential profits today).
- reduces informational asymmetries between suppliers, which can lower procurement cost by inducing more aggressive bidding in subsequent winner-take-all tendering processes.
- gives the buyer more leverage over non-contractible dimensions of product quality: the buyer has additional disciplinary power with respect to product attributes that are difficult to specify in a contract.

---

[23] Anton and Yao, 1989.

[24] Furthermore, contracting many suppliers (instead of only two) has the advantage of ensuring continuity of supply. Kranton and Minehart (2001) analyses the case of a buyer who uses a supplier network to remove the risk of interrupting the supply. Having many suppliers, additional to keeping up the level of competition, covers against the risk of firms' failure.

[25] Lyon (2000). He analysed a panel dataset of tactical missiles, focusing on the price benefits of competition.

[26] In a winner-take-all tendering process all production will be awarded to only one supplier. Therefore, there will be only one contract and only one price.

7.7.7.2. Rotating purchases among rival suppliers

Another method useful to minimize the risk of lock-in is awarding the procurement contract to rotating suppliers.[27] When economies of scale are remarkable, the buyer may initially rotate and then end up with the most experienced supplier. Otherwise, the buyer may continue with supplier rotation. When a supplier becomes dominant, the procurer benefits from lower production costs due to the economies of scale. On the other side he has to consider the risk related to the reduction of competition in the market.

The procurer shall consider the trade-off between the exploitation of the economies of scale and the decrease of competition due to a dominant player.[28]

Experimental studies indicate that supplier rotation may indeed be successfully used in order to stimulate dynamic competition among rival suppliers, that is, to exploit learning effects while minimizing the costs of becoming locked-in to one producer.[29] In a setting where the procurer does not always have to choose the best offer these empirical studies find that

- sellers aggressively compete with each other in the early periods, even offering lower prices than their supply costs (*penetration price*), in order to penetrate the market and reduce costs exploiting the economies of scale,
- the buyer obtains a large surplus even at early stages (when suppliers do not yet exploit economies of scale) because of the suppliers' penetration pricing strategy,
- the buyer occasionally selects another than the lowest price seller to allow him to move down its learning curve and to maintain cost parity with the other suppliers (*rotation among participants*),
- in the end, only one supplier finally gains a sufficient cost advantage to become the dominant supplier (*market tipping*).

7.7.7.3. Cost and risks of multi-sourcing

On the one hand, multi-sourcing allows the procurer to choose from a big pool of potential and experienced suppliers over the whole life of the procurement

---

[27] This part is borrowed from the empirical study implemented by Lewis and Yildirim (2002).

[28] Note that rotating suppliers does not require abandoning auctions as a method to award contracts. For example, it is possible to award the contract on the basis of the best price offered, but under the condition that some suppliers can not win twice (or three, four times) in a row.

[29] See Lewis and Yildirim (2002).

contract. Moreover, competition spurs greater efforts to reduce cost and thereby speeds up the learning process.

On the other hand, scale economies will hardly be completely exploited if production volumes are split among more than one producer (or if they are rotated continuously). In markets where high idiosyncratic investments are required, the efficiency loss when splitting the production probably outweighs the savings from multisourcing. Awarding the contract to more than one supplier moreover raises the procurer's fixed cost. In addition, relying on simultaneous competing suppliers implies a higher potential for collusive behaviour upon (and before) sharing the contract. It is crucial to carefully analyse the trade-off between cost and benefits from multisourcing before using it.

> **Practical conclusion 5 (Multisourcing)**
>
> Before resorting to multisourcing, compare the following:
> - Costs: loss of scale economies, higher fixed cost for the procurer, higher risk of collusion
> - Benefits: lower risk of lock-in, steeper learning curve

7.8. Conclusion

In this chapter we analysed how the division of the procurement contract into lots may influence actual as well as future tendering results.

We argued that the number of lots and the number of participants in the procurement are interdependent variables, and that their interdependence has to be taken into account carefully in the tendering design. The division into lots should ideally strengthen the incentives to participate without increasing the risk of collusion during the tendering process (too much). We proposed two ratios that allow to evaluate alternative designs by measuring expected competition in the competitive procurement as a function of the number of lots and the distribution of firms in terms of their eligibility to bid for certain lots. We then discussed in detail the implications participation and potential collusion have on the lot division. Finally, we showed that the division into lots may also be important to deal with dynamic aspects of competition. We analysed the consequences multi-market contact of large firms should have on the tendering design, in particular on the lot division. We moreover analysed the problem of lock-in over repeated tendering processes and discussed several alternatives to maintain multiple firms in the market.

Bibliographical notes

An excellent general treatment of multi-unit competitive bidding is in Milgrom (2004), and a brilliant discussion on the number of lots and competition is in Klemperer (2002). Optimal bundling has been analysed first by Palfrey (1983), and most recently by Grimm (2006), who also discussed the effects on participation. Farrel and Gallini (1988) first showed the benefits of dual sourcing, while Lewis and Yldirim (2002) recently showed how to minimise the risk of lock-in.

References

Anton, J. and D. Yao, (1987). Second Sourcing and the Experience Curve: Price Competition in Defense Procurement, *RAND Journal of Economics*, 18 (1), Spring.

Anton, J. and D. Yao, (1989). Split Awards, Procurement, and Innovation, *RAND Journal of Economics*, 20 (4), Winter.

Armstrong, M. (2000). Optimal Multi-Object Auctions, *Review of Economic Studies*, 67, 455–481.

Avery, C. and T. Hendershott, (2000). Bundling and Optimal Auctions of Multiple Products, *Review of Economic Studies*, 67, 483–497.

Binmore, K. and P. Klemperer, (2002). The Biggest Auction Ever: The Sale of the British 3G Telecom Licences, *Economic Journal*.

Chakraborty, I. (1999). Bundling Decisions for Selling Multiple Objects, *Economic Theory* 13, 723–733.

Farrel, J. and N. Gallini, (1988). Second Sourcing as a Commitment: Monopoly Incentives to Attract Competition, *Quarterly Journal of Economics*, 103 (4), 673–694.

Grimm, V. (2006). Sequential versus Bundle Auctions for Recurring Procurement *Journal of Economics*, forthcoming.

Klemperer, P. (2004). *Auctions: Theory and Practice*, Princeton University Press.

Kranton, R. and D. Minehart (2001). A Theory of Buyer-Seller Networks, *American Economic Review*, 91(3), 485–508.

Krishna, V. (2002). Multiple Object Auction in *Auction Theory*, Academic Press, 2002.

Ivaldi, M., B. Jullien, P. Rey, P. Seabright, and J. Tirole, (2003). The Economics of Tacit Collusion, *Final Report for DG Competition*, European Commission.

Jehiel, P., M. Meyer-ter-Vehn and B. Moldovanu (2003). Mixed Bundling Auctions, *Journal of Economic Theory*, Forthcoming.

Lewis, T. and H. Yildirim, (2002). Managing Dynamic Competition, *American Economic Review*, 92, (4), September.

Lyon, P. T. (2000). Competition and Technological Complexity in Procurement: An Empirical Study of Dual Sourcing, Mimeo, Stephen M. Ross School of Business, University of Michigan, 2000.

Milgrom, P. (2004). *Putting Auction Theory to Work*, Cambridge University Press, Cambridge, United Kingdom.

OECD (1999). Competition Policy and Procurement Markets, Paris.

Palfrey, T. (1983). Bundling Decisions by a Multiproduct Monopolist with Incomplete Information, *Econometrica* 51, 463–484.

Richardson, J. (1993). Parallel Sourcing and Supplier Performance in the Japanese Automobile Industry, *Strategic Management Journal*, 14 (5), 339–350.

Shepard, A. (1987). Licensing to Enhance Demand for New Technologies, *RAND Journal of Economics*, 18 (3), Autumn.

8 Multi-contract tendering procedures and package bidding in procurement

Nicola Dimitri, Riccardo Pacini,
Marco Pagnozzi and Giancarlo Spagnolo

8.1. Introduction

In practical procurement, the most common way to purchase multiple supply contracts – of different types, say, or for different geographical areas – is probably the simultaneous sealed-bid competitive tendering of several distinct contracts. In this competitive bidding procedure, when tenders are only economic, suppliers make a separate bid for each contract and each contract is awarded to the supplier who makes the lowest bid, at a price equal to his bid. Typically, the chance that a supplier is awarded a particular contract is independent of the bids he submits on any other contract.

This simple way of awarding supply contracts may be appropriate when the cost of supplying each contract is independent of which other contracts a supplier is serving. But, in reality, a supplier's cost of serving a contract often depends on how many, and which, other contracts he also supplies. When this is the case, the procurer should allow suppliers to submit offers that can take such relations into account. For example, when the average cost of serving two adjacent regions is substantially lower than that of serving just one of the two areas – say because part of the fixed investment required can be used for both areas – bidders should be allowed to tender offers whose conditions are valid only if they are awarded the service contracts for both adjacent regions.

In this chapter, we discuss methods for procuring multiple contracts when there are 'complementarities' among them – that is when a supplier's cost of serving each contract depends on which other contracts the same supplier is also serving. We mainly focus on sealed bidding and on situations where the private-cost component of serving contracts prevails (see Chapter 6). Multi-contract dynamic auctions are discussed in Chapter 9.

We argue that the nature and magnitude of complementarities should drive the choice of the most appropriate form of competitive tendering for the procurer.

Positive complementarities, the most common and interesting in procurement, arise when, for some potential suppliers, the total cost of serving a set of contracts is lower than the sum of the costs of serving each single contract in the set alone. An example of products with strong positive complementarities is ICT devices and software, where large suppliers can offer very low prices thanks to significant economies of scale.

Negative complementarities, more rare in procurement, arise in the opposite situation, when for a supplier the cost of serving a group of contracts is higher than the sum of the costs of the single contracts. This is normally the case when a bidder's capacity constraints are relatively tight so that, as the number of contracts supplied increases towards this capacity, total cost increases steeply. An example of negative complementarities is energy provision: since energy cannot be stored and power plants have limited capacity, production constraints represent rather rigid bounds for a producer, who has to drastically increase production costs in order to provide a quantity beyond such limit.

When two contracts generate strong positive complementarities for a supplier, he may be willing to lower his offer for one of the contracts only if he is sure he will also be awarded the other contract. Therefore, the procurer should adopt a tendering procedure in which bidders are also allowed to bid for a group, or a 'package', of contracts, as well as for single contracts, in order to increase his saving.

We first discuss the simultaneous ascending auction (adapted to procurement), which has been successfully used around the world, for example, to allocate radio spectrum for mobile-phone licences and pollution licences. Although this tendering format does not allow package bidding, it does allow bidders to place their offers while observing their competitors' bids and, hence, helps them in selecting which contracts to bid on in the presence of mild complementarities. However, if complementarities are sufficiently important, suppliers may still be unwilling to bid aggressively in a simultaneous ascending auction and, therefore, other formats that allow package bidding should be considered.

We briefly discuss the procurement version of the Vickrey auction, which has been widely analysed theoretically and which enjoys remarkable efficiency properties. However, because of the practical problems related to its implementation (due, e.g., to its complicated pricing rule), the Vickrey auction is not in general advisable for procurement. We then consider the procurement version of the sealed-bid 'menu auction', a sealed-bid tendering procedure in which bidders are allowed to bid on packages of contracts, and winning bidders receive the price they bid for the contract(s) they are awarded. This competitive tendering procedure is becoming increasingly popular for procurement, because it is relatively easy to implement and its rules are readily understood by bidders.

Package auctions can become computationally complex because a large number of possible packages arises from the combination of even a small number of initial contracts. We suggest some practical solutions to mitigate such complexity. Package bidding may also bring in other inefficiencies, because it may induce suppliers only interested in single contracts to bid less aggressively.

When negative complementarities among contracts are likely to prevail, in a standard sealed-bid tendering that allows offers only on individual contracts, a supplier may be exposed to the risk of winning more contracts than he desires at a given price because, even if he is interested in winning just one of several similar contracts, he may still want to bid on more contracts in order to increase his chance of winning. As with positive complementarities, the procurer should favour tendering procedures where bidders can explicitly submit offers conditional on being awarded a certain set of contracts, so that the price a winning supplier is paid can depend on which contracts he is awarded. This encourages bidders to submit competitive offers for single contracts, without facing the risk of being assigned too many contracts at a low price.

When contracts are homogeneous 'shares' of a whole supply and complementarities are negative, as for example in electricity supply, the procurer may choose simpler versions of sealed-bid tendering procedures with package bidding, where suppliers are asked to bid 'supply schedules' – that is, combinations of quantities (number of contracts) and prices at which they are willing to supply those quantities. These 'competitive tendering of shares' are simple to implement and can award contracts using different rules to determine prices. We discuss which pricing rules are appropriate in different situations, taking into account their potential costs and benefits for attracting participants and inducing strategic/collusive bidding ('demand reduction').

Chapters 7 and 11 argue that, when there are capacity constraints, the higher the number of contracts procured and the smaller their size, the greater is the number of small suppliers that can participate in the tendering. But although many small contracts can increase competition, in the absence of package bidding they also reduce the ability of larger supplier to exploit economies of scale, by exposing them to the risk of only winning few very small contracts. There is then a trade-off, in choosing the number and size of contracts to tender, between encouraging participation of small suppliers and allowing large suppliers to exploit economies of scale. Allowing for package bidding helps resolving this trade-off, because even if only very small contracts are offered, large firms can still exploit economies of scale by bidding for large packages of contracts. So package bidding with many small contracts may be the ideal solution to foster participation of many heterogeneous suppliers, allowing each of them to express their competitive strength by offering on their own ideal combination of contracts, improving the outcome for the procurer.

The rest of the chapter is structured as follows. Section 8.2 discusses auctions and sealed-bid tendering procedures which are appropriate when contracts display positive complementarities. The case of negative complementarities is discussed in section 8.3. Section 8.4 analyses the effects of the tendering rules on bidders' participation. A few examples conclude the chapter.

8.2. Contracts with strong positive complementarities

Positive complementarities arise when two or more contracts are worth more together than separately or when, equivalently, due for example to economies of scale, a bidder's total cost of supplying a group of contracts is lower than the sum of the costs of supplying each of the contracts in the group separately. This, in principle, can allow bidders to supply contracts at relatively low prices, and the procurer to obtain substantial savings.

In the sealed-bid tendering most commonly used to award heterogeneous contracts in procurement, suppliers are not allowed to offer on groups of contracts (or, in general, to place a bid on a contract conditional on also winning another contract).

But with strong positive complementarities, a bidder may be willing to lower his price for a particular contract only if he is sure to be also awarded another contract (or even more than one), because the cost of a single contract when both of them are supplied is lower than when only one of the contracts is supplied. In this case, in a competitive tendering where suppliers are not allowed to bid for a specific *group* of contracts, the bidder may be unwilling to offer aggressively on a single contract because he is unsure whether he will also be able to win the other contract. This is often called *exposure* problem, because the bidder is exposed to the risk of winning only some components of a desired package for which the price offered was calculated. Should such risk be perceived as too high, suppliers may be discouraged from bidding aggressively. In this situation, allowing package bidding could lead to much higher savings for a procurement agency.

To evaluate the potential extreme consequences of the exposure problem, consider the following example with two bidders, 1 and 2, and two different lots A and B. Figures in the cells represent the lowest prices that bidders' are willing to accept for supplying the single lots or the two lots together.

	Lot A	Lot B	Package (A,B)
Bidder 1	300	300	300
Bidder 2	100	100	500

As the figures suggest, the two lots are positive complements for bidder 1: due, for example, to substantial economies of scale, bidder 1 can provide the two lots at the same cost at which he is able to provide a single lot. This is the case if, for instance, bidder 1 has a fixed cost of production equal to 300 and marginal cost equal to 0. Bidder 2 can provide each one of the lots at price 100, but because of a binding capacity constraint, his cost for providing both lots is higher than the sum of the costs of producing each single lot. So bidder 2 has decreasing returns to scale in production. Assume that bidders know each other's production costs.

Suppose that, as it is standard in procurement practice, the procurer is buying the two lots simultaneously, asking bidders to place sealed-bids for the lots. Suppose also that bidders are only allowed to bid for single lots, and not for the package of two lots.

Bidder 1, who is the most efficient bidder (for the two lots), could provide the highest savings for the procurer. So the efficient (i.e., cost-minimizing) allocation consists in awarding both lots to bidder 1. However, bidder 2 is willing to bid a price as low as 100 for at least one of the lots. Therefore, in order to be sure to win both lots beating bidder 2, bidder 1 has to offer a price no higher than 100 for each lot. But this is not profitable for him (because the total price he would receive would be lower than his cost of supplying the two lots). So the allocations of the contracts cannot be efficient (even if there is no incomplete information on the costs). As a consequence, bidder 1 may prefer not to participate in the competition at all, which would drastically increase the price paid by the procurer.

This extreme conclusion depends on bidder 1 facing a bidder with sharply decreasing returns to scale. But the exposure problem also arises in much more general contexts. Suppose, for example, that bidder 1 participates in the competitive tendering without any information about bidder 2's costs. Then bidder 1 may be unwilling to offer a price lower than 300 (i.e., his cost of production for one lot) on any single lot, for fear of ending up winning that lot only (and hence having to supply it at a price lower than his cost), in case bidder 2 places a lower winning bid only on the other lot. (Notice that this argument does not depend on the actual costs of bidder 2 and, in particular, on whether bidder 2 has increasing, decreasing or constant returns to scale).

As a consequence, even if bidder 1 is able to supply both lots at a cost of 300, the sum of his bids on each lot may be much higher than that, and possibly not lower than 600. This, again, could increase the price paid by the procurer and generate an inefficient allocation.

8.2.1. Simultaneous ascending auction (SAA)

A simultaneous ascending auction (SAA) is a dynamic auction format that can also be used to partially address the exposure problem (besides the problems addressed in Chapter 6). This format allows bidders to place their offers while observing their competitors' bids and, hence, helps them in selecting which contracts to bid on in the presence of complementarities.

The SAA, developed by Milgrom, Wilson and McAfee, is the format successfully adopted by the American Federal Communications Commission in a number of auctions that, starting from 1994, have been used to sell radio spectrum for mobile-phone licences. The format was also used by various European governments to sell 3G mobile-phone licences in 2000/2001. This auction is very similar to a standard ascending auction (used, e.g., to sell paintings by Sotheby's and Christies), except that several items are auctioned at the same time and bidders can choose which object(s) to bid on. In procurement auctions, the price decreases on each contract independently, but none of the contracts is awarded until no one is willing to bid again on any of the contracts. So the auction only stops when no further offer is submitted on any contract, and each contract is assigned to the highest proposed price discount.

This auction is organized in rounds, with the procurer communicating, at the end of each round and for each contract, the lowest price received and the highest acceptable offer for the next round. Typically, though not necessarily, the highest acceptable offer is fixed by decreasing of a certain percentage the lowest price submitted in the last round. To avoid bidders remaining idle during the auction (because, for example, a bidder may be reluctant to place offers until he first observes his rivals' bids), an activity rule can be introduced. This rule requires a bidder in each round to hold the lowest bid on a certain number of contracts, or else make a new lower bid. This induces participants to bid from the beginning of the auction and reduces the auction length.[1] The activity rule may vary during the auction. For example, to facilitate price discovery when bidders are uncertain about the contracts' values, it may be less strict in the early stages of the auction and tighter in later rounds.

The SAA has many advantages. First, it is a simple and transparent procedure which encourages price discovery. As the auction progresses, bidders can observe the price offered by their opponents' and, hence, they can condition subsequent bids on this new information. And if the contracts to be procured have common and uncertain cost components, a dynamic mechanism such as the SAA better reveals a supplier's private information on this component to his opponents and, therefore, reduces bidders' information rents. This induces more aggressive bidding and allows the procurer to pay a lower price.

The second main advantage of the SAA is that bidders can choose the most desirable subsets of contracts on which to bid, given their opponents' offer. And since bidders have the flexibility to shift their bids across groups of contract when relative price levels change, a supplier can stop offering on a group of complementary contracts he initially intended to obtain if he realizes, as the auction progresses, that he will not be able to win one of the contracts in that group. This mitigates the exposure problem and helps bidders assemble the most desirable group of contracts they can obtain. For example, suppose a bidder considers two contracts to be positive complements (and, hence, is willing to receive a lower price if he is awarded both contracts). The bidder may confidently start bidding on both contracts because he knows that, if the price of one of the contracts becomes too low, he may stop bidding on the other contract too and/or switch to other

---

[1] A further way to keep under control the pace and length of the auction is to fix the daily number of rounds.

contracts that are more attractive at the new prices.[2] Moreover, since during the auction participants can shift their bids across substitute contracts, the final prices of contracts with similar characteristics should be similar.

But although the SAA limits the exposure problem, it does not completely solve it. Consider again the example discussed in the previous paragraph. Assume the procurer is running a SAA auction and the price has reached 300 on each of the lots. At this point bidder 1 may prefer not to bid any further and drop out of the auction because, although he is willing to provide both lots at a price lower than the current total price of 600, he may be afraid of bidding less than 300 on a single lot, in case he fails winning the other lot too. In general, even in a SAA, bidder 1 may fail to bid aggressively for fear of being unable to win both lots and having to take one lot only. The reason is precisely that the SAA does not allow suppliers to place bids on groups of contracts. As discussed above, this may discourage aggressive offers and induce an inefficient allocation.

Two other problems which emerged in running a SAA are *demand reduction* and *collusion*. Demand reduction, which will be discussed in more detail in section 8.3.1, arises when a bidder prefers to bid on fewer contracts than he actually desires in order to reduce competition and maintain high prices on the contracts he is actually bidding on. Collusion is typically easy in the SAA just because of its transparency. Participants may use their bids during the auction to coordinate on a collusive outcome by, for example, signalling their willingness to concentrate on a certain subset of contracts. And since a bidder can observe his opponents' bids, he can detect and punish during the auction another bidder who tries to deviate from a collusive agreement. This reduces the competitiveness of the auction and generates higher prices for the procurer. This theme is the subject of Chapters 14 and 15 and therefore will not be discussed any further here.

8.2.2. Sealed-bid tendering with package bidding

When there are strong positive complementarities between contracts, because of the exposure problem suppliers may be unwilling to bid aggressively, even in a SAA. In this case, the procurer should consider

---

[2] Moreover, to further mitigate the exposure problem, a supplier is sometimes allowed to withdraw a bid, paying a fee equal to the difference between the final winning bid and his withdrawn bid, if this difference is positive.

allowing package bidding. In a package (or combinatorial) tendering procedure, a bidder can make offers conditional on being awarded a specific group of contracts, called a package, as well as for a single contract.

Package bidding has often been used in practice. For example, it has been employed in the assignment of airport slots, in truckload transportation, bus routes and procurement. In the United States, package bidding was also proposed to allocate radio spectrum for mobile-phone licences.

Clearly, combinatorial offers allow bidders to better express their preferences and eliminate the exposure problem because, by only bidding for a package of contracts that he considers complements, a supplier can be sure that he will be awarded a contract if and only if he is also awarded the other contracts in the package. This induces suppliers to bid more aggressively and can lead to lower prices paid by the procurer.

> ### Practical conclusion 1
> Package bidding should be introduced if it appears likely that, for a significant number of bidders, there are substantial positive complementarities among some of the contracts/lots.

We are now going to analyse the specific rules that can be adopted in a combinatorial tendering procedure. In this chapter we will concentrate on sealed bidding. Dynamic package auctions will be analysed in Chapter 9.

8.2.2.1. Vickrey auction in procurement

In a procurement version of the Vickrey auction, the sealed-bid tendering procedure should be such that the buyer asks each bidder to report his production cost, for each contract to be procured and for each possible group of contracts. Then the buyer awards the contracts in order to minimize the total price (i.e., the sum of the winning bids). A winning bidder receives for each contract or group of contracts that he wins a price equal to the cost he declared, less the total (called social) cost for all contracts, plus the total cost for all contracts that would have been paid if that bidder had not been present.[3]

It is the multi-contract Vickrey auction (rather than the uniform-price auction discussed later in this chapter) that incorporates the main strategic

---

[3] Equivalently, the price received by a winning bidder is the difference between (i) the sum of the bids that would win if that bidder does not participate in the auction and (ii) the sum of the other bidders' actual winning bids.

feature of the second-price single-contract tendering competition; namely that, when bidders have private valuations, it is the dominant strategy for them to submit an offer equal to their true cost for each of the contracts, and each group of contracts to be procured (see Chapter 1). So bidders' strategies are very simple and the tender always efficient, as it awards the contracts to the bidders who value them the most. And, since suppliers are allowed to bid on packages of contracts, the Vickrey auction solves the exposure problem arising when contracts exhibit positive complementarities.

It's worth showing the auction pricing rule considering the following example.

	Lot A	Lot B	Package (A,B)
Bidder 1	300	300	350
Bidder 2	250	250	400

If both bidders behave according to their dominant strategy and report their true costs, the procurer awards both lots to bidder 1 (which is the efficient allocation). The total cost of the contracts is 350; while, if bidder 1 had not been present, the total cost of the contracts would have been 400 (bidder 2's cost for the two contracts). Therefore, bidder 1 is paid by the procurer a price equal to $350 - 350 + 400 = 400$.

Given the above considerations, it could be tempting to believe that the Vickrey auction is the perfect solution to purchase multiple contracts because of its remarkable theoretical properties. However, due to its complexity the design is not used in procurement activity. Moreover, like in the single-contract case, bidders may be unwilling to report their true cost to the procurer, because they may fear he will exploit this information in future negotiations. Furthermore, the Vickrey auction may also result in more efficient bidders with a low production cost receiving a lower price for a contract than bidders with a high production cost (which often appears unfair). Finally, it may result in the procurer paying a high price. The Vickrey auction also has the undesirable property that increasing the number of bidders may actually *increase* the price paid by the procurer.[4] For all these reasons, it is probably better for a procurer to consider other

---

[4] E.g., Milgrom (2004).

types of combinatorial tendering procedures, when he has to purchase multiple contracts in the presence of positive complementarities.

8.2.2.2. Sealed-bid tendering with menu (pay-as-bid) package bidding

This is a sealed-bid tendering in which each bidder submits a separate price for each contract or package of contracts he may want to supply. The word menu derives from the fact that packages on which suppliers can submit offers are defined by the procurer who, in so doing, may introduce some constraints on possible bids, a point which is discussed in the following paragraph. The buyer selects the feasible combination of offers that maximises his savings (i.e., minimises the total price tendered). Each winning supplier receives the price he bids for the contract or package of contracts he is awarded. This procurement mechanism has been used, for example, in the London Bus Routes auction.

To understand how this competitive tendering works, consider again our previous example. In a menu package bidding tendering, if bidder 1 knows the production costs of bidder 2, he can place a bid slightly lower than 400 for the package of two contracts, so that it will never be profitable for bidder 2 to underbid him. Then the contracts are efficiently allocated to bidder 1, who has an incentive to participate in the auction. Even if, more realistically, bidder 1 does not know the production cost of his opponent, he is still willing to bid aggressively even in the presence of positive complementarities, because he knows that, by placing a bid for the package of two contracts which is not lower than 350 (his total production cost), he will never be awarded the two contracts at a price which is unprofitable for him, regardless of his and his opponent's bids for the individual contracts.

From a theoretical point of view, this form of competitive tendering has been analysed under the restrictive hypothesis that each bidder knows his opponents' production costs. Its properties under the more realistic assumption that bidders do not know their opponents' costs have not been fully analysed yet. However, when compared to the Vickrey auction, the pricing rule of the menu package bidding tendering is much more intuitive and easier to understand for bidders. Therefore, from a practical point of view, such tendering procedure should be preferred to the Vickrey auction to procure multiple contracts in the presence of complementarities and small, or absent, common and uncertain cost components.

We recapitulate the main considerations made in the following practical conclusion.

Practical conclusion 2
When positive complementarities among contracts are likely to prevail, and common and uncertain cost components are small or absent, favour sealed-bid tendering with menu package bidding.

Example 8.1. Procurement of fresh fruit and vegetables in Italy.

In 2005, Consip, the Italian Procurement Agency for Public Administrations, designed a competitive tendering with package bidding to procure fresh fruit and vegetables for the Public Administration. The end-users of this purchasing service were wide-ranging, as they were from different PA sectors and differed in size and location. Thus, logistics was a major concern for an effective supply execution, which induced Consip to look at the wholesale market as the relevant one when designing the competitive tendering. The Italian wholesale market was characterized by a geographically homogeneous firm distribution, large fragmentation both at the regional and the provincial level, and strong competition. Given the underlying competitiveness of the market, in order to achieve high savings, Consip needed to allow larger players to exploit geographical synergies within the macro-area level. However, the strength of geographical synergies was not clear, and with weak synergies a combination of small local suppliers might have been more efficient. For this reason supply was divided into 24 geographical lots, grouped in 6 macro-areas. Package bids were allowed for these macro-areas, to let large suppliers exploit synergies within such areas and compete against local suppliers bidding on single contracts. Bidding competition was then established and contracts were efficiently allocated to large suppliers, when positive synergies were strong, and to small local suppliers otherwise.

8.2.2.3. Issues with package bidding

Constraints on bids

A distinguishing feature of competitions with package bidding is their potential computational complexity, since even in very simple procurement designs the number of packages to be considered may be extremely high, and the number of bids that suppliers report to the procurer very large. More specifically, with combinatorial bidding the number of offers is an exponential function of the number of contracts being procured: if n is the number of contracts, then 2^n-1 is the total number of possible bids that a participant can submit. So if N is the number of bidders, the number of offers that can be received by the procurer is $N(2^n-1)$. For example, if $N=3$ and $n=4$, the buyer can receive $15\times3=45$ bids. And when the number of contracts increases from $n-1$ to n, the number of possible bids increases by $N2^{n-1}$, namely linearly in N but much faster, exponentially, in n.

It should then be clear that managing a combinatorial tendering procedure can in principle be highly demanding for the procurer, because of the cost of processing a high number of offers and determining the winners. For this reason, the computational tractability of the design could be, in principle, a concern when allowing combinational bids.

These considerations may justify the introduction of an upper bound to the total number of bids that a participant can place. Constraints on bids to reduce the complexity problem can take different forms; in what follows we exemplify few possible ones.

1. If (2^n-1) is the maximum possible number of offers, a generic upper bound, say $n^*<(2^n-1)$, can be imposed independently of where bids are made. The bound can further specify whether offers can all be combinational or not.

2. A limit on bids for packages can be introduced. For instance, if $n=5$, bidders could be allowed to submit at most one offer for each package with 5, 4, 3, 2 and 1 items.

3. A structure of offers, such as the so called 'Sunflower', can be introduced. In this case, bidders may be asked to submit as many offers as they want, but with a unique non-empty common intersection. The idea is simple: with regard, for example, to bus routes, bidders would be asked to identify their most important routes (the non-empty intersection) so that all (possibly package) offers that they make will have to include those routes.

Free-rider problem

With package bidding, suppliers seeking only a single contract may *free ride* – that is, they may prefer to submit high prices, relying upon other participants bidding aggressively. Free riding may allow a package bidder to win the competition even when it would be more efficient to allocate the contracts separately and, hence, it may result in low savings for the procurer. To illustrate the issue, also known as the *threshold problem*, consider the following example with three bidders and two lots. (As usual, numbers represent bidders' production costs.)

	Lot A	Lot B	Package (A,B)
Bidder 1	90	90	300
Bidder 2	90	90	300
Bidder 3	0	0	200

In this example, total savings for the procurer would be maximized by bidder 1 winning lot A (or B) at price 90 and bidder 2 winning lot B (or A) at price 90.

Consider a dynamic reversed auction with package bidding, a generalization of the SAA, and suppose that the following table summarizes the bidding situation at round t, where a 0 stands for no offer having been submitted.

Bids at round t

	Lot A	Lot B	Package (A,B)
Bidder 1	110	0	0
Bidder 2	0	110	0
Bidder 3	0	0	210

Given the current bids, both contracts would be allocated to bidder 3. This allocation, however, would be inefficient and economically unattractive for the procurer.

Bidders 1 and 2 could win the auction, beating bidder 3, by reducing their offers so that the total price for the two lots is lower than 200; but each bidder would prefer the other to bear the cost of doing so. As a consequence, bidder 1 may be unwilling to lower his own offer, if he expects bidder 2 to lower his offer down to 90. In general, to win one of the lots, each bidder may rely upon the other supplier offering a low price, to induce bidder 3 to drop out of the competition. But if none of them lowers his offer, the two lots may end up being assigned to bidder 3.[5]

When the possibility of free riding is a major concern, and if an open auction is not too costly to implement, the procurer should favour the SAA with no package bidding.

---

[5] When the lots to be procured are identical, even if bidders 1 and 2 do not want to *free ride*, they may still fail to coordinate their bids on different lots and, hence, they may induce an inefficient allocation.

8.3. Contracts with strong negative complementarities

As we observed above, supply contracts that exhibit strong negative complementarities are somewhat less common in procurement. They typically arise when suppliers have limited and rigid production capacities, so that their costs are steeply increasing in the quantity supplied, even at relatively low production levels. An example is given by procurement for electricity, where firms have a rigid production capacity that makes it extremely expensive or even impossible for suppliers to extend electricity provision beyond a certain level.

With negative complementarities suppliers prefer to be awarded few contracts. But since bidders are now exposed to the risk of winning more contracts than they wish at a given price, in multi-contract lowest price sealed-bid competitions, where offers made on separate lots are independent, they might bid very cautiously (or not participate at all). Therefore, to encourage entry and competition the buyer should choose tendering processes where suppliers are not exposed to the risk of winning different number of contracts at the same per-contract price. Again, both dynamic auctions and package bidding should reduce bidders' exposure to such risk.

As suggested in section 8.2.1 (for positive complementarities) one possibility would be to choose a simultaneous ascending auction. This would allow observing which lots each supplier is likely to win and take this into account when formulating new bids. Such auction would partially protect suppliers from the risk of being awarded the 'wrong' set of contracts relative to their price bid. However, the implementation of dynamic auctions, such as a SAA, can be too expensive and complex for some procurements, and may facilitate collusive behaviour (see Chapter 14.). If the SAA is too costly, collusion is a problem, and dynamic auctions are not needed for the reasons discussed in Chapter 6, then sealed-bid tendering with package bidding should be considered.

8.3.1. Sealed-bid conditional tendering

When lots are different, a sealed-bid tendering competition similar to the *menu package tendering* procedure described in section 8.2.2.2 is probably the easiest way to reduce bidders' exposure to the risk of winning too many contracts at the wrong price. As discussed above, in a lowest price *menu tendering* competition a bid on a package prevails on the sum of single bids made on the lots underlying the same package bid if the bidder is awarded all such lots in the package. However, while with *positive complementarities* a package bid prevails because of a buyer's savings optimisation, with *negative complementarities* such priority should be made an absolute rule, namely should apply independently of price considerations, in order to effectively 'protect' bidders against the risk of winning too many contracts at the price offered to serve one of them.

The allocation procedure then minimizes the buyer's expenditure taking into account such a constraint, that is, the package bid (absolute) priority.

In this 'constrained' *menu (pay-as-bid) package tendering* bids on single contracts will of course be more aggressive than those on packages of several contracts, which will have the 'insurance' function mentioned above, and the efficient outcome for the procurer will be likely to involve many suppliers simultaneously serving one or very few of the contracts/lots each.[6]

To understand the working of this tendering format, consider the following example with two bidders, 1 and 2, and two different lots A and B. Figures in the cells represent the lowest prices that bidders are willing to accept for supplying the single lots or the two lots together.

	Only A	Only B	(A,B)
Bidder 1	290	320	1,000
Bidder 2	330	370	1,300

In this example supplying both lots for bidder 1 and 2 implies much higher production costs than the simple sum of supplying lots singularly. Then the 'constrained' *menu (pay-as-bid)* package tendering allows suppliers to bid aggressively on each of the lots without running the risk of being awarded both lots at the prices bid for the single lots: by submitting a package bid on lot A and B, bidders can 'protect' themselves against such a risk. Bidder 1, who can offer the lowest price on each of the two single lots, knows that he can bid competitively both on lot A and lot B, whatever his knowledge about bidder 2's costs, since he is aware that, by placing a package bid on the two lots no lower than €1,000,000 (his total production cost), he will never be awarded the two contracts at a price

---

[6] However, this form of competitive tendering suffers for the same problem of the standard *menu (Pay-as-Bid) package tendering* procedure described in section 8.2.2.2, i.e., it has not been fully analysed from a theoretical point of view yet.

which is unprofitable for him, regardless of his and his opponent's bids for the individual contracts.

As the example showed, also in the context of *negative complementarities* the presence of package bidding (but in this case strengthened with an absolute priority rule) reduces the exposure of suppliers to the risk of winning too many contracts. Once eliminated the risk of winning too many contracts, bidders would be willing to compete aggressively on both lots in order to increase the likelihood of winning a contract.

> **Practical conclusion 3**
>
> With negative complementarities, if contracts/lots are not homogeneous, collusion appears unlikely (see Chapters 7 and 14), and the common-cost component is important and uncertain (see Chapter 6), favour SAA. Otherwise, use sealed-bid tendering with menu package bidding.

8.3.2. Homogeneous supply contracts and 'tendering on shares'

When contracts are perfect substitutes for suppliers the negative complementarities are simply 'negative returns to scale', that is, per-unit production cost that are increasing in the supplied quantity. Then only the number of awarded lots matters (not exactly which ones) and a tendering competition with package bidding becomes simpler since it can be implemented by letting each bidder tender a 'supply function' – that is a schedule of prices that depends only on the number of contracts/lots awarded. To see how such a supply function implicitly expresses package bidding, consider how it can be expressed using the same format employed for the example above (where lots were different). Consider the following supply function submitted by bidder 1:

$$B(1) = (200, 500).$$

The supply function is increasing and indicates that bidder 1 is willing to serve the first contract at €200,000 and the second one at €500,000; or, in other words, one contract at €200,000 and two contracts at €700,000. Then, this supply function can be expressed by the table format used above in the following way (remember that lots A and A' are now identical):

	Only A	Only A'	Package (A,A')
Bidder 1	200	200	700

This is precisely what happens in most electricity supply tendering processes (as well as in Treasury auctions for selling government bonds). When lots are homogeneous, there are negative complementarities (decreasing return to scale) and suppliers can submit a whole supply function, the procurer can select the parts of the supply functions of the lowest cost suppliers until total supply equals total demand. When the auctioneer is selling a good, these competitive tendering mechanisms are called 'auctions of shares', hence in our procurement applications we can name them 'tendering on shares'.

The price at which contracts are awarded in tendering on shares may differ. Specifically, if each winning supplier is paid a price equal to his bid for the contract he is awarded, the tendering is called 'discriminatory'; if each winning supplier is paid the same price, the tendering is called 'uniform'.

8.3.2.1. Discriminatory tendering on shares

To illustrate how a discriminatory tendering on shares works, suppose a buyer wants to procure in a single competition five identical contracts/shares/lots for the provision of electricity. There are three potential suppliers and each of them is required to submit his, sealed bid, supply schedule specifying the price at which he is willing to provide each of the lots.

For example, assume that supplier 1 bids the following supply price schedule:

$$B(1) = (150; \ 200; \ 400; \ 700; \ 1{,}200).$$

This means that supplier 1 is willing to provide a first lot at the price €150,000, a second additional lot at €200,000, and so on up to €1,200,000 for the fifth lot. Similarly, assume that suppliers 2 and 3 bid the following schedules:

$$B(2) = (100; \ 200; \ 400; \ 700; \ 1{,}300).$$

$$B(3) = (150; \ 300; \ 500; \ 500; \ 1{,}100).$$

The procurer then ranks all the bids for the single lots from lowest to highest, and awards the five lots to the suppliers who made the five lowest bids. Therefore, in our example suppliers 1 and 2 obtain two lots each and supplier 3 obtains one lot. Each winning supplier receives a price equal to his bid. Hence, supplier 1 receives €150,000 for providing the first lot and a price of €200,000 for the second lot; supplier 2 receives a price of €100,000 for the first lot and a price of €200,000 for the second lot and supplier 3 receives a price of €150,000 for the only lot he wins.

A problem with a discriminatory-price tendering is that suppliers may be paid different prices for lots that are identical. First, this may be considered unfair by bidders and may be a potential source of legal problems, particularly in public procurement. Second, when significant and uncertain common-cost components are present, and bidders are highly heterogeneous in terms of available information, less informed bidders may pay much higher prices than better informed ones, and this risk (of a winners' curse) may induce them not to participate or to bid extremely cautiously.

8.3.2.2. Uniform price tendering on shares

The term 'uniform' refers to the fact that with this mechanism the procurer buys all contracts at the same price, which is determined by equating demand and supply (the price is then equal to the lowest losing bid, or the highest winning bid).

Consider again the previous example with the same set of supply functions tendered (note though that in general the same set of suppliers will make different bids under different tendering rules). After having ranked from lowest to highest all the bids for the single lots, the procurer awards the five lots to the suppliers who made the lowest bids, but now all suppliers are paid for each of the awarded contracts the same price, equal to the sixth lowest bid. Therefore, suppliers 1 and 2 obtain two lots each and supplier 3 obtains one lot, and the 'uniform price' is given by €300,000.

More in general, if the procurer is interested in buying K contracts, the K lowest bids will win and, for each lot, the winners will all pay a price equal to the $(K+1)$st lowest offer.

An important characteristic of uniform-price tendering is that, when the contracts have relevant and uncertain common-cost components, it encourages participation by small and less-informed suppliers. Since the final price is the same for all the assigned lots, and depends on the bids and the information of all winning suppliers, including better-informed ones, less-informed suppliers (like new entrants or smaller firms) are less exposed to the risk of a winner's curse – which is particularly intense when firms are heterogeneous and some of them are better informed – and, hence, are willing to bid more aggressively. For these reasons, less-informed suppliers are also more likely to participate in a uniform-price tendering.[7]

---

[7] Though rather obvious, it is worth remarking again that one should not deduce from the example we discussed that the discriminatory-price tendering is always preferable to the uniform-price tendering simply because in the former each winning bidder is paid a price equal to his bid, which is lower than the marginal losing bid (paid by all winners in a uniform-price tendering). This is because different

The distinguishing feature of uniform-price tendering, that all lots are assigned at the same price, is also usually perceived as fair, since all awarded contracts are perfect substitutes both for the buyer and the suppliers.

8.3.2.3. Unilateral and coordinated demand reduction

With both the pricing rules described, suppliers' exposure problem is greatly reduced, because they can specify the minimum price at which they are willing to supply a given group of contracts. However, a well-known bidding phenomenon that might occur in uniform-price tendering is the so called 'demand reduction', which in case of procurement becomes 'supply reduction'. This arises when participants shift their supply schedule upwards and therefore bid higher prices.[8]

Consider, for example, a buyer offering two identical contracts for electricity provision, and two bidders: bidder 1 is an efficient firm who can supply one lot for €300,000 and a second lot for €300,000 and bidder 2 is a less efficient firm who is capable of supplying one lot for €500,000 and a second lot for €1,000,000. Moreover, suppose each bidder knows his competitor's costs. Bidders' lowest acceptable prices for supplying the single lots or the two lots together are then the following (remember that lots A and A' are still identical):

	Only A	Only A'	(A, A')
Bidder 1	300	300	600
Bidder 2	500	500	1,500

Suppose supplier 2 bids competitively and, hence, offers to supply the first lot at price €500,000 and the second lot at price €1,000,000. Then if bidder 1 too bids competitively (i.e., he offers to supply the first lot at price €300,000 and the second lot at price €300,000), he is awarded both lots and receives the tendering price of €500.000 for each of them, making a total profit of €400,000. However, bidder 1 could do better by manipulating his bid and offering, for example, to supply the first contract at price €300,000 and the second at price above €1,000,000. Because of the uniform price rule, in this case bidder 1 is awarded one lot only, but receives a price of €1,000,000, making a higher total profit of €700,000. Clearly, the strategic behaviour of

designs will induce different bidding behaviour and, in particular, suppliers would be willing to offer lower prices in a uniform-price tendering, which may well yield higher savings for the procurer.

[8] Wilson (1979) and Ausubel and Cramton (1998).

bidder 1 greatly increases the price paid by the procurer, and also reduces efficiency as the second lot is then served by a supplier with higher costs.

In procurement, demand reduction is particularly likely when there is a large supplier among bidders that, by manipulating its supply, can produce a substantial effect on the final price. In particular, a large supplier realizes that bidding aggressively (i.e., close to her production cost for each contract) lowers the price of all contracts that she wins. This induces him to bid less aggressively, which in the case of procurement consists in offering to supply lower quantities at higher prices. This strategic behaviour – that leads to fewer contracts won at higher prices and higher profits – is akin to that of a monopolist, who prefers to sell a lower quantity charging a higher price.

In the example described above, one of the bidders has an incentive to unilaterally manipulate his bid. However, bidders may also find it attractive to coordinate their strategies. In a uniform-price tendering there can also be outcomes that appear collusive, because they induce a price that is much higher than if contracts were sold as an indivisible package. This happens because bidders can implicitly (or explicitly) agree to determine a very high price for the procured contracts, by each submitting very steep supply functions – that is, by both bidding very high prices for a small number of contracts and very low prices for a large number of contracts. This makes it unprofitable for other bidders to try to obtain a number of contracts higher than their collusive share, by deviating from the collusive agreement.

Consider the following example, in which bidders are now symmetric. Figures in the cells represent the lowest prices that bidders are willing to accept for serving the single lots or the two lots together (with lots A and A' still identical):

	Only A	Only A'	(A, A')
Bidder 1	300	300	600
Bidder 2	300	300	600

If both bidders behave competitively (offering for each lot the minimum price they are willing to obtain) they are awarded one lot each at price €300,000. Therefore, they both make no profits. But bidders can do much better by coordinating to manipulate their bids. If, for example, they offer to supply one contract at price €300,000 and a second contract at price €1,000,000, they are still awarded one lot each, but they are paid €1,000,000 each (which is the marginal losing bid), making a higher profit of €700,000. Notice that no bidder has an incentive to deviate from this behaviour and try to win two lots, because in doing so it would reduce the price to €300,000 and, hence, obtain no profit. Once again, this strategic behaviour greatly increases the price paid by the procurer. As a consequence, in a uniform-price tendering suppliers' bids can be much higher than their costs and, from the point of view of a procurer, expected savings can be particularly low.

There is evidence of demand reduction in electricity markets, spectrum auctions, and in experiments.[9] Typically, the presence of a large supplier bidding against smaller firms suggests a higher risk of unilateral demand reduction. Coordinated demand reduction is more likely when suppliers are able to implicitly or explicitly collude.

In discriminatory auctions demand reduction is less of a problem. For example, assume, as in our previous example, two bidders are trying to sustain a 'collusive' division of the lots being procured by bidding a low price for their share of the lots, and much higher prices for the other lots. (This makes it unprofitable for a bidder to try to obtain more lots than his 'collusive' share). In a discriminatory auction, this strategy is much less profitable than in a uniform-price auction, because each supplier is simply paid the price she offers on the lots she wins.

We can now suggest the following practical conclusion, concerning the two formats discussed above.

Practical conclusion 4

With strong negative complementarities and homogeneous supply contracts, if the common-cost component is relevant and uncertain, potential suppliers are heterogeneous in terms of available information and/or participation is a major concern, then favour uniform-price tendering. Otherwise, favour discriminatory tendering.

Both the uniform-price and discriminatory tendering procedures can be easily implemented when the number of identical contracts is very large and their size very small. In electricity procurement (as well as in sales auctions of Treasury bonds) the size of a single contract is typically very small, and this is why the procedures are denominated tendering/auctions of shares.[10]

---

[9] Kagel and Levin (2001), List and Lucking-Reiley (2000), Wolfram (1998), and Wolak (2003).
[10] Wilson (1979).

In this kind of tendering bidders have the opportunity to submit their supply schedule with a very high degree of accuracy, which attracts potential suppliers and helps the procurer in selecting the best providers from a large set of possibly very heterogeneous market suppliers.

8.4. Number of lots, package bidding and participation

When designing a procurement, the buyer must decide the number and size of lots/contracts in which the supply is split (see Chapter 7). The procurer is usually facing many heterogeneous potential suppliers, typically very many small ones, several medium-large sized ones, and a few very large ones. Also, the procurer typically does not know exactly which type of potential supplier is more efficient for a specific procurement, nor the strength of economies or diseconomies of scale and of other possible complementarities among potential lots/contracts.

When positive complementarities are expected to be relevant for larger suppliers, in the absence of package bidding there is a natural tension between lots aggregation, which allows larger suppliers to fully exploit economies of scale, and lots fragmentation, which favours entry by many smaller firms. Note that small firms are often more flexible and innovative, and so may sometimes be more cost effective than large ones, even if they cannot exploit economies of scale.

The flexibility in lots aggregation allowed by package bidding lets the market endogenously choose the optimal aggregation of contracts and scale of supply, at the same time encouraging participation of small potential suppliers and allowing the exploitation of economies of scale. The buyer can greatly reduce the minimum size of contracts/lots, and thereby maximize the number of smaller suppliers otherwise excluded, without hindering the ability of larger suppliers to bid on large sets of contracts in case they are characterized by positive complementarities. This allows all types of firms to express their different competitive advantages and the market to effectively decide who should be awarded the contracts.

Practical conclusion 5
When package bidding is allowed, reducing the size of the contracts to be procured encourages the participation of small firms without preventing large firms from exploiting economies of scale.

Example 8.2. The procurement of road paintings in Sweden.

The Swedish National Road Administration (SNRA) usually awards 50–60 contracts per year for the updating of road markings on national roads and each contract is valid for one year. In 2001, the SNRA implemented a field test applying a combinatorial tendering procedure. There were 8 potential bidders in the market. Two firms were relatively large and operated on a national basis. The other firms were more or less local, operating in adjacent counties only. The main aim behind the test was to make it easier for firms – both SMEs and large firms – to express in their bids the true production costs for various packages of contracts. This would in turn have the potential of lowering the SNRA's costs and increase economic efficiency. The SNRA set bidding rules which made the combinatorial bidding possible, allowing firms to submit offers on individual contracts and on any arbitrary number of contracts bundled at the bidder's discretion. In addition, the SNRA gave individual firms the option to put an upper bound on the maximum number of lots a firm could take on in case it won 'too many contracts'. On average 4.7 bids were submitted on each contract. The SNRA's cost was reduced and the number of firms that won contracts increased. In sum, the result indicates that combinatorial bidding increases competition because, compared to more conventional mechanisms, it allows SMEs to enter the auction lowering the procurer's cost.

Example 8.3. The procurement of telecommunication services in Italy.

In 2002, Consip implemented a combinatorial tendering procedure to procure telecommunication services. Two different lots were purchased: lot A was for fixed telecommunication services and lot B was for mobile tele-communication services. The market was characterized by two incumbents, Telecom Italia and Wind, which were the current providers respectively for fixed and mobile telecommunication services, and some potential entrants, among which the larger ones were Albacom and Vodafone. Furthermore, the two incumbents were active both in the fixed and mobile tele-communication service markets, whereas all the potential entrants were active either in the fixed or in the mobile telecommunication services market. With such bidders, the main goal was to design a tendering mechanism to encourage both participation of potential entrants and the emergence of synergies, if any, between fixed and mobile telecommunica-tion services. Therefore, Consip decided to keep mobile and fixed telecom services as distinct lots, so that Albacom and Vodaphone could participate, and implement a combinatorial tendering design that allowed Telecom and Wind to express possible cost synergies. (For legal reasons the best non-combinatorial offer for the single lot had the preference. Hence, a combinatorial bid could win only if it was the best both in lot A and B.) The design was successful: all four potential participants placed a bid and the threat of a competitive offer by potential entrants pushed the incumbents to offer aggressively. Both Telecom and Wind submitted package bids which were slightly lower than their offers on single lots and which lost to a combination of bids on single lots (because of the rule described above). This revealed that only small synergies existed between the two services.

Bibliographical notes

The theory and practice of multi-object competive bidding has long been focused on how to sell perfectly divisible assets such as state bonds (Wilson, 1979; Back and Zender, 1993). For an exposition to the main themes, such as the exposure and the threshold problems, and results on multi-object competitive bidding see the excellent books by Krishna (2002), Klemperer (2004), Janseen (2004) and Milgrom (2004). The work by Rassenti, Smith and Bulfin (1982) has been pioneer on combinatorial bidding while Rothkopf, Pekec and Harstad (1998) later analysed the issue of computionally complexity. Menu-Auctions, a sealed-bid specification of package bidding, were first introduced by Bernheim and Whinston (1986). For a more general, and recent, discussion on package bidding see Pekec and Rothkopf (2003) and Milgrom (2004). The volume by Cramton, Shoham and Steinberg (2006), is the most exhaustive effort on combinatorial tendering procedures, putting together practical as well as theoretical contributions by economists, computer scientists and operations reasearch experts. Applications of package bidding to procurement are more recent; an interesting and successful example is illustrated in the paper by Epstein et al. (2004).

Bibliography

Ausubel, L. and P. Cramton (1998). *Demand Reduction and Inefficiency in Multi-Unit Auctions*, Mimeo, University of Maryland, Working Paper No, 96–07, July 2002 revision.

Ausubel, L. and P. Cramton (2004). Auctioning Many Divisible Goods, *Journal of the European Economic Association*, 2, 480–493.

Ausubel, L., P. Cramton and P. Milgrom (2006). The Clock-Proxy Auction: A Practical Combinatorial Auction Design, in Cramton, Y. Shoham and R. Steinberg (Eds), *Combinatorial Auctions*, MIT Press.

Back, K. and J. Zender (1993). Auctions of Divisible Goods, *Review of Financial Studies*, 6, 733–764.

Bernheim, D. and M. Whinston (1986). Menu Auctions, Resource Allocation, and Economic Influence, *Quarterly Journal of Economics*, 101 (1), 1–31.

Bonaccorsi, A., B. Codenotti, N. Dimitri, M. Leoncini, P. Santi and G. Resta (2003), Generating Realistic Data Sets for Combinatorial Auctions, *Proceedings IEE Conference on Electronic Commerce (CEC)*, Newport Beach, CA, June 331–338.

Borgers, T. and E. Van Damme (2004). Auction Theory for Auction Design, in Maarten Janssen (Ed.) *Auctioning Public Assets: Analysis and Alternatives*, by Cambridge University Press, Cambridge, United Kingdom.

Cantillon, E. and M. Pesendorfer (2006). Auctioning Bus Routes: The London Experience, in P. Cramton, Y. Shoham and R. Steinberg (eds.), *Combinatorial Auctions*, MIT Press.

Cramton, P., (2006). Simultaneous Ascending Auctions, in *Combinatorial Auctions*, by Cramton, Shoham and Steinberg (eds), MIT Press.

Cramton, P., Y. Shoham and R. Steinberg (2006). Introduction to Combinatorial Auctions, in *Combinatorial Auctions*, by Cramton, Shoham and Steinberg (eds), MIT Press.

Cramton, P., Y. Shoham and R. Steinberg (2006). *Combinatorial Auctions*, MIT Press.

Engelbrecht-Wiggans, R., J. List and D. Lucking-Reiley (2006). Demand Reduction in Multi-Unit Auction with Varying Number of Bidders, *International Economic Review*, 97, 203–231.

Epstein, R., L. Henriquez., J. Catalan, G. Weintraub, C. Martinez, F. Espejo (2004). A Combinatorial Auction Improves School Meals in Chile: a Case of OR in Developing Countries, *International Transactions in Operational Research*, 11, 593–612.

Holzman, R. and D. Monderer (2004). Characterization of ex post Equilibrium in the VCG Combinatorial Auctions, *Games and Economic Behavior*, 47, 87–103.

Holzman, R., N. Kfir-Dahav, D. Monderer and M. Tennenholtz (2004). Bundling Equilibrium in Combinatorial Auctions, *Games and Economic Behavior*, 47, 104–123.

Kagel, J. and D. Levin (2001). Behaviour in Multi-Unit Demand Auctions: Experiments with Uniform Price and Dynamic Vickrey Auction, *Econometrica*, 69, 413–454.

Kelly, F. and R. Steinberg (2000). A Combinatorial Auction with Multiple Winners, *Management Science*, 46, 586–596.

Klemperer, P. (2004). *Auctions: Theory and Practice*, Princeton University Press.

Krishna V. (2002). *Auction Theory*, Academic Press.

Kwasnica, A., J. Ledyard, D. Porter and C. DeMartini (2005). A New and Improved Design for Multi-Object Iterative Auctions, *Management Science*, 51, 419–434.

List, J. and D. Lucking-Reiley (2000). Demand Reduction in Multiunit Auctions; Evidence from a Sportscard Field Experiment, *American Economic Review*, 4, 961–972.

Milgrom, P. (2004). *Putting Auction Theory to Work*, Cambridge University Press, Cambridge, United Kingdom.

Pekec, A. and M. Rothkopf (2003). Combinatorial Auction Design, *Management Science*, 49, 1485–1503.

Porter, D., S. Rassenti., A. Roopnarine and V. Smith (2003). Combinatorial Auction Design, *Proceedings of the National Academy of Sciences*, 100, 11153–11157.

Rassenti, S. V. Smith and R. Bulfin (1982). A Combinatorial Auction Mechanism for Airport Time Allocation, *Bell Journal of Economics*, 13, 402–417.

Rothkopf, M., A. Pekec and R. Harstad (1998). Computationally Manageable Combinatorial Auctions, *Management Science*, 44, 1137–1147.

Wilson, R. (1979). Auctions of Shares, *Quarterly Journal of Economics*, 94, 675–689.

Wolfram, C. (1998). Strategic Bidding in a Multi-Unit Auction: An Empirical Analysis of Bids to Supply Electricity in England and Wales, *RAND Journal of Economics*, 29, 703–725.

Wolak, F. (2003). Measuring Unilateral Market Power in Wholesale Electricity Markets: The California Market 1998 to 2000. *American Economic Review, Papers and Proceedings*, 93 (2), 425–430.

Dynamic auctions in procurement

Lawrence M. Ausubel and Peter Cramton

9.1. Introduction

Procurements for many related items are commonplace. Dynamic auctions have many advantages in such environments. We consider both the purchase of many related items and the purchase of many divisible goods, such as energy products or environmental allowances, or other procurement contracts. In such auctions, the bids specify quantities of each of the items: the megawatt-hours of electricity or the tons of emissions. Often, related goods are – or could be – auctioned at the same time. In electricity markets, products with several durations or locations may be auctioned together. In environmental auctions, emission reductions for each of several different pollutants or time periods may be bought at the same time. This chapter explores how procurement auctions for many divisible or indivisible goods should be conducted. Of course, the answer depends on the objective of the buyer and the bidding environment.[1] Here we focus on a few of the important issues of auction design in a setting where the buyer cares about some combination of efficiency (procuring the goods from the lowest-cost suppliers) and minimization of the payment for purchasing the goods. Our purpose is to motivate a sensible design in a realistic environment, rather than to prove the optimality of a particular design, which would require more restrictive assumptions than we care to make.

One of the initial design decisions is whether to conduct a static (sealed-bid) competitive tendering or dynamic (descending-bid) auction. A frequent

Department of Economics, University of Maryland, College Park, MD 20742, USA. Authors' websites: www.ausubel.com and www.cramton.umd.edu. We gratefully acknowledge the support of National Science Foundation Grant SES-0531254.

[1] As this is a volume on procurement, we will study dynamic auctions to procure, in which the auctioneer is a buyer, the bidders are suppliers, and the price typically descends. Analogous results apply in auctions to sell (i.e., the standard auctions studied in auction theory), in which the auctioneer is a seller, the bidders are buyers, and the price typically ascends.

motivation for the use of dynamic auctions is reducing common-value uncertainty, thereby enabling bidders to bid more aggressively with less fear of the 'Winner's Curse' (see also Chapter 6). However, in the context of buying many goods, the price discovery of a dynamic auction plays another, often more important, role. By seeing tentative price information, bidders are better able to make decisions about the quantity of each good to sell. This is particularly useful because the goods being procured are related. Some may be substitutes; others may be complements in production (see also Chapter 8). Bidding in the absence of price information makes the problem much more difficult for bidders. Furthermore, practical constraints can make bidding in a sealed bid tendering exceedingly difficult unless the buyer allows the bidders to express these constraints in their sealed bids, whereas, in a dynamic auction, the bidder can see tentative prices and assignments, allowing the bidder to make decisions that are consistent with the bidder's constraints.

The case for dynamic auctions is further strengthened when we recognize that it is costly for bidders to determine their preferences. A dynamic auction, by providing tentative price information, helps focus the bidder's decision problem. Rather than consider all possibilities from the outset, the bidder can instead focus on cases that are important given the tentative price and assignment information. Although this point is already valid in auctions for a single good,[2] it becomes more critical in the context of many goods, where the bidder's decision problem is much more complicated. Rather than simply decide whether to supply, the bidder must decide which goods to supply and what quantity of each. The number of possibilities grows exponentially with the number of goods. Determining costs and then bids for each of these possibilities is difficult at best, whereas, in the presence of transparent price information the decision problem becomes relatively more straightforward.

Given the increased importance of price discovery when auctioning many divisible or indivisible goods, we focus on dynamic auctions. The question then becomes: How can the auction designer best promote effective price discovery? For divisible goods, simultaneous clock auctions are both effective and simple. In a simultaneous clock auction, there is a price "clock" for each divisible good indicating its tentative price per unit quantity. Bidders express the quantities they wish to supply at the current

---

[2] See Compte and Jehiel (2002).

prices. The price is decremented for goods with excess supply, and bidders again express the quantities they wish to supply at the new prices. This process repeats until supply is made equal to demand. The tentative prices and assignments then become final. For indivisible goods, the simultaneous descending auction may be preferred, especially if the number of items is large. The simultaneous descending auction is analogous to the simultaneous ascending auction used by the US Federal Communications Commission (FCC) and other countries for selling radio spectrum. The only difference between the simultaneous descending auction and a clock auction is that in the simultaneous descending auction, the bidders specify both a price and quantity for each item they wish to supply. In the clock format, the buyer names prices and the bidders only express quantities at the announced prices.

Discrete rounds, rather than bidding in continuous time, are used in real-world situations which implies that issues of bid decrements, ties and rationing become significant. We argue that this complication is best handled by utilizing "intra-round bids," allowing bidders in each round to express their supply curves along a line segment between the starting and ending price vector for the round. Allowing a rich expression of preferences within a round makes bid decrements, ties and rationing less important. Since preferences for intermediate prices can be expressed, the efficiency loss associated with the discrete decrement is less, so the buyer can choose a larger bid decrement, resulting in a faster and less costly auction process.

Natural linkages among goods often exist in practice. For example, in the case of an auction of electricity capacity, the goods may differ by the duration of the contract (e.g., three months, one year, or multiple years). Such products are natural substitutes: a two-year contract is simply a sequence of two one-year contracts. Hence, the relative prices of such products are closely related. The auction can exploit this linkage by enhancing substitution possibilities across these products.

Market power is a final practical consideration. Although some auction settings approximate the ideal of perfect competition, most do not. The auction design needs to address limited competition. Three useful instruments are information policy, reserve pricing and efficient pricing. By controlling the information that bidders receive, the buyer can enhance price discovery while limiting the scope for collusion. Reserve pricing serves two roles, providing price discipline in the absence of competition and discouraging collusion by limiting the maximum gain from successful collusion. Finally, since uniform pricing inevitably leads to supply reduction,[3] the resulting inefficiency can be avoided by instead using the efficient pricing rule of the Ausubel auction.[4]

We now address each of these issues in detail. Section 9.2 briefly outlines the simultaneous descending auction, which is suitable for the purchase of many related *discrete* items. The remainder of the chapter focuses on clock auctions, which are best suited for the procurement of *divisible* goods. The chapter then proceeds with considerations of practical implementation, treating discrete rounds (section 9.3), natural linkages among goods (section 9.4) and limited competition (section 9.5). Finally in section 9.6 we describe the clock-proxy auction, which is a practical method for procuring many related goods in a package auction.

In the Technical Appendix, we formalize the advantages of the clock-proxy auction.

9.2. Simultaneous descending auction

One of the most successful methods for auctioning many related items is the simultaneous ascending auction – and its counterpart for procurement, the simultaneous descending auction (see also Chapter 8). This auction form was first developed for the FCC spectrum auctions, beginning in July 1994, and has subsequently been adopted with slight variation for dozens of spectrum auctions worldwide, resulting in revenues in excess of $200 billion. The method, first proposed by Paul Milgrom, Robert Wilson and Preston McAfee, has been refined with experience, and extended to the sale or purchase of divisible goods in electricity, gas and environmental markets. Here we describe the method and its extensions.

The simultaneous descending auction is a natural generalization of the English auction when procuring many goods. The key features are that all the goods are purchased at the same time, each with a price associated with it, and the bidders can bid on any of the items. The bidding continues until no bidder is willing to reduce the price on any of the items. Then the auction ends with each bidder supplying the items on which it has the low bid, and is paid its bid for any items supplied.

The reason for the success of this simple procedure is the excellent price discovery it affords. As the auction progresses, bidders see the tentative

---

[3] See Ausubel and Cramton (2002).   [4] See Ausubel (2004).

price information and condition their subsequent bids on this new information. Over the course of the auction, bidders are able to develop a sense of what the final prices are likely to be, and can adjust their purchases in response to this price information. To the extent price information is sufficiently good and the bidders retain sufficient flexibility to shift toward their best package, the exposure problem[5] is mitigated – bidders are able to piece together a desirable package of items, despite the constraint of bidding on individual items rather than packages. Moreover, the price information helps the bidders focus their efforts on estimating their production costs only in the relevant region of the price space.

To further mitigate the exposure problem, most simultaneous descending auctions allow bidders to withdraw bids. This enables bidders to back out of failed aggregations, shifting bids to more fruitful packages. However, we find that bid withdrawals often facilitate undesirable gaming behaviour, and thus the ability to withdraw bids needs to be constrained carefully. It is our view that price discovery – not bid withdrawal – is the more effective limit on the exposure problem in simultaneous descending auctions.

There is substantial evidence that the simultaneous ascending auction design has been successful. Cramton[6] provides a detailed examination of the early FCC spectrum auctions. The auction format performed well on both revenue and efficiency grounds. Although there is less experience with the simultaneous descending auction in procurement, the limited evidence that we do have is promising, and there is no reason to think that the positive results for auctions to sell would not carry over to the procurement context. By revealing information in the auction process, bidder uncertainty is reduced, and the bidders safely can bid more aggressively. Also, costs may decrease to the extent the design enables bidders to piece together packages of items that they can more efficiently supply.

Despite the general success, simultaneous descending auctions have experienced a few problems from which one can draw important lessons. One basic problem is the simultaneous descending auction's vulnerability to cost-increasing strategies in situations where competition is weak. Bidders have an incentive to reduce their supply in order to keep prices high, and to use bid signalling strategies to coordinate on a split of the items.

---

[5] The exposure problem is the problem of winning some – but not all – of a complementary collection of items in an auction without package bids. The bidder is "exposed" to a possible loss if his bids include synergistic gains that might not be achieved.

[6] See Cramton (1997).

We begin by motivating the design choices in a simultaneous descending auction. Then we describe typical rules, including many important details.

9.2.1. Auction design

The critical elements of the simultaneous descending auction are (i) open bidding, (ii) simultaneous purchase, and (iii) no package bids. These features create a desirable competitive process provided (i) items are substitutes, (ii) bidders are price takers, and (iii) bid increments are negligible.[7] Of course, these conditions do not hold in practice. Some degree of market power is common, at least some items are complements, and bid decrements in the 5 to 10 percent range are required to get the auction to conclude in a manageable number of rounds.

Still the simultaneous descending auction does perform well in practice largely because of the benefits of price discovery that come from open bidding and simultaneous sale. These benefits take two forms. First, in situations where bidder costs are positively related, price discovery may mitigate the Winner's Curse and thereby reduce procurement costs.[8] Bidders are able to bid more aggressively since they have better information about the items' costs. More importantly, when many items are purchased, the price discovery lets bidders adapt their bidding and analysis to the price information, which facilitates the aggregation of a complementary package of items to supply.

The alternative of sequential auctions has the effect of limiting the information that is available to bidders and of limiting how bidders can respond to information. With sequential auctions, bidders must guess what prices will be in future auctions when determining bids in the current auction. Incorrect guesses may result in an inefficient assignment when item costs are interdependent. A sequential auction also eliminates many strategies. A bidder cannot switch back to an earlier item if prices fall too low in a later auction. Bidders are likely to regret having sold early at low prices, or not having sold early at high prices. The guesswork about future auction outcomes makes strategies in sequential auctions complex, and the outcomes less efficient.

Almost all the simultaneous descending auctions conducted to date do not allow package bids. Bids are only for individual items. The main

[7] See Milgrom (2004).   [8] See Milgrom and Weber (1982).

advantages of this approach are simplicity and linear prices. The auction is easily implemented and understood. The disadvantage is the exposure problem. With individual bids, bidding for a synergistic combination is risky. The bidder may fail to supply key pieces of the desired combination, but receive payment based on the synergistic reduction in costs. Alternatively, the bidder may be forced to bid below its costs in order to secure the synergies and reduce its loss from being stuck with costly individual items. Individual bidding exposes bidders seeking synergistic combinations to aggregation risk.

Not allowing package bids can create inefficiencies. For example, suppose there are two bidders to supply two items, which the buyer values at $150 for the two items together. One supplier has a technology which can produce both items for a cost of $100, but cannot produce a single item. Thus, it costs her $100 to supply both items, and it also costs $100 to supply just one; the items are perfect complements. The second supplier uses a different technology, which allows her to supply either item, but only one item at a cost of $25; the items are perfect substitutes. Note that the efficient outcome is for the first bidder to supply both items at a total cost of $100. Yet any attempt by the first bidder to supply both is foolhardy. The first bidder would have to drop its bid to $25 on each item in order to be selected to supply both, but then the bidder would be paid only $50 and have costs of $100. The final outcome is for the second bidder to provide a single item at the opening price. The outcome is inefficient, and fails to procure the required items.

This example is extreme to illustrate the exposure problem. The inefficiency involves large bidder-specific complementarities and a lack of competition.

Unfortunately, allowing package bids creates other problems. Package bids may favour large suppliers due to a variant of the threshold problem. Continuing with the last example, suppose that there is a third bidder who has a cost of $60 to supply either item. Then the efficient outcome is for the individual bidders to provide both items, resulting in total costs of $25 + $60 = $85 < $100. But this outcome may not occur when costs are privately known. Suppose that the second and third bidders have placed individual bids of $65 on each of the two items, but these bids are beaten by a package bid of $110 from the first bidder. Each bidder hopes that the other will bid lower to beat the package bid. A reduction of at least $20 is required from the individual bidders. However, the second bidder has an incentive to overstate her costs. She may refrain from bidding, counting on the third bidder to break the threshold of $110. But the third bidder cannot come through, so the auction ends with the first bidder supplying both items for $110.

Package bidding also adds complexity. Unless the complementarities are large and heterogeneous across bidders, a simultaneous descending auction without package bids may be preferred.

9.2.2. Typical rules

The simultaneous descending auction works as follows.[9] A group of items with strong cost interdependencies are up for auction at one time. A bidder can bid on any collection of items in any round, subject to an activity rule which determines the bidder's current eligibility. The auction ends when a round passes with no new bids on any item. This auction form was thought to give the bidders flexibility in expressing costs and building packages of items. Common rules are described below.

Quantity cap   To promote competition in the supply chain, a bidder often is limited in the quantity it can supply.

Payment rules   Often suppliers will be required to post a bid bond or letter of credit, or pass some credit review process. The bid bond and credit review typically define the bidder's maximum eligibility. A bidder interested in supplying a large quantity of items would have to post a large bid bond. The bid bond provide some assurance that the bids are serious. Suppliers are paid at the time of delivery.

Minimum bid decrements   To assure that the auction concludes in a reasonable amount of time, minimum bid decrements are specified. Bid decrements are adjusted in response to bidder behaviour. Typically, the bid decrements are between 5 and 20 percent.

Activity rule   The activity rule is a device for improving price discovery. It forces a bidder to maintain a minimum level of activity to preserve its current eligibility. As the auction progresses, the activity requirement increases, reducing a bidder's flexibility. The lower activity requirement early in the auction gives the bidder greater flexibility in shifting among packages early on when there is the most uncertainty about what will be obtainable.

Number of rounds per day   A final means of controlling the pace of the auction is the number of rounds per day. Typically, fewer rounds per day

---

[9] See Cramton (2006) for more details.

are conducted early in the auction when the most learning occurs. In the later rounds, there is much less bidding activity, and the rounds can occur more quickly.

Stopping rule   A simultaneous stopping rule is used to give the bidders maximum flexibility in pursuing backup strategies. The auction ends if a single round passes in which no new bids are submitted on any item.

Bid information   The most common implementation is full transparency. Each bidder is fully informed about the identities of the bidders and the eligibility of each bidder. Low bids and bidder identities are posted after each round. In addition, all bids and bidder identities are displayed at the conclusion of each round, together with each bidder's eligibility.

Bid withdrawal   To limit the exposure problem, the low bidders can withdraw their bids subject to a bid withdrawal penalty. If a bidder withdraws its low bid, the buyer is listed as the low bidder and the maximum bid is the second-lowest bid for that item. The second-lowest bidder is in no way responsible for the bid, since this bidder may have moved on to other items. If no firm bids on the item, the procurer can increase the maximum bid. To discourage insincere bidding, there are penalties for withdrawing a low bid. The penalty is the larger of 0 and the difference between the final purchase price and the withdrawn bid. This penalty is consistent with the standard remedy for breach of contract. The penalty equals the damage suffered by the buyer as a result of the withdrawal.

We now turn to the clock format for procuring divisible goods.

9.3. Simultaneous descending clock auction

When goods are divisible, such as electricity or emission allowances, the simultaneous descending clock auction yields desirable outcomes. A simultaneous descending clock auction determines the market clearing prices and the suppliers for each product procured. The descending clock auction is an iterative auction procedure in which the auctioneer announces prices, one for each of the products being procured. The bidders then indicate the quantities of each product offered at the current prices. Prices for products with excess supply then decrease, and the bidders again express quantities at the new prices. This process is repeated until, for each product, supply equals demand. This auction format has been used to procure greenhouse gas emission allowances in the United Kingdom and will be used to procure electricity capacity in New England.

9.4. Accommodating discrete rounds with intra-round bidding

Although in theory one can imagine implementing a descending clock auction in continuous time, this is hardly ever done in practice. Clock auctions inevitably use discrete rounds for two important reasons. First, communication is rarely so reliable that bidders would be willing to be exposed to a continuous clock. A bidder would find it unsatisfactory if the price clock swept past the bidder's willingness to provide the good because of a brief communication glitch. Discrete rounds are robust to communication problems. Discrete rounds have a bidding window of significant duration, rarely less than ten minutes and sometimes more than one hour. This window gives bidders time to correct any communication problems, to resort to back-up systems, or to contact the buyer and have the round extended. Second, a discrete round auction improves price discovery by giving the bidders an opportunity to reflect between rounds. Bidders need time to incorporate information from prior rounds into a revised bidding strategy. This updating is precisely the source of price discovery and its associated benefits.

An important issue in discrete-round auctions is the size of the bid decrements. Larger bid decrements enable the auction to conclude in fewer rounds, but they potentially introduce inefficiency from the use of a coarse price grid. Large decrements also introduce incentives for gaming as a result of the expanded importance of ties and rationing rules. But using small decrements especially in an auction with many clocks can greatly increase the number of rounds and, hence, the time required to complete the auction (see also Chapter 6). Bidders generally prefer a shorter auction. A short auction reduces participation costs. A short auction also reduces exposure to price movements during the auction. This is especially relevant in securities and energy auctions for which there are active secondary markets in close substitutes, and for which underlying price movements could easily exceed the price decrements.

Fortunately it is possible to capture nearly all of the benefits of a continuous auction and still conduct the auction in a limited number of rounds, using the technique of *intra-round bids*.[10] With intra-round bids,

---

[10] Intra-round bidding, activity rules, indifference tables, and other aspects of the practical implementation of clock auctions are described in greater detail in Ausubel, Cramton, and Jones (2002).

bidders express their supply in each auction round at all price vectors along the line segment from the start-of-round price to the end-of-round price. In a traditional clock auction, price may decrease from say $11 to $10 in a round, but the bidder is only able to express the quantity it wishes to provide at $11 and at $10. With intra-round bids, the bidder expresses the quantity it wishes to provide at all prices between $11 and $10. This avoids the inefficiency associated with a coarser price grid. It also avoids the gaming behaviour that arises from the increased importance of ties and rationing with coarser prices. The only thing that is lost is the within-round price discovery. However, *within-round* price discovery is much less important than the price discovery that occurs between rounds.

More specifically, with intra-round bids, in each round, the procurer announces a start-of-round price and a (lower) end-of-round price. Each bidder then expresses its supply curve for all prices between the start-of-round price and the end-of-round price. Supply curves are constrained to be increasing step functions: as the price falls, a bidder can maintain or decrease the quantity; the quantity cannot increase in response to lower prices. In every round, the bidder names the prices between the start-of-round and end-of-round prices at which it wishes to reduce its quantity. For example consider an energy auction where quantity is measured in megawatts (MW). Let $11.00 be the start-of-round price and $10.00 be the end-of-round price in round 6. Suppose the bidder's quantity at $11.00 is 800 MW, and the bidder wishes to reduce quantity to 600 MW at $10.63 and to 350 MW at $10.17. Then the bidder's bid consists of two price-quantity pairs: ($10.63, 600 MW) and ($10.17, 350 MW) as shown in figure 9.1. The bidder is offering the quantity of 800 MW for prices from $11.00 to $10.63, 600 MW for prices from $10.63 to $10.17, and 350 MW from $10.17 to $10.00. At each step, we assume that the bidder is indifferent among all quantities between the two end points. Thus, at $10.17, the bidder's bid is satisfied by any quantity between 350 MW and 600 MW.

At the end of the round, the buyer forms the aggregate supply curve from the individual bids. Then, if there is excess supply at the end-of-round price, the auctioneer reports the excess supply at the end-of-round price and a new round begins. Otherwise, the auctioneer reports the clearing price and each bidder is informed of the quantity it is obligated to provide.

Figure 9.2 shows a sample auction, which lasts six rounds. The auction begins with a starting price P0 = $20.00. At the end of round 1, no bidder reduced quantity, so the aggregate supply curve is vertical between P0 and P1. At P1, there is substantial excess supply indicated by the distance

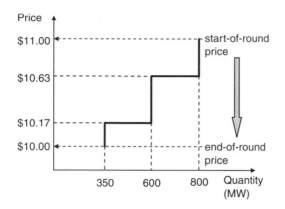

Figure 9.1. Individual supply bid, round 6

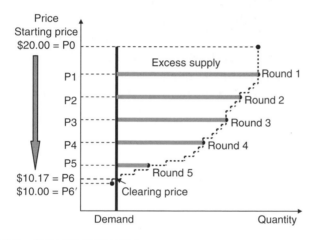

Figure 9.2. Aggregate supply curve

between the vertical demand curve and the aggregate supply curve. In each subsequent round, one or more bidders reduces quantity at prices between the start-of-round price and the end-of-round price, and the excess supply shrinks. As a result of the intra-round bidding, the reductions are at numerous prices and are small relative to the total demand. In round 6, the tentative end-of-round price is $P6 = \$10.00$, but at this price, demand exceeds supply. Thus, the buyer backs up to the price $P6 = \$10.17$ at which supply and demand intersect. The procurer reports that the auction concluded at the clearing price $P6 = \$10.17$.

The experience from a number of high-stakes clock auctions indicates that intra-round bidding enables the buyer to conduct auctions with ten or more products in about ten rounds, with little or no loss from the discreteness of rounds. These auctions can be completed in a single day. By way of contrast, early spectrum auctions and some electricity auctions without intra-round bids took weeks or even months to conclude. In a few extreme instances, the longer duration was warranted due to the enormous uncertainty and extremely high stakes, but generally speaking, intra-round bids would have reduced the bidding costs without any meaningful loss in price discovery.

9.5. Exploiting the natural linkages among goods

The motivation for auctioning many products together is that the products are related. The bidders may view some of the goods as substitutes and others as complements. At the same time, there may be substitution possibilities as to what is procured in the auction. Given the natural linkages among goods, a second important issue in the implementation of a simultaneous clock auction is the amount of flexibility given to bidders in switching across products and to the buyer in the determination of supply.

9.5.1. Bidder flexibility

To promote price discovery, *activity rules* are generally imposed in clock auctions. The simplest clock auction is for a single homogeneous good. There, the activity rule takes the simple form of a monotonicity constraint: each bidder's quantity supplied is not permitted to increase as the price decreases, consistent with upward-sloping supply curves. Without the monotonicity constraint, a bidder might bid as a 'snake in the grass' – grossly understating supply at high prices and then jumping in with large supply near the end of the auction. Widespread use of a snake-in-the-grass strategy would undermine the very purpose of utilizing a dynamic auction.[11] A monotonicity constraint prevents this form of strategic behaviour,

---

[11] One motivation for a bidder to use a 'snake-in-the-grass' strategy is to avoid conveying information to rivals in an environment where bidders exhibit *interdependent costs*. If each bidder's estimate of cost is based in part on rivals' information, one bidder demanding large quantities might induce her rivals to reduce their cost estimates and bid more aggressively. A second motivation for a bidder to use a snake-in-the-grass strategy arises from bidders' limited capacities to provide items. The bidder holds back on bidding for the good she wants most to provide, instead bidding for the goods her rivals want to provide, in the hopes of exhausting the competitors' limited capacities. The bidder then shifts to bidding on her true interests late in the auction, now facing weakened competition for providing these goods.

thus encouraging better price discovery and facilitating rapid convergence to equilibrium.

In situations with multiple goods that have relatively independent supply curves, a monotonicity constraint may be applied independently to each good. However, in situations where the interdependencies across goods are substantial, applying monotonicity constraints independently to each good may be overly restrictive. For example, if two products are close substitutes, it is natural for the bidder to supply the product with the more attractive price. Thus, the bidder may want to decrease the quantity she bids on the product with a faster falling price, and *increase* her quantity on the product with a slower falling price. Such bids would be excluded by the simplest application of monotonicity constraints.

In some applications, identifying and exploiting the natural linkages among goods may resolve these issues. Goods are organized into *product groups*. Substitute goods are assigned to the same group; while complementary goods are assigned to different groups. The activity rule is crafted to permit bidders to freely substitute among goods contained in the same product group. However, monotonicity is applied independently across groups, so that no substitution is permitted between products in different groups.

The quarterly Electricité de France (EDF) Generation Capacity Auctions, the first practical implementation of simultaneous clock auctions, has successfully taken this approach. Broadly speaking, two types of goods are offered: baseload capacity contracts, and peakload capacity contracts. These goods would be expected to be complements, since a new entrant in the French electricity market can best meet the needs of customers with a particular combination of baseload and peakload capacity. However, baseload and peakload capacity are each offered in multiple durations – three-month, six-month, one-year, two-year and three-year contracts, with the same starting date – and the various durations of the same type of contract are close substitutes. Consequently, the goods are organized into two product groups, each containing five products. Since the goods within a group are denominated in comparable units (MW of power), the activity rule applied to all products within a group is simply a monotonicity constraint on the sum of the respective supply curves.[12]

---

[12] As many as five product groups have been offered in some of the EDF auctions. An additional Power Purchase Agreement product has sometimes been offered, in addition to the basic baseload and peakload product. Moreover, in some of the auctions, contracts with different starting dates have been

9.5.2. Supply flexibility

In many applications, the evident substitutability of goods makes it desirable to give flexibility to the buyer, as well as to bidders. For example, financial securities may be bought in a variety of durations, but the only real constraint on the buyer is that the total quantity bought must equal the buyer's total demand. Or energy products may be offered with a variety of delivery locations, but the principal requirement is again on the total quantity bought. The objectives of efficiency and procurement cost minimization are both served by allowing "the market to decide" the demand of each of the substitute products to be procured.

Again, the EDF auctions have successfully taken this approach. As described in section 9.4.1, both baseload and peak capacity are offered in many durations. EDF recognized that different bidders would prefer different durations, but EDF did not have a reliable method for predicting the demands for the various durations other than through the auction itself. By way of contrast, EDF had excellent information about its own willingness to substitute quantities among durations, as a function of price.

Observe that, if both the supplies and the relative prices of the various durations were allowed to be determined endogenously, then the entire system would be underdetermined. Since the supplies were intended to be market driven and since the buyer's tradeoffs on price were well understood, the decision was made that the prices of the various products within a group would be linked together and would decrease in lockstep. (However, the prices associated with different product groups move independently of one another). Before the start of the auction, the buyer determines an *indifference table* expressing the price differentials (i.e., a yield curve) amongst the various products within a group that would make the buyer indifferent between obtaining one product or another. With two product groups containing five products each, there are effectively just two clocks (baseload and peak), and ten prices, with the prices for each product group determined by the clock and the indifference table. The clearing condition is that the aggregate supply for each product group is no greater than the total demand. The bidders then determine endogenously the division of purchases across the various durations, contributing both to efficiency and to procurement cost minimization.

offered as separate product groups. For further information, see EDF's website (www.edf.fr) and the websites listed in the Bibliographical notes.

9.6. Addressing limited competition

In most auctions, competition is limited. Either the number of bidders is small or some bidders are significant in size relative to the auction volume. In these auctions, the auction designer needs to address the potential exercise of market power in the auction design. Three of the most important instruments available to the auction designer are: the information policy, the use of reserves, and the pricing rule.

9.6.1. Information policy

In a competitive auction, price is used to resolve the assignment problem. Those bidders willing to provide at lower cost, get to provide more. However, when there is a lack of competition, a major concern is that bidders will agree on a division of the goods by means other than the auction price.

Most spectrum auctions have used a fully transparent simultaneous ascending auction, in which the complete history of bids (including the identities of the bidders making the bids) has been reported after every round. This has enabled bidders to adopt collusive strategies in spectrum auctions where competition was especially weak.[13]

In clock auctions, a useful information policy for mitigating collusive possibilities is to report only the aggregate supply for the goods after each round. In many situations, the aggregate supply contains most of the information needed for price discovery. If, instead, the buyer revealed the individual supply curves of the bidders, this detailed information could be used to facilitate a coordinated reduction of supply at high prices. For example, the bidders might cooperatively reciprocate the quantity reductions of competitors, and punish those who do not reciprocate by shifting quantity toward products that the non-reciprocating bidder wishes to provide. In order to avoid such possibilities, in all real-world clock auctions of which we are aware, the buyer has reported only end-of-round aggregate demand or supply, and not the individual demands or supplies of bidders.

---

[13] See Cramton and Schwartz (2002), Brusco and Lopomo (2002), Grimm, Riedel, and Wolfstetter (2002).

9.6.2. Reserve pricing

A reserve price is a second important instrument to address limited competition. It does this in two ways. First, it reduces the incentive for collusion by limiting the maximum gain from collusion. Bidders must provide the good at no higher than the reserve price no matter how effective their collusion. Second, the reserve price guarantees that the price paid by the buyer is not unreasonably high, even when competition is weak. Reserve prices are easily implemented in clock auctions. Most commonly, the initial clock price serves as a reserve. Bidders are not permitted to express supply at prices above the reserve.

Alternatively, the procurer can start the auction at a high price but apply a secret reserve. A given product does not clear until the supply is less than or equal to the demand *and* the reserve price (which is not announced) is met. This approach was applied successfully in the September 2003 EDF auction.

More generally, the buyer may wish to adjust demand in response to bids.[14] In a clock auction, a demand adjustment is most easily accomplished by specifying an explicit downward-sloping demand curve. This has the effect of expanding the quantity demanded when there is ample competition, but reducing the quantity demanded (and implicitly introducing a reserve-like mechanism) when there is insufficient competition.

9.6.3. Efficient pricing

The pricing rule is a final instrument to address market power. Most auctions for divisible goods use uniform pricing: all units of a given product are bought at the same market-clearing price. The difficulty with this pricing rule is that it creates the incentive for bidders to engage in supply reduction – bidding a quantity less than true supply at every price.[15] Moreover, the supply-reduction incentive increases in the quantity supplied; larger bidders shade more and smaller bidders shade less. This differential shading creates an inefficiency in which small bidders supply too much and large bidders supply too little.

This inefficiency can be completely avoided in a clock auction by making a simple change in the pricing rule, as proposed by Ausubel.[16] For homogeneous goods, each unit is procured at the price at which it is 'clinched,'

---

[14] See Ausubel and Cramton (2004b), McAdams (2005).
[15] See Ausubel and Cramton (2002).   [16] See Ausubel (2004, 2006).

that is, at the point where it becomes mathematically impossible for the bidder not to be selected to provide the unit. For example, suppose that there are four identical items and three bidders, each offering to supply two units. If one bidder reduces its quantity bid from two units to one, then each of the other two bidders 'clinches' one unit at the current clock price. The clock continues to descend in order to determine the allocation and price of the remaining two units. Under this modified rule, the clock auction yields the same pricing as in the (sealed bid) Vickrey auction, adjusted to procurement.[17] Bidders now have an incentive to bid their true supply curves and an efficient allocation is obtained.

Although the Ausubel auction eliminates the assignment inefficiency created by supply reduction, it does not solve the excessive procurement cost problems stemming from market power. Under either uniform or Vickrey pricing, bidders are paid more when there is less competition. Hence, the other tools – information policy and reserve pricing – need to be used in combination with Vickrey pricing to address the excessive procurement cost problems created by limited competition.

9.7. Clock-proxy auction

In settings where complementarities are both strong and varied across bidders, package bids are needed to improve the efficiency of the auction mechanism. In this section we describe the clock-proxy auction of Ausubel, Cramton and Milgrom[18] as a practical package auction. A typical application is a procurement in which different bidders combine items in different ways. Some pairs of items may be substitutes and others may be complements. Indeed, a given pair of items may be substitutes for one bidder but complements for another, and may change between substitutes and complements for a single bidder as the prices of the other items change. The method combines two auction formats – the clock auction and the proxy auction – to produce a hybrid with the benefits of both.

The clock auction is just as described earlier – an iterative auction procedure in which the buyer announces prices, one for each of the items being procured. The bidders then indicate the quantities of each item that they wish to provide at the current prices. Prices for items with excess supply

---

[17] See Vickrey (1961).   [18] See Ausubel, Cramton, and Milgrom (2006).

then decrease, and the bidders again express quantities at the new prices. This process is repeated until there are no items with excess supply.

The descending proxy auction is a particular package bidding procedure with desirable properties.[19] In the procurement context, the bidders report their true costs to their respective proxy agents. The proxy agents work just like proxy bids on eBay, where a bidder submits his maximum willingness to pay and eBay then automatically raises the bidder's bid as needed. Here proxy agents iteratively submit package bids on behalf of the bidders, selecting the best profit opportunity for a bidder given the bidder's inputted costs. The buyer then selects the provisionally winning bids that minimize costs. This process continues until the proxy agents have no new bids to submit.

The clock-proxy auction is a hybrid auction format that begins with a clock phase and ends with a final proxy round. First, bidders directly submit bids in a clock auction, until there is no excess demand for any item. Then bidders have a single opportunity to input proxy values. The proxy round concludes the auction. All bids are kept live throughout the auction. There are no bid withdrawals. The bids of a particular bidder are mutually exclusive. There is an activity rule throughout the clock phase and between the clock phase and the proxy round.

There are three principal motivations behind the clock-proxy auction. First, Porter et al.[20] describe a particular version of a 'combinatorial' clock auction, and they provide experimental evidence in its support. Second, the recent innovation of the proxy auction provides a combinatorial auction format suitable for related items. Unlike pure clock auctions, whose anonymous linear prices are not generally rich enough to yield efficient outcomes even with straightforward bidding, the proxy auction leads to efficient outcomes and it yields competitive procurement costs when bidding is straightforward. It also has some desirable individual and group incentive properties. However, the theoretical development of the proxy auction treats only a sealed bid procedure, omitting opportunities for bidder feedback and price discovery. Third, the empirical success of the simultaneous clock auction in the field suggests that the clock phase would be a simple and effective device for providing essential price discovery in advance of a final proxy round. During the clock phase, bidders learn approximate prices for individual items as well as packages (summing the

---

[19] See Ausubel and Milgrom (2002, 2006a).
[20] See Porter, Rassenti, Roopnarine, and Smith (2003).

individual prices). This price information helps bidders focus their cost analysis on packages that are most relevant.

The clock-proxy auction has important advantages over the simultaneous descending auction described earlier. The simultaneous descending auction performs well when items are substitutes and competition is strong. The clock phase by itself also does well in this simple setting and, in particular, the outcome is similar to that of a simultaneous descending auction. However, the addition of the proxy auction round should be expected to handle complications, such as complements, collusion, and market power, much better than the simultaneous descending auction. In environments where such complications are present, the clock-proxy auction is likely to outperform the simultaneous descending auction both on efficiency and procurement cost.

9.7.1. Proxy phase

Since the clock phase has already been described at length, it remains to describe the proxy phase. Like the clock auction, the proxy auction is based on package bids. However, the incentives are quite different. The main difference is the absence of anonymous linear prices on individual items. Only packages are priced – and the prices may be bidder specific. This weakens price discovery, but the proxy phase is not about price discovery. It is about providing the incentives for efficient assignment. All the price discovery occurs in the clock phase. The second main difference is that the bidders do not bid directly in the proxy phase. Rather, they submit costs to the proxy agents, who then bid on their behalf using a specific bidding rule. The proxy agents bid straightforwardly to maximize profits. The proxy phase is a last-and-final opportunity to bid.

The proxy auction works as follows.[21] Each bidder reports its costs to a proxy agent for all packages that the bidder is interested in supplying. The proxy agent then bids in a descending package auction on behalf of the real bidder, iteratively submitting the allowable bid that, if accepted, would maximize the real bidder's profit (price minus cost), based on the reported costs. The auction in theory is conducted with negligibly small bid decrements. After each round, provisionally winning bids are determined that minimize the buyer's cost from compatible bids. All of a bidder's bids are

---

[21] See Ausubel and Milgrom (2002, 2006a).

kept live throughout the auction and are treated as mutually exclusive. The auction ends after a round with no new bids.[22]

Two important advantages of the proxy auction over the Vickrey auction are that the prices and procurement costs are monotonic (increasing the set of bidders leads to lower prices) and the procurement costs are competitive. More details about this format can be found in the Technical Appendix.

9.8. Conclusion

A simultaneous descending auction is a powerful tool to procure many related items. When the items are divisible goods, a clock auction format is best. The buyer announces a price for each good, and bidders express the quantities of goods that they wish to provide at the current prices. The prices of the goods are decremented in relation to their respective excess supply. The process repeats until there is no excess supply for any good. At that point, bidders are selected to supply their quantities offered at the final prices.

While the underlying theory utilizes continuous clocks, bidding in real-world dynamic auctions normally occurs in discrete rounds. This, however, does not pose much of an obstacle to efficiency. What is needed is a mechanism for bidders in each round to express supply at intermediate prices between the starting and ending prices. This intra-round bidding enables the efficiency gains of continuous clocks. All that is lost is the within-round price discovery, but this is much less important than the price discovery between rounds, which is retained – and even enhanced – by a pause in the bidding, allowing time for the bidders to update their strategies in light of the new information.

An important element of the auction design is the activity rule, which limits bidding behaviour in a way that is consistent with reasonable economic incentives. This promotes price discovery. In clock auctions for a single good, all that is required is a monotonicity condition – as prices fall, bidders can maintain the same quantity or reduce quantity, but cannot increase quantity. Thus, the bidding must be consistent with an upward-sloping supply curve. With many goods that are close substitutes, such a condition would be excessively harsh. In such auctions, it is best to group

---

[22] See Hoffman et al. (2006) and Day and Raghavan (2004) for practical methods to implement the proxy phase. Further details of the clock-proxy auction are described in Ausubel et al. (2006) and Ausubel-Milgrom (2006b).

goods together that are strong substitutes and impose the monotonicity on the bidder's total quantity within the group. This enables bidders to arbitrage freely across goods within the group. Buyer substitution also can be addressed. For example, the buyer can specify price spreads across goods in a group and only specify the total quantity for the group. The quantity procured of each good within a group is then determined by both the suppliers' and buyer's preferences.

Market power is a final practical concern. This is addressed with three instruments available to the buyer. An information policy is established to limit the bidders' ability to adopt collusive strategies. Reserve prices and demand adjustments are used to limit the incentive for collusion and to guarantee reasonable procurement costs even if competition is weak or collusion is effective. Finally, the buyer can switch from uniform pricing to Vickrey pricing to avoid the inefficiencies created by market power under uniform pricing. When combined properly these three tools can address both the efficiency and procurement cost increases arising from market power.

Although simultaneous clock auctions are new, they have already been applied in high-stakes auctions in many countries. Applications have included electricity auctions in France, the United States and Belgium, gas auctions in Germany, France and Austria, and environmental auctions in the United Kingdom.

For highly competitive auctions of items that are mostly substitutes, a simultaneous clock auction will perform well. Indeed a simultaneous clock auction may be the best approach, as it offers the greatest simplicity and transparency, while being highly efficient.

For more complex environments, we recommend the clock-proxy auction – a simultaneous clock auction followed by a last-and-final proxy round. The basic idea is to use anonymous linear prices as long as possible to maximize price discovery, simplicity, and transparency. The clock phase also greatly facilitates the bidders' cost analysis for the proxy round, because the analysis can be confined to the relevant part of the price space identified in the clock phase. Finally, unlike the simultaneous descending auction, the clock-proxy auction does not suffer from an exposure problem.

With limited competition or items with a complex and varied structure of complements, adding the proxy phase can improve the auction outcome. In particular, a core outcome is achieved. Buyer procurement costs are competitive and the allocation is efficient. The supply reduction incentive present in the clock phase is eliminated. Most importantly, adding the proxy round does no harm: in the simplest settings where the clock auction alone performs well, adding the proxy round should not distort the outcome. The proxy round simply expands the settings in which the auction performs well.

We conclude with the following summary:

Practical conclusion 1

When many items or services are to be purchased, consider
- the simultaneous descending auction if items are not divisible
- the simultaneous clock auction if goods are divisible
- the clock-proxy auction if complementarities among items are strong and varied across bidders.

Bibliographical notes

This chapter is adapted from several of our papers, especially Ausubel and Cramton (2004a). Further materials on the theory and practical implementation of auctions are available on the websites of Market Design Inc. (http://www.marketdesign.com), Efficient Auctions LLC (www.efficientauctions.com) and Power Auctions LLC (http://www.powerauction.com), as well as in the recent books by Milgrom (2004) and Cramton, Shoham, and Steinberg (2006).

Technical appendix

We will see that the proxy auction ends at a 'core' allocation for the reported preferences. Denote the coalition form game (L, w) where L is the set of players ($l = 0$ is the buyer and the rest are the bidders) and $w(S)$ is the value of coalition S. Let x denote the set of feasible allocations $(x_l)_{l \in L}$. If S excludes the buyer, then $w(S) = 0$; if S includes the buyer, then

$$w(S) = \max_{x \in X} \Sigma_{l \in S} v_l(x_l).$$

The Core (L,w) is the set of all imputations π (payoffs imputed to the players based on the allocation) that are feasible for the coalition of the whole and cannot be blocked by any coalition S; that is, for each coalition S, $\sum_{l \in S} \pi_1(x_l) \geq w(S)$.

Theorem 1. (Ausubel and Milgrom 2002, Parkes and Ungar 2000). *The payoff vector π resulting from the proxy auction is a core imputation relative to the reported preferences: $\pi \in Core\ (L,w)$.*

Core outcomes exhibit a number of desirable properties, including: (i) efficiency, and (ii) competitive procurement costs for the buyer. Thus, the theorem shows that the proxy auction is not subject to the inefficiency of supply reduction: no bidder can ever reduce the price it pays for the package it wins by withholding some of its losing bids for other packages. The theorem also includes the idea that the buyer obtains competitive procurement costs: no bidder or coalition of bidders is willing to bid less to supply the buyer's goods. Ausubel and Milgrom (2002, theorems 2 and 14) establish the core outcome result, whereas Parkes and Ungar (2000, theorem 1) independently demonstrate the efficiency of outcomes of an ascending proxy auction without addressing the issue of the core.

A payoff vector in the core is said to be *bidder optimal* if there is no other core allocation that all bidders prefer. If the items are substitutes, then the outcome of the proxy auction coincides with the outcome of the Vickrey auction and with the unique bidder-optimal point in the core. If the goods are not substitutes, then the Vickrey payoff is not generally in the core and the proxy auction yields an outcome with lower buyer cost.

Theorem 2. (Ausubel and Milgrom 2002). *If π is a bidder-optimal point in the Core (L,w), then there exists a full-information Nash equilibrium of the proxy auction with associated payoff vector π.*

These equilibria may be obtained using strategies of the form: bid your true cost plus a non-negative constant on every package. We emphasize that this conclusion concerns full-information Nash equilibrium; bidders may need to know π to compute their strategies.

References

Ausubel, Lawrence M. (2004). An Efficient Ascending-Bid Auction for Multiple Objects, *American Economic Review*, 94 (5), 1452–1475.

Ausubel, Lawrence M. (2006). An Efficient Dynamic Auction for Heterogeneous Commodities, *American Economic Review*, 96 (3), 602–629.

Ausubel, Lawrence M. and Peter Cramton (2002). Demand Reduction and Inefficiency in Multi-Unit Auctions, Working Paper 96–07, University of Maryland.

Ausubel, Lawrence M. and Paul Milgrom (2002). Ascending Auctions with Package Bidding, *Frontiers of Theoretical Economics*, 1, 1–45, www.bepress.com/bejte/frontiers/vol1/iss1/art1.

Ausubel, Lawrence M. and Paul Milgrom (2006a). Ascending Proxy Auctions, in Peter Cramton, Yoav Shoham and Richard Steinberg (Eds.), *Combinatorial Auctions*, Chapter 3, 79–98, MIT Press.

Ausubel, Lawrence M. and Paul Milgrom (2006b). The Lovely but Lonely Vickrey Auction, in Peter Cramton, Yoav Shoham and Richard Steinberg (Eds.), *Combinatorial Auctions*, Chapter 1, 17–40, MIT Press.

Ausubel, Lawrence M. and Peter Cramton (2004a). Auctioning Many Divisible Goods, *Journal of the European Economic Association*, 2, 480–493, April–May.

Ausubel, Lawrence M. and Peter Cramton (2004b). Vickrey Auctions with Reserve Pricing, *Economic Theory*, 23, 493–505.

Ausubel, Lawrence M., Peter C. Cramton, and Wynne P. Jones (2002). System and Method for an Auction of Multiple Types of Items, International Patent Application No. PCT/US02/16937.

Ausubel, Lawrence M., Peter Cramton, and Paul Milgrom (2006). The Clock-Proxy Auction: A Practical Combinatorial Auction Design, in Peter Cramton, Yoav Shoham, and Richard Steinberg (Eds.), *Combinatorial Auctions*, Chapter 5, 115–138, MIT Press.

Brusco, Sandro and Giuseppe Lopomo (2002). Collusion via Signalling in Simultaneous Ascending Bid Auctions with Heterogeneous Objects, with and without Complementarities, *Review of Economic Studies*, 69, 407–436.

Compte, Olivier and Philippe Jehiel (2002). Auctions and Information Acquisition: Sealed-bid or Dynamic Formats? Working paper, CERAS-ENPC.

Cramton, Peter (1997). The FCC Spectrum Auctions: An Early Assessment, *Journal of Economics and Management Strategy* 6(3), 431–495.

Cramton, Peter (2006). Simultaneous Ascending Auctions, in Peter Cramton, Yoav Shoham and Richard Steinberg (Eds.), *Combinatorial Auctions*, Chapter 4, 99–114, MIT Press.

Cramton, Peter and Jesse Schwartz (2002). Collusive Bidding in the FCC Spectrum Auctions, *Contributions to Economic Analysis & Policy*, ,1(1), www.bepress.com/bejeap/contributions/vol1/iss1/art11.

Cramton, Peter, Yoav Shoham and Richard Steinberg (2006). *Combinatorial Auctions*, Cambridge, MA: MIT Press.

Day, Robert W. and S. Raghavan (2004). *Generation and Selection of Core Outcomes in Sealed-Bid Combinatorial Auctions*, Working paper, University of Maryland.

Grimm, Veronika, Frank Riedel, and Elmar Wolfstetter (2002). Low Price Equilibrium in Multi-unit Auctions: The GSM Spectrum Auction in Germany, *International Journal of Industrial Organization*, 21, 1557–1569.

Hoffman, Karla, Dinesh Menon, Susara van den Heever, and Thomas Wilson (2006). Observations and Near-Direct Implementations of the Ascending Proxy Auction, in Peter Cramton, Yoav Shoham, and Richard Steinberg (Eds.), *Combinatorial Auctions*, Chapter 17, 415–450, MIT Press.

McAdams, David (2005). *Adjustable Supply in Uniform Price Auctions: The Value of Non-Commitment*, Working paper, MIT.

Milgrom, Paul (2004). *Putting Auction Theory to Work*, Cambridge: Cambridge University Press.

Milgrom, Paul and Robert J. Weber (1982). A Theory of Auctions and Competitive Bidding, *Econometrica*, 50, 1089–1122.

Parkes, David C. and Lyle H. Ungar (2000). Iterative Combinatorial Auctions: Theory and Practice, Proceedings of the 17th National Conference on Artificial Intelligence (AAAI-00), 74–81, Austin, Texas, 2000.

Porter, David, Stephen Rassenti, Anil Roopnarine and Vernon Smith (2003). Combinatorial Auction Design, *Preceedings of the National Academy of Sciences*, 100, 11153–11157.

Vickrey, William (1961). Counterspeculation, Auctions, and Competitive Sealed Tenders, *Journal of Finance*, 16, 8–37.

PART IV

Attracting and screening participants

10 Pricing and other business strategies for e-procurement platforms

Bruno Jullien

10.1. Introduction

The pace of innovation in information and communication technologies over recent decades had a dramatic impact for the organization of industries. Traditional vertical relationships are now challenged by new forms of electronic intermediation proposed by e-marketplaces, exploiting the possibilities offered by the Internet. Foreseen improvements in reliability, security and process innovation open the prospect for a complete reshaping of supply chain management via e-commerce. According to the European e-Business Report (*e-Business W@tch*) in 2004, and based on the five largest EU countries, 23 percent of firms were buying more than 5 percent of their supply on-line. Eleven percent of the firms were using some e-marketplace for procurement, with leading figures for ICT, transport equipment, chemicals and electronics.

Behind these figures lies a huge diversity of situations, with services ranging from simple search and matching services to fully integrated supply chain management. For instance *eMarket Services* (www.emarketservices. com) describes an e-marketplace as 'an aggregation of information portals, trading exchanges and collaboration tools.' This diversity comes with equally large attrition rates, highlighting the 'winners-take-all' nature of electronic intermediation activities. While there is a high rate of entry, few remain after some years, and the collapse of the Internet bubble is a reminder to all that profitability may not be at the initially expected level. To some extent these changes can be traced back to a drastic change in the cost structure of intermediation, with a huge reduction in the variable costs of information processing. The reduction in costs comes along with a reduction in prices and an increase in the relative importance of scale economies as a driving force for market evolution. This evolution of cost alone cannot explain, however, the key features of the markets for electronic intermediation. A second consequence of the reduction in information processing costs and of the increase in the ability to manage complex systems is that it has created new scopes for interaction. In particular e-procurement allows the elimination of some bilateral relationships between buyers and the intermediary, or suppliers and the intermediary, and their replacement by electronically assisted direct negotiations between buyers and suppliers, in a new mix exploiting the best of intermediation and of direct vertical relationships. This highlights the role of the service as a communication platform as opposed to buy-and-resell services. Indeed most platforms attempt to shape the design of the service to improve the quality of interactions between participants. Increased interactions between buyers and suppliers on e-marketplaces raise the importance of externalities among users of the service to such a level that it becomes crucial for success to understand their role. Indeed the value of communication being the joint outcome of the parties involved, each participant will care about the behaviour of the other potential participants. While this remark is trivial for system designers, it is of great relevance for economic dimensions such as pricing. The reason is that, as prices affect the behaviour of economic agents, there is a potential for using them to induce efficient usage of the service. New marketplaces then design complex pricing schemes with different prices targeted to different activities (membership fees, transaction fees, options) or different actors (buyers, suppliers, advertisers, privileged buyer). Moreover they also rely on non-price instruments such as free services and gifts.

10.2. Two-sided markets and e-procurement

These market developments have brought to the forefront of research in economics the analysis of intermediation services such as e-procurement, auction houses, matching services. These services are part of a broader range of activities that economists include in the concept of two-sided platforms. To build on a definition that I used in another paper, the concept refers to 'situations where one or several competing platforms provide services that are used by two types of partners to interact and operate an exchange.' This includes e-procurement platforms, and also activities as diverse as exchanges, credit cards, shopping malls, dating agencies or operating systems. They all have these characteristics in common: one can identify two sides of the markets, the value creation requires the two sides, and each side can receive a specific treatment.[1] This new perception of the nature of the business is clear from the following statement by Jeff Bezos (CEO, Amazon. com):[2]

'Ultimately we're an information broker. On the left side we have lots of products; on the right side we have lots of customers. We're in the middle making the connections. The consequence is that we have two sets of customers: consumers looking for books and publishers looking for consumers. Readers find books or books find readers.'

While there remains much to understand about these markets, all of which have their specificity, some recent progress has been made by economists in their understanding of their two-sided nature, in particular concerning pricing strategies and efficiency, as well as some other aspects such as bundling, vertical integration and antitrust issues. The object of this chapter is to present some of these results and their implications.

Launching a successful e-procurement service requires solving of classical chicken and egg problem. A downstream firm will be willing to rely on the service for its supplies only if it is confident that it will find an adequate offer. On the other hand securing the offer requires convincing suppliers that their investment in the relationship with the platform will meet adequate demand for their products. The key difficulty is then to start the process, to get one side 'on board.' This calls for specific pricing strategies that differ from strategies followed in more conventional businesses. Before turning to that, it is worth discussing the underlying logic.

10.3. The dual nature of the customers of a platform

Like any other business, platforms sell a service to customers who pay in order to access the platform. However, the nature of the economic transaction involved is slightly different from the more conventional lines of business. In a typical exchange, the consumer is not involved in the production process that is carried on by the firm. The payment then remunerates the firm who buys inputs on other markets. In the case of a platform, the product is the outcome of the interaction between the

---

[1] Clearly, there can be more than two sides involved. Focusing on two sides simplifies the reasoning but the principles apply to multi-sided markets.

[2] Quoted in Leadership Online: 'Barnes & Noble vs. Amazon.com', Harvard Business School (1998), p. 11.

customers of the platform. The traditional distinction between the input of the production process and the output becomes to some extent irrelevant. When two agents A and B use a platform to conduct a transaction, a key service that the platform offers to agent A is the access to agent B, and vice versa. Agent A is thus a customer willing to pay for access to B through the platform, but at the same time, the operator of the platform should be aware that the willingness to pay of agent B is determined by the participation of agent A in the process. Following this logic, a customer of a platform is both a client buying a service and an input for the service offered to other clients.

This dual nature of the customer is key to understanding the specificities of the pricing strategies followed by platform, as well as other business practices such as bundling of services, exclusivity rules, free services, etc. For instance, while traditional monopoly pricing results from a trade-off between increasing the margin and reducing the volume of sales, this is not the case for platforms as we shall develop below. This leads to a different approach to the relationship between the firm and its clients. Instead of just asking 'what can I bring to the client that has some value to him?', the firm should also enquire 'what value can the client bring to other clients'?

For instance, one consequence of this greater interest for coordination with clients is that one should expect more vertical integration for platforms which is indeed the case: there are numerous cases of platforms owned by their customers or by not-for-profit associations set-up by users. For instance *VISA* is a not-for-profit association, members being the banks issuing credit cards; up to 2005, *NYSE* was a not-for-profit corporation controlled by 1366 'regular members.'

10.4. Balancing the tariffs

As we shall see, the price structure has to be assessed globally (including participation fees and transaction fees) and may involve some form of cross-subsidy.

For the moment, let us focus on the total tariff charged to each side to set some general principles. For the sake of clarity think about prices as charged for participating in the platform activity (although one can develop similar reasoning when the tariff is affected by the level of activity). Prices reflect the price-elasticity of demand but also the extent to which the participation of the customer is valued by others. Typically raising the participation of one side through lower prices allows raising the price charged to the other side without affecting its participation level. This has several consequences for pricing.

First considering a non-profit platform, the standard marginal cost pricing rule for efficient usage of a facility does not apply. If the platform set prices for suppliers equal to the marginal cost of servicing them, suppliers will participate up to the level where their benefit equates this cost. However they will not account for the extra benefits that buyers on the platform derive from their participation. In the context of a platform that is not subject to congestion, the consequence is that at prices equal to marginal costs, the level of participation of each side is too low. If this is achievable, the optimal price structure would require setting all prices below marginal cost.

Subsidizing both sides occurs for instance on platforms that are free of charge and financed by governmental organizations, such as *AcquistinRete* (www.acquistinretepa.it), the marketplace set up by *Consip*, that aims at providing goods and services to the public administrations in Italy.

This conclusion reflects the fact that there are positive externalities between participants that must be tempered in general for two reasons. First there may be congestion or other types of negative externalities (for instance suppliers may prefer to face little competition). Second this means that the platform would operate at a loss which implies that it receives a subsidy, usually from the government.

Given that such subsidies generate bureaucratic costs, tax distortions and organizational inefficiencies, an alternative is to rely on tariffs that balance the budget. Still, even for tariffs that balance the budget some price will typically remain below marginal cost. For a budget-balanced platform, it is not the case that each customer should be charged an amount that covers the cost of its participation. The reason is that rebalancing the tariff in favour of one side of the market, thus with a small subsidy, may benefit all participants. Raising the participation of suppliers to the platform through subsidy requires increasing the fees paid by buyers so as to cover the total cost. But they may be willing to pay this extra amount if the benefits they derive from the increase in the participation level of suppliers compensate them for the extra payment. This is similar to other network situations, although here there are different types of customers and it is rather easier to identify the nature of the externality, being participation or usage.

The resulting price structure is thus one involving cross-subsidies between participants.

For instance, *eBay* doesn't charge buyers to participate in an auction. Implicitly this corresponds to a small subsidy (although the variable cost in this case is very small). On the other hand it charges complex tariff to suppliers. The supplier must pay a fee when the good is put to auction which is a non-linear function of the starting price, and a fee once the transaction is concluded which is a function of the closing price. Clearly the business model aims at boosting the participation of buyers by generating only revenue from suppliers.

Let us now point to the fact that the above reasoning applies as well to a for-profit platform with some variation. The key difference is that when considering whether lowering the price for some participants to the platform is profitable or not, the firm will not consider the impact on the welfare of participants but the enhanced ability of extracting more revenue from other participants. But as pointed above, raising the participation level of side A raises also the willingness to pay of members of side B. This can thus be leveraged by charging higher fees on side B. In so far as this increase in profits generated on side B is larger than the reduced benefits on side A, the firm may be willing to sacrifice the revenue on side A. This implies that the profit margins on both sides of the market may differ substantially and not reflect the price elasticity of the demand of each side in a conventional way. Moreover the effect may be so strong that the firm may end up servicing one side with an apparent loss: the price charged will not cover the direct cost of servicing these customers. This apparent contradiction can be explained by noticing that there is an 'opportunity' gain associated with the participation of this group of agents which corresponds to profits on the other side. To build on the discussion of the dual nature of customers, subsidized customers are treated more like input than like buyers: the platform buys their participation and 'resells' it to other clients.

This is in particular the case for free services that are very common. To give an example, *ZDNet* (www.zdnet.com) a leading information portal on information technologies, provides substantive advice and information for free. On the other side it raises revenue from advertising and sponsoring. The advertising revenue is directly related to the frequency of visits to the site, justifying the provision of the service for free. Because frequency of visits is also affected by quality, this provides incentives for *ZDNet* to provide good-quality advice. According to this reasoning, the fact that a service is free is by no means a sign that it is of poor quality.

Such pricing strategies typically occur for platforms that operate in a competitive environment and thus will have low profit margin. But even in the case of a monopoly this may result in some side being subsidized.

Practical conclusion 1

The tariffs must be assessed globally, accounting for the externalities between participants. Efficient price structures involve some form of cross-subsidy between different types of participants and may require pricing below cost for some participants or even subsidizing their participation.

Indeed when looking at platforms in general, there are many instances where it is possible to identify one side of the market as a loss-leader while the platform generates profit on the other side. This is for instance always the case when access to the platform is offered for free to one side.

As a particular case of this general pattern, the platform may wish to attract some customers with direct subsidies, very much like a night club offering not only free entry but also free drinks to women. Monetary subsidies raise obvious issues but, as we shall see below, the platform may offer in-kind subsidies that are tailored to the needs of specific customers. The practice that includes free information services is much more common.

Given that the prices charged to all sides are inter-related, the main question is then to understand which side should be treated more favourably. The answer lies in the reasoning followed to explain cross-subsidies. The intellectual exercise involves evaluation of the impact of rebalancing the tariffs between the two sides of the market. Clearly if side B attaches a large value to an increase in the participation of side A, while members of side A do not care so much, it should be optimal to reduce the fees charged to side A. As a general principle the platform should compare the externalities generated on both sides and set relatively lower prices where they are perceived to be small.

Practical conclusion 2

Favour a price reduction or a subsidy for the side of the market where members are less subject to participation externalities (smaller benefits derived from the participation of members of the opposite side).

This general principle must be pondered by price sensitivity considerations. Indeed when reducing the price on side A, the corresponding increase in prices on side B is directly related to the change in volume of participation on side A. This volume is affected by the price sensitivity of side A. To give an example, suppose that we start from equal profit on each side and that the platform targets a 1 percent increase in participation of buyers. Suppose that this allows raising the profit on suppliers by 1 percent. This is profitable only if the profit on buyers is reduced by less than 1 percent, which occurs when the reduction of the price-cost margin on buyers is less than 2 percent. Thus price elasticity matters. The more elastic the demand the smaller will be the price reduction necessary to achieve a given volume target, and the more incentive there will be to boost the participation of the targeted group. Thus the above effect of externalities may be mitigated if the price elasticity is lower for the low externality side. This is related to but different from the standard analysis of monopoly pricing. In particular this applies also in competitive contexts.

Practical conclusion 3
Favour a price reduction for the side of the market where the participation level is the most sensitive to the fees charged (high price-elasticity).

While the main application of these principles concerns balancing the tariffs between the two sides of the market, it also has implications for differentiated treatments within one side. For instance, if potential suppliers are particularly eager to gain access to a particular category of buyers, then the platform may find it optimal to design special offers targeted to this category.

More generally this points to the fact that customers of platforms will receive much contrasted treatments. E-marketplaces should rely extensively on price-discrimination. Cross-subsidy between buyers and suppliers on the platform is just one and the most obvious form of such discrimination schemes.

Unlike more conventional markets, these price-discrimination schemes need not reflect the exercise of market power and be alleviated by competitive pressure. The reason is that they are motivated by an efficiency concern: they aim at inducing agents to participate for the benefits of other users of the service. This means that unlike other markets, one cannot take the observation of price-discrimination or the fact that some prices are seemingly below cost as a sign that the platform is not facing competition

In traditional output markets, competition puts pressure on prices and tends to align them with costs. Firms will reduce the price of any individual product under the pressure of competitors, and this process will end when their profit vanishes on each product or service, that is, when prices equal costs. This is not true for platforms as they may be willing to incur a loss on one side in order to secure the other side of the market. Thus one cannot treat the service sold to firms using a procurement platform for their supply, and the service sold by the platform to suppliers, as two different services sold on distinct markets. Even if competition reduces overall profit, this concerns the total profit of the platform and this should not result in prices equal to the cost of providing the service, for each individual service.

Indeed as we have discussed above, prices that reflect marginal costs are not efficient because the economic decisions of members of a platform affect the other users of the platform. Typically competition will force platforms to try to offer the best services and to be efficient. But this requires some subsidies, and in a competitive environment one should expect that some services will be sold at prices below costs.

> ### Practical conclusion 4
>
> Competition between platforms raises both the degree of cross-subsidy between sides and the tendency to price-discriminate within sides.

Indeed competition should favour strategies that are referred to in the literature as 'divide and conquer.' These strategies aim at attracting one side of the market through very advantageous conditions (divide) and then to generate revenues by charging high prices on the other side of the market (conquer). The ability to use these 'divide and conquer' strategies seems to create much more scope for competition in a two-sided market than in other more traditional markets with network effects or scale economy. This suggests that even successful marketplaces will remain under strong competitive pressure and that markets for e-procurement may be more contestable than was thought probable at the infant stage.

10.5. Transaction vs. membership fees

While the discussion above focuses on the balance between the two sides of the market, when the pricing instruments are rich enough, one should consider also other types of balancing. It is traditional to distinguish at least two types of fees: membership fees and transaction fees. Membership fees, or subscription fees, are typically paid once, and renewed at regular intervals, and give the right to access the platform. As we shall discuss below, they may also give access to various information services that are not directly related to transactions concluded on the platforms (advice, news, electronic tools). Transaction fees are fees that are paid per effective transaction. These fees can be fixed or proportional to the price at which the transaction takes place. Their main characteristic is that the total payment is affected by the extent of usage of the platforms, measured either by the number of transactions or by the value of transactions.[3]

Here the issue when designing the tariffs is a trade-off between inducing efficient usage of the platform and income. Membership fees affect the size and the composition of the population that will be active during a given period of time on the platform. But for a fixed population of members, they do not affect the activity on the platform. On the other hand, transaction fees affect the activity of members on the platform. When choosing the transaction fees, the platform should keep in mind two things. First rebalancing the transaction fees so as to improve the usage by a customer indirectly benefits the users on the other side of the market. Second a reduction of transaction fees that raises the expected benefits of customers can be compensated by a proportional increase in the membership fee paid by this customer.

This suggests that membership fees are preferable to transaction fees as candidates for raising revenue and balancing the tariffs between the two sides of the market.

Practical conclusion 5
A well-established platform with a stable homogeneous clientele and no competition should aim at designing transaction fees so as to maximize the volume of trade per member and use membership fees as the primary source of profit.

However there are many caveats to this idea. A key issue is that customers may be reluctant to pay up-front a membership fee if they are not confident that the quality of the service will meet their expectation. In this case, transaction fees provide more insurance to the customers, as they anticipate

---

[3] One could add also fees per item put to sell by suppliers, or items put for tender by buyers.

that they will not have to pay if they do not find buyers for their products, or a supplier in case of a tendering firm.

Practical conclusion 6

A platform that needs to provide some insurance to its customers should favour financing through transaction fees and low membership fees.

Notice that insurance needs may be due to the intrinsic nature of the procurement activity of the clients, such as volatile needs, or stem from a lack of reputation of the platform and the fear that the service turns to be of poor quality. In particular, newly established procurement platforms should rely much more extensively on transaction fees than established ones.

As an example illustrating these conclusions, the leading automotive vertical portal, *Convisint* (www.covisint.com) relies on membership fees. But this is not the case of other automotive e-procurement services. *Partsforindustry* (www.partsforindustry.com) is a platform that relies most extensively on volume-related payment. As of September 2005, it charged a 10 percent commission fee on the final price of any transaction plus a fixed fee per item listing (US$ 2.5). In addition the platform proposed options allowing unlimited listing for a fixed period. The subscription may last from one month to twelve months with a degressive subscription fee.

A related advantage of payment systems based on transaction fees is that they give incentives to the platform to generate a large volume of transaction. A client may fear that if he pays only fixed fees, the platform may favour other clients at his expense, either large clients or others paying for transaction. Charging a transaction fee is thus a way to commit to act in the best interest of the client.

A second point illustrated by the example above is that in general the population of clients is heterogeneous on both sides. As we have argued above, price discrimination or targeted offers are normal and efficient business practices for platforms. When direct discrimination is not possible, the platform should rely on indirect mechanisms. An alternative will then be to rely on the flexibility offered by complexity of tariffs on procurement platforms to achieve such discrimination. One possibility for instance is to tie transaction fees to membership fees, but let suppliers choose between several pricing schemes: suppliers anticipating a large volume of transaction may prefer to pay up front and to have low transaction fees, while other users anticipating few transactions may prefer to be charged per transaction. This is a fairly standard practice in industries relying on non-linear tariffs (economists refer to such schemes as 'second degree price discrimination'). In the context of platforms this may be an effective way to raise the level of participation and thus to improve efficiency.

10.6. Bundling and free services

Most information services include a complex mix of services. In particular they usually involve bundling of services. Bundling refers to the practice of selling several goods together in a bundle; it can be pure when goods are only available together, or mixed when the bundled goods are available separately. A particular form consists in forcing consumers who buy a good A to buy also an alternative good B, referred to as tying.[4] Bundling is a common and well-known phenomenon on the Internet that has received considerable attention. One main example has been the emergence of large portals such as *Yahoo* or *AOL*. Notice that a portal like Yahoo proposes a B2C marketplace and an on-line travel agent. An initially very specialized search service like Google is moving toward integrating various activities. Typically e-procurement platforms that rely on membership fees offer a large bundle of services to their customers.

Indeed a typical evolution for e-procurement platforms is to start at small scale and then to extend their activity to become an information portal. For example a service like *Esteel* (www.esteel.com) started as a simple matching service for steel suppliers and buyers into a large scope vertical portal that offers integrated on-line supply chain management solutions to several industries.

The prominence of bundling in information services relates in part to the fact that these services incur very small variable costs. Once a service is designed, the cost is not very sensitive to the volume of usage.[5] Most of the costs of a platform (at least in the short run) are fixed costs. The same is true for adding a service, as once the fixed cost of offering the service is sunk, the variable cost is very small. This means there is very little cost to offer a service to all the population using a platform rather than to a sub-population. In this context, it may be more profitable to offer all the services

---

[4] For instance, recent antitrust Microsoft cases were concerned with tying of various programmes with windows (internet explorer, media player).

[5] For software distributed on-line, the variable cost is close to zero. For platforms there are costs related to computing capacity, congestion and delays, energy.

in a bundle with a single total price, than setting a price per service and letting customers choose which services they want.[6]

More generally it has long been acknowledged that using various combinations of tying and bundling is the way to achieve some form of price-discrimination. For example, suppose that there are two types of suppliers using the platform. The suppliers of the first type are only interested in listing their product to find clients and can manage all the transactions themselves. Suppliers of the second type are also interested in value-added services such as billing or accounting. Suppose that the platform cannot identify the members of each group of suppliers. If both services are sold separately, both types of suppliers will pay the same listing price. By bundling the value-added services and listing, the platform can differentiate the two groups. In particular when the listing price is constrained by a low willingness to pay of the second type of suppliers, the platform can bundle listing and value-added services, and raise the price for listing. The interested suppliers (second type) will buy the bundle, but provided that the price of the bundle remains above the price for listing alone, suppliers of the first type who are only interested in listing will prefer to buy the service alone. Such a mechanism allows the platform to raise its price for the first type of suppliers without loosing the participation of the second type of suppliers.

Ariba (www.ariba.com) bundles buyers' procurement applications ('Spend Management') and access to an e-procurement platform (*Ariba Supplier Network*) with more than 120,000 referenced suppliers. Clearly the initial business model aimed at raising revenue from firms seeking procurement solutions and buying applications. On this platform suppliers have the option between free access and a subscription based service with support and enhanced features, as in the example above. Moreover, until recently access to the platform came as a bundle with *Ariba*'s software. These combinations of value services, price discrimination, and bundles have allowed the building of the network of suppliers and buyers. It allows *Ariba* now to extend its scope: in 2005 Ariba has unbundled the service by launching a service providing access to the network to customers not using Ariba Buyer™ software.

For platforms such as e-marketplaces, bundling may also have a different dimension. As was discussed before, efficient pricing rules for platforms

---

[6] See Bakos, Y. and E. Brynjolfsson (1999), 'Bundling Information Goods: Pricing, Profits and Efficiency', *Management Science* 45(12), 1613–1630.

may require subsidizing some agents. In this context, the ability to offer bundles of information services has several advantages. The first point is that monetary subsidies are very difficult to implement. Typically individuals who do not intend to use the service at all may claim the subsidy so that identifying the right target may be very cumbersome. One alternative is to give the subsidy through the form of a free service provided to members of the platforms. Providing a free service is de facto equivalent to tying access to services and based intermediation services. To the extent that it is only of interest for a specific category of potential users of the platform, and not to free-riders, this may be an efficient way to target a subsidy toward this category. This applies in particular when the subsidy is targeted to one side of the market.

Practical conclusion 7

Offering free services may be used as a means to subsidize the participation of one side.

Second, as we have seen above, the two-sided nature of the market intensifies the benefits of using bundles in order to discriminate between users of the benefits.

Practical conclusion 8

Offering free services targeted to specific buyers or suppliers of strategic importance may raise efficiency or profit, by improving the ability to discriminate and to coordinate the various sides of the market.

Given that the market for e-procurement may be subject to tipping and be rather concentrated, successful e-procurement platforms should devote special care to antitrust issues. Traditional antitrust analysis of tying emphasizes the fact that a motivation for tying may be grounded in an attempt to raise barriers to entry. The firm using tying does not maximize the current profit but this is justified because by limiting entry, it raises its future market power which allows recovering this 'loss.' From this perspective, the current situation need not be viewed as one with dynamic recovering. Costly tying of the services offered to one side of the market is justified for the firm by the possibility of instant recovery on the other side of the market through higher participation rates. It is clearly a competitive tool that should be used by platforms in the contest against other platforms. Moreover it has a rationale in terms of improved efficiency through better coordination between users of the platform. From an antitrust perspective this means that the usual legal standard for exclusionary practices should not apply as such to platforms. The same holds true for predatory tests, as a price below variable cost for some side of the market (violating the Areeda–Turner rule for predation[7]) can be efficient.

Still the treatment of these practices is not settled yet, and platforms with strong market power should use these instruments with caution.

10.7. Incentive issues

Key to success is the ability to design the platform services and tariffs so as to provide adequate incentives to trading partners to contribute and internalize externalities. The degree of satisfaction of a user of the service, say of a supplier, depends on the behaviour of the client it will meet. Typically this buyer will act on its own interest and will not account for the fact that misconduct may penalize the platform, as the supplier may decide to switch to another platform. This 'moral hazard' issue can undermine the functioning of the platforms. In the case of procurement platforms, this may take the form of buyers who cancel orders or do not pay, and of suppliers who do not deliver, or deliver affer a long delay, or with a lower quality than announced.

This issue of poor quality due to a lack of incentives of the partner in a business relationship is probable when the duration of the relationship between the two trading parties is short. Indeed it is known to be one of the benefits of long-term relationships, along with better coordination and investment in relation to specific assets. As moving to an electronic marketplace for procurement may imply a larger turnover of suppliers, these institutions are particularly sensitive to this issue.

Practical conclusion 9
The platform should devote special care in monitoring and preventing misconduct by participants.

---

[7] Noticing that a firm should not rationally price below marginal costs P. E. Areeda and D. F Turner proposed that a price below average variable cost be considered as unlawful, 'Predatory Pricing and Related Practices under Section 2 of the Sherman Act', *Harvard Law Review*, 88, 697–733.

For instance many procurement platforms rely on a code of good practice that goes beyond the mere applications of legal rules.

Electronic marketplaces have been very imaginative in using the new technologies to invent solutions to this problem. The most famous is probably the information feedback system that has been used by eBay. Part of the success of eBay has been attributed to its ability to overcome quality concerns through adequate and innovative information systems.[8]

Another example is presented by *PriceMinister* (www.priceminister.com), a French B2C website. While the transactions are negotiated and concluded by the suppliers and buyers, *PriceMinister* acts as a payment system, receiving the payment from the buyers at the time of the order but releasing the payment to the supplier only after confirmation of delivery. This mitigates buyers' opportunism as well as moral hazard issues on supply delays. Still *PriceMinister* relies on a feedback mechanism with grading by buyers to monitor sellers.

This issue of incentive also sheds light on the role of vertical integration. If a firm owns shares of a platform it uses for procurement purpose, it has more incentives to maintain the profit of this platform and thus to act in the best interest of the platform. Joint ownership by key users of the platforms may help to address incentive issues and improve the quality of the service offered.

Bibliographical notes

For an introduction on the economics of information goods, see the excellent book by Shapiro and Varian (1998). The economic literature on two-sided markets is rather new, with leading articles by Caillaud and Jullien (2001, 2003), Rochet and Tirole (2003), Armstrong (2002). General presentations are provided by Rochet and Tirole (2004a) and Jullien (2005). For a friendly introduction to two-sided markets, see Evans and Schmalensee (2005).

---

[8] eBay has set up a forum where trading partners can grade each other once the transaction is completed and provide comments. Each potential buyer then observes a summary of the grades of the seller he faces, and can access the comments, and vice versa. This works as a reputation mechanism where poor performance of suppliers is penalized through low grades. The interested reader can refer to Dellarocas C. (2004) 'Sanctioning reputation mechanisms in online trading environments with moral hazard', MIT Sloan WP 4297–03.

General pricing formulas for monopoly platforms are derived in Armstrong (2002), Gaudeul and Jullien (2001), Rochet and Tirole (2004a), Jullien (2005). Papers differ in the nature of the interactions and the number of pricing instruments but they are all consistent with the idea of a mark-up over 'opportunity cost'.

Competition between platforms is analysed in Caillaud and Jullien (2003) with a study of usage and subscription fees, in Rochet and Tirole (2003) with a study of usage fees in a model of credit cards, and in Armstrong (2002) with a study of subscription fees.

A good reference for bundling of information goods is Bakos and Brynjolfsson (1999), while tying by platforms is addressed in Rochet and Tirole (2004b). Commitment and incentives of platforms are discussed from a two-sided market perspective in Hagiu (2004).

Selected bibliography

Armstrong, M. (2002, revised 2005). Competition in Two-Sided Markets, forthcoming *Rand Journal of Economics*, University College London.

Bakos, Y. and E. Brynjolfsson (1999). Bundling Information Goods: Pricing, Profits and Efficiency, *Management Science*, 45 (12), 1613–1630.

Caillaud, B. and B. Jullien (2001). Competing Cybermediaries, *European Economic Review Papers & Proceedings*, 45, 797–808.

Caillaud, B. and B. Jullien (2003). Chicken & Egg: Competition among Intermediation Service Providers, *Rand Journal of Economics*, 34, 309–328.

Damiano, E. and H. Li (2003). Price Discrimination in Matching Markets, mimeo, University of Toronto.

Delarocas, C. (2004). Sanctioning Reputation Mechanisms in Online Trading Environments with Moral Hazard, MIT Sloan WP 4297–03.

Evans, D. and R. Schmalensee (2005). The Industrial Organization of Markets with Two-Sided Platforms, forthcoming in W. D. Collins Ed., *Issues in Competition Law and Policy*, American Bar Association, 2005.

Gaudeul, A. and B. Jullien (2001). E-commerce: Quelques éléments d'économie industrielle, *Revue Economique*, 52, 97–117.

Hagiu, A. (2004). Optimal Pricing and Commitment in Two-Sided Markets, mimeo, Princeton University.

Jullien, B. (2000). Competing in Network Industries: Divide and Conquer, IDEI Working Paper 112.

Jullien, B. (2005). Two-Sided Markets and Electronic Intermediaries, *CESifo Economic Studies*, 51 (2–3), 235–262.

Kaplan, S. and Sawhney, M. (2000). B2B E-Commerce Hubs: Towards a Taxonomy of Business Models, *Harvard Business Review*, May–June.

Katz, M. and C. Shapiro (1994). System Competition and Network Effects, *Journal of Economic Perspective*, 8, 93–115.

Pashigan, P. and E. Gould (1998). Internalizing Externalities: The Pricing on Space in Shopping Malls, *Journal of Law and Economics*, 41, 11–142.

Resnick, P. and R. Zeckhauser (2002). Trust Among Strangers in Internet Transactions: Empirical Analysis of eBay's Reputation System, in *The Economics of the Internet and ECommerce*. Amsterdam, Elsevier Science.

Rochet, J. C. and J. Tirole (2003). Platform Competition in Two-Sided Markets, *Journal of the European Economic Association*, 1, 990–1029.

Rochet, J. C. and J. Tirole (2004a). Two-Sided Market: an Overview, *IDEI Working Paper*.

Rochet, J. C. and J. Tirole (2004b). Tying in Two-Sided Market and the Honor-all-Cards Rule, *IDEI Working Paper*.

Shapiro, C. and H. Varian (1998). *Information Rules: A Strategic Guide to the Network Economics*, Harvard Business School Press.

The Economist (2000). Survey on E-Commerce, *The Economist*, 24th Feb. http://www.economist.com/surveys/showsurvey.cfm?issue=20000226.

Fostering participation

Gian Luigi Albano, Nicola Dimitri,
Isabelle Perrigne and Gustavo Piga

11.1. Introduction

Participation in tendering processes is a crucial dimension of procurement. A commonly accepted view is that a large pool of suppliers has to be attracted in order to obtain economically advantageous conditions. The main intuitive reason is that, in most circumstances, a large number of participants induces tough competition which, in turn, translates into high savings and attractive standards of quality. Suppliers, however, differ in various respects. Market shares, access to the credit market, and information on the nature of the procurement contract are just a few dimensions of heterogeneity among them. Thus, if large participation may be *per se* a desirable feature of a procurement tendering process, the final outcome will eventually be affected by the individual characteristics of participants. If only a few large suppliers participate it is likely that they will attempt to reach a tacit agreement to soften price–quality competition. If, instead, the pool of potential suppliers includes a large number of big and small firms, then anti-competitive behaviour becomes more difficult to sustain.

The buyer then faces a double task: attracting a large number of participants and affecting the pool of suppliers in order to stimulate the participation of the most efficient ones in the market. Pursuing the two goals becomes even more compelling when the outcome of the tendering process determines the degree of competition among firms in a downstream market.

The authors would like to thank Vijay Krishna for helpful insights on 'optimal reserve prices', and R. Calandruccio and P. Pacchione of the Energy group at the Italian Procurement Agency (Consip S.p. A.) for useful conversations on the practice of setting reserve prices in energy competitive tendering processes.

One noticeable example is provided by the celebrated 3G spectrum auction that took place in the United Kingdom in 2000. The number of licences was the crucial dimension in determining the number of competitors in the after-auction market. In order to favour entry into a market with four big incumbents, five licences were put up for sale, one of the most valuable of which was reserved for new entrants. Eventually, the presence of new entrants was considered one of the successful features of the UK auction and certainly contributed to fostering competition.

These introductory considerations address the fundamental point of this chapter, namely, whether from the procurer's standpoint more suppliers are always better than fewer and, if so, how the design of a tendering process might facilitate entry and active participation, especially by those potential candidates with characteristics which are of interest for the procurer.

In the ensuing discussion, section 11.2 will elaborate on how some aspects of the design of a tendering process can affect participation. In particular, we will emphasize that when suppliers differ from each other with respect to their levels of intrinsic efficiency then the 'exclusion principle' holds. This principle says that the buyer pursuing the minimization of the awarding price may find it in her interest to set a reserve price at the tendering stage that (i) reduces the expected numerical participation – the number of effective participants is lower than the number of suppliers in the market that could perform the contract – but (ii) induces a more aggressive bidding strategy of participating suppliers. Section 11.3 will further investigate how the buyer's optimal reserve price is affected by several characteristics of the procurement market. Suppliers are often likely to differ with respect to many other dimensions: size, experience as contractors in previous procurement contracts, ease of access to the credit market. In such circumstances the buyer may pursue other objectives than price minimization. Promoting entry of new suppliers and favouring the participation of small and medium enterprises (SMEs) call for the adoption of discriminatory policies in favour of objectively disadvantaged suppliers. These goals are not necessarily in conflict with the minimization of awarding prices as we will see in section 11.4.

11.2. The design of a tendering process and participation

In this section we explore the links between the design of a competitive tendering and participation. In most circumstances, aspects of the design such as the presence and the level of a reserve price, the magnitude of participation costs, the number of supply contracts being procured and the format of the tendering process determine both the level of participation and the characteristics of participating suppliers. In this sense, participation should be generally considered as an endogenous decision by competing suppliers.

The link between design and participation is instrumental in answering a more fundamental question: what are the buyer's most effective solutions in attracting a specific class of participants such as small and medium enterprises, or new entrants, in a procurement market with a stable number of, possibly, strong incumbent firms?

11.2.1. Competitive tendering formats and participation

To what extent does the choice between a dynamic auction and a sealed bid tendering format affect participation? A received view on this is that sealed-bid procedures generally induce higher participation relative to dynamic (descending in prices or ascending in discounts, with respect to the reserve price, or scores) procedures, when participants are likely to be asymmetric. Asymmetry may come from different sources. In oil-lease sale auctions, where the quantity of oil is the relevant (common) uncertain component companies do not necessarily have access to the same information (seismic explorations, drilling samples etc.) before bidding takes place. Similar environments arise in procurement contracts for the provision of food and beverages to public schools, where transportation cost is the relevant (private) component of the contract evaluation. Big suppliers with a larger distribution network bear, on average, lower transportation costs than small suppliers.

Whether stemming from a common rather than a private value component, asymmetries may keep small (weak) suppliers from participating when the format is dynamic. The argument is fairly simple. In a dynamic (say, ascending in discounts) format a weak participant anticipates that the contract will always be won by a stronger supplier and thus he will surely quit the contest at some point, before the auction ends. Indeed in such an auction a strong supplier, upon observing the offer from a weaker rival, can always slightly outbid him and eventually win.

With such a conviction in mind, since participation in a dynamic auction always entails some positive cost on bidders, given by the sum of both organizational expenses and possible entry fees, a weak potential applicant may get discouraged and simply avoid entering the auction. This is because a very low chance of winning the contest would render expected advantages from participation lower than the overall cost.[1]

Sealed bid procedures, instead, generate an element of uncertainty on the final outcome that may benefit weak suppliers. Consider, for instance, a procurement tendering procedure to award a contract for the maintenance of a hospital's central heating and electric equipment. If the contract has already been assigned in the past, it is likely that the pool of potential participants will include some (if not all) of the past winners ('incumbents') and other suppliers ('entrants'). The contract surely involves a firm-specific (private) component in the production costs (individual firm's efficiency in performing the task), but also requires an accurate knowledge of water pipes, electric wires, the structure of the building, etc. Suppliers may be similar as to the private component, but they are not quite likely to be so as to the second one. If at least one incumbent supplier participates, then the latter has access to better information about the intrinsic characteristics of the task. In formulating his offer the incumbent will include a positive mark-up that, however, leaves room for a more aggressive bid by one of the entrants. A sealed bid format does make the outcome of a competitive tendering uncertain by not guaranteeing to strong participants the ability to outbid systematically weaker ones. Such an uncertainty makes the prospect of positive profit rosy even to weak participants, which would render the latter suppliers more inclined to participate.

To sum up, sealed bid procedures appear to be more appropriate than open procedures to favour participation of weak suppliers, without typically discouraging participation on the part of stronger ones. This leads to the following practical conclusion.

---

[1] It should be borne in mind, however, that advantages from participation are not always confined to direct returns (such as the supplier's expected revenue) but also to indirect ones. For example, in a dynamic auction even if a supplier correctly anticipates that his chances to win are nil, he might still want to compete (and pay a price for it) so as to make stronger rivals pay more than what they would have paid had he not entered. As a general principle, however, a participant should be careful not to bid below the expected cost for performing the contract in order to avoid losses *ex post*. To sum up, participation could be justified also when the expected economic costs imposed on the opponents are higher than own costs. Finally, participation by weak suppliers with thin chances of winning could also be interpreted as a way to signal their presence and their willingness to be active in the relevant market.

> **Practical conclusion 1**
> Sealed bid tendering procedures tend to favour participation with to dynamic auctions when participants are heterogeneous in their characteristics or their degree of information regarding the procured good/service.

A remarkable example illustrating the above conclusion is given, once more, by the celebrated 3G UK spectrum auction. When at first it seemed that there were going to be only four licences on sale with four incumbents, Paul Klemperer, one of the UK Government advisors proposed to include a final, sealed-bid session after the first, dynamic (ascending) phase of the auction: the so-called Anglo-Dutch format.[2] In particular, the original proposal for the 3G auction was to allow the first five highest bidders of the ascending phase to make sealed bid offers for the four licences, in the second and final stage of the contest. While the first dynamic phase would help suppliers learn more about the net benefits of the licences, the final sealed bid stage was conceived to have two functions: to countervail possible collusive behaviour as well as to provide new entrants with a concrete possibility of winning one licence, if they could make it to the final stage. The underlying conviction was that such a format would have induced entry of new firms thus enhancing competition among bidders. Eventually, the Anglo-Dutch solution was discarded because licences became five, and a simultaneous ascending auction was adopted (see chapters 8 and 9).

11.2.2. Reserve prices, entry costs, entry fees and financial guarantees

Reserve prices, entry costs, entry fees and financial guarantees represent other dimensions of procurement competitive tendering design that might have a significant effect on participation. In what follows, we will discuss how these aspects can affect the composition of the pool of suppliers willing to compete for a procurement contract.

11.2.2.1. Reserve price

Consider a sealed bid lowest price tendering procedure for awarding a single contract for cleaning services. The buyer has a very high opportunity cost for not awarding the contract. This cost captures, for instance, the

---

[2] See Chapter 6 for more details about the Anglo-Dutch format. Klemperer (2004) discusses in greater detail the design issues raised by the UK spectrum auction.

procurer's option of entering a bilateral negotiation with a well-known, but not very efficient, contractor who does not belong to the competing pool of suppliers. The cost might also capture the possibility for the buyer to organize an in-house supply of the same services. In either case, letting a pool of suppliers compete for the project implies that the buyer will never be willing to accept any bid above her opportunity cost, since she can always discard that price offer and have the project performed at a lower cost. The buyer, although unable to distinguish more efficient from less efficient suppliers, is reasonably confident that suppliers' private costs (measuring their efficiency levels) are all below her opportunity cost. Such a conviction reinforces her decision to set a tendering procedure to award the contract rather than negotiating it with the well-known, inefficient, contractor (or resorting to in-house production).

The buyer publicly announces a reserve price determining the highest acceptable offer (maximum bid), so bids above the reserve price are rejected. Consequently, those firms with production costs *above* the reserve price cannot participate. Should they submit an acceptable bid and win they would suffer losses. Thus any supplier efficient enough to be able to submit an acceptable offer knows that his competitors will belong to a pool of participants with expected costs below the reserve price. While the number and the heterogeneity of the pool of competing firms are reduced, submitted offers are normally more aggressive than in the absence of a reserve price. The simple reason is that the reserve price 'informs' each bidding supplier that his competitors are on average more efficient than what they would be otherwise. Thus each active supplier has to compensate the lower chances of winning, due to more efficient competitors, by submitting a more aggressive (i.e., lower) price offer.[3]

This simple example forces us to add a crucial caveat to our discussion in the introduction on the buyer's desirability of a large participation. From the buyer's perspective, announcing a reserve price makes it more likely that each single firm is unable to participate. However, the degree of competition among those suppliers which do participate is enhanced, thus the buyer expects better economic offers and a lower expected awarding price. Such a

---

[3] Asker and Cantillon (2004) show that an optimal bidding strategy in scoring auctions inherits the same properties of the one in price-only auctions provided that the scoring rule is quasi-linear and bidders' efficiency levels are independent from each other. A quasi-linear scoring rule can be written as $v(Q) - p$, where $v(Q)$ is an increasing function of the quality of the supply and p is the price bid by the supplier.

sophisticated line of reasoning makes us wonder how people in real competitions interpret the presence of a reserve price. A noticeable example is provided by a series of auctions for selling cards from the game *Magic: The Gathering*[4] that were manipulated to modify the reserve price. As a sale, price offers were ascending rather than descending. One of the strengths of such a 'field experiment' was the pool of participants who had heterogeneous demographic backgrounds, but shared an intense interest in the items being sold. They were then valuable subjects for testing the presence of strategic behaviour while competing. Recall that in a sale auction the buyer *reduces* the expected number of valid price offers by *raising* the reserve price. The results of this experiment fully confirmed the predictions just described: increasing the reserve price decreased the number of bids received and the chances of selling the good, *but* increased revenue for cards which were actually sold. Even more interestingly, bidders reacted strategically to the existence of a reserve price, that is, they bid more aggressively when the minimum bid was raised.

It is worthwhile summarizing the nature of the competitive framework we have considered so far. The fixed number of competitors captures a procurement market where entry is basically limited over time,[5] while idiosyncratic private costs are the relevant source of uncertainty (e.g., managerial skills) among firms. Then, by lowering the level of maximum bid, the buyer *lowers* (expected) participation but raises her savings thanks to a lower expected awarding price. The factors affecting the 'optimal' choice of the reserve price will be further investigated in section 12.3.

There exist different circumstances under which the buyer may *increase* participation by simply *announcing* a reserve price. Consider a situation in which suppliers' production cost for performing a contract is affected by an unknown component common to all suppliers, such as uncertainty about the composition of different tasks in the final demand.[6] If uncertainty about the actual production cost is such that inexperienced firms fear they are likely to incur the winner's curse, that is, to realize losses *ex post*, participation may be seriously deterred. However, a publicly announced reserve price may convey some of the buyer's information about the cost of

---

[4] See Reiley (2005) for further details on the game and for a more detailed analysis of the results of the field experiment sketched in the text.

[5] This might be the case, for instance, when specific know-how is necessary in order to formulate a valid offer for the project.

[6] This framework is further developed and analysed in Chapter 6.

performing the contract, thus helping suppliers form a less imprecise estimate of that cost. This may encourage entry, hence participation.

11.2.2.2. Entry costs and entry fees

We turn now our attention to participation costs that comprise entry costs
and entry fees. Entry costs typically include all expenses borne by a supplier
to 'prepare' a bid. These comprise efforts by specialized personnel ranging
from technical staff to lawyers, but also resources spent in estimating the
value of the contract as in the case of geological surveys for oil drilling rights
bidding competitions. Consider first those entry costs that are necessary to
formulate a bid. They exert an effect on participation similar to the one
induced by a reserve price. In this last case, the set of potential suppliers is
divided into two sub-groups: those with an efficiency level guaranteeing
positive expected profits from bidding, and those less efficient suppliers
with production costs above the reserve price. Analogously, when there are
sizeable entry costs, potential suppliers will become *active* participants only
if their expected profit at the tendering stage compensates entry costs. Since
less efficient firms expect on average lower profits than more efficient
competitors, those unable to compensate entry costs will not become active
participants.

Other kinds of entry costs, such as those incurred in obtaining information on the value of the contract, may generate an additional effect on a
supplier's decision as to whether or not to participate. In oil-lease auctions,
the quantity of oil underneath the ground, which determines the value of
the contract, can only be estimated by conducting costly geological surveys.
Before this is done, each potential participant has hardly any idea about the
value of the contract. Investing resources upfront is, however, not sufficient
to estimate the profitability of the lease contract since this depends also
upon the awarding price which, in turn, depends upon the number of firms
that are willing to make similar investments. In such circumstances, a
potential participant becomes uncertain about the number of competitors
that will *eventually* submit an offer. Thus, proceeding with the analogy,
while the introduction of a reserve price makes it less likely that each
potential participant is efficient enough to participate, the reserve price itself
allows each participant to estimate the level of efficiency and aggressiveness
of those who *will* participate.

Such estimates however become even more imprecise when entry costs
have to be borne for obtaining information about the value of the contract.
In this case each participant, before deciding whether or not to bear such

costs, has to evaluate several scenarios that differ with respect to the number of competitors who have paid similar costs and have become active participants.

Participation costs may also include entry fees, namely a non-refundable payment due to the buyer that allows potential suppliers to submit their bids. Each potential participant will be willing to submit a bid if his efficiency level guarantees expected profit high enough to compensate the amount paid to the buyer. Entry fees then cut off all potential participants whose production costs are above a threshold value.

Participation costs (e.g., entry fees and entry costs in the form of expenses to prepare a bid) and reserve price have a similar effect on participation. However, there are substantial differences that are worth emphasizing. First, entry fees consist in payments from the participants to the buyer while entry costs are simply deadweight losses. A reserve price does not directly affect participants' profit although there is an indirect effect since participants become more aggressive than in the absence of a reserve price, thus they expect lower profit. Second, participation costs differ from a reserve price with respect to the consequences arising after competition for the contract has taken place.

Suppose that a small supplier has borne sizeable organizational costs to submit his bid, but discovers he has not been awarded the contract. This supplier, together with all other losers, will suffer losses *ex post*, although all of them expected positive profits before submitting their bids. When participation costs are negligible a losing supplier suffers no loss if the buyer has introduced a reserve price. A losing supplier is basically as well off before the competitive tendering as after it. Losses due to the presence of either entry costs or entry fees, although sunk once competition is over, may have a dramatic impact on participation in *future* procurement tendering contests. Small and medium enterprises that bear substantial participation costs but hardly win any contract may decide, at some point, to exit the procurement market.

Whenever participation is viewed in a dynamic perspective, considerable entry costs and entry fees may have a potentially dangerous drawback. The possibility that some small suppliers leave the procurement market may justify, whenever possible, reduction of entry costs and entry fees to enhance long-term competition by sustaining participation. Since e-procurement often reduces participation costs, it could be part of a policy fostering participation. This issue will be further developed in section 11.4.

We conclude this section with a brief discussion on the role of financial collaterals. Financial deposits, and more in general guarantees, are normally used by procurers to screen financially solid and reliable suppliers. These deposits typically constrain the amount of financial resources that suppliers can allocate to the competitive tendering. Financial deposits may be assimilated to entry fees, but some of their features require a brief separate discussion.

Financial deposits, whenever requested, could both prove a supplier's reliability and represent a signal of commitment. In procurement markets, they are frequently used to prevent phenomena such as abnormally low bids submitted by suppliers who may find themselves in financial distress.[7] If one of these suppliers is able to win the contract he would try to renegotiate with the buyer better contractual clauses in order to remain afloat in the market. This may happen thanks to managers' limited liabilities, and the buyer's potentially high costs for replacing the contractor who does not carry out the agreed performance. While reducing the risk of abnormally low bids, financial collaterals may reduce the participation of SMEs since they normally suffer from a limited access to the credit market relative to bigger suppliers.

The discussion developed so far leads us to formulate the following

Practical conclusion 2

Reserve prices, entry costs and entry fees typically reduce expected numerical participation, generally enhance the intensity of price competition among those suppliers who decide to participate, and may lower the expected awarding price in a single competitive tendering.

The buyer should, however, adopt effective policies to reduce entry fees and entry costs as they may seriously hamper the participation of small firms when competitive procurement is repeated over time.

11.2.2.3. Number of contracts-lots

Although most of the issues concerning single vs. multi-contract tendering have already been touched upon in Chapters 7 and 8, we focus here on the relationship between the number of lots and participation. Contracts normally differ under a variety of perspectives such as quantity, geographical location and nature of products. In procurement, contracts typically refer to

---

[7] This seems to be a recurrent problem in the construction industry. See Chapter 13 for more on this.

the same type of product and may differ according to geographical location and/or quantity.

We start with the simple consideration that, for a given value of the procurement contract, the higher the number of lots, say geographical lots, the higher the expected number of participants. The immediate argument is that a higher number of small suppliers will possess the capacity of performing the contract in a specific lot (i.e., a specific geographical area). There exist, however, circumstances under which raising the number of lots alone may not increase participation. This may happen when the production cost for performing the contract has a component which is common to all suppliers, but is unknown to them at the time of the competitive bidding. For instance, the contract comprises low- and high-cost tasks, but their relative weight in the final demand is not known in advance. Incumbent suppliers, that is, those who have been active in related procurement contracts in the past, are likely to be more informed on the common uncertainty than those suppliers participating for the first time. Incumbent suppliers are then in a position to bid more accurately than entrants, thus the latter suppliers, especially the smallest ones, may be discouraged from entering even if the buyer divides the contracts in a higher number of lots. Participation might be increased if the buyer releases valuable information on the composition of the final demand so as to 'level the playing field' between incumbents and new entrants.

We finally observe that there exists another exception to the positive relationship between the number of lots and participation. In certain sectors the number of qualified bidders is limited, so increasing the number of lots beyond a certain threshold cannot increase participation and actually even induce, in some cases, greater collusion.[8] For example, the fragmentation of contracts in high number of lots in the pharmaceutical industry is not likely to increase participation in a competitive tendering, at least in the short run.

Practical conclusion 3

In many circumstances, the higher the number of contracts/lots the higher participation in a competitive tendering.

---

[8] See Chapter 7 on the relationship between the number of lots and the risk of collusion among suppliers.

11.3. Optimal reserve price

In the previous section we have emphasized that the buyer's adoption of a reserve price generates two opposite effects. It makes it more likely that each single supplier is unable to participate. However, the degree of competition among those suppliers which do participate is enhanced, thus the buyer expects better economic offers and a lower expected awarding price.

The aim of the current section is to investigate what factors influence the buyer's choice of the 'optimal' reserve price. Optimality requires the exact specification of a goal to be pursued. Here, we proceed by assuming that the buyer's main motivation is to minimize the expected cost for performing the contract. In public procurements, this seems a reasonable assumption. Nonetheless, the buyer may face other constraints such as political constraints when the contract has to be allocated to a local supplier because of employment issues or time limits when the contract has to be allocated in a short period of time. These constraints may invalidate some of the practical conclusions we are going to derive. There are also other competitive tendering processes such as the sequential and the multi-unit ones as well as other downstream interactions among suppliers, as the case of subcontracting, for which the buyer's optimal reserve price policy is yet unknown. Hence, we will highlight those circumstances under which we are in a position to derive robust guidelines for a public procurer or a private company.

The basic idea of an optimal reserve price is a trade-off between foregone transactions because of a low reserve price and gains from increased pressure on bidders to extract their rents.[9] The exact computation of the optimal reserve price would require the knowledge of the underlying distribution of the suppliers' efficiency levels (that are crucial in determining production costs), and other idiosyncratic characteristics of the same suppliers. In general, the buyer may have a rough idea of the degree of heterogeneity of suppliers in terms of efficiency, but she is very unlikely to be able to draw a precise distribution of suppliers' efficiency levels. This makes in principle the computation of the optimal reserve price a difficult task.

Recent developments of statistical techniques have, however, made feasible such a computation.[10] For instance, the buyer could now use data

---

[9] This section mainly relies on the excellent review of auction theory by Krishna (2002).
[10] See Guerre, Perrigne and Vuong (2000).

(i.e., bids) from previous similar procurement contests to compute the optimal reserve price.[11] These methods are now being integrated in some decision tool packages. Any firm interested in participating in or designing itself a competitive tendering process needs to enter a few parameters concerning the procurement environment, and the package will provide an optimal reserve price and the estimated probability of not concluding the transaction, that is, the chances that all tenders will be higher than the reserve price. Nonetheless, these packages are expensive and require some computer skills.

As explained above, the buyer finds it profitable to exclude high-cost firms from the procurement process. In order to achieve this objective[12] the procurer sets the reserve price at a value below her opportunity cost to perform the contract. One of the most celebrated results in the economic analysis of competitive procurement is that the optimal reserve price does not depend on the number of suppliers when suppliers' efficiency levels are firm-specific, that is, independent from each other. Hence, the buyer need not worry about the number of active suppliers in the procurement market since this information does not enter the relevant computation.

This result is no longer valid when some correlation, or more generally dependence across suppliers' costs, is expected. Consider, for instance, a group of suppliers assembling computers and providing a helpdesk service. The cost of performing the contract comprises the costs of computers' components and those for setting up and running the helpdesk service. It is reasonable to expect that suppliers do not know the helpdesk-related costs since these depend upon the final users' computer skills, although suppliers may get an estimate by looking at earlier similar contracts. In this scenario, suppliers' production costs are certainly correlated. With such a dependence (or correlation), it is unclear how the optimal reserve price should vary with the number of participants though some results suggest that it should increase with the number of suppliers in the relevant procurement market. When this dependence is strong it is then optimal for the procurer to adopt a less aggressive strategy with the reserve price, namely to set it at a level equal to her opportunity cost. The exclusion principle, defined in the introduction, holds because the gain on bids from having a lower reserve price outweighs the foregone transactions. This is due to the difference in value between the lowest and the second-lowest cost. With a strong

---

[11] This is explored in Li, Perrigne and Vuong (2003).
[12] Financial guarantees, which are widely used in procurements, can play a similar role.

dependence among suppliers' costs, this difference becomes very small, leaving little room for an optimal reserve price lower than the buyer's opportunity cost.

Practical conclusion 4

It is optimal for the buyer to set a reserve price below his opportunity cost when suppliers' costs can be considered independent from each other. If suppliers' costs are expected to be dependent the optimal reserve price tends toward the buyer's opportunity cost.

Consider now a procurement environment where suppliers' production costs are significantly affected by a common component, that is, the *ex post* cost for performing the contract is unknown to suppliers at the time of the competitive tendering and this cost is expected to be the same whatever the contractor's identity. As we explain in more detail in chapter 6, this situation typically arises when the procurement contract comprises high-cost tasks (such as cleaning medical laboratories) and low-cost tasks (such as cleaning large halls), but suppliers do not know the weight of each task in the final demand.[13] In such circumstances the optimal reserve price is higher than in the environment where suppliers only differ with respect to the private component of production costs.[14] The reason is quite simple. In a common value environment, winning the competitive tendering reveals some 'bad news' as it is likely that the winner underestimates the real cost for performing the job. This effect is known as the winner's curse.[15] To correct for the winner's curse, competing suppliers need to adjust their bids upward. The optimal reserve price follows the same strategy. Indeed, a strong common component in the suppliers' production costs is equivalent to a strong correlation among suppliers' costs. Thus we can exploit the discussion preceding practical conclusion 4 to derive the next conclusion.

Practical conclusion 5

When some common value is expected in the competitive tendering, the reserve price should be set at a larger value than when private information is the norm.

---

[13] This is a very stylized description of the main feature of a 'frame contract.'

[14] See Chapter 6 for a more detailed analysis of the private and common components in the suppliers' production costs.

[15] The interested reader is referred to Chapter 6 where a stylized procurement contract illustrates how the Winner's Curse may arise and what precautions the procurer may adopt to limit its negative consequences on suppliers' bidding strategies at the tendering stage.

Suppliers may face many uncertainties and may prefer a certain outcome to an uncertain one. Uncertainty is pervasive in procurement. It is intrinsic at the tendering stage where bidders do not know whether they are going to be awarded the contract; it also arises after the tendering stage since the costs of performing the contract may be affected by exogenous events. As we argue in section 2 of Chapter 4, a supplier may undertake actions that provide some 'insurance' against the fear of risk. Although the insurance markets do not offer contracts against the vagaries of a procurement contract, any supplier could resort to 'internal insurance policies' such as the value of the contract being only a tiny fraction of the contractor's turnover, a high degree of diversification of his activities, and, more generally, by the supplier's ease of access to the credit market. For instance, the higher the level of centralization in public procurement the more any single contract accounts for a supplier's overall turnover, thus the less diversified the supplier's activity and the higher the latter's fear of risk. When deciding to participate in a competitive tendering such a supplier anticipates that getting (at least a share of) the contract may have a substantial impact on his ability to remain in the market.

This uncertainty at the bidding stage would make the supplier accept to pay a premium or, equivalently, to reduce his profit to avoid the risk of not being awarded the contract. Suppliers' fear of risk causes them to bid more aggressively (i.e., lower bids) than when they are insensitive to risk. Therefore the procurer does not have to exercise the same pressure on suppliers to extract their rents or profits. Indeed suppliers are willing to give up a part of their expected profits since they dislike the risk arising at the bidding stage. Consequently, the optimal reserve price can be set at a larger level than when suppliers are indifferent to risk. This discussion leads us to

Practical conclusion 6

When suppliers fear the risk of not being awarded the contract, the reserve price should be set at a larger value than when risk does not matter.

Procurement contracts often involve important transportation costs of heavy material. This gives suppliers located in the proximity a clear advantage in terms of costs. Thus suppliers cannot be treated alike and have to be considered as heterogeneous or *asymmetric*. In this case, the procurer can take further advantage of such an asymmetry by using discriminatory policies such as discriminatory reserve prices in favour of disadvantaged or high-cost suppliers, namely a higher reserve price could be set for disadvantaged suppliers. Observability is needed to make sure that no supplier takes undue advantage of a discriminatory policy that is not meant in principle to favour him. In the same spirit, a price preference policy can be used to discount[16] the bid of disadvantaged bidders as further explained in the next section.

Practical conclusion 7

When suppliers are asymmetric or heterogeneous and disadvantages are objectively identifiable the procurer should use discriminatory policies in favour of disadvantaged suppliers such as different reserve prices or price preference.

Collusion is known to be a latent problem in procurements. A bidding ring or cartel hampers competition since the bidding ring typically submits only one serious bid.[17] The use of reserve prices can mitigate the negative effects of collusion, which tends to increase the procurer's expected awarding price. When collusion is suspected to take place among most of the suppliers, the procurer should set the reserve price at a lower level than in the absence of collusion. This simple policy forces the bidding ring to submit a lower bid.

Practical conclusion 8

When collusion among suppliers is suspected, the reserve price should be set at a lower value than in the absence of collusion.

Announcing a reserve price implies a strong commitment of the buyer. The discussion on the 'exclusion principle' of the optimal reserve price at the beginning of the current section implicitly assumed that the buyer accepts the possibility that the transaction does not occur. Thus, the buyer can perform the job or contract on her own and/or can postpone the allocation of such a contract. If the commitment is weak, that is, if the buyer is open to bargaining after the competitive tendering when the contract has *not* been allocated because no offer was under the reserve price, rational

---

[16] This practice is widely used in procurements when the government wants to favour local firms, national firms or firms owned by minorities. See Flambard and Perrigne (2005) for the simulation of discriminatory policies in snow removal procurements.

[17] This is the most commonly observed collusive mechanism in a competitive tendering. This is the main topic of Chapter 15.

suppliers will wait in the prospect of obtaining a better deal later and will not participate in the competitive tendering.

Practical conclusion 9

A weak commitment in the reserve price will induce lower participation and will raise the buyer's expected awarding price.

In the same spirit, it is usually better to announce the reserve price rather than keeping it secret. In a procurement environment where suppliers' production costs are mainly affected by firm-specific components a secret reserve price becomes a factor that 'randomly' determines whether or not a supplier's bid will be rejected. Suppliers are most likely to react to such an additional uncertainty by submitting higher bids, thus raising the buyer's expected awarding price of the contract.

There exist, however, some circumstances under which a secret reserve price may allow the buyer to *lower* the expected awarding price. When suppliers are known to be sensitive to procurement risk, an unknown reserve price represents indeed an additional dimension of uncertainty to bidding. We have seen earlier in the section that those suppliers who dislike risk tend to bid more aggressively as they are willing to pay a premium to reduce the impact of uncertainty. A secret reserve price magnifies the effect of uncertainty on bidding and induces suppliers to lower their bids, thus benefiting the buyer.

A secret reserve price may also encourage suppliers' participation or entry as it increases their *ex ante* probability of being awarded the contract. When suppliers face some (sunk) entry costs to evaluate the feasibility of the contract, they may find it unprofitable to participate as the announced reserve price is too low in view of their expected performance. When such information is not revealed, the unknown reserve price will raise their expectation and induce their participation. Lastly, a secret reserve price may give some discretion to the buyer to refuse the lowest offered bid. This is rational for the buyer if she anticipates that rejecting the lowest offer today will induce suppliers to bid more aggressively in future competitive procurements.

Practical conclusion 10

When suppliers have fear of risk, or when they face some entry costs, a secret reserve price can be a better option than a publicly announced reserve price.

11.4. Methods to increase participation

In the previous sections we have explored the circumstances under which a higher number of participants does not necessarily induce a more desirable outcome for the buyer, namely higher savings. Nevertheless, in a number of instances the buyer is interested in inducing a higher level of participation than the one that would otherwise arise. For instance, when participation costs are sizeable or when big incumbent suppliers enjoy informational advantages, SMEs may anticipate a low chance of winning. Thus entry of small suppliers may be inhibited if the buyer does not take appropriate actions.

In what follows we will discuss how to foster participation of weaker suppliers by operating on the auction design.[18] The general and common principle underlying these methods is to encourage weaker participants to enter by increasing their chances to win, sometimes even by reserving for them some of the lots. Adopting discriminatory policies in favor of weaker suppliers may force stronger suppliers to bid more aggressively and eventually lead to lower awarding prices.

11.4.1. Awarding limits and limited bidding in a multi-contract competitive tendering

Tendering rules may specify a maximum number of contracts that a supplier is entitled to win (awarding limits), or on which contracts participants are allowed to bid (limited bidding). Clearly, bidding behaviour may be very sensitive to these differences and, in turn, originate rather different final outcomes.[19]

While favouring entry of smaller suppliers, limiting the number of lots that any single supplier in entitled to win may induce stronger suppliers to use a selective strategy in choosing lots to bid for. Hence 'awarding limits' may reduce competition and raise expected awarding prices.

Within this class of discriminatory policies lies the one that reserves a subset of lots/contracts to SMEs. The most famous policy experiment in establishing set-asides for small firms is the one launched in 1953 by the United States through the Small Business Act, the purpose of which is

---

[18] The main references from which we borrow some of the ideas developed here are Klemperer (2004) and Milgrom (2004).

[19] See Ayres and Cramton (1996), and Milgrom (2004).

described in the first lines of the Act:

The essence of the American economic system of private enterprise is free competition. Only through full and free competition can free markets, free entry into business, and opportunities for the expression and growth of personal initiative and individual judgment be assured. The preservation and expansion of such competition is basic not only to the economic well-being but to the security of this Nation. Such security and well-being cannot be realized unless the actual and potential capacity of small business is encouraged and developed. It is the declared policy of the Congress that the Government should aid, counsel, assist, and protect, insofar as is possible, the interests of small-business concerns in order to preserve free competitive enterprise, to insure that a fair proportion of the total purchases and contracts or subcontracts for property and services for the Government (including but not limited to contracts or subcontracts for maintenance, repair, and construction) be placed with small business enterprises, to insure that a fair proportion of the total sales of Government property be made to such enterprises, and to maintain and strengthen the overall economy of the Nation.

The goal of the SBAct (see *http://www.sba.gov*) is to promote the development and the competitive capacity of small firms also through the increase in their participation and competition in public procurement, limiting – when possible and advantageous – contract bundling. Limiting contract bundling is considered advantageous if it does not bring discounts, for contracts under $75,000 at least 10 percent of the contract value and, for those above $75,000, at least 5 percent of the value of the contract.

As for shares assigned to federal prime contracts in procurement, the goal is to reach at least 23 percent of the total procured value. There is also an automatic quota reserved to small firms for contracts whose value is between $2,500 and $100,000, but for the case in which it is not possible to find two or more small firms that are competitive in terms of price and quality.

In Europe such shares are prohibited by EU Directives. Nevertheless some supranational agencies for which Directives do not apply are sensitive to the issue. The European Space Agency (ESA), for example, has a 4-tier procurement policy it applies on technology contracts:

- C1 contracts: activities in open competition, limited to non-Large System Integrators;
- C2 contracts: activities in open competition where a significant participation of non-Large System Integrator is requested;
- C3 contracts: activities limited to SMEs and R&D organizations, preferably in cooperation;

- C4 contracts: activities in open competition subject to the SME subcontracting clause.

It is worth noticing that the goal of C3 contracts is to increase the efficiency and flexibility of the system by facilitating the access of interesting and innovative industrial and R&D partners.

In sale auctions such as the UMTS spectrum auctions in the United Kingdom and the United States, similar measures were adopted for a series of reasons among which are the need to promote entry of non-incumbent bidders and the effects of the auctions on downstream market interaction. In particular, the rules in the simultaneous ascending auctions, which were eventually adopted by the UK Government, for five licences on sale included that no bidder was allowed to win more than one licence, and that one of the largest licences (in terms of spectrum size) was reserved for new entrants. Behind such a rule one could easily see a concern for both auction participation and market structure, in the sense of avoiding dominant market positions. The presence of a *set-aside* licence, reserved to new entrants favoured entry. Moreover, it forced the four incumbents to compete only on four licences, together with new entrants who were allowed to bid on all licences. The competitive bidding behaviour on the four licences reserved to incumbents, was probably due to the new entrants making offers on all of them, in so doing forcing all the bidders to genuinely compete. The presence of new entrants was probably due to the set-aside licences that were reserved for them.

More in general, set-aside items can increase the level of competition among stronger bidders, due to lower number of objects for which the latter can compete. Although smaller bidders may generate lower revenues on the set-aside licences, more aggressive competition among stronger bidders might imply an increase in revenue on the licences that are not set aside, which would render the total returns higher in this case.[20]

As an alternative, the UK government could have set aside two licences, not necessarily the two largest ones, thus increasing even further the competition among the incumbents, with their number now being strictly higher than the available supply contracts (three).

Observe, however, that set-asides per se do not necessarily imply that enough competition would arise on the reserved lots. More concretely, suppose that, everything else being equal, in the UK 3G auction only a few and weak entrants had entered rather than the nine who actually

[20] Ayres and Cramton (1996) discuss this case in a purely private value case.

participated. Then in such a scenario competition could have been weak on *all* licences. With maximization of expected revenue as one of the main goals, the final outcome in this case could have been even worse than without set-aside licences. Indeed, had those few entrants been too weak, bidding on the reserved licence could have generated lower revenues than if incumbents had been also allowed to bid on all licences.

Setting contracts aside in procurement, and so reducing the number of lots available to strong bidders, can also have the further consequence of protecting weak participants such as SMEs which may run the risk of disappearing from the market altogether if they are unable to get a share of sizeable procurement contracts. Economic as well as political reasons may sometimes suggest this prospect to be undesirable in procurement, and so a set-aside policy may become recommendable.[21]

11.4.2. Bidding credits

In order to induce small suppliers to enter, the procurer may introduce bidding credits.[22] The mechanism is very simple. It consists in applying monetary *discounts* to the bids of smaller suppliers, provided they win a contract. This clearly implies that those bidders who can benefit from monetary discounts have to be well identified before the contest begins. In a dynamic auction the right might, in principle, be assigned also in the course of the auction, but this procedure may suffer from a number of complications and would presumably be unable to achieve the same results. More specifically, if bidding credits are meant to induce entry then the announcement that such credits may or may not be given in the course of the auction has to take place before the contest starts. Without such an announcement, the goal of inducing higher participation would clearly fail.

The possibility of enjoying a discount of, say, $100t$ percent, with $0 \leqslant t \leqslant 1$, of the winning bid in a sale of competitive tendering, with an exclusively private component, allows a bidder with value v to raise his price up to $v/(1-t)$. In a procurement competitive tendering, discounts become credits. If the winning bidder is awarded the contract at a price p, he receives a payment of $p(1+t)$ from the buyer. To see the possible consequences of bidding rewards in a procurement competitive tendering, consider, as an

---

[21] The link between the number of lots and the degree of competition is explored in more depth in Chapter 7.

[22] Ayres and Cramton (1996), and Milgrom (2004).

example, a sealed bid lowest price format for a single contract. There are two firms, 1 and 2, with costs for serving the contracts equal to $c_1 > c_2$ respectively. Thus firm 1 is the 'weak' bidder while firm 2 is the 'strong' one. If $c_1/(1 + t) < c_2$, namely $t > (c_1 - c_2)/c_2$, then the weak bidder could in principle outbid the strong one. Since the buyer typically does not know bidders' costs, and so the lowest price that they are willing to offer, the problem is the correct calibration of t, that is, of the size of the credit. A fundamental trade-off then arises. If t is too high then a weak participant has a high chance of outbidding a strong one. However, the resulting allocation would be inefficient in the sense that the contract would not be awarded to the most efficient (lowest cost) supplier. On the other hand, if t is too small, weak participants may perceive the probability of outbidding strong ones as too low and thus decide not to participate.

One noticeable example of the competition-enhancing effect of bidding credits is the 1994 'regional narrowband' auction of thirty licences in the United States. Relying on a statutory mandate by the Congress, the Federal Communication Commission (FCC) granted substantial bidding preferences to firms controlled by women and minorities ('designated bidders'). The overall effect of bidding credit was that favoured bidders had to pay only 50 percent of a winning bid. At first blush one is inclined to believe that allowing designated bidders to enjoy a 50 percent discount of a winning bid would necessarily reduce the government's revenue. This, however, does not take into account that subsidizing designated firms created extra competition in the auctions and induced the established, unsubsidized firms to bid higher. In fact, it was estimated that the FCC's affirmative action increased the government's revenue by 12 percent – an increase in total revenues of nearly $45 million.[23]

In multi-contract tendering processes, bidding credits may produce effects similar to those generated by set-aside contracts.[24] To illustrate this point, consider a dynamic ascending (in discounts with respect to the reserve price) auction with two lots and three bidders, one strong and two weak, A and B. Moreover, assume that the strong bidder is willing to offer a discount for each lot equal to 10 percent, while A is willing to offer a 3 percent discount for the first object, and 8 percent for the second. If $t = 0.05$ (namely 5 percent), bidder A cannot outbid the strong one on the first lot, but he is in principle able to win the second lot. Obviously, bidders do not

---

[23] Ayres and Cramton contain all relevant details about this auction.

[24] See Ayres and Cramton (1996).

know each other's strategies in terms of discounts at the time of bidding. However, the strong bidder anticipates that both A and B are more likely to win so he is induced to bid more aggressively on both lots. If, eventually, A is awarded the second lot the outcome of this auction with bidding credits is the same as that of an auction without bidding credits, but where the second lot is set aside for the two weak bidders.

11.4.3. Anglo-dutch

The Anglo-Dutch format was briefly touched on in section 11.2 and is investigated in more detail in Chapter 6. Our aim here is to emphasize that the final sealed bid stage may encourage the participation of weaker suppliers. Indeed even if a weak supplier is systematically outbid in the dynamic phase by a stronger competitor, he can profit from the uncertainty arising in the last sealed bid session provided that he is able to reach that stage. As argued in more detail in Chapter 6, the main reason for having a first dynamic phase is to favour bidders' learning on a potentially relevant common component in the production costs for performing the contract.

The exact rules of the Anglo-Dutch format may depend upon a variety of factors. We thus conclude the chapter by describing some of the potential problems that may arise when the buyer adopts an Anglo-Dutch format.

Suppose that the buyer wishes to procure 900 PC monitors. We first consider the case where all monitors are of the same size, say 15 inches, and then the case of monitors of three different sizes. In both situations there are 3 lots of 300 monitors each; however, the two cases differ with respect to the composition of lots. In the former each of the three contracts is made of 300 monitors of 15 inches, while in the second the three lots are respectively 300 monitors of 15 inches, 300 of 17 inches and 300 of 19 inches. Hence in the first case lots are perfect substitutes, whereas in the second case they are not.

Consider first the case of perfect substitutes. Bids are expressed in terms of discounts for each single lot with respect to a reserve price. Owing to perfect substitution, the reserve price is the same for all lots. The number of bidders is strictly greater than three, namely strictly higher than the number of lots.

Within this multi-lot context, the first open ascending phase ends when a predefined number of bidders for all three lots have remained in the contest, while all others have dropped off. Exit can be observed when bidders stop obeying the activity rule. Suppose that, say, four bidders for all three lots are admitted to the second phase. Then in this sealed bid phase of the Anglo-Dutch contest bidders submit discounts with respect to the reserve price which must be higher than what they proposed in the dynamic phase. The three highest bidders win the three lots, and are paid a price equal to the reserve price minus the submitted discounts according to a discriminatory criterion. There are, however, variations of the tendering format that may have a different impact on participation. For instance, the buyer may admit more than four bidders to the sealed bid phase and make a transfer to the winners (the contractors) of this last phase equal to the reserve price minus the highest rejected (i.e., the fourth) discount according to a uniform price criterion.

In the second situation, namely when the three lots differ in terms of the monitor size, the buyer would normally set different reserve prices, and participants bid separately on each of them. Suppose that those bidders submitting the highest two discounts in each lot are admitted to the sealed bid phase. Notice that if there are less than four different bidders admitted to the second phase, some corrections have to be adopted in order to reduce the risk of collusion among bidders. To illustrate this point consider the following table (table 11.1) where on the columns the numbers 1,2,3 and 4 stand, respectively, for the highest, second highest etc. offer made on the relevant lots, which are indicated on the rows. Capital letters in the cells indicate bidders' identities.

According to the entries in table 11.1, in the sealed bid phase bidders A and B should compete for the 15-inch, C and B for the 17-inch and B and A for the 19-inch lots. Overall, only subjects A, B and C will participate in the sealed bid final phase and there could be a clear potential for collusive behaviour, with participants coordinating on low offers in all the three lots. A possible remedy against the risk of collusion could be to allow the third-highest offer, in the three lots, to participate in the sealed bid phase unless the first three positions are occupied by the same three subjects in all lots. In this case, the fourth-highest offer will be allowed to bid for the existing lots. In table 11.1, it is in the 17- and 19-inch lots that new participants appear, namely D and E. Although in the 15-inch lot there is no third competitor, the presence of a third bidder in the other two lots is likely to reduce the risk of collusive behaviour.

11.4.4. Competitive tendering with premium

As an instrument to encourage entry as well as aggressive bidding behaviour, giving a premium bears some analogies with bidding credits.[25] In a single-lot competitive tendering, for example, it may consist in

---

[25] See Milgrom (2004).

Table 11.1.

	1st	2nd	3rd	4th
15 inches	A	B	C	D
17 inches	C	B	D	E
19 inches	B	A	E	A

Table 11.2.

	1st	2nd	3rd	4th
Bids	50	70	80	85
Premiums	0	0.30(80−70)	0.30(85−80)	0

providing losing bidders with a money premium corresponding, in percentage, to the difference between a losing bid and the one immediately lower.

A possible premium structure could be like the one summarized by table 11.2, reporting the offers of a lowest price sealed-bid competitive tendering.

In table 11.2, the top row describes, in Euro, the four bids while the bottom row the premium scheme. This specifies that the best loser – that is, the bidder who submitted the second lowest price – is awarded 30 percent of the difference between the third and the second losing price, while the second best loser obtains a 30 percent fraction of the difference between the fourth and the third highest price offer.

Hence, the premium going to the second best offer is 0.30 (€80−€70) = €3, where €70 is the second lowest bid and €80 the third lowest bid. By a similar reasoning, the premium going to the third best offer is 1.5.

Competitive tendering with premium and bidding credits differ in that the former awards a premium to losers whereas the latter awards a credit to the winner conditional on this last belonging to a predefined subset of (disadvantaged) bidders. However, both premiums and credits provide disadvantaged bidders with an extra incentive to bid more aggressively. Strong bidders then are forced to react by bidding more aggressively as well. Consequently, it may then be the case that the expected amount of transfers that the buyer will award is outweighed by the additional savings stemming from the more aggressive behaviour of both weak and strong bidders. If this is the case the buyer is able to pursue two apparently conflicting goals: using additional financial resources to promote entry of disadvantaged suppliers and minimize the expected cost for having the contract performed.

Bibliographical notes

The result that a revenue-maximizing seller or a cost-minimizing buyer should use a binding reserve price is a milestone in auction theory. The first seminal contributions trace back to Myerson (1981) and Riley and Samuelson (1981). Krishna (2002) provides an excellent analytical survey of auction theory.

The design of spectrum auctions in Europe and the United States has raised new issues such as the participation in sale auctions of disadvantaged and/or budget constrained firms, and entry of new firms in the market. Our discussion of the methods to foster participation is inspired by Klemperer (2004) and Milgrom (2004).

References

Asker, J. and E. Cantillon (2004). Properties of Scoring Auctions, CEPR Working Paper No. 4734, London.

Ayres I. and P. Cramton (1996). Deficit Reduction Through Diversity: How Affirmative Action at the FCC Increased Auction Competition, *Stanford Law Review*, 48, 761–815.

Flambard, V. and I. Perrigne (2005). Asymmetry in Procurement Auctions: Some Evidence from Snow Removal Contracts, *The Economic Journal*, forthcoming.

Guerre, E., I. Perrigne and Q. Vuong (2000). Optimal Nonparametric Estimation of First-Price Auctions, *Econometrica*, 68, 525–574.

Klemperer, P. (2004). *Auctions: Theory and Practice*, Princeton University Press.

Krishna, V. (2002). *Auction Theory*, Academic Press.

Li, T., I. Perrigne and Q. Vuong (2003). Semiparametric Estimation of the Optimal Reserve Price in First-Price Auctions, *Journal of Business and Economic Statistics*, 21, 53–64.

Milgrom P. (2004). *Putting Auction Theory to Work*, Cambridge University Press.

Myerson, R. (1981). Optimal Auction Design, *Mathematics of Operations Research*, 6, 58–73.

Reiley D. H. (2005). Field Experiment on the Effects of Reserve Prices in Auctions: More Magic on the Internet, *The RAND Journal of Economics*, forthcoming.

Riley J. G. and W. F. Samuelson (1981). Optimal Auctions, *American Economic Review*, 71, 381–392.

12 Scoring rules

Federico Dini, Riccardo Pacini and
Tommaso Valletti

12.1. Introduction

Competition for procurement contracts is widely recognized to have a multidimensional nature. The buyer often cares about both the price and other non-monetary attributes, including various measures of quality. The typical mechanism that can be used in these circumstances is a scoring-based competitive bidding. In such a competitive bidding format, participants bid for price and non-price attributes (quality). The buyer then selects the winner using a scoring rule that weights price and quality, with the aim of achieving best value for money. Hence, scoring competitive bidding involves the choice of a scoring rule that allows the buyer to rank offers and to determine the final contractor. Scoring competitive bidding can be more costly to design and run than price-only mechanisms, since it requires the evaluation of potentially complex quality attributes. However, it also guarantees more flexibility when handling the trade-off between price and quality.

In this chapter we investigate several practical issues concerning scoring rules that should inform the choices of private and public procurers. First, we examine how the procurer should choose the scoring rule according to her preferences. This explains how to solve the possible tension between low prices and high quality. Second, we describe different scoring rules and we analyse their properties paying particular attention to features such as simplicity, predictability and ability to promote competition. We identify the settings where a particular scoring rule is likely to work better than others do, providing some practical conclusions. Third, we briefly mention the problem of abnormally low tenders, which is treated in more detail in Chapter 13, and show how scoring rules may be adapted to prevent risks associated with extremely low bids.

12.2. What are scoring rules?

When quality is a crucial component of a procurement contract and flexibility is needed to handle the trade-off between price and quality, scoring mechanisms are particularly appropriate. Should this be the case, procurement contracts for goods and services are awarded taking into account some non-price attributes that include various measures of quality. We refer to these attributes simply as 'technical aspects' to emphasize the fact that they are quite easy to measure and contract upon.[1] For instance, in the procurement of personal computers, hard disks, screen dimension, weight, etc., are valuable technical aspects for end-users, and the buyer is likely to take them into account in the design of the procurement strategy. The assessment of relevant technical aspects in a procurement contract involves a weighting scheme allowing the buyer to award the contract not simply to the lowest price but to the best price–quality combination.[2] Weighting technical aspects implies the set-up of a *scoring rule*, that is, a mechanism assigning a score to each dimension of the contract. The sum of these scores determines the bidder's total score. The total score is the crucial 'number' that allows a ranking of the suppliers' price–quality offers in order to determine the winner (i.e., the contractor).

By way of illustration, suppose a buyer wants to procure screens for PCs, taking into account only the price and the dimension of the screen. A natural scoring rule for this two-dimensional procurement context is the following:

$$\text{Total score} = \text{price score} + \text{screen dimension score}$$

The total score is composed of two 'sub-scores', one for each dimension of the contract. Sub-scores are essentially weights that the buyer attaches to the attributes evaluated.

The scoring rule should reflect the buyer preferences, namely the relative importance of each aspect considered in the contract. In the spirit of the example illustrated above, if the dimension of the screen (quality) is

---

[1] In this chapter we refer to non-price attributes as 'technical aspects', namely those measures of quality that are observable by the contracting parties and verifiable by a third party (a court). Since these measures of quality can be easily regulated and enforced within a contract, they are often called 'contractible' by economists. Chapter 3 is devoted to the analysis of non-contractible aspects of quality, such as the originality of a tender, the reputation of the contractor, etc.

[2] The European Directive 2004/18 on public procurement refers to this as the 'most economically advantageous' offer.

perceived as very important, the buyer will attach a considerable weight to it (e.g., she will award many technical points to large screens). Instead, if price matters much more, for instance because the main buyer's concern is cost saving, the buyer will attach a large weight to price and reduce the relative importance of quality.

12.2.1. Price–Quality Trade-off in Procurement

Imagine one bid is first on *all* dimensions of the contract, that is a bidder offers both the cheapest price and the best technical performance. This bidder will win the contract under different scoring rules, even if they differ in their weightings. However, this situation is not a general one since *price–quality trade-offs* are likely to exist. Indeed, high-quality goods and services usually involve higher costs, so that good technical offers are more likely to be associated with high price offers. Low-quality goods and services mean the opposite situation and are likely to be offered at a cheap price. Since buyers want to procure valuable products at the lowest price, quality and price are in general conflicting goals. Therefore, buyers face a price – quality trade-off between cheap – low-quality and expensive – high-quality products and it is expected that different scoring rules determine different rankings of the same price – quality combinations and then different winners. This is shown in the following example.

Example 12.1

Three bidders, A, B and C wish to bid for a procurement contract. The reserve price for the contract is €100. The price offers are expressed in percentage discount on the reserve price. There is a total of 100 points available, 50 for the price offer and 50 for the technical aspects. The price score is given by the rule: '(discount)*50'. Suppose the bidders offer the following discounts: 10 percent (A), 15 percent (B) and 35 percent (C) and that the technical points obtained are 20 (A), 10 (B) and 7 (C). These offers yield the following final ranking: A is first (25 total points), C comes second (24.5 points) and B comes third (17.5 points). Now, suppose the price scoring rule is changed to: '(Lowest bid/Price bid)*50' and that the bidders still offer the same bids as before. It is easy to verify that with the new scoring rule C is first (57 total points), A comes second (56.1 points) and B is third (48.2 points). Therefore, different scoring rules can give different final rankings.

To solve the price–quality trade-off, the buyer should look at her preferences and set the scoring rule accordingly. In the next sections we provide some indications useful to manage this problem. For this purpose we address the following questions: what amount of money is the buyer willing to pay for quality? What price–quality combinations can be considered equivalent from the standpoint of the buyer? What price discount does the buyer require to award an extra point? The process through which the scoring rule is chosen and calibrated is just the way the buyer answers these questions.

12.2.2. The Monetary Value of a Point (MVP) and the Buyer's Monetary Equivalent (BME)

What amount of money is the buyer willing to pay for quality? What price discount does the buyer require to award an extra point? These are the key questions the buyer faces when designing multidimensional procurement strategies. We show how the respective answers to both questions, namely the *buyer's monetary equivalent* for quality (henceforth, BME) and the *monetary value of a point* (henceforth, MVP), allow to solve the price–quality trade-off. We start from the concept of MVP, which is easy to grasp by way of a simple example.

Example 12.2

A buyer has to choose a contractor for the provision of a good/service and has to evaluate economic offers (price offers) and quality (technical offers). She sets a total of 100 points available, 50 for the price offer and 50 for the technical aspects. Suppose bidder A gets 50 points for a price of €100,000, while bidder B gets 40 points for a price of €110,000 (we do not consider yet the technical aspects). Bidder A is awarded 10 extra points for a discount of €10,000 on B's bid: this is as if each point is worth €1,000. Thus, €1,000 is the monetary value of a point in this example.

The MVP is the money discount necessary for a bidder to obtain one additional point. Therefore, the notion of MVP has several important implications. First, the buyer reveals the points value of a discount. Second, the MVP incorporates the buyer's preferences since it allows calculating the monetary value the buyer attaches to non-price attributes. In the example above the MVP (€1,000) would be multiplied by all the points allocated to non-price attributes (a maximum of 50 points), yielding up to €50,000. This value is the *buyer's monetary equivalent* (BME) of all the technical aspects taken into consideration in the auction. As we shall see, the knowledge of BME is the first necessary step for the buyer to set the scoring rule since it allows to rank price – quality combinations, and to define the MVP in the scoring rule.

Practical conclusion 1

When you are able to evaluate *a priori* the non-price attributes considered in the bidding process, you can set the scoring rule so that a point awarded to bidders on the price-side is monetarily equivalent to a point awarded on technical aspects.

The procedure to follow in order to apply practical conclusion 1 is simple:
1. set the total points available (e.g., 100 for simplicity) and divide them between the price and non-price aspects according to the relative importance you give them;
2. evaluate your BME of each non-price attribute;
3. allocate the points you set for non-price aspects in step 1 to each non-price attribute proportionally to its own BME;
4. divide the BME of all non-price attributes by the points assigned to non-price aspects to obtain the MVP;
5. set the price scoring rule so that every point costs the bidders the same MVP (consistency).

This procedure makes it possible for all technical aspects to have the same MVP. The price score is such that the monetary discount necessary to obtain one additional point from price reductions equals the money necessary to obtain (at the buyer's valuation) one additional point from technical improvements.

It is always possible to determine the MVP in any procurement contest once the buyer has received and assigned a score to all the bids (i.e., *ex post*, as we did in Example 12.2), however, not all the scoring rules allow us to fix the MVP, as recommended above in step 5, so that it is possible for bidders to know it *a priori*. Indeed, the possibility for *a priori* knowledge of the MVP depends on the scoring rule.

Practical conclusion 2

Favour scoring rules which allow calculating the MVP *a priori* to promote predictability of the score for suppliers.

When a scoring rule allows to calculate the MVP *a priori*,[3] bidders are provided with a clear and certain relationship between the price bid and the score (predictability): if the score associated with any price offer is known before the bidding phase takes place, participants can easily calculate the MVP and bid accordingly. By comparing his monetary cost of a technical point with the MVP, a bidder can optimally allocate his budget for the contract among all attributes that are subject to assessment. Consider the following example.

Example 12.3

Consider a buyer wishing to procure a screen for PCs where the non-price dimension concerns the size of the monitor. Suppose the buyer adopts a scoring rule which attributes up to 30 points to the non-price attribute and up to 70 points to the price offered. The former are awarded to the technical improvements in this way: 0 points to a 14" monitor, 10 points to a 15" monitor, 20 points to a 16" monitor and 30 points to a 17" monitor. The latter are awarded to price discounts in this way: one point is given for every reduction of €50 in the price bid. This setting then assumes that the buyer's monetary equivalent (BME) for one additional inch is €500. Table 12.1 illustrates the above weighting scheme.

We assume the participants define their bidding strategy by allocating their budget among price and non-price attributes. Consider a 'representative' supplier, A. Suppose that A's internal cost reporting says that every inch added starting from 14" costs €400, and that the Head Office of A gives to the sales manager a budget of €1,000 to spend to win the contract.[4] The objective of the manager is to allocate the budget in the way that achieves the highest net score for A. Suppose he strategically decides to spend the whole budget. Then he finds that the best offer for A consists in a €200 price discount plus a 16" monitor, since the internal cost for 10 extra technical points is €400, which is less than €500 (the cost for obtaining 10 extra points from the price side). If instead of €400, every inch added had cost more than €500, the sales manager would have found the best offer for A to consist in a €1,000 price discount, thus spending the whole budget on price discounts rather than on technical improvements.

---

[3] This is the case of all those scoring rules where a bidder's score does not depend on the bids submitted by other bidders.

[4] Here we abstract from arguments of optimal strategic behaviour relating to competitive bidding formats (See Chapter 6 for more on this).

Table 12.1. Point allocation among price and non-price attributes: an example for PCs

Price		Non-price attribute	
Bid	Points	Monitor	Points
€5,000	0	14″	0
€4,500	10	15″	10
€4,000	20	16″	20
€3,500	30	17″	30
€3,000	40		
€2,500	50		
€2,000	60		
€1,500	70		
Max points $= 70 + 30 = 100$			

Predictability benefits the buyer as well, since it reduces the risk of losing potential best value for money, as shown in the following example.

Example 12.4

Consider the same setting of Example 12.3, where the buyer has two offers that differ in price by €500 and for a 1″ difference in size of monitor: that is, an offer of A consisting in a 14″ monitor at €2,000 and an offer of B consisting in a 15″ monitor at €2,500 are equivalent for the buyer. The buyer should keep the scoring rule with the above setting if and only if her actual monetary equivalent (BME) for one additional inch is €500. Otherwise, this scoring rule would not reflect the buyer's preferences, thus raising the risk of losing potential value for money. In fact, if her 'true' BME for one additional inch was €300 instead, and the winning bidder was the representative supplier A of Example 12.3 with a budget of €1,000 and internal cost of €400 per inch, the buyer would have lost €200. This is because, if the scoring rule implies a MVP of €50, thus implicitly yielding a BME of €500, A offers €200 in price discounts plus a 16″ monitor, which means €800 for the buyer (€200 + €300 + €300). If the scoring had assumed instead the correct BME of €300, then A would have offered a €1,000 price discount for a 14″ monitor (hence, potential lost savings are €1,000 − €800 = €200).

Finally in the following example we show why scoring rules which do not allow calculating *a priori* the MVP[5] may harm both the bidders and the buyer.

Example 12.5

Consider the same setting of Example 12.3, where the buyer has to decide between two offers that differ in price by €500 and for 1" monitor (that is, she values each inch added at €500), except for the scoring scheme concerning the price offers. Assume there are two bidders, A and B, who have respectively a budget of €1,050 and €900 to spend in the tendering, and production costs equal to €550 and €350 when they add an inch to a monitor (thus ten technical points cost €550 to A and €350 to B). Suppose the price score now depends on the 'state of the world' which occurs ex post, for instance because the scoring rule adopted depends on the price bid by both firms. This implies the MVP is unknown *a priori* as it depends on the state of the world realized *ex post*. Thus, suppliers' bidding strategies can only rely upon 'expectations' about the state of the world. Suppose, for instance, there are only two possible states of the world, say high-value MVP ('H') and low-value MVP ('L') and the corresponding MVP is €50 and €25, respectively (thus ten extra points could cost €500 or €250 from the price side). Uncertainty on the MVP may harm both bidders and the buyer. Suppose, after bids are opened, the state of the world which occurs is the one consistent with the BME, that is, H. If both suppliers had the right expectations (i.e., 'H'), A would offer €1050 in price discounts, B would offer €200 in price discounts plus a 16″ monitor, and the buyer would choose B since €1,050 < €1,200 (= €500 + €500 + €200). But if both suppliers expected 'L', A would still offer €1,050 in price discounts, B would instead offer €900 in price discounts, and the buyer would choose A since €1,050 > €900. Hence, uncertainty on the MVP can make the buyer loose potential value for money if bidders expect 'L' instead of 'H'. Furthermore, if the state of the world which occurs is L, thus not consistent with the BME, then we fail in what was described in Example 12.4.

12.2.3. *Ex post* Evaluation of Non-Price Attributes

There are circumstances when the buyer can also opt for *ex post* evaluation of some or all non-price attributes. *Ex post* evaluation is involved whenever automatic scoring is not possible, that is, the precise way points are awarded

---

[5] For example, this occurs when the scoring rule depends on the minimum (on the maximum, on the average, or on any other) bid submitted.

to technical improvements and non-price attributes is not defined completely before the bidding phase takes place. This method can be appropriate when the buyer is not sufficiently informed about the value (or the characteristics) of some non-price attributes to give them a precise weight when designing the scoring rule. In this case it may be better to wait for the bidders' offers as they can reveal *ex post* to the buyer the existence of particular solutions, technical features etc., which could be useful for the actual procurement although they could not be anticipated in details. Bidders can also derive some advantages when the non-price attributes are only indicated in broader terms. Indeed, they have more freedom to enrich and articulate their offers, especially for the procurement of particularly complex goods/services. The downside is that flexibility creates room for discretion.

Detailed *ex ante* specifications increase the predictability of procurement competition, minimizing risks of discretionary behaviour and abuses of the evaluating committee (e.g., corruption). This comes at the cost of losing some flexibility. Therefore, the buyer should carefully evaluate and compare case by case costs and benefits of both flexibility and predictability. When corruption is not a particular concern[6] and participants can offer different valuable solutions for the good or service to be procured, it is more likely that benefits from flexibility prevail. In this case, there can be much to gain from *ex post* evaluation. In contrast, if corruption during the evaluation process is a concern, *ex post* flexibility should be minimized either by adopting an *ex ante* BME (automatic scoring) or, in case this were not possible, by reducing the weight given to technical attributes.

Practical conclusion 3

When opting for *ex post* evaluation of non-price attributes, consider the trade-off between flexibility and predictability. If corruption during the evaluation process is of potential concern, it is more appropriate to reduce either *ex post* evaluation flexibility through automatic scoring or the weight attributed to technical aspects.

Ex post evaluation of non-price attributes does not make it possible to follow the mechanical procedure we proposed in practical conclusion 1. In the absence of corruption concerns, it is still possible to assign points to

---

[6] For instance, in private procurement the issue of corruption appears to be less important than in public procurement. This may explain why the private sector usually has (and uses) more discretion and flexibility in selecting suppliers. See Chapter 4 for more on corruption. See also Chapter 16 for an analysis of methods able to prevent corruption.

bidders on the price side that are monetarily equivalent to points assigned on technical aspects, acting in the following modified way. Technical aspects should be evaluated first, before opening the sealed envelopes with the price offer that should, therefore, be kept separate from the technical offer. After studying the technical offers, the committee determines an ordinal ranking of all the technical offers, that is, it establishes who is 'the first, the second, the third, ..., the last' on purely technical grounds. Then, technical offers are evaluated cardinally; in other words, they are attached a monetary value. Suppose for simplicity there are only two offers, say 'A' and 'B', and that the quality of 'A' is considered higher than the quality of 'B'. Therefore, if both 'A' and 'B' were offered at the same price, 'A' would be awarded the contract. What if 'B' offered a price P while 'A' offered a higher price $P + X$? If the value of X is sufficiently small, 'A' would still be preferred to 'B' as its better technical performance more than compensates the more expensive price. However, as X is increased, there will be a value $X = X^*$ such that 'A' and 'B' are equivalent, that is, X^* is the *monetary equivalent* that places 'A' and 'B' on an equal footing. X^* provides a monetary measure of the quality differential of the two offers. Given her preferences, the buyer can determine her monetary equivalent for any technical attribute offered by a bidder. At this stage, the evaluating commission would consider the price bids. If the price offered by 'A' turns out to be more expensive than the price offered by 'B' $+ X^*$, then 'B' would win, otherwise 'A' would get the contract.

12.2.4. Predictability of scoring rules and collusion: is there a relationship?

We argued that simplicity and predictability are good properties of procurement rules, since the buyer's preferences are revealed to the market and participants are able to better define their bidding strategies. These objectives are met when the relationship between the price offered and the score attained is made explicit to the participants, that is, when suppliers know *ex ante* the MVP. Example 12.5 showed some adverse effects arising from the uncertainty about the points associated with bids: bidders could only base their bidding strategies upon expectations. Uncertainty can make worse off both the buyer (less savings) and bidders (risk of losing the contract).

One particular concern about predictability, though, is related to collusion (See Chapters 14 and 15 for more on this topic). In general, transparent processes tend to favour collusive behaviours, since cartels are more likely to be sustainable. The basic argument is that if procurement rules are predictable, the cartel can always observe its members' actions and punish any behaviour deviant from the agreed (collusive) behaviour. Therefore, more predictability may help sustain the stability of collusive agreements. This is a concern for the procurer. However it is not clear whether and how the degree of predictability specifically related to scoring rules can have collusive effects, also because there are several important aspects of the procurement contest that may affect the bidders' decision to collude (e.g., the number of lots, information disclosed to participants during the bidding phase, market structure, etc.), which are treated in other chapters, and that have very little to do with scoring rules.

We present a simple case to discuss the relationship (if any) between predictability in scoring rules and collusion. We imagine a procurement competition where participating suppliers agree to collude and one supplier wins the contract and rewards the others for withdrawing. We compare two alternative scoring rules with different degrees of predictability, namely with and without *a priori* knowledge of the MVP. An extremely simple and predictable scoring rule we can think of is the one that assigns the points proportionally to price reductions: *linear scoring*. In contrast, a less predictable rule is the *lowest bid scoring* where the score of all bidders depends on the lowest bid: for instance, '(lowest bid)/ (bidder's "i" bid)'.[7] What can we say about the collusive effects of these two scoring rules? Can we argue that the former gives more incentives to collude than the latter because of its higher predictability?

Imagine that a buyer wants to procure one laptop, and that he fixes the reserve price at €1000. N bidders wish to bid for the contract and collude as follows: one of the N bidders, say '1', wins the contract bidding €999 and all other N-1 participants bid the reserve price. Profits are then shared. Moreover, all participants agree to offer the same quality of laptop (e.g., the same screen dimensions, RAM, etc.), so that they get the same technical points. Collusion concerns price. With either linear scoring or lowest bid scoring, non-winning bidders can break the cartel by just offering €998. The cost of breaking the cartel is the same for all bidders and does not depend on the predictability of the scoring rule adopted: by reducing the price

---

[7] We provide more details about the properties of these scoring rules in section 12.3.

by €1, any bidder is effectively able to break the agreement and win the contract. The cartel can break down under both scoring rules, with predictability playing no major role. Therefore, in this simple case, the degree of predictability of the scoring rule has no effects on collusion. See Chapter 14 for more on collusion.

12.3. Scoring rules for price bids: some general features

In this section we analyse the properties of some price scoring rules that allow the buyer to transform price offers into a score. We focus on five scoring rules:

- Linear scoring (Ls)
- Parabolic scoring (Ps)
- Lowest bid scoring (Lo)
- Highest bid scoring (Hs)
- Average scoring (As)

We look at these scoring rules in terms of predictability, complexity and possible impact on competition. Before entering the details, we group the scoring rules into two families that have common features. The grouping of the scoring rules can be made on the basis of many different criteria (for instance, the ability to promote competition). Here, we propose the criteria of simplicity and predictability:

1 Simple scoring rules: the score of any bidder depends on his price bid only.

   With this type of rules the relationship between the score, the price and the MVP are well known *a priori*. This property makes scoring rules belonging to this family predictable and simple. However, implementation is possible only if some parameters can be pre-defined (e.g., a reserve price is used). Linear scoring and parabolic scoring belong to this group.

2 Alternative scoring rules: the score of any bidder also depends on other bidder's price offers.

   In this family, the relationship between the score, the price and the MVP is *not* known *ex ante*. Lowest bid, highest bid and average bid scoring belong to this group. These scoring rules are sensitive to the bid distribution. Within this family, the decision to accept/reject abnormally low tenders can influence the score achieved by all bidders and change the ranking.

12.3.1. Simple scoring rules: linear and parabolic scoring

Linear Scoring (Ls).[8] The linear scoring rule is a very simple way to transform price bids into a score. This rule is described by the following expression:

$$\text{Price score} = \text{nn} * [\text{Reserve price} - \text{Price bid}] \, / \, [\text{Reserve price} - \text{Price threshold}]$$

where 'nn' is the maximum number of points (typically out of 100) available to bidders for price offers. The remaining (100 − 'nn') points are attached to technical aspects. The reserve price is the price above which bidders get no points. The price threshold is a lower bound: the bidder cannot improve his score with further price reductions.[9] In the absence of the price threshold (price threshold = 0), this scoring rule becomes a very simple linear rule which awards the maximum score 'nn' only if the good is offered for free (a price discount of 100 per cent).

The linear scoring rule has the following features:
- the score awarded to a single price bid does not depend on the bids distribution. This allows all participants to know *a priori* the score associated to their bid;
- it allows to know *a priori* the MVP;
- the MVP is constant;
- the reserve price must be pre-defined;
- the score given to a price offer is not sensitive to the rejection of abnormally low tenders;
- a price threshold can be introduced and tuned to optimize price competition;
- the maximum score ('nn') is achieved for a price offer equal to the price threshold; the minimum score of '0' is achieved for a price offer equal to the reserve price.

Because of these features, the linear scoring rule is very simple and predictable, which allows both the buyer and the participants to better define their strategies. The MVP is obtained directly from the previous formula:

$$\text{MVP} = [\text{Reserve price} - \text{Price threshold}]/\text{nn}.$$

---

[8] In a recent contribution Asker and Cantillon (2005) argue that the optimal scoring rule would be quite complex to implement for the buyer. For this reason they suggest, as we do in this chapter, to use simple scoring rules. They further argue that, with respect to other scoring rules, one that is linear in prices fits well the optimal scoring rule when the number of suppliers competing for the procurement contract is high enough.

[9] The price threshold can be an important tool for the buyer to manage the intensity of price competition and to prevent abnormally low tenders (see figure 12.1).

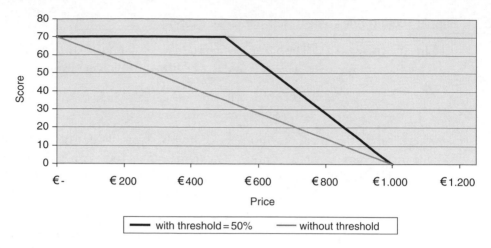

Figure 12.1. Linear scoring rule: the role of the price threshold

---

Example 12.6.

Consider the procurement of a good with a reserve price of €1,000, no threshold, and 70 points reserved to price offers. The MVP in this case is 1,000/70 ≈ €14.3. For instance, in order to get 20 points, a bidder has to offer a discount of approximately €286 below the reserve price.

Notice that the higher the MVP the more costly it is to get a point for any given price reduction, thus making a bidder more reluctant to concentrate his bidding strategy on price cuts compared to quality improvements. Conversely, a small MVP implies that a price discount can guarantee many points, thus making bidders more aggressive in their price bidding. From the above formula it is then clear that aggressive price bidding is more likely the higher the 'nn', the lower the reserve price, the higher the price threshold. We expand below on the latter, but similar arguments would also apply to the role of 'nn' and the reserve price.

Figure 12.1 shows the shape of two hypothetic linear scoring rules, one without price threshold and another one with price threshold equal to 50 percent of the reserve price. In this example, we assumed again a reserve price of €1,000, with 70 and 30 points attached to price and technical aspects, respectively. It is straightforward to notice that, other things equal, the introduction of a threshold *increases* the slope of scoring rule and lowers the MVP. The slope has a special meaning: it measures how the score increases as price declines. In other words, the slope provides a measure of the *incentive for participants to bid on price*. The lower the MVP, the steeper the scoring rule, the higher the incentive to bid on price.

Practical conclusion 4

Linear scoring is particularly appropriate in competition for procurement contracts. Once you set the reserve price and the maximum points available, you can use the price threshold to fine-tune the intensity of price competition.

Notice that the price threshold splits the scoring line in two regions with different levels of price competition. Prices ranging between zero and the threshold involve no price competition since the maximum score is achieved when the price offered is equal to the threshold. Instead, intense competition arises in the intervening range between the threshold and the reserve prices. Therefore, the higher the price threshold, the more intense competition price is, but the smaller the region involving such a competition. Thus the buyer has to be careful to avoid selecting a threshold level which is 'too high' since it can eliminate competitive bids.

Parabolic scoring (Ps). Ps can be thought as an extension of linear scoring in that the score increases but at decreasing rates with further price reductions. Parabolic scoring takes the following expression when the price threshold is equal to 0:

$$\text{Price Score} = nn \, ^* \, [1 - (\text{Price bid} / \text{Reserve price})^2]$$

This is the simplest way to describe Ps. It is also possible to introduce a price threshold by slightly re-writing the formula.[10]

This rule has the same properties of the linear scoring, except that:

- the MVP is not constant, more precisely it is decreasing in price. This makes the rule a bit more complicated compared to the linear one. Suppliers need to calculate the MVP for any price bid and define their bidding strategy accordingly, while in linear scoring the MVP is constant;
- the rule stimulates aggressive bidding for prices close to the reserve price. As the price offered decreases, the price score increases as well but at a decreasing rate. Thus the incentive for additional discounts decreases (the curve tends to be flat and the MVP becomes relatively larger);

---

[10] The standard equation of the parabolic scoring rule is: *Price score* $= nn^*[a^*(\text{Price bid})^2 + b^*(\text{Price bid}) + c]$, where the parameters 'a', 'b', and 'c' are appropriately set in order to obtain a scoring rule consistent to the chosen price threshold.

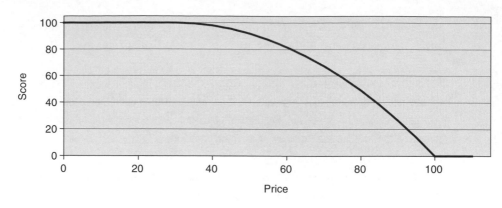

Figure 12.2. Parabolic scoring

These features allow the buyer to fine-tune price competition by giving milder rewards to high discounts, thus progressively favouring bidding on technical improvements.

Practical conclusion 5

Favour parabolic scoring if bidders are expected to bid aggressively on price and to neglect quality.

Figure 12.2 shows an example of parabolic scoring with price threshold equal to 70 percent of the reserve price.[11] The scoring line shows that there are no incentives to reduce bids below €30, as under linear scoring with the same threshold. However, incentives are already low for bids below €50, thus making additional discounts unlikely to occur.

12.3.2. Alternative scoring rules

The scoring rules we treat here are more complex and less predictable compared to linear and parabolic scoring rules. These rules prevent bidders from knowing *a priori* the exact relationship between the price offered and the score, which, in turn, implies uncertainty about the MVP. We discussed in section 12.3.1 that both the linear and the parabolic scoring rules need an 'anchor' represented by the reserve price. In some circumstances, this may not be easy to set. For instance, the buyer may be poorly informed about the market value of a complex project (e.g., IT architecture or facility

---

[11] Notice that the price threshold is achieved rather smoothly in parabolic scoring while it is identified with a kink in linear scoring.

management services), therefore it may be better not to fix the reserve price and allow market forces to determine the final contract price. The reserve price may also be difficult to set when the market value of the good or service to procure is volatile (e.g., energy supply), since the price prevailing in the bidding phase can differ much compared to the one used to construct the reserve price in the earlier phase of the procurement strategy design. In what follows we review some scoring rules which do not need an *ex ante* setting of parameters, except for the weight 'nn'.

Lowest bid scoring (Lo). Lo takes the following general expression:

$$\text{Price score} = nn * [\text{Lowest bid} / \text{Price bid}]$$

This scoring rule has the following features:
- the difference between the highest and the lowest score is always lower than the maximum score 'nn'.
- the score given to each bidder is crucially linked to the best price offer;
- if the best price offer is found to be abnormally low and rejected, the new ranking may change in unpredictable ways with little resemblance to the original ranking;
- this scoring rule can induce 'aggressive' price bidding because participants, by bidding low, increase the likelihood to get the highest score reducing at the same time the score obtained by all other competitors.

Highest bid-lowest bid scoring (Hs). Hs takes the following general expression:

$$\text{Price score} = nn * [\text{Highest bid} - \text{Price bid}] / [\text{Highest bid} - \text{Lowest bid}]$$

This scoring rule has the following main features:
- the score assigned to each price offer depends on both the lowest and the highest price offers;
- it is 'aggressive': regardless of the price distribution, the lowest bid is awarded the maximum score, while the highest bid is awarded zero points.

Hs is independent of the *whole* bid distribution, that is, its slope and the position are only determined by the highest and the lowest bid, while all bids in between are irrelevant. Hs assigns the maximum possible score differential between the lowest and the highest bid, scoring all other bids proportionally. This is indeed a straight line connecting the lowest and the highest bid.

Average scoring (As). As can take the following general expression:

$$\text{If bid} < \text{Average bid} \rightarrow \text{Price score} = \text{nn}$$
$$\text{otherwise:}$$
$$\text{Price score} = \text{nn}^* \ [\text{Highest bid} - \text{Price bid}] \ / \ [\text{Highest bid} - \text{Average bid}]$$

This scoring rule has the following characteristics:
- when the price offered decreases, the score grows linearly up to its highest level as soon as the price offer equals the average bid;
- all bids below the average bid obtain the maximum score;
- particularly low prices are not rewarded in terms of score with respect to the other best offers, since they get the same score of the tender which is just below average;
- the score assigned to any price offer depends on all the price offers submitted.

If the market value of the good/service is unknown and volatile this scoring rule ensures that the contract is awarded to the average bid, which may proxy the true market value of the good/service at that moment. This rule discourages low tenders since no additional score is obtained bidding below the average. Average scoring has been used in several countries, such as Italy, Peru and Taiwan, to deal with abnormally low tenders (see section 12.4.1 for a short discussion of scoring rules and low tenders). However, as it will be clarified in Chapter 13, As should not be used for that scope, since the attempt to prevent low tenders may come at the considerable cost of high prices. Lower-than-average prices do not increase the chance to win the contract. Therefore, bidders will not be encouraged to submit their lowest price, rather, they will try to forecast the average and bid that value. This destroys the price competition and can lead to significant loss of savings for the procurer. Buyers should be aware of such adverse effects when using As and other similar scoring rules.

Practical conclusion 6

When the reserve price is difficult to set, you can use with caution one of the alternative scoring rules Lo and Hs.

12.3.3. Scenario analysis

We now compare the above scoring rules on the basis of different assumptions about the price bids distribution. This comparative analysis attempts to highlight how, under different bid distributions, these scoring rules behave in terms of: (i) the score achieved by bidders, (ii) the score differential among bidders, (iii) the incentives to compete on price, and (iv) the final ranking, taking as given the technical points. Notice that the analysis does *not* take into account that bids depend on the scoring rule. Indeed, different scoring rules provide participants with different incentive structures. Therefore we expect bid distributions to somewhat vary according to the scoring rule adopted. This element is not considered here. Nevertheless, this kind of comparative analysis allows the buyer to gather useful information for the choice and the set-up of the scoring rule, since it shows how bidders' incentives to compete on price vary in response to both different scoring rule settings and bids distributions. This information can help the buyer to optimally balance, according to her preferences, the potentially conflicting goals of high quality and low price. With this type of exercise the buyer can also understand how much discount is necessary for a 'cheap' – low quality offer to defeat a 'more expensive' – higher quality offer.

We focus on two possible bid distributions, which are representative of two alternative kinds of markets:

1 Uniform distribution (asymmetric bidders).

Suppliers' price bids are uniformly distributed along the price line. This distribution is characterized by a large variance of bids indicating that bidders are heterogeneous with respect to some relevant characteristics. For instance, bidders may experience significant differences in cost structures.

2 Concentrated distribution on high prices and a very low tender (all symmetric bidders except one).

Suppliers' price bids are concentrated except one very low price bid. In this context, bidders are substantially symmetric, but there is one 'maverick' bidder posting a very aggressive bid that may correspond to an abnormally low tender (ALT).

We assume the reserve price, the maximum number of points awarded to price offers ('nn'), and the threshold price to be equal to €1,000,000, 30 and €0 respectively, for both linear and parabolic scoring rules.

12.3.3.1. Uniform distribution

In comparing the scoring rules (see table 12.2 and figure 12.3) we find the following:

- With As, Hs and Ls the score grows linearly as the price decreases; in As the score grows up to the average bid, while in Hs the score grows up to the lowest bid and in Ls it grows up to the zero price bid;
- Lo and Ps are non-linear;

Table 12.2. Uniform distribution

	Score				
	As	Lo	Hs	Ls	Ps
€1,000	0.0	3.0	0.0	0.0	0.0
€900	6.6	3.3	3.3	3.0	5.7
€800	13.3	3.7	6.6	6.0	10.8
€700	20.0	4.2	10.0	9.0	15.3
€600	26.6	5.0	13.3	12.0	19.2
€500	30.0	6.0	16.6	15.0	22.5
€400	30.0	7.5	20.0	18.0	25.2
€300	30.0	10.0	23.3	21.0	27.3
€200	30.0	15.0	26.6	24.0	28.8
€100	30.0	30.0	30.0	27.0	29.7
△Points (best bid – worst bid)	**30.0**	**27.0**	**30.0**	**27.0**	**29.7**
△Points (best bid – 2nd worst bid)	**0.0**	**15.0**	**3.3**	**3.0**	**0.9**

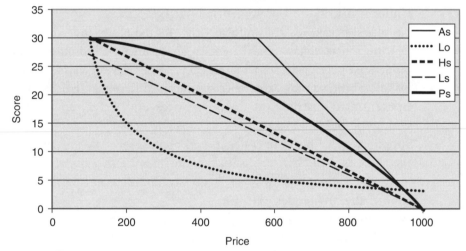

Figure 12.3. Uniform distribution

- As and Hs assign all the score differential available; As assigns a score of zero to the highest bid, and the highest score to all bids equal or below the average bid; Hs assigns a score of zero to the highest bid, and assigns the maximum score only to the lowest bid;
- Lo, Ls and Ps do not assign all the score differential available. In general Lo never assigns all the score differential because it always awards a strictly positive score to the highest bid, whereas Ls and Ps allocate all the

Table 12.3. Concentrated distribution on high prices and an abnormal low tender

Bids	Score				
	As	Lo	Hs	Ls	Ps
€900	0.0	10.0	0.0	3.0	5.7
€890	3.1	10.1	0.5	3.3	6.2
€880	6.2	10.2	1.0	3.6	6.7
€870	9.4	10.3	1.5	3.9	7.2
€860	12.5	10.4	2.0	4.2	7.8
€850	15.7	10.5	2.5	4.5	8.3
€840	18.8	10.7	3.0	4.8	8.8
€830	22.0	10.8	3.5	5.1	9.3
€820	25.1	10.9	4.0	5.4	9.8
€810	28.2	11.1	4.5	5.7	10.3
€300	30.0	30.0	30.0	21.0	27.3
ΔPoints (best bid – worst bid)	**30.0**	**20.0**	**30.0**	**18.0**	**21.6**
ΔPoints (best bid – 2nd worst bid)	**1.8**	**18.9**	**25.5**	**15.3**	**17.0**

score differentials only when the highest bid equals the reserve price and the lowest bid equals the price threshold.

With a uniform bids distribution, these scoring rules are quite heterogeneous with respect to the incentive they provide on price competition. Therefore, when bidders are asymmetric, incentives to compete on price may vary significantly according to the scoring rule adopted.

12.3.3.2. Concentrated distribution on high prices and a very low tender

When the bid distribution is concentrated on high prices but there is one abnormally low tender (see table 12.3 and figure 12.4), we have that:
- As, Lo and Hs still assign the maximum score available, whereas Ps and Ls respectively assign slightly less than the maximum score and about 2/3 of it;
- the score differential between the ALT and the second best bid is zero with As, it is similar with Ls, Ps and Lo, and it is very large with Hs;
- the ALT does not change the score differentials among all the other bids under Ls and Ps, while it affects them under the alternative scoring rules, especially with Hs.

12.3.4. Price scoring, suppliers' behaviour, and incentives

The incentive to bid on price changes under different scoring rules. Incentives to compete on price and thus price bids effectively submitted can

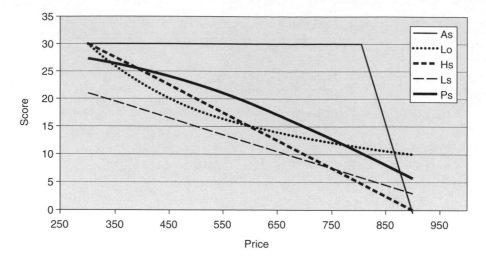

Figure 12.4. Concentrated distribution on high prices and ALT

Table 12.4. Comparing scoring rules on the basis of some key feautures

| Feature | Scoring rule | | | | |
	As	Lo	Hs	Ls	Ps
Simplicity	0	3	1	3	2
Predictability	0	0	1	3	3
Competition	0	3	3	1	2
Sensitivity to bid distribution	2	3	1	0	0

Notes: 0 denotes minimum level; 3 denotes maximum level

be rather different: other things being equal, we expect lower prices from 'competitive' scoring rules. In table 12.4 we report a summary of the results that emerge from the relative comparison of the scoring rules. Each scoring rule is compared on the basis of four features: simplicity, predictability, competition and sensitivity to bid distribution. Comparisons are conducted in relative and not absolute terms. The scale of evaluation ranges from 0 to 3. Ls and Ps that we recommend to procurers are the simplest and most predictable, mainly because they are not sensitive to bid distributions. Although they tend to give weaker incentive on price competition with respect to Lo and Hs, we remind procurers that price competition can be fine-tuned by using the price threshold and the maximum number of points ('nn').

12.3.5. Scoring rules and contract penalties

The scoring rule plays a key role in determining the penalties the buyer imposes in case of contract violations. Again, the property of predictability is particularly useful. Imagine a contractor that had promised a certain quality X (e.g., a 15″ PC screen) but delivered less than X, say Y (e.g., a 14″ screen). What penalty should be imposed? The answer depends on the MVP. If the difference between X and Y corresponds to Z points in the scoring rule, then the penalty should be equal to MVP*Z. In this way the buyer is compensated for the reduced quality delivered with the corresponding monetary value. In Example 12.3 (see section 12.2.2) the correct penalty should be €500 per inch. Penalties and scoring rules should be set in a consistent manner, and such a consistency is clearly ensured only if the MVP is known *a priori*.

Another important point is that penalties imposed on various technical aspects should reflect their relative importance. For example, if the screen dimension weights 60 points and the power (RAM) weights 30 points, then the penalty on the screen should be twice the one on the power aspect, otherwise the 'nominal' *ex ante* point value 2:1 of technical aspects is different from the 'real' *ex post* penalty value, which may generate perverse incentives for the bidders. For instance, if the relative penalty value between screen and RAM is 3:1, then the relative penalty value of RAM is 'too low' compared to the penalty value of screen. The bidder might be inclined to promise *ex ante* a very powerful PC, which awards many points in relative terms, but then delivers *ex post* a less powerful one, as the corresponding penalty is not burdensome. This has negative consequences both for the buyer and for the suppliers. One bidder particularly efficient in the production of large screens is penalized with the incorrect penalty rule. This can have a negative impact on the tendering results, since the buyer is not actually rewarding the bids that fit most her preferences. Chapter 4 is devoted to the analysis of contracting issues and penalties.

12.4. Links to other chapters

The problem of abnormally low tenders (ALTs) can be of particular concern in the context of procurement for two main reasons. Firstly, firms that bid very low prices to win the contract may incur in default risks during the execution of the supply, which results in damage for both the buyer (non-completion of the supply) and the contractor (bankruptcy). Problems of and solutions to ALTs are treated extensively in the next chapter: truncated auctions and surety bonds are some tools suggested to deal with them. Secondly, aggressive bidding may lead firms to reduce *ex post* non-contractible quality, thus undermining overall quality of the supply and reducing customer satisfaction. Chapter 4 deals with non-contractible quality.

12.4.1. Scoring rules and abnormally low tenders

We briefly discuss whether and how scoring rules might be used as an additional tool to deal with low bids. The simple and general principle is that tough competition on price does not help much to prevent ALTs and, on the contrary, it may exacerbate it. Hence, competitive tendering formats and scoring rules that put less emphasis on the price aspect may help to some extent. The clear downside is that the buyer loses out on potential cost saving if price competition is muted. For instance, average scoring rules (As) can prevent ALTs, as every bidder does not have any incentive to deviate from the average price. But this eliminates completely any competition among bidders, and the buyer may not be able to screen participants if they all submit the same price bid. Thus scoring rules such as As are not recommended in general.

Other scoring rules are better suited to limit ALTs without giving up the positive aspects arising from price competition. In particular, parabolic scoring and linear scoring with a price threshold are two scoring rules that can be fine-tuned by the buyer, while still preserving their useful properties of simplicity and predictability. The price threshold is a lower bound on price, since it does not allow bidders to increase their score with further price reductions. By introducing a price threshold the buyer can achieve the goal of avoiding too low tenders, if she believes that there is a critical price level below which the profit margins are insufficient for the contractor to provide *ex post* acceptable performances.[12]

Parabolic scoring can also be adjusted to limit the additional score one bidder obtains through a marginal reduction of price. The buyer can set the parabolic scoring rule in a way such that below a certain level of price, say P, the curve is made sufficiently flat so that the score grows even more slowly as the price declines. This ensures that further discounts on price below P give the bidder a negligible additional score (or, symmetrically, to increase the score the bidder needs to lower the price considerably below P). Indeed,

---

[12] As shown in section 12.3, the MVP depends on the price threshold. In particular, the higher the price threshold the lower the monetary value of a point and the higher the incentive to compete on price up to the threshold.

with parabolic scoring, the monetary value of a point is decreasing in the price. Then it becomes more and more costly for the supplier to bid on the price side as the price declines, while it is relatively more convenient for him to bid on the technical side. Since parabolic scoring makes marginal price reductions more costly at lower prices than at higher prices, it can be one way to discourage aggressive bidding at low prices.

12.4.2. Non-contractible quality

Scoring rules are used to manage contractible quality, namely aspects of quality that can be specified in a contract and verified *ex post*. For instance, the gigabytes and the screen dimension of a PC are technical aspects that can be specified and evaluated in a procurement contract for PCs. Crucially, they are verifiable *ex post* since the procurement agency can directly check, and prove in court, that the PCs bought meet the promised technical characteristics. Quality is non-contractible when it is impossible for the buyer to define in the contract some important aspects, because it is too costly or too difficult to monitor or to be verified by third parties. For instance, in the procurement of consultancy services, if consultants are less skilled and experienced than promised/expected, it is hard for the buyer to demonstrate the gap in court. The second part of Chapter 3 treats these problems in greater detail with examples.

Unfortunately, non-contractible quality cannot be managed through scoring rules. Appropriate scoring rules allow the buyer to deal effectively only with contractible quality. We said earlier that scoring rules can be adjusted (e.g., with price thresholds) to limit contractors' default risk. However, they do not ensure satisfactory *ex post* performances over the non-contractible dimensions of quality. Regardless of the payment received, the contractor can always increase profits by minimizing the level of quality of goods/services provided, if such quality is non-verifiable. What the price threshold does is to prevent contractors from going bankrupt as a consequence of extremely low bids, but it is ineffective to ensure good *ex post* performances when quality is non-contractible. Chapter 3 shows that adequate dynamic (e.g., dual-sourcing, reputation) and/or within-contract incentives (e.g., renewals, bonuses, penalties) can effectively reduce the incentive for suppliers to under-perform on non-contractible aspects of quality. The problem of non-contractible quality is also discussed in Chapter 18 in the context of the optimal design of reputation mechanisms (feedback) for e-platforms.

12.4.3. Scoring rules versus minimum quality standards

Scoring-based competitive tendering is used when quality is an important component of the procurement contract. However, quality can also be taken into account by performing a price-only competitive tendering when *minimum standards* are introduced. Minimum standards allow bidders to compete on price only if they meet some minimal technical/quality requirements. Bidding takes place in two stages. In the first state, technical requirements are evaluated. Bidders not meeting the requirements in the first stage are excluded, while all bidders meeting the requirements are allowed to compete on price in the second stage.

Minimum standard/price-only bidding is recommended each time the buyer can specify *ex ante* all the required technical parameters that are essential to her, and she does not really face a price – quality trade-off. If, instead, there is a price – quality trade-off, then scoring-based bidding is a more flexible format that the procurement agency can exploit to its advantage.[13]

12.5. Concluding remarks

Procurement contracts are often awarded taking into account attributes other than just price. Awarding these contracts involves the use of a scoring-based bidding and the definition of a precise scoring rule. Scoring rules allow the buyer to find the appropriate balance between the price and the non-price attributes (quality) according to her preferences.

This chapter has dealt with the choice and design of scoring rules. We have discussed how the buyer can set the scoring rule to solve the typical price – quality tension arising in any procurement context. One effective way to do it is to define a simple and predictable linear scoring rule. We provided some practical conclusions to compare various common types of scoring rules. Scenario analysis can help to understand which scoring rule might perform better in what context.

---

[13] A common misconception is that quality is low in price-only competitive tendering with minimum quality standards. On the contrary, they can accommodate very high standards, in which case all prices are likely to be high as the buyer renounces to the price–quality trade-off typical of scoring mechanisms.

Bibliographical notes

The seminal work of Laffont and Tirole (1987) studied a procurement problem with private information over a single dimension (the marginal cost of production is known by the firm/supplier but not to the buyer). They establish that, under standard conditions, the optimal competitive mechanism (from the standpoint of maximizing the buyer's payoff) takes the form of a competitive bidding in which each firm makes a monetary bid to become the sole supplier, and the winner is the high bidder and pays the second-highest bid. Furthermore, they find a result of 'separation between screening and selection'. The effect of competition is to reduce (but not eliminate) the net payment that is made to the winner; in particular, the winning firm's effort put in delivering the good is the same as if it had no competitors. Dasgupta and Spulber (1990) and Che (1993) complement their results by focusing on how to implement the optimal mechanism via a score-based system.

Dasgupta and Spulber (1990) consider implementation by per-unit bid auctions, where firms offer per-unit bids against a given quantity. Che (1993) develops the case in which firms bid on both price and quality, and bids are evaluated by a scoring rule. He considers three competitive bidding schemes, 'first score', 'second score' and 'second preferred offer'. In a first score scheme, each bidder submits a sealed bid and, upon winning, produces the offered quality at the offered price. In the other two schemes, the highest scorer is the winner and is required to match the highest reject score (under the second preferred offer, the winner has to match the exact quality–price combination of the highest rejected bid, while no such constraint is imposed in the second score scheme). Schemes similar to these are related to practices of the US Department of Defense. Che (1993) emphasizes the crucial role played by the buyer's commitment power to a scoring rule that may not fit her true preferences. If such a power does not exist and the only feasible and credible scoring rule is the buyer's true preference schedule, then the three schemes proposed by Che (1993) are worth the same to the buyer. This is a two-dimensional (price/quality) equivalent of the Revenue Equivalence Theorem. He also finds that first- and second-score auctions induce the best level of quality, which turns out to be excessive from the buyer's point of view since the buyer bears costs due to her inferior informational position. If, instead, the buyer can commit to a scoring rule, she should under-reward quality relative to her true preferences. By acting as if she did not care too much about quality, the buyer is able to increase competition among suppliers along the price dimension and pay a reduced price overall. This is a 'bias against quality' result. Branco (1997) extends the result of Che (1993) to the case of affiliated costs for the suppliers.

Asker and Cantillon (2005) consider optimal procurement when each supplier has private information about two components of his cost structure (fixed and marginal cost of providing quality). Multidimensionality adds considerable complication to the problem. They show that many results from one-dimensional settings change in a multidimensional setting. For instance, the 'separation' result of Laffont and Tirole no longer holds. Also the 'bias' result of Che (1993) changes in multidimensional environments because the optimal scheme now sometimes requires a high marginal cost supplier to win more often that what is dictated by efficiency. They also compare the performance of the optimal scheme to that of two buying procedures used in practice: a 'quasilinear' scoring rule and negotiation. A score is quasilinear when it uses a scoring rule linear in price (see Chao and Wilson (2005) for an application of a quasilinear scoring rule used for the procurement of electricity reserve supply in the United States). Asker and Cantillon find that negotiation performs poorly and the buyer is better off holding a competitive mechanism than negotiating. They also find that the optimal quasilinear competitive mechanism is a better proxy for the optimal mechanism than other mechanisms as the number of suppliers increases.

Burguet and Che (2004) consider a setting where procurement is administered by a corrupt agent who can manipulate his evaluation of proposals in exchange for bribes. The optimal scoring rule for the buyer in this context should deemphasize quality relative to price to mitigate the distortionary effects of corruption. The case of abnormally-low tenders and how to remedy them is considered by Calveras et al. (2004).

References

Asker, J. and E. Cantillon (2005). Optimal Procurement When both Price and Quality Matter, *mimeo*.

Branco, Fernando (1997). The Design of Multi-dimensional Auctions, *Rand Journal of Economics*, 28 (1), 63–81.

Burguet, R. and Y.-K. Che (2004). Competitive Procurement with Corruption, *Rand Journal of Economics*, 35 (1), 50–68.

Calveras, A., J. Ganuza and E. Hauk (2004). Wild bids. Gambling for Resurrection in Procurement Contracts, *Journal of Regulatory Economics*, 26, 41–68.

Chao, Hung-po and Robert Wilson (2002). Incentive-Compatible Evaluation and Settlement Rules: Multidimensional Auctions for Procurement of Ancillary Services in Power Markets, *Journal of Regulatory Economics*, 22 (2), 161–183

Che, Yeon-Koo (1993). Design Competition through Multi-dimensional Auctions, *Rand Journal of Economics*, 24 (4), 668–680.

Dasgupta, S. and D.F. Spulber (1990). Managing Procurement Auctions, *Information Economics and Policy*, 4, 5–29.

Laffont. J.-J. and J. Tirole (1987). Auctioning Incentive Contracts, *Journal of Political Economy*, 95 (5), 921–937.

13 Managing risky bids

Andreas R. Engel, Juan-José Ganuza,
Esther Hauk and Achim Wambach

13.1. Introduction

Public procurement is plagued by bankruptcy. In the United States more than 80,000 contractors went bankrupt between 1990 and 1997, leaving unfinished private and public construction projects with liabilities exceeding US\$ 21 billion.[1] Bankruptcy is very costly for the buyer: the direct bankruptcy costs (e.g., administrative costs or lawyers) vary between 7.5 and 20 percent of the liquidation proceeds, and indirect costs (e.g., delays and other losses) are estimated to be even larger.[2] Bankruptcy may arise when the payment (and therefore the winning bid) lies below the possible realized cost of the project. Why are suppliers willing to bid below the possible realized cost of the project? There are three main answers to this question: (i) the winning supplier underestimates the cost and bids too optimistically; this phenomenon is known as the 'Winner's Curse' and is studied in Chapter 6; (ii) the selected supplier expects to renegotiate the contract later on when it is very costly for the buyer to replace the incumbent contractor; this renegotiation generates cost overruns for the buyer and rents for the incumbent that are discounted in the bid and are discussed in Chapter 5;[3] and (iii) aggressive bids might also be due to suppliers in a bad financial situation struggling for survival by taking a risky strategy. The possibility to file for bankruptcy implies that supplying firms have limited liability. If things go too badly, the supplier simply shuts down. Hence, the supplier's

---

[1] Cited from Calveras et al. (2004).

[2] See White (1989).

[3] More than 60% of the failures in the US construction industry are due to cost overruns that are not covered by the contracted payment and the financial assets of the contractor (Arditi et al. (2000)). 77% of the largest public work projects in Spain led to cost overruns, with an average cost overrun of 22% of the calculated budget (Ganuza, 1997). The average cost overrun in a sample of US defence programmes was more than 120% of the budget (Peck and Scherer (1962)). Theoretical models of cost overruns include Lewis (1986), Arvan and Leite (1990), Ganuza (2000) and Bajari and Tadelis (2001).

possible losses are bounded while its possible gains are not. This affects the supplier's bidding behaviour and leads to risky bids for the buyer. In this chapter we focus on the third source of aggressive bidding behaviour: limited liability. We will describe the effects of limited liability on bidding in detail and we will discuss and suggest possible remedies.

13.2. Effects of limited liability on bidding

The logic that limited liability leads to an increase in the probability of bankruptcy is as follows: as the cost of a project is uncertain when the contractors enter the procurement process, the contractors face the risk that the realization of the cost is higher or lower than calculated.[4] Due to the possibility of declaring bankruptcy, the losses of a winning supplier are limited in case of high costs. However, if the project is going well, the contractor participates fully. Limited liability therefore changes the attitude toward the risk.[5] In most economic activities, firms dislike risk. As we have seen in Chapter 5, in this case the buyer designs the contract so as to account for the suppliers' fear for risk. However, in procurement with limited liability 'good news' (low cost realizations) is always good news while 'bad news' may not matter so much. Thus, suppliers become prone to risk, and bid more aggressively. Therefore, the winning bid and also the expected payment will be lower than those under unlimited liability. This leads to an even higher probability of bankruptcy.[6]

> Remark 1: The limited liability effect: Limited liability leads to more aggressive bidding than unlimited liability as the supplier's losses are limited but the profits are not.

---

[4] This may be caused by the uncertainty of the project in general, errors in the calculation or potential financial need to cover losses of other projects that are still in process.

[5] This is similar to the so-called problem of asset subsitution or risk shifting in corporate finance and banking.

[6] A famous example for such a behaviour in the context of a selling auction was the sale of the C-block spectrum licences in 1996 by the Federal Communications Commission (FCC) in the United States. To attract smaller firms, winners were allowed to delay their payment at a below-market borrowing rate. It turned out that the (selling) auction prices were three times as high as in previous auctions, leading to a revenue of US\$ 10.2 billion. However, soon after the auction, many buyers declared that the licences were overvalued. Even worse for the FCC, these buyers did not make their payments and declared bankruptcy. Following the bankruptcy of the most aggressive contractor NextWave, the company's obligations were reduced by the FCC from US\$ 4.74 billion to US\$ 1.02 billion. This ruling was overturned by an appeal court in 1999. In 2004, eight years after the auction, the case was finally settled, with NextWave receiving approximately 1/6 of the contracted frequency for US\$ 504 million.

We will now illustrate the phenomenon and consequences of limited liability in the simple setting of a second-price sealed bid (SPSB) competitive bidding.[7]

Example 13.1.

A buyer uses a SPSB competitive bidding format to procure a project with 50 percent probability of being low cost 2 or high cost 4. There are many identical potential suppliers. If there is no problem of limited liability because suppliers have 'deep pockets' (big budgets) so that they can fully accommodate losses without risking bankruptcy then each supplier will bid the expected cost of 3. In case of low costs the contractor makes a positive profit of 1, in case of high costs the supplier makes losses of 1. If, on the contrary, suppliers have no budget and therefore cannot incur any losses, at a payment of 3 there will be bankruptcy with 50 percent. However, at a payment of 3 the supplier will make positive profits: with 50 percent probability there will be low costs and suppliers make a profit of 1, while in the case of high costs they declare bankruptcy and make no losses at all. Competition among suppliers will drive the bids down to 2. Notice that this price reduction is not good news for the buyer as additional costs will follow non-fulfillment (in addition to the direct and indirect costs mentioned above, these can be costs of renegotiation or re-procuring the contract): if the cost realization is low, the buyer just pays the cost to the next supplier. However, if the realized costs are high, the buyer will have to search for a new supplier to whom he will have to pay 4 to be able to complete the project. Hence, the costs for the buyer are always higher under limited liability than under unlimited liability.

    Example 13.1 is very simple; especially since all firms have the same cost. In general, firms are heterogeneous. One of the main advantages of using competitive tendering for procurement projects besides the rent reduction is that competition helps the buyer to select the most efficient supplier to undertake the project. We will introduce a modification into the previous example to illustrate that limited liability may destroy this virtue.

---

[7] In the SPSB competitive bidding the supplier with the lowest bid wins the contract at a payment equal to the second lowest bid. In this competitive bidding format the best strategy ('weakly dominant' in the economists' jargon) for each supplier is to bid the opportunity cost of building the project.

Remark 2: If suppliers have similar budgets but different costs, limited liability may destroy the capability of the competitive tendering to select the most efficient supplier.

In example 13.2 an inefficient supplier with a risk of bankruptcy has the same probability of winning as an efficient supplier without a risk of bankruptcy. If we consider a situation in which suppliers differ in budget the situation could be much worse: the competitive tendering may not only fail in selecting the best supplier; in fact, we will show that it may select the worst supplier, namely the one with the highest probability of bankruptcy.[8]

Example 13.2.

Imagine the same situation as in example 13.1 with the following modification. Now there is one supplier with a different cost structure: namely, the same low cost of 2, but a high cost of 6. If there is no problem with limited liability this inefficient supplier will never win the contract. Let all suppliers have a budget of 1. For simplicity assume that the competitive tendering is of the form SPSB. The efficient suppliers will bid the expected cost of 3: in case of high costs they can compensate the losses of 1 with their budget of 1. The inefficient suppliers will also bid 3: with low costs it makes a profit of 1, with high costs its losses are limited to its budget, namely -1. Since all suppliers bid the same, the inefficient supplier has some possibility of getting the contract. In this case limited liability destroys the screening capability of the competitive tendering while allowing for the possibility of bankruptcy at the same time.

Example 13.3.

Consider our example 13.1 with the following modification: all suppliers have a budget of 1 but one supplier has a budget of 0. As explained before the supplier with a budget of 1 will bid 3 and will never go bankrupt. However, the supplier with the budget of 0 will bid more aggressively since it has less to lose in case of a high cost realization. In fact, she will bid 2: with 50 per cent probability cost will be low and the supplier makes a profit of 1 (as all the others bid 3, the payment will be 3); with 50 percent costs will be high and the supplier declares bankruptcy, losing its budget of zero.

---

[8] See Zheng (2001) and Calveras et al. (2004).

Remark 3: If suppliers have different budgets but similar costs, the supplier with the lowest budget and consequently the highest risk of bankruptcy will also be the supplier most likely to win the contract.

Example 13.3. describes a situation that is very common in procurement: on the one hand, there is a number of healthy suppliers (those bidding 3 in the example) that could always finish the project and bid around expected cost. On the other hand, there are some potentially insolvent suppliers who will win the contract by bidding clearly below the expected cost. These low bids are referred to as *abnormally low tenders (ALTs).*[9]

13.3. Managing risky bids

A natural remedy for many economic problems is to increase competition. However, for ALTs and other situations where risk taking under limited liability matters, the motto "the more the competition, the better" does not work. As more competition will reduce the payment this naturally will increase the probability of bankruptcy. Since the cost of bankruptcy is potentially very large, this reduction in price can be worse for the buyer. Furthermore, in a situation in which suppliers have different budgets (financial strengths) and the competitive tendering adversely selects the least solvent firm, the fiercer the competition, the more likely it is that the selected contractor is a firm in a very bad financial situation. Thus, competition might even aggravate the problem of ALTs. On the other hand, if suppliers differ in efficiency, then competition is the main instrument to select the more efficient supplier over the less efficient ones. Thus, there is a trade-off. There are basically three strategies for reducing the problem of ALTs: (i) weakening competition to increase the procurement payment, (ii) designing the procurement process in such a way that the probability of winning by more solvent suppliers is higher than by less solvent ones, and (iii) reducing the impact of bankrupt contractors. In the following we will discuss some remedies based on these strategies for dealing with abnormally low tenders.

---

[9] The intuition why less solvent suppliers bid more aggressively than more solvent suppliers is similar to that in the corporate finance literature where limited liability causes shareholders of 'risk-indifferent' (or risk neutral) firms in financial distress to choose riskier projects. This phenomenon is called the *gambling for resurrection strategy.*

13.3.1. Choosing the right competitive bidding format

Since suppliers are prone to risk under limited liability the standard competitive bidding formats are no longer revenue equivalent[10]: they will deliver different payments and therefore different probabilities of bankruptcy. To illustrate this we will compare the bidding behaviour in the English and the Dutch auction.[11] In the Dutch auction the price is steadily increased and the first supplier to accept the called price obtains the contract. In both auctions the bidding behaviour will be driven by the opportunity cost of undertaking the project. This cost includes the expected cost of finishing the project in case it is finished and the expected loss of budget in case of bankruptcy. Notice that this opportunity cost will be 'optimistic' for potentially insolvent suppliers since it is lower than the expected cost of the project in the absence of bankruptcy. However, the auctions differ in the way the payment is set. The English auction stops at a price when the second lowest bidder exits. Therefore, from an *ex ante* point of view, the payment is uncertain conditional on winning. In the Dutch auction the payment is the bid of the winning bidder; therefore, the payment is certain conditional on winning. As the limited-liability effect makes the suppliers prone to risk, less risk means less profits and therefore the Dutch auction will generate less competition. Thus, the suppliers will bid more aggressively in the English auction and as the bids are lower, the expected payment is lower as well. For this reason, the probability of bankruptcy in an English auction is in general at least as high or even higher than in a Dutch auction.[12] As the limited liability effect makes suppliers prone to risk, the English (SPSB-auction) auction leads to more aggressive bidding than the Dutch auction (FPSB-auction), because the payment in the English (SPSB-auction) auction incorporates more risk. This insight can be generalized beyond the comparison of the English and the Dutch auctions. Procurement processes that lead to high uncertainty on the bidders' side make them behave more aggressively, which increases the bankruptcy risk.

---

[10] "Standard" competitive tendering formats are all those that award the contract to the supplier that bids the lowest price (or the best price/quality combination). Almost all competitive bidding formats are of this kind; only particular and rare scoring rules are "non-standard" (see Chapter 14 on this). Under certain conditions, standard tendering formats yield the same expected payment for the buyer. For more on this see Milgrom (2004), Klemperer (2004) or Krishna (2002).

[11] The English auction starts with a very high price which is lowered gradually until there is only one supplier left willing to accept the price. The remaining supplier is awarded the contract at the exit-price of the last supplier that dropped out. In the Dutch auction the price is steadily increased and the first supplier to accept the called price obtains the contract.

[12] For more details see Board (2005), Engel and Wambach (2006a) and Parlane (2003).

Hence, the Dutch auction will deliver a higher payment and a lower risk of bankruptcy than the English auction. However, in a procurement process there are other factors that can influence the choice of the competitive tendering format. For example, if there are common value components in the cost structure and uncertainty and consequently the Winner's Curse problem arises, the English auction tends to outperform the Dutch auction.[13] More importantly, the ranking of the firms is the same in the two formats. In other words, the winning supplier will always be the supplier with the lowest opportunity cost which could be the one with the lowest budget and the highest probability of bankruptcy. Both auction formats fail in selecting the healthy firms.

13.3.2. Modifying standard competitive bidding formats: the truncated english auction

We can adapt standard competitive bidding formats to deal specifically with the problem of ALTs. One possibility is to use a truncated English auction, which works as follows: the procurement process will have two stages. In the first stage the procurement payment will be determined. This is done via an English auction, which is carried out until $m(m > 1)$ suppliers are left. The auction stops when the supplier with the $m + 1$ lowest offer exits. Consequently, the procurement payment will be higher than in an English auction. In the second stage the final contractor will be chosen. As further price competition in the second round would increase the probability of bankruptcy, the buyer should – without negotiating any further – check the offers of the pre-qualified m suppliers in more detail (e.g., screening or due diligence) and award the contract to the most appropriate supplier. In this case the buyer has to invest screening costs for only a small number of suppliers and learns more about them. A rather simple selection procedure (with the same consequences on the payment) would be a "lottery" between the remaining suppliers. A lottery is a special form of rationing, where at the given price the demand for contracts (the suppliers) exceeds the supply (the

---

[13] Chapter 6 illustrates in more detail the problem of the winner's curse and the links between information and competitive tendering formats.

single contract to be awarded).[14] While a lottery is often referred to as a fair allocation process, it can also mitigate the problem of ALTs. Following the logic from above, an English auction with rationing leads to a higher price and a lower probability of bankruptcy than an English auction.

Example 13.4.

Five suppliers with zero budget and different costs enter an English auction for one input factor. Each supplier has the cost of either c or $c + \Delta$ for the good as shown in the table below. Each cost realization has 50 percent probability.

Supplier	A	B	C	D	E
Low cost	2.5	2.8	3.1	3.4	3.7
High cost	3.0	3.3	3.6	3.9	4.2

Each supplier is willing to remain in the auction until the lower realization of the cost is reached. In the English auction supplier A wins at the payment 2.8. As the realization of supplier A's cost can be 2.5 or 3.0, the probability that she goes bankrupt is 50 percent. Consider now a truncated English auction with $m = 2$. The auction stops as soon as the third lowest supplier exits the auction. In this case, suppliers A and B will enter the second round and the payment will be 3.1. If the allocation procedure is a lottery, the probability that A wins is 50 percent. A's probability of bankruptcy is zero as the payment is always higher than the realization of the cost. B wins with probability of 50 percent and has bankruptcy probability of 50 percent (cost is higher than the payment). Thus, the truncated English auction yields less probability of bankruptcy (25 vs. 50 percent) at higher prices (3.1 vs. 2.8) than the English auction.

A drawback of this method is that the second round could be regarded as arbitrary. The mechanism loses transparency which is a major advantage of any competitive tendering. Moreover, while this mechanism reduces the probability of winning of less solvent supplier, it does not give priority to more solvent suppliers.

---

[14] Lottery as a rationing device is a common method in an environment with excess demand – take, for instance, equity IPOs and Central Bank Tenders. See Gresik (2001) or Gilbert and Klemperer (2000).

13.3.3. Multi-sourcing

Risk diversification means that a buyer *should not put all eggs into one basket*. Using the same principle, the buyer can reduce the risk of bankruptcy by sourcing to more than one contractor. As an example, automobile manufacturers often use more than one contractor for their components. When multi-sourcing (also called split award contracts) is used, a contract will be split up into m sources ($m>1$) and contractors will win a share of the contract. The advantage of multi-sourcing in terms of procurement risk is the flexibility that a solvent contractor can finish the lot of a bankrupt contractor. The disadvantage is that the price is in general higher than with single sourcing. Multisourcing has other advantages and disadvantages discussed in Chapters 4, 7 and 17. For example, if the buyer procures say two equal shares, the two winners of the contract have to beat the third best firm. There is no competition among the winning two.[15]

There are several issues to be addressed by multi-sourcing. One is to determine whether the environment is such that multi-sourcing is indeed risk reducing. In this context we discuss capacity constraints and the correlation between risks. The other issue refers to the degree of competition and the trade-off between price and risk. Here, we give guidelines for the sharing rule, that is, how many shares and the size of the shares.

The major advantage of multi-sourcing from a risk management point of view is the flexibility to let a solvent contractor finish a bankrupt contractor's part. So, as a first step it has to be investigated if such a switch of contractors is possible. Switching might be impossible (or very costly) due to capacity constraints on the side of the contractors. If two contractors get an order of 50 percent each of the total business, but both can provide only say up to a maximum of 70 percent each, then the risk reduction effect of multi-sourcing is very much reduced. Another problem occurs, if the risks of the contractors are correlated. For example, the risk of bankruptcy of firms in one country is to some degree correlated as these firms face the same political risks, the same business cycle, perhaps the same risk of suffering from an earthquake, etc. Thus, when one contractor goes bankrupt, it is quite likely that the other is bankrupt as well. As a consequence, if an intra-group correlation of risk is given (e.g., firms from the same country), the buyer should source by means of different criteria (e.g., firms from different countries).

---

[15] For this and more results on the competition in multi-share procurement see Wambach (2002).

Once the decision to do multi-sourcing is made, the buyer has to decide upon the number and the size of the shares. In the example above (50/50), the expected payment is the third lowest bid. But the buyer can do better than this, that is, the buyer can award the contract at a lower price with a similar probability of bankruptcy. If the buyer procures two unequal shares, say 70/30, the expected price of the whole contract will be lower, while the two winning contractors will also compete with each other. With the 50/50 sharing rule, the contractors compete to be among the two lowest. With the 70/30 sharing rule, the contractors not only compete to be among the two lowest, but also to get the larger share. Therefore, the (theoretically) best case of multi-sourcing would be to award according to the following rule: The winner gets 100 percent of the share and all others get 0 percent of the share and if the first goes bankrupt, the second lowest can finish the project and so on. In that case the price will be the lowest possible price, as all contractors compete as aggressively as possible for the 100 percent share. And also the probability of bankruptcy is minimized, as there are many potential contractors who can step in to finish the project if necessary.[16] This extreme case shows the trade-off a buyer faces. If switching costs are low, it pays for the buyer to make the split between the larger shares to foster competition.

13.3.4. Entry fees

The buyer can also introduce additional features in the procurement process such as entry fees. Entry fees were used, for instance, in most European UMTS spectrum licence auctions.[17] To see how entry fees work in a framework with limited liability consider the following: With respect to cost efficiency, suppliers with high costs and an expected profit lower than the entry fee do not enter the competitive bidding process. But low cost suppliers with a higher expected profit do enter. Thus, the more inefficient suppliers are excluded and the payment, due to less competition, is higher on average (*ceteris paribus*) which reduces the probability of bankruptcy. But entry fees will also affect the bidding behaviour: bidders with less capital will not enter, if the fee is higher than the budget. However, the others that

---

[16] Surely this extreme case is not easy to implement but it is done occasionally. See also Chapter 4 for more on contracting and quality.

[17] Taken literally, entry fees are monetary fees that the suppliers have to pay for the right to participate in the competitive bidding. However, entry fees can also be interpreted as a cost of preparation for the bidding process. Examples might be the construction of a prototype, investment in qualification for the contract or internal costs for the calculation of the project costs.

enter have to pay the fee and become poorer. This will lead to more aggressive bidding and a higher probability of bankruptcy. Thus, the effect of entry fees on the probability of bankruptcy is ambiguous. As entry fees are paid in advance they are similar to the instruments we will discuss in the section, namely letters of credit.

13.3.5. Third-Party guarantees: letters of credit versus surety bonds

Another possibility to deal with the risk of bankruptcy is to require third-party guarantees from the suppliers. These guarantees are meant to compensate the buyer in case of default and are only provided by the final selected contractor. However, all potential suppliers know in advance which type of guarantee is required by the buyer and negotiate the potential fee for the required guarantee before the actual bidding takes place. Only the winning bidder actually pays the fee and deposits the guarantee once awarded the project. During construction the winner learns the true costs of the project. He either finishes the project on his own (if costs are not too high) or the buyer is compensated according to the guarantee.

> **Definition 1** A letter of credit (typically issued by a bank) is a cash guarantee to the owner. The letter of credit is secured by pledging sufficient assets from the firm. If the letter is rightfully called upon by the owner before its expiring date, the owner receives the amount specified in the letter as a cash payment. The fee the firm has to pay to obtain a letter of credit depends on the size of the letter but is identical for all firms.

> **Definition 2** A surety bond (typically issued by a surety company) is a guarantee that the firm will perform the obligation stated in the bond. Surety bonds are secured by the financial strength (assets) of the surety company. No assets of the firm are pledged. In case of default, the issuer of the bond (the surety company) has two options: it can either take up the contract (complete the project) or pay the amount specified in the bond to the buyer. The fee the firm has to pay to obtain the surety bond is firm-dependent.

The most common forms of guarantees used in practice are cash guarantees or letters of credits and surety bonds. The exact nature of a letter of credit and of a surety bond varies in different countries. To facilitate the discussion we will therefore define what we mean by each type of guarantee. We will use the definitions that make these two instruments for dealing with ALTs as distinct as possible.

According to these definitions issuing a letter of credit is a riskless activity for the bank. The task of the bank is to pledge sufficient assets from the firm and to check, should the letter be called upon, that this call is correct. Issuing a surety bond is risky: the surety company compromises its own assets and therefore has incentives to screen the supplier, that is, it will try to learn about the efficiency of the supplier and his financial strength. The advantage of the surety firm over the buyer for doing this screening comes not only from specialization but also from the possibility to use soft information to assess the supplier's quality. To issue the bond the surety company will request a fee from the supplier, which is determined individually for each supplier and depends on the supplier's risk of bankruptcy. The higher the risk, the higher the likelihood that the surety might have to intervene and hence the higher the fees.[18]

How do these different guarantees affect the supplier's bidding behaviour? Letters of credit pledge firms' assets and thereby exclude suppliers with a budget lower than the one required by the letter from the bidding process. But at the same time letters of credit diminish the financial strength of the remaining suppliers: fewer assets are available for completing the project.[19] By reducing their financial liquidity letters of credit can convert good firms into potentially insolvent suppliers with some risk of bankruptcy. Moreover, if the required letter of credit is of a fixed size, among those suppliers who can afford the letter of credit, the lowest bid will still be from the firm with the lowest budget and therefore the highest risk of bankruptcy. To see this point, we assume that all suppliers are equally efficient. The buyer requires a letter of credit of size. We also assume that pledged assets cannot be used in production. In this case, all suppliers with assets less than L will be excluded from the competitive bidding while each remaining supplier's accessible assets will be reduced by L and each supplier will bid more aggressively according to these accessible assets. Since the supplier with the fewest assets has the least to lose, its bid will be the lowest.

---

[18] As we said before there exist intermediate instruments like letters of credits in which banks do not require collateral and behave more like surety companies. In that case a letter of credit would be close to the surety bond and will achieve a similar result.

[19] This argument requires that at least some of the pledged assets cannot be used in production. Typically, these assets are liquid and remain deposited in the bank.

On the contrary, a surety bond lowers the risk of bankruptcy by making the surety company co-responsible for the completion of the contract. The surety company influences supplier's bidding behaviour by conditioning the fees required for the bond on their financial situation. A worse financial situation implies a higher opportunity cost for issuing the bond and therefore a higher fee. Since the fees are passed to the buyer, all bids will be higher. But, due to higher fees the bids of less solvent suppliers will be greater than that of more solvent suppliers. This partially counterbalances the effect that less solvent suppliers bid more aggressively since they have less to lose. Logically, suppliers with a restricted financial status (lower budget) have to pay a higher fee, since it is riskier for the surety to issue the bond. Therefore, suppliers with lower budgets have to raise their bid to recover the fees and get some profits. This reduces the probability of ALTs. This implies that the probability of bankruptcy is reduced and sometimes even completely eliminated. Moreover, some potentially insolvent suppliers are converted into solvent suppliers from the buyer's point of view. The surety will finish the project if the contractor gets into financial difficulties whenever the bond is larger than the missing budget for finishing the project.

While surety bonds mitigate and sometimes even eliminate the problem of abnormally low tenders, letters of credit tend to worsen it.[20] Therefore,

Practical conclusion 2

Default insurance/surety bonds (which involve risk taking, screening, and individual fees): YES; default deposits/letters of credit (which involve no risk taking and the same fee for all): NO

If suppliers are free to choose the guarantee themselves, it is unlikely that they choose the socially efficient one, since they have no incentives to internalize the "externalities" inflicted on the administration by their choice. In countries where surety bonds are not well developed, the fee for a surety could be very high and a construction firm might prefer to present a letter of credit since it has lower costs and consequently permits a more aggressive bid. The buyer should therefore not just require any kind of guarantee from contractors but a surety bond. However, since the price of the bond is passed onto the buyer, the question arises how sureties set the price and how it depends on the organization of the market for surety bonds. Moreover, the argument in favour of surety bonds assumes that surety

---

[20] This strong claim is made in accordance with the above definition of letters of credit and surety bonds.

companies actually fulfil their obligations should the contractor default. This requires some regulation on who can act as a surety and the organization of the surety's collateral.

Practical conclusion 3

Only use surety bonds if the regulatory setting guarantees that surety companies have sufficient financial strengths to fulfil their obligations.

What should this regulatory setting look like? It will be very similar to the regulation of banking and other financial institutions. Competition is a desirable goal but protecting the rights of the less informed party (customers of the bank or the buyer in our setting) is a MUST. Hence, the regulatory framework has to guarantee that surety bonds are riskless for the buyer. This discussion leads us to a more general question why regulating sureties is better than regulating bidders directly.

It is easier to regulate sureties than bidders for several reasons: (i) there are fewer sureties than bidders and (ii) the financial strength of a surety is easier to observe. The accounting of the surety captures most of the relevant information while in the case of the bidder the complexity of the technology and pre-existing commitments are also relevant. Hence, screening the bidders requires one to rely on soft information and it is difficult to characterize efficient regulatory rules. Finally, given the complementarity of the surety business with the financial business in general there should be regulatory synergies.

To illustrate the previous discussion we will briefly describe the organization of the market for surety bonds in the United States where surety bonds are commonly used and are legally required for all Federal construction contracts over $100,000 (Miller Act).

In the United States the Treasury approves a list of corporate sureties. For each corporate surety the Treasury determines its financial strength and sets an underwriting limit, also called bonding limit. This limit states the maximum amount of money that can be compromised in surety bonds by the company and thereby guarantees the firm's financial soundness. However, only few firms will be able to issue large bonds, hence competitiveness of the surety market decreases with the size of the bond. Three measures are taken to mitigate this problem: (i) co-bonding is allowed, that is, for very large projects smaller bonds are issued by several surety companies; (ii) a corporate surety company can compete for too large a bond since it can exceed its bonding limit by contracting surety bonds from other surety companies; and (iii) competition is increased by allowing individuals and non-approved companies to act as a surety. In order to do so, they need to pledge certain assets (cash, readily marketable assets or irrevocable letters of credit) equalling the amount of the bond. This last measure has the drawback that individuals might lack the necessary experience to screen suppliers and might therefore assess supplier's bankruptcy risk badly. Screening should be left to specialized firms whose experience allows them to reduce screening costs and improve the efficiency of screening tools.

Bonding limits or cash guarantees are necessary to avoid default by the surety but they necessarily reduce the competitiveness for large surety bonds to some extent and thereby increase its price. This leads to the question of the optimal size of the bond. This question is important even if there was full competition for every bond size. We assume that there is some opportunity cost for issuing the bond. This implies that even the completely solvent supplier will have to pay some fee for receiving the bond. Therefore, it is costly for the buyer to increase the size of the bond.[21] On the other hand, a higher bond improves the solvency level of the selected contractor in two ways: (i) if the bond is very large, the surety will always prefer to finish the project than pay the bond; and (ii) the potentially insolvent contractor has to pay a higher fee to receive the surety bond. The larger the bond, the larger this fee: hence the larger the probability that the contractor will be a solvent firm. The optimal size of the bond for the buyer is a trade-off between increasing the price and increasing the expected solvency of the selected contractor. From this trade-off we can conclude that the optimal size of the bond will depend on the riskiness of the project: it increases with the underlying uncertainty and the costs of bankruptcy and decreases with the solvency level of the industry, since firms are financially stronger.

Practical conclusion 4

Increase the size of the surety bond with the riskiness of the project where riskiness is captured by the underlying uncertainty and the buyer's costs of bankruptcy.

In general it might be difficult to get a precise estimate of the underlying uncertainty of a project and consequently it could be difficult to set the size of the optimal surety bond. However, a broad classification of projects

---

[21] This opportunity cost of the surety bond lies between zero and the riskless interest rate. This two extreme scenarios have been analysed by Engel et al. (2005) and Calveras et al. (2004) respectively.

according to their uncertainty should be possible. For example, the buyer should require lower bonds for projects that have been undertaken in a similar way many times before and a larger bond for innovative projects where there is little historical experience. This broad classification will improve the existing regulatory mechanism for fixing the size of the surety bond. For example, the US system requires a bond equal to the price of the project. This system has its weakness because it links the size of the bond to the expected costs of the project which can be easily improved. Think for example of two projects: one is very costly but basically riskless and one has a lot of uncertainty but it is considerably cheaper. The US system puts a higher surety bond on the first project, while the optimal system would require the opposite: the second project is riskier and therefore the bond for the second project should be higher.

13.4. How NOT to deal with abnormally low tenders

In this section we discuss some commonly used rules to prevent ALTs from having unintended negative consequences. We first discuss attempts to identify ALTs and exclude them from the competitive bidding. We then turn to the average-bid method and to explicitly supporting weaker suppliers.[22]

13.4.1. Mechanisms to identify abnormally low tenders

The working group on ALTs of the European Commission (1999) suggested a statistical method for identifying ALTs. It consists of a statistical analysis of former bids offered for similar projects. The idea is to infer from past projects with similar characteristics what an ALT is in the present contest. We do not recommend this mechanism mainly due to two drawbacks: (i) what was efficient or possible in the past need not be efficient today. Also many public projects are highly idiosyncratic and therefore it will be difficult to find projects that serve as a reference point. More subtle is the second drawback. (ii) If such a rule leads to different treatments of bids submitted, firms will presumably bid differently which in turn changes what should be considered an ALT. Take, for instance, a method that is used in many countries,[23] which defines a tender as abnormally low if it lies a

---

[22] See also Chapter 12 for some discussions about average-based scoring rules.

[23] E.g., Italy, Belgium, France, Portugal, Romania and Spain. See also Chapter 2 for more on the methods used by public procurement agencies.

certain percentage below the average of all bids or below the second lowest bid. Such tenders are either automatically excluded or checked in detail before exclusion.[24] However, the mechanism fails to be successful since it has strategic effects on the bidding behaviour. Anticipating exclusion, firms will bid higher. It is also not guaranteed that a financially healthy supplier is chosen. Indeed, less solvent suppliers will not be excluded from the competitive bidding. It implies that less solvent suppliers can always reproduce the bids of financially healthy suppliers (since their minimum bid is higher) and hence become indistinguishable from the financially healthy suppliers. While the probability of bankruptcy is reduced due to a higher payment, the competition does not exclude suppliers with the higher probability of bankruptcy from the competitive tendering. This insight is discussed in more detail in the next section.

13.4.2. Average bid wins

Excluding the lowest bids from the competitive bidding is similar to the average bid method where the average bidder wins the contract. Such a method or similar methods were used in Italy, Peru and Taiwan. Alternatively, one might think that taking the second lowest bid to be the winning bid is the appropriate procurement rule (as reported to us as being used in Switzerland). Again suppliers' bidding behaviour will be affected by this change in rules. In a procurement environment, this rule implies that if the rules specify that the second lowest bid (or the average bid) wins the contest, no one will want to deliver a low bid. As this is anticipated by everyone, everyone will raise his bid even further, which might lead to very high bids. Bankruptcy might be eliminated but at a very high price.[25]

The argument for the average bid method is similar. Suppose every supplier bids the same high price, then everyone makes the average bid, and everyone has the same chance of winning the contract. And, if one wins, she

---

[24] Usually, the firm is automatically excluded but has the opportunity to justify its bid and be readmitted if the justification is satisfactory. In practice readmission is very rare.

[25] The following story from cycling nicely illustrates how. In the quarter final of the individual pursuit World Championships in Milan in 1955, the Dutch cyclist Jan Derksen had to compete with the Italian Antonio Maspes. After the first round, Maspes was in first position and Derksen had the advantage of the windbreak, in which he needs about 20 percent less energy. With the disadvantage of being first, Maspes stopped and tried to force Derksen to the first place, but the latter also stopped. After 32 minutes and 20 seconds without moving the officials stopped the race. After it was started again, Maspes won the race. As it turned out, the desire to be second and not first, made the cyclists to move very slowly.

will make a decent profit as the price is quite high. Offering any other bid implies moving away from the average, thus the supplier will lose the contest for sure. Therefore, bidding this price is an equilibrium. As everyone tries to be just average, this will take the competition out of the contest. These attempts to deal with ALTs lead to undesirable results as it pays not to be among the lowest suppliers. In general, these designs will lead to lower (or zero) bankruptcy rates but at very high prices.

Practical conclusion 5
Do not design your procurement such that it pays not to be among the first.

One issue which complicates this analysis even further is the possibility of fake bids. In some cases the buyer does not control who offers a bid and how many bids someone offers. If the rule is such that the average bid wins, it may pay for a contractor to offer one extremely high bid to raise the average, and then a second bid close to the expected average. Fake bidding, also known as shill bids, is very hard to analyse theoretically. However, as the strategic behaviour in competitive bidding with shill bidding is very complicated to determine, it does not seem to be a good advice to design the procurement such that shill bids might become attractive.

13.4.3. Subsidizing weaker firms

The buyer might have some information about who might be a weak supplier (e.g., the local contractor, a small and medium sized enterprise, etc.), which has less financial means. Suppose that the buyer wants to keep the weaker supplier in the contest, either for political reasons or to foster competition. One might argue that in order to lower the risk of bankruptcy, it is useful then to subsidize the weaker bidder. This subsidy can take the form of a price preference, a bonus or a discount. Such a scheme is used, for instance, in some countries which favour domestic companies by giving them discounts (e.g., the Buy American Act in the US public procurement gives domestic firms a discount of 6 percent and small domestic firms a discount of 12 percent). This rule is at first glance risk reducing – subsidizing a weak bidder will make him go bankrupt less often. However, a closer look at the consequences shows that a subsidy has three effects on the outcome, two of which might increase the risk for the buyer. The positive effect is that, as the subsidy is paid in case of winning to the weak supplier, the supported firm has to cover less costs. Thus, the supported supplier goes bankrupt less often. The two negative effects are as follows. First, as the subsidized supplier can bid lower than without the subsidy, there is more competition in the contest and prices are lower in general.[26] Following the logic of section 3.1 (weaken competition to reduce the risk), using a subsidy to foster competition will increase the risk of bankruptcy. Thus, this effect is good in terms of lower prices but it is does not improve the outcome from a risk point of view. Second, as the subsidy makes the weak supplier more aggressive, it can be the case that a weak supplier only wins because of the discount. Then, a less efficient and less solvent supplier wins over a more efficient and more solvent supplier, which is again bad news for the buyer. As the two negative effects can offset the positive effect, subsidizing weaker bidders does not help to reduce the risk of bankruptcy.[27] As subsidizing weaker bidders makes them bid even more aggressively this increases the risk of bankruptcy.

Practical conclusion 6
In the presence of limited liability do not subsidize weaker competitors.

13.5. Conclusion

In this chapter we have explained why low bids can be bad news for the buyer. Potentially insolvent firms protected by limited liability bid very aggressively for a project with uncertain costs since they have little to lose in case of bankruptcy. If the cost turns out to be low, they make profits; however, if the cost turns out to be high, their losses are limited since they close down the firm. This aggressive bidding known as the problem of abnormally low tenders leads to a high risk of bankruptcy and destroys the screening capability of competitive bidding to select the most adequate supplier. Moreover, strong competition can even worsen the outcome. On the other hand some competition might still be necessary to select the more efficient supplier and to keep prices under control.

The potential remedies for this problem try to reduce the risk of bankruptcy by increasing the procurement payment and by designing the procurement

---

[26] This is the argument used by McAfee and McMillan (1989) to justify the use of the Buy American Act, as it leads to lower prices.

[27] See Engel and Wambach (2006b) for more details.

mechanism such that the more solvent supplier is selected. They also try to reduce the impact of bankruptcy to the buyer.

Increasing the payment is an easy task: measures like minimum bids or a competitive tendering format, which weaken competition (such as the truncated English auction) might be appropriate. Designing the mechanism to select the right supplier is more difficult. While typical competitive bidding formats are likely to select the supplier with the lowest budget, most of the remedies (entry fees, truncated English auction) eliminate this bias in favour of the less solvent supplier but do not select a healthy firm for sure. The cost for the buyer in case of bankruptcy might be reduced by letters of credits or multi-sourcing. But these instruments also have drawbacks. Multi-sourcing is not always possible and, in case of capacity constraints or correlation between suppliers, might not be risk reducing. Letters of credits tend to worsen the financial situation of the competing supplier and might convert some good suppliers into potentially insolvent suppliers.

While there does not exist any perfect remedy for abnormally low tenders, a surety bond seems to be a fairly good remedy: screening is delegated to the private sector (some surety company) that is made co-responsible in the case of bankruptcy. The surety company will base the surety fee on the financial status of the firm and might even deny the bond to less solvent firms. The fees for the bond are higher for less solvent firms whose bid are therefore increased considerably. Hence, the bias of the competitive mechanism towards less solvent suppliers is reduced. Moreover, if the selected contractor runs into financial difficulties this does not necessarily imply a bankruptcy cost for the buyer because the surety company might finish the project. Otherwise, the costs of bankruptcy are reduced by the size of the surety bond. Surety bonds thus combine the three potential ways to reduce the problem of abnormally low tenders.

Bibliographical notes

The limited liability effect is derived in different settings by Zheng (2001), Calveras et al. (2002, 2004), Parlane (2003), Board (2005), Engel and Wambach (2006a). Calveras et al. (2002, 2004) in procurement auctions and Zheng (2001) in standard selling auctions analyse the bidding behaviour of bidders with different budgets and show that the most aggressive bidder is the bidder with the lowest budget. The performance of different auction formats under limited liability is evaluated in Parlane (2003), Board (2005) and Engel and Wambach (2006a). To learn more about letters of credit and surety bonds see Calveras et al. (2004). The functioning of surety bonds in practice (mainly in the United States) is described in Donohue and Thomas (1996) or at the surety information office (http://www.sio.org/). The European and in particular the Spanish regulation on dealing with abnormally low tenders is discussed in Calveras et al. (2002). For the truncated English auction, multi-sourcing, entry fees and further means to weaken competition see Engel and Wambach (2006a). For the analysis of national discrimination (supporting weaker contractors) and its consequences for the insolvency of contractors see Engel and Wambach (2006b).

References

Arditi, D., A. Koksal and S. Kale (2000). Business Failure in the Construction Industry, *Engineering, Construction and Architectural Management*, 7 (2), 120–132.

Arvan, L. and A. Leite (1990). Cost Overruns in Long-Term Projects, *International Journal of Industrial Organization*, 8 (3), 443–467.

Bajari, P. and S. Tadelis (2001). Incentives Versus Transaction Costs: A Theory of Procurement Contracts, *RAND Journal of Economics*, 32 (3), 287–307.

Board, S. (2005). Bidding into the Red: A Model of Post Auction Bankruptcy, working paper, University of Toronto.

Calveras, A., J. Ganuza, and E. Hauk (2004). Wild Bids. Gambling for Resurrection in Procurement Contracts, *Journal of Regulatory Economics*, 26 (1), 41–68.

Calveras, A., J. Ganuza and E. Hauk (2002). Las bajas temerarias en las subastas de obras públiucas. Un análisis de la regulación española, *Hacienda Pública*, 162-(3), 135–153.

Donohue, D. and G. Thomas, (1996). Surety Bond Basics, Construction Briefings, Federal Publications, Inc.

Engel, A. and A. Wambach (2005). Insuring Abnormally Low Bids, working paper, Univerisity of cologne.

Engel, A. and A. Wambach (2006a). Public procurement under limited liability, forthcoming in the Journal (this year!): Rivista di Politica Economica.

Engel, A. and A. Wambach (2006b). A Note on National Discrimination in Procurement, working paper, University of Cologne.

European Commission, working Group on Abnormally Low Tenders (1999). Prevention, Detection and Elimination of Abnormaly Low Tenders in the European Construction Industry, resport.

Ganuza, J. (1997). Los sobrecostes en las obras publicas. Un analisis economico del caso español, *Economia Industrial*, 318, 111–122.

Ganuza, J. (2000). Competition and Cost Overruns. Optimal Misspecification in Procurement Contracts, working paper 471, Universitat Pompeu Fabra.

Gilbert, R. and Klemperer, P. (2000). An Equilibrium Theory of Rationing, *RAND Journal of Economics*, 31, 1–21.

Gresik, J. (2001). Rationing Rules and European Central Bank Auctions, *Journal of International Money and Finance*, 20, 793–808.

Klemperer, P. (2004). *Auctions: Theory and Practice*, Princeton University Press: Princeton, NJ.

Krishna, V. (2002). *Auction Theory*, Academic Press: San Diego, CA.

Lewis, T. (1986). Reputation and Contractual Performance in Long-Term Projects, *RAND Journal of Economics*, 17, 141–157.

McAfee, P. and J. McMillan (1989). Government Procurement and International Trade, *Journal of International Economics*, 26, 291–308.

Milgrom, P. (2004) Putting Auction Theory to Work, Cambridge University Press: Cambridge, UK.

Parlane, S. (2003). Procurement Contracts under Limited Liability, *The Economic and Social Review*, 34, 1–21.

Peck, M. and F. M. Scherer (1962). The Weapons Acquisition Process: an Economic Analysis, Harvard University Press: Cambridge, MA.

Wambach, A. (2002). A Simple Result for Revenue in Share Auctions, *Economics letters*, 75, 405–408.

White, M. J. (1989). The Corporate Bankruptcy Decision, *Journal of Economic Perspectives*, 3 (2), 129–151.

Zheng, C. Z. (2001). High Bids and Broke Winners, *Journal of Economic Theory*, 100, 129–171.

PART V

Preventing collusion and corruption

14 Preventing collusion in procurement

Gian Luigi Albano, Paolo Buccirossi,
Giancarlo Spagnolo and Matteo Zanza

The system of sealed bids, publicly opened with full identification of each bidder's price and specifications, is the ideal instrument for the detection of price-cutting. (Stigler, 1964, p. 48.)

14.1. Introduction

Competitive procurements are commonly designed to select the most efficient contractor in a pool of competing firms and to maximize the buyer's savings. Competition is not, however, firms' preferred scenario. Firms dislike cutthroat behaviour. They would rather coordinate their actions in order to soften price competition and raise joint profit. Coordination, whether explicit or tacit, is both tempting and feasible since most procurements are repeated over time. In oligopolistic markets it typically takes a rather simple form. Firms set a high price and keep it stable over time only if no one undercuts its rivals at any point in time. Cheating is normally deterred by the threat of a possibly ever-lasting price war. The emergence of 'bidding rings' in procurement, that is, collusive agreements in tendering processes, is driven by forces very similar to those governing cartel formation in oligopolistic markets. As Stigler pointed out, transparency of procurement processes may facilitate collusion since a cartel can promptly identify and punish defecting firms.

Successful bidding rings greatly increase supply price or reduce supplied quality at a given price and are therefore a central concern in procurement design. As John Vickers, Chairman of the UK Office of Fair Trade (OFT), puts it with: Collusive tendering deprives customers of the benefits of competition.[1]

Cartel formation is far from being a theoretical speculation. France recently fined twenty-one construction companies €17.3 million for

---

[1] This is taken from: http://www.oft.gov.uk/News/Press+releases/2005/126-05.htm

concerted practices involved with bidding for the building of a highway. In the Netherlands, 344 companies were fined for bid-rigging in connection with public work contracts relating to the high-speed rail link to Belgium and France. In the United Kingdom, on 12 July 2005 the Office of Fair Trading announced that it had fined six roofing contractors in western-central Scotland for price-fixing through collusive tendering in breach of Chapter 1 of the Competition Act. In December 2005, OFT investigators reported that they had uncovered evidence of more than 1,000 suspect cases of bid-rigging among construction companies, involving contracts worth £500 million, in the previous eleven months alone.[2] In 2004 the Finnish and the Swedish Competition Authorities uncovered a cartel in the asphalt market that had run for almost ten years. According to the Swedish Competition Authority, following the exposure of the asphalt cartel, the National Road Administration, who was the main 'victim' of the cartel, has recorded a 25–30 percent drop in prices in some regions. In 2001, the Italian Competition Authority (ICA) fined a collusive agreement among some of the participants in a competitive tendering for the provision of 'Lunch Coupon.' Eight out of ten firms were convicted for bid-rigging. The investigation proved that the cartel members had agreed on the composition of bidding consortia, which varied across lots, on the bids that each group had to submit, and on the identity of the firm in each group that had to become the only active participant in the tendering process. These are just a few examples of the most recent cases of collusion in competitive procurement.

What does 'collusion' means? For practical purposes, collusion can be thought of as any conduct adopted by a group of firms that aims at reproducing or approximating the market outcome induced by a single, dominant firm. To achieve such an objective, firms need to coordinate their strategies either tacitly or explicitly. They face then a non-trivial problem of choosing a profile of coordinated strategies. In competitive procurements, such coordination may take several forms:

1. price-fixing or 'bid-rigging', whereby colluding firms select the winning bidder and the winning bid. All other cartel members are instructed to bid higher prices or less favourable conditions ('phoney bids'). This collusive scheme requires the definition of a sharing rule according to which the winning bidder transfers some of the rent to other cartel members. This could be achieved in a scenario of repeated competitive

---

[2] see *The Times*, 2 December 2005.

bidding, for example, by a rotating mechanism that selects a different winner at each single date;

2. market-sharing agreements, whereby customers are divided according to some relevant characteristics (e.g., location) and assigned to a predetermined winning bidder. Each cartel member apart from the designated winner agrees to submit a phoney bid.

3. 'Bidding fees', whereby a trade association (or a consortium) charges a fee for the privilege of submitting a bid. Bidders add this fee to their bid. Funds accumulated through bidding fees are later returned to the cartel members according to some predetermined sharing rule.

Even if firms are able to agree on a mechanism to 'share the pie', collusion still entails a second fundamental problem, that is, the enforcement of the collusive scheme. Although gains from collusive coordination are evident, each single firm (or at least some of them) can raise its short-run profits by deviating unilaterally from the coordinated action and stealing business from colluding rivals. Obviously, firms cannot rely on the legal system to enforce their illegal collusive scheme. Therefore they are bound to use self-discipline, that is, a market mechanism that punishes defections. When suppliers are long-run competitors, an effective enforcement mechanism consists in firms monitoring each other's market conduct. Any deviation from the coordinated strategy is usually punished by phases of price wars generally involving all conspiring firms. Thus if the present value of short-run gains from a deviation is lower than the present value of the long-run loss caused by the subsequent phase of harsh competition, each firm would find it rational to adhere to the collusive scheme and never deviate from it.

We can conclude, as a general statement, that a factor facilitates collusion if (i) it helps firms solve the 'coordination problem' by providing some simple rule to 'share the pie'; or (ii) it reduces the short-run profits a firm can gain by reneging on the collusive agreement; or (iii) makes punishment swifter or more severe; or (iv) it increases the level of collusive profits. The opposite statement is true if conditions (i)–(iv) are reversed. This brief discussion has highlighted that some factors may have ambiguous effects on collusion. For instance, they may loosen the coordination problem but reduce the scope for enforcement, or increase both collusive and deviation profits. The assessment of the impact of these factors on collusion must follow a case-by-case analysis.

The chapter is organized as follows. In section 14.2, we investigate how structural factors of the procurement market affect the sustainability of collusion. We put forward some arguments developed by economic analysis for standard oligopolies, and then discuss their specific application to procurement. In section 14.3 we discuss how the buyer's appropriate choice of the tendering format, awarding rule and of the admissibility of bidding consortia and subcontracting may reduce the risk of successful bid-rigging. Appendix 14.1 contains a detailed account of how the ICA uncovered (and convicted) an active cartel in the Meal Coupons Procurement, while Appendix 14.2 explores some of the potentially pro-collusive features of the recent EU Directive 2004/18/EC concerning framework agreements in procurement.

14.2. Structural factors affecting collusion

14.2.1. Number of competitors

In oligopoly the number of competitors affects collusion for two main reasons.

1. The higher the number of competitors in a market the more difficult the coordination among them. Reaching an agreement on market shares and on prices becomes more complex as the number of firms increases.

2. The higher the number of collusive firms, the smaller the share of the 'pie' they get. This implies that the gains from deviating from a collusive agreement increase with since the 'residual market' a firm could steal by undercutting the collusive price increases relative to the defective firms' collusive share.

The forces just highlighted are also at work in competitive procurements. As a general rule, a high number of participants hinders collusion because it makes both the coordination and the enforcement problem of a collusive scheme more difficult.[3]

14.2.2. Entry barriers

Strictly related to the number of participants is the issue of entry barriers. Actual and potential entry of new competitors in a market is probably the most important force that limits collusion. Entry hinders collusion because

---

[3] This rule admits, however, some exceptions. There are circumstances under which increasing the number of bidders may end up facilitating a coordinated behaviour. For instance, one of the more frequently advocated reasons for splitting procurement contracts in several smaller lots is to foster participation. However, the absolute number of participants provides only a partial indicator of the expected level of competition. The crucial aspect that any procurer should take care of is the relationship between the number of participants and the number of lots. For a more detailed discussion, see Chapter 7.

potential competitors, attracted by above-the-normal rate of returns, will tend to disrupt an existing collusive scheme. Only if there are barriers to entry incumbent firms may enjoy supra-competitive profit without fearing the threat of new competitors. Moreover, entry diminishes the scope for retaliation, which in turns limits the sustainability of collusion. More in detail, even if future entry does not affect short-run benefits deriving from deviation, it reduces the potential cost of deviation in terms of foregone future profits thus making retaliation against a deviating firm less effective.

This applies to standard oligopolies as well as to procurement markets. There are many ways to ease entry in procurement, including simplifying tender procedures, reducing entry fees, or using on-line auctions.[4] The procurer may also foster participation by augmenting the number of lots and, consequently, by lowering their individual economic value (thus lowering a possible barrier to entry); smaller firms should then find it easier to participate in the competitive bidding.[5] Another factor that may limit entry is the strategic advantage an incumbent acquires over time due to the ownership of complementary assets.[6] For instance, Italian Local Health Authorities ran a series of tendering to acquire blood glucose test devices. These are made of two complementary products, a test strip and an optical reader, that are incompatible across the different devices. Although the tendering required bidders to submit a bid for the entire system, the incumbents had a strong advantage in that they already had their optical readers distributed to the Local Health Authority. According to the Italian Competition Authority, this aspect helped the major producers of blood glucose test devices coordinate their response to the competitive procedures adopted by the Local Health Authorities.[7]

14.2.3. Frequency of interactions

The more frequently the same group of competitors interact the more easily sustainable collusion becomes since deviations can be punished more promptly. If, instead, firms compete more infrequently, they have a lower

---

[4] A variety of instruments to facilitate participation is examined in Chapter 11.

[5] This recommendation should, however, be coupled with a warning. A higher number of smaller lots may encourage participation, but if the number of participants does not increase substantially, it may facilitate collusion. For this reason, it may be worth using the competition indexes developed in Chapter 7 to evaluate the effects of different division in lots on participation and collusion.

[6] For more detailed analysis on the problem of lock-in see Chapters 7 and 17.

[7] See Decision No. 19946 of the ICA of 30 April 2003, Bollettino No. 18/03.

ability to sustain collusion as deviations can be punished only in a distant future.[8]

In procurement, the frequency of interaction can be identified with the frequency of tendering processes held by the procurer. Typically, the frequency of interaction is negatively related to the length of the supply contract: the longer the duration of contracts the less frequent are the contacts among firms. This feature is likely to affect bidders' collusive behaviour. Short contracts do not induce firms to deviate from the cartel since punishment would be inflicted in the near future; long contracts can hinder collusion since deviating becomes more profitable.

Practical conclusion 1
When risk of collusion is high, favour a longer contract length.

In designing tenders, the procurer should consider the market for procurement as a whole rather than treating each type of goods and services as distinct markets. The main reason is that many of the suppliers are multi-product firms which meet repeatedly in procurements for different goods.

14.2.4. Market transparency: disclosure and collusion

Market transparency facilitates collusion by making deviations from the collusive agreement more easily detectable by rivals who can promptly retaliate. Therefore, collusion becomes easier to sustain when prices are readily observable. The nature of information that can be inferred from market data is then a crucial factor in determining the degree of market transparency.

Transparency in competitive procurements for multiple contracts refers mainly to the amount of information disclosed to bidders across different phases of the same tendering process. A completely opaque disclosure policy, hiding all information to bidders, would make collusion difficult to sustain. It is almost impossible to sustain collusion if each firm is unable to observe its competitors' strategies. If cheating cannot be detected, there is no ground to decide whether and when to punish a defector since firms do not know if a defection has taken place. The same logic applies to those competitive

---

[8] A similar logic applies to the frequency of price adjustments: the more frequent adjustments the easier it is to sustain collusion since non-defecting firms can retaliate quickly after a defection has taken place.

procurements in which several goods or services are bought *sequentially*. If the risk of collusion is high, the only disclosure policy with a strong impact is no disclosure, that is, keeping all information on bids and winners on each lot secret to all bidders.[9] However, since procurement agencies generally operate on behalf of the public, they simply cannot afford a fully opaque disclosure policy owing to the risk of corruption. Obvious reasons impose the procurer to reveal to the winning bidder that he has been selected and to the other bidders that they have lost. Thus the degree of transparency concerns the amount of information released to non-winning bidders. Among all possible partial disclosure policies, publicly disclosing only the selling price(s) may affect the cartel's ability to detect and punish internal deviations. All other partial disclosure policies are practically equivalent to a fully transparent one.[10]

Again, a partial disclosure policy that reveals only the selling price(s) would appear too opaque in terms of the risk of corruption it may generate. So, if a buyer is bound to adopt a transparent format, one could still make collusion somewhat harder by altering the timing of disclosure. Delaying publication of information as much as possible, thereby hiding as long as possible the identity of possible deviant(s) from the cartel's prescribed bidding strategies, may increase gains from undercutting cartels and possibly destabilize some of them.

Practical conclusion 2
Delaying information disclosure hinders collusion among bidders. Partial disclosure policies have often little effect.

14.2.5. Demand growth

Procuring goods and services often takes place in rapidly evolving markets such as computers and energy. To what extent does an expanding market affect firms' ability to collude? It is intuitive that, for a fixed number of participants, collusion is easier to sustain in growing markets. Since future profits will be much higher than current ones, the gains from complying with the collusive agreement grow over time, so the temptation of cheating becomes lower. This logic, however, does not take into account that growing markets usually attract new entrants whose presence is disruptive

---

[9] The pro-collusive features of sequential auctions is explored by Albano and Spagnolo (2005) who also analyze how the seller (the buyer in procurement auctions) can counterbalance these effects by varying the degree of transparency of the auction mechanism.

[10] See also Blume and Heidhues (2004).

for operating cartels. Hence, growing markets generate two forces: the first is pro-collusive, the second anti-collusive. The resulting outcome is generally unpredictable. The level of barriers to entry is then the crucial factor to assess the relative strength of the two opposite forces. When barriers to entry are low, growing markets may attract a large number of new firms compared to the ones already active (and colluding). The anti-collusive effect is likely to more than compensate the pro-collusive effect generated by a growing market. When barriers to entry are high, instead, existing firms are protected from new entrants, so the prospect of higher collusive gains in the future produces an overall pro-collusive outcome.

14.2.6. Demand fluctuations and business cycle

Collusion is generally considered more difficult to sustain when markets are subject to demand fluctuations. The idea is simple. When the market is at a peak, deviating from the cartel brings the maximum gains while the potential cost of retaliation is at minimum. This means that when demand is higher than average, deviations are more tempting and therefore collusion is more difficult to sustain. The same analysis is valid for seasonality and business cycles.

14.2.7. Asymmetry in market shares

It is often argued that asymmetry in market shares hinders collusion since smaller firms have higher gains from deviating (and a larger fraction of the market to steal). However, this argument is exposed to the criticism that market shares are endogenous, since they depend on more fundamental asymmetries such as production costs, capacity, product range or quality. Moreover, smaller firms are more financially fragile and, therefore, more easily deterred from cheating by the prospect of a price war. Consequently, market shares seem not to constitute a relevant factor for a detailed analysis. In procurement, however, market shares may play an important role in the sustainability of collusive agreements. Indeed, market shares often determine a supplier's ability to compete for procurement contracts and, consequently, a cartel's ability to allocate lots among its members.[11]

---

[11] The Italian Procurement Agency (Consip S.p.A.), for instance, awards contracts only to suppliers with sufficiently high market shares (measured by the supplier's yearly turnover in an analogous business).

14.2.7.1. Coordination

Supply contracts are often split into several lots. Suppliers' decisions regarding which lots to compete for typically depend on their preferences but are constrained by their production capacities which, in turn, may determine their market shares. If the contracts are split in small lots and a potentially large number of both large and small firms may participate, coordination for agreeing on specific 'pie sharing' may become too complex. Hence, if firms are asymmetric, that is with different market shares, symmetric (i.e. of similar value) lots may constitute an anti-collusive device.[12]

14.7.2.2. Enforcement

Market shares determine the number of active participants and thus the size of a potential cartel. Therefore, strong asymmetry in market shares may imply low participation of smaller firms. This may in turn facilitate collusion by preventing small firms to threaten larger ones.

14.2.8. Cost asymmetries

Cost asymmetries make collusion more difficult to sustain for three related reasons:

1. Firms may find it difficult to agree on a common pricing policy. Low cost firms would be inclined to choose a lower price than the one that high cost firms are willing to sustain. This makes the choice of the collusive price ('focal point') difficult.

2. Even if firms are able to overcome the problem of coordinating on a collusive price, it is nonetheless more difficult to discipline low cost firms since they can obtain higher gains from undercutting the cartel and are less worried about price wars.

3. Since the incentive to deviate is linked to the collusive profit, in order to prevent low cost firms from undercutting the cartel price colluding firms should agree to share profits asymmetrically: low cost firms should get a bigger share of collusive profit. However, high cost firms would get lower shares of the collusive profit which, in turn, increases their incentive to deviate from the collusive agreement.

Consequently, cost asymmetries reduce the possibility of sustainable collusive agreements when compared with symmetric costs.

---

[12] See Chapter 7 for a more in-depth analysis of this issue.

In procurement cost asymmetries may produce an additional effect that inhibits collusion. Since a procurement contract is not a perfectly divisible object, asymmetric firms may find it impossible to implement an asymmetric market sharing agreement whenever the contract is split into several, homogenous lots.

14.2.9. Asymmetries in capacity

When suppliers have symmetric capacity constraints, the impact of these constraints on collusion is generally ambiguous. On the one hand, a capacity constrained firm has less to gain from undercutting the cartel price since it can serve demand only up to its capacity (pro-collusive effect); on the other hand, a capacity constrained firm has a limited power of retaliation (anti-collusive effect).

Asymmetries in capacities have less ambiguous effects. A firm with larger capacity than other competitors has a strong incentive to undercut the cartel price since its rivals have a low retaliatory power. In this sense asymmetries in capacity constraints tend to mitigate collusion in oligopolistic markets as well as in procurement.

The asymmetries discussed in this and the previous sections (market shares, costs and capacity) generally do not depend on the design of a single tendering process and, therefore, cannot be directly influenced by the procurer. However, the procurer may take them into account when designing a tender in order to reduce the risk of collusion.

> ### Practical conclusion 3
> If the potential bidders have asymmetric market shares, costs or capacity, a division of the contract in homogeneous lots may discourage collusion.
> If the potential bidders have symmetric market shares, costs or capacity, a division of the contract in heterogeneous lots may discourage collusion.

14.2.10. Product differentiation

In most markets, suppliers produce goods and services that consumers do not consider as perfect substitutes. Products may differ in terms of an intrinsic attribute (quality). Thus, consumers are willing to pay a higher price for a high-quality product. This is normally called 'vertical differentiation'. Another source of differentiation is generated when products are offered, possibly at comparable prices, in different combinations of characteristics (colour, shape, location). This form of product differentiation, called 'horizontal differentiation', aims at creating brand loyalty. The consequences of horizontal product differentiation on collusion are, in general, unclear. Horizontally differentiated firms gain less from deviating from a collusive agreement since they can attract a potentially tiny fraction of rivals' customers. At the same time, they are less vulnerable to retaliation because some of their customers will not be lured by competing offers. Reduced gains from deviation make collusion more stable, whereas a less severe punishment hinders collusion. Overall the impact of horizontal differentiation appears quite ambiguous.

The consequences of vertically differentiated products on collusion are more clear-cut. Vertical differentiation creates asymmetries that can disrupt collusion. To some extent, a firm that offers a better quality is situated as if it were enjoying a cost advantage. Thus vertical differentiation can be assimilated to cost asymmetries, and some of the conclusions drawn in section 14.2.8 would hold true here as well. However, while the supply of a low quality substitute creates a welfare inefficiency, it may be considered welfare increasing if it allows price discrimination. That is, some consumers, who are not willing to pay the high price of the high-quality product, may buy the low quality product at a price that is below their willingness to pay and above the economic cost of production. Therefore, a producer must decide whether or not she wants to buy low-quality goods to satisfy part of the demand that would not be served by the high-quality firm. In the first case a division of the contract in lots defined according to the quality of the product may serve this efficiency purpose, but may strongly increase the risk of collusion.

14.2.11. Multi-market contact

It is well known that multi-market contacts can facilitate collusion in obligopoly. There are two main reasons that explain this proposition.
1. Firms that meet in more markets interact more frequently and can therefore coordinate more easily.
2. These firms can level asymmetries that may arise in a single market. For example, using the threat of abandoning collusion in one market to enforce collusion in other markets, where this would not be sustainable in the absence of this additional threat.

This is valid in procurement activity as well. This is the reason why, in the section about frequency of interactions, we wrote that, while evaluating the frequency of competitive procurements it is important to look also at every market in which large suppliers are active and not only at the single market for each good.

In the next sections we discuss some specific factors of a tendering process that may facilitate or hinder collusion. These are the tendering format, simultaneous and sequential tendering processes, some relevant tendering rules, and the admissibility of bidding consortia and subcontracting.

14.3. Tendering formats

A procurer may choose among several tendering format which are mainly defined according to the possibility for bidders to improve their bids (dynamic, auction vs. sealed-bid tendering), and to the way the buying price is determined (lowest price vs. second-lowest price competitive tendering). Other tendering rules are discussed in section 14.3.4.

14.3.1. Dynamic auction vs. sealed-bid competitive tendering

A dynamic auction makes collusion more likely as a defector faces the threat of immediate retaliation by the designated winner.[13] Indeed, if some firms form a ring and designate the most efficient firm as the winner of the contract, any member of the ring cannot offer a lower price (or a higher rebate) without triggering the immediate response by the designated winner. This will provoke a further reduction of the price so that the deviating form cannot gain from its behaviour. In a sealed-bid competitive tendering, once a bidding ring identifies the designated winner, all other bidders must withdraw from the competitive tendering or submit phoney bids, while the designated winner submits a bid above his valuation. In this case a designated loser, by deviating, has a chance to win as the designated winner cannot immediately react to his deviation. For a more detailed analysis and practical conclusion on this see Chapter 15.

---

[13] See Klemperer (2004).

14.3.2. Lowest price vs. second-lowest price

An active cartel would use different strategies in a lowest and a second-lowest price competitive tendering to secure the same amount of collusive profit. In a lowest price competitive tendering, the collusive agreement would call the most efficient firm in the cartel to submit an offer equal to the reserve price while other cartel members do not participate. Alternatively, the most efficient firm may submit a bid marginally below the reserve price while other cartel members submit offers equal to the reserve price. In a second-lowest price competitive tendering, instead, the most efficient firm would submit a bid equal to its production cost while other members submit offers equal to the reserve price. Thus, in a second-lowest price competitive tendering, it is not profitable for a cartel member to defect from the collusive strategy since this would require undercutting the most efficient firm and would result in negative profit for the defector since the awarding price coincides with the marginal cost of the most efficient firm.[14] In a lowest price competitive tendering, the most efficient firm pays a price equal to the reserve price (or marginally below), so it is still possible that a defector slightly undercuts the collusive price and makes positive profit.

Practical conclusion 4

A second-lowest price competitive tendering is highly exposed to the risk of collusion.

Second-lowest price competitive tendering in procurement takes almost always the form of descending competitive processes (if bids are absolute prices, alternatively they become ascending in discounts). Such mechanisms may also facilitate collusion with respect to sealed-bid tendering in that defections can be immediately detected and punished.[15]

14.3.3. Simultaneous vs. Sequential competitive tendering

Sequential lowest price tendering processes of multiple objects are very common in publich procurement. Supply contracts for different but related goods (for example printers, laptops, desktops, monitors, servers) are typically awarded separately, i.e. sequentially rather than simultaneously. For multi-product bidders active on several of the goods procured by the

---

[14] See Graham and Marshall (1987).
[15] This point is investigated in more depth in Chapter 15.

buyer, the procurement process turns into a sequential, lowest price tendering of multiple objects.

There are two ways in which a sequential format may facilitate collusion among bidders relative to a simultaneous one.[16] In many real world sequential competitive procurements there is full information disclosure after each object is awarded, so we maintain this assumption during this discussion.[17]

The first intuitive collusive drawback of a sequential competitive procurement is linked to the ability of ring members to identify defections and react faster, within the same sequence. This limits the short-run gains a bidder can obtain by undercutting his cartel, facilitating the enforcement of collusion with respect to a simultaneous format. In case of procurement of related goods, this effect can be seen as an increase in the frequency of interaction. It is stronger when the number of related goods sequentially procured is large (or when the lots are small).

The second effect is linked to the possible asymmetry within a ring of colluding suppliers. The viability of cartels is often limited by the presence of so called 'mavericks', that is firms that are difficult to discipline as they have more to gain from undercutting a cartel (or less to gain from being part of it).[18] If firms are asymmetric, a sequential competitive tendering can facilitate collusion by allowing the ring to soften the maverick's aggressiveness by allocating to him the last object(s) in a given sequence. This minimizes the maverick's incentive to defect and improves the viability of the ring.

Practical conclusion 5

Sequential competitive procurements facilitate collusion. If collusion is a major concern, try to procure simultaneously all supply contracts on which the same bidders are active.

14.3.4. Alternative rules for dynamic auctions

Dynamic auctions for multiple contracts are particularly susceptible to the so-called 'in-auction' collusion. The dynamic feature of this kind of competitive procurements embeds a particular form of repeated interaction that

---

[16] See Albano and Spagnolo (2005).

[17] Disclosure policies that may counteract this effect are discussed in Section 14.2.4.

[18] See, for instance, Baker (2002).

allows bidders to adopt more sophisticated strategies than in simultaneous tendering formats. The more transparent dynamic auctions, that is, the more information the buyer releases about bidders' behaviour, the more likely various forms of tacit coordination arise since deviations can be easily detected and punished. However, the transparency of bidding process also allows extensive information revelation that favours bidders' efficient aggregation of objects. The trade-off between efficiency and tacit collusion has characterized the assessment of the long series of the FCC auctions that were designed in the United States since 1995. In what follows, we summarize the main communication devices used by participants in the various FCC auctions, and we come to some conclusions that might limit the occurrence of such coordination.

Code bidding. Code bidding was one of the more obvious forms of signalling. Since bids were expressed in dollars and since, at least in the FCC auctions, most objects displayed six-digit prices, bidders could use the last digits to encode messages. Code bids had different natures. Some bidders used the last three digits to 'disclose' their identities. For example, in the AB competitive bidding (Auction 4), GTE frequently used '483' as the last three digits; this number corresponds to 'GTE' on the telephone keypad. In other circumstances code bidding had a *reflexive* nature. The last three digits were used by a bidder both to signal an object of special interest to him and the object on which the same bidder was punishing competitors for not bumping the first market.[19] Such communication devices may become ineffective if the procurer (i) publishes only a subset of anonymous bids (say, the highest five bids out of ten), (ii) limits the bidders' degree of freedom in choosing the last digits.

Jump bidding. In dynamic auctions, it is not always in the bidders' interest to lower prices at the minimum pace required by the tendering rules. A bidder can benefit by using jump bids as a signal of a low cost (or high valuation), possibly causing other bidders to drop out earlier. This may lead to lower savings for the buyer.[20] The use of such a strategy may be limited by imposing an upper bound to the bids increase. Interestingly, the FCC took a similar decision in the LMDS competitive tendering (Auction 17).[21]

---

[19] See Cramton (1997) and Cramton and Schwartz (1999, 2000) for detailed accounts of collusive behaviour in the actual FCC auctions. See also FCC Report 1A, 1997.

[20] See Gunderson and Wang (1998). Avery (1998) also constructs equilibria involving jump bids in the context of one-object English auctions with affiliated values.

[21] See Cramton and Schwartz (2000).

Bid withdrawals. While the FCC originally allowed unlimited number of bid withdrawals for the bidders to make more efficient aggregations of objects, it was soon noticed that they could be used as signalling devices. Withdrawal bids were used in FCC auctions[22] as part of a warning or of retaliation strategies, as well as part of cooperative strategies, where bidders attempted to split objects among themselves. In order to reduce the use of such a strategy, the seller may either limit the number of bid withdrawals or make it costly. The FCC's decision to limit their number to two, for example, in the LMDS auction (Auction 17) provides an example of the first option.

Closing rules. In order to promote price discovery and efficient aggregation of bundles of licences, the FCC auction rules specified that bidding would remain open on all objects until there were no new bids on *any* object. This simultaneous closing rule allows each losing bidder to switch at any time from the lost object to a substitute or to stop bidding on a complement. However, it has been pointed out that such rule is also vulnerable to collusion.[23] Bidders might 'split the market' by remaining active only on a small subset of objects. With two bidders and two contracts to be procured, such a strategy implies that only supplier 1 submits the highest possible bid on contract A and supplier 2 does the same on contract B. Any deviation by either bidder is punished by the other bidder reverting to a competitive bidding on both contracts. The collusive outcome is that the two contracts are awarded at the highest possible prices.

The collusive strategy depends heavily upon the simultaneous closing rule. Thus the low saving scenario constructed above would be avoided if closing were not simultaneous, but rather object-by-object. According to such a closing rule, bidding would stop on an object if at any round there is no new bid on that object.

The discussion above leads to the following practical conclusions to prevent collusion in dynamic auctions.

Practical conclusion 6

If collusion is the major concern in designing a dynamic auction, the following precautions might be adopted:
- Publish anonymous bids;
- Limit the number of bids published

---

[22] See, again, Cramton and Schwartz (2000).
[23] See Milgrom (2000).

- Limit bids in their last digits
- Make withdrawals costly
- Limit the amount of bid increments (i.e., the value of a tick)
- Adopt object-by-object closing rule

14.3.5. Awarding rules

Simplicity and transparency are generally considered good properties of tendering rules. If the buyer's preferences are clearly revealed to the market, participants can more easily formulate their bidding strategies. Transparency is a crucial attribute of scoring rules that assign a score to each bidder on the basis of both a technical and an economic offer. Transparent scoring rules are those allowing participants to compute their score before submitting their offers. In particular, bidders are able to compute the monetary value of a technical point (MVP) that captures the value of the trade-off between quality and price. If, instead, participants are unable to predict their score then the scoring rule is non-transparent. Chapter 12 deals with the possible relationship between the degree of transparency of a scoring rule and cartel's ability to sustain a collusive scheme. Here, we emphasize that a class of non-transparent scoring rules, namely average scoring rules, possesses a pro-collusive feature that is not shared by other transparent and non-transparent scoring rules. The class of average scoring rules comprises a series of awarding rules in which suppliers' score depends upon the distance from the average score. To see this in more detail, consider a procurement contract for supplying 10,000 identical laptops, with a reserve price of €1,000 each. Suppose, for the sake of simplicity, that competition takes place on the price of the laptop only, so there are no technical points related to the various quality dimensions. $N > 2$ firms participate in the competitive procurement and adopt a simple collusive mechanism: firm '1' wins the contract by submitting an offer of €999/laptop while all other $(N-1)$ firms bid the reserve price.[24] Surplus is then shared. With either linear scoring or lowest bid scoring,[25] non-winning bidders can break the cartel by just offering €998. The cost of breaking the cartel is the same for all bidders and does not depend on the transparency of the scoring rule adopted; by reducing the price by €1/laptop, any bidder is effectively able to break the agreement and win the contract.

---

[24] We assume that prices have to be formulated as multiples of €1.

[25] See Chapter 12 for a formal definition of the two scoring rules. Linear scoring is transparent whereas lowest-bid scoring is a non-transparent scoring rule.

Consider now a form of average scoring[26] that awards the contract to the supplier whose bid is closest to the average, *but* below the average. Again, the cartel selects bidder '1' to win by submitting €999. The remaining $N-1$ bidders bid the reserve price. What is the amount a deviating bidder should submit in order to win the contract? How much does the deviation cost to him? Notice first that bidder 1 is indeed the winner since €999 is the only bid below the average, where the latter is equal to $(1/N)$ €999 + $[(N-1)/N]$ €1000. To win the competitive procurement a defecting bidder, say bidder '2', needs to place a bid such that all other bids remain above the average. It is easy to see that €998 is not low enough as under linear and lowest-bid scoring. To see this more clearly, consider the situation where $N=5$. Should bidder '2' submit €998 the average would be $(998 + 999 + 3(1000))/5 =$ 999.4. With such an average bidder '1' is still the winner. As a result, €998 is not sufficient for bidder '2' to win the competitive procurement. In order to be the winner, bidder '2' needs to bring the averge below €999. Then he needs to bid a price b_{def} such that $(b_{def} + 999 + 3(1000))/5 \leq 999$, which implies $b_{def} \leq$ €996. More generally, when the number of colluding firms is N, then $b_{def} \leq (N-1)$ €999$-(N-2)$ €1000.

The simple pro-collusive feature of average-bid scoring stems from the higher cost borne by a defecting bidder to break the collusive scheme with respect to linear and lowest-bid scoring rules. This cost of defection is high when the number of colluding firms is high since the defecting bidder must counterbalance the weight of other $(N-2)$ identical bids in order to be the only below-the-average bidder. Our conclusion is at odds with a basic force that is at work in cartels in oligopolistic markets. There, other things being equal, the greater the cartel size the higher the incentive to defect since the *gains* from defection typically grow with the cartel size. Here, a greater cartel size provides a lower incentive to deviate through the higher cost of deviation.

14.3.6. Bidding consortia and subcontracting

Bidders may form bidding consortia (BCs) to participate in a competitive procurement or may assign part of the awarded contract to a different (non-winning or non-participant) supplier (subcontractor). Both contractual relationships have ambiguous effects on collusion. On the one hands, they may solve efficiency problems and foster competition by either allowing

---

[26] Since there are no technical points, the mechanism should be named 'average-bid' tendering.

participation of firms that would otherwise be excluded, or more aggressive bidding by some participants or both. On the other hand, these contracts may be instrumental to coordination as they implement distribution of profits that would otherwise be unfeasible. The complex task of a procurer is then to devise rules on the admissibility of such contracts that limit their pro-collusive utilization, without preventing their adoption for efficiency purposes.

One simple rule is to admit BCs or subcontracts if and only if they involve firms that individually would not be in the position to take part in the tendering process. This rule calls for a specification. The impossibility for individual firms to participate in the competitive bidding may either refer to the formal discipline of the tendering process, where it defines the conditions for eligibility, or to the actual economic capabilities required to provide the procured products. The two conditions may not coincide. In this case, there is a tension between rules on eligibility and rules on BCs and subcontracting. If the procurer, in order to encourage entry, softens the conditions some firms might individually satisfy the formal requirements even if their scale is insufficient to cope with the volume and type of procured products. If we apply the rule on BCs formally, these firms will be *de facto* excluded by the competitive bidding for they cannot individually participate in the tendering process because of lack of economic requisites. Moreover, they are prevented to group together by the BCs admissibility rules of the competitive procurement.

Practical conclusion 7

A bidding consortium might be considered non-admissible only if each single firm has the economic capabilities to supply the procured products.

This conclusion defines a necessary but not a sufficient condition. Even if two or more firms are economically able to supply the procured products, a bidding consortium may induce them to become more effective competitors. Consider, for instance, a market where four firms are active: two large and equally efficient firms and two firms that operate at a lower scale and face increasing marginal costs. Suppose that the two small firms are not an effective competitive constraint for the large firms. The latter are then in a position to devise a collusive mechanism to maximize their joint expected profit without compensating the small firms. If the two small firms form a BC, they can combine their production facilities and possibly obtain the same level of efficiency of the large firms. In this situation, collusion becomes more difficult because the large firms are challenged by the competitive threat of the BC and must include it in the ring to keep colluding. Hence, to the previous rule we must add the following:

Practical conclusion 8
A bidding consortium should not be considered admissible only if it does not improve the efficiency of less efficient participants.

Combining these two rules we can state that a bidding consortium should be admitted if it is either

1. composed of firms that individually do not have the economic capabilities to undertake the procured contract; or if it
2. improves upon the participants' efficiency.

The implementation of this rule may prove extremely difficult because it imposes on the procurer (or some other administrative authority) the demanding task of assessing the efficiency properties of a BC. However, one can try to approximate this result by adopting more simple rules. For instance, the procurer could declare inadmissible a BC in which participants are:

1. the incumbent operator(s);
2. the market leaders (defined with a threshold market share); or
3. the winner of competitive procurements of the same size for the same products.

Antitrust authorities (at least in Europe) have a more stringent approach in admitting BCs. Since a BC is an agreement whereby participants agree on any dimension of their commercial strategies, at least with respect to a well-defined client, it violates antitrust norms such as Article 81 of the EC Treaty, unless it concerns firms that are not actual competitors. The latter condition is satisfied only if the two firms cannot individually participate in the competitive bidding. This seems to indicate that the 'Practical Conclusion 7' may provide the necessary and sufficient condition to decide on the inadmissibility of BCs. However, if we adopt this viewpoint it must still be specified whether, in order to exclude a BC, it is sufficient that one firm is able to participate on its own or at least two firms are in the same position. If we neglect efficiency considerations and restrict our attention to a static analysis, it seems that a BC formed by a firm able to act alone and other firm(s) who can not participate by themselves is at best neutral. Suppose that, as in the previous example, there are four firms in the market, two large and two small firms, and that the two small ones cannot participate in the tendering process. If a large firm forms a BC with one of the two small firms, competition (and collusion) is bound to occur between the two large firms. If the two small firms cannot participate also by grouping, the BC between the large and the small firm does not affect the degree of competition exixting in the market and the conditios for collusion to merge. However, if the two small firms could compete by forming a BC between themselves, then a BC that binds one of the small competitors to large firm rules out the formation of this third rival and facilitates collusion among the remaining two. This situation occurred, for instance, in a case investigated by the ICA.[27] The proceeding originated from a complaint filed by the Municipality of Milan, following an unsuccessful tendering organized by the Municipality to contract the insurance coverage for a number of areas. The Municipality alleged the existence of a collusive agreement among the insurance companies which were invited to participate in the tendering. Following the boycott of two public tendering processes and a third unofficial one, the Municipality proceeded to negotiate privately with a group of companies led by Assitalia, who were the only one to take part in the tenders. The ICA found that, after the call for tender, some of the main insurance companies formed a pool of companies in order to make a co-insurance bid to the Municipality. The ICA noted that the co-insurance bid made by the BC, besides eliminating the rivalry between the members of the BC, had as its main effect the prevention of other competitive bids. These insurers, through the co-insurance provision, took part in the tender in a cooperative way, by replacing competition with collusion and preventing the contracting Municipality from receiving other competitive bids and selecting the most convenient.

14.4. What after uncovering a cartel?

An extremely important instrument to prevent collusion is to vigorously fight it *ex post*. Recent successful antitrust investigations, as those discussed in the introduction, show that suppliers are often able to devise and put in place collusive schemes to limit competition. They do so when the expected gain from colluding exceeds the expected loss stemming from an antitrust conviction. Hence, the threat of severe sanctions may discourage bidders from forming bidding rings in the first place. The dissuasive impact of a

---

[27] See ICA Decision No. 5333 of 25 September 1997, Bollettino No. 39/97.

sanction depends on two factors: its absolute level and the probability of being exposed to it. While procurers cannot affect the level of the public sanctions, they can increase the expected loss suffered by cartel participants when their illegal scheme is uncovered by claiming damages. A second way procurers can affect the cartelists' expected loss is to increase the probability that a cartel is discovered and convicted. Therefore, procurers should always report to antitrust agencies suspected bidding behaviours. Some examples of suspected behaviours are reported in the section below. By creating a reputation of being tough on cartels, the buyer can substantially reduce the risk of being subject to collusion.

A different issue is whether the procurer should add 'private sanctions' to those provided by the public enforcement of antitrust law when an antitrust investigation uncovers an existing cartel. In particular, should convicted firms be excluded from future competitive procurements? Should they be penalized, by imposing extra-costs or 'scoring handicaps'? These measures can have high deterrence effects. However they entail the unwarranted costs of distorting future competition. Therefore, the procurer should consider them only if other, less distorting, means (for example, low-suits for damages) are not available and only if the advantage stemming from a lower expected level of collusion is not offset by the social cost of distorted market. We believe that, in most developed countries, these conditions are rarely satisfied, particularly if the Competition Authority has not introduced effective leniency programmes.[28]

Practical conclusion 9

A procurer should always claim damages when a cartel is uncovered and convicted. A procurer should always report suspect bidding behaviour to antitrust authorities.

14.4.1. Examples of suspected bidding behaviour

In 2000, the ICA fined five pharmaceutical companies for bid-rigging in the Italian market for radiopaque agents. These are pharmaceutical specialties that are procured virtually in their entirety by Italian public hospitals and Local Health Authorities (LHA) to be used for radiological examinations. The investigation was triggered by a complaint from a LHA which reported that there was an anomalous similarity in the prices charged by all the

---

[28] On the role of leniency programmes in deterring bid-rigging see Aubert et al. (2005), and Spagnolo (2006).

Table 14.1. Submitted discounts at the radiopaque agents sealed-bid tendering (2000).

Company	Commercial name of the drug	Retail price	Retail price minus compulsory discount (50%)	Discount offered	Actual price
Bracco	iopamiro	74,363	37,181	58.31	31,000
	iomeron	91,545	45,772	66.13	31,000
Schering	ultravist	68,909	34,454	55.01	31,000
Nycomed	imagopaque	62,000	31,000	50	31,000
	omnipaque	74,363	37,181	58.31	31,000
	visipaque	62,273	31,136	50.21	31,000
Byk	optiray	73,545	36,772	57.85	31,000
Farmades	xenetix	77,909	38,954	60.21	31,000

companies for non-ionic radiopaque agents for radiological use. A quite striking example of this suspect behaviour is reported in table 14.1. According to the Italian law, pharmaceutical companies must offer hospital and other public health institutions a minimum discount of 50 per cent of the drug retail price. In one procurement tendering run by a LHA the five companies, some of which had several products with different commercial names, offered very different discounts ranging from the minimum required by law (50 per cent) to over 66 per cent. The 50 per cent discount was offered by the company with the lowest retail price, while all the other companies offered a higher discount. Strange enough, by applying the very different discounts all companies ended asking the same identical price which was *de facto* the maximum price they could charge.

Some years before, in 1996, the ICA had uncovered another collusive agreement among the four main security guard companies operating in the province of Cagliari (Sardinia). The evidence collected by the ICA proved that none of these companies had exerted any competitive pressure in tendering for any of the contracts awarded in the period in the 1990–1995. However, when two smaller companies challenged the position of two of the four incumbents, these reacted in a coordinated way by bidding below cost so as to foreclose the emerging competitors. An example of this bidding behaviour is reported in table 14.2. It shows the bids of the two incumbents (Sicurezza Notturna, SN, and Vigilanza Sardegna, VS) and those of the new entrant (Sant' Elena, SE). The highlight grey bid identifies the winning bid. In 1991 SN submitted a bid of 22,184 ITL[29] in some lots and a bid of 22,358

---

[29] This value identifies the hourly rate of a security guard.

Table 14.2. Repeated coordinated bidding in Sardinia (1990–95)

Lot	1991 SN	1991 VS	1992 SN	1992 VS	1993 SN	1993 VS	1993 SE	1994 SN	1994 VS	1994 SE
A	22,184	22,477	25,200	25,477	26,500	n.b.	n.b.	8,900	8,950	n.b.
B	22,358	22,177	25,800	25,477	n.b.	26,350	n.b.	9,000	8,950	16,000
C	22,358	22,177	25,800	25,477	n.b.	26,350	n.b.	9,000	8,950	15,500
D	22,358	22,177	25,800	25,477	n.b.	26,350	n.b.	9,000	8,950	14,700
E	22,358	22,177	25,800	25,477	n.b.	26,350	n.b.	9,000	8,950	n.b.
F	22,358	n.b.	25,200	25,477	26,500	n.b.	n.b.	8,900	8,950	n.b.
G	22,184	22,477	25,200	25,477	26,500	n.b.	n.b.	8,900	8,950	n.b.
H	22,184	22,477	25,200	25,477	26,500	n.b.	n.b.	8,900	8,950	n.b.
I	n.b.	22,477	25,800	25,477	n.b.	26,350	16,950	9,000	8,950	12,200
L	22,184	22,477	25,200	25,477	26,500	n.b.	16,950	8,900	8,950	12,200
M	22,184	22,477	25,200	25,477	26,500	n.b.	n.b.	8,900	8,950	n.b.

ITL in all other lots. It won all the lots where it had submitted the lower of these two figures and lost all other lots with the exception of lot F where its 'competitor' had not submitted any bid. VS behaved similarly. It won all lots where it had submitted a low bid (22,177 ITL) and lost all lots where it had submitted a high bid (22,477 ITL) but one where SN had not presented any offer. The same exact allocation of lots occurred in 1992. That year, however, the two companies had envisaged a different scheme whereby VS submitted the same identical bids in all lots (25,477 ITL) and SN submitted a low price (25,200 ITL) in the lots already won the previous year, and a high price (25,800 ITL) for all other lots. In 1993, the two companies decided to share the market as usual, but thought that submitting phoney bids was not worthwhile so that the designated loser did not bother bidding. However, a newcomer, SE, disrupted their plan, at least partially, and was able to steal two lots from the incumbent companies. Note that apart from this, the repartition of the lots won by the two companies was exactly the same as the one that resulted from the tendering of the previous years. In 1994, SN and VS organized their response to SE. They both undercut the new entrant by offering a price that, according to the ICA, was below cost. They followed the same scheme as in 1992, whereby VS submitted a uniform bid of 8,950 ITL and SN submitted a low bid of 8,900 ITL for all its 'historical' lots and high big of 9,000 ITL for all lots 'belonging' to SN. By doing so, they were able to obtain the allocation of lots that resulted from the previous tendering before the aggressive entry of SE.

14.5. Conclusions

Economic theory, empirical studies and casual observations all indicate that collusion is more likely to emerge in a stable and predictable environment. Whatever specific rules a procurer adopts to hinder collusion, it should be coupled with a meta-rule: do not let the tendering design crystallize over time so as to provide a reliable context for would-be conspirators. Changing the design of the competititve bidding over time might prove extremely useful to create uncertainty, which would destabilize existing cartels.

An aphorism might be: Whatever the appropriate rule to fight collusion, change it frequently!

Bibliographical notes

The classic study about collusion in oligopoly markets is Stigler (1964). A recent accessible overview on how tacit collusion can threaten competition is Ivaldi et al. (2003). Early analysis on collusion in auction and procurement can be found in Robinson (1985) and Graham and Marshall (1987) while recent analysis includes Pesendorfer (2000) and Albano and Spagnolo (2005). A general analysis on collusion and competitive bidding is in Klemperer (2004). For other references see Chapter 15.

References

Albano G. L. and G. Spagnolo (2005). The Collusive Drawbacks of Sequential Auctions, University College London, Mimeo.

Antitrust Division, United States Department of Justice, (1999). Annual Report FY.

Aubert, C., W. Kovacic and P. Rey (2005). The Impact of Leniency and Whistleblowers Programs on Cartels', *International Journal of Industrial Organization*, forthcoming.

Blume, A. and P. Heidhues (2004). Private Monitoring in Auctions No SP II 2003–14, CIC, Working Papers, Wissenschaftszentrum Berlin.

Graham, D., and R. Marshall (1987). collusive Bidder Behavior at Single-Object Second-Price and English Auctions, *Journal of Political Economy*, 95, 1217–1239.

Klemperer, P. (2004). *Auctions: Theory and Practice*, Princeton University Press.

Ivaldi, M., B. Jullien, P. Rey, P. Seabright and J. Tirole (2003). The Economics of Tacit Collusion; Final Report for DG Competition, European Commission.

Pesendorfer, M. (2000). A Study of Collusion in First-Price Auctions, *Review of Economic Studies*, 67, 381–411.

Rey, P. and J. Tirole (1986). The Logic of Vertical Restraints, *American Economic Review*, 76, 921–939.

Robinson, M. (1985). Collusion and the Choice of Auction, *Rand Journal of Economics*, 16, 141–145.

Spagnolo, G. (2006). Leniency and Whistleblowers in Antitrust, forthcoming in P. Buccirossi (Ed.), *Handbook of Antitrust Economics*, MIT Press, Cambridge, MA.

Stigler, G. J. (1964). A theory of Oligopoly, *Journal of Political Economy*, 72, 44–61.

Vickers, J. (2004). www.oft.gov.uk

Appendix 14.1. Scoring rule and collusion in the meal coupons procurement

In this section we present a Case Study related to the results of the first meal coupon procurement performed by Consip in March 2001. In this competitive tendering eight over ten participating companies joined a cartel in order to defend market shares, as stated in the decision of the Italian Competition Authority (ICA). The study aims at highlighting potential collusive effects of particular types of scoring rules.

Characteristics of the tendering procedure

Meal coupons are very often used by private companies and public administrations that cannot or are not willing to provide lunch directly to employees. The aim of this procurement was to provide meal coupons to Italian Public Administrations, including Central Authorities, Regions and Municipalities. The object of the competitive tendering was a contract for a 2-year provision of meal coupons to all Italian Public Administrations. The winner of the tendering process stipulated a frame-contract with Consip, that is, a contract regulating the key terms of the supply (price, quantity and other contract details etc.).

Coupons were of nominal unitary value of €4.65, for a total amount of about €418 millions (35% of the total market value). The contract was split in five geographical lots of identical amount and it was awarded using the most economically advantageous offer criterion. The price and technical aspects were attached equal weights (50 points each). In particular, technical points were attached on the basis of:

1. the supplier's number of affiliated shops (up to 40 points) in capital cities;

2. the number of capital cities in which the supplier is affiliated with at least one shop (up to 6 points);
3. proposals of the suppliers for the management of electronic orders.

The scoring rule

The scoring rule adopted for the price was the following:

> If bid < average bid → price score = 50* Lowest bid/Price Bid
> otherwise:
> price score=50*(Lowest bid/Price bid)*[1-(Price bid-Average bid)/Reserve price-Average bid)]

where 50 is the maximum number of points achievable on price offers, while the reserve price is equal to the nominal unitary value of coupons (€4.65).

The rule works as follows: the lowest bid obtains the highest price score (50 points). All price bids below the average bid obtain a score proportional to the lowest bid, while all other bids obtain a score which depends on the average and the lowest bid.

The technical points were assigned through a nonlinear scoring algorithm. We report the scoring rule computing the score for affiliated shops, since the remaining points (4) are attached on a discretionary basis.

- Technical score $1 = 40^*(U_k/U_{max})^{1/2}$
- Technical score $2 = 6^*(A_k/A_{max})^{1/2}$

where:

- U_k is the number of affiliated shops of a generic supplier 'k';
- U_{max} is the suppliers' highest number of affiliated shops;
- 40 is the maximum number of points a supplier can achieve for affiliated shops;
- A_k is the number of capital cities in which a generic supplier 'k' is affiliated with at least one shop;
- A_{max} is the suppliers' highest number of capital cities with at least one shop;
- 6 is the maximum number of points a supplier can achieve for affiliated shops.

This rule has two key features. The first one is that price competition is quite intense for price bids below the average. Price reductions above the

Table 14.3. Market share in the meal ticket industry (1999)

Company	Brand	Number of affiliated shops	Revenues (Millions of Euros)	Market share 1999 (based on revenues) %
Gemeaz Cusin S.r.I.; Serial S.r.I.	Ticket restaurant; City time	60,000	596.5	45.31
Sodexho Pass S.r.I., Agape card S.r.I.	Sodexho pass; Agape card	30,000	142.0	10.79
Day Ristoservice S.r.I.	Day	30,000	114.1	8.67
Pellegrini S.p.A.	Pellegrini card	25,000	98.1	7.45
Ristomat S.r.I. Lunch Times S.r.I.	Ristomat Lunch time	25,000	88.3	6.71
Qui! Ticket Services S.p.A.	Qui! ticket service	25,000	77.5	5.88
Ristochef S.p.A.	Buonchef	20,000	62.0	4.71
Repas S.r.I.	Lunch coupon	15,000	38.7	2.94
Sagifi S.p.A.	Meal ticket	15,000	25.8	1.96
Cascina S.c.a.r.I.	Break time	15,000	27.4	2.08
Cir S.c.a.r.I.	Bluticket	3,000	7.2	0.55
Others		n.a.	38.7	2.95
Total			1316.4	100.00

Source: Balance sheets of La Cascina SRL (year 2000).

average yield very small increments of the score. This is the important motivation that drove the use of such a scoring rule: stimulating sufficient price competition but avoiding poor quality potentially produced by aggressive bids. Second, bids are interdependent, with the average bid playing a crucial role. This is because any participant is able to affect the average bid and thus not only her score but also the score all other participants. As we will see, this last characteristic of the scoring rule might have been determinant for the dynamics of collusion.

The Italian meal coupon industry

Table 14.3 illustrates some data about companies operating in the meal coupon industry. The industry is composed of eleven identified companies and some other operators with very small market shares (less than 3%). The market is rather concentrated, with one Company, GEMEAZ, facing more that 45% of the market share in terms of revenue and over 60,000 affiliated shops. Notice that ten out of eleven companies participated in the competitive bidding.

Results of the tendering process and collusion

The decision of the ICA established that collusion occurred with the goal to maintain market shares of companies involved in the cartel. As indicated in the last column of table 14.4, except Ristochef and Qui!, all other companies in the cartel increased or maintained market shares with respect to the previous meal coupon competitive procurement run by Consip in 1996. The two leading Companies substantially maintained their positions, while market shares of non-colluding Companies, Pellegrini and Repas, were dramatically reduced by 7.4 per cent and 3.2 per cent, respectively. Table 14.5 shows the winning companies for each lot. Firms unable to participate as solo bidders in one or more lots are allowed by the Italian law to group together to create a larger and more competitive 'participant': the group. This aggregation mechanism is allowed in all competitive bidding to facilitate participation of small firms.

The aggregation of colluding participants was such that each firm had to be included in at least one of the winning group. Table 14.5 provides some information about the compositions of groups as well as the results of the tendering process. Collusion involved eight Companies out of the ten participating. The cartel represents almost the whole market of meal coupons. The antitrust authority documents accurately describe the process of firms' coordination. The three largest Companies (Gemeaz, Sedexho and Ristoservice) initially willing to create a simple competitive group, decided to give life to a larger but non-competitive agreement among all other participants (except Pellegrini and Repas). The agreement took shape in several steps. The first problem was to maximize the probability to win in each lot, assuming that Pellegrini and Repas, the only two companies that did not take part to the cartel, would have behaved competitively. The solution to this problem was identified in the creation of one single strong group for each lot, as witnessed by table 14.5. The second problem was determining how to share profits. Accordingly, the cartel appropriately chose the composition of groups and the allocation of revenues within the winning group for each lot in order to allow each firm to substantially maintain its position in the market.

Example of coordination: the case of lot 1

Defining the five winning groups for each lot was strictly related to coordination of price and technical offers. We focus here on the case of lot 1, since coordination for all other lots occurred following similar logics.

Table 14.4. Market shares in the meal ticket auction

Company	Market shares in the 2001 auction %	Market share before 1996 auction %	Variation 1996–2001
Pellegrini	0.0	7.4	−7.4
Repas	0.0	3.2	−3.2
Sagifi	3.0	0.0	3.0
La Cascina	5.0	2.1	2.9
Ristomat	8.9	4.8	4.1
Ristochef	9.5	11.7	−2.2
Qui	9.8	11.2	−1.4
Ristoservice	11.6	7.4	4.2
Sodexho	20.2	20.2	0.0
Gemeaz	32.0	31.9	0.1

Source: Data pertaining to 1996 have been taken from the corresponding balance sheet of 'Gemeaz SRL'. Data pertaining to 2001 have been taken from the corresponding balance sheet of 'La Cascina SRL'.

Lot 1 has been awarded to a group composed of three firms: Ristochef-Ristomat-Qui!. We can see from table 14.5 that this group offered a discount of 6.75 per cent while all other colluding participants (Gemeaz, Ristoservice and Sedexho) offered very small (and losing) discounts (0.33%, 0.89% and 0.56%, respectively). Pellegrini bid competitively with a discount on price equal to 9.5 per cent. The resulting average discount was 3.59 percent. Colluding companies coordinated their offers simulating the results of the competitive bidding for an aven more aggressive bid of Pellegrini (12% of discount). Such a discount corresponded to the limit price below which it was reasonable that no company could have gone. Given this assumption, the group coordinated price offers. The discount of 6.75 per cent was considered a good (competitive) price offer, that combined with other collusive discounts, determined a limited score differential between the aggressive bid of Pellegrini (12%) and the one of the winning group. This is because the discount of 6.75 per cent is equivalent to a price of 4.33, which is below the average price 4.48: since all prices offers below the average obtained a score equal to '50* (lowest bid/bid)', the price score differential between Pellegrini and the collusive group was quite limited. Instead, the score differential on the technical offer was quite strong in favour of the winning group. The technical part played a key role in the dynamics of collusion. This role has been enhanced by the fact that colluding firms had a good estimation of the number of affiliated shops of the two competitive firms. Thus, colluding firms were able to simulate with sufficient accuracy the

Table 14.5. Participating suppliers and discounts offered

Lot 1 (North-west)	Percentage of discount over the reserve price
Winning Group: Ristochef, Ristomat, Qui!	6.67
Gemeaz	0.33
Ristoservice	0.89
Sodexho	0.56
Pellegrini	9.50
Average discount	3.59
Lot 2 (North-east)	
Winning Group: Ristoservice, Ristomat, Sodexho	3.89
Gemeaz	0.67
Ristochef	0.56
Qui!	1.11
Pellegrini	9.50
Average discount	3.15
Lot 3 (Centre)	
Winning Group: Gemeaz, La Cascina	5.22
Repas	8.00
Ristochef	1.67
Qui!	2.22
Ristomat	1.89
Ristoservice	1.39
Sodexho	1.00
Sagifi	1.22
Pellegrini	9.50
Average discount	3.57
Lot 4 (Centre-south)	
Winning Group: Gemeaz, Sagifi	5.00
La Cascina	0.44
Ristochef	1.11
Qui!	1.11
Ristomat	0.67
Ristoservice	0.89
Sodexho	0.56
Pellegrini	9.50
Average discount	2.41
Lot 5 (South and Islands)	
Winning Group: Ristoservice, Ristomat, Sodexho	6.67
Gemeaz	0.11
Ristochef	0.56
Qui!	0.22
Pellegrini	9.50
Average discount	3.41

results of the competitive bidding and to define bidding strategies in order to minimize the risk of defeats.

Notice the following. At the beginning, the winning group for the first lot was composed of Ristochef and Qui! only, while Ristomat should have been included in the winning group of another lot. The group faced a clear trade-off in including Ristomat. With exclusion, Ristomat would have placed her collusive bid contributing to maintain a low average discount (high average of price offers), thus limiting the score differential between Pellegrini and the group itself. However, if included, Ristomat would have had no role in terms of price offers, but would have added a considerable number of affiliated shops. The ICA showed that the group gained much more by including Ristomat in the cartel, since the gain in terms of increase of points was larger for the technical side over the price side.

Despite complexity of the scoring rule, most of the participants were able to coordinate their offers to share procurement contract and maintain market shares. Even though collusion may have occurred regardless of the scoring rule at work, it is quite reasonable that the interdependent nature of the particular rule adopted facilitated the coordination of collusive firms and the exclusion of competitive ones.

Appendix 14.2. EU Framework agreement and collusion

The first article of the Directive 2004/18/EC states that a 'framework agreement is an agreement between one or more contracting authorities and one or more economic operators, the purpose of which is to establish the terms governing contracts to be awarded during a given period, in particular with regard to price and, when appropriate, the quality envisaged'. The statement makes it clear that this contractual solution permits awarding the contract to more than one economic operator. The contracting authorities can choose the supplier (economic operator) offering the most advantageous good/service. When contracts written according to framework agreements are signed with several economic operators (at least three), Article 32, clause 4 of the Directive 2004/18/EC establishes that they may be awarded either by application of the terms laid down in the framework agreement without reopening competition, or (if not all the terms are laid down in the framework agreement) by opening a new stage of competition on the basis of the same and, if necessary, more precisely formulated terms, and, where appropriate, other terms referred to in the specifications of the framework agreement.

The EU framework agreements (FAs henceforth) make room to a two-stage selection of contractors. At the first stage, the procurer (contracting authority) may select a subset of suppliers. At the second stage, the latter may be invited to revise/update their offers possibly according to more precisely formulated economic conditions.

In what follows, we attempt to put forward some explorative thoughts concerning the potential procollusive and anti-collusive features of the FAs. More precisely, consider one of the most common schemes used by active cartels in procurement whereby the cartel selects one supplier to submit an offer marginally lower than the reserve price while all other cartel members submit offers equal to the reserve price. How would conspirators' lives be affected by the implementation of a selection process that (i) may allow for more than one winner and (ii) a possible second stage of competition?

In order to evaluate the impact of the EU FAs on the sustainability of collusive schemes, it may be instructive to explore how FAs are likely to modify the cartel members incentives to adhere to a collusive scheme.

According to the FAs, if more than one supplier has to be selected at the first stage, they must be at least three. This implies a potentially higher frequency of interactions among the suppliers admitted to the second stage of competition with respect to a standard frame contract that is divided in several lots and is awarded to different winners. In the latter situation the supplier of, say, high-quality laptops will be providing the same exact good throughout the duration of the frame contract. The same will apply to the suppliers of medium- and low-quality laptops. Under a FA, instead, selected suppliers may, in principle, be required[30] to satisfy the demand for any quality of laptops following further stages of competition.

The effects of further stages of interactions among selected suppliers may be illustrated by using a simple example. Suppose that the group of suppliers admitted to the second stage includes firms A, B and C and that firm A is the cartel's selected winner of a three-year contract. If the procurer organizes, say, three new rounds of competition among the selected suppliers,[31] deviations by either firm B or C would be detected and punished more promptly than under a standard frame contract in which one winner is selected at the tendering process stage and awarded a three-year contract. In other words, multiple rounds of competition among those suppliers admitted to the second stage imply lower gains from deviations than under

---

[30] This is indeed highly speculative since, to the best of our knowledge, the content of the directive 2004/18/EC neither states nor rules out such a clause.

[31] This implies that a three-year contract is split in three one-year contracts.

a frame contract. Moreover, multiple rounds of competition may become instrumental to implement side transfers from firm A to all other cartel members. If, for instance, the selected suppliers are not forced (alternatively, they do not commit) to serve demand, they have full freedom in allocating market shares. Hence, firm A is able to reward firms B and C for their adherence to the collusive scheme. In this respect, the EU framework agreements may have a pro-collusive effect. If, instead, firms A, B and C have to commit to serve demand whenever it arises, then market sharing agreements cannot be implemented with certainty. In this case, firm A would be forced to design side transfers similar to those under a frame contract. The picture drawn so far thus illustrates a more pro-collusive nature of FAs with respect to frame contracts.

There exist, however, an additional effect of FAs on existing cartels. If a deviation from a collusive scheme were to take place at the first stage of competition, those suppliers admitted to the second stage may be tempted to avoid a price war and coordinate on a new collusive scheme. This temptation to renegotiation is more likely when the suppliers competing at the second stage are the most efficient ones within the set of applicants. If more efficient firms have an incentive to deviate in order to renegotiate a 'new' collusive scheme, the initial cartel may be destabilized by the two-stage competitive process implied by the FAs.

As it reads, the content of the Directive 2004/18/EC does not allow a more detailed investigation of its pro- and anti-collusive effects. The main reason is not, however, the lack of details on the actual selection procedures implied by the Directive, rather than the difficulty, at this stage, to predict how the collusive schemes themselves might change in response to the adoption of the Directive throughout Europe.

Bidding rings and the design of anti-collusive measures for auctions and procurements

William E. Kovacic*, Robert C. Marshall,
Leslie M. Marx* and Matthew E. Raiff

15.1. Introduction

Since the mid-1990s, the enforcement of competition laws against cartels has drawn considerable attention to the means by which buyers or sellers establish and manage collusive schemes.[1] High-profile lawsuits against cartels in the food additives and vitamins sectors have made public an unprecedented wealth of information about how cartels operate.[2] Complementing this stream of data is a modern body of scholarship that,

* William E. Kovacic is a commissioner with the US Federal Trade Commission. The views expressed here are his alone and not necessarily those of the Federal Trade Commission or its individual members.
* This chapter was completed while Marx was visiting the US Federal Communications Commission, but the views expressed do not necessarily reflect those of the FCC, its staff, or Commissioners.

[1] See Grossman (2004) (collection of essays examining operation of collusive agreements); Marshall and Meurer (2004) (discussing how competition policy toward cartels should account for the form of auctions and procurements and for the means used by firms to coordinate behavior).

[2] See Evenett et al. (2002). Considerable information appears in court opinions and publicly available court records dealing with the prosecution of individual and corporate cartel participants. See e.g., *United States* vs. *Andreas*, 216 F.3d 645 (7th Cir. 2000) (affirming conviction of Archer Daniels Midland executives who helped orchestrate food additives cartel; describing cartel's operation); Gavil et al. (2002, 1017–21) (statement presented by the Department of Justice in connection with the sentencing of Hoffmann-La Roche for its participation in the vitamins cartel). Public statements by government prosecutors (e.g., Guersant 2002; Kolasky 2002) also supply informative accounts of these and other cartels. Further insight is provided by publicly available statements prepared by witnesses who testified in private treble damage cases against the vitamins cartel participants (e.g., Bernheim 2002). The recent secondary literature on the food additives and vitamins prosecutions is varied and voluminous. See e.g., Connor (2001) and Eichenwald (2000) (discussing food additives cartel); First (2001) (reviewing public prosecution of food additives and vitamins cartels).

working extensively with reported judicial decisions and other materials, has provided informative perspectives on the methods of cartel coordination.[3]

For the most part, discussions inspired by modern enforcement developments and scholarly contributions have addressed the optimal design of *public* policies against cartels.[4] Key focal points for debate have included the formulation of strategies for improving the detection of cartels (e.g., providing inducements for cartel members or employees of cartel members to inform public authorities about the existence of the cartel);[5] the establishment or enhancement of private rights of action to supplement anti-cartel enforcement by public agencies;[6] and the choice of remedies (e.g., civil damages and criminal punishment, including imprisonment for individuals).[7]

In this chapter, we explore the implications of the modern data and literature on cartel coordination with a different orientation. Rather than assess refinements in public enforcement policy, we analyze possibilities for precautions that contracting parties can take independently, without necessarily invoking public laws that condemn cartels, to defeat or discourage collusion by bidders. The strong tendency to emphasize public policy responses to collusion obscures the degree to which a successful anti-cartel campaign might engage the efforts of potential cartel victims to forestall or inhibit successful coordination.[8] The context in which we examine possible anti-cartel precaution-taking by purchasers and sellers is the event that is integral to the implementation of a collusive scheme: the individual auction or procurement. Cartel agreements ultimately are executed through the behavior of the cartel's participants in the day-to-day episodes of

---

[3] See e.g., Genesove and Mullin (2001) (discussing how participants in Sugar Institute collusive scheme detected cheating); Marshall and Meurer (2004; 96–99) (describing operation of bidding rings for used industrial machinery). The more recent literature adds to an older collection of popular and scholarly accounts dealing with the organization and operation of cartels, such as the electrical equipment price-fixing conspiracies of the 1950s. See Fuller (1962); Herling (1962).

[4] See Marshall and Meurer (2005); 101–09.

[5] On the development and application of leniency and bounty systems for detecting cartels, see Aubert et al. (2005), Chen and Harrington (2005), Kovacic (2001), Motta and Polo (2003), Spagnolo (2005), Spratling (2001).

[6] Calkins (1997b); Wils (2003).

[7] On the strengths and weaknesses of various types of civil and criminal sanctions, see Baker (2001); Breit and Elzinga (1986); Calkins (1997a); Connor (2005); OECD (2005); Wils (2005)

[8] Our approach is roughly analogous to the perspective embodied in the law and economics literature (Cooter 1985) that considers how the frequency and total cost of accidents and failed contracting episodes might be reduced by adopting tort and contract rules, respectively, to give both parties (the tort feasor and the tort victim, the promisor and the promisee) incentives to take appropriate precautions. On the contributions of auction design as a supplement to antitrust enforcement in deterring collusion, see Klemperer (2002); Marshall and Meurer (2004; 110–117).

buying and selling through which parties routinely transact business. These individual auction and procurement transactions supply the settings in which the cartel members must translate their ambitions for coordination into practical, operational techniques for curbing rivalry. The capacity of a cartel's members to manipulate and orchestrate the outcome of auctions and procurements determines the success of the entire collusive venture.

In studying the operation of auctions and procurements, we describe some common structures used by bidding rings to support collusion with an eye toward providing recommendations for auction designers to combat collusion. By understanding the types of mechanisms that bidding rings commonly use to suppress rivalry and increase their profits, the designers of auctions and procurements may be able to make choices that deter collusion. Some choices may make it more difficult for bidding rings to operate effectively in the first place, and other choices may make it easier to detect and prosecute collusion after the fact.

We begin this chapter by providing some background on bidding rings that have been prosecuted in the past and the different type of cartel organization used in those cases. For ease of exposition our discussion will focus on auctions, although when appropriate, procurements will be explicitly discussed.[9]

In general, our concern is with allocation schemes where offers are considered simultaneously. Housing transactions do not fit within this context since offers are usually considered sequentially, and without recall. Posted price markets do not fit either. However, many transactions do fit within this context.

15.2. The role of procurements in collusion

It is natural for bidders to attempt to suppress rivalry and thus capture some of the rents that otherwise would be transferred to the seller (or to the buyer in a procurement). The uniquely large body of US case law is replete with examples of Sherman Act violations for bid rigging (American Bar Association 2002, 89–91), and recent enforcement experience in other jurisdictions underscores the extent and apparent universality of the

---

[9] It is simply cumbersome and distracting each time the word auction is used to say, 'or a procurement in the case of a single buyer with multiple sellers'. This being said, there often are significant differences between auctions and procurements, especially when the commodity being procured is multi-dimensional in nature and bids are scored over the many dimensions.

Table 15.1. US penalties for cartel offenders – 1970 and 2005 compared

Sanction	1970	2005
Status of offense	Misdemeanor	Felony
Maximum prison term	One year	Ten years
Maximum corporate fine	$50,000	$100 million, twice the loss to victims, or twice the gain to the violator

phenomenon.[10] The record of reported judicial decisions and public enforcement matters cases does not capture the full dimensions of the problem, as these sources only involve episodes of collusion in which the bidders were detected and prosecuted.[11]

In addition, many industrial cartels are characterized by activities that appear to be unrelated to bid rigging, such as market share allocations. But, for many of these cartels, the buyers obtain the commodity from cartel firms through 'competitive' procurements where the cartel members have rigged bids. In other words, cartels are often characterized by how members divide the collusive gain (market share allocations, geographic divisions, customer allocations, etc.), but at the transaction level, cartel members will benefit from preventing competition among themselves when interacting with buyers. When buyers use competitive procurements, the cartel firms are likely to rig bids.

Since 1940, the US courts have made clear that cartels would be treated as per se offenses under Section 1 of the Sherman Act.[12] Yet it is only in recent decades that the antitrust hazards for cartel participants have become genuinely severe. In that period, among other measures, the United States has boosted sanctions and strengthened leniency mechanisms that

---

[10] See e.g., Scott (2004) (reviewing experience in Canada and other jurisdictions with enforcement of competition law provisions against cartels).

[11] The actual frequency of cartel activity defies accurate calculation, although estimates of frequency often figure into the establishment of penalties.

[12] The watershed in this development is *United States* vs. *Socony-Vacuum Oil Co.*, 310 US 150 (1940). The historical development of the strict prohibition in US law and policy against cartels is reviewed in Kovacic and Shapiro (2000). By speaking of 'cartels', we refer to arrangements that are unsupported by valid efficiency rationales. The trend in modern competition policy analysis has been to make careful distinctions between 'naked' agreements to restrict output and agreements for which the participants advance cognizable, plausible efficiency rationales. For a recent synthesis of the relevant US jurisprudence on this subject, see *Polygram Holding, Inc.* vs. *FTC*, 416 F.3d 29 (D. C. Cir. 2005).

give cartel members incentives to report their misconduct.[13] Table 15.1 above compares key features of the US regime of sanctions in 1970 and 2005. These reforms have coincided with significant improvements in the effectiveness of the private plaintiffs' bar in obtaining treble damages from cartel offenders.[14] Noteworthy achievements in recent years have included nine-figure recoveries against large auction houses and vitamins cartels.[15]

In the past decade, numerous other jurisdictions have embraced a policy norm that favors aggressive measures to police cartels. With the encouragement of the United States and various multinational organizations, a growing number of competition systems today treat cartels as an extremely serious offense.[16] The US experience with the enhanced leniency regime introduced in the 1990s has inspired many jurisdictions – among them, Australia, Brazil, Canada, the Competition Directorate of the European Union, and many of the EU member states – to adopt or bolster their own leniency measures.[17] One major jurisdiction (the United Kingdom) has revised its laws to treat cartels as crimes, and many nations are experimenting with measures to increase the power of private rights of action to recover damages on behalf of cartel victims (Global Competition Review 2004).

Despite these developments, many bidders may still tend to regard the possibility of prosecution under the antitrust laws of the United States or other jurisdictions as simply an acceptable cost of doing business. Whenever new auction mechanisms are proposed or designed, there seems to be remarkably little attention paid to the issue of bidder collusion. Yet, in terms of foregone revenue, bidder collusion is probably the most serious practical threat to revenue.[18]

---

[13] The modern sequence of enhancements in methods for detecting cartels and punishments for cartel offenders is reviewed in Kovacic (2003).

[14] The US antitrust laws permit private rights of action and allow private plaintiffs to recover three times their actual damages. See Gavil et al. (2002; 999–1000) (describing US legal framework governing private enforcement). The victorious plaintiff also is entitled to recover its attorneys' fees and costs from the defendant.

[15] See First (2001) (documenting success of private litigants in vitamins cartel cases); Anderson (2001) (reporting on agreement by Christie's and Sotheby's auction houses to pay total of $512 million to settle private class action antitrust claims).

[16] See ICPAC (2000); OECD (2005).

[17] Vann and Litwin (2004) (reporting that, since enhancement of antitrust leniency programs by United States in 1990s, at least twelve jurisdictions have adopted similar policies).

[18] The theoretical auction literature addresses revenue differentials that can arise between schemes due to risk aversion or affiliated values, to name two prominent emphases. The revenue issue typically concerns whether the second-highest valuation, or something bigger than it (up to the highest

At first glance, the extent and apparent success of cartel activity in the United States – even in the face of strong legal prohibitions – and in other jurisdictions over the past half-century might seem surprising in light of the literature that has catalogued the obstacles to effective coordination among buyers or sellers. It is the rare competition attorney or economist who has not studied Stigler's (1964) article on the tasks of cartel formation and operation. Stigler pointed out that in order to succeed, cartels had to reach a consensus on the terms of their cooperation, detect deviations from their agreement, and punish defectors. To this list could be added the challenge of co-opting or forestalling entrants who might be attracted to the market by the high prices fostered by the cartel.[19] As Stigler observed, the accomplishment of these tasks in many settings could be difficult. Thus, many cartels eventually – perhaps quickly – would disintegrate as the centrifugal forces generated by efforts to form and sustain a consensus flung the participants apart.

One possible implication of this literature was that the typical cartel was too unstable and short-lived, even in the absence of antitrust laws that condemned such coordination by rivals, to be a serious concern for contracting parties or for public policy generally. By focusing on the problems of cartel formation and operation, commentators and policy makers may have overlooked a separate body of learning that, at least indirectly, suggested that the obstacles in question were not as formidable as believed. In many episodes of contracting, the parties may face strong temptations to renege on their initial commitments. For various reasons, recourse to enforcement in the courts may provide an ineffective means to ensure performance. Thus, parties have experimented with a variety of mechanisms to improve the monitoring of performance and to improve incentives to fulfill the originally specified terms of agreements.[20]

One might expect that, in facing the obstacles identified by Stigler, the same creativity that firms brought to bear in solving contracting problems in legitimate transactions could be applied to promoting the success of illegitimate ventures.[21] Such expectations would be appropriate. The revelation in recent years of detailed information about conspiracies such as the

---

valuation), is what gets paid to the seller. Effective collusion can drop the price paid down to the seller's reserve price, or to the highest value of a non-colluding bidder, which could be quite low.

[19] See Marshall and Meurer (2004), 92–93.

[20] This is a central insight of the transaction costs literature associated with the work of Ronald Coase (1937) and elaborated by scholars such as Williamson (1975). See Chapter 4 for a detailed discussion on contracting strategies to ensure performance in procurement.

[21] See also Baker (2002, 160–162) (reviewing means by which rivals tacitly coordinate conduct).

vitamins cartel indicates the ingenuity and perseverance of the participants in finding ways to overcome coordination problems. The durability and success of these illicit collaborations underscore the effectiveness of the chosen methods for covert coordination.[22]

In what follows, we will distinguish between two types of competitive mechanisms: dynamic auctions and first-price sealed bidding.[23] At a dynamic auction for selling a good, the bidders gather at the time of the auction, typically together in a room, but also possibly online. Each bidder can submit multiple bids, and the current price continues to rise (to fall in case of procurement) until no bidder is willing to raise it further. Bidders are able to observe the current high price. The bidder submitting the final bid wins the object and pays the amount of its bid. With first-price sealed bidding, each bidder submits only one bid, typically in writing, and typically in secret from the other bidders. Once all bids are submitted, they are evaluated by the auctioneer, and the high bidder wins and pays the amount of its bid.[24]

Intuitively, dynamic auctions are more susceptible to collusion than first-price sealed bidding. At a dynamic auction, the cartel can use a very simple rule – if a cartel member is actively bidding, then no one else from the cartel can bid. If a cartel member withdraws from the bidding, then another cartel member can bid, but no cartel member can bid against it. In this way the cartel suppresses all intra-cartel competition at the auction. Furthermore, there is no need for ex-ante communication among the cartel members about their values and thus no concern about misrepresentation of information. Note that the cartel member with highest value is prepared to bid up to its value, which is exactly what it is prepared to do acting

---

[22] The vitamins cartel took shape in the early to mid-1980s and functioned successfully until the late 1990s. Reported decisions involving the prosecution of numerous other cartels highlight the longevity of the challenged collusive scheme – a result that confidently can be attributed at least in part to the success of the participants in devising solutions to coordination problems that threaten to unravel efforts to formulate and execute a common plan. See e.g., *United States* vs. *Hal Brown, Jr.*, 936 F.2d 1042 (9th Cir. 1991) (collusive arrangement to suppress competition for billboard sites began in 1964 and operated until attacked by Justice Department in 1988); *United States* vs. *Pippin*, 903 F.2d 1478 (11th Cir. 1990) (conspiracy by dairies to rig bids on school milk contracts in Florida operated from the early 1970s until 1988); *United States* vs. *Portsmouth Paving Corp.*, 694 F.2d 312 (4th Cir. 1982) (road paving conspiracy began in mid-1960s and ran effectively until challenged in early 1980s).

[23] Our focus is on single-object auctions or procurements. Additional issues arise when considering multiple-object auctions or procurements, and different auction designs may be appropriate. For example, on the use of a 'clock-proxy' auction for auctioning many related items, see Ausubel, Cramton, and Milgrom (2004).

[24] This is first-price sealed bidding. There are other sealed-bid competitive mechanisms, such as second-price sealed-bidding, where the high bidder wins and pays the amount of the second-highest bid.

non-cooperatively. Most importantly, note that there is no incentive for ring members to cheat on this collusive arrangement. Even if a ring member employs a shill bidder[25] to act on its behalf, it cannot profitably beat the highest-valuing ring member.[26]

In contrast, with first-price sealed bidding, in order to secure a collusive gain the cartel must drop the bid of its highest-valuing member below what it would have bid acting non-cooperatively. The reduction in this bid opens the door for deviant behavior and misrepresentations by bid members. After all, by slightly outbidding this reduced bid, a ring member may realize a gain that it never could have realized when the highest-valuing bidder acted non-cooperatively. Collusion is therefore more difficult with first-price sealed bidding than dynamic auctions. It almost surely requires ex-ante communication that is not needed with collusion at a dynamic auction, and there is the possibility of profitable deviant behavior that may not be easily traced to the deviator.

Practical conclusion 1
When bidder collusion is a potential concern, use first-price sealed-bidding.

There is another issue of significance pertaining to enforcement. For many cartels, the people who take actions to implement the conspiracy are the owners of the firms. However, when the conspiracies involve large corporate entities, and those companies are engaged in bidding in hundreds of procurements around the world, the high-level managers who are running the conspiracy cannot submit all bids for all procurements. They must leave this to their sales forces which of course, have usually not been informed that there is an explicit cartel in operation. Prior to the existence of an explicit cartel, the sales force is likely to have incentive schemes that reward expansion of market share.

Once the cartel is in place, these incentives are likely to change, emphasizing price elevation subject to maintaining market share. There may be explicit directions to the sales force not to bid certain accounts if their bid is being solicited because a competitor has tried to raise a price. Although these are not direct statements by management that an explicit

---

[25] A shill bidder is an agent of a given bidder who is not recognizable as such by the auctioneer/procurer and the other bidders.

[26] There are environments where consideration of a shill bidder is sensible and others where it is not. It is not reasonable to think of a major aircraft manufacturer using a shill bidder in a defense procurement, but it is certainly reasonable to think of an antique dealer using a shill bidder at an estate auction.

cartel is functioning, these statements should be viewed as a strong indication by the sales force that the nature of interfirm rivalry has changed substantially and that explicit collusion is likely. It may be that if the sales force unexpectedly wins a large account, management does not react positively but, rather, treats the event as a mistake. This is also an indication that an explicit cartel is at work.[27]

Practical conclusion 2

For those conducting a private or public antitrust investigation, check whether the incentive scheme of the sales force of suspected firms has changed to emphasize price over market share (sometimes referred to as 'price before tonnage' or 'price before volume').

In practice, prior to the submission of collusive bids, a cartel often finds it necessary to make price announcements so as to prepare buyers for higher bids and reduce buyer resistance to the ensuing increases.[28] Of course, price increase announcements are also made when factor costs, or demand shifts, warrant it. The key to understanding whether a communication is non-collusive or collusive is to see if the price announcement is explained by market-relevant events. If non-market factors, such as the time between price announcements, are more relevant, perhaps reflecting regular cartel meetings, then collusion looms as a potential explanation.

Practical conclusion 3

For those conducting a private or public antitrust investigation, analyze the communications by suppliers used to implement price increases. Investigate if cost and demand factors can explain the observed price increases or, if instead, the time elapsed between price announcements better explains the observed price increases.

15.3. Prosecuted bidding rings

We begin by considering bidding rings that operated at dynamic auctions and then consider rings that operated with first-price sealed bidding. We

---

[27] The sales force will recognize the regime shift, and there is a way for enforcement authorities to take advantage of their information for enforcement of antitrust laws. As noted earlier, a growing modern literature has explored the possibility of creating incentives for those engaged in collusion, and employees of colluding firms, to reveal the collusion to antitrust authorities.

[28] See Marshall, Marx, and Raiff (2005) (showing how public price announcements by the vitamins cartel facilitated collusive price increases).

focus on a selection of bidding rings that were prosecuted in the United States and for which the legal record provides a description of the organization of the ring. Then we discuss the extent to which cartels, such as market share cartels, must also rig bids.

15.3.1. Bidding rings at dynamic auctions

One way to operate a bidding ring at a dynamic auction is for the ring members to meet prior to the auction and designate one of the bidders as the one who will win. Bidders who are not designated as winners do not bid at the auction (or they may submit very low bids in an attempt to disguise the presence of the bidding ring). Bidders can also agree on payments or other arrangements to compensate losing bidders for their participation.

One case in which this type of arrangement was used is *Finnegan* vs. *Campeau Corp.*[29] In 1988, R. H. Macy & Co., Inc. and Campeau Corp. were engaged in a bidding war to buy Federated Department Stores, Inc. According to the reported decision in the case, 'Macy and Campeau agreed that Macy would cease bidding and let Campeau be the buyer, thereafter dividing the benefits of their conduct between themselves.'[30] This is an example of a bid suppression scheme, which the US Department of Justice (DoJ) defines as a scheme in which one or more competitors who otherwise would be expected to bid, or who have previously bid, agree to refrain from bidding or withdraw a previously submitted bid so that the designated winning competitor's bid will be accepted.[31]

Another way to operate a bidding ring at a dynamic auction is for the ring members to designate one ring member to bid on behalf of the ring at the auction, and then, assuming the designated ring member wins the object, the ring can meet after the auction to decide which ring member should receive the object and how much should be paid to each ring member as compensation for their participation in the ring.

We now provide three examples in which the collusive mechanism used by the bidding ring involved no communication prior to the auction, except

---

[29] *Finnegan* vs. *Campeau Corp.*, 722 F.Supp. 1114 (S.D.N.Y. 1989) (dismissing antitrust complaint filed by shareholders; dismissal granted on ground that US securities laws permitted challenged conduct), affirmed, 915 F.2d 824 (2nd Cir. 1990).

[30] 722 F. Supp. at 1115.

[31] US Department of Justice, 'Price Fixing & Bid Rigging – They Happen: What They Are and What to Look For, An Antitrust Primer for Procurement Professionals,' available at http://www.usdoj.gov/atr/public/guidelines/pfbrprimer.pdf.

possibly to establish the identity of the cartel members or, in the case of *District of Columbia* vs. *George Basiliko* (described below), to designate a cartel member who would then bid on behalf of the cartel. Then the ring members met after the auction to finalize details of the allocation and transfer payments.

The first example is the case of *US* vs. *Pook*,[32] in which a bidding ring operated at antique auctions. As stated in the 1988 decision in the case,

> When a dealer pool was in operation at a public auction of consigned antiques, those dealers who wished to participate in the pool would agree not to bid against the other members of the pool. If a pool member succeeded in purchasing an item at the public auction, pool members interested in that item could bid on it by secret ballot at a subsequent private auction ('knock out') . . . . The pool member bidding the highest at the private auction claimed the item by paying each pool member bidding a share of the difference between the public auction price and the successful private bid. The amount paid to each pool member ('pool split') was calculated according to the amount the pool member bid in the knock out.[33]

This is an illustration of another type of bid suppression scheme. In the scheme used by the antique dealers, the dealers would not compete against one another at the auction, and then, if a dealer in the ring won the object, it would be offered for sale at a secondary auction, the knock out, to the ring members. If a ring member bid more at the knock out than was paid at the initial auction, then the difference between the two prices was divided up among the ring members. In the absence of collusion, the difference between the two prices is money that would have been received by the auctioneer.

Our second example of a bidding ring that did not communicate prior to the auction is the case of an industrial machinery purchasing cartel in *US* vs. *Seville Industrial Machinery*.[34] The mechanism used by the cartel in *Seville* resembled the scheme used in *Pook*. The ring members agreed not to bid against one another at the auction and then used a knock out to allocate objects won and determine payments between ring members. Prior to 1970, members of the industrial machinery cartel did meet prior to the auction, but in this meeting the ring members only made vague indications of interest in the various objects being offered for sale. Then only the cartel organizer would submit bids at the auction based on its educated guess about the likely high value for the object from among the ring members.

---

[32] *United States* vs. *Pook*, No. 87–274, 1988 US Dist. LEXIS 3398 (E.D. Pa., 18 April 1988).
[33] 1988 US Dist. LEXIS 3398 at 2.
[34] *United States* vs. *Seville Industrial Machinery Corp.*, 696 F.Supp. 986 (D.N.J. 1988).

The final allocation of the object and transfers among ring members were again determined by a knock out.

The third example is the case of *District of Columbia* vs. *George Basiliko*, [35] which involved a real estate cartel. There are many similarities between this cartel and the previous two examples. The reported decision in *Basiliko* states that:

The defendants and the co-conspirators discussed and agreed ... not to compete with one another to win the bid; selected a designated bidder to act for the conspirators ...; discussed and agreed on specific payoffs that conspirators present would receive for not bidding, or discussed and agreed to hold a private, secret auction among themselves after the designated bidder won the public real estate auction ...; in many instances, held a secret auction in which the conspirators bid solely among themselves to acquire the property for a price higher than the price paid by the designated bidder at the public real estate auction and agreed to divide the difference between the public real estate auction price and the secret auction price by making payoffs among the conspirators; arranged by contract or other means for the secret auction winner to take title or ownership of the property; and made the payoffs that they had agreed to make.[36]

These examples show that at dynamic auctions, some bidding rings choose to use collusive mechanisms that operate prior to the auction, and others choose to use mechanisms that involve meetings after the auction is over. There are advantages and disadvantages (from the perspective of the bidding ring) associated with each of these types of mechanism. One goal of a bidding ring would be to win the object whenever there is some ring member who values it more than the non-ring members, and to allocate the object to the ring member who values it most highly.

In general it is not possible to achieve this goal using a post-auction mechanism.[37] To see why, note that when a ring operates a post-auction mechanism, it must provide two sets of incentives to ring members. First, it must provide incentives for ring members to bid appropriately at the auction. Typically, this means not bidding against fellow ring members, but bidding against non-ring members if a ring member values the object more than those non-ring members. Second, the ring must provide incentives for ring members to truthfully reveal their values for the object at the post-auction mechanism. In general, one cannot construct a mechanism that provides both types of incentives. So a post-auction mechanism will result

---

[35] *District of Columbia* vs. *Basiliko*, 1992 US Dist. LEXIS 1260 (D.D.C. 10 Feb. 1992).

[36] 1992 US Dist. LEXIS 1260 at 6–7.

[37] See Lopomo, Marshall, and Marx (2005).

in some type of inefficiency – either non-ring members sometimes win the object when there is a ring member who values the object more, or the ring wins the object but awards it to a ring member who is not the highest-valuing ring member, or some combination of the two.

In contrast, a ring can avoid the problem of inefficiency by using a pre-auction mechanism, but this approach has distinct drawbacks, as well. A pre-auction mechanism requires a meeting and transfers prior to every auction, and so it may be easier to detect. In contrast, a bidding ring using a post-auction mechanism need only meet if a cartel member wins the object, and transfers may not be necessary under all circumstances. In addition, a bidding ring using a pre-auction mechanism either needs to be able to control the bids of its members, for example by explicitly preventing some bidders from participating in the auction, or the ring needs to have someone willing to act as a 'banker' to hold and pay out money for the ring members,[38] and finding a person willing to play the role of a banker for an illegal bidding ring might be difficult.

Another choice for a ring is to avoid using transfer payments completely, but in this case the ring has few options other than to agree to a bid rotation scheme. The DoJ defines a bid rotation scheme to be one in which con-spirators take turns being the winning bidder.[39] According to the DoJ, "The terms of the rotation may vary; for example, competitors may take turns on contracts according to the size of the contract, allocating equal amounts to each conspirator or allocating volumes that correspond to the size of each conspirator company." But as one might expect, a rigid bid rotation scheme produces a pattern of bidding that could not arise by chance and so may be relatively easy to detect and prosecute.

15.3.2. Bidding rings with first-price sealed bidding

In the absence of a pre-arranged bid rotation scheme, bidding rings with first-price sealed bidding have no choice but to meet prior to bidding since

---

[38] More formally, in the language of Marshall and Marx (2006), there exist efficient pre-auction mechanisms if either (i) the ring operates a bid-submission mechanism under ex-post budget balance (Mailath and Zemsky, 1991), or (ii) the ring operates a bid-coordination mechanism under ex-ante budget balance.

[39] The DoJ describes a bid rotation scheme for a procurement as one in which 'all conspirators submit bids, but take turns being the low bidder'. But at an ascending-bid auction (or descending-bid auction for a procurement), all conspirators need not submit bids. They need only agree on the rotation. US Department of Justice, 'Price Fixing & Bid Rigging–They Happen: What They Are and What to Look For, An Antitrust Primer for Procurement Professionals,' available at http://www.usdoj.gov/atr/public/guidelines/pfbrprimer.pdf.

the ring must decide what bids each ring member should submit. This typically involves figuring out which bidder has the highest value for the object, deciding how much that bidder should bid, and then assigning losing bids to all the other ring members.

In this section, we provide six examples of bidding rings with first-price sealed bidding. Three of the examples, *US* vs. *Addyston Pipe*, *US* vs. *Lyons*, and *US* vs. *Inryco*, involved repeated interaction among the colluding firms, but the illegal behavior described in the other three, *US* vs. *A-A-A Electrical*, *US* vs. *Brinkley & Son*, and *US* vs. *Metropolitan*, involved only a single sale or purchase.

In *US* vs. *Addyston Pipe & Steel Co.*,[40] colluding cast-iron pipe manu-facturers met prior to the procurement, determined which one of the colluding firms would participate, and agreed on transfer payments:

> When bids are advertised for by any municipal corporation, water company, and gas company, the executive committee determines the price at which the bid is to be put in by some company in the association, and the question to which company this bid shall go is settled by the highest bonus which any one of the companies, as among themselves, will agree to pay or bid for the order. When the amount is thus settled the company to whom the right to bid upon the work is assigned sends in its estimate or bid to the city or company desiring pipe, and the amount thus bid is 'protected' by bids from such of the other members of the association as are invited to bid, and by the bidding in all instances being slightly above the one put in by the company to whom the contract is to go. . . . Settlements are made at stated times of the bonus account debited against each company, where these largely offset each other, so that small sums are in fact paid by any company in balancing accounts.[41]

The protecting bids described above are also sometimes referred to as complementary bids or cover or courtesy bids.[42] They are not intended to win, but are designed to create the appearance of competition. With regard to procurements, according to the DoJ, "Complementary bidding schemes are the most frequently occurring forms of bid rigging and they defraud

---

[40] *United States* vs. *Addyston Pipe & Steel Co.*, 78 F. 712 (E.D. Tenn. 1897). See also, *Addyston Pipe & Steel Co.* vs. *United States*, 171 US 211 (1899).

[41] *United States* vs *Addyston Pipe & Steel Co.*, 78 F. 712 (E.D. Tenn 1897) at 713–14.

[42] See *United States* vs. *Mobile Materials, Inc.*, 881 F.2d 866, 869–74 (10th Cir. 1989) (describing arrangements made by road paving conspirators across a number of procurements to orchestrate presentation of complimentary bids to government purchasing authorities); *United States* vs. *Portsmouth Paving Corp.*, 694 F.2d 312, 320–21 (4th Cir. 1982) (discussing use of complimentary bids by road paving conspirators).

purchasers by creating the appearance of competition to conceal secretly inflated prices."[43]

Another issue facing the bidding ring in *US vs. Addyston Pipe* is the issue of how to arrange transfer payments among the ring members without creating a detailed paper trail of the ring's activities. In this case, the bidding ring was active for a long period of time and participated in many procurements, so the participants were able to solve the problem by maintaining records of what payments were owed and then only occasionally clearing the accounts. As mentioned above, many of the required payments offset each other, so that the payments actually made were small.[44]

In the bidding ring of the next example, all payments were made to a single ring organizer. In *US vs. Lyons*,[45] when a sheet metal project came up for bid, Lyons would arrange for a meeting with the other contractors. "The group chose the low bidder and determined the amount of its bid. This was calculated by averaging the cost estimates of interested contractors, then adding a mark-up and an additional amount known as the 'burden' which was a cash payment to [Lyons]. The system provided a financial incentive for contractors to refrain from truly competitive bids on a particular job because of the assurance that conformity to the conspiratorial procedure would keep them eligible to benefit from future allocations." The *Lyons* participants were willing to share part of the profit associated with participating in the ring with the organizer (Lyons) in order to ensure that they would be allowed to participate in the bidding ring in the future. So the on-going nature of the interaction among the ring members was an important aspect in this case.

In contrast, the next case relates to a single interaction among electrical contractors. (Of course, it may be that the parties involved had other illegal interaction that was not prosecuted.) In *US vs. Λ-Λ-Λ Elec. Co.*,[46] contractors bidding for work at the Raleigh-Durham Airport discussed their bids before submitting them and designated A-A-A as the one who would submit the lowest bid. After receiving final payment for the work, A-A-A

[43] US Department of Justice, 'Price Fixing & Bid Rigging–They Happen: What They Are and What to Look For, An Antitrust Primer for Procurement Professionals,' http://www.usdoj.gov/atr/public/guidelines/pfbrprimer.pdf.

[44] See also *United States vs. MMR Corp.*, 907 F.2d 489 (5th Cir. 1990), which provides a fact-intensive narrative of steps that electrical contractors took to track and account for amounts owing among themselves from their participation in past episodes of collusion.

[45] *United States vs. Lyons*, No. 81–1287, 1982 US App. LEXIS 22194 (7th Cir. 1 Feb. 1982).

[46] *United States vs. A-A-A Elec. Co., Inc.*, 788 F.2d 242 (4th Cir., 1986).

made payments to its co-conspirators. In this example, the cartel met prior to bidding to discuss bids, but the transfer payments made by the designated winner to the bidders who agreed to suppress their bids were not finalized until later. The willingness of bidders to wait for their transfer payments may suggest that there was repeated interaction among the firms since otherwise one might expect firms would be concerned that A-A-A would renege on its promise to pay them.

Another concern of a bidding ring is whether bidders who agree to submit non-winning bids will actually do so. In *US vs. W. F. Brinkley & Son Construction Company, Inc.*,[47] Brinkley's competitors for a pumping station and pipeline contract discussed their bids prior to the procurement, agreeing that Brinkley would submit the winning bid. The ring solved the problem of monitoring the bids of Brinkley's competitors by, in at least one case, having the competitor fill out his bid and give it to Brinkley to turn in for him. The threat that ring members who agree prior to bidding to submit a non-winning bid might not do so when they actually bid plays an important role in how economists think about the differences between collusion at a dynamic auction and collusion with first-price sealed bidding. However, in *Brinkley*, it seems the bidding ring was able to overcome this problem.

Finally, the DoJ describes subcontracting arrangements as potentially an important part of bid-rigging schemes (see also Chapter 14). In particular, bidders who agree not to bid or to submit a losing bid might be compensated by being awarded a subcontract by the winning bidder. In *US vs. Metropolitan Enterprises, Inc.*,[48] Broce Construction Company met with a group of other highway paving companies prior to bidding for a number of Oklahoma repaving contracts. These companies agreed not to bid against Broce, which then outbid the remaining bidders for the contracts. In compensation, Broce subcontracted with one of the companies agreeing not to bid against Broce. A subcontracting arrangement is also described in *US vs. Inryco, Inc.*,[49] where concrete construction firm Inryco subcontracted with its competitor Western in compensation for Western's submitting artificially high bids at certain procurements.[50]

---

[47] *United States* vs. *W. F. Brinkley & Son Construction Company, Inc.*, 783 F.2d 1157 (4th Cir. 1986).

[48] *United States* vs. *Metropolitan Enterprises, Inc.*, 728 F.2d 444 (1984).

[49] *Unite States* vs. *Inryco, Inc.*, 642 F.2d 290 (1981).

[50] See also *State of New York* vs. *Hendrickson Brothers, Inc.*, 840 F.2d 1065, 1069–72 (2nd Cir. 1988) (discussing use of subcontract awards as means for cartel members to sustain the commitment of all participants to the collusive scheme).

> **Practical conclusion 4**
> Subcontracting can be pro-collusive. If possible, bids should be absent of subcontracting arrangements.

In summary, bidding rings with first-price sealed bidding typically meet prior to each auction to discuss the bids each ring member will submit. The ring may have to take steps to ensure that ring members who are supposed to submit losing bids actually do so. And, payments among ring members (to compensate ring members who agree to submit losing bids) may be arranged prior to the auction, or after the auction, or may be consummated through subcontracting arrangements.

15.3.3. Bid rigging by 'standard' cartels

The bidding rings discussed above had no overarching agreement other than the agreements related to collusion at individual auctions. In contrast, some cartels do have broader agreements, such as market share agreements or customer allocations, even though buyers procure the product through competitive procurements.

For example, the recent vitamins cartel[51] was centered upon a market share agreement, under which each cartel firm received a fixed relative percentage of the within-cartel global market. Output of each cartel firm was carefully monitored by the cartel. If firms wavered from their agreed market shares, then within-cartel redistributions occurred to 'true-up' shares to the cartel agreement.[52] But despite this level of organization and coordination, cartel members still had to elevate bids at competitive procurements in order to realize a collusive gain.

Although bidder collusion may not seem to be a big part of cartels using market share agreements or customer allocations, it is still the case that most buyers run competitive procurements to buy product. No matter what the cartel does in terms of organization and coordination as a preamble to interaction with individual buyers, the conspirators must elevate bids in order to realize a collusive gain. But this raises the question: If each and every bid is elevated then why bother with market share agreements, output monitoring, and redistributions?

---

[51] The European Commission (2003) decision provides an excellent detailed description of the cartel and its inner workings.

[52] European Commission (2003) paragraph 196.

In the case of the vitamins cartel, the market for the commodity was global and the buyers were numerous. On occasion, some buyers would elect to extend contracts with incumbent suppliers rather than conduct competitive procurements, and there were third party vendors in the market, brokers, who could supply product on a regular basis. These features of the market imply that each firm participating in the cartel would be uncertain as to whether their co-conspirators were secretly selling product to brokers at discount prices, secretly offering discounts to customers in order to secure contract extensions, or secretly chiseling on the terms of their nominal bids at procurements so that, even though they had bid a high amount, they were still awarded the contract under the guise of some superior non-price attribute. In other words, secret price cutting behavior would be a constant suspicion by the conspirators of one another.[53]

One way for that suspicion to be removed is to have a global market share agreement among co-conspirators, monitor the output of all conspirators, and conduct interfirm redistributions as needed. With a market share agreement and output monitoring in place, if a given conspirator attempted to cheat on the agreement (oversell their assigned market share), its behavior would be detected and appropriate redistributions would occur. In this context, once the firms have agreed on the collusive price then collusion at the procurements is a relatively straightforward matter. The firms simply try to get the quantities won at each procurement to aggregate in a way that each cartel firm receives its assigned market share.

In the vitamins industry, procurements were repeated regularly. Any given procurement was tiny relative to the market. There was no reasonable possibility of a shill bidder. Deviations would all be addressed at year's end through redistributions that brought all cartel members to their appropriate market share. Thus, even though the procurements were sealed-bid procurements, where collusion might be more difficult, the repetition, monitoring, market share agreement, and redistributions made bidder collusion feasible, profitable, and stable.

15.4. How auction formats affect bidding rings

In this section, we discuss a number of dimensions for which auction or procurement formats affect bidding rings. We begin by noting that it may

---

[53] In addition, in the absence of a market share agreement, collusion at any given procurement would entail significant bargaining costs as firms tried to argue that it was their turn to win.

be easier to prosecute collusion at sealed-bid tendering versus dynamic auctions. We then continue by discussing how different formats, sealed bid versus dynamic, affect the ability of a ring to induce its members to comply with the instructions of the ring on how they should bid. We then discuss the role of information provided by the auctioneer in facilitating collusion and how the auction format affects the incentives for bidders to participate in a ring in the first place. And we discuss the effects of shill bidders on bidding rings and the effects of having more or less frequent auctions on bidding rings.

15.4.1. Prosecution of collusion

With first-price sealed bidding, typically all participating bidders submit bids, and the auctioneer should have a written (or electronic) record of all of these bids. Having fewer than the normal number of competitors submit bids suggests the possibility of collusion, so colluding bidders with first-price sealed bidding can be expected to arrange for ring members, who are not designated as the winning bidders, to submit complementary bids to disguise the presence of the cartel. Thus, with first-price sealed bidding, the auctioneer will have a record of the participants and all of their bids. This paper trail may facilitate the prosecution of collusion with first-price sealed bidding.

At a dynamic auction, such a paper trail typically does not exist. First, the bids themselves may be submitted orally, and so it may be that no formal record of submitted bids exists. Second, depending on the auction format, many bidders may not submit bids at all, even in a non-collusive environment, if the price rises (falls in case of procurements) to a level above their willingness to pay before they have an opportunity to enter a bid.[54] So the observation that only a small number of bidders actually submit bids at a dynamic auction may not be suggestive of collusive activity the way it is with first-price sealed bidding. One may not even be able to identify all the participants in a dynamic auction, since one may only know about those who actually submitted bids. These issues mean that it may be more difficult to prosecute collusion at a dynamic auction than with first-price sealed bidding.

15.4.2. Susceptibility of auction formats to collusion

It is commonly thought that dynamic auctions are more susceptible to collusion than first-price sealed bidding. For example, the US Forest Service

---

[54] Some auction formats include participation rules that require bidders to participate in early rounds of the auction in order to be eligible to participate in later rounds.

held this view and mandated a move towards more first-price sealed bidding in an attempt to deter collusion among bidders at its timber auctions.[55] Theoretical models in the academic literature have formalized the result that in many environments bidding rings can more easily organize and can be more profitable at dynamic auctions than with first-price sealed bidding.[56]

The reasoning behind a dynamic auction being more susceptible to collusion than a first-price sealed bidding is explained with a simple example. Suppose there are four bidders – A, B, C and D – who have the following privately known values for the one item being sold:[57]

A:80, B:60, C:40, and D:20.

Acting non-cooperatively at an oral ascending bid auction, D will bid up to 20 before dropping out, C will bid up to 40, B to 60, and A to 80. Thus, A will win the item for a price of 60. With first-price sealed bidding, the bidders need to shade their bids below their values in order to have any positive expected payoff. Suppose they bid as follows.

$b_A = 60$, $b_B = 45$, $b_C = 30$, $b_D = 15$

Bidder A wins the item for a price of 60.

Now we consider collusion under each scheme. At a dynamic auction, a ring must suppress the bids of all members except the bidder with highest value. The ring member with highest value goes to the auction and bids as if it were acting non-cooperatively. In the example above, if A, B, and C collude, but D does not, then B and C suppress their bids while A remains ready to bid up to 80. The ring wins the item for a price of 20. Any ring member who thinks of breaking ranks and competing at the auction faces the highest ring bidder and the highest non-ring bidder, each submitting bids that are the same as if all were acting non-cooperatively. Thus, there is no gain to deviant behavior. In our example, potential deviant behavior by bidder B will not result in B winning the item – A stands ready to bid up to 80 which exceeds B's value for the item.

---

[55] US Senate. Timber Sales Bidding Procedures: Hearings before the Senate Subcommittee on Public Lands and Resources. 95th Congress, 1st Sess. 1077.

[56] Robinson (1985) provides this formalization for the case in which there is perfect communication among ring members (ring members' values are common knowledge within the ring). Marshall and Marx (2006) provide this formalization for the case in which ring members' values are private information.

[57] Each bidder knows their own value but not the value of any other bidder, although they will each know the distribution from which bidders draw their values. In the example considered here, the distribution is uniform on the interval from 0 to 100.

First-price sealed bidding is quite different. In order to secure a collusive gain, the ring member with the highest value must lower its bid below what it would have bid acting non-cooperatively, and other ring members must suppress their bids. In our example where A, B, and C collude but D does not, suppose that B and C again suppress their bids and that A submits a bid of 20. This bid will prevail against D.[58] But when the highest-valuing ring member lowers its bid, the opportunity is created for a non-highest-valuing ring member to secure the item by entering a bid at the auction, either on its own or through a shill (for example, it may be possible for a ring member to have another person or firm submit a bid on its behalf, thereby disguising its identity and potentially avoiding any penalties that the ring would impose on it if the ring discovered it had not followed the instructions of the ring). This possibility jeopardizes the feasibility of a cartel with first-price sealed bidding. In other words, if B were to deviate from the agreement and bid 30, they would win the item and secure a relatively large surplus. For the ring to guard against such deviant behavior requires bidding behavior that mitigates the collusive gain. This a fundamental difference between the oral ascending and first-price sealed bidding.[59]

At this point, we emphasize our previous recommendation that first-price sealed bidding should be used instead of a dynamic auction if collusion is a potential concern.

In addition, the auctioneer or procurement official can oppose the collusion through some strategic actions. A reserve price, more aggressive than would be used were bidders not suspected of collusion, can be employed in many circumstances.[60] Their threat of using such a reserve will deter collusion. This leads to the following additional recommendation.

Practical conclusion 5

The auctioneer or procurement official can use an aggressive reserve price policy to increase their payoff and simultaneously help deter collusion.

---

[58] We have not specified how D bids when confronting a cartel but it will never be as much as 20 since bidding 20 or more leaves D without the hope of any positive surplus.

[59] The issue described here has nothing to do with an oral auction being 'open outcry'. The same contrast in susceptibility discussed here is present if the oral ascending bid auction is replaced with a second-price sealed-bid auction.

[60] In a procurement context, there are circumstances where an aggressive reserve price is not possible because it is not credible that the procurement official will not procure. Alternative strategies can be employed in these cases, such as securing a supply agreement from a seller who acts as a producer of last resort and thus makes credible the threat not to buy from others.

15.4.3. Role of information

Another aspect of auction formats that affects the ability of bidders to collude is the amount of information provided by the auctioneer on auction outcomes. For example, if the auctioneer reveals the identity of the winner and the price paid at the auction, then a bidding ring might be able to operate with greater efficiency, or with less risk of detection, by utilizing that information.[61] If an auctioneer with first-price sealed bidding reveals the amounts of the bids of all the bidders, then the problem that a bidding ring faces in policing the bids of its members is made much easier. In general, the less information provided on auction outcomes, the more difficult it is for a bidding ring to operate. Unfortunately, in many settings it will be impossible to hide the identity of the winner, but certainly the full range of bids with first-price sealed bidding need not be revealed.

Practical conclusion 6

Losing bids made with first-price sealed bidding should not be revealed

Although it may be possible to deter collusion by not revealing information from auctions, from the standpoint of detecting and prosecuting collusion, it is important that auctioneers retain all available information from the auctions held. In particular, complete information on all bids submitted should be retained. This is particularly true when a bidding ring does not include all the bidders since the bids of the ring members may not be the highest bids submitted, but those bids may still be used to identify the presence of the ring and reveal the identity of its members.[62]

Practical conclusion 7

Whenever possible, every aspect of the auction/procurement should be documented, and the records should be retained for a long period. The recording and documentation should include, but not be limited to, announcement of the auction/procurement, who was invited to bid, who actually bid, all discussions and conversations, and all bids. All bidders should be notified ex ante that the entire record of all auctions/procurements will be made available to public enforcement authorities and/or private litigants should an investigation of collusive bidding occur.

---

[61] For a mechanism that uses the identity of the winner and the price paid at the auction, see Graham and Marshall (1987).

[62] See Marshall and Marx (2006) for a characterization of ring members' bids at a sealed-bid auction when the ring is not all inclusive.

Losing bids with first-price sealed bidding can contain information of relevance for inferring collusion. Although a bidding ring always attempts to suppress bids, for collusion to be effective with first-price sealed bidding a ring must prevent its own ring members from cheating on the collusive agreement. The incentive for ring members to cheat is mitigated if bidders elevate their bids somewhat, but to enforce these elevated bids the cartel may need to have a ring bidder submit a bid that is just underneath the highest ring bidder's bid. This implies that sequential bids may be very close to one another, even when they are losing bids. Bids of this nature are an indication of potential collusion.[63]

In a procurement setting, it is often the case that the incumbent supplier is given a right of last refusal. In other words, before the close of the procurement, the incumbent is notified of the leading competitive bid and offered the opportunity to meet the bid to retain the business. Notifying an incumbent of the bids of others before the procurement is over provides the incumbent with a way to monitor the bidding behavior of potential co-conspirators and react in real time to deviations from agreed collusive bidding. It deters deviations by ring members.

> **Practical conclusion 8**
>
> If the costs of switching suppliers are not very high, the practice of offering 'right of last refusal' should be avoided since it is pro-collusive.

Finally, there are auction/procurement environments in which bidders have considerable expertise relevant to the evaluation of the item or project. For example, antique dealers have expertise in assessing the authenticity of a period piece or timber mills have expertise in assessing the quality of standing timber in a particular drainage area. In such cases, bidders will have an extra incentive to collude since their competitive bidding will transfer all expertise rents to the seller/buyer. The auction or procurement official can mitigate this incentive by providing detailed and high quality information to the entire bidding public prior to the auction/procurement. Providing this information has the added benefit of reducing the "winner's curse".[64] Reductions in

---

[63] This bidding behavior is discussed in Marshall and Marx (2006).

[64] See Chapter 5 for an introduction and Hirschleifer and Riley (1993, p. 395) for a discussion of the winner's curse.

the winner's curse lead to more aggressive bidding, especially by less well-informed bidders, which might typically be the non-cartel bidders.[65]

Practical conclusion 9
All information of relevance known to the auctioneer/procurer about the item for sale/ procurement should be revealed ex ante to the entire bidding public.

15.4.4. Participation

With first-price sealed bidding, in order for there to be any gains from collusion, the ring member designated as the winner must submit a lower bid (higher bid at a procurement) than it otherwise would. If the ring member submits the same bid as it would in the absence of collusion, then there is no benefit from the collusion. But, if there are bidders who are not included in the ring, then the selected ring member must be careful not to distort its bid too much since the bid must still be competitive relative to the bids of the non-ring bidders.

This problem is not faced by a bidding ring at a dynamic auction since in that case the designated ring member can respond in real time to any bids made by bidders not in the ring. With first-price sealed bidding, the designated ring member must commit to a bid without knowing the bids of the non-ring bidders. This potentially reduces the gains from collusion with first-price sealed bidding relative to a dynamic auction. And this reduction in the gains from collusion may mean that with first-price sealed bidding, some bidders would prefer not to participate in the ring – they might prefer to bid on their own rather than participate in the ring, and potentially have to make transfer payments to the other ring members in exchange for the suppression of competition. This is particularly true for bidders with first-price sealed bidding with very high values for the object being sold (very low cost suppliers of the object being procured). It is these high-value bidders who are most likely to decline to participate in a bidding ring with first-price sealed bidding.[66] In contrast, even high-value bidders would be expected to be willing to participate in a bidding ring at a dynamic auction.

---

[65] See Marshall and Meurer (2004) for the details of this argument, and see Hendricks and Porter (1988) for the role of the winner's curse in OCS auctions.

[66] See the results on individual rationality constraints in Marshall and Marx (2006).

15.4.5. Role of shill bidders

As mentioned above, if ring members with first-price sealed bidding have the ability to submit bids under disguised names, it may make it more difficult for a bidding ring with first-price sealed bidding to police the bids submitted by its members. In particular, ring members who have been instructed by the ring to submit losing bids may have an incentive to try to win the item under a disguised name, thereby avoiding any retaliation from the ring. For dynamic auctions, there exist collusive mechanisms that are not susceptible to the ability of ring members to use shill bidders.[67] Thus, the ability or inability to use shills need not affect bidding rings at dynamic auctions.

Because of the potentially destabilizing effect of shill bidders on bidding rings, particularly with first-price sealed bidding, the auctioneer may have an incentive to facilitate the use of shill bidders. For example, the auctioneer might keep private the identities of the bidders, perhaps referring only to bidder numbers. The auctioneer might allow bids to be telephoned in, or mailed in, rather than requiring that bidders turn in their bids in person at a designated time and place where all can observe. And, the auctioneer can allow a bidder to submit more than one bid under different bidder numbers, or under different identities.

15.4.6. Frequency of auctions

As discussed above, some bidding rings make transfer payments among themselves after the auctions at which they collude, or perhaps keep records of amounts owed and only infrequently make payments to clear the accounts. Such behavior is made easier if the bidding ring knows there will be a regular stream of auctions in which they can participate (for more on this see section 14.4). When there are auctions at regular intervals, a bidding ring can more easily implement a bid rotation scheme and can threaten to punish ring members at future auctions if they do not follow instructions. If the value of the items being sold at any individual auction is small, then ring members may have little incentive to disobey the instructions of the ring because the gains to doing so are small relative to the threat of future punishment.

---

[67] See Marshall and Marx (2006).

For these reasons, an auctioneer concerned about collusion may prefer to hold fewer auctions, each with a larger number of items being sold. Or the auctioneer may prefer to create higher-valued items by bundling a number of lower-valued items. And an auctioneer may prefer not to announce a fixed schedule for future auctions, instead bringing objects up for sale at irregular intervals. Longer time intervals between auctions may encourage ring members to defect from the ring since the potential for retaliation by the other ring members is pushed farther into the future.

15.5. Conclusion and discussion: auction design and countermeasures

Collusive schemes are typically executed through individual auctions and procurements. The manner in which sellers conduct auctions, and buyers conduct procurements, can increase or reduce their vulnerability to collusion, regardless of the availability of antitrust statutes or other legal commands that forbid such forms of coordination. Thus, the design of auctions and procurements provides an important opportunity for firms to supplement, by private means, safeguards against collusion embodied in public law.

As discussed in this chapter, modern experience in prosecuting cartels has generated a valuable body of information that can inform the design of collusion countermeasures in auctions. Among other steps, auctioneers can take the following measures to deter collusion. We summarize the main points below:

1. If collusion is a major concern for auction designers, then use first-price sealed bidding rather than a dynamic auction. Auctioneers and procurement officials should use an aggressive reserve price policy whenever possible.

2. Auctioneers and procurement agents should maintain a record of all bids, not just those of winners, as well as all other aspects of the auction/procurement. It should be made known ex ante that these records will be made available to public enforcement authorities and/or private litigants should an antitrust investigation occur.

3. To the extent possible, auctioneers and procurement agents should limit the amount of information provided to bidders regarding the auction outcomes or the bids of their competitors. In addition, in the absence of a compelling reason, the right of last refusal should not be granted to an incumbent supplier. However, auctioneers and procurement agents

should provide detailed information to the entire bidding public prior to the auction about the item being sold/procured.

4. To the extent possible, auctioneers should allow bidders to submit multiple bids, with some under disguised identities.

5. To the extent possible, auctioneers should hold auctions at long, irregular time intervals.

These steps have potential benefits for all categories of auctioneers and procurement bodies, but they have special significance for public purchasing authorities. A striking number of cartel cases prosecuted by antitrust agencies in recent decades have involved scenarios in which the victim of the collusive scheme is a public purchasing authority.[68] The apparent attractiveness of government auctions and procurements as targets for collusion suggests the gains to be had for public agencies by strengthening anti-cartel countermeasures, including the safeguards suggested here.

In addition to the points discussed above, there are a number of other ways in which an auctioneer or procurement official can attempt to mitigate collusion. Although a detailed discussion of these is beyond the scope of this article, we provide some general discussion below.

A number of tactics for mitigating collusion involve the use of market power and/or discretion by the auctioneer or procurement official. Examples include the use of an aggressive reserve price or the right not to sell. The latter could be invoked through an ambiguously defined scoring function, which then a judicious procurement official uses to assess the non-cooperative nature of the bids, penalizing apparent collusive bidding. Although good discretion is common, when discretion is retained in the hands of an auctioneer or procurer who is working as an agent of the owner or ultimate buyer, bad decisions can occur because of a breakdown in the agency relationship. Much of the US Federal Acquisition Regulations are about controlling discretion by government procurement officials. We recognize that the retention by public officials of discretion to oppose collusive bidding would conflict with some features of existing procurement regulations in the United States and in other countries.

One tactic used by auctioneers and procurers to mitigate potential collusion by bidders involves the use of protecting bidders. These bidders are available to the auctioneer or procurer on a favored basis. Firms who have demonstrated aggressivity in the past, sometimes referred to as 'maverick' bidders, are a good potential choice for this role.

---

[68] See Haberbush (2000) (examining experience with cartel prosecutions involving government procurement in the United States).

It is often the case that procurers point to split awards and 'benchmarking' as safeguards of their buying process. In general, not only is neither robust to collusion, but each is inherently susceptible to manipulation by a cartel. Benchmarking, whereby a firm would obtain information from a third party about what others in the market are typically paying for the items being purchased, allows detection of inadequacies of a procurement official or some other idiosyncratic shortcoming of a firm's procurement practice, but it does not allow a procurer to detect collusion since a cartel will elevate bids for all buyers in the industry. In other words, benchmarking is particularly poor at providing information about highly correlated events that similarly impact procuring firms.

Split awards suffer from a significant deficiency as well. Namely, split awards or multi-sourcing in a procurement context can produce results that look like collusion, which is counter-intuitive.[69] Maintaining multiple sources of supply simultaneously seems to suggest that one supplier can be used to implicitly monitor another. But, initial bidding behavior can be dramatically distorted by split awards. Consider two firms, A and B, who can each produce three units. For each, the first two units can be produced at a marginal cost of 5, while the third unit can be produced at a marginal cost of 100. Suppose a buyer wants two items. If the buyer runs a sole-source procurement, then the bidders pay a total of 10 for two objects. A split award also results in the purchase price being 10 for two objects. The issue arises if each of the suppliers can produce one fewer object so that the marginal cost of producing the first item is 5, but the marginal cost of producing the second item is 100 for each. In this case, a sole-source procurement results in the buyer paying 105 for two objects. However, a split award results in the buyer paying 200 for two objects. This outcome is counter-intuitive and looks like collusion, but we arrive at it through wholly non-cooperative bidding. The collusion comes before the procurement through the restriction of supply to the market. Thus, two safeguards that are often used in practice, benchmarking and split awards, are not without significant limitations.

Bibliographical notes

The revenue equivalence theorem is the benchmark result of auction theory. The seminal papers in this area include Riley and Samuelson (1981)

---

[69] See Anton and Yao (1992).

and Myerson (1981). Deviations from the basic assumptions have been investigated for the last two and a half decades. One vein of investigation has been relaxation of the assumption of non-cooperative play. Initial work in this area includes Robinson (1985), Graham and Marshall (1987), McAfee and McMillan (1992), and Mailath and Zemsky (1991). Interest has also been partially fueled by the importance of bid-rigging and collusion for competition policy. The comparative robustness of different auction schemes to collusion garners attention from both those engaged in competition policy and those designing auctions and procurements. A paper that provides an overview of the main issues is Marshall and Meurer (2004). Recent theoretical work dedicated to the contrast, especially when collusion may not include all bidders, can be found in Marshall and Marx (2006).

References

American Bar Association, Section of Antitrust Law (2002). *Antitrust Law Developments* (5th Ed.).

Anderson, Mark R. (Fall 2001). Settle or Roll the Dice?, *Litigation*, 28 (1), 37–41.

Anton, James and Dennis Yao (1992), Coordination in Split Award Auctions, *Quarterly Journal of Economics*, 57, 681–707.

Aubert, Cecile, Patrick Rey and William E. Kovacic (2005). The Effect of Leniency and Whistleblowing Programs on Cartels, *International Journal of Industrial Organization* (forthcoming).

Ausubel, Lawrence M., Peter Cramton and Paul Milgrom (2004). The Clock-Proxy Auction: A Practical Combinatorial Auction Design, forthcoming in Peter Cramton, Yoav Shoham, and Richard Steinberg (Eds.), *Combinatorial Auctions*, MIT Press, 2006.

Baker, Donald I. (2001). The Use of Criminal Law Remedies to Deter and Punish Cartels and Bid-Rigging, *George Washington Law Review*, 69, 663–720.

Baker, Jonathan B. (2002). Mavericks, Mergers, and Exclusion: Proving Coordinated Effects Under the Antitrust Laws, *New York University Law Review*, 77, 135–203.

Bernheim, Douglas (2002). Expert Report of B. Douglas Bernheim, M.D.L. No. 1285, in Re: Vitamins Antitrust Litigation, Misc. No. 99–0197 (TFH), 24 May 2002.

Breit, William and Kenneth G. Elzinga (1986). *Antitrust Penalty Reform – An Economic Analysis*, Washington and London: American Enterprise Institute.

Calkins, Stephen (1997a). Corporate Compliance and the Antitrust Agencies' Bi-Modal Penalties, *Law & Contemporary Problems*, 60 (3), 127–167.

Calkins, Stephen (1997b). An Enforcement Official's Reflections on Antitrust Class Actions, *Arizona Law Review*, 39, 412.

Chen, Joe and Joseph E. Harrington, Jr. (2005). The Impact of the Corporate Leniency Program on Cartel Formation and the Cartel Price Path, in Vivek Ghosal and Johan Sennek, (Eds.), *Political Economy of Antitrust* forthcoming, North-Holland.

Coase, R. H. (1937), The Nature of the Firm, *Economica*, 4, 386–405.

Connor, John M. (2005). Price-Fixing Overcharges: Legal and Economic Evidence, Working Paper #04–05 American Antitrust Institute.

Connor, John M. (2001). *Global Price Fixing: Our Customers Are the Enemy*. Series: Studies in Industrial Organization, vol. 24, Boston: Kluwer Academic Publishers.

Cooter, Robert (1985). Unity in Tort, Contract, and Property: The Model of Precaution, *California Law Review*, 73, 1–51.

Eichenwald, Kurt (2000). *The Informant: A True Story*, New York: Broadway Books.

Evenett, Simon J., Margaret C. Levenstein and Valerie Y. Suslow (2002). International Cartel Enforcement: Lessons from the 1990s, OECD Global Forum on Competition.

European Commission (2003). The Commission of the European Communities Decision of 21 November 2001, Case COMP/E-1/37.512-Vitamins, *Official Journal of the European Communities*, 1 October 2003.

First, Harry (2001). The Vitamins Case: Cartel Prosecution and the Coming of International Competition Law, *Antitrust Law Journal*, 68, 711–734.

Fuller, John G. (1962). *The Gentleman Conspirators: The Story of the Price-Fixers in the Electrical Industry*, New York: Grove Press.

Gavil, Andrew I., William E. Kovacic and Jonathan B. Baker (2002). *Antitrust Law in Perspective: Cases, Concepts and Problems in Competition Policy*, St. Paul: West Group.

Genesove, David and Wallace P. Mullin (2001). Rules, Communication and Collusion: Narrative Evidence from the Suger Institute Case, *American Economic Review*, 91, 379–98.

Global Competition Review (2004), Cartel Regulation, www.globalcompetitionreview.com.

Graham, Daniel A. and Robert C. Marshall (1987). Collusive Bidder Behavior at Single-Object Second Price and English Auctions, *Journal of Political Economy*, 95, 1217–1239.

Grossman, Peter Z. (Ed.) (2004). *How Cartels Endure and How They Fail: Studies of Industrial Collusion*, Northhampton, MA: Edward Elgar.

Guersant, Olivier (2002). European Commission Adopted Ten Decisions Imposing Heavy Fines on Hard Core Cartels in 2001, Directorate for Competition, European Commission.

Haberbush, Kara L. (2000). Limiting the Government's Exposure to Bid Rigging Schemes: A Critical Look at the Sealed Bidding Regime, *Public Contract Law Journal*, 30, 97–122.

Hendricks, Kenneth and Robert H. Porter (1988). An Empirical Study of an Auction with Asymmetric Information, *American Economic Review*, 78, 865–883.

Herling, John (1962). *The Great Price Conspiracy: The Story of the Antitrust Violations in the Electrical Industry*, Washington: R. B. Luce.

Hirshleifer, Jack, and John G. Riley (1993). *The Analytics of Uncertainty and Information*, Cambridge: Cambridge University Press.

International Competition Policy Advisory Committee (ICPAC) to the Assistant Attorney General for Antitrust (2000), Final Report, US Department of Justice.

Klemperer, Paul (Winter 2002). What Really Matters in Auction Design, *Journal of Economic Perspectives* 16, 169–189.

Kolasky, William J. (2002). Antitrust Compliance Programs: The Government Perspective, Antitrust Division, US Department of Justice. Available at http://www.usdoj.gov/atr/public/speeches/11534.htm.

Kovacic, William E. and Carl Shapiro (2000). Antitrust Policy: A Century of Economic and Legal Thinking, *Journal of Economic Perspectives*, 14, 43–61.

Kovacic, William E. (2001). Private Monitoring and Antitrust Enforcement: Paying Informants to Reveal Cartels, *George Washington Law Review*, 69, 766–797.

Kovacic, William E. (2003). The Modern Evolution of US Competition Policy Enforcement Norms, *Antitrust Law Journal*, 71, 377–478.

Lopomo, Guiseppe, Robert C. Marshall and Leslie M. Marx (2005). Inefficiency of Collusion at English Auctions, *Contributions to Theoretical Economics* 5 (1), Article 4.

Mailath, George, and Peter Zemsky (1991). Collusion in Second Price Auctions with Heterogeneous Bidders, *Games and Economic behavior*, 3, 467–486.

Marshall, Robert C. and Leslie M. Marx (2006). Bidder Collusion, forthcoming in *Journal of Economic Theory*.

Marshall, Robert C., Leslie M. Marx and Matthew E. Raiff (2005), Cartel Price Announcements: The Vitamins Industry, Working paper, Duke University.

Marshall, Robert C. and Michael J. Meurer (2004). Bidder Collusion and Antitrust Law: Refining the Analysis of Price Fixing to Account for the Special Features of Auction Markets, *Antitrust Law Journal*, 72, 83–118.

McAfee, R. Preston and John McMillan (1992), Bidding Rings, *American Economic Review*, 82, 579–599.

Motta, Massimo, and Michele Polo (2003). Leniency Programs and Cartel Prosecution, *International Journal of Industrial Organization*, 21, 347–379.

Myerson, Roger B. (1981). Optimal Auction Design, *Mathematics of Operations Research, 6*, 58–73.

Organization for Economic Cooperation and Development (OECD) (2005). Cartels: Sanctions Against Individuals. Available at http://www.oecd.org/dataoecd/61/46/34306028.pdf.

Riley, John G. and William F. Samuelson (1981). Optimal Auctions, *American Economic Review*, 71, 381–392.

Robinson, Marc S. (1985). Collusion and the Choice of Auction, *RAND Journal of Economics*, 16, 141–145.

Scott, Sheridan (2004). Cartel Enforcement: International and Canadian Developments, in B.Hawk, (Ed.), *International Antitrust Law and Policy*, Fordham Corporate Law Institute (2005), 33–56.

Spagnolo, Giancarlo (2005). Leniency and Whistleblowers in Antitrust, forthcoming in P. Buccirossi, (Ed.), *Handbook of Antitrust Economics*, MIT Press.

Spratling, Gary. R. (2001). Detection and Deterrence: Rewarding Informants for Reporting Violations, *George Washington Law Review*, 69, 798–823.

Stigler, George J. (1964). A Theory of Oligopoly, *Journal of Political Economy*, 72, 44–61.

Vann, David E., Jr. and Ethan E. Litwan (2004). Recent Developments in International Cartel Enforcement, in *Getting the Deal Through: Cartel Regulation* (Global Competition Review).

Williamson, Oliver E. (1975), *Markets and Hierarchies: Analysis and Antitrust Implications*. New York: The Free Press, 1975.

Wils, Wouter P. J. (2005). Is Criminalization of EU Competition Law the Answer?, *World Competition*, 28 (2), 117–159

Wils, Wouter P. J. (2003). Should Private Antitrust Enforcement Be Encouraged in Europe?, *World Competition*, 26, 473–488.

16 Corruption in procurement auctions

Yvan Lengwiler and Elmar Wolfstetter

16.1 Introduction

Auctions are an efficient mechanism to procure. This is why they have been used for centuries and are being used ever more frequently. But they are not immune to manipulations through collusion and corruption. Collusion means that bidders coordinate their actions with the intention to increase the price. Corruption means that the person who runs the auction, the auctioneer, twists the auction rules in favor of some bidder(s) in exchange for bribes. Corruption and collusion are sometimes interlinked. However, in this chapter, we focus exclusively on corruption.

We describe with the term corruption all kinds of behavior where a person who is in a position of trust misuses this position to her own advantage. In its procurement guidelines, the World Bank defines a "corrupt practice" as "The offering, giving, receiving, or soliciting, directly or indirectly, of any thing of value to influence the action of a public official in the procurement process or in contract execution".[1] In the specific circumstances of an auction, the person of trust is the auctioneer, who acts on behalf of the procurer, and the bidders who have pledged to play by the rules. Obviously, if the procurer and the auctioneer are one and the same person, there is no room for corruption. However, if the procurer is a firm with a broad ownership (a publicly traded company, for instance), there will necessarily be an agent who takes on the role of the auctioneer on behalf of the procurer. The same is true if the procurer is a public organization, such as a nation state. It is immaterial if the auctioneer is an external outside

We would like to thank Gustavo Piga for his detailed comments and Giancarlo Casartelli for sharing his insight into modern procurement. Financial support was received by the *Deutsche Forschungsgemeinschaft (DFG)*, SFB Transregio 15, Governance and Efficiency of Economic Systems.

[1] See The World Bank (2004a).

expert or a public servant. In both cases, the auctioneer and the procurer are not identical, and corruption is potentially an issue.

Corruption is a widespread problem in procurement all over the world. Recently, the World Bank estimated the volume of bribes exchanging hands for public sector procurement alone at roughly $200 billion per year.[2] Therefore, procurers must be alerted to the different forms of corruption, and one must design mechanisms that eliminate corruption or at least make it more difficult. Different forms of corruption have been observed in procurement:

- bid rigging,
- bid orchestration, and
- distortion of quality ranking.

In each of these kinds of corruption, the auctioneer may or may not have an existing relation with one favored bidder or the auctioneer establishes a corrupt relationship only with that bidder who offers the highest bribe. In the following we explain the major types of corruption and sketch the means to restrain them.

16.2 Bid rigging

Bid rigging happens whenever the auctioneer allows a favored bidder to adjust his bid after receiving information about rival bids.

16.2.1 Favored bidder selection independent of the bids

Suppose the auctioneer has already established a relationship with one of the bidders before the auction. The auctioneer allows this preferred bidder to match the lowest bid of his competing bidders.

This can mean one of two things:

- In the event in which the preferred bidder submitted the lowest bid, the auctioneer allows him to raise his bid and still win the auction, thereby increasing his payoff.
- If the preferred bidder did not submit the lowest bid, the auctioneer allows him to match the lowest bid so as to win the auction anyway.

In all cases, the paid price is the lowest bid of the non-preferred bidders. The preferred bidder wins whenever he has an incentive to adjust his bid,

---

[2] See Kaufmann (2005).

which occurs if and only if the lowest bid of the non-preferred bidder exceeds his own cost.

Evidently, the original bid of the preferred bidder is irrelevant, because it can be adjusted in either direction. Therefore, the auction with a preferred bidder is equivalent to a sequential auction in which the non-preferred bidders first submit their bids and then the preferred bidder can respond and has the right to match the lowest rival bid. In other words, the preferred bidder is granted the Right of First Refusal.

Generally, if this kind of corruption occurs, the auction will not always select the least-cost bidder as winner; hence it is generally inefficient. Moreover, it tends to reduce the payoff of the procurer.[3]

This type of corruption can be remedied by running an open auction[4] or a sealed-bid second-price (Vickrey) auction.[5] Indeed, in the Vickrey auction everyone submits a bid equal to his true cost; similarly, in the English auction everyone stays active until the price reaches his cost. Therefore, the preferred bidder is treated just like all the other bidders and the outcome is the same as without corruption.

The corruption issue is slightly different if the selection of the favored bidder is based on bribe competition. Suppose the auctioneer asks bidders to simultaneously offer bribes and submit bids, with the understanding that he will collect the highest bribe in exchange for granting the preferred bidder status.

If the auction is first-price, in equilibrium, bidders submit maximum bids and at the same time submit bribes that are such that their payoffs are the same as in a regular first-price auction without corruption. The outcome is efficient in the sense that the lowest-cost bidder is awarded the contract, but the entire surplus is pocketed by the auctioneer. From the procurer's point of view this situation is most unsatisfactory.

Again, this corruption problem can be remedied by running an open-bid or a sealed-bid second-price (Vickrey) auction, because in that case being a

---

[3] This follows from two facts: (i) Bidders quote a price above their cost, because otherwise they cannot benefit from winning. (ii) Suppose the favored bidder's cost is higher than the lowest-cost of all bidders but lower than the price quoted by the least-cost bidder, then, the favored matches the lowest bid and wins. This shows that the auction result can be inefficient. See Arozamena and Weinschelbaum (2004), Bikhchandani, Lippman, and Ryan (2005).

[4] This could be an open, descending-bid English or an ascending-bid Dutch auction.

[5] The Vickrey format is, however, not popular because it is vulnerable to other manipulations. For example, the auctioneer has an incentive to invite a shill bidder to close the gap between the two lowest bids, and bidders may engage in self-enforcing collusion.

preferred bidder has no value, as above, and therefore it is an equilibrium to offer no bribe and make a bid equal to one's cost.

Practical conclusion 1

Favor a sealed-bid second-price (Vickrey) or an open-bid auction if you suspect that the auctioneer has established a favored bidder relationship before the auction or invites bribes during the auction.

16.2.2 Favored bidder selection based on bids

In the cases we have studied so far, the selection of the favored bidder does not use information revealed to the auctioner from observed bidding behavior. Yet, it may be more advantageous for the corrupt auctioneer to delay that selection until he has observed the bids, for the following reasons:

• The auctioneer may infer the maximum gain from corruption from observed bids, and then select the most profitable bidder as favored bidder.

• By approaching only one or a few bidders, the auctioneer minimizes the number of illegal contacts and thus the risk of detection.

As before, in a first-price auction a corrupt deal can take one of two forms.[6] The auctioneer can invite the lowest bidder to raise his bid to the second highest bid, in exchange for a bribe. Alternatively, the auctioneer can invite the second highest bidder to lower his bid to the lowest submitted bid (that is, the auctioneer grants this bidder the Right of First Refusal), again in exchange for a bribe. Because the auctioneer has good information about bidders' willingness to pay (by inferring their true cost from the submitted bids), he can choose that form of corruption that gives rise to the highest possible bribery income. This form of corruption is very hard to detect – and thus involves little risk for the corrupt coalition – because only two parties have hard evidence on it.

In a second-price auction, a corrupt coalition consisting of only one bidder and the auctioneer cannot change the price paid to the seller, and thus they have no possible gain from corruption to share among themselves. The minimum size of the corrupt coalition involves the auctioneer and the two lowest bidders. They can agree that the second lowest bidder withdraws his bid, so that the lowest bidder wins the auction but has to pay only the third lowest bid to the seller. We therefore conclude that he Vickrey auction proposed in Practical conclusion 1 is not sufficient to prevent this form of corruption.

---

[6] This case has been analyzed by Lengwiler and Wolfstetter (2005).

Larger coalitions are also possible and they make greater gains from corruption possible. But the detection risk obviously increases with the number of people who know about the corruption.

The corruption schemes that follow this pattern rely on the ability of the parties to change the bids after they have been submitted. If this is not possible, this form of corruption will no longer be feasible. One way to make this impossible is to make the bidding process public. As a consequence, the open auction, which is also featured in Practical conclusion 1, suffices as an anti-corruption device simply because it destroys the secrecy required for this type of corruption.

Practical conclusion 2

Favor an open auction if you suspect that the auctioneer tries to make a secret deal with a small number of bidders after the bidding round in an attempt to collect side payments.

An open auction may not be desirable for other reasons, such as fear of collusion. In that case one should try to make the sealed-bid auction corruption-proof. This requires technology that makes it impossible to tamper with bids.

One could require that the auctioneer breaks the seals of all bids in public, after the bidding time window is closed.[7] Yet, the bidders have an interest to inform the auctioneer about their bids, because they also profit from corruption. The auctioneer could therefore invite each single bidder to come to his office with his unsealed bid. The auctioneer decides which bidder will be allowed to change his bid, and contacts him. The first bid of this bidder is simply destroyed and replaced by the new, rigged bid.[8] Therefore, the conventional practice of sealing bids and requiring the seals to be broken in public is not sufficient to exclude bid rigging. What is required in addition is that no bid can be destroyed and replaced.

It is often thought that one can solve the problem of corruption by employing a safe-keeper of bids such as a notary public, who is paid a

---

[7] This is a requirement of procurements funded by the World Bank and the Asian Development Bank.

[8] However, such a scheme exposes the corrupt auctioneer to high risk since he has to establish illegal contact with each bidder.

sufficiently high "wage of trust",[9] to whom all bids are submitted. However, this is not true as a bid can be replaced without leaving trace of it.[10]

The latter feature can be implemented with an electronic bid submission system. Such a system must contain a logbook that records who made the submissions at what time and who viewed them at what time. This requires the use of digital signatures and time stamps. Because of the logbook, the auctioneer can no longer replace a bid without leaving a trace. As a result, a bid, once submitted, can no longer be altered.

Practical conclusion 3

If you suspect the auctioneer to collect bribes in exchange for favorable treatment of bidders but still want to use a sealed-bid auction format, run the auction on an electronic submission system with a secure logbook. This remedy also works if the special relationship already exists before the auction (the case of Practical conclusion 1).

16.2.3 Bid orchestration

Even if bids cannot be changed after having been submitted, corruption may still occur in the form of bid orchestration. There, the auctioneer serves as a "ring manager" of a collusive cartel among the bidders who coordinates bids before they are submitted.

A widely publicized example is the recent insurance broker scandal in the United States. The Attorney General of New York, Eliot Spitzer, sued a leading insurance brokerage firm, alleging that it "steered unsuspecting clients to insurers with whom it had lucrative payoff agreements, and that the firm solicited rigged bids for insurance contracts."[11]

---

[9] The idea of paying a surplus above the competitive wage to those who are put into a position of trust is succinctly described already in Smith (1776, Book I/8).

[10] An interesting early case of corruption in auctions in Goethe's dealing with his publisher Vieweg concerning one of his publications. Eager to know the true value of his manuscript, Goethe designed a clever scheme. He handled over a sealed note containing his reservation price to his legal Counsel Böttiger. At the same time he asked Vieweg to make a bid and send it to Böttiger, promising publication rights if and only if the bid is at or above Goethe's reserve price, in which case Vieweg would have to pay Goethe's reserve price (Moldovanu and Tietzel 1998). However, Böttiger was not reliable. He opened Goethe's envelope, and maliciously informed Vieweg, about its content, before he made his bid. Not surprisingly, Vieweg's bid was exactly equal to Goethe's reserve price, and thus Goethe failed to find out how much his writings were valued by his publisher.

[11] The Economist, Just how rotten? October 21, 2004.

Apparently, the accused insurance brokers collected compensation for steering business to their insurance company partners, and some even solicited fake bids, which deceived their customers into thinking that true competition had taken place.

Major insurance companies in the United States were named in the complaint as participants in steering and bid rigging. The immediate victims of the illegal practices were the brokers' customers.

16.3 Distortion of quality ranking

In many procurements of goods and services a bid has many dimensions. Apart from price different quality characteristics matter and require judgment. In these cases the typical procedure is the "Quality-and-Cost-Based Selection" (QCBS). There, bidders are asked to submit two bids in two separate sealed envelopes: one specifying the price ("financial proposal") and the other specifying the product or service to be delivered ("technical proposal"). The technical proposal is then reviewed by an evaluation committee that assigns quality scores without knowing the financial proposal. The financial proposals remain sealed and deposited with a public auditor or independent authority until they are opened publicly after all technical proposals have been evaluated, and then price and quality scores are aggregated using a pre-specified scoring rule. Finally, the bid with the highest aggregate score is selected.[12]

A typical scoring rule as it is used in practice is the following: Each member of the evaluation committee rates the technical proposals on a score between 0 and 100; the *quality score* of the bid is then computed as the arithmetic mean of the individual evaluators' scores; in a second step, the financial proposals are opened and the quoted prices are transformed into relative *price scores*, according to the following formula,

$$\text{price score} = 100 \times \frac{\text{smallest submitted price}}{\text{submitted price}}.$$

---

[12] The terms employed here are used in the World Bank Guidelines which offer a good example for a set of well thought out procurement rules for goods and services. See The World Bank (2004a,b), and for similar rules The Asian Development Bank (2002).

Thus, the cheapest proposal gets a price score of 100; all other bids get a smaller price score. Finally, quality and price scores are combined into a total score using a convex linear combination of the two, for example by giving 80 percent weight to quality and 20 percent to price, as in the following formula:

$$\text{total score} = 80\% \times \text{quality score} + 20\% \times \text{price score}.$$

Finally, the proposal with the highest total score is selected.[13] The winner is typically paid the price he requested in his financial proposal. Alternatively, and in analogy to the Vickrey rule mentioned before, the winner may be paid the price that makes his total score equal to the score of the highest losing bidder.[14]

In dealing with the corruption problem, first we need to take care of the bid rigging, as discussed in the previous sections. This is relevant here both with respect to the financial and the technical proposal. Note that the use of an open auction (Practical conclusion 2) is generally not applicable to the technical proposal because that bid is typically a complex document rather than a single number. Therefore, the technical proposal has to be an electronically secured sealed-bid auction (Practical conclusion 3), as explained above.

For the financial proposal there are more options. One can either also use the same electronic bid submission system with a secured logbook or use an open auction format. An open, decreasing-price auction should take place after the technical proposals are evaluated and the quality scores are published. The best way to run it is a clock action in which, however, the usual price clock is replaced by a score clock. Given his quality score, each bidder can then compute the price that corresponds to a given score.

---

[13] This rule differs considerably from the standard model of scoring actions in the economics literature (Che 1993, Asker and Cantillon 2004). That literature assumes that the procurer computes the total score of a proposal by estimating the value of the technical proposal and deducting the price quoted in the financial proposal. In practical applications it is, however, often impossible to compute the economic value of the technical proposal. This has lead to the adoption of problematic scoring rules like the one described in the text (see Wolfstetter 2006).

[14] As an example, suppose the smallest submitted price is 28, and the financial proposals of the two bidders with the highest total score are 40 and 35, respectively. Thus, their price scores are 70 and 80, respectively. Suppose the quality scores are 80 and 76, respectively. Then, the winners' total score is 78 and the highest losing score is 76.8. The price that makes the winners proposal reach the same score as the highest losing score is 43.75. This is the price that would be payed to the winning bidder if this version of the Vickrey rule is used.

Practical conclusion 4

Make the technical proposals tamper-proof by using an electronic bid submission system with a secure logbook. Make the financial proposals either in the same form or use an open score-clock format, where price bidding takes place after all technical proposals have been evaluated.[15]

Even after bids have been made tamper-proof, corruption may still be an issue in the evaluation of technical proposals. Bidders may attempt to bribe members of the evaluation committee in exchange for biased quality scores. Having brided one or more evaluators allows the bidder to ask for a higher price.

We believe that there is no perfect remedy for this problem. Yet, there are ways to make this type of corruption more difficult, more costly, and more risky for the involved parties.

One way is to reduce the weight of quality to account for the fact that the quality signal is less reliable due to the possibility of manipulation.[16] Another way is to draw evaluators at random form a large pool after bids have been submitted. This decreases the influence of a single member of the pool of evaluators and thus makes it more costly for bidders to "buy" a good quality assessment.

Practical conclusion 5

If possible, draw evaluators at random from a large pool of potential evaluators *after* bids have been submitted. Of course, one should always make sure that evaluators are not in conflict with past or present obligations with any bidder.

One should also analyze the distribution of quality scores in order to detect bias in the assessment of individual evaluators. If evaluators agree on a quality ranking, it will be unlikely that an evaluator has been bribed.[17] If an evaluator has been bribed, he will submit an assessment that is biased in favor of his client. In principle, such a bias could be detected with a

---

[15] For example, the World Bank permits electronic bid submission but insists that "the system is secure, maintains the confidentiality and authenticity or proposals submitted, uses an electronic signature system ... and only allows proposals to be opened with due simultaneous electronic authorization of the consultant and the Borrower" (The World Bank 2004b, 21).

[16] This has been suggested by Burguet and Che (2004).

[17] It could of course mean that all evaluators have been bribed by the same bidder, but this would be hard to detect unless one can observe the transfer of bribes.

statistical test. However, in practice, the power of such a test will be weak because the number of evaluators is typically small.

There is a simple way to reduce the effect of such outliers. It is usual to compute the quality score as the simple average of the assessments of the individual evaluators. Simple means that each evaluator's score is given the same weight. Yet, we would like to give less or even no weight to outliers.

One can do this by using a *trimmed* mean instead. The x percent-trimmed mean is the mean calculated after removing the extreme x percent of the observations from the top and bottom of data sets.[18] For instance, a simple implementation of this idea would be to remove for each proposal, the highest and the lowest quality score of all evaluators, and then compute the mean of the remaining evaluators.

Going one step further, one can compute the *median* of the quality score of all evaluators. The median is the quality score of the evaluator who is "in the middle": one half of the evaluators rate the proposal higher, the other half rate it lower than the median evaluator. Unlike the mean, the median is not affected by outliers. An extreme evaluation by a single, biased evaluator (possibly because he has been bribed) has no effect on the median score.

Table 16.1 illustrates the effect of this alternative aggregation method. There are three proposals and seven evaluators. The evaluators cannot measure the objective quality of the proposals precisely, so their quality scores are not perfectly precise. We simulate this by adding some noise when simulating the evaluators' quality scores.[19] As we can see from the true quality scores, proposal A has the highest quality. It is also the most expensive, but according to the scoring rule, it is this proposal that should be chosen. Proposal B is of somewhat lower quality but is also cheaper. According to the scoring rule, it comes in second. In the example, evaluator 1 has been bribed by the suppliers of proposal B: he inflates his quality score for proposal B and biases his quality score against the strongest competitor, proposal A, in an attempt to turn the decision in favor of B.

The average quality scores of the three proposals, using simple averages over all seven evaluators, are 56.1 for A, 58.1 for B, and 48.4 for C, respectively. The total scores are 56.9, 60.0, and 58.7, respectively, so that proposal B is chosen. Evaluator 1's bias has tipped the balance away from the better choice A. If, however, the aggregate quality score would have been

---

[18] Bryan and Cecchetti (1994) have used this idea to compute inflation rates that are less affected by extreme price fluctuations of single commodities.

[19] Specifically, we add normally distributed noise to the evaluators' quality scores, plus some bias in evaluators' scoring while truncating scores to [0, 100].

Table 16.1 Mean vs. median aggregation in scoring auctions

Proposal	A	B	C
Price	45	40	27
Price score	60.0	67.5	100
True quality score	60	55	45
True total score	**60.0**	57.5	56
Quality score evaluator			
1	46	75	44
2	53	53	45
3	65	48	58
4	59	64	63
5	58	49	50
6	60	67	42
7	52	51	37
Result using mean aggregation			
Quality score	56.1	58.1	48.4
Total score	56.9	**60.0**	58.7
Result using median aggregation			
Quality score	58.0	53.0	45.0
Total score	**58.4**	55.9	56.0

evaluated using the median instead of the mean, evaluator 1 would not have been able to make a difference, as can be seen from the table. In this case, the aggregate quality scores are 58.0, 53.0, and 45.0, respectively, and proposal A wins with a total score of 58.4 against 55.9 for proposal B.

We have estimated the robustness of this finding with a Monte-Carlo simulation.[20] We find that, with the particular parameters we have chosen, the aggregation of the quality scores using simple means correctly selects proposal A with 23 percent probability only. This probability will increase to 47 percent if the median is used instead.[21] However, the flip side is that

---

[20] We ran 10,000 draws using R. B. Myerson's Sim Tools utility, see http://home.uchicago.edu/~rmyerson/addins.htm. The worksheet that contains the specifications of evaluators' bias and the assumed random errors is available for download from our websites.

[21] One caveat is in order here: we do not model the strategic aspects of the evaluators' assessments. A corrupt evaluator may behave differently depending on whether the mean or the median is used for computing the quality score. What remains true, nonetheless, is that the median is much less affected by extreme points of view. Because corrupt evaluators are more likely to make extreme (i.e., biased) assessments, using the median reduces the power of corrupt evaluators, and thus decreases the bidders' willingness to pay for corruption.

median aggregation also chooses the least attractive proposal C with higher probability, which is of course undesirable.[22]

> **Practical conclusion 6**
> In scoring auctions, consider using the median of the evaluators' quality scores instead of the usual mean.

Even if a statistical test is not available, inspection of the scores in Table 16.1 makes evaluator 1 appear suspicious. In such circumstances, one obvious course of action is to start an investigation. Independently, one should ask for a second opinion from a separate team of evaluators. An investigation could involve questioning the evaluators and possibly checking their recent bank transactions. Once an evaluator has aroused suspicion he should be blacklisted. Moreover, second opinions should be routinely solicited at random even if there is no indication of a bias. Of course, this policy should be advertised to all involved parties as a deterrent.

> **Practical conclusion 7**
> Inspect the individual quality scores and check for indications of an outlier. If manipulation is suspected, consider soliciting a second opinion or initiating a criminal investigation. It is also advisable to make this policy known to all involved parties before the auction takes place, as a deterring device.

Apparently some agencies do not record the scores of individual evaluators and their evaluation committees report only their average score. Evidently, this hides important information, which is not advisable.

16.4 The special case of objective quality measures

In some rare cases, the relevant quality is readily measurable without complex evaluation. In these cases one can execute a scoring auction essentially in the same manner as a standard one-dimensional auction, where bidding in scores takes place of price, and all the issues and advice we gave in section 16.2 apply with some slight reinterpretation.

---

[22] Mean aggregation selects project C with 4 percent and median aggregation with 10 percent probability.

A case in point is the so-called "A+B Bidding" procedure employed by Federal and State Highway Administrations in the United States in their selection of contractors for highway repair work.[23] There, a major quality concern is the duration of construction work, which causes costly traffic delays.

"A+B Bidding" requires bidders to submit a financial proposal (estimated cost) and a time completion estimate. It uses the following linear scoring rule

$$\text{total cost score} = \text{estimated cost}$$
$$+ \text{ time completion estimate} \times \text{time unit cost},$$

based on a stipulated completion time unit, and then awards the contract to the proposal with the lowest total cost score.[24]

In such an auction bidding can be viewed (and could actually be implemented) as a one-dimensional auction, where each bidder submits a score, the lowest score bid wins, with the understanding that the winner is free to select his preferred combination of cost and time for completion as long as it delivers the promised total score. Of course, the bidding of scores can be either in a sealed-bid or an open-bid format. And the pricing rule can be either first- or second-"score", where second-score means that the winner must match the lowest of all losing total cost scores (generalized Vickrey pricing rule). Manipulation of the quality assessment is not an issue, and therefore corruption can only take the form of bid rigging which we have discussed in section 16.2.

16.5. Further issues

In QCBS based procurement one usually requires a short list of a given size, typically six bidders, regardless of how many bidders have submitted their Expression of Interest.[25] This rigid requirement is made with the intention

---

[23] The US Federal Highway Administration (FHWA) initiated this format already in 1990, and it is now widely and successfully used (see for example the performance evaluation by the State of Arizona 1999).

[24] Of course, the rules also stipulate an incentive/disincentive for early/late completion of the construction job.

[25] See for example the shortlisting requirements of the European Community, the World Bank, and the Asian Development Bank.

to assure transparency, fairness, and competition. However, it is often counterproductive because it brings low-quality bidders into the bidding.

A low-quality bidder is a bidder who has a low level of technical expertise and is unable to deliver a high-quality product or service. If high-quality bidders participate in the bidding, a low-quality bidder has little or no chance of winning without corruption. Therefore, he is particularly inclined to bribe evaluators in exchange for a favorable quality assessment or for insider information concerning unspecified yet desired product characteristics. This is how low-quality bidders may turn into "rotten apples", and thus rigid shortlisting requirements may contribute to corrupt the procurement process.

A potential remedy for this problem is to keep the size of the short list somewhat flexible, and allow a shorter list when not enough high-quality bidders have submitted their Expression of Interest.

Practical conclusion 8

In QCBS procurement keep the size of the required short list of bidders who are invited to submit their technical and financial proposals flexible. In that short list you should not include bidders who are known or suspected of low quality, because they are most likely to corrupt the procurement process.

Permitting some flexibility in choosing the size of the short list runs counter to the philosophy that is currently prevalent at the EC and various international agencies. They firmly believe in rigid prescriptions of competitions as the best safeguard against corruption. However, practical experience suggests that these very rules often open the door to bidders who are particularly prone to corruption.

Of course, the following precaution should be taken.

Practical conclusion 9

The short list should not be prepared by those who serve later as evaluators of technical proposals. Otherwise, evaluators may be tempted to include "rotten apples" with the expectation that these will most likely offer bribes to them.

Efforts to curb corruption have been increased in recent years, due to new legislation that makes companies liable for bribes paid by their branches and affiliates and also for bribes paid to third parties. Another important milestone is the US Foreign Corrupt Practices Act (FCPA) passed by the Congress in 1977 and later ratified by several other countries. That act prescribes the prosecution of companies involved in corrupt practices in and outside their home country.[26] In the past many countries permitted their national firms to tax deduct bribes paid abroad as business expenses. In view of this practice the proliferation of legislation like the FCPA is an important change of direction.

Finally, we mention that corruption often extends to the time after the contract has been awarded, during the execution of the job. There, corruption takes the form of granting the contractor generous change orders that inflate the price above the level stated in the original financial proposal. The door for this kind of corruption is generally wide open if the Terms of Reference (TOR) that state the technical specifications and cost estimate are imprecise. Therefore, one should always insist on a carefully worked out and detailed Terms of Reference.

> **Practical conclusion 10**
>
> Make sure that the Terms of Reference for the technical proposal are well researched and worked out in detail. Consider setting up a review process for all change orders that may be requested by the contractor during the contract execution. Without these precautions the door is open for excessive change orders and subsequent cost overruns.

Of course, the need for change orders can never be ruled out altogether. Depending upon the nature of the procured good or service, it is more or less common that the contractor's tasks must be adjusted to unforeseen events.[27] Therefore, the relationship between contractor and procurer needs constant governance.

Bibliographical notes

The theoretical literature views corruption in auctions as a manipulation of the quality assessment in complex bids or as bid rigging, and it distinguishes

---

[26] See http://www.state.gov/p/inl/rls/rpt/c6698.htm

[27] Change orders are particularly frequent in construction, engineering, and architectural services. For an interesting case study of private sector building contracts in Northern California see Bajari McMillan, and Tadelis (2002).

between corruption based on a predetermined relationship between the procurer and a favored bidder and an endogenous selection of the favored bidder.

The first theoretical contribution is probably by Laffont and Tirole (1991). They assume that the auctioneer has some leeway in assessing complex multidimensional bids, and is predisposed to favor a given bidder. That framework was later adopted and extended by several authors (e.g., Celantani and Ganuza 2002, Burguet and Che 2004).

A second branch of the literature considers a particular form of bid rigging, in which the auctioneer grants the Right of First Refusal to a favored bidder. This right gives the favored bidder the option to match the highest bid and win the auction (see, for example, Burguet and Perry 2003, Arozamena and Weinschelbaum 2004, Koc and Neilson 2005). This scheme implies that *all* bidders know about the corruption, and thus entails a large risk of detection. An auctioneer who cares about the risk of detection should consider proposing corruption only to a small set of bidders.

This takes us to the third branch of the literature which assumes that bid rigging is arranged by the auctioneer after he has observed all the bids. This allows him to approach only a minimum number of bidders, and select the bidder(s) whose collaboration delivers the highest profit (see Lengwiler and Wolfstetter 2005, Menezes and Monteiro 2003). Another paper on bid rigging by Compte, Lambert-Mogiliansky, and Verdier (2005) assumes that bribes cannot exceed a small upper bound. This is meaningful in some contexts; however, bribes are often accepted only if they are sufficiently high to compensate for the risk of detection and punishment.

The practical problems of fighting corruption in procurement are documented in many publications by international agencies such as the World Bank, the Asian Development Bank, the WTO, and the European Community (see, for example, Aguilar, Gill, and Pino 2000, Trepte 2004). Awareness of corruption and efforts to curb it – ranging from hot lines and rewards for "whistleblowing," to blacklisting of contractors who were caught in corruption, and staff rotation – have increased both in the private and in the public sector. An interesting collection of case studies drawn from private and public sector experience, including an account of the remarkable case of the reform of the public sector in Singapore by Lee (1999), is in Stapenhurst and Kpundeh (1999) and Arvis and Berenbeim (2003).

References

Aguilar, M., J. Gill, and L. Pino (2000). *Preventing Fraud and Corruption in World Bank Projects. A Guide for Staff.* Washington, DC: The World Bank.

Arozamena, L. and F. Weinschelbaum (2004). The Effect of Corruption on Bidding Behavior in First-Price Auctions, Discussion paper, Universidad de San Andrés.

Arvis, J.-F. and R. Berenbeim (2003). *Fighting Corruption in East Asia: Solutions from the Private Sector.* Washington, DC: The World Bank.

Asker, J. and E. Cantillon (2004). Properties of Scoring Auctions, Working paper, Harvard Business School.

Bajari, P., R. McMillan, and S. Tadelis (2002). Auctions vs. Negotiations in Procurement: An Empirical Analysis, Working paper, Department of Economics, Stanford University.

Bikhchandani, S., S.A. Lippman, and R. Ryan (2005). On the Right-of-First-Refusal, *Advances in Theoretical Economics*, 5, 1–42.

Bryan, M.F. and S.G. Cecchetti (1994). Measuring Core Inflation, in N.G. Mankiw, Ed., *Monetary Policy*, 195–215. Chicago: University of Chicago Press.

Burguet, R. and Y.-K. Che (2004). Competitive Procurement with Corruption, *Rand Journal of Economics*, 35, 50–68.

Burguet, R. and M. Perry (2003). Bribery and Favoritism by Auctioneers in Sealed-Bid Auctions, Discussion paper, Institute of Economic Analysis, UAB, Barcelona.

Celantani, M. and J.-J. Ganuza (2002). Corruption and Competition in Procurement, *European Economic Review*, 46, 1273–1303.

Che, Y.-K. (1993). Design Competition through Multidimensional Auctions, *Rand Journal of Economics*, 4, 669–680.

Compte, O., A. Lambert-Mogiliansky, and T. Verdier (2005). Corruption and Competition in Public Market Auctions, *Rand Journal of Economics*, 36, 1–15.

Kaufmann, D. (2005). Six Questions on the Cost of Corruption with World Bank Institute Global Governance Director Daniel Kaufmann, in *News*. Washington, DC: The World Bank.

Koc, S. and W. Neilson (2005). Bribing the Auctioneer in First-Price Sealed-Bid Auctions, Discussion paper, Texas A&M University.

Laffont, J.-J. and J. Tirole (1991). Auction Design and Favoritism, *International Journal of Industrial Organization*, 9, 9–42.

Lee, T.A. (1999). The Experience of Singapore in Combating Corruption, in R. Stapenhurst and S. Kpundeh (Eds.), *Curbing Corruption. Toward a Model for Building National Integrity*, pp. 59–66. Economic Development Institute of Washington, DC: The World Bank.

Lengwiler, Y. and E. Wolfstetter (2005). Bid Rigging. An Analysis of Corruption in Auctions, Discussion paper, Humboldt University at Berlin.

Menezes, F. and P. Monteiro (2003). Corruption and Auctions, Discussion paper, Australian National University.

Moldovanu, B. and M. Tietzel (1998). Goethe's Second-Price Auction, *Journal of Political Economy*, 106, 854–859.

Smith, A. (1776/1937). *The Wealth of Nations*, Cannan Edition, Modern library, New York.

Stapenhurst, R. and S. J. Kpundeh (Eds.) (1999) *Curbing Corruption. Toward a Model for Building National Integrity*. EDI Development Studies, Washington, DC: The World Bank.

State of Arizona (1999). Arizona Department of Transportation A+B Bidding, Performance Audit, Discussion paper report No. 99–22, Office of the Auditor General.

The Asian Development Bank (2002). *Handbook for Users of Consulting Services: Procedures and Practices*. Manila: The Asian Development Bank.

The World Bank (2004a). *Guidelines: Procurement of Goods and Services by World Bank Borrowers*. The International Bank for Reconstruction and Development. Washington, DC: The World Bank.

The World Bank (2004b). *Guidelines: Selection and Employment of Consultants by World Bank Borrowers*. The International Bank for Reconstruction and Development. Washington, DC: The World Bank.

Trepte, P. (2004). *Regulating Procurement*. Oxford: Oxford University Press.

Wolfstetter, E. (2006). Procurement of Goods and Services. Scope and Government, in S. Qi and X. Li (Eds.), *Corporate Governance, Firm Performance, and Economic Growth*, Beijing: Economic Science Press.

PART VI

Dynamic forces and innovation

17 Managing dynamic procurements

Tracy R. Lewis and Huseyin Yildirim

17.1. Introduction

Recently we considered which laptop computer to purchase for the new and returning faculty at our business school. The choice was between an old proven brand that we had been using and a new brand that was attractively priced but unfamiliar to our people. The old brand was reliable but it had not been updated much recently, whereas the new brand incorporated some advanced technology and attractive design features. Overall the new brand seemed like a better buy than the old one. But, there was a cost to switching from the old to the new brand. We would have to learn new skills to operate the new brand and our technicians would need additional training to repair and service the new machines.

We decided after much deliberation to remain with the old brand. The cost of switching computers was too high. We realized the school had become so dependent on the old technology that we were locked in. Switching to a new one was not feasible, at least not in short run. But, this was just the tip of the iceberg. We discovered there were many more products and services that we were locked into buying, including computer software, reproduction equipment, communication services, and information technology. In each case, we would need to retrain our employees and adjust our operating procedures to switch products. We were unwilling to bear these costs and so we continued to use the old products.

From this experience we learned the importance of formulating a dynamic procurement strategy for buying products that entail switching costs. Switching costs occur with many of the high technology products including computer software and hardware, communications services, and information technology we have come to rely on. One can reduce the life

We thank Gian Luigi Albano, Giancarlo Spagnolo and Matteo Zanza for helpful comments.

cycle costs of procurement by understanding how suppliers of high technology goods compete to attract and maintain their customer base and how the switching costs that result can be minimized.

We lay out some best practice rules of procurement for goods with switching costs in this chapter. These recommendations are based on research on managing dynamic competition we have conducted for the last five years that is summarized in Lewis and Yildirim (2002, 2005). In the analysis to follow we first describe the factors to consider when purchasing services with switching costs. We indicate how optimal procurement tendering procedures are designed to manage dynamic competition in section 17.2. In section 17.3 we identify the essential tradeoffs between *conservation* of switching costs and *diversification* of supply. Conservation leads one to renew service from an incumbent supplier to avoid switching costs. Purchasing from a new supplier maintains future options for diversification of services from independent providers. In section 17.4 we discuss long-term strategies for training employees and organizing production to manage long-term procurements of goods with switching costs. We identify instances when the creation of switching costs within an organization may actually reduce the life cycle costs of procurement by forcing suppliers to price more competitively to maintain their incumbency advantage. section 17.5 concludes with some summary observations.

17.2. The procurement setting

To fix ideas, suppose a government or private procurement agency needs to purchase computer equipment or software on a regular basis. There are several qualified suppliers for the agency to select from but their products are not necessarily compatible with each other. To effectively employ a product may require employees to develop a new set of skills, to reconfigure hardware and software to be compatible, and to acquire other complementary services. All of these are time consuming and costly activities. These skills employees acquire to operate new equipment are likely to be retained if the organization continues with the same product. However, these skills may deteriorate if the product is not used for some time or is replaced with an alternative.[1] As a result, when an incumbent supplier is

---

[1] There is a vast empirical literature that document the presence of learning-by-doing in various industries. See, for instance, Alchian (1963) and Asher (1956) on aircraft production; Hirsch (1952) in

replaced, employees may incur short-term and long-run switching cost. In the short term employees need to invest in learning new skills to operate the new equipment. In the long run the employees' skill at operating the old equipment must be reacquired as operating skill deteriorates with non-use. The task for the procurer then is to optimally manage these short-and long-term switching cost while minimizing the price of acquisition over time.

The procurer may acquire equipment like computer hardware or software by various means. One way, perhaps the ideal one, is to integrate with the suppliers and make the products in house. Here the 'integrated buyer' would minimize the switching cost and choose the efficient product in each period since the purchase price would not be marked up above production cost. The only reason the procurer would switch products is if it were warranted by changing production costs or by varying effectiveness of different products. Despite its apparent efficiency, supplying itself with goods and services is typically not feasible for a government agency due to the costs of establishing supply sources.[2] Nonetheless, we will retain the integrated buyer case as a benchmark for comparison with other procurement strategies.

When self-supply is not feasible, the procurer must outsource the product. An outsourcer is unlikely to know the exact cost of production for outside suppliers because monitoring costs is difficult. This gives outside suppliers an incentive to exaggerate their costs of production to increase profits. To reduce acquisition costs, the outsourcer needs to carefully negotiate the terms of purchase prices that also reflects the costs of switching suppliers. One plausible strategy is to negotiate a long-term sole source contract with one supplier to govern the terms of exchange for an extended period of time. Sole sourcing minimizes switching cost, but restricts the procurer's flexibility to adopt new products when appropriate. Besides this, it is notoriously difficult for a government agency to write long-term procurement contracts. Administrative and legal rules typically constrain public officials from making commitments for purchase of goods and services beyond their term in office. Similar concerns are also present for private procurements. Incompleteness of contracts and enforcement problems render long-term contracts difficult to write for a buyer and seller.

machine tools; Gruber (1998) and Nye (1996) in semi conductors; Thompson (2001) on shipbuilding. There is also an emerging literature that report the importance of forgetting or depreciation of knowledge in manufacturing, industrial and service sectors. See, for instance, Argote et al. (1990), Benkard (2000), and Darr et al. (1995).

[2] Imagine the setup cost of making laptop computers in house.

When long-term agreements are not available sole sourcing works less well because the supplier is unwilling to discount price without the guarantee of future purchases.

Absent the ability to make long-term commitments, the procurer must resort to short-term competitive bidding mechanisms to manage his supply This is the topic we now turn to.

17.2.1. Procurement tendering procedures

Imagine a setting where the procurer designs a sequence of tendering procedures to purchase goods and services. Here our goal is to describe the optimal feasible tendering format, so we will not restrict attention to a particular tendering form such as a dynamic ascending (in discounts) auction. At the beginning of each tendering procedure suppliers are privately informed of their cost of production. The procurer wishes to purchase the product at lowest cost, but he must also account for the costs of switching he will incur if he adopts a new supplier. The procurer requests the competing producers to simultaneously submit a supply price. The sellers independently and without consultation select a supply price based on their knowledge of the buyer's skill in employing their product and any switching costs that might occur.[3] The buyer selects one supplier to produce the desired good based on the submitted prices and the subsequent switching costs involved. After the winning supplier is determined the product is provided at the price bid, whereupon the process moves on to the next tendering procedure which is held during the next procurement cycle.

17.3. Factors in choosing suppliers

The procurer's objective is to minimize the discounted sum of switching costs and purchase prices. There are two conflicting factors that govern the procurer's optimal choice of supplier in each tendering procedure that we refer to as *conservation* and *diversification*. The conservation factor argues for the procurer to continue purchasing from the incumbent supplier to

---

[3] In many settings, suppliers will be able to observe directly or to infer the buyer's current skill with their product. The buyer will often reveal his skill state and knowledge in operating products during material specifications for procurement. Moreover, Appleyard (2002) indicates that suppliers often work with buyers to help them use their product. Given that we have in mind large power buyers, such a close relationship seems reasonable.

conserve employees' skill in using this product. This is important when expertise in operating sophisticated equipment is easy to lose during periods of non-use. The diversification factor argues for procuring from alternative suppliers to enable employees to acquire skill with other products. Diversifying enables employees to switch more readily between suppliers to take advantage of lower cost products in future periods. The procurer also increases future competition among suppliers when he diversifies his purchases.

The procurer's optimal purchasing policy is shaped by these two factors: conservation and diversification. The procurer's concern for diversification is generally outweighed by his concern for conservation.[4] This implies the procurer must contend with positive switching costs in each tendering procedure that he conducts. This brings us to our first Practical conclusion.

Practical conclusion   1

Favor the incumbent supplier in any given tendering procedure. That is, the procurer should generally purchase from the incumbent unless one of the other suppliers offers a significantly lower price than the incumbent's price to compensate for the costs of switching suppliers.

Practical Conclusion 1 indicates that all else equal, the procurer is more likely to purchase from the incumbent.[5] To appreciate the extent of the incumbency advantage, next we compare this with integrated buyer's procurement strategy. Recall the integrated buyer who self-supplies is not concerned about the purchase price since he knows the cost of production. Like the procurer the integrated buyer is also concerned with conservation and diversification. Unlike the integrated buyer though, the procurer wishes to promote price competition. This means the procurer has a stronger diversification motive than the integrated buyer and will therefore discount some of her switching cost to foster greater price competition among rival suppliers. This leads to our second Practical conclusion:

Practical conclusion   2

When outsourcing, ignore part of the switching cost to increase price competition.

---

[4] Lewis and Yildirim (2002, 2005) show this point in a formal model.

[5] In his study of U.S. Government procurement of mainframe computers, Greenstein (1995) finds that 73% of procurements were awarded to incumbent suppliers.

To rationalize practical conclusion 2, recall the outsourcer is concerned with limiting price markups of suppliers. These markups are especially high for the incumbent, who knows the buyer is partially locked into his product (practical conclusion 1). The buyer is willing to ignore part of his switching cost to signal that the incumbent's lead is not insurmountable. This allows the outsourcer to counter the incumbent's (partial) monopoly power. practical conclusion 2 implies the outsourcer switches suppliers too frequently compared to the integrated buyer who takes full account of switching cost.[6]

17.4. Organizing production to reduce switching costs

The procurer can adopt various ex ante measures to reduce switching costs. First, he can adopt a flexible production technology to adapt to different inputs at a small cost, or require suppliers provide compatible products. Second, he can train his employees to learn new technologies and to invest in organizational memory by documenting best practice procedures to reduce the loss of skill during periods of non-use.

Before we discuss the procurer's incentives to invest in these measures, let us clarify how switching costs affect multiperiod procurements. The procurer becomes biased toward the incumbent's products when there are costs to switching (Practical conclusion 1). This creates an asymmetry between the incumbent and other suppliers, which benefits the procurer in two ways. On the one hand, non-incumbent suppliers discount their price to take over production, while the incumbent supplier reduces price to maintain its place as the primary supplier. Both incentives for discounting price increase with switching cost and the incumbency bias that results. Thus while an increase in switching cost has an adverse direct effect on the overall cost of procurement, this is offset to a degree by its beneficial strategic impact on competition that arises. To determine how these countervailing effects of switching costs impact on procurement costs, note that the strategic effect is absent for an integrated buyer and a sole-sourcing procurer and likely to be

---

[6] This excessive switching contrasts with other motives for switching. For instance, Taylor (2002) indicates that consumers with private costs of switching may engage in excessive switching to signal they have low switching costs. This enables them to gain a favorable bargaining position in future exchanges. Cabral and Greenstein (1990) find a buyer may commit to switching often by ignoring switching costs altogether.

small for an outsourcing procurer with many suppliers.[7] This leads us to

Practical conclusion   3

Try to avoid switching costs whenever (i) products are made in-house, (ii) sole-sourcing is feasible, or (iii) there is strong competition among numerous suppliers.

According to practical conclusion 3 the procurer will want to reduce switching costs whenever there is effective competition among suppliers. For instance, the procurer may install a flexible production technology that adapts readily to the inputs from different suppliers. He may procure from suppliers with substitute products or require suppliers to produce compatible products.

When the buyer is unable to procure from a competitive group of suppliers the strategic benefits from switching cost may outweigh their direct costs. The procurer will want to facilitate the creation of the switching cost in such cases. For instance, the procurer may use a dedicated production technology that is costly to adapt to different inputs. He may purchase from suppliers whose products are not compatible with each other. With regards to organizing production, the procurer may not document best operation practices for different types of equipment or retain skilled employees able to switch between different production processes. We summarize this observation in

Practical conclusion   4

If an outsourcing procurer faces a small number of non competitive suppliers, investing to reduce switching cost may not be profitable.

Practical conclusion 4 may appear counterintuitive. After all, the extant literature on switching cost economics[8] concludes that switching costs are generally harmful to consumers, who should avoid them if possible. An important assumption driving this conclusion is that consumers are small and passive price-takers. Our analysis reveals that this prescription may be reversed when buyers are large and powerful with the ability to affect prices as in the case of a government procurement agency, the department of defense, a university or a large corporation. Indeed, switching cost can be a

---

[7] Recall that the integrated and sole-sourcing buyers are not concerned with competition. In addition, the outsourcer with many alternative suppliers should already be able to obtain a reasonably low price due to competition.

[8] See, e.g., Klemperer (1995), and Farrell and Klemperer (2004) for excellent surveys.

useful strategic tool for a power buyer in negotiating price when there are few suppliers who don't compete directly with each other. A buyer who can, for instance, regulate the degree of compatibility between competing products will wish to retain some incompatibility to insure there are costs to switching from the incumbent supplier. This establishes an advantage for the incumbent that other suppliers will compete to attain and the incumbent will attempt to defend by reducing price.[9]

Another implication of practical conclusion 4 is that the outsourcer will be less concerned about turnover in skilled labor as compared to an integrated buyer. Letting go of skilled employees signals to the incumbent supplier that he will lose his stature as the favored producer unless he discounts his price to maintain the buyer's interest. Although there is a direct cost to losing skilled workers, the signal value of this strategy is very valuable to the outsourcer. We further illustrate this point with a numerical example.

Example 17.1.[10]

Consider the procurement decision our business school faces as to which brand of laptop computers to buy for the new and returning faculty. This is a decision the business school (buyer) needs to make almost annually. Suppose there are two suppliers. Although each supplier produces a different brand, both serve the buyer's purpose. We assume the unit production cost for each supplier changes from year to year and it is an independent draw from two values, $800 and $1200, with equal probability. Each supplier privately knows its current cost draw but it is uninformed of the rival's or its own future costs. Finally, all parties discount future costs and profits with a common discount factor $\delta \in [0,1]$. To highlight the strategic role of switching costs, we start with a benchmark case where there are no switching costs from changing suppliers. In this case, without the benefit of long-term contracts, the best the buyer can do is to hold a tendering procedure each year, and a simple second price tendering format will achieve this objective. The buyer's expected cost will be $[800 + 3(1200)]/4 = 1100$. This means the buyer's expected discounted cost for the lifetime product purchases is $1100/(1-\delta)$.

---

[9] Standard theory of oligopoly with passive price-taking consumers suggest that consumers might benefit from compatibility and standardization of products to avoid switching costs. However, the theory also suggests that suppliers are better off differentiating their products to prevent head-to-head competition, unless standardization and compatibility improve market demand.

[10] A more general version of this example can be found in Lewis and Yildirim (2005).

Now, consider the case with switching costs. In particular, suppose the buyer incurs a one period switching cost of $200 every time he switches products. At any point in time, the buyer is skilled at using the incumbent supplier's product, while he is unskilled at using the product of the other supplier, who we will call the potential entrant. Note that it is optimal for the buyer to switch brands only when the entrant actually has a lower supply cost than the incumbent, which occurs with probability 1/4. This is the only case where the switching cost is justified. In the remaining three cases of cost draws, the buyer purchases from the incumbent. From here it is immediate that the buyer will pay an expected discounted switching cost of $(1/4)[200/(1-\delta)] = 50/(1-\delta)$ and production cost of $(3/4)[800/(1-\delta)] + (1/4)[1200/(1-\delta)] = 900/(1-\delta)$ for the lifetime of purchases. These are however not the only payments the buyer has to make. Since suppliers' actual costs are unobservable, these costs can be exaggerated. This is however possible only for the incumbent with an actual cost $800. Such an incumbent will be tempted to ask for a price $1200 and win the tendering procedure with probability 1/2.[11] Hence, the incumbent earns an expected profit of 1/2 $(1200-800) = 200$, whereas the entrant earns 0. As a result, the buyer pays a total discounted cost of $50/(1-\delta) + 900/(1-\delta) + 200 = 950/(1-\delta) + 200$. Comparing total procurement costs in the two cases, we see that the buyer is better off in the presence of switching costs as long as $\delta \geq 0.25$, that is, as long as the buyer as well as suppliers sufficiently care about future costs and returns. By breaking the symmetry between suppliers, switching costs create rents to the incumbent, which induces a fierce competition early on.

17.4.1. Frequency of procurement and make-or-buy decision

The make or buy decision is an important one for all organizations. Self-provision requires costly investment in production capacity but it allows the firm to control the acquisition price of the good. Outsourcing of products is typically preferred when the procurer can effectively control the purchase price through careful design of the acquisition process. Incumbent suppliers will price more competitively when they fear being replaced by a rival producer. The likelihood of being replaced is greater the shorter the procurement cycle. If supply contracts are rebid more frequently, say annually

---

[11] The incumbent who asks for $1200 will win the tendering procedure if the entrant draws a high cost. Otherwise, the buyer will find it optimal to switch.

rather than every five years, there is greater pressure on the incumbent to discount price to retain his business. This leads us to

Practical conclusion 5
The more frequently the product is procured, the more preferable it is to outsource it.

Practical conclusion 5 highlights the importance of switching costs in determining the boundaries of the organization. The organization literature[12] argues how buyers may integrate with suppliers to overcome production inefficiencies. Our analysis suggests in contrast that switching costs lead to less integration when procurements are frequently repeated. The incentives to self-supply are smaller and the benefits to outsourcing are greater, when goods are replaced more often.

17.5. Conclusion

This chapter provides some guidelines for designing on-going procurement tendering procedures to acquire products with switching costs. Although both the outsourcer and integrated buyer occasionally will choose to switch products the outsourcer will change suppliers less frequently (Practical conclusion 1). The outsourcer buyer deliberately ignores part of the switching cost to foster greater price competition between the incumbent and rival suppliers (Practical conclusion 2). Whereas the integrated buyer tries to avoid switching costs, the outsourcer buyer may employ switching cost to facilitate greater competition with repeated acquisitions (practical conclusions 3 and 4). The incumbency advantage is fragile in this setting, requiring constant price discounts from the current producer to avoid being displaced by rivals. Unlike the integrated buyer, the outsourcer has little incentive to lower switching cost by standardizing his sources of supply, employing a flexible technology or investing institutional memory to document best practices. Finally, we find that switching costs are easier to manage, the greater is the frequency of procurement (Practical conclusion 5). The incumbent must discount price with each acquisition cycle to maintain his prominent supply position. Frequent replacement of products tilts the choice of make or buy-decision towards outsourcing as switching costs are less problematic in this setting.

---

[12] See, for instance, the seminal studies by Williamson (1975) and Klein et al. (1978).

We can extend this analysis to address other important conceptual and policy issues. The current analysis does not address the possibility that rival suppliers may collude – a major concern in repeated procurements as discussed in Chapters 14 and 15. A topic for future research is how the outsourcer optimally designs procurements when suppliers may collude in setting price. The current analysis also presumes production is awarded to a single supplier. A further extension would be to incorporate split award tendering procedures into our analysis. Dual sourcing becomes an attractive option for supply when there are small fixed costs to production with different goods and operating skills deteriorate rapidly through non-use. A third extension of our work would be to identify standard tendering formats including English and Dutch tendering procedures that one could implement to manage multiperiod acquisitions of goods with switching costs.

Bibliographical notes

The recommendations for optimal procurement tendering procedures we discuss in this chapter are based on our two papers Lewis and Yildirim (2002, 2005). These papers contain a formal model and rigorous derivation of the five practical conclusions presented here. A related analysis in which procurers are assumed to be small passive price takers is Cabral and Riordan (1994).

Our analysis is at the intersection of the two literatures on repeated procurement with a large buyer and switching cost economics with small passive buyers. A classic reference on procurement theory is the book by Laffont and Tirole (1993). Klemperer (1995) and Farrell and Klemperer (2004) provide excellent surveys of switching cost literature. Also the economics of lock-in and learning by doing and the policy questions associated with these processes are reviewed in Benkard (2000), Darr et al. (1995), Dudley (1972) and Greenstein (1995, 1997).

An analysis of split award tendering procedures and dual sourcing is in Anton and Yao (1987).

References

Alchian, A. (1963). Reliability of Progress Curve in Airframe Production, *Econometrica*, 31 (4), 679–693.

Anton J. and D. Yao (1987). Second Sourcing and Experience Curve: Price Competition in the Defense Procurement, *RAND Journal of Economics*, 18 (1), 57–76.

Appelyard, M. (2002). Cooperative Knowledge Creation: The Case of Buyer–Supplier Co-Development in the Semiconductor Industry, Working Paper, University of Virginia.

Argote, L., S. Beckman, and D. Epple (1990). The Persistence and Transfer of Learning in Industrial Settings, *Management Science*, 36, 140–154.

Asher, H. (1956). *Cost–Quantity Relationships in the Airframe Industry*, Report 291. Santa Monica, CA: RAND Corporation.

Benkard, L. (2000). Learning and Forgetting: The Dynamics of Aircraft Production, *American Economic Review*, 90 (4), 1034–1054.

Cabral, L. and S. Greenstein (1990). Switching Costs and Bidding Parity in Government Procurement of Computer Systems, *Journal of Law, Economics, and Organizations*, 6 (2), 453–469.

Cabral, L. and M. Riordan (1994). The Learning Curve, Market Dominance, and Predatory Pricing, *Econometrica*, 62 (5), 1115–1140.

Darr, E., L. Argote, and D. Epple (1995). The Acquisition, Transfer, and Depreciation of Knowledge in Service Organizations: Productivity in Franchises, *Management Science*, 41(11), 1750–1762.

Dudley, L. (1972). Learning and Productivity Changes in Metal Products, *American Economic Review*, 62, 662–669.

Farrell, J. and P. Klemperer (forthcoming). Coordination and Lock-In: Competition with Switching Costs and Network Effects, in *Handbook of Industrial Organization*, vol. 3, M. Armstrong and R. Porter (eds.), North Holland.

Greenstein, S. (1995). Sole Source Versus Competitive Bidding: US Government Agencies' Procedural Choice for Mainframe Computer Procurement, *Journal of Industrial Economics,* XLIII (2) 125–140.

Greenstein, S. (1997). Lock-in and the Costs of Switching Mainframe Computer Vendors: What Do Buyers See, *Industrial and Corporate Change*, 6 (2), 247–273.

Gruber, H. (1998). Learning by Doing and Spillovers: Further Evidence for the Semiconductor Industry, *Review of Industrial Organization*, 13 (6), 697–711.

Hirsch, W. (1952). Manufacturing Progress Functions, *Review of Economics and Statistics*, 34 (2), 143–155.

Klein, B, R. Crawford, and A. Alchian (1978). Vertical Integration, Appropriable Rents, and the Competitive Contracting Process, *Journal of Law and Economics*, 21 (2), 297–326.

Klemperer, P., 1995. Competition When Consumers Have Switching Costs: An Overview with Applications to Industrial Organization, Macro Economics, and International Trade, *Review of Economic Studies*, 62, 515–39.

Laffont, J. J. and J. Tirole (1993). *A Theory of Incentives in Procurement and Regulation*. Cambridge, MA: The MIT Press, 1993.

Lewis, T. and H. Yildirim (2002). "Managing Dynamic Competition", *American Economic Review*, 92 (4), 779–97.

Lewis, T. and H. Yildirim (2005). Managing Switching Costs in Multiperiod Procurements with Strategic Bugers, *International Economic Review*, 46 (4), 1233–69.

Nye, W. (1996). Firm-Specific Learning by Doing in Semiconductor Production: Some Evidence from the 1986 Trade Agreement, *Review of Industrial Organization*, 11 (3), 383–394.

Taylor, C. (2002). Supplier Surfing: Competition and Consumer Behavior in Subscription Markets, *RAND Journal of Economics*, 34 (2), 223–246.

Thompson, P. (2001). How Much Did the Liberty Shipbuilders Learn? New Evidence for an Old Case Study, *Journal of Political Economy*, 109 (1), 103–137.

Williamson, O. (1975). *Markets and Hierarchies: Analysis and Antitrust Implications.* New York: The Free Press.

18 Designing reputation mechanisms

Chrysanthos Dellarocas, Federico Dini
and Giancarlo Spagnolo

18.1. Introduction

A common problem in procurement is the presence of relevant aspects of
an exchange that cannot be fully specified in an explicit contract, because
for example they are not verifiable by a third party (like a court or an
arbitrator) at reasonable cost. Non-contractibility opens the door to two
well-known forms of opportunism: 'ex-ante' and 'post-contracting'
opportunism. Ex-ante opportunism takes place at the supplier selection
stage, when the valuation of a good or service by the buyer depends on some
unobservable characteristics of the seller or the good/service it provides.
This often results in an undesirable matching between buyers and sellers,
that is, in situations where a buyer may end up interacting with a seller (or
buying a good) that does not have the desired characteristics (e.g., quality),
even though sellers (goods) with the desired characteristics are present in
the market. Post-contracting opportunism refers to possible opportunistic
behaviour of one trading party during the procurement transaction that
reduces the welfare of the other; for example, a contractor or a seller who,
after having been selected, reduces below the level agreed upon the quality
of service (or the effort exerted) on those aspects of the supplied good/
service that are difficult or costly to monitor.

Appropriate explicit incentive contracts[1] can partly overcome these
informational problems when indicators correlated to the non-contractible
features exist. Procured goods and services often present important qualitative aspects that are difficult to specify and enforce contractually and
buyers have limited contractual tools to control opportunism.

Concerns about supplier quality and opportunism may be particularly
severe in electronic marketplaces because of the reduced contractual

---

[1] See Chapter 4 for a discussion on properties and advantages of incentive contracts.

guarantees imposed by the geographical separation and relative 'anonymity' of the trading partners. Long distance makes the resolution of contractual disputes much more complex and costly than in traditional 'face-to-face' transactions; this may increase a trader's incentives to behave opportunistically.

Moreover, trading relationships in large e-markets are often occasional and not part of repeated supply relationship where the promise of gains from future cooperation may curb one's temptation to 'cheat'.

These problems have led several electronic marketplaces to adopt mechanisms that collect information about individual traders' past behaviour and disseminate it across the community of potential future trading partners.[2] Such *feedback* or *reputation mechanisms* aim at exposing a trader's opportunistic behaviour to potential future partners, and to allow each trader to build up a publicly observed reputation for trustworthiness and being thereby recognized as a reliable trading partner. The objective of such mechanisms is to discourage opportunistic behaviour, drive out unveiled dishonest traders, and foster trust and cooperation within the trading (virtual) community.

The above objective is surprisingly tricky to achieve. In this chapter we discuss the most important issues that are of practical relevance to the design of effective feedback mechanisms for e-platforms, and raise some novel issues that have not yet received sufficient attention but which, we believe, will become important elements of future feedback mechanisms.

We also pay special attention to the specificities of the increasingly important public e-platforms,[3] some of which (like particular legal constraints) may increase or reduce the complexity of designing feedback mechanisms. Most of the problems raised and solutions proposed turn out to be equally relevant to private and public e-procurement systems though.

---

[2] The interest on the topic among economists, computer scientists and practitioners, has grown so rapidly that it led to the creation of the *Reputation Research Network*, (http://web.si.umich.edu/reputations/index.html) an online discussion network for researchers and experts who are 'studying how reputation systems should in theory, how they actually work in practice, and how they could work better'.

[3] In the united kingdom the *OGC Buying Solutions* (Office of Government Commerce) provides e-procurement services to public administrations. In the United States the *GSA* (General Service Administration), provides a large variety of goods and services for the federal Government. Several Governments in America, for example Brazil (*Comprasnet*), Chile (*Chilecompra*), Mexico (*Compranet*), recently developed e-procurement systems. Consip, the Italian Public Procurement Agency, allows public administrations to buy several types of goods in the *Public Administrations' Marketplace*.

The chapter is organized as follows. Section 18.2 discusses the general features of feedback mechanisms. Section 18.3 describes and compares the feedback mechanisms of eBay and Amazon, two of the best-known examples of feedback mechanisms in use today. In section 18.4 we discuss the main issues related to the design of effective feedback mechanisms we are aware of, and provide some 'Practical Conclusions' for e-platforms. Concluding remarks are in section 18.5. The appendix reports a case study on the feedback mechanism proposed for the Public Administration's Marketplace managed by Consip, the Italian Centralized Public Procurement Agency.

18.2. Feedback mechanisms for private e-markets

Several e-markets are currently using feedback mechanisms as the primary means of building trust and facilitating efficient transactions. Table 18.1 lists several noteworthy examples of such mechanisms in use today.

The primary objective of feedback mechanisms in e-markets is to enable efficient transactions in environments where cooperation is compromised by traders' opportunism. Feedback mechanisms can deter post-contracting opportunism by acting as sanctioning devices. If the community follows a norm that punishes traders with histories of bad behaviour (by refusing to buy from them, or by reducing the price they are willing to pay for their products) and if the present value of punishment exceeds the gains from cheating, then the threat of public revelation of a trader's cheating behaviour in the current round provides rational traders with sufficient incentives to behave honestly towards their partners.

Ex-ante opportunism is present in situations where sellers have information (about some aspect of their innate ability, product quality, etc.) that buyers don't (or vice versa).[4] Such situations often arise in markets for 'experience goods', that is, goods and services whose quality can only be evaluated after having consumed them. Consider, for example, an online hotel booking site where hotels of different qualities advertise rooms. Consumers cannot be certain about the true quality offered by each hotel until they have actually stayed there. On the other hand, hotels do not have an incentive to advertise any of their weak points. Knowing this, consumers believe that all hotels are of 'average' quality and will not be willing to pay more than the 'average' price. Such a situation will eventually drive all,

---

[4] See the seminal contribution of Akerlof (1970).

Table 18.1. Examples of online feedback mechanisms (as in use of June 2005)

Web site	Category	Summary of feedback mechanisms	Format of solicitated feedback	Format of published feedback
eBay	Online marketplace (service for users: auctions and direct purchase)	Buyers and sellers rate one another following transaction (two-sided feedback mechanism); Short comments (only if rating is provided)	Numerical ratings (scale −1, 0, +1); Short comments; Ratee may post a response	Sum of ratings received during past 6 months
Amazon	Online marketplace (service for users: auctions and direct purchase)	Buyers and sellers rate one another following transaction (two-sided feedback mechanism); Short comments	Numerical ratings (scale 1–5); Short comments	Average of ratings: only ratings as a seller are included in the reputation (substantial one-sided feedback mechanism)
Google	Search engine	Search results are ordered based on how many sites contain links that point to them	A web page is rated based on how many links point to it, how many links point to the pointing page, etc.	No explicit feedback scores are published: ordering acts as an implicit indicator of reputation
Slashdot	Online discussion board	Positing a prioritized or filtered according to the ratings they receive from readers	Readers rate posted comments	

Citysearch	Entertainment guide	Users rate restaurants, bars, clubs, hotel, shops (one-sided feedback mechanism)	Numerical ratings (scale 1–10); Qualitatve feedback as 'useful', 'not useful'	Weighted averages of ratings per aspects reflecting both user and editorial ratings; Users' reviews can be sorted according to 'usefulness'
eLance	Professional services marketplace	Contractors rate their satisfaction with subcontractors (one-sided feedback mechanism)	Numerical ratings (scale 1–5); Comments; Ratee may post a response	Averages of ratings received during past 6 months
Ep nons	Online opinions forum	Users write reviews about products/services; Other members rate usefulness of reviews (recursive -information	User review with unmerical ratings (scale 1–5); Readers rate reviews as 'useful', 'not useful'	Averages of item ratings; % of readers who found a review 'useful'

Source: Elaboration on Dellarocas (2006).

except the lowest quality sellers, out of the market. Demanding consumers seeking for high-quality hotels are not willing to spend money for a lower quality and thus will not participate in the market.

Feedback mechanisms alleviate ex-ante opportunism issues by acting as signalling devices. For example, by soliciting and publishing experiences of consumers who have stayed in advertised hotels, they help the community learn the true quality of each hotel. This, in turn, allows a better matching of buyers and sellers and a more efficient market.

Both forms of opportunisms are simultaneously present in many circumstances: Sellers differ in their intrinsic ability levels but, in addition, have a choice of behaviour (which is partially, but not completely, conditioned by their ability). For example, certain attributes of the customer experience (location, size of rooms, etc.) can be considered as part of a hotel's immutable 'type', whereas other attributes (cleanliness of facilities, professionalism and politeness of staff, etc.) are the result of the hotel's level of 'effort' and can be varied strategically on a daily basis. In such settings, feedback mechanisms play both a sanctioning and a signalling role, revealing the hotel's true immutable attributes while providing incentives to the hotel to exert reasonable effort.[5]

In other circumstances, one of the two roles is dominant. For example, Amazon Reviews primarily serves a signalling role: it spreads information about the (initially privately known, but essentially 'immutable') qualities of the products (books, CDs, DVDs, etc.) being reviewed. eBay, on the other hand, is an example of a mechanism that primarily acts as a sanctioning device. Under the assumption that all eBay sellers are equally capable of acting in honest and dishonest ways, eBay's problem is to deter post-contracting opportunism. Accordingly, eBay users do not rate sellers on the absolute quality of their products but rather on how well they were able to deliver what was promised on the item description. The role of eBay's feedback mechanisms is to promote honest trade rather than to distinguish sellers who sell high quality products from those that sell low quality products.

Initial evidence suggests that a well-designed feedback mechanism can have significant positive impact on trade. For example, several studies have shown that eBay's feedback mechanism seems to affect both prices and demand for a wide variety of goods, such as office equipment (1% of an increase in positive feedback increases selling prices by 36% above their

---

[5] As we have seen in the second part of Chapter 4, reputation and performance indicators play a key role in any procurement relationship, at the selection stage and during the execution of supply contracts.

average level), electric guitars (a 10% increase in positive feedback increases selling prices by 17%, while a 10% of increase in negative feedback decreases selling prices by 24%), collectible stamps (20 additional positive ratings determine a 5% increase in auction price) and collectible dolls (reputable sellers get prices 5% higher than no-feedback sellers). It is also shown that the growth rate of a seller's transactions can drop considerably after the first negative feedback (from about 7% per week to about −7%) and so does the selling price (a 1% level increase in the proportion of negative feedback is followed with a 9% decrease in price).[6]

18.3. Feedback mechanisms in use: eBay vs. Amazon

This section describes and compares two of the best-known feedback mechanisms in use today, the one used by eBay, and that of Amazon auctions.

With more than 190 millions of registered users who buy and sell goods eBay is now the most popular online intermediary in the world, absorbing 14% of global e-commerce. In 2005, the number of listings is above 1.9 billion and eBay's gross merchandise volume accounted to more than 44.3 billion US dollars.[7]

As in many other online communities, eBay transactions are not backed by typical legal/contractual guarantees. Cooperation and trust among trading parties mainly rely on their honesty and on a simple feedback mechanism.[8] The eBay's feedback system is two-way (or two-sided) mechanism through which users can rate one another at the end of any transaction. The ratings

---

[6] See Cabral and Hortacsu (2004) for more on these and other results. For other empirical findings consistent with theory see: Ba and Pavlou (2002), Melnick and Alm (2002), Kalyanam and McIntre (2001), Houser and Wooders (2006), Dewan and Hsu (2004) and Mc Donald and Slawson (2002). Other works, such as Jin and Kato (2004), Eaton (2002), Kauffman and Wood (2000), Bajari and Hortacsu (2004) and Yin (2003) provide results not consistent with theory and indicate that reputation does not affect prices or it affect them but in the 'wrong' direction with respect to the one predicted by the theory.

[7] See the eBay's announcement of 2005 full year results at http://investor.ebay.com/news/Q405/EBAY0118-123321.pdf and the Annual Meeting of Stockholders at http://investor.ebay.com/downloads/2006ShareholderMeeting_060106.pdf

[8] Trade may also be supported by an intermediary, Escrow. The scope for opportunism in big transactions can be reduced by this intermediary, that collects the payment from the buyer (gross of intermediation fees) and diverts it to seller only when the buyer confirms his satisfaction for the good. In case the buyer is not satisfied, he can return the good to the seller and recover his payment, at the cost of Escrow's fees.

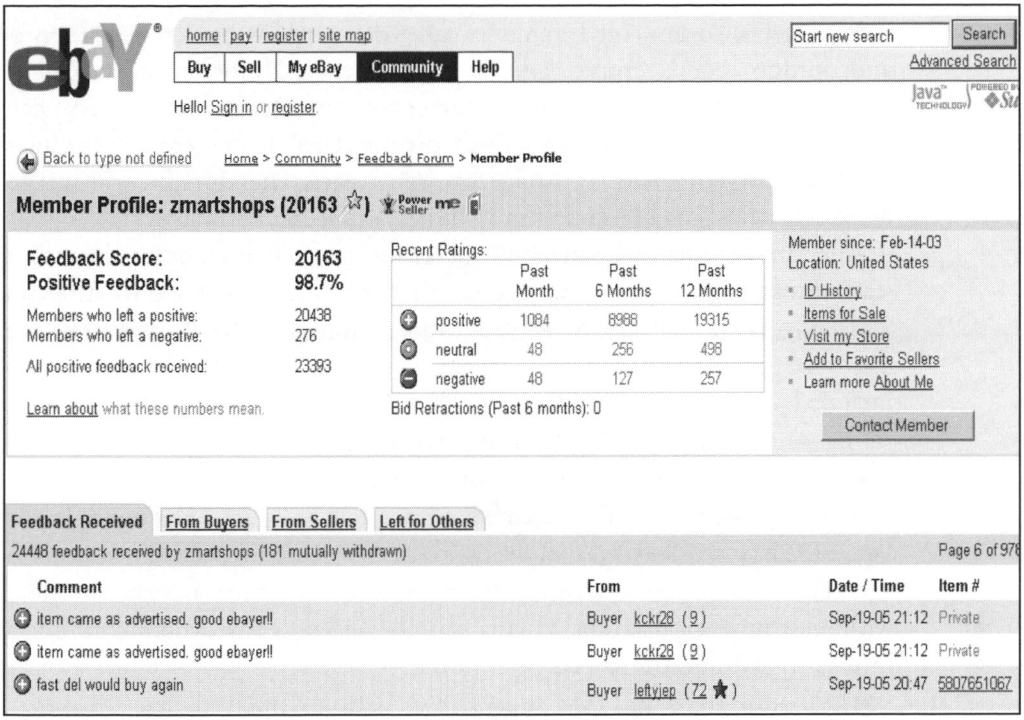

Figure 18.1: an example of eBay's member card.

can be positive (1), neutral (0) or negative (-1), and are usually accompanied by short text comments.

Ratings are summarized into a reputation indicator, the *feedback score.* This indicator is the sum of positive ratings minus the sum of negative ratings, with the caveat that multiple ratings received by the same user are counted only once (see section 18.4 for more details about this aspect). For instance, as the figure 18.1 illustrates, the user achieved a score of 20.163, with a percentage of successful transactions of 98.7%. Despite 23.393 positives received only 20.438 are counted in the score, since 'only' 20.348 *different* members posted a positive feedback.

The figure 18.1 displays a typical user's ID card and member profile (as of September 2005).

Amazon was founded in 1995 primarily as an online bookstore. In the fiscal year 2005 net sales accounted for $8.49 millions and the number of active customers achieved 57 million.[9] Amazon offers millions of unique

[9] See the Annual Shareholder Meeting at http://media.corporate-ir.net/Media_files/irol/97/97664/ 2006_shareholder_Meeting_Final_Web.pdf

new, refurbished and used items in categories such as books, food, sports and outdoor goods, music, DVDs, electronics and office, toys and baby items, jewellery and watches (see Amazon.com Inc., March 2005). Items can be purchased from amazon.com or by private sellers who merchandize their products through e-shops on Amazon web spaces. Therefore, in contrast to eBay, Amazon is at the same time a seller and a market maker.

After any transaction, Amazon enables users to rate each other through a star rating system, from 5 stars (best) to 1 star (worst). As stated by Amazon 'both buyers and sellers may leave feedback ratings. All feedback entries are displayed on the site, but only feedback ratings submitted by buyers are included in a seller's overall feedback calculations'. In eBay, instead, all ratings are included in a trader's final score regardless of whether they have been posted when the trader was acting as a buyer or as a seller.

A seller's reputation is the arithmetic mean of all his ratings. For example, the figure 18.2b (p. 455) reports that the user collected 60 ratings, with a mean of 4.7.

Buyers and Sellers on Amazon are allowed to leave a text comment without a numerical rating. This is not allowed on eBay, where comments must always be accompanied by a rating.

The figure 18.2a (p. 455) shows information displayed in an Amazon user's page (as of September 2005).

These are the two main differences between Amazon and eBay feedback mechanisms. First, Amazon's rating scale is more granular than that of eBay (1–5 against −1,0,1, respectively), although Amazon summarizes the ratings also in eBay's scale to facilitate information processing. As we will see in the next section, the granularity of ratings is one key dimension of the feedback mechanism design. The choice of Amazon to report ratings also in a 'positive, neutral, negative' mode, as eBay does, may indicate that users find it easier to process.

Second, on eBay a trader's reputation is given by the sum of ratings regardless of whether they have been received when the trader was acting as a buyer or as a seller. On Amazon, instead, only ratings provided by buyers enter in a seller's reputation. This policy substantially reduces the two-sided system of Amazon to a one-sided system.

18.4. The design of online feedback mechanisms

Before proceeding with the discussion of the various aspects linked to the design of feedback mechanisms, we would like to underline that in most

Figure 18.2a. Example of an Amazon's member profile.

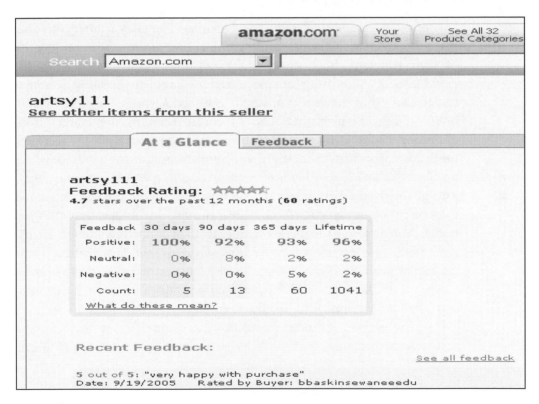

Figure 18.2b. Example of feedback card of an Amazon's member..

public and private e-markets the informational problems are less severe than in the, somewhat extreme, context of eBay and Amazon and other online (anonymous-trade) communities. Formal contracts, standard warranties, more restricted or better controlled participation, as well as procurement laws ensure that some issues, for example partner anonymity, are not of great concern for the market maker. Despite the less severe informational problems, feedback mechanisms may obviously help dealing with non-contractible dimensions of the transactions, to achieve more adequate level of customer satisfaction. As widely discussed in Chapter 4, in many procurement situations, customer satisfaction heavily depends on non-measurable aspects of quality. These qualitative aspects cannot be regulated by explicit contractual specifications, but can be elicited by a well-designed feedback mechanism able to stimulate parties to put more effort in the execution of supply contracts.

18.4.1. Anonymity of transacting partners

Part of the uncertainty of trading in e-markets like eBay is due to trading partners' 'anonymity'. People trading online do not know the real identity of their counterparts, since everyone operates through nicknames (or pseudonyms). Anonymity can be a serious problem because dishonest traders can avoid the effects of negative feedback with a new registration under a different nickname. This of course prevents the market from punishing 'bad' traders and it undermines the effectiveness of the feedback mechanism. Fortunately, there are some possible solutions to overcome this problem.[10] The first solution is to require users to reveal their true identity. This is clearly the best solution, but it is not always feasible. A second solution is requiring entry fees.[11] Fees would discourage opportunistic traders from entering the market frequently to avoid bad reputation. At the same time, however, entry fees may discourage overall participation to the market, which is a crucial point for the success of any e-platform (see Chapter 10). The third one is to assign an 'introductory' low reputation to new market entrants who would then have to 'pay their dues' (i.e., undergo a period of lower profits and demand) before they become reputable participants. Such an approach also discourages opportunistic

---

[10] This problem is outlined by Resnick et al. (2000).

[11] The role of entry fees is discussed in Dellarocas (2005) and in Friedman and Resnick (2001), who also illustrate cryptographic authentication technologies.

identity changes, as traders understand that, with every identity change, they will have to 'pay their dues' once again. This solution does not come without cost: a very low entry reputation may also deter new potential entrants (see section 18.4.9).

The access to public e-markets is typically not free as is in eBay or Amazon, which only require free and quick registration. While buyers (public administrations) are only required to register as in eBay, sellers (vendors) may have to meet some specific requirements. Public and several private platforms do select entrants on the basis of some criteria, precisely to avoid participation of 'unreliable' vendors. These features make anonymity and all related problems much less relevant. While a public market maker usually imposes buyers and sellers to be identifiable registered users because of legal prescription, a private market maker can choose to do so to increase security, without compromising the participation to and the function of the platform.

18.4.2. Feedback provision

Sufficient feedback provision is crucial for the mechanism to produce reputational effects. This issue refers to the problem of *free-riding*, which arises for particular types of goods, namely *public goods*. Public goods are such that the consumption of a good by one agent does not preclude (non-excludable condition) and does not diminish (non-rival condition) its consumption by another. Examples of public goods are (the construction of new) roads. Free-riding occurs because a person (free-rider) knows that although he does not contribute to fund the road he is not prevented from driving on it. If everyone who should finance the construction of the road does this reasoning, it is clear that the road does not have big chances to be constructed. In general, the public nature of a good determines the under provision of that good.

In most cases feedback contribution does not directly benefit its provider, who knows the performance of her partner whether or not he incurs the cost of leaving a feedback. Only other individuals benefit from an agent's decision to leave a feedback,[12] by using this information in their future trading decisions. Feedback produce therefore a pure *positive externality*, benefiting all agents *but* the provider, so they are an extreme type of public good.

---

[12] Sometimes the provider also may benefit from leaving the feedback. Gazzale (2005) shows how buyers can benefit from providing feedback in terms of acquiring a reputation for *gossiping*.

As for other public goods, or even more than for them, individuals have no economic incentives to provide feedback, given that they incur their cost but enjoy no benefit from them, so feedback underprovision, free-riding on giving feedback should be expected. Despite free riding, eBay faces a remarkable rate of feedback provision: 52 per cent of buyers post a feedback after trading, while 60 per cent of sellers do. Still, more (truthful) feedback would improve the functioning of the mechanism, while it is unclear whether the observed 52 per cent of feedback are given for altruistic or strategic reasons (see section 18.4.3).[13] Free-riding may prevent traders from collecting sufficient feedback to produce reputational effects. This problem is particularly severe for new users, since incumbent users may be discouraged to trade with a new user, whose reliability is completely unknown to the market. The lack of a reputation results then in an entry barrier for new operators who are likely to find more difficulty in trading in comparison to the incumbents. This may also limit the overall level of competition in the market.

18.4.2.1. Possible solutions

Recent work[14] suggests possible solutions to the problem of *free-riding*. One is paying feedback providers and taxing non-providers. A similar method, which also deals with the problem of feedback reliability, rewards feedback depending on how well it predicts the feedback of other buyers. The idea is that feedback referring to one seller tend to be correlated (good sellers will get on average positive evaluations, bad sellers will instead get negative ones) and any feedback that is much different from the others should be considered unfair and thus subject to penalty. If this system applies, rational traders are expected to provide honest (and also frequent) feedback because this way they maximize their expected payment.[15]

Payment-based systems seem to be difficult to implement, especially in public contexts, so most current feedback mechanisms do not make use of such incentive mechanisms. Nevertheless, evidence has, so far, not confirmed the (rather pessimistic) predictions regarding free-riding. Consumer participation in online feedback mechanisms is surprisingly high, ranging from 50 to 60 per cent on eBay as mentioned above. Sites can stimulate voluntary feedback

---

[13] These data and several other statistics are provided by Resnick and Zeckauser (2002).

[14] See, for instance, the interesting contributions of Avery et al. (1999) and Miller et al. (2005).

[15] Other methods for eliciting honest feedback in peer-to-peer environments are investigated by Papaioannou and Stamoulis (2005) and Jurca and Faltings (2004). These methods are essentially based on the agreement between the parties' feedback.

provision by maximizing the user-friendliness of their feedback mechanisms and by using pro-active IT solutions, such as e-mail feedback solicitation.

18.4.3. Two-sided feedback mechanisms: reciprocation and retaliation

Feedback mechanisms are very often two-sided (or two-way), in the sense that sellers and buyers are given the chance to rate one another. In theory, bilateral rating is used to ensure that *both* parties fulfil their obligations. In practice, however, two-sided mechanisms may produce adverse effects on the informational content of posted feedback because they allow for *retaliation* and *reciprocation*. These effects stem from the *ex-post* opportunity for users to reply to the received feedback.

18.4.3.1. Retaliation

Even after an unsatisfactory transaction, a party that values her own reputation may be reluctant to post a 'negative' feedback (first) for fear that the partner could retaliate leaving a negative feedback in response, even if unjustified. Retaliation could also be used strategically to discourage future negative feedback: a party may build a reputation for always retaliating against negative feedback, and thereby deter future partners that care about their reputation from leaving a negative feedback when performance was poor. Recent works[16] show that the fear of retaliation is present in eBay, is the most likely cause behind the scarce number of negative feedbacks, and induces parties that do leave a negative feedback to do it at the 'last minute', so that the likelihood of negative retaliation is reduced. Retaliation of course compromises the reliability of information: neutral and potentially missing feedback are counted as 'neutral' even when they result from *poor* transactions that have not been negatively rated for the fear of retaliation.

18.4.3.2. Reciprocation

An early positive feedback from a seller following a not too problematic transaction may create in the mind of the buyer a simple reciprocal obligation to return the feedback, even though the seller's performance was not terribly good. At the end of the transaction traders may also implicitly or explicitly agree to exchange positive feedback, even though none of them

---

[16] See Klein et al. (2005) for an in depth analysis of retaliation and last minute feedback; see also Chwelos and Dhar (2005), who find that Amazon's one-way reputation system performs better than eBay's one, and suggest the eBay failure is linked to retaliation/reciprocation.

performed particularly well (fortunately, these kinds of agreements are likely to be hard to enforce, as once the first party has left feedback the second is free to behave as he wishes). For example, at eBay, it is common practice to negotiate first before resorting to negative feedback. This may induces traders to report only really bad performance.[17]

An agent can choose to always reciprocate positive feedback in order to build a reputation of being a 'reciprocator' that encourages future partners to give positive feedback first. Whatever the driving force might be, reciprocation compromises the effectiveness of feedback mechanisms by unfairly inflating the reputation of users. Recent studies show that the problem is empirically relevant.[18]

18.4.3.3. Possible solutions

The above discussion seems to indicate that *one-sided feedback mechanism* might be preferable to two-sided mechanisms, as no retaliation/reciprocation can take place.

The choice of a one-sided feedback mechanism is supported on the ground that reputation is typically more relevant for the supply side. Private companies and public procurers using e-procurement platforms are likely to care more about the vendors' performance than their local structure 'performance'. In eBay things are different since many traders are both buyers and sellers and eBay is a just a third party (market maker).

The primary role of reputation is to adjust selling prices and chances to do business according to the sellers' performance. While sellers' past behaviour can have effects on them, buyers' past behaviour often cannot. The final price of the products auctioned in eBay is likely to depend on the sellers' reputation but hardly depend on the buyers'. Reputation of buyers has little influence on market prices in auction-driven platforms (but not in general).

The creation of reputation on the demand side appears in general less relevant, although there may be some scope for this as buyers (private

---

[17] See Resnick et al. (2000).

[18] See Klein et al. (2005) and Chwelos and Dhar (2005). Resnick and Zeckhauser (2002) show that in eBay almost all feedback are positive. A recently noted puzzling regularity is that the many positive feedback are reciprocated by another positive most of the time, while the scarce negative feedbacks are not. This puzzle has been noted first by Dini and Spagnolo (2005) in Resnick and Zeckhauser's (2002) data; Klein, Lambertz, Spagnolo and Stahly (2005) find the same puzzle in a much larger data-set. The strong correlation between positive feedback due to generalized good performance, but also to reciprocation. Similarly, the few negatives could be due to the fear of retaliation or to good market performance. To distinguish among these explanations the authors focus on the timing and the sequence of different feedback partners.

company divisions, and more likely public administration) may delay in payments and sometimes engage in imprecise online ordering, which is costly for the vendor. Then, one-sided feedback mechanisms may come at some costs: the market does not evaluate buyers' performance, thus missing the opportunity to 'discipline' them.[19]

An alternative policy that avoids the drawbacks of reciprocation and retaliation without giving up two-sided mechanism is 'feedback anonymity' (See also Section 18.4.10.1). This solution may require randomizing the disclosure time of feedback and expanding a lot the period when feedback can be given. Feedback anonymity however comes at the cost of not allowing to leave comments, and not to know the characteristics of a former partner (e.g., experienced or not) that left a given feedback and the size and type of transaction to which the feedback relates (see section 18.4.8 on the value of this information).

The most efficient way to curb the retaliation/reciprocation problems is probably one suggested recently, consisting simply in keeping the feedback secret until the period in which feedback can be given/modified/withdrawn expires. Then agents cannot react anymore, and the feedbacks (if any) can be made public.[20] This solution also implies some costs. Sellers' behaviour during the time lag is not observable immediately. Thus, sellers may be induced to misbehave during the time lag when buyers cannot yet observe negative feedback.

As a result, buyers cannot account for recent negative feedback (if given) in their actual trading decision. Note, however, that eliminating the ability of agents to react to received feedback has its own drawback: it greatly reduces the agents' ability to complain and deter 'unfair' feedback.

18.4.4. The input side of feedback mechanisms

Several questions arise when we want to appropriately design a feedback mechanism. For instance: should feedback be numerical (ratings), qualitative

---

[19] Notice that many of the buyer's obligations (essentially payment schedules) can be easily specified in the contract and thus enforced by courts of justice. In this case, reputation mechanisms are less useful since the contract itself is able to protect the seller from buyer's misbehaviours. Reputation forces are much more important when relevant aspects of the trade are not specifiable in the contract. See also Chapter 4 for more on non-contractible dimensions in procurement.

[20] See Klein et al. (2005). Reciprocation/retaliation requires the possibility to observe and react to a feedback, which is possible only when feedback are observed before the end of the period when feedback can be given.

(text comments), or both? Should assessments be given to the transaction as a whole or should they refer to specific aspects (shipping, quality, etc.). What should be the granularity (1–5, 1–10, etc.) of numerical feedback?

The answers to these questions partially come from the experience of the most important e-markets, such as eBay and Amazon, and Yahoo! and Citysearch. There exist two main approaches. On eBay, for example, traders collectively rate all aspects of a transaction with a single rating. Other websites, such as Citysearch, allow users to provide (qualitative) assessments on several aspects of a service, such us 'useful', not 'useful', 'comfortable', 'uncomfortable', 'pros' and 'cons' etc.

The choice between these two approaches can be done according to the nature of the service provided by the platforms. When the good/service is more complex (e.g., hotel evaluation in Citysearch) and composed of many different aspects (comfort, efficiency, usefulness, etc.) it may be appropriate to distinguish the various aspects and rate them separately. Instead, when the product is not that complex, the choice of eBay to allow for only one rating is probably the best.

The choice between qualitative and quantitative feedback is not of particular concern. If the problem is quantifying the performance, qualitative aspects can be attached a numerical value.

Concerning the granularity of ratings, as shown in section 18.3, eBay adopts a scale −1, 0, 1 while Amazon adopts a scale 1–5, Yahoo! a scale 1–10. However, some contributions on the topic[21] suggest that more granularity does not improve the efficiency of the mechanism: Binary feedback mechanisms (1,−1), can be efficient and are very simple.

When designing a feedback mechanism public procurers may be constrained by some factors. For instance, the presence of constraints due to procurement legislation and vendors' scepticism to performance evaluation – vendors may refuse mechanisms allowing for 'negatives' and may threat legal disputes in case they receive a bad report – suggest that one should focus on particular types of mechanisms (as we will see in the case study presented in section 18.6, this is the case of the Italian Public Procurement

---

[21] See for instance the work of Dellarocas (2005). The author discusses whether it would be more efficient for eBay to switch to the Amazon scale. Dellarocas (2005) analyses a family of eBay-style mechanisms and he shows that a binary feedback mechanism (transaction 'positive' or 'negative') that publishes the sum of recent ratings yields high level of cooperation between traders and that such cooperation is stable over time. The efficiency of the mechanism cannot be improved by a more complex rating scale (such as the one adopted by Amazon) or by publishing the whole feedback history.

Legislation). Furthermore, the nature of the mechanism itself can be a potential source of conflict: feedback mechanisms provide a 'subjective' measure of reputation that aims at capturing non-verifiable aspect of quality that formal contracts are not able to enforce. Vendors may refuse the idea that business can be affected by subjective measures of performance, even though this is what happens in everyday market transactions.

When these concerns are perceived important, the procurement agency could design mechanisms with only non-negative ratings. To avoid the potential fall in participation, agencies should maximize the perception that the feedback mechanisms can be a business opportunity for firms and not a 'punishment' tool. This choice may allow the agency to achieve two important goals simultaneously: increasing participation, by attracting 'reliable' vendors, and increasing quality.

> **Practical conclusion 1**
> Favour simple non-negative feedback scales like (0,1) or (0,1,2) when 'negative feedbacks' may reduce participation.

18.4.5. Reputation metrics

Ebay calculates the reputation as the sum of the ratings provided by other users (feedback score). However, as mentioned in section 18.3, feedback provided by the same user is counted only once. The reason is in what follows. Suppose someone buys more than once from the same seller and that he is always satisfied of him. A trustworthy long-run relationship between the two parties may develop over time. Therefore, it is likely that feedback the buyer posts to the seller will be positive. Feedback are counted only once to avoid that the reputation is boosted by collecting many feedback in the context of long-run relationships between the parties. Long-run relationships are sustained by the prospect of future gains from further cooperation with the particular partner and should not be considered in the reputation, as eBay correctly does. Indeed, feedback mechanisms aim at measuring how people perform when involved *in single occasional* interactions and not in self-enforcing long-run relationships.

18.4.5.1. Average reputation

The reputation users acquire in eBay depends on the number of transactions they complete. This raises two concerns. First, it favours old users who have a longer history. Second, it does not allow a comparison of the reputation profile across users. One simple solution to overcome these problems can be measuring the reputation with the following index:

Reputation (1) = sum of ratings and provided by single users in the most recent (N) transactions.

This is a simple sum of ratings and can be interpreted as an *implicit* measure of (average) reputation since the set (N) of transactions over which it is calculated is fixed and equal for all users. This sum does not vary according to history, solving automatically the second problem. Such a sum of ratings can be a basic tool for measuring reputation: It is simple to compute and is easily processable by users.

Consider now the following index of average reputation:

Reputation (2) = sum of the recent ratings provided by single users in the most recent N transaction/N.

With respect to the former index, this one makes *explicit* the weight of good reports over the total reports, thus immediately providing users information about the user's relative level of performance.

The indexes proposed can be further refined to obtain a more accurate and customized measure of reputation.[22]

18.4.5.2. Median reputation

As discussed in the previous section, reputation measured through averages (or appropriate sums) of ratings can be good reputation measures. However, they still far away from overcoming the reputation bias produced by undeserved ratings and to strategic manipulation of feedback. Fortunately, there are alternatives to account for this problem.[23] For

---

[22] For instance, we may also account for the number of feedback providers. Suppose one seller encountered K buyers for a total of N transactions. The seller may have interacted more than once with some or all of the K buyers. Now, compute the average rating of the last M transaction for each of the K users. Then, compute the average of these averages. We then obtain a sort of generalized formula, in which K and M can be appropriately chosen. By fixing particular values for K and M we get back to special cases: for example, by setting $N = 1$ we obtain the average rating provided by the last K single users. Setting $N = K = 1$ we are in the special case in which only the last rating matters. If necessary, N and K can be chosen large arbitrarily in order to consider a longer feedback history. For example, suppose 3 buyers, A,B,C traded 4,3,4 times with a seller D, posting (0, 0, **1**, **0**), (1,**1**,**1**) and (1,−1,**−1**,**−1**), respectively. If we restrict the attention to the average of the most two recent ratings (in bold), then the average rating for each user is 0.5 for A, 1 for B and −1 for C. The simple average of these ratings is $(0.5 + 1 − 1)/3 = \mathbf{0.16}$. Notice that reputation based on the last rating would be $(0 + 1–1)/3 = \mathbf{0}$.

[23] See Dellarocas (2000), (2003), (2004) and (2006) for discussions and formal analysis of feedback immunization methods. See also Douceure (2002) and Cheng and Friedman (2005).

instance, reputation can be measured using the *median rating* instead of the mean of ratings. As is well known, one important statistical property of the median is that it is less sensitive to extreme values with respect to the mean. As an example, take the eBay scale of ratings and suppose that one user faces with the following sequence of ratings $(-1, 0, 1, 1, 1)$. This sequence comes with a mean of 0.4 and median of 1. The 'friends' of the user ("ballot stuffer") can artificially improve profile with a 'flood' of positive feedback as to generate a better sequence of ratings as $(-1, 0, 1, 1, 1, 1, 1, 1, 1)$. This new sequence has a median equal to 1 and a mean equal to 0.67. Thus, while reputation measured by the median does not vary as ballot stuffers unfairly rate partners, reputation measured by the mean increases up to 0.67, thus biasing the reputation. Similar arguments hold in the case of 'bad-mouthers', that is, users willing to destroy reputation of competitors.

Measuring reputation through the median should impact the strategic behaviour of feedback manipulators. If manipulators know in advance that reputation is median-based and not mean-based, they will face fewer incentives to provide unfair ratings because such ratings will not bias reputation. As a result, we should expect fewer manipulations.

Notice that manipulations can take place in several other ways (some of which are discussed in section 18.4.10.1). For instance, in Usenet – a discussion forum where people share information about goods and services – competing firms influence the consumer beliefs regarding the quality of their respective products by posting costly 'fake' promotional messages in Usenet groups. Such a manipulation can seriously compromise the informativeness of the forum. However, this is not true in more general settings where ex-ante and post-contracting opportunism are both relevant (in Usenet the major concern is the ex-ante opportunism). Strategic manipulation can increase forum informativeness. The presence of honest consumer opinions can induce firms to reveal their own, more precise, knowledge of product qualities by manipulating the forums at relative intensities that are proportional to their actual qualities. The impact of manipulation then is to further separate the published ratings of the high quality firm from those of the low quality firm, making it easier for consumers to infer each firm's true quality.[24]

---

[24] See Mayzlin (2006) and Dellarocas (2006b) for further details on manipulations in settings where adverse selection is the major concern.

18.4.5.3. Comparing median and average

Likewise the average, the median can be computed over the recent N ratings to eliminate young-old discriminations and to allow for reputation comparisons. Although it overcomes the problem of artificial ratings, the median gives a less accurate measure of reputation – it can be only equal to −1, 0, 1 – and it can provide biased information like the average. Suppose, in the example illustrated above, that 'friends' are instead honest traders and that they provided a 'flood' of feedback. The average captures this (fair) reputational improvement, while the median does not. Under this point of view, the two approaches follow opposite directions. While the median does not account for further reputational improvements at all (additional feedback are considered unfair), the average fully accounts for those improvements (additional feedbacks are considered fair). Since both the measures are not robust to potential informational bias, it is convenient to use average. We then conclude:

Practical conclusion 2

A simple and effective measure of reputation is the sum of ratings provided by single buyers in the most recent N transactions.

18.4.6. How much information should be published?

The type and amount of information that is disclosed to the market are key elements of the feedback mechanism design. In this section we discuss what information should be disclosed to optimize a feedback mechanism. Most well-known e-markets usually disclose many detailed information. However, these are not easily processable by users. Publishing less but informative data may be a more effective disclosure policy. eBay publishes the users' reputation, and many other statistics about ratings. It has been argued that it may be optimal for eBay to 'hide' details and to implement a *feedback mediator*.[25] Feedback mediators provide highly customized information and meet the potentially heterogeneous informational need of the users. What we find missing in the eBay's disclosure (and also in Amazon) policy is the *number of transactions* completed by the user. This information could be

---

[25] Resnick et al. (2000) and Dellarocas (2003) provide a critical discussion on disclosure policies and feedback mediators.

very useful to assess how many traders are active in the market and how many transactions are left 'unfeedbacked'.

Interestingly, the practice of public e-platforms provides examples of other potentially useful information that might be disclosed. For instance, since 1995, the GSA – the US federal procurement platform – is endowed with the *EPLS* (Excluded Parties List System), which makes available on the GSA web site the list of vendors excluded from federal procurement. The web site also discloses the causes of the exclusion and the relative treatment. Everyone has free access to the 'black list' of suppliers who are not allowed to do business with the federal Government. Publishing such information can have considerable (negative) reputation effect and should be a further deterrent to firms' misbehaviors.

Another important aspect concerning disclosure policies is the optimal length of feedback history. In eBay each user has a feedback history, reporting feedback and comments from the oldest transaction to the most recent one. The question we address here is the following: is it better for a platform to publish the entire history or to limit it to the recent past? The debate on the 'right' length of feedback history reveals the existence of a trade-off between effectiveness of the feedback mechanisms and completeness of information disclosed. Publishing the entire feedback history is fully informative about traders' past behaviours but implies that the most recent feedbacks have negligible effects on reputation: observing only one or few negative rating over a long history may not be determinant for a trading decision. Conversely, reducing the history to the recent feedbacks provides incomplete information about users' past behaviours but it increases the power of the mechanisms since the impact of single ratings on reputation is now greater. At an extreme limit, publishing only the last rating minimizes the amount of information disclosed but maximizes the power of the mechanism. Indeed, it strengthens the incentives to cooperate and eliminates the temptation to 'stay on the laurels', when traders exploit the good reputation acquired in the past.[26]

Practical conclusion 3

Disclose the following key and easily processable information: the reputation index; the total number of ratings received; and the number of transactions completed.

---

[26] For more on the topic of reputation dynamics see Holmstrom (1999) and Cripps et al. (2004).

18.4.7. Portability of reputation

It is widely recognized that the effectiveness of feedback mechanisms crucially depends on the mass of users to whom information is disseminated. The power of feedback mechanisms can be limited if information is not sufficiently spread.[27] *Portability*, namely the possibility for traders to use the reputation in markets other than the one it was acquired can yield further improvements of feedback mechanisms.

Despite its importance, the two largest private e-markets, Amazon and eBay, decided to interrupt reciprocal portability of reputation. eBay threatened to sue Amazon claiming the property of its users' reputation. This episode highlights that the absence or limited portability results in a substantial exit barrier. Limiting the use reputation only to the market where it was acquired has two main negative effects. At the individual level, it prevents honest sellers to freely enter in other markets, since this can occur only at the cost of *losing* reputation and building up a new one. At the aggregate level, these markets miss the chance to register new good sellers, which may improve the overall quality of trade.

Portability may also favour multi-homing, stimulating users to rely on more platforms to buy/sell several goods (see Chapter 10 on business strategies for e-platforms).

Portability may take different forms:

- It can be *within* e-procurement agencies with multiple platforms, e.g., managing an electronic marketplace and auctioning traditional supply contracts (paper-based competitive tendering); or working for different jurisdictions or firm division with some suppliers in common;
- It can be *across* different e-markets: vendors may 'export' the reputation acquired in a (private or public) e-market to another (public or private) e-market.
- It can be *discretional*, so that agents have *the option* to disclose/use in other markets their reputation developed in a first market.
- Or it can be automatic, in the sense that anybody outside the platform can easily check an agent's reputation in a platform.

Practical conclusion 4

Increasing portability tends to increase the effectiveness of reputation mechanisms

---

[27] See Resnick et al. (2000).

18.4.8. Value of transactions

Is it useful for traders to know the value of transaction associated to feedback?[28] Information on the value of the transaction may be important to discover/prevent asymmetric behaviour with respect to transactions of different size. The temptation to 'cheat' on an unusually valuable transaction tends to be stronger, hence satisfactory performance in more valuable transactions should have higher reputational value. On the other hand, if more valuable transactions are intermediated by third parties like Escrow, then the scope for 'cheating' may in fact be lower. Then feedback mechanisms may well take into account the value of transactions and whether it was guaranteed by Escrow or similar additional mechanisms. One simple way to do so is giving feedbacks a weight proportional to the value of the underlying transaction, but appropriately reduced for the seller if Escrow was used, so that *ceteris paribus* large transaction feedback weight is more than small transaction ones. However, recent experimental works on the topic suggests that transaction value plays a limited role.[29]

18.4.9. Reputation for new suppliers

People may be sceptic to interact with (new) traders who do not have a feedback history. Since the market 'knows' only the incumbent, the new-comers may face fewer business opportunities. This may result in an entry barrier that can discourage participation, limit competition, and force new traders to enter at lower prices to fill the 'reputation gap'. Moreover, in public contexts the presence of entry barriers may be in contrast with the procurement legislation, for instance because platforms are required to ensure equal trade opportunity among vendors.[30]

To soften the entry barrier new entrants may be endowed with an introductory or entry reputation, a free asset they can spend in the market.[31]

---

[28] This issues is raised by Resnick et al. (2000).

[29] Chwelos et al. (2005) performed an experiment in which eBay's reputation profiles have been adjusted to provide information about transaction value to test how individuals respond. Surprisingly, the additional information does not make much of a difference to how people perceive the trustworthiness of other traders.

[30] This is the case of the Italian public procurement legislation.

[31] However, this strategy is effective only if the number of transactions is a 'hidden' information. If the number of transactions is publicly observable new entrants can be perfectly distinguished from incumbents and the entry barrier is not removed by the introduction of the entry reputation. High degree of transparency allows one to know whether a trader is new. But this prevents them from 'hiding'. In contrast, when transparency is low, it is not easy to distinguish new entrants from

But what is the optimal entry reputation? We discuss three possible (not exhaustive) alternatives: (i) the lowest reputation in the market; (ii) the average market reputation; and (iii) the highest market reputation.

Several aspects must be considered to determine the optimal level of reputation among these three alternatives. First, high starting reputation encourages *all* vendors to enter the market, hence attracting low-quality vendors as well (ex-ante opportunism). Moreover, the higher the entry reputation the higher the likelihood for opportunistic behaviours to occur: vendors face higher incentives to increase profits by lowering performances (post-contracting opportunism). Second, in environments where name changes cannot be avoided, high entry reputation provides incentives to sellers to change their identity as soon as they get a single negative rating. Third, the larger the entry reputation the higher the relative 'costs' for incumbents. The effort incumbent put in acquiring a good reputation is somehow 'wasted' since a new entrant can get it for free. Further, the higher the entry reputation the higher the overall market average reputation. Endowing new entrants with the highest reputation increases the market average reputation: this will further penalize incumbents because their actual reputation is even lower than the (increased) average reputation. This problem appears particularly relevant at the beginning stages of the platform. Instead, when the platform is sufficiently developed and the number of participants is large new entries have negligible effects on average reputation and do not affect the relative positions of incumbents. However, penalization of incumbents can be limited by setting the entry reputation equal to the market average reputation; or by preventing entry reputation higher than the average from entering the computation of the market average.

18.4.9.1. Benefits and effects of average entry reputation
The idea to endow new entrants with an intermediate reputation instead of extreme reputation finds support in studies and practice.[32]

---

incumbents, but this reduces the value of reputation for the incumbents, and consequently the disciplining power of the feedback mechanism. Therefore, maximizing transparency and reputation effects conflicts with reducing informational entry barriers: The higher transparency, the higher the value of incumbents' reputation, the higher the informational entry barriers, and vice versa.

[32] See Mailath and Samuelson (2001) for economic insights on the topic. Concerning practice, the OGC (the UK Office of Government Commerce) uses a 'traffic lighter' a supplier rating model (green, amber, red). Suppliers are given the rate of amber (the average) at the beginning of the contractual relationships and the rate is updated depending on the performances.

With respect to high reputation, the average reputation is less attractive for low-quality sellers because they do not gain much by exploiting it, while it is attractive for high-quality sellers because they can improve it at low costs given their (good) characteristics.

Low reputation is worse than the average reputation because it attracts only low-quality sellers. High-quality sellers are not interested in low reputation because it is too costly to rise. Thus, the average is preferable to extreme reputation because it attracts high-quality sellers and minimizes ex-ante opportunism.

From the standpoint of the procurer/market maker, high entry reputation seems appropriate in the early stages of the marketplace, that is, when benefits from attracting users overwhelm costs of inefficient assignment of reputation. The long term optimal strategy consists in bringing the entry reputation towards zero when benefits from attracting new users are likely to be offset by inefficiency costs.

From the standpoint of suppliers, new e-markets are attractive only if the value of entry is high, since risks are counterbalanced with the asset of high reputation. However, in the long-run e-markets are likely to be populated by many traders and sellers who will find entry much more valuable regardless of the entry reputation.

Practical conclusion 5

Endow new entrants with the market average reputation when platform population is still an issue.

Reduce the entrants' endowment towards zero as the number of users grows.

18.4.10. Other issues

In this section we discuss two issues that seem not yet to be the object of attention by feedback mechanism designers, but they appear to be of practical relevance in feedback mechanism design. These issues are money for reputation and feedback withdrawal.

18.4.10.1. Money for reputation

Rating, feedbacks, and the reputation indicators they generate will improve the performance of an e-procurement platform if they contain information on agents' real past performance, that is, if feedbacks are 'truthful'. Unfortunately, there are several reasons why agents' feedback may often not be truthful, one of which is the possibility that untruthful good feedback are exchanged against money or favours.

As explained in section 18.4.2, giving feedback in itself entails, in general, no immediate gain for an agent, as the agent that gives the feedback already has the information he is transmitting to other participants.[33] Leaving truthful feedback is in large part an altruistic act. If the reputation system is working, on the other hand, a good feedback has economic value for the party that receives it (truthful feedbacks have of course economic value also for other future potential trading partners of the evaluated party). Given that the rated agent values the feedback more than the rater, there are potential 'gains from trade' (from 'collusion' against future trading partners): the rated party may be willing to pay for an additional, untruthful good rating, and the rating party may be willing to sell an untruthful positive rating.

Suppose one more positive feedback is worth $X to a seller. The seller may share the fraction of $X with a buyer to be sure to get a positive feedback. But if paying for feedback is easy, reputation will lose value progressively. Buying feedback today lowers its informational content, and hence the value of reputation tomorrow, since everyone will know that some feedbacks are bought rather than 'conquered'. The additional value of reputation goes below $X at the next stage, and tends to zero over time. Reputation measures end up having little information content and market value, but for 'naïve' agents. When a 'market' for feedback arises, or could arise, their likely informational content falls, undermining the functioning of the original market the reputation mechanism was supposed to support.[34] Therefore, one must be very careful in designing the feedback mechanism so that feedbacks cannot easily be traded/exchanged.

Practical conclusion 6

Design the reputation mechanism so that trading untruthful feedback against money or favours is as difficult/costly as possible.

Remedies. When are transactions of money (or favours) against reputation feedback cheap and easy to enforce? Certainly, when the seller and the buyer need to meet personally to conclude the transaction started online

---

[33] Giving feedback may provide utility when an agent can build a reputation for giving a certain kind of feedback, but this requires that the platform is designed so that it is easy to track information of the feedback given (rather than received) by each participant.

[34] Dini and Spagnolo (2005) provide a more detailed analysis of the problem.

(billing phase). For instance, in the case of services, or of goods that need installation/maintenance, buyer and seller meet repeatedly and can easily trade money for reputation simultaneously, at no costs, when installation/maintenance is being realized. When the various phases of the purchase are not fully supported online (from ordering to billing) or cannot be so because the seller and the buyer have to meet at least once, a 'market for reputation' is more likely to arise.[35]

When instead the exchange is fully executed online, by distant traders, as is often the case, it is more complicated for the parties to enforce a contract whose object is money for reputation. In this case the market for reputation is *less likely* to occur. Still, in global platforms like eBay, with very distant traders and moderate value of feedback, there are several other ways in which feedbacks can be (and are currently) traded, at the expense of reputation-driven efficiency. For example, in eBay users sell for less than $1 a book titled 'Get 100% positive feedback quick'. The book is circulated in pdf format; therefore it can be costlessly transferred by e-mail. This is simple a chain through which users collect positive feedback simply by buying and re-selling the book in exchange for a positive feedback. With few cents one user can buy the book and get a very cheap positive feedback. By reselling the book the seller can get another positive feedback. Any user can buy and resell the book as many times as he desires to collect positives. This results in a completely artificial way to acquire reputation.[36]

The birth of a 'market for reputation' is harder when more persons are involved in the decision to give feedback. Buying reputation is more costly when more people are in charge to evaluate performance since the vendor must bribe all of them. It is obviously more difficult to convince more than one person to accept the bribe in exchange for an untruthful report, and the additional value of the feedback should be shared among several persons, thus lowering the bribe per-capita. This reduces the convenience for the vendor to corrupt procurement agents and the procurement agents to be corrupted for little money.

---

[35] A fully analogous problem emerges when the buyer wants to collects information on 'customer satisfaction' from procured goods' users, and is linked to the information collected being 'soft', that is subjective and not verifiable. The provided information cannot be shown to be false to a court, hence providing false information cannot be punished. See also Chapter 4 for more on this problem and Dini and Spagnolo (2005b).

[36] http://scams.flipshark.com/safefeedback.html illustrates other ways through which 'scammers' acquire artificial reputations.

More generally, remedies to fight 'feedback trade' include:

- Forbid all forms of rating sales (many of them are very easy to discover).
- When trading partners are organizations, use many individuals as joint raters, and advertise the chosen rating between all users of the rated good or product; this increases the number of people that the rated party must 'bribe' and of those who can complain against untruthful reports.
- Make ratings anonymous for the sellers, so that a rated person can never be sure who rated her; this may require randomizing the disclosure time of left feedbacks and expanding a lot the period when feedback can be given (see below for more on this). The informational costs of this possible solution are that specific comments that explain what was good or bad in each transaction – often containing important explanations – cannot be left; and that other parties cannot check the 'type' of a former partner (e.g., experienced or not) who left a feedback to a potential prospective partner.

18.4.10.2. Deadlines to provide feedback and withdrawals

eBay allows users to provide the feedback within 90 days after the trade is completed.[37] This time is believed sufficient for users to complete the exchange of commodities (shipping and payment) and to evaluate the counterpart's performance.

It can be important for any platform to decide whether the feedback should be provided within a certain time (deadline). This is particularly true for procurement of services with long duration. For long-term services one could think of letting the buyer evaluate the supplier more than once, during and after the end of the contract, provided feedback trading can be avoided. Fixing the feedback deadline according to shipment and payment can be quite difficult, since these two parameters may vary according to the category of supply and to the type of purchase.[38] Note, though, that in two-sided mechanisms, a well-chosen and sharp deadline together with the rule that feedback are made public to parties only after the deadline expires and cannot be withdrawn, tends to reduce reciprocity-based feedback

---

[37] To be precise, eBay only guarantees that feedbacks can be left for 90 days after the auction, but feedback can be left later, although at the risk that they are not recorded. See Klein et al. (2005) for a discussion of the likely effects of this possibility.

[38] For instance, in case of 'direct purchase', the Italian Public Administration's Marketplace requires Administrations to pay within 60 days, while payments schedules are freely established by the parties in case of 'Request for Quotation'. Moreover, the execution of services takes much more time than the delivery of goods.

trade and stimulate truthful negative feedback provision by making it impossible for agents to retaliate, that is, to observe and react to each other's feedback.[39]

The issue of feedback withdrawal does not appear to be of concern for feedback mechanism designers. This is probably because, once posted, feedback is usually irreversible. However, eBay recently modified its system introducing the possibility to withdraw feedbacks. For this to happen, both parties have to agree to remove their feedback. If they do so, the feedbacks are erased from the reputation index although the words 'withdrawn feedback' continues to be displayed in the history of the user.

In general, feedback changes might be desirable. For instance, a buyer may recognize that the negative feedback posted to the seller is unfair. A buyer may decide to withdraw a negative feedback after the seller replaced a faulty good, or after it awarded a fair price discount. In these cases removing the feedback is good since it goes with transaction improvements.

However, not always is feedback withdrawn for fair reasons. For example, a seller may *ex-ante* post an unfair negative feedback in order to propose *ex-post* profit increasing-removal deal. This is likely to be the dominant behaviour when feedback is only observable after the deadline for giving them has expired, but it can be withdrawn if both bidders agree: better to have something to exchange, just in case your partner is surprisingly unsatisfied. However, if the buyer anticipates this and behaves the same way there will be no gains from the trade since it would only result in a non-profitable common feedback withdrawal. Ex-ante negative feedback motivated by potential ex-post gains does not seem to be an optimal strategy because they are not completely erased from feedback profiles. The option to display removed feedbacks may be just motivated by the need to minimize undesirable ex-post trade in eBay. In any case to minimize this problem we suggest the following:

Practical conclusion 7

In two-sided feedback mechanisms: Favour a sharp deadline for providing feedback; Make feedback public only after the deadline has expired, and do not allow for feedback withdrawals.

---

[39] Klein et al. (2005) for empirical evidence on the fear of retaliation pushing sophisticated agents to post negative feedbacks in the 'last minute'.

18.5. Concluding remarks

E-procurement practice and many recent studies show the importance of feedback mechanisms in generating efficient exchange and cooperation among trading partners. Worldwide e-markets such as eBay, Amazon, and Yahoo! use differently designed feedback mechanisms to build trust and facilitate exchanges in online communities with little contractual instruments available. In the absence of formal contacts or when these are incomplete, reputation generated by feedback mechanisms can play a key role in attracting good suppliers and in mitigating opportunistic behaviours in e-platforms.

This chapter has discussed the main issues affecting the optimal design of feedback mechanisms. In discussing the issues we provided practical indications to designers for e-procurement platforms of different types.

18.6. Case Study: feedback mechanisms for Consip

Here we present a proposal for the Italian Public Administration Marketplace (henceforth IPAM) and frame-contracts managed by Consip. The proposals reported below could in general apply for any public (but also private) procurement platform.

18.6.1. Proposals for the Italian Public Administrations' Marketplace

The goal of the feedback mechanisms is to allow public administrations to provide a voluntary and subjective feedback about vendors' performances in each transaction.

We suggest a one-sided feedback mechanism based on irreversible feedback. Pre-defined answers will guide administrations in providing feedback. For this purpose, we considered 3 possible formats:

We suggest to:

- use the format 'B';
- measure the reputation as the average of recent K ratings provided by different administrations in the case of format 'B';
- measure the reputation as the average of recent K rating provided by different administrations with respect to the recent N transactions in the case of format 'C';

(eBay model)	Rating
Format A	
Positive transaction	1
Neutral transaction	0
Negative transaction	−1
Format B	
Excellent transaction	2
Good transaction	1
Neutral transaction	0
Format C	
Excellent transaction	2
Good transaction	1

- disclose the following information about vendors: the reputation, the number of transaction completed, the total number of ratings;
- allow public administrations to motivate ratings with short comments;
- endow each new vendor with an 'entry reputation' equal to the market average reputation;
- set-up an ID vendor card disclosing the information indicated in the fourth bullet;
- To stimulate the feedback provision we suggest to set-up a 'pro-active' system through which administrations are reminded to post their feedback. The reminder is an e-mail that links to the ID vendor card, which overviews for the Administration all the purchases completed and evaluated and those not evaluated.

18.6.2. Discussion

In formats 'A' and 'B' administrations face a more granular scale than with respect to 'C'.[40] Thus they can differentiate performance's evaluation in great detail. In both 'A' and 'B' administrations are given the opportunity to post non-positive feedback, even though negative feedback in 'B' are not explicit and much softer than 'A'. As already shown in section 18.4.4, despite efficiency, mechanisms including negative feedbacks may be a source of vendor's reluctance and legal problems.[41] Whether these problems

---

[40] The value of reputation obtained with the format 'C' can be rescaled by multiplying it for a factor of 50 or 100, working as a 'magnifying glass' of the reputation measure.

[41] See section 18.4.4.

are relevant, at least in the first stage, the application of format 'B' or 'C' appears preferable.

In cases 'B' and 'C' possible misreporting may be due to the impossibility to post (explicit) negative feedback, by simple omissions or by the willingness of the administration to post no feedback (regardless of the vendor's performance). In contrast to 'C', format 'B' gives the opportunity to post a non-positive feedback. For this reason it is more likely that misreporting in format 'C' hides a negative feedback in comparison with format 'B'. Under this point of view 'B' can be better than 'C'. At least in the first stage, the suggestion for Consip is to adopt the format 'B', because it is as efficient as 'C' and 'A' but it complies more with the procurement legislation.

In format 'B' reputation is measured differently with respect to 'C'. In 'B' (but also in 'A') reputation is based on provided feedbacks only, because administrations can (softly) signal with a '0' a vendor's poor performance. Instead, with format 'C' there is the need to consider all those negative but informative feedbacks that are part of the mass of unevaluated transactions. For this reason, in format 'C' the reputation measure takes into account the recent transactions. The effect is the following: any additional transactions left unevaluated reduces the reputation since it is believed to be substantially negative.

In either format 'B' or 'C' strictly negative feedbacks can however be collected for monitoring purposes. This allows one to follow-up problematic transactions and to establish some tolerance limits for possible reminders to vendors. Notice that, monitoring transaction without using the information collected may be risky; reputation is overestimated by collecting but not computing negative feedbacks. This may also create discrimination with respect to all vendors recognized to be good contractors.

18.6.2. Feedback mechanisms and frame-contracts

Consip is mandated by the Ministry of Economy and Finance to stipulate frame-contracts with national relevance. Frame-contracts allow all Italian public administrations to buy a wide range of goods and services at the fixed awarding price and up to a maximum pre-defined quantity. The frame-contract regulates the relationship between Consip and the contractor and the other general conditions at which public administrations can apply and the contractor attains to (length contracts, shipment schedules, minimum purchase, etc.).

As remarked in the introduction, procurement supply contracts, as many others, are subject to incompleteness and may contain several non-verifiable quality dimensions. In very competitive environments vendors may submit aggressive bids and ex-post recover the profits lost by minimizing non-contractible quality. When contracts are long lasting and involve large quantities of goods or services quality problems are more important because vendors may perform poorly on large scale and for a long time.

These arguments suggest that in frame-contracts also feedback mechanisms can play a key role: to stimulate vendors' 'flight to quality'. One simple and effective way to achieve this goal is to allow for portability from the marketplace to frame-contracts. This is obtained straightaway by making the information about reputation accessible to users and non-users. If reputation is published in the Consip web page it is clear that vendors will be induced to put more effort in carrying out the contract's activities to create a good image of them.

The reputation acquired can also be used by the vendor in private commercial relationships. Portability will be automatically effective. The vendor may increase his business opportunity by using the good reputation acquired in the public sector to maintain actual customers and to convince new ones to deal with him.

Bibliographical notes

The literature on online feedback mechanisms expanded considerably in the recent years. Economists, and also computer scientists, contributed much to the development of the research and applications in this field. Dellarocas (2003) and (2006) provide an interesting survey on theoretical and practical issues on the design of feedback mechanisms. Dellarocas (2005) presents a formal analysis of eBay-style feedback mechanisms and their robustness to missing feedback and manipulations. Friedman and Resnick (2001) focus on the problem of anonymity and name changes.

Resnick and Zeckhauser (2002) presents an interesting outlook and some empirical findings on the eBay's reputation system paying particular attention to the problem of feedback provision and reciprocation. Empirical analyses on the effectiveness of reputation systems, with particular emphasis on eBay, are in Bajari and Hortacsu (2004), Cabral and Hortacsu (2004), and Klein et al. (2005). The contribution of Mailath and Samuelson (2001) is quite useful for the problem of introductory reputation. Dini and

Spagnolo (2005a) and (2005b) focus on feedback mechanism design with particular concern for public e-procurement platforms, also discussing several new issues that we also illustrated in this chapter. Avery et al. (1999) and Miller et al. (2005) present pricing and subsidy mechanisms to induce sufficient and honest provision of evaluations.

The Reputation Research Network, an online discussion network for researches and feedback designers, makes available on its web site many of the papers reported in the footnotes of this chapter.

References

Akerlof, G. A. (1970). The Market for Lemons: Quality Uncertainty and the Market Mechanisms, *The Quarterly Journal of Economics*, 84 (3), 488–500.

Avery, C., P. Resnick, and R. Zeckhauser. (1999). The Market for Evaluations, *American Economic Review*, 89 (3), 564–584.

Ba, S. and P. Pavlou. (2002). Evidence of the Effect of Trust Building Technology in Electronic Markets: Price Premiums and Buyers Behaviour, *MIS Quarterly*, 26 (3), 243–268.

Bajari, P. and A. Hortacsu. (2004). Economic Insight from Internet Auctions, *Journal of Economic Literature*, 62, 457–492.

Bolton, G. E., E. Katok and A. Ockenfels (2004). How Effective are Online Feedback mechanisms? An Experimental Investigation, Discussion Paper 25–2002, Max Plance Institute for Research into Economic Systems, Jena, Germany.

Cabral, L. and A. Hortacsu. (2004). The Dynamics of Seller Reputation: Theory and Evidence from eBay (April 2004). CEPR Discussion Paper No. 4345. http://ssrn.com/abstract=541161.

Cheng, A. and E. Friedman (2005). Sybilproof Reputation Mechanisms, Proceedings of 3d Workshop on the Economics of Peer-2-Peer Systems (P2PECON), Philadelphia, PA.

Chwelos, P. and T. Dhar (2005). Caveat Emptor: Differences in Online Feedback mechanisms, manuscript, Sauder School of Business, University of British Columbia.

Chwelos, P., M. Brydon and I. Benbasat (2005). Fooling Most of the People Most of the Time: Combating Reputation Manipulation on eBay, Working Paper, Sauder School of Business, University of British Columbia. 05-MIS-001.

Cripps, M., G. Mailath and L. Samuelson. (2004). Imperfect Monitoring and Impermanent Reputations. *Econometrica*, 72 (2), 407–432.

Dellarocas, C. (2000). Immunizing Online Reputation Reporting Systems against Unfair Ratings and Discriminatory Behavior, Proceedings of the 2nd ACM Conference on Electronic Commerce, Minneapolis, MN, 17–20 October.

Dellarocas, C. (2003). The Digitization of the Word of Mouth: Promise and Challenges of Online Feedback Mechanisms, *Management Science*, 49 (10), 1407–1424.

Dellarocas, C. (2004). Building Trust On-Line: The Design of Robust Reputation Mechanisms for Online Trading Communities, in G. Doukidis, N. Mylonopoulos and

N. Pouloudi (Eds.), *Information Society or Information Economy? A Combined Perspective on the Digital Era*, Idea Book Publishing 95–113.

Dellarocas, C. (2005). Reputation Mechanism Design in Online Trading Environments with Pure Moral Hazard. *Information Systems Research* 16 (2), June, 209–230.

Dellarocas, C. (2006). Feedback Mechanisms, in T. Hendershott (ed.), *Handbook of Information Systems and Economics*. Elsevier Publishing.

Dellarocas, C. (2006b). Strategic Manipulation of Internet Opinion Forums: Implications for Consumers and Firms. *Management Science* 52 (10), October.

Dewan, S. and V. Hsu. (2001). Addverse Selection in Reputations-Enabled Electronic Markets: Evidence form Online Stamp Auctions, *Journal of Industrial Economic,* 52(4), 497–516.

Dini, F. and G. Spagnolo (2004). Meccanismi Reputazionali per Mercati Elettronici: Problematiche Economiche e Possibili Soluzioni per il Public Procurement, *Quaderno Consip N. 2,* Novembre (available for download from http://www.consip.it/sc/uff_studi. htm).

Dini, F. and G. Spagnolo (2005). Feedback mechanisms and Electronic Markets: Economic Issues and Proposals for Public Procurement, ch. 12 in Khi Thai et al. (Eds.), *Challenges in Public Procurement: an International Perspective*, PrAcademic Press, 227–247.

Dini, F. and G. Spagnolo (2006). Manipulating Soft Performance Indicators in Procurement, Procerding of the 2nd International Public Procurement conference.

Douceur, J. (2002). The Sybil attack. Proceedings of the 1st International Workshop on Peer-to-Peer Systems (IPTPS '02), Cambridge, MA.

Eaton, D. H. (2002). Valuing Information: Evidence from Guitar Auctions on eBay, Working paper 0201, Department of Economics, Murray State University, Murray, KY.

Friedman, E. and P. Resnick. (2001). The Social Cost of Cheap Pseudonyms, *Journal of Economics and Management Strategy,* 10 (2), 173–199.

Gazzale, R. (2005). Giving Gossips Their Due: Information Provision in Games with Private Monitoring. Williams College Working Paper. http://lanfiles.williams.edu/~rgazzale/research/rgazzale_gossips.pdf

Holmstrom, B.. (1999). Managerial Incentive Problems: A Dynamic Perspective, *Review of Economic Studies*, 66 (1), 169–182.

Houser, D. and J. Wooders. (2006). Reputation in Auctions: Theory and Evidence from eBay, *Journal of Economics and Management Strategy*, 15(2), 353–396.

Jin, G. Z. and A. Kato. (2004). *Blind Trust Online: Experimental Evidence from Baseball Cards*, Working paper, University of Maryland.

Jurca, R. and B. Faltings (2004). CONFESS: Eliciting Honest Feedback without Independent Verification Authorities. Sixth International Workshop on Agent Mediated Electronic Commerce (AMEC VI 2004), New York, USA, 19 July 2004.

Kalyanam, K. and S. McIntyre. (2001). Returns to Reputation in Online Auction Markets, Retail Workbench Working Paper W-RW01–02, Santa Clara University, Santa Clara, CA.

Kauffman, R. J. and C.Wood (2000). Running up the Bid: Modelling Seller Opportunism in Internet Auctions, Proceedings of The American Conference on Information system (AMCIS 2000). Association for information systems, Long Beach, CA: 929–935.

Klein, T., C. Lambertz, G. Spagnolo, and K. Stahl (2005). *Last Minute Feedback*, manuscript, University of Mannheim and Stockholm School of Economics.

Mailath G.J and L. Samuelson. (2001). Who Wants a Good Reputation? *Review of Economic Studies*, 68, 415–441.

Mayzlin, D. (2006). Promotional Chat on the Internet. *Marketing Science*, 25 (2), 157–165.

McDonald, C. G. and V. Carlos Slawson. 2002. Reputation in an Internet Auction Market, *Economic Inquiry*, 40, pp. 633–650.

Melnik, M. I. and J. Alm. (2002). Does A Seller's eCommerce Reputation Matter? Evidence from eBay Auctions, *Journal of Industrial Economics*, 50, 337–30.

Miller, N., P. Resnick and R. Zeckhauser. (2005). Eliciting Honest Feedback: The Peer-Prediction method, *Management Science*, 51 (9), 1359–1373..

Papaioannou, T. and G. D. Stamoulis (2005). An Incentives Mechanism Promoting Truthful Feedback in Peer-to-Peer Systems, in Proceedings of IEEE/ACM CCGRID 2005 (Workshop on Global P2P Computing), May 2005.

Resnick, P., R. Zeckhauser, E. Friedman and K. Kuwabara. (2000). 'Reputation Systems', *Communications ACM*, 43 (12), 45–48.

Resnick, P. and R. Zeckhauser (2002). Trust Among Strangers in Internet Transaction: Empirical Analysis from eBay Reputation Systems, in Michael R. Baye (Ed.), The Economics of the Internet and E-Commerce, *Advances in Applied Microeconomics*, vol. 11. JAI Press.

Yin, P. (2003). Information dispersion and auctions prices, Working Paper, Harvard Business School.

19 | Procuring Innovations

Luis Cabral, Guido Cozzi, Vincenzo Denicoló, Giancarlo Spagnolo and Matteo Zanza

19.1. Introduction

Innovation is a key source of competitive advantage, for both firms and nations.[1] Though internal research and development (R&D) is widely acknowledged as a primary source of innovation, it is less often remarked that a firm can secure innovative products from its suppliers. Innovative procurement is somewhat hidden in the popular press, but practitioners know all too well that a carefully designed procurement policy is often the key to success in the most innovative markets. The recent history of the Formula One championship nicely demonstrates how crucial the role of suppliers and procurement of innovative goods can be in determining a firm's eventual success or failure.[2] In our 'age of outsourcing', in which all non-core activities are increasingly being outsourced, firms must know how best to procure innovative inputs from strategic suppliers. This involves selecting the suppliers, choosing how to reward them, designing property rights for on-demand innovation, and ensuring that suppliers do not gain too much bargaining power, creating hold-up problems.

On the other hand, public procurement can strongly impact firms' profitability in innovative industries. It is well known, for example, that the US government's defence procurement has been a major driving force for

We would like to thank Bob Hunt, Stephen Maurer, Gustavo Piga and Susanne Scotchmer for comments and stimulating discussions.

[1] This was forcefully recognized by the Lisbon European Council of March 2000 in setting the objective of making Europe a more competitive and, therefore, innovative economy.

[2] In 2005, the rules of Formula One races changed in that the same set of tires had to be used for an entire race. Japanese manufacturer Bridgestone, that supplied tires to Ferrari and other minor teams, apparently was much less able than its French rival Michelin in developing products coping with the new rules and, as a result, Michelin-supplied teams dominated the 2005 championship after five years of persistent leadership by Ferrari.

the development of such innovations as large passenger jets[3], semi-conductors,[4] and the Internet.[5] These examples highlight that public procurement mechanisms can play a crucial role in stimulating or hampering private innovative activity.[6] Since governmental large-scale purchases can be oriented toward goods with different R&D contents, governments must take into account the effects of their procurement decisions on R&D investment in the private economy. Although the appropriate design of procurement contests may entail substantial gains in terms of static efficiency, any contribution it may give to faster technical progress will compound over time and potentially can result in benefits of a larger order of magnitude.

In this chapter we draw from frontier economic research to offer practical answers to these crucial questions. In particular, we consider different ways to induce potential suppliers to produce and sell innovative products. Many of our arguments and practical conclusions are equally valid when the procurer is public or private, but some apply only to public or only to private procurers.

We will also try to answer important macroeconomic questions on how to use public procurement in order to stimulate aggregate R&D expenditure and to incentivize the formation of human capital in the sector or country. Note that, at the private level, large firms are often the most important buyers for several specialized suppliers, which raises at the industry or

---

[3] The US military sector provided large amounts of funds to research on jet engines that greatly facilitated the development of commercial wide body jets. During the interwar period commercial aircraft have been developed and introduced more slowly in the absence of defence-related R&D and military procurement (see e.g. Ruttan, 2005).

[4] The microelectronics industry attracted a considerable amount of government investment effort (by the 1953 the Army Signal Corps was funding approximately 50% of transistor research at Bell Telephone Laboratory, see Holbrook, (1995). There is a consensus among industrial analysts that the USA government through its direct or indirect procurement polices stimulated an early market, promoting R&D investments and allowing firms to learn and decrease production cost.

[5] The Advanced Research Projects Agency (ARPA) of the American Department of Defence played a crucial role for the development of Internet. Since 1966 ARPA began to fund a multi-computer network that would have interconnected time-sharing computers. From that year ARPA continued to finance research in the field and in the late seventies procured to Western Union an updated version of the Automatic Digital Network – that was developed for exclusively military use (see Litan and Rivlin, 2001a, b).

[6] A recent study by Cozzi and Impulitti (2004) suggests that the US Government dramatic shift in procurement choices in favour of high-tech sectors was a main determinant of the wave of innovation that the US economy in the 1980's and 1990's. For less technical discussions on the role of the US technology policy, and in particular of innovative procurement policy, see Branscomb and Florida (1998) and Hart (1998). The EU also recognized now the importance of procurement as an instrument to stimulate innovation, and among other actions commissioned an experts' report on the subject (EU Expert Group, 2005).

district level questions that are similar to the analysis of the growth effect of public procurement.

Innovative knowledge is a particular good, and its procurement is possible but rather tricky, whether at the public or private level. Section 19.2 will deal with methods to procure such a special good as knowledge.

Other goods that buyers want to procure are often new or innovative. New knowledge must be created to produce these goods, and therefore the buyer must ensure that the suppliers have enough incentives to invest in the innovative knowledge that will eventually be incorporated in the goods it needs. In section 19.3 we discuss what changes in the structure of optimal procurement contests are implied by this additional objective that must be pursued.

Procurement policy can have important indirect effects on innovative activity, for example by enlarging the market for new goods, by facilitating the adoption of new standards, by changing the input and output market structure and prevailing prices so as to make them conducive to faster innovation etc. Section 19.4 discusses the effects on innovation races of standard setting activities by large, often public, procurers. It also considers how to optimize the degree of competition between suppliers, and other more practical indirect ways to stimulate innovation. Section 19.5 discusses how public and large private firm's procurement may induce innovation and growth at the national, industry or network level by affecting input market prices and the return to investments in human capital. Section 19.6 discusses how risk management methods used in procurement should be modified when innovation is a central concern for the buyer.

19.2. Procuring knowledge

Innovative knowledge can in principle be procured like any other good. To be sure, knowledge is 'non-rival', once it has been created, it can be used by many people simultaneously at almost no cost: any number of people can simultaneously apply Pythagoras' theorem without 'consuming' it. Similarly, once a new idea about what to produce (a new product) or about how to produce (a process innovation) has been invented and successfully tested it can be applied to the production of an indefinite number of products. For example, given the chemical formula for a new drug, a firm can implement it to manufacture an indefinite number of drugs; given a project for a new engine, it can be embedded in an indefinite number of cars, etc.

In the absence of intellectual property rights, secrecy, or other means of appropriation, innovative knowledge also tends to be 'non-excludable', that is it is hard or impossible to control who has or is using a certain innovative knowledge. This means that knowledge tends to be what economists name a 'public good',[7] which however does not preclude the public procurement of innovative knowledge. Even private procurement of knowledge is possible, either for philanthropic reasons, in which case knowledge is put in the public domain as soon as it is acquired, or else when the buyer can somehow exclude others from the innovative knowledge he has procured from the original inventor or author and thus can profit from his monopoly. This section reviews the main tools for the procurement of knowledge and compares procurement with other means of fostering innovative activity, like intellectual property.

Society procures innovative knowledge in various ways. First, innovative knowledge is often publicly provided: for example, a considerable amount of basic research is conducted in public universities and laboratories. However, ideas tend to be widely distributed among individual researchers.[8] This implies that effective public provision of innovative knowledge can be very costly, since it requires that the government hires a large number of researchers in order to avoid the risk that valuable ideas are not pursued. Although costs can be somewhat reduced by using various incentive mechanisms to elicit adequate research effort, like performance-based research grants and promotions, public provision tends to be practical only if the number of potential innovators is limited, because the expertise required to contribute innovative knowledge is difficult to achieve.

The main alternative to public provision is intellectual property. Through intellectual property rights or trade secrecy, authors and inventors obtain a temporary monopoly over the commercial use of the innovative knowledge they have created. The prospect of reaping monopoly rents, albeit for a limited time period, stimulates innovative activity. Although intellectual property and trade secret protection can be viewed as special forms of procurement in which the monetary payment is replaced by the right to exercise monopoly power temporarily, the optimal design of intellectual property falls outside the scope of this book and will be dealt with only cursorily.

---

[7] The notion that knowledge can be viewed as a public good dates back at least to Arrow (1962). For a critique of such a view, see Boldrin and Levine (2005)

[8] Menell and Scotchmer (2005).

Another mechanism to foster innovative activity, and one that is most akin to standard procurement, is the granting of monetary prizes to innovators; any innovative knowledge elicited by the prospect of winning the prize is then put in the public domain. One can distinguish between ex-ante and ex-post prizes. *Ex-ante prizes* are posted in advance and can be claimed by the first to solve a well-defined problem, for example, proving Fermat's conjecture. *Ex-post prizes* reward discoveries that may not even have been conceived of before they occurred to someone. Still, if ex-post prizes are systematically and consistently awarded when useful innovations occur, the prospect of winning such prizes may elicit substantial research effort. In both cases, the nature of the innovation must be clearly and objectively defined, either ex ante or ex post, so that the prize can be awarded if and only if the innovation is achieved.

Private firms can procure knowledge in much the same way as society does: they can conduct research in-house, obtain licences from independent holders of intellectual property rights or trade secrets, and post prizes. Both ex-ante and ex-post prizes can be used by private firms: for example, pharmaceutical firms normally reward with bonuses their researchers that find solutions to pre-specified health market needs,[9] whereas IBM used to reward with a monetary prize any patent obtained by one of its employees. Clearly, posted prizes can be privately profitable only if the firm can appropriate the result of the research, for example, through intellectual property. Although we will mostly focus on public procurement of knowledge, many conclusions reviewed in this section readily extend to the case of private procurement.

19.2.1. Ex-ante prizes

Monetary prizes financed out of general fiscal revenue have sometimes been used to reward innovators. In particular, ex-ante prizes are posted in advance and can be claimed by anyone that is first to invent. They differ from ex-post prizes in that the latter are granted discretionally as a reward for achievements that could not be foreseen in advance. In both cases, the prospect of winning the prize will elicit some research effort. Famous examples of ex ante prizes include the eighteenth century 'longitude' prize,[10]

---

[9] See also Chapter 4 for a discussion on how bonuses can be designed to provide performance incentives.

[10] In 1714, in order to create an instrument able to determine the longitude, the British Government designed a contest with a final fixed prize of £20,000 (equivalent to millions of pounds today) for the

'America's most energy-efficient refrigerator' prize,[11] and the X Prize for space technology.[12]

In some cases, innovations originally spurred by the prospect of a monetary prize turned out to be patented;[13] on other occasions, the government acquired newly granted patents in exchange for a monetary prize[14] (such patent-buy-outs resemble ex-post prizes and will be discussed more fully later).

19.2.1.1. Problems of ex-ante prizes

Ex-ante prizes are impractical unless the invention society wants to procure is easily describable, like for example 'a vaccine against AIDS which is effective in at least 70 per cent of the population', and it is verifiable whether the invention has been achieved or not, for instance through monitored clinical tests.[15] Even assuming that these conditions are met, however, three shortcomings of prizes as compared to intellectual property – patents, in the vaccine example – come immediately to mind:

1. When the procurement of innovations is financed out of general fiscal revenue, some individuals may end up paying for something they do not use or value. In contrast, with patents no one pays more than he benefits from what he buys.

2. Individual countries must reach an international agreement to divide the burden of funding the prize amongst them. With patents, a similar

---

winner. John Harrison presented the eventual solution: a clock that could withstand storms, changes in temperature, and salt air. He received an initial payment of 10,000 and the remaining sum of money after the first successful test. See the entertaining account in Sobel (1995).

[11] A prize incentive was proposed for developing new vaccines, new ICT and other technologies. In 1991, a $30 million prize was sponsored to build 'America's most energy-efficient refrigerator'. Whirlpool won the contest but to receive payment Whirlpool had to sell 250,000 copies of new refrigerators by 1997 (the prize was established in 1992). Only 200,000 units have been sold and, therefore, the prize was not paid. See Langreth (1994).

[12] The X-Foundation in 1996 posted a 10 million dollar prize for to the first private firm to carry three passengers to a sub-orbital height of 100km twice within a single to two-week period. Many teams representing several countries have entered the race. The prize was awarded in 2005 (see www.xprizefoundation.org).

[13] John Hyatt's invention of celluloid was spurred by the prospect of a monetary prize posted by a manufacturer of billiard balls, but Hyatt eventually decided to patent his innovation (Porter, 1994).

[14] As an example, Louis Daguerre, the inventor of photography, sold his rights on the invention to the French government in exchange for a pension. The French government then put the invention in the public domain.

[15] Regulatory agencies like the FDA in the US and EMEA in Europe routinely decide whether a new drug is effective and safe or not; this means that the achievement of this particular innovation in principle would be verifiable.

problem might also arise (i.e., each country might be tempted to free ride on research incentives provided by others), but this problem has already been addressed and solved by various international treaties, like TRIPS. (Presumably, with patents an agreement was simpler to reach precisely because with a fully harmonized patent system each country pays in proportion to what it benefits from the innovation.)

3. 'The reward conferred by [patents] depends upon the invention being found useful, and the greater the usefulness, the greater the reward.'[16] With incomplete information on the value of the innovation, in contrast, it is difficult to choose the 'correct' prize, that is the prize that aligns the private incentive to invest with the social value of the innovation; consequently, a prize system is bound to over-incentivize certain innovations and under-incentivize others.

19.2.1.2. Advantages of ex-ante prizes

On the other hand, a prize system has two important advantages over a patent system. First and foremost, generally the deadweight loss from monopoly pricing of new goods is greater than the excess burden from an optimally designed tax system – and probably from most of the existing tax systems. For example, in the AIDS vaccine case, monopoly pricing of a patented vaccine might result in some people being excluded from the cure, with social costs that might amount to thousands if not millions of deaths. With prizes, the vaccine would be immediately priced at marginal cost and a much smaller number of people would be excluded. Second, typically the private value of a patented innovation falls short of its social value[17] and thus a patent system may provide insufficient incentives to invest in research, whereas in principle there is no upper bound on the size of a monetary prize.

19.2.1.3. Choosing between ex-ante prizes and intellectual property rights

Leaving aside distributional concerns, assuming that international agreements are easy to reach, and assuming that the optimal patent life is finite,[18]

---

[16] See Mill (1848).

[17] There are various reasons why the private value is lower than the social value: limited protection, the fact that the patentee may not be able to extract all the surplus from consumers, technological spillovers, monopoly deadweight losses.

[18] This is not to suggest that with a finite optimal patent life there is no under-investment in research; quite to the contrary, an optimized patent system must lead to under-investment in research because

the comparison between patents and prizes boils down to a comparison between the distortion created by asymmetric information on the one hand and those associated with monopoly pricing on the other hand. Note that, to the extent that potential innovators are uncertain about the value of the innovation, incomplete information will distort the decision to invest in research also under a patent system. The extra cost of a prize system is due to the asymmetry of information between the government (that sets the prize) and innovators, and vanishes when information is symmetric – even if it is incomplete. Therefore, in a world of symmetric information it would be preferable to reward innovators through monetary prizes. This conclusion continues to hold if informational asymmetry is limited and the monopoly deadweight loss (the social loss induced by the exercise of market power, with higher prices and reduced output) is large, for example the demand for the new good is very elastic. A patent system would be preferable if the asymmetry of information is substantial and/or demand is inelastic.[19]

Practical conclusion 1

Procuring innovations through monetary prizes tends to be preferable to intellectual property when the innovation is easily describable in advance, the expected costs of monopoly prices are high, the occurrence of the innovation is verifiable, and there is little informational asymmetry on the value of the innovation.

When the procurer is a private firm, a similar trade-off may arise. Consider a private firm that is the sole potential user of an innovation that can uniquely be supplied by an independent inventor. The private firm can wait for the inventor to achieve and patent the innovation and then bargain for a licence, or it can post a prize which it commits to pay to the successful inventor, retaining any intellectual property right that might be granted on the innovation. Bargaining ex-post for a licence is costly, however, and the licensing agreement may involve distortionary clauses such as unit royalties. On the other hand, the procurer may not know the value of the innovation

increasing patent protection is socially costly and so it is desirable to stop raising the strength of patent protection before the socially optimal level of investment in R&D is reached. However, when the optimal patent life is finite, any under-investment in research is due to the monopoly deadweight losses created by the patent, and therefore are already encompassed in the first reason why prizes can be better than patents.

[19] See Wright (1983). The monopoly deadweight loss may be small even if demand is elastic, provided that the patentee can engage in price discrimination.

that the independent inventor will eventually supply. Again, a trade-off arises and the procurement of innovative knowledge through a monetary prize posted ex-ante tends to be preferable if information is symmetric or informational asymmetry is limited.

Coming back to the case of public procurement, consider next self-selection mechanisms that combine prizes and intellectual property. One such mechanism is an optional patent system in which the supplier (that is better informed on the value of his innovation than the government) can choose between a patent and a monetary prize.[20] The reward obtained by a successful supplier will be constant if he chooses the prizes, but will increase with the value of the innovation if he opts for patent protection. Consequently, more valuable innovations will end up being patented, and only innovators holding less valuable innovations will claim the monetary prize. Such a sorting means that suppliers will retain some informational rents. Nevertheless, a properly designed optional system dominates a pure patent system and may be preferable to a pure prize system.[21]

An optional patent system can be further improved upon by allowing for the possibility that innovators are granted both a prize and a patent. In particular, the government could offer a menu comprising a monetary prize and, alternatively, a lower (and possibly negative) prize augmented by a patent of positive length. If optimally designed, this two-option menu is preferable to an optional patent system. Furthermore, it turns out that offering to innovators two options suffices to achieve a constrained optimum under weak regularity conditions.[22]

---

[20] Shavell and van Yperseele (2001). Note that when the procurer is a private firm, even if only a monetary prize is offered, the supplier retains the option to patent and therefore effectively faces an optional system. To rule out the option to patent, the procurer should require participants to the competition for the prize to assign in advance any intellectual property rights they may obtain to the procurer itself.

[21] To see this, consider a fully optimized patent system and take the lowest possible value of the innovation. Offering a menu with the same patent length and a prize slightly greater than the lowest private value of the innovation (i.e. the private value in the worst possible case, calculated on the basis of the optimal patent length) will raise the incentive to innovate and reduce the expected deadweight loss. Similarly, consider the optimal prize in a pure prize system. Now reduce the prize but offer a patent of positive length, in such a way that the expected deadweight loss remains constant. Such a move reduces the investment in relatively low-value innovations, and increases the investment in relatively high-value innovations; thus, this move tends to be welfare improving. There is no guarantee, however, that such a move will indeed be welfare improving, because the changes in equilibrium investments brought about by this move are discrete, not infinitesimal. The move will be welfare improving if there is enough uncertainty on the value of the innovation. See Shavell and van Ypersele (2001) for details.

[22] See Scotchmer (1999) and Chiesa and Denicolò (2005) for more on these more elaborate schemes.

Practical conclusion 2

When the innovation is easily describable in advance and the occurrence of the innovation is verifiable, the supplier should offer a menu comprising two options: a monetary prize, and a lower prize coupled with patent protection.

19.2.2. Ex-ante prizes with sequential innovations

So far, we have considered the case where each innovation is independent of the others. However, innovation is cumulative in nature: typically each innovation builds on the previous ones, and in turn constitutes the basis for subsequent developments. With cumulative innovation, intellectual property rights run into problems, which potentially enhance the desirability of ex-ante prizes.

In particular, the cumulative nature of technical progress has two important consequences. First, with sequential innovations the social value of an innovation now includes also the option value of investing for obtaining the subsequent improvements. Second, the occurrence of the next-generation innovation tends to kill the market for the current innovation. This means that when path-breaking innovators are protected by intellectual property, instead of being compensated for the option value they have created, they suffer from competition from second-generation innovators.

Basic innovations therefore need forward protection, because otherwise future innovators could compete away the original innovators' profits, and because the first innovator should be rewarded for opening the way to the subsequent improvements.[23] The patent system provides forward protection in two ways: first, any patent application must meet certain novelty requirements; second, even patentable improvements may constitute infringement on the original patent, depending on the first-generation patent's leading breadth. Both the novelty requirement and leading breadth, however, entail a social cost in that they impede the achievement of the second-generation improvements, which can be substantial and socially valuable.[24]

---

[23] See Scotchmer (1991).

[24] In fact, the novelty requirement and leading breadth protect early innovators in different ways. The fact that an innovation must satisfy novelty requirements may block or impede second-generation improvements, thus lengthening the first-generation innovators' monopoly. On the other hand, by finding that an improvement infringes on a basic patent, the courts can force the patentees to bargain

A prize system is in principle immune from these defects, because prizes can be calculated taking into account the option value of basic innovations, and because business stealing from second-generation innovators is not an issue when any innovative knowledge is immediately put in the public domain. However, ex-ante prizes must be properly designed in order to cope with the sequential nature of the innovative activity. For example, when it is important for cumulative innovation that individual innovations are disclosed early, so that other researchers can use them, it may be optimal to abandon the classic 'winner-takes-all' design, select a group of innovators, and ensure that the prizes each of them wins is shared with the others in the group.[25]

19.2.3. Ex-post prizes

When the innovation is not easily and precisely describable, or cannot even be conceived of in advance, ex-ante prizes are unfeasible. However, if the occurrence of the innovation is verifiable ex-post, in principle a procurer could commit to offer ex-post prizes to successful innovators. In an ex-post framework, describing the innovation is no longer at issue, but the problem remains of guessing the value of the innovation and hence the appropriate prize.

19.2.3.1. Uncertainty and discretion

With ex-post prizes two distinct problems in fact arise: the uncertainty over the value of the innovation, which raises issues similar to those discussed in the preceding subsection, and the fact that the value of the innovation is typically unobservable. Generally speaking, in a public procurement case, once the innovation has been achieved the government has an incentive to renege on its promises, be it the award of a prize or an intellectual property right. Whereas with ex-ante prizes and intellectual property it is easy to observe whether or not the government has kept its promises, and so simple

over profit shares, thus allowing the original innovator to capture some of the rents from the improvement. This means that the novelty requirement has a 'blocking effect', and leading breadth a 'sharing effect'. The sharing effect of leading breadth, however, automatically entails also a blocking effect: if the second innovation is small and infringes, the profit left to the second innovator may be too low for investment to be profitable (R&D costs are sunk when bargaining between the patent holders takes place). This means that even leading breadth inevitably prevents some second-generation improvements. See Denicolò and Zanchettin (2002) for a more detailed discussion of these two effects of forward patent protection.

[25] See e.g., Lewis and Talley (2005).

reputation mechanisms[26] can provide enough incentives for the government to stick to the commitment, with ex-post prizes the government is not committed to any particular size of the prize. As a consequence, if the value of the innovation is unobservable to third parties, reputation mechanisms do not work efficiently to induce the government to match its promises. Ex post, the government is therefore systematically tempted to under-reward innovators; such a temptation will be anticipated by potential innovators and results in under-investment in research.

The fact that the value of the innovation is not observable or verifiable also means that the procurer can set the prize quite discretionally, implying that innovators have an incentive to engage in opportunistic behaviour and lobbying. As a consequence, the whole system of ex-post prizes can be prone to corruption. These reasons explain why ex-post prizes are rarely observed in practice. The Nobel prizes, and other similar prizes, are in fact awarded at pre-specified dates, and are of a pre-specified size; thus, they resemble research contests (discussed later) more closely than ex-post prizes.[27] Examples of ex post prizes are medals, honour mentions, and similar recognitions that heads of state award every now and then to successful people.

19.2.3.2. Kremer's mechanism and collusion

These problems with ex-post prizes could be overcome, however, if a mechanism to set the prize could be found that leaves little or no discretion to the procurer. A recently proposed patent-buy-out mechanism may achieve this goal and at the same time solve the problem of informational asymmetries that plague even ex-ante prizes.[28] The proposal is that suppliers initially rely on the protection conferred by intellectual property, but at a subsequent stage the government acquires the intellectual property rights it just granted, using an appropriately designed competitive procurement, and then puts the innovative knowledge in the public domain.

The fundamental premise of the Kremer patent-buy-out mechanism is that even if the government is poorly informed about the value of

---

[26] See also Chapter 4 on contracting issues, and Chapter 18 on feedback mechanisms for further discussions on the role reputation in procurement

[27] Even so, the Nobel Prize has, on occasion, 'cheated': in the early '30s the physics prize was not awarded for several years.

[28] This mechanism is known as Kremer's patent-buy-out mechanism after Kremer (1998).

innovations, the patentee's competitors are typically better informed. To extract this information at a low social cost, the government implements a standard first-price sealed-bid tendering process for the patent, with the proviso that almost always the winner will not receive the patent, which will instead be acquired by the government, at the price determined by the tendering process. In order to preserve the incentives to bid correctly, however, in a small fraction of cases the winner of the competitive bidding should really get the patent and pay his bid.

The main problem with the Kremer patent-buy-out mechanism is that it is hardly collusion-proof. Although almost any competitive procurement is subject to the risk that bidders collude (See Chapters 14 and 15), typically some competition among bidders will remain unless all bidders participate in the cartel. The Kremer competitive tendering, in contrast, can be undermined by agreements involving only two bidders, even if the number of bidders is quite large; in addition, the collusive agreement is always self-enforcing, even if players discount the future heavily.

To see this, suppose that firms A and B enter a bilateral agreement whereby firm B systematically bids in excess of the value of A's patents, and A does the same when it comes to B's patents to be competitively procured. Even if there are many bidders and no other firm participates in the agreement, firm B's (over-valued) bids will determine the price that the government pays for A's patents, and in like manner A will determine the price that B gets for its own patents. In the rare event that B must really purchase A's patent, the patent can be re-sold to A; alternatively, B can wait for A to over-pay one of B's patents to be compensated. Because such bilateral agreements are easier to reach than multilateral agreements, are self-enforcing irrespective of the size of the discount factor (there is no temptation to deviate), and there can be several bilateral agreements in place, the government may very often end up paying an excessive price for the patents it buys out.

Because of this weakness of the Kremer patent-buy-out mechanism, it would be prudent not to apply the mechanism systematically, especially in those industries – like the pharmaceutical industry – in which there is a relatively small set of players that remain active for a long time. However, the patent-buy-out mechanism possesses nice properties if bidders behave non-cooperatively, and thus it can be useful when collusive agreements can somehow be prevented – for example, if the mechanism is used quite rarely, the probability that the winning firm must acquire the patent is not negligible, and re-sale of the patent is prohibited.

> **Practical conclusion 3**
> The Kremer patent-buy-out mechanism must be used with caution, making sure that it is not employed frequently in the same industry, choosing a sufficiently large probability that the winning supplier must acquire the patent, and prohibiting re-sale of the patents.

Table 19.1 summarizes the effects of ex-ante and ex-post prize systems.

19.2.4. Research contests

Often the outcome of innovative activities is neither describable in advance nor verifiable ex post.[29] Because a minimal requirement for a prize system to be feasible is that the occurrence of the innovation is verifiable, in these circumstances the procurer must resort to other mechanisms to obtain innovative knowledge.

19.2.4.1. Contests are easy to implement

Research contests are informatively less demanding than both ex-ante and ex-post prizes, and thus often constitute a feasible option. In a research contest, the procurer sets both a prize and a time deadline, and pays the prize to whoever has made the largest progress when the deadline is reached. There is no need of ascertaining whether a prescribed target has been reached or not; all that matters is that the prize is awarded to a contestant at the conclusion of the research contest. The incentive to award the prize may be provided by reputational mechanisms, or else the procurer's obligation may be enforced by the courts. In any event, the court need not be called to decide whether the winner has been properly selected, since the procurer has little incentive to manipulate the outcome of the contest given that he must pay the prize to someone.[30]

The main difference between research contests and research prizes is that research contests end on a specified date, whereas an innovation race for a prize ends whenever the innovation is achieved. As a consequence, in a

---

[29] The longitude prize example illustrates that verifiability is often an issue: it took several decades, the construction of several prototypes and several replication tests to the watchmaker that won the longitude prize to actually receive his prize, because the prize-awarding commission was composed of astronomers that were looking more for new *knowledge* useful to establish longitude with precision, that being non-rival could be freely used by a large number of navigators, rather than for a hard to replicate and expansive object physically incorporating the solution to the longitude problem (in fact, such a knowledge did materialize later on, see the discussion in Scotchmer 2004).

[30] Taylor (1995, p. 973).

Table 19.1. Effects of *ex ante* and *ex post* prize systems

	Ex ante prizes	*Ex post* prizes	Results
Asymmetrically informed contractual parties	• Difficulty in choosing the 'correct' prize • *Ex ante* prizes are impractical	• Uncertainty over the value of the innovation • The procurer can set the prize quite discretionally	• *Ex post* prize is the only practicable prize system
Symmetrically informed contractual parties	• No need for information over the value of the innovation • With *ex ante* prizes and intellectual property it is easy to observe whether or not the procurer has kept its promises	• No need for information over the value of the innovation • The procurer has an incentive to renege on the award of a prize	• Government is systematically tempted to under-reward innovators • *Ex ante* prize system preferable

research contest the timing is fixed but the amount of innovative knowledge produced is variable, whereas in an innovation race the R&D output is fixed but the timing of innovation is variable.[31]

Because research contests are informatively parsimonious and easily implementable, they are used frequently both by private and public procurers. The prize can be a sum of money, a procurement contract, and so on. Over the years, contests have played a major role in the procurement of many innovations. One of the most famous research contests was sponsored in 1829 by the Manchester and Liverpool Railway to choose an engine for the first passenger service between the two cities, Liverpool and Manchester. Two different engines were proposed. One of them reached a speed record of 51.5 kilometres per hour but collapsed. So the railway paid to the other proposal a prize of £500. However, both the engines had impressive performances and this spawned an explosion of innovation in locomotives.[32] Relative performance evaluation systems for laboratory researchers that pay

---

[31] Under this respect, research prizes are similar to patent races. Although innovators have some latitude in determining when to apply for a patent, which they may be tempted to exploit strategically, such a latitude is limited by various legal rules and so for many practical purposes one can assume that intellectual property rights are awarded as soon as a pre-specified innovation is achieved.

[32] See Day (1971) and Fullerton and McAfee (1999).

yearly bonuses to the best performing research teams are other common forms of research contests.

19.2.4.2. Research versus Sport contests

Research contests are remarkably similar to sport contests which have been analysed in a large and burgeoning literature.[33] However, in a research contest the procurer is typically interested in maximizing the performance of the winning supplier, that is, the innovative knowledge supplied by losers duplicates that supplied by the winner and thus is useless to the procurer, whereas in sport contests more complex objectives seem appropriate, like maximizing the suppliers' average performance or guaranteeing that sport events are sufficiently levelled. These differences can have notable consequences on the optimal design of sport contests as compared to research contests, and mean that one must use caution in applying to research contests conclusions drawn from the rich experience that has been gained in the design of sport contests.

Designing a research contest requires several careful choices: How many suppliers should the procurer invite to participate in the contest? Should the prize be awarded entirely to the winner, or should it be divided amongst several suppliers (presumably, the best performers)? Should suppliers compete on equal footing, or should the procurer handicap the most able? Although there are no clear-cut answers to these questions, a few general principles emerge from the rich experience from sport contests and a rigorous economic analysis of these issues.

19.2.4.3. The optimal number of participants

In sport contests, the number of participants is often restricted. In the Olympic Games, only one team per country is admitted in team sports, and only three participants per country are admitted in individual sports. In most European countries, about twenty football teams are admitted to the national premier league. Less than two hundred cyclists participate in the Tour de France or the Giro d'Italia. Many similar examples readily come to mind; often, there are complicated rules to determine who should be invited to participate in such elite sport events.

Some of the reasons why participation in sport contests is restricted do not have an immediate counterpart in research contests. For example, participation in the Tour de France by two thousands cyclists would be

---

[33] See Smylianski (2002) for an excellent survey.

impractical or even dangerous, whereas in a research contest adding one participant hardly impedes the performance of the others. In sport contests, selecting a restricted number of ablest athletes guarantees that the game is more levelled than with free participation, but the procurer of a research contest is rarely interested in the levelness of the contest per se.

Other reasons to restrict participation, however, do extend to research contests. Consider a chrono race, where the performance of each athlete depends on his ability, effort and a random component, and where each participant is incompletely informed of the performance of his rivals while he is performing. In such a race, the marginal value of effort is the prize to the winner multiplied by the increase in the probability of winning the race associated with a unit increase in effort. Because the latter decreases with the number of participants, the incentive to exert effort will also decrease with the number of participants. As a consequence, if the procurer wants to maximize the best performance, he might benefit from restricting participation in the race to only the ablest athletes. By the same logic, in a research contest the incentive to invest of any one participant may decrease with the amount of research conducted by others. In this case, if the procurer wants to maximize the total amount of research (i.e. the expected quality of the winning innovation), he may want to limit the number of participants.[34]

However, two countervailing effects may undermine this restricted-participation result. First, imagine a research contest with two suppliers, 1 and 2, and consider the effect of supplier 3's entry into the contest, starting from the two-supplier equilibrium. If supplier 3 wins with positive probability, its entry will reduce the value of the investments made by suppliers 1 and 2. However, it is the marginal value, and not the total value of research effort that determines the best responses of suppliers 1 and 2, and the marginal value may well go up. This is most clear when each competitor can observe the progresses made by its rivals. Suppose that firm 3 would win by a small

---

[34] See Taylor (1995) and Fullerton and McAfee (1999). While Taylor shows that the optimal number of participants can be finite, Fullerton and McAfee arrive at the much stronger conclusion that entry into a research contest should be restricted to two participants. The explanation of these different results is that whereas Taylor implicitly assumes that firms are capacity constrained in their research activity (in his model, the research activity consists in making draws from a probability distribution, and firms can only make one draw per period), Fullerton and McAfee assume that each firm can conduct an arbitrarily large amount of research, with a constant marginal cost of research. Furthermore, Fullerton and McAfee assume that there is a fixed cost of conducting research, and limiting the number of participants in the contest prevents wasteful duplication of the fixed costs. The result that it is optimal to restrict participation to just two firms has also been found in the more structured framework analysed by Che and Gale (2003).

margin if firms 1 and 2 did not change their effort levels after 3's entry. In this case, probably suppliers 1 and 2 would be willing to exert more effort after 3's entry. If, however, supplier 3 would win by a large margin, this may well induce suppliers 1 and 2 to reduce their efforts. Likewise, in sport contests more intense competition can make rivals perform harder when they are neck-and-neck, whereas it can even induce laggards to completely stop investing if one contestant has a very large advantage over the others.[35]

Second, innovative ideas are widely distributed among individual suppliers and inventors,[36] implying that more effort exerted by any one firm may not compensate for the exclusion of another supplier from the contest. Also, restricting participation in a research contest risks eliminating very promising lines of research. As a matter of fact, research contests rarely involve substantial entry fees, as procurers frequently are concerned that there is enough competition in research. For example, the DoD has often subsidized the suppliers selected to participate in research contests in order to ensure their financial stability.[37]

Assuming that restricting participation is, nevertheless, desirable, the number of participants can be restricted by the introduction of an entry fee rather than by fiat. Using entry fees has the advantage of allowing the procurer to extract some (or even all) of the rents that otherwise would be obtained by the participants, but may result in excessive entry or, even worse, in entry by only one firm – if the procurer is not fully informed. To solve this problem, it is possible to run an entry competitive tendering procurement.[38] Like contests, competitive procurement has low informational requirements and, if properly designed, is likely to select the most efficient contestants. In addition, and like entry fees, they allow the procurer to collect some revenue.

19.2.4.4. The division of the prize

In a contest, should the prize be awarded entirely to the winner, or should it be divided between several contestants? In sport contests, the-winner-takes-all principle is the exception rather than the rule, although typically the size of the prize is rapidly decreasing in the rank order of the contestants. With

---

[35] Similarly, the patent race literature has shown that reaction functions can slope either upward or downward, depending on the specific assumptions made (compare Loury (1979) and Lee and Wilde (1980)).

[36] Menell and Scotchmer (2005).

[37] Che and Gale (2003).

[38] See Fullerton and McAfee (1999).

intellectual property, in contrast, only the first inventor has a right on the innovation.

There are two main reasons why in sport contests typically the winner does not take all. First, if the contestants' ability is the main determinant of their performances, rewarding only the winner will likely induce the less able athletes to exert little effort. This is not appropriate if the procurer sponsoring the contest wants to maximize aggregate effort. Second, in a multi-stage race the winner-takes-all principle may result in most of the effort being exerted in the first stages; once the rank order of the participants starts being clear, and laggards have little chances to overcome the leader, efforts may decline dramatically, especially if the leader can monitor the performance of the laggards.

> **Practical conclusion 4**
> In multi-stage research contests, it is important to ensure that there is effective competition even in later stages. This can be achieved by splitting the prize between the contestants.

19.2.4.5 Handicapping contestants

Strong chess players often concede a pawn, or even a rook, when they play against a weaker opponent. This makes the game more levelled and therefore more enjoyable to both players, who have stronger incentives to play carefully than if they compete on equal footing. The same principle holds true in research contests: if contestants are asymmetric, it is optimal to handicap the most efficient one.[39] The reason is again that contestants perform harder when they are neck-and-neck; if they differ in their ability, handicapping the most efficient contestants results in a more levelled race. Note that the procurer is not interested in levelness per se; rather, he wants suppliers to be neck-and-neck in order to elicit more effort. However, this instrument has to be used with much care: it is crucial not to handicap suppliers too much. One has to be sure that a more levelled competition is worthwhile despite the decrease in the average productivity of research it inevitably entails. Suppose, for example, that in the economy there were two firms like ACER and DELL competing with a large number of extremely backward competitors. Severely handicapping the most efficient contestants

---

[39] Che and Gale (2003).

to level the battle field might be highly detrimental to aggregate innovative performance.

Practical conclusion 5

When contestants differ in their ability, handicap the most efficient contestants in order to guarantee that the contest is more levelled if and only if the resulting level is not too low.

Box 19.1. Ex-ante prizes, ex-post prices, and research contests

Ex-ante prizes are posted in advance and can be claimed by the first to solve a well-defined problem, like proving Fermat's conjecture. Ex-ante prizes are impractical unless the invention society wants to procure is easily describable, like 'a vaccine against AIDS which is effective in at least 70 per cent of the population', and it is verifiable whether the invention has been achieved or not, for example, through monitored clinical tests. They differ from ex-post prizes in that the latter are granted discretionally as a reward for achievements that could not be foreseen in advance.

Ex-post prizes reward discoveries that may not even have been conceived of before they occurred to someone. If the occurrence of the innovation is verifiable ex-post, in principle the procurer could commit to offer ex-post prizes to successful innovators. In an ex-post framework, describing the innovation is no longer at issue, but the problem remains of guessing the value of the innovation and hence the appropriate prize.

Research contests are informatively less demanding than both ex-ante and ex-post prizes, and thus often constitute a feasible option. In a research contest, the procurer sets both a prize and a time deadline, and commits to pay the prize to whoever has made the largest progress when the deadline is reached. Thus, there is no need of ascertaining whether a prescribed innovation has been obtained or not; all that matters is that the pre-specified prize is awarded to one of the contestants at the conclusion of the research contest.

The main difference between research contests and research prizes is that research contests end on a specified date, whereas an innovation race ends whenever the innovation is achieved. As a consequence, in a research contest the amount of innovative knowledge produced is variable, whereas in an innovation race it is pre-specified.

19.3. Procuring innovative goods

We have already remarked that in a research contest the prize for the winner may be an amount of money, a procurement contract, the positive advertising associated with the mere fact of winning the contest and so on. When the prize is pre-specified ex ante, any benefit associated with winning the contest can be given a monetary evaluation; the sum total of these benefits then represents the prize to the winner.

However, when the winner of the research contest is rewarded through a procurement contract for the supply of the innovative good or service, the procurer has another instrument that can be used to improve upon the outcome of the contest, namely the price of the good. Imagine a two-stage competition, in which in the first-stage suppliers invest to obtain an innovative good of variable quality, and then in the second stage they bid for the right to sell the innovative good to a procurer. As compared to a simple research contest with a pre-specified prize there are two main differences. First, the prize is not specified in advance, but is determined as a result of the second-stage competitive bidding. Second, the highest quality innovator is not sure of getting the prize; the winner of the contest will instead be the supplier that bids the lowest price per unit of quality supplied.[40]

Since a recurrent theme of the preceding section was that allowing the procurer to set the prize ex-post leaves room for opportunistic behaviour, it may sound surprising that now the procurer does not want to commit to a pre-specified prize when commitment is possible. Note, however, that in the proposed mechanism the prize is the outcome of a competitive bidding, and thus it is not left to the procurer's discretion. This means

---

[40] In principle such competitive bidding-augmented research contests could be used even with monetary prizes: i.e., suppliers first invest in research and then bid the prize they ask for the innovative knowledge they have created. However, for the mechanism to work suppliers must disclose their innovative knowledge to the procurer, who could then have access to all of the knowledge by paying only the low prize asked by a low-performance supplier. This difficulty can be overcome if suppliers can somehow communicate to the procurer the quality of their research outcome without disclosing all of the knowledge. Typically, this is possible when production of the good requires some tacit knowledge that suppliers cannot or need not transmit to the procurer, in which case the procurer cannot directly use the innovative knowledge but must procure the innovative good from the contestants.

that there is no room for opportunistic behaviour on the part of the procurer.

It is important to note that this ability to separate between good and bad innovations is achieved at a cost: the competitive bidding inevitably reduces the prize contingent on winning the race, thereby reducing the benefits from investing in R&D. If R&D responds to incentives, this may lower the innovative effort of all suppliers participating in the race. For this reason, if the suppliers are homogeneous, competitive bidding-augmented research contests promote R&D less than research contests with the same pre-specified price. However, with heterogeneous suppliers they may be preferable despite the negative incentive effect on R&D expenditure.

Why can competitive bidding-augmented research contests be preferable to research contests with pre-specified prizes? There are at least three answers to this question.[41]

1. One advantage of competitive bidding is that it requires little information: when suppliers are symmetric, the procurer needs no information at all concerning supplier' costs to properly design the contest. In a standard research contest, in contrast, the procurer needs some information on the technology of research to optimally determine the prize. (When suppliers differ in their ability, and it is desirable to handicap the most efficient contestants, some information about firms' ability is nevertheless required.)

2. With heterogeneous suppliers, the efficiency gap between the most efficient contestant and the second most efficient contestant can be so large that the outcome of the contest is largely independent of research efforts, which reduces the incentives to invest of all suppliers. Letting less efficient suppliers bid for a lower price in case they produce a low-quality innovation enhances the competitive pressure on the efficient firm, and makes the contest more similar to a neck-and-neck race. (This is also the intuitive reason why, with heterogeneous firms, the most efficient firms should be handicapped.)

3. Competitive bidding-augmented research contests allow one to achieve a better alignment of the social and private incentives to invest in the innovative activity.

---

[41] See Che and Gale (2003) and Fullerton et al. (2002).

Let us summarize our results in Table 19.2 and in the following Practical conclusion.

Practical conclusion 6

When suppliers can communicate to the procurer the quality of their research outcome without disclosing all of the innovative knowledge, it is desirable to employ competitive bidding-augmented research contest in which suppliers first invest in research, and then bid a price for the innovative good that the procurer wants to procure.

19.4. Using procurement to stimulate innovation

Procurement design can have indirect effects on innovative activity by enlarging the market for new goods, by facilitating the adoption of new standards,[42] or by changing the market structure so as to make it more conducive to faster innovation. In this section we analyse these more indirect ways in which procurement can stimulate innovation.

19.4.1. Procurement and standards setting

Many innovative goods and services exhibit network effects: each user's value increases when the number of other users increases as well. Sometimes, these effects result from 'physical' networks, such as a telephone network (the value of a phone is greater the greater number of people I can call). In most cases, however, we are faced with 'virtual network' effects. For example, the more users buy the Windows operating system, the more complementary products and services (e.g., software) will be available for Windows users.

Strong network effects can potentially lead to market failures that public procurement can help alleviate.[43] Two particularly important forms of market failure in markets for innovative goods that exhibit network effects are excess inertia and inefficient lock-in. Excess inertia refers to the situation when a new, superior technology fails to displace an older, inferior one due

---

[42] Chapter 3 discusses how centralized procurement is able to magnify network effects and the adoption of common standards.

[43] A few economics scholars, however, passionately disagree with such a statement. See for example Liebowitz and Margolis (1990).

Table 19.2. Competitive bidding-augmented research contest vs. standard research contest

	Competitive bidding-augmented research contest	Standard research contest (Pre-specified prize)	Results
Asymmetrically informed contractual parties	• Little information needed	• The procurer needs much more information on the technology of research to optimally determine the prize	• Competitive bidding-augmented research contest reduces the effect of asymmetric information • Competitive bidding-augmented research contest is preferable
Symmetrically informed contractual parties	• No need for information concerning suppliers' costs to properly design the contest • Competitive bidding-augmented research contests discourage research activity	• No need for information concerning suppliers' costs to properly design the contest	Standard research contest is preferable
Heterogeneous bidders	• Possibility of very large efficiency gaps among suppliers • Competitive bidding-augmented research contest makes the contest more similar to a neck-to-neck race	• Possibility of very large efficiency gap among suppliers • The incentives to invest of all suppliers are reduced	• In a standard research contest, the outcome from the contest is largely independent of research efforts, whereas in competitive bidding-augmented research

	- Better alignment of the social and private incentives to invest in the innovative activity	
Homogenous suppliers	- In case of asymmetrically informed contractual parties, the competitive bidding-augmented research contest reduces the effect of asymmetric information When the contractual parties are symmetrically informed, the competitive bidding-augmented research contest reduces suppliers' innovative activity	- In case of asymmetrically informed contractual parties, the procurer needs some information on the technology of research to optimally determine the prize
		- contest suppliers compete neck-to-neck - Competitive bidding-augmented research contest is preferable - Standard research contest is preferable

to network effects. Inefficient lock-in refers to the situation when market dynamics lead to the adoption of an inferior version of a new technology or standard.

The mechanism behind excess inertia is that users of the old technology or standard fear that they will be among the few to switch to the new one. If network effects are very strong, a new technology with few followers is worse than an old one with a good solid installed base, especially when there are costs in switching to a new technology or standard. Historical examples of excess inertia include the aborted attempt at switching from AM to FM radio broadcasting in the 1950s; and the failed launch of quadraphonic sound technology in the 1970s.

Inefficient lock-in typically results from the self-reinforcing (or 'snow ball') dynamics of network effects. A classic example is that of video-cassette recorders (VCRs). Many industry experts agree that Sony's Betamax system was superior to JVC's VHS (in fact, until the advent of digital recording technology, Betamax remained the technology of choice for TV professionals). However, the VHS standard found itself on the right side of the wave when, during the 1980s, video rental stores and consumers needed to coordinate on one standard. Once most video stores were carrying mostly VHS tapes, even users who would otherwise prefer the Betamax system caved it and opted for the JVC-sponsored standard.

Whenever there is a market failure, there is a potential for welfare-improving public policy intervention. In the context of network effects, this can take on various forms. Governments can mandate a standard or a technology. For example, several governments have decreed deadlines for switching to digital television broadcasting. Alternatively, governments may subsidize investments in a particular standard or technology. In this section, we are particularly interested in public policy through procurement.

When public administrations purchase sizeable amounts of innovative goods and services, choosing a new technology or choosing a particular version/standard of a new technology may have significant effects in the eventual outcome of the technology adoption process.

The adoption of a new technology by the public sector as a whole may also stimulate private demand through the reduction of the risk of isolation. More generally, by adopting new technologies the public sector can play a key role in coordinating the demand and avoiding lock-in. By increasing the installed base of the good that it purchases, the public sector's action increases the value of that good, thus inducing greater adoption by other users. Moreover, a choice made by such a large agent as a government agency may act as an important focal point of coordination whenever there are several options available.

There are a variety of examples where government procurement had an influence in the direction of the standard setting processes. Nuclear power reactors is one such example. By the late 1950s, there were about a dozen relevant alternative technologies. According to Cowan (1990), 'light water is considered inferior to other technologies, yet it [currently] dominates the market for nuclear reactors'. The reason for this inefficient lock-in can be traced back to a major procurement effort by the US Navy in the 1950s.

Wide body aircraft provides an instance of an indirect network industry. An airline (the typical buyer) has an incentive to buy the same type of aircraft as other buyers. Otherwise, maintenance and other complementary services may become prohibitively costly. During the mid 1970s, the McDonnell Douglas DC-10 was in serious danger of being taken over by the Boeing 747 (and, to some extent, the Lockheed 1011). However, when the US Air Force ordered sixty units of the KC-10 (the military version of the DC-10), the programme was given a new life and was able to compete for a few more years.[44]

A final example is given by computer operating systems, which, as shown above, are subject to strong 'virtual network' effects. The Brazilian government has recently decided to expand the use of open source software in the public sector. In September 2004, an agreement with IBM led to the establishment of a knowledge and technology centre to promote and develop open source and GNU/Linux solutions in Brazil. Brazil is just the latest of a long list of government agencies that are actively promoting GNU/Linux through their procurement decisions. Others include, in the United States, the Air Force, the Federal Aviation Administration, the Postal Service, and the Departments of Defense, Agriculture and Energy, in Europe, the European Commission, various government offices in Germany, and France's Ministries of Culture, Defense and Education, and China's Post Office.[45]

---

[44] Eventually, a series of crashes considerably reduced public confidence in the DC-10, which was discontinued in 1980. In retrospect, the DC-10 panic was blown out of proportion. By the end of the century, the statistics on the rate of hull losses per million departures show 1.90 for the 747 (early models); 0.77 for the L-1011; and 2.57 for the DC-10 (see *The Wall Street Journal*, 19 September 2000, p. A18). Though certainly the highest among the three, the DC-10 number hardly justifies the public's reaction.

[45] *Sources:* http://www.ZDNet.com on 04/06/2002; http://www.usatoday.com on 30/05/2002.

In sum, the public sector is likely to be a large buyer in whatever market it establishes a procurement process.[46] And to that extent its choice of supplier, in particular its choice of standard, is bound to have an effect on market outcomes. What guidelines should the public sector follow to account for this potential influence?

Cabral and Kretschmer[47] analyse the situation when two different versions of a given technology battle for market dominance – what some refer to as 'standards competition' or 'standards war'. Two polar cases are considered. At one extreme, the life cycle of the innovative standard is expected to be relatively long. This implies that the cost of a mistake in the standard-selection process is likely to be very high. It follows that a long experimentation phase is optimal, as the higher experimentation costs are outweighed by the reduced likelihood of selecting a worse standard. The study refers to this as the 'patient planner' case and show that the best policy is to support the lagging technology (a bit like what the US Force did in the widebody aircraft race during the 1970s and many governments are currently doing in the operating systems race).

At the opposite extreme, when the life cycle of the innovative standard/technology is expected to be short, the costs of a protracted standards war are not justified by the benefits of a better selection. This is the 'impatient planner' case. The optimal policy is then to intervene early and in support of the already leading standard.

This analysis ignores the issue of investment in technology improvement: the underlying assumption was that two technology designs are available and that the goal is to standardize on the optimal one. However, many (most?) situations present us with evolving technologies. The goal is then not only to select an appropriate technology but also to create incentives for investment in its improvement. If the potential for technology improvement is significant enough, then there may be benefits from delaying the standardization process.[48] The intuition, in broad strokes, is that early standardization may lead to a sort of 'tragedy of the commons', whereby the key players have lower incentives to invest in technology improvement than they would if a standards war were still being waged.

---

[46] For more examples, see Cabral and Kretschmer (2004).
[47] See Cabral and 3alant (2006).
[48] See Cabral and Kretshmer (2004).

Practical conclusion 7
- If the life cycle of the innovative standard is expected to be relatively long and the potential for technology improvement is significant enough, favour a long experimentation phase by supporting lagging technologies.
- Otherwise, intervene early and in support of the already leading standard.

19.4.2. Procurement, competition and innovation

Procurement can be designed in such a way as to create more or less competition among potential suppliers. For example, contracts can be awarded through negotiations, beauty contests, or many different types of competitive mechanisms and tendering processes. The degree of competition induced by the chosen procurement design may affect suppliers' incentives to invest in R&D and innovate.

The relationship between the degree of competition in a market and the firms' incentive to innovate is a complex issue. Traditional economic analysis suggests that there exists a positive correlation between innovation and market power: tougher competition erodes the innovator's prospective monopoly rents, and is therefore detrimental to his incentives to invest in research for innovation.[49]

However, in oligopolistic industries the relation between competition and incentives to innovate is generally non-monotone. Although diverse results have been found in the literature, based on different assumptions on the nature of technical progress (tournament or non-tournament) and on who conducts the research (incumbents or outside firms), two robust effects emerge. On the one hand, almost any definition of competition involves the idea that more intense competition reduces the equilibrium price, thus exerting downward pressure on the innovator's prospective rents and incentives to invest. On the other hand, in more highly competitive industries the technological leader has a larger market share, implying that competition tends to be good for innovation. The market share effect may or may not outweigh the negative effect of more intense competition on the equilibrium price.

---

[49] See the classical contributions of Schumpeter (1942). This argument is not uncontested though. See e.g., Arrow (1962).

To get a flavour of the subtle issues involved, consider one commonly accepted measure of the degree of competition, namely the number of incumbent firms. An increase in the number of competitors for a given total market size, will tend to:[50]

- Decrease price and individual firm output. This effect will tend to reduce R&D effort because a unit cost reduction will benefit a diminished output (size effect).
- Increase the amount of business a firm can steal from competitors through cost saving innovation (due to the elasticity effect). This increase competition effect will tend instead to increase R&D effort, because a unit reduction in costs will allow the firm to increase its output more than with weak competition.

The existence of opposing effects means that the overall impact of more intense competition on the incentive to innovate is generally ambiguous, perhaps making the relationship between the intensity of competition and innovation non-monotone. Some recent studies find that the relationship between competition and innovation has, indeed, an inverted-U shape: ceteris paribus, the market share effect (whereby competition stimulates innovation) tends to dominate at lower levels of competition, whereas the 'Schumpeterian' effect (competition erodes expected profits from the innovation hence the incentives to invest in R&D) tends to dominate at high levels of competition.[51] When procurement can be designed to induce more or less competition among suppliers, in light of the discussion above, we can conclude that:

Practical conclusion 8
- If in the past procurement was not very competitive, fostering competition in procurement tends to increase suppliers' innovation.
- If procurement is already highly competitive, and the leading supplier has a strong advantage on followers, a further increase in competition may reduce suppliers' incentives to innovate.

---

[50] See e.g., Vives (2004). For a given total market size, competition - in terms of a larger number of competitors – affects the effective market of a firm that is: its residual demand (a 'level' or 'size' effect) and the elasticity of the residual demand faced by the firm (an 'elasticity' effect).

[51] See for instance Aghion et al. (2005). However, consistently with Schumpeter (1942), Aiginger and Falk (2005) find that R&D intensity is higher where the competition is lower.

19.4.3. Procurement and the demand for innovative goods

The larger the market for an innovative good, the stronger the incentive to invest in it. Recent empirical research on the effect of market size on drug entry and pharmaceutical innovation clearly shows that there is a strong response in terms of emergence of innovative drugs to market size.[52] For example, only a handful of the 1,400 new drugs approved over the last forty years target so-called 'tropical' diseases like malaria or tuberculosis, although such diseases are responsible for the death of millions of people every year. [53]

By affecting the size of the market, procurement design can therefore significantly impact the development of innovative products. Centralized procurement of large bundled contracts for innovative products or services provide the prospect of a sufficiently large and certain demand to recover large investments in R&D. Moreover, the larger the demand a producer can satisfy with his innovation, the more intensively economies of scale can be exploited (this effect relates to the industry cost structure).[54] These effects suggest that split-award procurement contracts can be bad for innovation.

However, when the research contest is bundled with a procurement contract for the supply of the innovative good, a large bundled contract makes it harder for small firms to participate in the contest. This is unfortunate as ideas tend to be widely distributed among individual firms, and important innovations are often achieved by small and medium enterprises (SMEs) and start-ups. When SMEs conduct most of the research, large bundles make the participation of SMEs in the research contest more difficult and so may in fact reduce overall innovation. Using large bundled contracts where the winner takes all, gives large, mature incumbents a competitive advantage and makes entry by small innovative firms more difficult. In the long run, it may also induce excessive *exit* from the market. Apart from the effect on competition (dealt with in Chapters 7 and 17 of this volume), this may:

- Reduce the 'diversity' of research paths thereby lowering the aggregate probability of success. A well-diversified research portfolio is important,

[52] Linn and Acemoglu (2004), for example, find that a 1% increase in potential market for a drug category leads to a 6% increase in the total number of drugs entering the US market; that a 1% increase in potential market size leads to approximately a 4% increase in the entry of new non-generic drugs; and that a 1% increase in potential market size is associated with a 4–6% increases in the entry of new molecular products.

[53] Kremer's proposal of creating a market for vaccines is based on the recognition that market size matters for innovation, and public policy can contribute to increasing the size of the market for innovative goods.

[54] This is one of the reasons behind the European project of a common market.

as is also recognized by venture capitals who often finance several start-ups working on similar projects, in order to maintain high technological variety and improve their selection of the best one.[55]

- Reduce the competitive pressure on the incumbent(s), which may induce him to rest on the laurels of his past success, and cut the investments for future innovation.
- Increase the distance between the technological leader and the follower. This reduces 'neck-and-neck' competition, which is bad for innovation, as both the laggard's reward to catching up with the technological leader and the latter's incentive to escape competition may fall.

These problems are exacerbated when firm size or experience are among the criteria of admission to procurement contests, as is often the case for a variety of reasons.

Licensing agreements can provide a solution to this problem. In principle, an innovator that does not participate in a procurement contest can nevertheless have an incentive to innovate if he can license the innovation to one or all of the participating firms. If the market for licences was perfect, the incentive to innovate would be independent of procurement design. However, a variety of transaction costs impede licensing agreements. To begin with, innovative technological knowledge can be difficult to codify and transmit to others. In addition, royalty licensing is possible only if the output is verifiable; when individual output is not verifiable, only fixed-fee licensing is feasible, but fixed-fee licensing is profitable only if the size of innovations is sufficiently small. Moreover, incomplete information over the size of the innovation can lead parties to introduce inefficient terms in the licensing agreement. These transaction costs may most likely result in an equilibrium outcome in which licensing does not allow the innovator to appropriate the value of his innovation fully. In these circumstances, procurement design matters.

When licensing agreements are difficult to reach, the sponsor may therefore want to split supply in smaller lots in order to allow small innovative firms to participate, even if this may dilute the incentive to innovate. The same outcome can be achieved through co-sourcing, dual-sourcing etc. Also, the procurer may want to delay the selection of the

---

[55] Venture capitalists typically finance pools of similar R&D-intensive projects precisely to maintain sufficient 'technological diversity', being then careful to implement cross-fertilization of ideas transferring useful knowledge from one project to the other (See Gompers and Lerner, 1999). Analogously, Allen and Gale (1999) forcefully argue that the main advantage of a large stock market in terms of R&D project financing is the diversity of ideas among the many independent investors.

winner to preserve diversity and maintain firms in a neck-to-neck competitive situation.

Another strategy that has been adopted to increase the share of R&D government contracts awarded to SMEs consists in reserving for them a part of these contracts. In 2001, for instance, the English Department of Trade and Industry launched a programme called Small Business Research Initiative (SBRI). The objective of the programme was to purchase at least 2.5 per cent; of their R&D from SMEs by 2004/05. Up to now over 230 companies have registered and received information about contracts suited to their capabilities.

However, this strategy reduces the size of the market captured by the winner, and therefore dilutes the incentives to innovate. The trade-off is therefore between admitting small innovative firm participation, having more than one contractor and technology variety in use, and enhanced competition, all of which may require multiple smaller lots; and the lower economies of scale exploited, and larger cost duplication incurred with small lots, which push to bundle supply (since production is or may be split among more firms).

The optimal size of supply contracts and number of contractors selected are therefore difficult to choose, as they depend on several economic variables which are hard to estimate (see Chapter 7). Given our limited knowledge of the strength of the various forces at play, one way out is to let competing firms endogenously determine the optimal demand size. This can be achieved by splitting competitive procurements in many small lots, but allowing for 'package bidding'. Package bidding means that bidders can condition their bids on the number, and possibly the type, of the lots awarded (Chapter 8 offers an overview of package bidding in procurement). The small size of lots allows small and perhaps more innovative firms to participate in the contest, but large suppliers can exploit economies of scale in R&D and production if these are substantial. Again, competitive tendering is an informatively parsimonious mechanism in that it allows the procurer to rely on the information held by suppliers to achieve the efficient solution.

Practical conclusion 9

When procuring innovation, if the relative importance of having small diverse innovators versus exploiting scale economies in R&D is not clear, unbundle total supply in more and smaller lots, and allow for package bidding.

19.4.4. Other procurement practices that stimulate innovation

So far, we have discussed how to stimulate innovation and R&D through different procurement tools. In this paragraph we describe some procurement initiatives promoted by governments or purchasing agencies in order to stimulate innovation. Procurement experiences and best practices taken into consideration show that some of the most important European and American centralized procurement units share common guidelines in order to promote innovation and stimulate suppliers in investing in R&D.

19.4.4.1. Involvement of suppliers in the procurement process

Suppliers have sometimes been involved at the beginning of the procurement process in order to facilitate creativity through the interaction between tendering designers and suppliers, to define shape requirements, provide feedback on feasibility and affordability, and gear them up to be able to respond to future procurements.[56] The UK Department of Trade and Industry (DTI) has applied this practice in the construction industry. The DTI and the National Health Service (NHS) have implemented the Pro-Cure21, a healthcare facilities construction project. The objective of Pro-Cure21 is to encourage a long-run cooperation between procurer and constructors in order to match users' needs. The programme aims at improving quality and safety, reducing costs and delivery date.

The new EU Directive (2004) on the procurement of goods and services introduces a new procurement procedure called 'competitive dialogue', to be used for public contracts considered 'particularly complex'. Thanks to this procedure the public authority can dialogue with pre-qualified tenderers for setting up *the* solution (which can be a combination of solutions). The aim of the dialogue shall be to identify and define the means best suited to satisfying the authority needs. They may discuss all aspects of the contract with the chosen candidates during this dialogue. Contracting authorities may not reveal to the other participants solutions proposed or other confidential information communicated by a candidate participating in the dialogue without his/her agreement. Finally, there is a tendering process limited to at least three participants without further negotiation based on the requirements issued from the dialogue

---

[56] See EU Expert Group (2005).

19.4.4.2. Requesting 'functionalities' rather than pre-specified solutions

Output or outcome specifications should be well constructed in order to stimulate suppliers in proposing innovative solutions. A well-defined outcome can go a long way towards challenging suppliers to generate ideas. A well-constructed output specification identifies the outputs from, rather than the inputs to, a requirement. An outcome specification takes this one step further and only specifies the end result to be achieved. It is equivalent to specifying the problem and inviting proposed solutions.

In allowing suppliers freedom to submit innovative bids, procurers should specify compliance with standards where appropriate, for example to ensure compatibility.[57] In order to stimulate innovative solutions (process, integration, production, or delivery), requirements as well as evaluation criteria have to be based on a set of functionalities that the contractor must provide, regardless of the technology used to implement them (making intelligent use of standards).

Of course a good management of the tendering process must ensure suppliers sufficient time and opportunity to develop innovative proposals. Often, tenders have to be submitted in a very short time, and this does not allow suppliers to find innovative solutions. The duration of the procurement process should be fine-tuned with the role played by innovative solutions.

19.5. Other effects of large buyers on innovation

When the amount of innovative goods needed by a big procurer is large, as in the case of repeated government procurement or big firms' procurement, it can have important indirect effects on the markets of the inputs needed for the R&D activities: it can impact the wages of scientists and technicians as well as other specialized knowledge workers, and, by inducing intersector reallocations of labour and changes in the educational choices of young students, it can affect the flow of new skilled workers in the district, industry, or economy at large. In this section we draw on theoretical and empirical analyses on innovation and growth to derive practical recommendations with a more macroscopic and long-term vision

---

[57] The experience of Consip shows that even the procurement of mature technological products may promote firms' investments in R&D. See also EU Expert Group (2005).

than in most of the chapter. There are several similarities between the larger buyers in the economy, and the distinction between 'public' and 'private' is often semantics, though in order to facilitate the reader, we will keep the corresponding practical conclusions formally separated in two different sections – 19.5.1 on public procurement and 19.5.2 on private procurement.[58]

19.5.1. Public procurement and innovation

Firms invest in R&D and innovation as long as it is profitable to do it. Given the probability of innovating per unit R&D investment and the cost of the R&D inputs, the expected value of such profits are the main driving forces of innovative activity. Since government expenditure can affect profits in a massive way, it has the potential to indirectly affect the total amount of private R&D expenditure at the macroeconomic level as well as its direction by merely changing the amount of public procurement and the sectors in which it is directed.

In some cases, the innovative sectors can easily raise capital from private investors (stock markets, banks, venture capitalists, etc.) to finance R&D expenditure. In other cases, firms find it difficult to get money from external sources and need to rely on internally generated funds (cash flows). To evaluate the effect of public procurement on R&D it is important to distinguish between these two cases: financially unconstrained and financially constrained R&D firms. In industries where innovative firms are severely financially constrained, R&D investments may not respond positively to the incentive of higher future profits, because of the difficulty in increasing internal funds, though of course they will negatively react to the expectation of lower future profits. Instead, their R&D normally reacts positively to an increase in current profits, because it immediately allows more internally generated funding.

Conversely, in industries where innovative firms are not financially constrained, R&D investments will respond positively to the prospect of higher future profits, because they do not need to increase internal funds, and they will negatively react to the expectation of lower future profits.

---

[58] Those interested in the efficient management of big firm procurement will find it useful, after glancing at section 19.5.2, to read section 19.5.1 for a better understanding of the logic underlying the practical conclusions appearing in section 19.5.2.

Instead, their R&D normally does not react at all to an increase in current profits.

Notice that, by increasing current profits through public procurement, the government would support the innovative activity of the firms ('incumbents') that are already manufacturing the current version of the good, and therefore the firms that are least interested in inventing a better version of it. While the incumbents are less motivated to cannibalize their products, the pure R&D firms ('outsiders') are the most interested in investing in drastic improvements of the existing products. However, in the presence of credit market imperfection, little can be done to help outsiders enter the market through public procurement.

Since the aggregation of public expenditure often impacts a relevant size of the market for the innovative goods, it can have a big impact on the profits of the innovative firms. Since profits are the main signal for R&D expenditure, public procurement indirectly affects the demand for R&D inputs, such as the highly skilled workers. Therefore, it may be the case that an increase in profits, by raising the demand for the R&D inputs, has an immediate major impact of the R&D input prices, while leaving R&D employment almost unchanged. This happens because increasing the supply of skilled workers takes time: years of college education and on the job learning, months of re-training by skilled workers specialized in different sectors, etc. Hence the supply of R&D workers is not elastic, if there are few unemployed skilled workers in the same sector or if it is difficult to attract skilled workers from other sectors, as often happens during economic booms. In such cases, it may not pay to try to stimulate R&D through procurement, unless the government accepts the initially higher wages as a signal for the production of future R&D inputs, for example by incentivizing the educational choices of future cohorts of college students.

We can summarize the discussion so far:

Practical conclusion 10

- To stimulate R&D and innovation in financially constrained sectors the government should increase the current cash flows of innovative firms, by buying more at higher prices.
- To stimulate R&D and innovation in sectors that easily raise external capital the government should commit to a policy that increases innovative firms' future expected profits. For example, by promising to buy future innovative goods more and at higher prices.

- Government expenditure should increase expected profits in sectors in which the supply of the R&D inputs is more elastic and reduce them where they are less elastic.
- Public procurement should increase expected profits in innovative sectors during recessions or, more generally, when there is excess capacity of R&D inputs (e.g., human capital).

In many cases, the ability of buyers to understand what new product is best for them is limited and the information about product qualities tends to disseminate too slowly. The decision by firms to invest in innovative activities becomes less motivated in markets in which the buyers do not respond quickly to the introduction of new goods, but instead keep demanding obsolete products for a while, due to habits, brand loyalty and imperfect knowledge. Besides aggregating demand, public procurement can also aggregate the search efforts of several single buyers, thereby allowing them to save on unit search costs and to promptly single out the best available products. More responsive public demand rewards the firms who innovate more and immediately penalizes laggards, thereby inducing more R&D effort. Such a policy would stimulate perpetual innovative efforts by firms in order to win future profitable opportunities and not to lose current profits.

It is often the case that, with sequential innovation, in some sectors the opportunities to innovate are becoming lower and lower. In fact, R&D difficulty tends to increase as a result of the previous innovative efforts by firms: the easiest ideas are normally invented first, and there is a progressive fishing-out of the remaining good ideas in some of the mature sectors. Despite more costly future innovations, firms may feel encouraged to invest in R&D anyway by the expectation that in case of success their next innovation would be subject to lower obsolescence. As a consequence, the private firm's time horizon being quite limited, the private R&D investment decisions fail to account for the increased complexity of future R&D generated by their current R&D. Therefore, it may be better to discourage R&D in those sectors and to stimulate the reallocation of R&D inputs into other more promising sectors in which complexity is increasing less intensely. Hence, we have reached the following:

Practical conclusion 11

- Government procurement should make prices and quantities demanded responsive to quality ranking modifications: top quality products should be guaranteed immediate

profits whereas for obsolete goods the public buyer should bargain for very competitive (zero profit) prices.
- Government expenditure should reduce expected profits in sectors in which the future innovative prospects are low and re-direct R&D towards the more technologically under-exploited sectors.

19.5.2 Large firms

In several industries there are big firms endowed with some degree of monopsonistic power vis-à-vis a large number of small potentially innovative suppliers. Each big firm may be interested in spurring the innovative activity of its suppliers as well as in inducing the acquisition of specialized skills by new workers entering their sector. Viewed in this light, as big procurers, they share some similarity with governments in national and international environments. They share with governments a good bargaining power in the procurement of its inputs, a macroscopic vision of their whole industry, and intertemporal considerations. With this in mind, the large firm might develop a reputation to use its bargaining power selectively in order to stimulate innovation by the multitude of its exclusive suppliers as well as to encourage the continual renovation and extension of the supply of human capital to its innovative suppliers.

Therefore the previous practical conclusions can easily be re-interpreted in this context, by replacing the word 'government' with 'big firms' and other obvious modifications. For example, big firms should try not to use their bargaining power to slash the profits of financially constrained but potentially innovative suppliers: this would depress their formal and informal R&D expenditures and therefore restrict their future opportunities to acquire highly innovative inputs (components, research tools, etc.) from their exclusive suppliers, thereby weakening the future competitive advantage of the big firms themselves and compromising their primacy.

Similarly, during recessions big firms should commit to buy more generously high technology inputs, because current R&D expenditure by potentially innovative suppliers would increase in real terms and not only get inflated by higher costs. Notice that, with efficient capital markets – in which suppliers are not financially constrained – such counter-cyclical commitment does not necessarily imply counter-cyclical expenditure: it is very likely that by the time the innovative inputs are finally introduced the economy would be recovering from the recession, if not booming, with excellent results for the big firm that encourage its exclusive suppliers' R&D.

Hence we can conclude that:

Practical conclusion 12

- To stimulate R&D and innovation in financially constrained input sectors a big firm should safeguard the current cash flows of its innovative suppliers, by accepting buying more at generous prices.
- To stimulate R&D and innovation in sectors that easily raise external capital the large firm should commit to a policy that increases innovative firms' future expected profits. For example, by promising to buy future innovative goods more and at higher prices.
- Large firm's procurement should increase expected profits in the input sectors in which the supply of the R&D inputs is more elastic and reduce them where they are less elastic.
- Large firm's procurement should increase expected profits in innovative sectors during recessions or, more generally, when there is enough excess capacity of R&D inputs (e.g. human capital).

Also, the large firms should react promptly to quality improvements in their input markets, by penalizing laggard suppliers to the advantage of the most innovative ones. However, in this case, the buyer should also be concerned with the survival – or at least the prompt potential entry – of enough supplier R&D firms, in order not to get captured by a too small number of exclusive suppliers.

Finally, large firms should not only monitor the quality of the existing inputs in order to buy the best ones at generous enough prices, but they should also consider the innovative prospects of each category of inputs. If for some inputs further innovation is becoming increasingly difficult at an abnormal pace, the firm should reconsider its input–output mix in order to try to spur its exclusive suppliers' investment in more easily improvable input categories.

To summarize:

Practical conclusion 13

- Large firm's procurement should make prices and quantities demanded responsive to quality ranking modifications: top quality suppliers should be guaranteed immediate profits whereas for obsolete goods the big buyer should bargain for very competitive (zero profit) prices.

- Large firm's procurement should reduce expected profits in sectors in which the future innovative prospects are low and re-direct R&D towards the more technologically under-exploited sectors.

19.6. Innovation and risk management in procurement

As discussed in detail in Chapter 13, risk management is an important component of successful procurement. The supply chain may break down if a contractor interrupts supply, say, because he is in financial troubles, hence – in normal situations – good procurement should select more reliable suppliers/offers and screen out more unreliable/risky ones.

When stimulating innovative activity is a concern, management of procurement risk remains important, but must be implemented rather differently. According to Rosemberg, "The essential feature of technological innovation is that is an activity that is fraught with many uncertainties. This uncertainty, by which we mean an inability to predict the outcome of the search process, or to predetermine the most efficient path to some particular goal, has a very important implication: the activity cannot be planned" (Rosemberg 1994). In particular, there are three policy issues. First, because the probability of failure is higher and much harder to evaluate for more innovative projects, to stimulate innovation more risk must be taken. There is, therefore, a trade-off between innovation and the risk of selecting bad suppliers: more innovation against less safe procurement. In addition, the risk management techniques discussed in Chapter 13 may have to be adapted to cope with the need of providing incentives for innovative activity.

Second, the uncertainty surrounding innovative activity may be resolved only at late stages in a multi-stage research contest. This means that there is a trade-off between selecting the winner at an early stage to save research costs and waiting for more uncertainty to be resolved, much as discussed in section 19.4 for standard setting activity.

Third, the market may be biased in favour or against risky research projects. Because of the 'winner-takes-all' nature of innovation races, the market may induce a research strategy that is too risky from the social point of view. In the procurement context, this means that contestants may choose research strategies that are more risky than those preferred by the buyer.

Among the instruments used for managing risky bids in public procurement, discussed in more detail in Chapter 13, there are screening 'Abnormally Low Offers', screening firms' financial health, and choosing 'less competitive' scoring rules to leave more resources to contractors and reduce the risk of cost overruns, bankruptcy, and so on. Let us discus them in turn.

19.6.1. Handling 'Abnormally Low Offers' (ALO)

A bidder that offers a price below a certain cut-off level, a percentage of the average offered price, may be asked to prove that the bid is not unrealistic. For example, in many European countries information is requested when the offer is below the 10–15% of the arithmetical average of offered prices.[59] However, when procuring highly innovative products, it is easier to receive highly heterogeneous offers, and the most effective innovations are likely to be those that offer the desired outcome at the lowest cost. It may be hard though to demonstrate how innovative, never implemented technologies are likely to deliver the estimated low cost. For this reason, a more innovative and competitive offer is more likely to be considered ALO. Hence, screening out ALO, that is not awarding procurement contracts to the lowest priced offer, might screen out precisely the more innovative (and risky) firms!

19.6.2. Scoring rules

In order to soften competition on price, which may aggravate indebted contractors' likelihood of going bankrupt, scoring rules are sometimes adopted that do not reward contracts to the best offer – but to offers closer to the average. For example, among the scoring rules applied around the world are:

- The winning offer is the closest to the arithmetic average of all submitted offers.

---

[59] In Italy details relating to components of the tender that are determined to be significant are requested when an offer presents a discount lower than 20% of the arithmetical mean of the all discounts considered valid (Art. 25, D. Lgs. 157/95). BESCHA (the German Federal Procurement Agency) follows a rule of thumb that a more than 20% deviation from the second best price demands an explanation of the price made from the first bidder. The Turkish Public Procurement Authority requires explanations about an offer when it is below a certain complex value called 'Boundary value' (an offer is considered abnormally low if the offer is below of a defined Boundary value obtained by multiplying a certain value 'K' by the 'Estimated cost' of the contract. To have the 'K' value, the procurement agency calculates the ratio between the arithmetical mean of the tenders (tenders 120% above or 40% below of the 'estimated cost' are not taken into account) and the 'Estimated cost'. To any value of this ratio between 1.2 and 0.4 there is a correspondent 'K' value.

- The winning offer is the closest to the average among those below the average.

Again, these methods incorporate a potential bias against innovation, apart from increasing the cost of procurement. Not to award contracts to the lowest priced offer might screen out precisely the more innovative (and risky) firms! The first type, this 'Average Price Competitive Procurement' is obviously the worst one: it eliminates all competition since each participant chooses its offer to be closer to the expected average. The winner is practically randomly selected. This is the opposite of what competitive procurement is constructed for: discriminating among efficient and inefficient suppliers. The second type is a bit 'less bad', but the interdependence among bids opens the door to incorrect bidding and possible manipulations (see Chapters 12 and 13 about the drawbacks of these scoring rules).

19.6.3. Screening suppliers through insurance schemes

The best way to avoid unsustainable offers, according to Chapter 13, is to use insurance schemes that screen suppliers, discriminating among firms depending on their financial condition and ability to perform the project. There are two main instruments usually applied to face this problem:

- Surety bonds: The winning contractors must have a surety bond to proceed with supply, but she can acquire it after winning the competitive procurement. If the contractor defaults, the surety firm has then to complete the project or cover the costs of finding another supplier. Surety firms screen bidders and projects, and the premium to the surety firm increases with risk. More risky firms expect to pay a higher fee for the surety bond, and will bid less aggressively, winning less often.
- Letters of credits: Contractors are admitted to bid for a procurement if guaranteed by a bank's letter of credit. If the contractor defaults the bank pledges an asset. Letters of credit exclude bidders with a very bad financial status but makes others more susceptible to bankruptcy.[60]

Both instruments have the property that they could prevent the most risky but innovative firms to participate, or substantially reduce their chances to win. If the primary object of the procurement is innovation, it is essential not to discriminate too much *a priori* against firms presenting innovative

---

[60] For more details about surety bonds and letters of credit See Chapter 13.

and risky projects. Procurers have other, better tools to increase the like-lihood to awarding the contract to innovative contractors or projects, while achieving some protection from risk. In particular, we suggest multi-sourcing, and a modified version of surety bonds without screening.

- Multi-sourcing: having several suppliers active in parallel and in back up reduces the risk of interruption of supply. Moreover, since ranking innovative products is typically very difficult in the beginning, by admitting more than one substitute innovation to be implemented prolongs the 'testing' period, delaying the final judgement on which among the substitute innovations is better, and therefore allowing the selection of the best innovation more often. Among the costs of this solution are the usual ones of multi-sourcing: reduced scale economies, fixed costs duplication, and so on. (See Chapters 7 and 13 for more on this).
- Surety bonds paid by the procurer: to reduce the risk of procurement but take the risk of selecting innovative firms, the price of the winning firm's surety bond could be paid by the procurer. This allows the procurer to be insured against non-performing contractors, but not to screen out the most risky and innovative ones.

Practical conclusion 14

When innovation is a priority both multi-sourcing and surety bonds paid by the procurer may be useful tools to increase the likelihood of awarding the contract to innovative contractors or projects, while achieving some protection from risk.

Because innovation is typically a very risky activity, managing risk is somewhat the opposite of innovating, of undertaking risky innovative activities. A final, obvious alternative when innovation is the main concern is of course that the procurer chooses not to manage risky bids. The procurer can just bear the risk that a contractor goes bankrupt. This alternative can be appealing particularly if the procurer is the government, a highly diversified procurer that is usually able to bear risk at low cost. Of course this strategy involves costs, but being the largest institution in a country, the government is clearly the most differentiated, hence the most able to pool risks from different activities; and the remaining costs may well be balanced by the benefits of more innovation.

19.7. Conclusion

In this chapter we have offered to firms and public agencies a number of practical suggestions on how best to manage the procurement of innovative goods, and how to use procurement to foster innovation. The uncertainty surrounding the innovative activity, and the dynamic perspective that it necessarily involves, make the procurement of innovation one of the most difficult issues in the theory and practice of procurement. The reader will have noticed that the strengths and weaknesses of each tool that could be used to procure innovative inputs depend on a number of variables. In real life, each procurer must take inevitably complex decisions, and we can only warn the reader that it is his or her own responsibility to mix the different ingredients we laid down on the table wisely. For example, the procurer's assessment of his or her ability to describe an innovative input in advance may tilt his or her preferences toward ex-ante prizes or ex-post prizes.

The range of potential applications of this chapter's suggestions is large, encompassing small and large lots, private and public procurers, symmetric and asymmetric procurer–supplier relationships and different degrees of competition and risk. We stress that real world procurement often involves a blend of the stylised hypotheses we made in the text, and so the procurer needs to resort to a mixture of our recipes. Any mechanical and non-critical application of our practical suggestions may lead to errors. Our guidelines are intended for astute and responsible readers, to whom they can give inspiration and hints for reflection. However, the optimal choice is up to the procurer to make, and guessing correctly is more of an active artwork than of a passive technique.

Bibliographical notes

An excellent, up-to-date and accessible source covering many of the themes treated in this chapter and providing references for further more technical analyses is Scotchmer (2004). For more on the role of public policy in standard setting battles see the forthcoming book edited by Greenstein and Stango (*forthcoming*). Branscomb and Florida (1998) and Hart (1998) offer interesting discussions of several technology policy issues related to this chapter from a US perspective. General reflections on practical procurement policies to foster innovation can be found in the EU Experts Group (2005) and in Maurer and Scotchmer (2004).

References

Acemoglu, D. and J. Linn (2004). Market Size in Innovation: Theory and Evidence from the Pharmaceutical Industry, *Quarterly Journal of Economics*, 119, 1049–1090.

Aghion, P., N. Bloom, R. Blundell, R. Griffith, and P. Howitt (2005). Competition and Innovation: An Inverted U Relationship, *Quarterly Journal of Economics.* 120 (2), 701–728.

Aiginger, K., and M. Falk (2005). The Inverted U: New Evidence on the Relationship Between Innovation and Competition, Working Paper, WIFO (Austrian Institute for Economic Research).

Allen, F., and D. Gale (1999). Diversity of Opinion and Financing of New Technologies, *Journal of Financial Intermediation*, Elsevier, 8 (1–2), 68–89.

Arrow, K. (1962). Economic Welfare and the Allocation of Resources for Invention. in R. Nelson (Ed.), *The Rate and Direction of Inventive Activity: Economic and Social Factors*, Princeton, NJ: Princeton University Press.

Branscomb, L. and R. Florida (1998). Challenges to Technology Policy in a Changing World Economy, in L. Branscomb and J. Keller (Eds.), *Investing in Innovation: Creating a Research and Innovation Policy That Works*, Cambridge, MA: MIT Press.

Cabral, L. and T. Kretschmer (2004). Standards Battles and Public Policy, Working Paper, forthcoming in S. Greenstein and V. Stango (Eds.), *Standards and Public Policy.* Cambridge UK: Cambridge University Press.

Cabral, L. and D. Salant (2006). *Evolving Technologies and Standardization*, Mimeo, New York and Columbia Universities.

Che, Y. and I. Gale (2003). Optimal Design of Research Contests, *American Economic Review*, 93 (3), 646–671.

Chiesa, G. and V. Denicoló (2005). *Patents, Prizes and Optimal Innovation Policy*, Mimeo, University of Bologna.

Cowan, R. (1990). Nuclear Power Reactors: A Study of Technological Lock-In, *Journal of Economic History*, 50 (Sept) 541–566.

Cozzi, G. G. and Impulitti, (2004). *Technology Policy and Wage Inequality*, Mimeo Rome and New York Universities.

Day, J. R. (1971). *Trains*, New York: Bantam Books.

Denicoló V. and P. Zanchettin (2002). How Should Forward Protection be Provided?, *International Journal of Industrial Organization*, 20, 801–827.

EC, (2004). On the coordination of procedures for the award of public works contracts, public supply contracts and public service contracts, Directive 2004/18/EC of the European Parliament and of the Council, 31 March.

EU Expert Group (2005). Public Procurement for Research and Innovation, Report of an Expert Group on measures and actions to assist in the development of procurement practices favourable to private investment in R&D and innovation. Available from http://europa.eu.int/invest in research/pdf/report_public procurement_research_innovation_en.pdf

Fullerton, R. L., B. G. Linster and M. McKee, (2002). Using Auctions to Reward Tournament Winners: Theory and Experimental Investigations, *RAND Journal of Economics*, 33 (I), 62–84.

Fullerton, R., L. and R. P. McAfee (1999). Auctioning Entry into Tournaments, *Journal of Political Economy*, 7, (3), 573–605.

Gompers, P. and J. Lerner (1999). *The Venture Capital Cycle*, Cambridge, MA: MIT Press.

Greenstein, S., and V. Stango (Eds.). *Standards and Public Policy*, forthcoming, Cambridge: Cambridge University Press, forthcoming.

Hart, D. (1998). US Technology Policy: New Tools for New Times, *NIRA Review*, Summer, 3–6.

Holbrook, D. (1995). Government Support to Semiconductor Industry: Diverse Approach and Information Flows, *Business and Economic History*, 24, (2), Winter.

Kremer, M. (1998). Patent Buyouts, A Mechanism for Encouraging Innovation, *Quarterly Journal of Economics*, 113 (4), 1137–1167.

Langreth, R. (1994). The $30 Million Refrigerator, *Popular Science*, 244, 65–7, 87.

Lee, T., and L. Wilde (1980). Market Structure and Innovation: A Reformulation, *Quarterly Journal of Economics*, 94, 429–436.

Lewis, T. R. and E. Talley (2005). Discovery Auctions and Optimal Cumulative Innovation, Mimeo, Fuqua School of Business, Duke University.

Liebowitz, S., J. and S. E. Margolis S. E. (1990). The Fable of the Keys, *Journal of Law & Economics*, 33 (1), 1–26 (April).

Litan R. E. and A. M. Rivlin (2001a). *The Economic Payoff from the Internet Revolution*, Washington DC: Brookings Institution.

Litan, R. E. and A. M. Rivlin (2001b). *Beyond the Dot.coms: The Economic Promise of the Internet*, Washington: Brookings Institution.

Loury, O. (1979). Market Structure and innovation, *Quarterly Journal of Economics*, 93.

Maurer, S., and S. Scotchmer (2004). Procuring Knowledge, in G. Libecap (Ed.), *Intellectual Property and Entrepreneurship: Advances in the Study of Entrepreneurship, Innovation and Growth*, vol. 15, 1–31. The Netherlands: JAI Press (Elsevier).

Menell, P. and S. Scotchmer (2006). Intellectual Property, in M. Polinsky and S. Shavell (Eds.), *Handbook of Law and Economics*. Vol. 1 Amsterdam: Elsevier.

Mill, J. S. (1872). *Principles of Political Economy with Some of Their Applications to Social Philosophy*, Boston: Lee & Shephard.

Ruttan, V. (2005). Military Procurement and Technology Development, Working Paper, Department of Applied Economics College of Agricultural, Food, and Environmental Sciences University of Minnesota.

Scotchmer, S. (1991). Standing on the Shoulders of Giants: Cumulative Research and the Patent Law, *Journal of Economic Perspectives*, 5, 29–41.

Scotchmer, S. (1999). On the Optimality of the Patent Renewal System, *Rand Journal of Economics*, 30 (2), 181–196.

Scotchmer, S. (2004). *Innovation and Incentives*, Cambridge, MA: MIT Press.

Sobel, D. (2005). *Longitude: The True Story of a Lone Genius Who Solved the Greatest Scientific Problem of His Time*, New York: Penguin.

Glossary

abnormally low bid/tender – In sealed-bid tendering or dynamic auctions, a particularly low price submitted to win a competition. Normally a tender is defined as abnormal when it is below, by a certain predefined percentage, the average of all prices bid by suppliers. Such very low tenders could be made by a very efficient supplier, by bidders who wrongly underestimated the uncertain cost of serving a contract, or by potentially insolvent suppliers who strategically chose to do so. In public procurement, bidders who submitted an abnormally low tender are asked to explain their offers by the buyer who, based on these justifications, could either accept or reject the offer.

activity rule – In dynamic auctions, a rule defining how participants have to bid in order to be allowed to remain in the auction.

asymmetric firms – In competitive procurement firms are considered asymmetric if they have a significantly different cost structure for performing a contract, and/or if they do not have access to qualitatively similar sources of information about a supply contract. Other possible sources of asymmetry could be the revenue or the number of employees.

auction – See dynamic auction.

awarding procedure – The procedure adopted by the procurer to assign a contract; in procurement, the two main awarding procedures are negotiations and competitive tendering.

bid – Offer made by a supplier in sealed-bid tendering or a dynamic auction. The proposal can consist of an economic as well as a technical component.

bidding consortium – A group of suppliers submitting a single bid.

bidding ring – A group of suppliers who illegally coordinate their bidding strategies in order to soften price competition, and bid prices higher than they would as compared to effective competition.

bundling – The practice of combining two or more contracts into a large single supply contract.

collusion – Explicit or tacit agreement among a group of suppliers aiming at softening price–quality competition, thus reproducing the behaviour of a single dominant firm.

collusive cartel – See bidding ring.

combinational competitive tendering – See combinatorial competitive tendering.

combinatorial competitive tendering – A multi-contract bidding competition where suppliers can submit prices for single contracts as well as for packages of contracts.

competitive tendering – Competition where suppliers submit tenders to be awarded the contracts being procured.

complementarities – For a supplier a group of contracts exhibit positive (negative) complementarities if the cost of serving all of them is lower (higher) than the sum of the costs of serving each single contract.

contract – See supply contract.

contractor – The supplier who is awarded a contract.

corruption – Illegal, wealth-seeking behaviour of the procurer when buying on behalf of a third party such as a public authority or a firm.

descending auction – See reverse auction.

dynamic auction – Bidding competition where participants can observe rivals' offers while the competition is running.

dutch auction – Used to sell quickly perishable goods, such as flowers and fish, and virtually absent in procurement. As adjusted to procurement it is a dynamic auction format whereby the procurer starts calling a very low price for a contract, which he raises until a supplier stops the increase. The bidder who does so is awarded the contract and paid the price he has bid. Dutch auctions can last very little time, which makes it possible to run a sequence of them in a limited amount of time.

e-auctions – Auctions which are conducted on-line.

economies of scale – The characteristic of a production process whereby the unitary cost of a product decreases as production increases.

e-platforms – Web portals working as mediators in two-sided markets.

e-procurement – Procurement activity conducted on-line.

externality – Any effect of a consumption or production decision on people not involved in the act.

free riding – Free riding occurs when one firm (or individual) benefits from the actions and efforts of another without paying for, or sharing, the costs.

heterogeneous bidders – See asymmetric firms.

incumbent – The actual contractor.

joint bidding – A bid made by a group of suppliers acting as a single participant in a competitive tendering.

letter of credit – A financial instrument, typically issued by a bank, working as a cash guarantee to the owner. The issuer is secured by the supplier's financial assets.

lot – A supply contract that is being procured.

lowest-price auction – A dynamic, reversed auction where the supplier offering the minimum price gets the contract and is paid his bid by the procurer. It is the English auction, used in sales, adjusted to procurement. One of the main features of the lowest-price auction is its end rule.

lowest-price sealed-bid tendering – A competitive tendering procedure where bidders compete for a supply contract by submitting a price in a sealed envelope to the procurer. The procurer opens the envelopes publicly and assigns the contract to the supplier who offered the lowest price. The contractor receives a payment equal to his bid. This is analogous to the first (highest)-price sealed-bid tendering used in sales. Sealed-bid tendering can also be conducted on-line.

most advantageous offer – The best price–quality combination received by the procurer. In competitive tendering procedures, the most advantageous offer is typically selected through a scoring rule.

multi-contract competitive tendering – Procurement competitive bidding where more than one contract is procured in the same sealed-bid tendering or dynamic action.

multiple-lot auctions – See multi-contract auctions.

multi-round auctions – A dynamic descending auction where each round comprises a sealed-bid session; after every round, and before the next one, the buyer publicly announces the offers received. Typically, at each stage the highest acceptable (reserve) price decreases.

negotiation – A procedure to award a contract whereby the procurer, to obtain the best conditions, entertains individual interactions with potential suppliers.

open procedures – Bidding competitions where all interested suppliers, provided they satisfy some preliminary requisites, can submit tenders.

package bidding – A competitive bidding mechanism in which suppliers can make offers on sets of contracts as well as on single ones.

procurement contract – See supply contract.

reserve price – In competitive tendering procedures, the maximum price acceptable by the procurer.

restricted procedures – Bidding competitions where the buyer selects the group of qualified potential suppliers that can submit a tender.

reverse auction – A dynamic auction where suppliers bid for a contract, which is awarded to the bidder who submitted the lowest price.

ring – See bidding ring.

scoring rule – A mathematical formula assigning a number (score) to the price and the other components of a multi-dimensional tender submitted by a supplier. Through a scoring rule the contract will be awarded to the supplier who obtained the highest score.

second-lowest-price sealed-bid tendering – The second price Vickrey auction, used in sales, adjusted to procurement. A competitive tendering procedure where bidders compete for a supply contract by submitting a price in a sealed envelope to the procurer. The procurer opens the envelopes publicly and assigns the contract to the suppliers who offered the lowest price. Unlike what happens in a lowest price sealed-bid tendering, the price that the buyer pays to the contractor is the second lowest price received by the procurer. In this format, when the cost of serving the contract is not uncertain for a supplier, submitting the minimum price a bidder is willing to be paid can be preferable to any other price that he could offer. The sealed-bid procedure could be conducted on-line.

sequential competitive tendering – A sequence of single-contract bidding competitions used to procure a certain number of contracts.

simultaneous competitive tendering – A multi-contract competitive tendering in which suppliers compete for a group of contracts which are procured simultaneously.

subcontracting – Agreement between a contractor (prime contractor) and another supplier (subcontractor) to share the supply contract, in which the prime contractor keeps responsibility for the completion of the contract.

supply contract – A contract that formalizes the relationship between buyer and supplier, specifying the conditions of the supply. Normally, a contract fixes a time horizon of validity and a precise quantity, or alternatively a maximum–minimum amount to be provided for the products being procured. The price for serving the contract can either be specified in the contract itself or determined as the outcome of a competitive tendering.

surety bond – A surety bond is a three-party instrument between a surety, the contractor, and the project owner. The agreement binds the contractor to comply with the terms and conditions of a contract. If the contractor is unable to successfully perform the contract, the surety assumes the contractor's responsibilities and ensures that the project is completed.

switching costs – Costs borne by the procurer when it changes the contractor.

tender – A supplier's offer, which can comprise a price as well as a technical proposal.

truncated English auction – As adjusted to procurement, a two-stage auction format in which the suppliers offering the $k > 1$ lowest prices are selected in the first stage. Among them, in the second stage, the procurer chooses the winning firm(s).

Vickrey auction – A competitive mechanism used in sales in which the winning supplier does not pay his bid, the highest price, but the second highest bid.

winner's curse – The phenomenon occurring when the winner of a contract submits too low a price having underestimated the uncertain cost of supply.

Index